Introduction to Interior Design

iNTRODUCTION TO

iNTERiOR dESiGN

Dorothy Stepat–De Van

Late Professor of Home Economics
Hunter College of the City University of New York

Darlene M. Kness

University of Montevallo

Kathryn Camp Logan

Interior Design Consultant

Laura Szekely

University of Kentucky

Macmillan Publishing Co., Inc.
NEW YORK

Collier Macmillan Publishers
LONDON

Macmillan Publishing Co., Inc.
866 Third Avenue, New York, New York 10022

Collier Macmillan Canada, Ltd.

Library of Congress Cataloging in Publication Data

Main entry under title:

Introduction to interior design.

   Previous editions by D. Stepat–De Van published under title: Introduction to home furnishings.
   Bibliography: p.
   Includes index.
   1. House furnishings. 2. Interior decoration.
I. Stepat–De Van, Dorothy   Introduction to home furnishings.
TX311.S76 1979   645   78-17412
ISBN 0-02-417090-9

Printing: 7 8   Year: 6

ISBN 0-02-417090-9

Preface

A primary purpose of Dorothy Stepat–De Van's writing was to aid students in developing an understanding of the home environment as it relates to personal development and affects relationships between family members. In her first edition she used the delightful French phrase *joie de vivre*, or "joy of living," to describe the happiness that is a direct result of our surroundings, of the aesthetic, functional living areas we create, design, and decorate. She emphasized the home as the sum of well-analyzed and selected ingredients, and also that such constitutients as furniture, decorations, and basic home products need to be chosen in relation to the family budget. This farsighted, total approach to home decorating was ahead of its time with her first edition in 1964.

She continued to keep her book timely with publication of the second edition in 1971. Recognizing societal changes that evolved during the sixties, Stepat–De Van revised her text to reflect the greater awareness of needs and rapidly emerging new technologies resulting in new requirements for living space along with innovative household products.

The current authors have learned much from her example, especially that a textbook should reflect a society's present and emerging needs. We think she would understand why the book itself has taken on a new look and a new title. It reflects not only the societal changes she recognized in her writing, but also college course changes toward an emphasis on interiors rather than home furnishings per se.

The word *interior* has many levels of meaning. It is an extension of the home as a shelter and has to provide for our needs for warmth, security, and coziness. Functionally, an interior not only serves physical but also psychological needs, representing the ideals, desires, dreams, and search for beauty of its inhabitants. Another meaning for an interior is to convey a sense of order, which we all require in our lives. This order is created through the arrangement of the space to control movement and activities within it. An interior also expresses personality; it can be friendly, open, or limiting. In addition to function, an interior has an aesthetic quality, conveying a sense of form, color, and design.

v

Teaching the reader to detect the many aspects of an interior and the many ways its users can reshape it is the principal object of this book. Families frequently give new looks and forms to their homes; this text presents basic information that will assist them.

One aspect of contemporary interiors and home furnishings is that there exist fewer rigidly defined rules and principles than in the past as to "proper" furniture selection or arrangement. We now have more freedom in making decorating choices and a larger selection of materials. Almost everyone today has a collection of some sort or interests that become part of interior displays. In one sense, decorating has become easier today because it presents few prescriptions. On the other hand, it has become more difficult because it makes more demands on individual judgement and taste. Thus instead of setting prescriptions for home furnishings and their arrangement, this edition discusses what can be considered the most important elements that go into making basic personal choices.

The authors were faced with numerous choices in preparing this new edition. We ultimately decided to follow Stepat–De Van's example by retaining those time-tested features that continue to be appropriate, while bringing coverage up to date where necessary. We have included a new chapter on mechanical systems and, to meet the needs of many instructors, a chapter on eclectic decoration. The chapter on American furniture styles now covers factors related to judging antiques, which are increasingly used to decorate the home. We also recognize the increased interest in do-it-yourself projects, which are popular because they are satisfying and save money in a time of shrinking family budgets; consequently, we have added appropriate coverage to the sections on paints, finishes, textiles, modern furniture, and budget decorating.

Illustrations are, of course, an important, integral part of this text. As styles change so must the photographs—the number of carefully chosen illustrations has increased in many chapters and out-of-date photographs have been deleted. The color plates we have selected provide suggestions, not prescriptions, for planning decorating schemes. In selecting the new illustrations, we have included decorating examples that should be available in many retail stores, as well as those considered "one of a kind" items. Students, therefore, have a wide range of visual material to select from and be inspired by. The ultimate choices and selections will be their's to make.

Other significant additions have been made to the text. A listing of periodicals is provided that students may consult for new developments and advances in the home furnishings field. Information on careers and competencies in interior design is included to acquaint readers with available opportunities and career requirements.

Acknowledgement is made to the many people who served as aides, advisors, and readers for this text. Gratitude goes to our editors, Mr. John Beck and Ms. Susan Greenberg, for their objectivity, proficiency, and patience, which contributed much to this revision. Many thanks to Professors Eloise Street, Faenelia Hicks, Betty McKee Treanor, Margaret Hassert, to Mr. Charles Bulnes (A.S.I.D.), and to Ms. Karen Schaeffer and Ms. Paula Swent Defore who read parts of the text and provided helpful suggestions. Gratitude is expressed to our families and friends who were patient, understanding, and encouraging to us throughout the process of writing this edition.

D. K.
K. C. L.
L. S.

Contents

viii

Contents

SECTION ONE

Planning a Home

Space for Living

We cannot talk about interior design unless we start at the beginning, and that beginning is people and the spaces that they occupy. The study of home furnishings is the study of the relationships between people and these surroundings. Interior design begins with the community, its streets and subdivisions, its outdoor furnishings, and its houses. Our interior spaces are only thinly separated by the membrane of walls from the exterior. In designing a structure the architect begins with an examination of the qualities of the exterior environment—its views, land formations, ground materials, and the existing community—and with the needs of the client. Home furnishings begin with the interior space—with an understanding of what the architect has defined—and alter it by choices in lighting, visual surfaces, and objects placed within the space.

Interior spaces silently communicate to people. Spaces can be not only beautiful in their shapes, colors, or feel but, by supporting behavior, organizing life styles, and even challenging imagination, can actually contribute to the enjoyment and growth of people within them. By promoting personal comfort, enhancing security, and encouraging personal communications spaces can become supportive human environments in which people may grow.

With the rapid rise of standardization in the building of homes and communities, it is most important today for one to gain a sense of control over and understanding of individual spaces, to feel comfortable in them and arrange them so as to express one's personal tastes. The trend in recent years has been to design for mass building projects such as large apartment houses or new suburban developments. Spaces for living are designed by "experts," by teams of specialists including architects, sociologists, psychologists, home economists, and land developers. Even if these experts succeed in providing people with satisfactory environments for living, the life and character of these spaces depends on the persons living in them. When we select a home, we should recognize that the start is a preshaped set of spaces that we may feel is comfortable or conflicting right from the beginning. Our introduction of objects, colors, or lights is a reaction to the limitations and suggestions given by the building's designer. Before we begin any discussion of furnishings, therefore, it seems desirable to consider a few basic factors involved in the selection of a home.

Housing is a worldwide problem, and there is a tremendous amount of housing that is neither safe nor sanitary. In most countries there are both short-range and long-range programs for improving conditions. However, our interdisciplinary approach to this problem reveals a new dilemma. We are becoming more cognizant of the fact that requirements vary with the individual and with the family at different stages of the life cycle, but there are also trends toward urbanization and more mass-produced housing. How, then, do we provide adaptable homes that truly meet needs and desires? Current research is attempting to provide some answers to this complex question.

There are no universally accepted standards with respect to what constitutes "adequate" housing. Many local communities have codes and laws that regulate building to some extent. Government-financed programs must meet certain specifications, but at the present time there is considerable controversy regarding this matter. Some authorities believe that standards are so low that we are merely creating new slums in a rather frantic effort to relieve the situation. The matter of minimum standards must be subjected to a great deal of further research.

What constitutes "desirable" housing poses quite a different question. Standards in this matter will naturally vary with the individual, and probably no two people have identical values. In addition to the many families who are forced to live in homes that are inadequate according to the most basic standards, there are many others who have homes that they do not consider desirable.

Most average families spend between one quarter or one third of their total income on either owning or renting a home.[1] Often the choices about how this money will be spent are more restricted than they are in other major areas of family economics, such as food, automobiles, insurance, and recreation.

Influences on Choice

What determines where people live and what kind of housing they purchase? There has been only limited research in this area, but simple observation points to some of the reasons.

Habit

Some of us are more migratory than others and perhaps more adaptable to different patterns of living. But many people find it difficult to change their way of life. There is an old cliché that goes, "It's a nice place to visit, but I wouldn't want to live here." The city dweller says it about the farm and the small-towner says it about the big city, and the probable reason is that each has become accustomed to the particular advantages of his or her own pattern. It is difficult to generalize about the different patterns of living because they vary to some extent with specific places.

There are advantages and disadvantages to living in either a city or a small town. Space is, of course, at a premium in most cities. One room in a convenient section may cost as much as a whole house with considerable ground around it in another area. Generally there is a more impersonal quality to city living than there is in a small town. Naturally the opportunities for entertainment, recreation, and other activities vary a great deal.

Suburbia has been the answer for many families. Living in a small community close to a big city would seem to solve all the problems because one can have the advantages of both types of living. But some families have found that suburbs also have the disadvantages of both types. The suburbanite who spends considerable time traveling to and from work may find that he or she cannot enjoy the advantages of either the city or the community. With rising transportation costs, city-center living areas are becoming increasingly attractive because of their proximity to places of work. This trend is helping in the rehabilitation of many inner-city areas.

[1] United States Labor Force Statistics, Pamphlet 18, (January 1978), p. 8.

Work

A particular job or type of work may force people to live in a certain area. A doctor who has established a practice or a person who owns a business may be bound to some special locality. Teachers, farmers, salespersons, lawyers, and diplomats must live where they will have the greatest satisfactions from their work. Industries are somewhat centralized in various parts of the country. Unskilled workers have more choice but still face problems of the labor market.

Family Ties

Some people stay in a particular locality simply because all their relatives live there. There may be dependent parents who cannot be moved easily to a different community. For some people, breaking close family associations is unthinkable. To others who have different sets of values, packing up and going may be a problem, but if the advantages outweigh the disadvantages, they can do it.

Transplanting children from one community to another is often a difficult problem. Once youngsters have established themselves in school it is not easy for them to become accustomed to a new way of life.

Status

Whether or not we like to face the fact, housing does represent a status symbol. In cities, people will often pay exorbitant rents for a tiny space simply because of a "good" address. Almost every town has a right and a wrong side of the tracks, even when there are no tracks. One can drive through almost any community and pick out the "elite" section.

Even in developments where hundreds of houses begin life on a par, owners begin to make improvements and the ball starts to roll. Some years ago it was the two-car garage and an outdoor patio that represented luxury and elegance. Now that these have become more generally available, the marks of the "upper strata" include a family swimming pool and/or tennis courts. The sauna is becoming a new status symbol as well. Who can tell what the next mark of distinction will be? Perhaps a private landing field for a family helicopter.

Mobility

People today change jobs and move more frequently than ever before. Most individuals will buy and sell several homes in their lifetime, purchasing each with a new perspective. The idea of a family "homestead," a cherished dwelling passed down from one generation to the next, is giving way to acceptance of less permanent and more easily disposed of dwellings such as mobile homes, prefabricated homes, and development units. Such homes are purchased with careful consideration of their possible resale.

Many contemporary homes are part of large-scale new developments whose construction is based on information from surveys and market studies indicating the types of exteriors and interiors that please the widest range of buyers. The home built for a specific family and its needs has given way to dwellings designed to please many potential owners. This type of home is not strongly committed to a particular school of design or style but is a simple unit with standardized decorations. Each home is slightly different; the units might vary in garage door color, type of railing, and so on. The interiors of these new homes are generally more open, with multipurpose spaces that allow for modification according to family needs.

Homes have changed in appearance, design, and construction. They look as light, simple, and streamlined as the cars and trailers in their driveways. Although there is still interest in columns and façade decorations referring to homes in the past, the basic forms of today's dwellings are simple boxes housing highly efficient mechanical systems. Because today's homes might house a succession of mobile families, they are seldom built to a particular family's specific needs and tastes. Added-on exteriors, modified interior walls, and raised roofs are common. The mobile family is also less likely to insist on permanent building materials such as brick or stone and will more readily accept prefabricated decorations or an entire prefabricated structure. Mobility has also spurred a desire to buy or own the finished product—homes complete with carpeting, fixtures, and appliances that in the past may have been slowly accumulated. In a mobile society, as people have become interested in do-it-yourself customization of dwellings, new owners more readily accept moving into homes completely decorated and left intact by previous owners.

Quality of Life

In selecting a home, prospective homeowners are placing increasing emphasis on the appearance of the building and its environment. With massive developments composed of identical housing units creating an endless sea of sameness, and with open landscape rapidly disappearing, people are becoming concerned with the quality of life their environment provides. This concern may be seen in the new interest in preserving older homes, in public interest in saving open spaces, and in the general process of neighborhood planning. With today's fast-paced construction and increased building density, people are more aware of and vocal about preserving the privacy and beauty of their environment through zoning laws and integrating the buildings to be erected with what already exists.

Needs in the Home

The primary purpose of shelter is, of course, to protect us from the elements, but beyond that we need and expect much more from our homes. Because what constitutes desirable living quarters is a very personal and individual matter, requirements and wants vary with each family. We are all consumers of shelter, and we have a certain number of dollars to spend for housing. Few of us can have all our wants satisfied, so our values determine how we spend those dollars. We sacrifice or compromise in one area to achieve something else that seems more important. One family might live in a small city apartment because it is convenient for the wage earner. Another similar family prefers to live some distance away from the city so that they have more space and a yard for the children, even though the wage earner has to travel back and forth. In each case the family might spend the same amount of money on housing, but each family spends it differently.

There are, however, certain basic needs and desires that we would like our homes to fulfill. Most of us want some degree of comfort, privacy, and convenience. We want our homes to be functional. And most of us also want our homes to be beautiful.

Standards

It has been pointed out that there are no real standards for adequate or desirable housing. Among the agencies and groups that either require or recommend certain qualities are the following:

Federal Housing Administration. The FHA is a government agency that was set up to insure mortgages; in an indirect manner it has established certain minimum standards. Before the FHA will approve a loan, the house must meet certain regulations, covering:

1. Materials and products.
2. Structural design.
3. Construction.
4. Exterior and interior covering materials.
5. Mechanical equipment.
6. Water supply and sewage disposal.
7. General planning.
8. Plot planning.
9. General criteria.

In some categories the requirements are quite specific, but they represent minimum rather than desirable standards.

Minimum standards for housing are both necessary and important, but they also present a dangerous threat. Instead of being regarded as a base below which the level must not fall, in practice they tend to become acceptable as pat standards.

American Public Health Association. In 1938 the association's Committee on the Hygiene of Housing defined certain requirements in a report, "Basic Principles of Healthful Housing." In the introduction to the second edition, it is pointed out that the report is a formulation of "basic health needs which housing should subserve." The introduction also says, "The

Principles and Specific Requirements are believed to be fundamental minima required for the promotion of physical, mental, and social health essential in low-rent as well as high-cost housing, on the farm as well as in the city dwelling." In a more recent report it was noted that "There is usually a considerable difference between 'optimum' and 'minimum' requirements; that there is a continuous, gradual movement from 'minimum' toward 'optimum.' Codes represent the level of conditions which the public and their representatives consider to be so economically, socially, and politically necessary and acceptable that they should be required by law for all people."[2]

Other organizations. Several agencies concerned with financing make recommendations for home construction—for example, the United States Savings and Loan League and the Metropolitan Life Insurance Company. In many communities local housing codes and building restrictions impose certain standards.

It has been pointed out that we are taking a new approach to housing research, and several universities have established centers for environmental studies. It is to be hoped that these centers will provide more useful guidelines for better housing programs.

Today most homes are designed for a pattern of living rather than for individual families. The requirements of each family vary with the different stages of family life. The beginning family with several young children will have different needs from those of the family with several teenagers. The special needs of retired couples and handicapped persons have received considerable attention in recent years.

Space

Space for specific needs and activities is of primary importance—but space is usually expensive in either bought or rented shelter. Except in luxury-type housing, some concessions must be made to costs. Also, space needs vary as a family grows and then decreases. In the

early years of family life, young children can share bedrooms, but as they grow older, it is often more desirable that they have private rooms. When the children mature and leave home, the parents are often left with excess space.

The FHA sets the following minimum standards for a three-bedroom living unit.

Living room	170 sq. ft.
Dining room	95 sq. ft.
Kitchen	70 sq. ft.
Total bedrooms	280 sq. ft.
(Minimum per bedroom	80 sq. ft.)

Remember that these are minimum standards. The total area for the rooms indicated adds up to 615 square feet. For a family of four, 1,500 square feet, not including closets and bathrooms can be a guideline.

Although adequate housing must include many other features, the proper amount of space is perhaps the most fundamental need. But the arrangement of available space is equally important. A matter of major concern today is planning for functionalism in this respect so that the normal activities of the family are served in the best possible manner.

Sleeping

A comfortable place to sleep is both physically and psychologically important. It is basic and imperative, therefore, for every home to have adequate sleeping quarters. The ideal of a private room for each member of the family who might want one is not always feasible. When people have to share sleeping quarters, every effort must be made to ensure maximum comfort and privacy for each person.

Eating

There is a curious association between the manner in which we partake of food and the general level of "standards of living." The arrangements that a home provides for feeding family and friends are, strangely enough, both a good indication of the values placed upon family life and a symbol of status.

[2] "Basic Health Principles of Housing and Its Environment," *American Journal of Public Health,* **69:**5 (May 1969), 841–851.

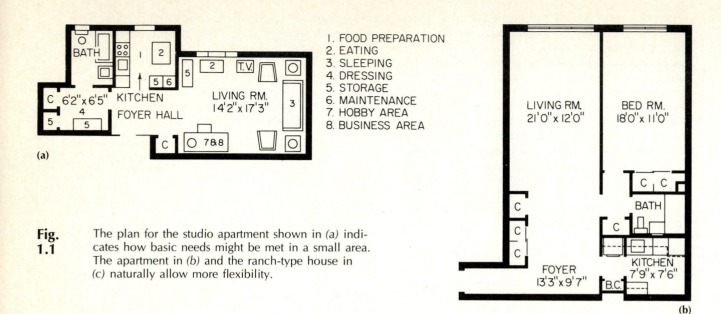

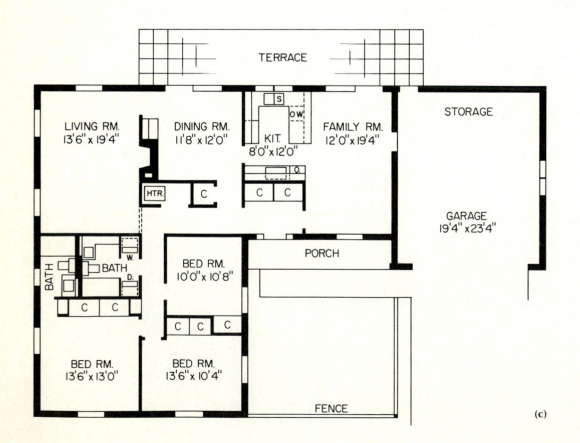

1. FOOD PREPARATION
2. EATING
3. SLEEPING
4. DRESSING
5. STORAGE
6. MAINTENANCE
7. HOBBY AREA
8. BUSINESS AREA

**Fig.
1.1** The plan for the studio apartment shown in (a) indicates how basic needs might be met in a small area. The apartment in (b) and the ranch-type house in (c) naturally allow more flexibility.

A separate room used exclusively for dining has almost become a thing of the past, although it should be noted that a dining room is one of the features listed as a desirable aspect for a home when the family can afford it.

A dining room affords the family a place to congregate; it also offers a place where friends may be entertained with ease and graciousness. The cost of maintaining such a room is often prohibitive, but if it is within reason, the family should not overlook the values received.

Dual-purpose dining rooms are gaining in favor. Such an area may be used in conjunction with the den. It may even be furnished to serve as a guest room, though such an arrangement may present several problems.

Various arrangements may be made in the home for providing meals of different types without a dining room. A snack bar in the kitchen for quick individual meals is sometimes useful. An alcove or a dining area as part of another room has become an accepted plan.

Outdoor eating and entertaining are part of the way of life in many areas of the country, and where the space and equipment for cookouts are available, this form of family dining and entertaining is both practical and enjoyable.

The kitchen is an important area in the home because of the specialized equipment and storage space. But it is such a major area of activity that the utilization and decoration of the room should be of primary concern to every family.

Some homes combine kitchen and laundry areas to economize on plumbing costs and for convenience purposes. In others, the kitchen is planned to become the "family room" or a second living room.

The kitchen of today is much more scientifically planned and executed than were yesterday's kitchens; even so, few families have the advantages of a kitchen that is efficient enough to meet all their needs in the best possible way. Although many studies have analyzed work-motion routines, storage needs, and the utilization of space, there are numerous homes being built with no recognition of the most practical arrangements.

There are also special kitchens planned for people with particular needs. The elderly person or the person with a heart condition should have a kitchen that is designed to meet specific requirements.

Privacy and Hobbies

It would be ideal to have a separate area for each member of the family. This is not always practical, but frequently some sort of compromise can be made whereby each person can at least use a corner or an area that provides a feeling of privacy. When there are several children in a family, it is usually necessary for them to share bedrooms. Even under these circumstances, various arrangements can be made to ensure the privacy of each individual. Every member of the household should have at least a corner that belongs to her or him alone, to do with as he or she wishes.

Group Living and Recreation

Certainly some area in the home must be devoted to the family as a group. The current tendency is to have two such areas—one a more formal "living room" and another "family room," also called a den, designed for informal use or as an adjunct to the group living quarters. Such an area is of particular advantage when the family includes teenaged children, or in any other situation where there may be two distinct interpretations of group living. Even within a small family unit there may be different ideas of enjoyable group association. Two or more living areas in the home make it possible for people to enjoy a variety of activities.

Bathroom Needs

Most families would prefer to have at least two bathrooms; a luxury standard would be a private bathroom for each member of the family, or a half bath located near the entertainment area for guests. Prohibitive costs of space, fixtures, and plumbing have forced the development of various kinds of new arrangements in bathrooms to make them more useful. Building each fixture into a compartment and including two sinks makes it possible to have a room that can accommodate more than one person at a time and yet afford some degree of privacy. Although this arrangement is not always the

Fig. 1.2 A one-room apartment can be elegant as well as functional. Lightweight furniture can be easily rearranged for entertaining. The game area may also be used as a work center. *(Designed by Barbara D'Arcy, A.I.D., Bloomingdale's, N.Y., photo by Richard Averill Smith)*

most desirable, it does at least extend the function of one bathroom to meet the needs of the family more adequately.

Maintenance

Various activities may be involved in maintaining the home. In a private home, a special laundry area is desirable, as is some type of workroom. The laundry may be part of the kitchen and the workroom may be part of the garage, or both areas may be in the basement. Where space is available, it is usually more desirable to have these areas separated.

Storage

Sufficient closet and storage space seems to be a problem in every home. Apartments are notable for having inadequate storage space. Even private houses fall short in this respect. An attic or a basement is, of course, very useful, but some homes have neither.

Ideally, each bedroom should have a walk-in closet, and any room that will be shared should have at least two large closets. In addition, general storage areas are necessary for linens, cleaning equipment, and so on. A house with a yard will need storage facilities for lawn mower, hose, and garden equipment. When there are children in the family, such items as bicycles, wagons, and sleds must be kept someplace when they are not in use. A garage is usually suitable for the storage of much of this equipment, but it should be large enough so that it can also accommodate the car. Many families in private homes neglect to provide storage space for such outdoor equipment and large toys. Frequently the garage becomes a storeroom while the car is left outside because it simply will not fit.

Business Center

Every household needs a special area for the business of managing a home. All sorts of records, bills, and stationery supplies should be convenient and readily accessible. This office might be merely a drawer in a chest or a desk in the living room, but it should be well organized and completely equipped. File drawers are a great asset, and some companies have recognized the need for filing cabinets that are attractive in the home. Wooden desks with file cabinets in them are available today. Good light, a comfortable chair, a typewriter, and an ample work surface are also desirable for the family office.

Choice of Housing

Although many families have extremely limited choices when it comes to making decisions about how they will use their allotments for shelter, there are still some choices that must be made:

1. To rent or to buy?
2. House or apartment?
3. One home or two?
4. Modular housing?

To Rent or to Buy?

There are general advantages and disadvantages to either renting or owning shelter, but for individual families the advantages of one may far outweigh the disadvantages. Renting a home is obviously more desirable for a family that may have to move frequently because of the work of the wage earners. But even for a more static family, renting shelter may provide a more desirable solution because of the comparative freedom from responsibilities. Usually the renter is absolved from the costs of and worry about major repairs and renovations. Although the rent may eventually be influenced by a change in tax rates and property values, a renter's expenses for shelter are more fixed and steady than those of a homeowner. The family that rents shelter is also more at liberty to keep the size of the home related to the needs of the family as it grows and disperses over the years.

Ownership, on the other hand, has much in its favor, as is witnessed by the growing number of families who prefer to buy housing rather than to rent it. Even in cities there is growing interest, especially in the middle-income group, in cooperatively owned apartment houses.

Most people have the idea that it is cheaper in the long run to own a home than to rent one, but such is not always the case; in some areas of the country it may be cheaper to own than to rent, but in other areas the opposite is true. Undoubtedly, the family income and the amount that can be spent for shelter are other determining factors. Families in very low income brackets are more likely to find the costs of ownership prohibitive.

Maintenance costs must be considered among the expenses for shelter. The ability of the homeowner to take care of the upkeep personally rather than to pay for the high costs of labor may well be another important consideration.

The homeowner may deduct some shelter expenses in computing his or her personal income tax, whereas the renter receives no such allowance; this may be an important consideration when comparing the economic advantages of ownership and rental.

The argument that after a period of years the

homeowner has "something to show" for the money spent does not always stand up under close economic analysis. If the property value depreciates and the homeowner includes all the expenses of his or her investment the homeowner may be far worse off from the monetary standpoint than the renter who preferred to invest capital in some other manner.

Aside from the seemingly unanswerable question of whether or not it is cheaper to own or to rent, there are other values that must be considered. Many families prefer the feelings of security and stability associated with home ownership. They sense a more integral relationship with the community, and they enjoy a certain status that is reflected not only in intangible ways but in a higher credit rating. Pride of ownership promotes greater interest in the appearance and maintenance of the home, but for the person who does not enjoy household tasks and chores these may soon become burdensome.

Most homeowners feel that through purchasing a home they can have a better quality of housing, with space and equipment more nearly designed to meet their needs.

House or Apartment?

The choice between a house and an apartment may be linked to the buy-or-rent problem because, in general, we buy houses and rent apartments. However, many people rent houses or buy apartments. In the past, an apartment that was owned was usually a cooperative venture with other tenants in the building. Today the condominium is becoming quite popular: one owns the apartment just as one might own a house. The condominium owner may buy and

Fig. 1.3

Habitat '67 in Montreal represents a pioneer experiment in modular housing. Units of precast concrete were hoisted in place to create a new type of futuristic architecture. *(Courtesy of National Film Board of Canada, photo by Central Mortgage and Housing Corporation)*

sell without the approval of the other tenants. This approval is usually necessary in the cooperative, which is another matter.

We have already discussed some of the relative merits of living in the city, country, or suburbs—and location may be the deciding factor—but there are other considerations, too. A house usually offers the advantages of a yard, with more opportunity for outdoor living and more play area for children. There is usually more space and a feeling of more freedom and privacy. For some people, apartment living carries an air of confinement; for others, the important factor in apartment living is freedom from chores and responsibilities.

One Home or Two?

Some families prefer to divide their housing allotment to cover a separate vacation home. Such an expense cannot be considered wholly shelter cost, because it can reduce the cost of vacations. But the costs of the regular home are likely to continue while the family is enjoying the vacation home. Of course, expense is an important factor to consider, but for many families two homes and two types of living have answered some of the questions already presented. An apartment that one rents during the year and a summer house that one owns may provide the advantages of almost all types of shelter. Vacation homes are often designed for easy maintenance so that it is possible to have the pleasures of ownership without the constant pressure of the chores.

Modular Housing?

Modular housing emphasizes the modular unit as a possible answer to some of our housing problems. A house or basic modules that can be transformed into apartments may be produced in a factory and transported to a building site where they are connected to utilities. Habitat, the complex shown at Expo '67 in Montreal, is a noted example of modular apartments.

Mobile homes, although not as new as apartment modules, are another example of modular housing. These units are becoming increasingly important, especially in meeting the housing needs of two particular groups: young married couples and elderly retired couples. Mobile homes differ from trailers in that they are usually larger; if they are to be moved at all, which is not usually the case, they must be hauled by professional transportation companies.

The average mobile home is 12 to 24 feet wide and 60 feet long and sells for about $30,000.00. There are expandable types that pull out to provide an additional 6 or 8 feet in width to a bedroom or a living room. The cost of a furnished mobile home is about $20 a square foot, as compared to about $35 or $40 a square foot for unfurnished conventional housing, depending on location.

In some areas of the country, location sites for mobile housing have been well developed and aesthetically planned. But according to one study, some communities have been reluctant to establish such sites because they are afraid of getting a poor image. Nevertheless, the study recommends modular units for apartments and houses as one answer to the national housing shortage.[3]

The houseboat is another type of mobile home that is becoming popular in certain areas. Some houseboats are quite luxurious, and living on the water seems to have a restful quality that appeals to many people. Although we have tended to think of a houseboat as a vacation home, it should be noted that even in colder climates there is a growing interest in the boat as an all-year-round home.

Owning a Home

Suppose that the decision has been made to own a home. The next decisions are important ones that will not only involve considerable sums of money but also influence personal and family life. There are so many things to consider about the home that planning and studying the project will take a great deal of time. Here again, one will have important decisions and choices, but it should be borne in mind that there probably is no house that is perfect in every respect.

[3] *The New Building Block,* Center for Housing and Environmental Studies (Ithaca, N.Y.: Cornell University, 1968).

14

**Fig.
1.4**

Modular housing answers some of the current needs for economy, space, and comfort.
(Courtesy of Stirling Homes Corporation, Avon, N.Y.)

(a) Above. Ceilings for the modules are made in a unique manner—upside down. After being constructed in giant forms, they are turned over by machine and set atop the modules on the moving production line.

(b) Below. Floor and wall units are carefully joined to form the basic module, which is moved down the production line on a rolling track.

(c) At the end of the production line, finished modules are covered with canvas and plastic sheets to protect them from the weather prior to being erected at the site. They are then loaded on haulers for transportation to the homesite.

(d) A module unit is dropped into position at the site. Each upper module is three feet longer than the lower unit in order to provide second floor overhang.

(e) The completed unit is dramatic evidence that this approach to "manufactured housing" can meet the challenge of today's housing crisis quickly.

An expandable mobile home opens to provide an additional room. *(Courtesy of Linda Schneider, Brooklyn, N.Y.)*

Fig. 1.5

One will usually have to make compromises between what is desirable and what is possible but weighing all the factors very carefully before making the decisions will certainly bring about more satisfying results.

The prospective homeowner may choose one of the following courses:

1. Buying a house that is already built.
2. Hiring an architect to draw up custom plans.
3. Buying a plan and having a house built.
4. Buying a prefabricated house.

Buying an Old House

There are some advantages to buying a house that already exists, since, of course, it is possible to see what one is purchasing. It is helpful to note the construction, the finishing, and the relationship of the house to the land. One can also see the space relationships and have a clearer picture of how they will meet the needs of the family.

A house that has already been occupied may have certain advantages by way of landscaping, storm windows, screens, and so on. Depending upon the age of the house, cracks from settling or needed repairs are evident. But one should try to find out the real reason the present owner wants to sell. If the house had some disadvantage for the present owner, it may have some for the new owner, too.

One of the reasons for selecting an old house may be the same as for buying antiques: preference for the aesthetic pleasures and the unusual or unique forms of the past. Most homes built before 1940, although subscribing to a general stylistic category, nevertheless have individuality and often have unique features. The charm, the nostalgia, and the association with the past may make such homes attractive to many among today's buyers. The houses may suggest a sense of roots, a feeling of stability, or a slower-paced life style that has come to be associated with earlier times.

In buying an old home, one generally expects that some changes and modifications may be necessary; these will generally be offset by a lower starting price than for a new home. The price of modernizing the utilities and services of the house must, however, be considered. One may frequently find old-fashioned kitchens and bathrooms, a lack of storage cabinets, inadequate wiring, and obsolete heating or cooling systems. Some of the common costs of repairs and improvements can be estimated by an expert before the house is purchased.

One usual advantage of the older house is its spaciousness, often affording 50 per cent more room than a new house for the same money; and allowing for wider choices in redesigning interior spaces. Most of these houses were not constructed in today's familiar box shape, so that there are a variety of interesting spaces to be found. On the other hand, rooms may have high ceilings in addition to their large sizes and thus require additional heating or insulation.

The settling of foundations in many old homes may cause the building to sag. Sagging may be visible in uneven floors and walls. Severely cracked plaster walls and windows may cause a problem, and it should be noted whether the first floor is level. Besides, the walls of older homes—especially those built before 1945—may have little or no insulation. As a principal building material of old homes may be wood, termite damage and wood rot should be checked. Old plumbing, which may be accompanied by poor water pressure, corroded pipes, or bad septic tanks, may have to be looked into. The age of the roof and the condition it is in must also be considered in the purchase price.

One should not assume that most older homes are beset with flaws. Of course, such houses require upkeep or remodeling. But the old home may have had several owners who have made changes and additions and have spent a lifetime of caring for it and investing in its upkeep. It will probably have existing landscaping and sufficient space for making further changes or additions. Many times the owner of a new home is caught almost immediately in a space squeeze and is forced to add or finish areas to increase storage facilities and space requirements.

Old homes generally mean an established neighborhood, one in which the purchaser knows what the area will look like. Trees and grass are already planted. Taxes are more stable. Old roads and sewers will not increase assessments. Existing schools, stores, and recreational facilities are usually near by. It is possible to move in immediately. Houses are less likely to increase in assessed value where schools and utilities already exist.

New Homes

A brand-new house will probably be more up to date in equipment and materials. However, all sorts of flaws may show up when one actually begins to heat it and use the plumbing. Buying from a reliable builder is, of course, essential, but one can almost always expect some unforeseen problems.

One may select a "model" home and have it built with some changes made from the original. This procedure has some advantages in that one can adapt the house to meet specific needs, but the more changes, the more expensive the house will be. "Optional" features on a model house can increase the costs considerably.

A new home is built to accommodate contemporary life styles, which are less formal and less defined than life styles of the past. Some basic qualities are included in the planning of contemporary houses.

"Open planning" allows space to flow from one area of use to another rather than being cut up into separate cubicles by partitions. The practical benefits are numerous; in many new homes, we find a flexibility in personal living, an adaptability to entertaining, an ease of housekeeping, and a simplicity of circulation throughout the house. New homes are increasingly offering a satisfying sense of space and a feeling of openness. Some of the faults of new houses may include a lack of the privacy afforded in old houses, where spaces were separated into cubicles by partitions. Today, houses are designed for the nuclear family and tend to revolve around the family's needs and interests. Rooms are multipurpose in nature, and each room is used extensively for several activities. For example, the same room might be called a game room, a family room, or a recreation room or den. Multipurpose rooms have reduced the size of the house, so that new homes tend to be smaller than older ones. In this respect, they are more efficient, easier to maintain, and less costly.

Frequently certain environmental controls are used in modern multipurpose spaces. Noise control, for example, is accomplished by acoustic ceilings, wall treatments, drapery arrangements, and flooring materials.

A major change has been that the basic machinery of the contemporary house is more efficient. Modern houses have often been compared to automobiles in that they provide for a climate-controlled inner space, well insulated from outside elements, using a variety of sophisticated mechanical devices. The changes in the modern home are most notable in its kitchen and bathroom equipment as well as its recessed channels for heating, air conditioning, and light.

A major concept in contemporary architecture is a feel of the openness of the interior to the outdoors. There is an emphasis on the relationship between the house and the site on which it is built—a relationship made visible by substituting glass in certain areas and introducing opaque walls in others.

In contemporary homes, types of finish and materials are chosen for their natural characteristics and ease of maintenance. The concept of exploring color, texture, and warmth through the materials themselves rather than by means of added or applied details is used extensively in today's homes.

Finally, contemporary architecture has tended to eliminate interior "ornaments," such as moldings, trims, and carvings. There is a new notion of providing a background of simple beauty so that good antiques, modern furniture, and paintings will fit in, no matter how styles or periods are mixed.

These features are generally not found in older homes unless they have been renovated. The new home, therefore, has a wide appeal because of its compatibility with contemporary life styles.

Buying or building a new home. There are at least two choices in acquiring a home: buying an old home or building a custom one. If you buy an existing home, your problem centers upon finding one that suits you in every way: appearance, size, arrangement, location, and price. If you decide on a custom house, your problems lie in organizing your desires concretely so that they may be clearly expressed to the architect or draftsman whom you will hire to work for you.

There are several options when one is buying a new home. One can purchase a home already erected by a commercial builder or real estate developer; one can buy stock plans or specifications and obtain bids from several contractors; one can work with an architect on the design of a home; or one can buy a standardized or prefabricated home after seeing a demonstra-

tion model. Those who are buying an existing house should take several things into consideration. In selecting an existing house, one sees what one is getting, although beneath the surface, of course, it is difficult to judge the quality of the materials and workmanship. The contractor is concerned with the entire building process, such as securing contracts for work and merchandise, observing local building codes, and cost increases in labor and supplies. The contractor alone has to worry about zoning and building permits. The best guarantee of quality is a contractor with a good reputation. Even so, one can protect oneself against hidden faults in the building by paying a fee to an outside expert to examine the house professionally and to render judgment.

The process of building one's own house may be more time-consuming, but individuality, taste, and needs may be reflected in both the exterior and the interior structure. The owner becomes a participant in the entire building process and works closely with the architect in achieving a custom-tailored house—one of a kind. In this case, owner and architect share many of the responsibilities that have been assumed by the builder in an existing home. Property or site must be selected, plans and contract must be negotiated, materials obtained, and a completion date fixed so that the owner can move in within a specified period. Delays caused by the weather often pose a problem.

The custom house. The major reason for having a house custom built is that everyone has slightly different needs and desires, and these can be incorporated into a house specifically designed for its user. Often people have a house custom built because they have been unable to find a home that suits them exactly.

A custom-built house is generally more expensive. Most development houses are designed with only a general knowledge of architecture and with minimal architectural supervision at the construction site. Advances in design that an architect may incorporate into a custom-built house take their time in filtering down to development models. Several statements will illustrate the advantages of the archi-

A custom house in a circular form designed to accommodate the individual pursuits of each family member. Designed by Peter Vanderklaauw. (*Courtesy of Letitia Baldrige Enterprises*)

Fig. 1.6

tect-designed home: "Our architect has a real regard for the way families live in houses"; "Throughout the planning stage, there was much give and take between us that was stimulating"; "The architect was able to design a satisfactory aesthetic environment that is a constant source of aesthetic pleasure, full of wonderful surprises and serenity." According to several owners, their architect "found" or "devised" something that was not expected, such as a sense of space even in a small house or materials that had not been contemplated. Of course, an added feature of a custom-designed home is its uniqueness and unusual beauty. As one owner says, "Everyone comes to see and admire our home."

Using an Architect. It is possible to engage an architect to draw up a custom-made plan. Then either the architect will be responsible for negotiating with a contractor to build the house or will turn over the plans to the prospective owner for the actual execution. Naturally, a custom-designed house is more expensive because more special services are involved. The well-devised plan wastes little space. The architect has ample experience concerning the proper size of rooms, the width of hallways, the spacing of doors and windows. Furniture placement will be considered so that a grand piano will not block a doorway. The sense of good design and

proportion and feeling for color and knowledge of materials and textures of the architect are very likely to exceed those of any amateur or any commercial builder.

Using an architect is important for designing as well as for overseeing work in progress. The architect is an expert in costs and financing; in knowledge of materials and their proper use; in building laws and ways to protect the owner's interests at every stage of building. He or she can help in evaluating a lot, obtaining zoning variances and building permits, and signing the building contract.

A blueprint will help those who are building a home to visualize what the house will look like; because the blueprint is only a plan, corrections are less expensive at this stage. Blueprints may have either white lines on a blue background, or blue lines on a white background. Eight or more sets of prints are usually prepared for the construction of an average house. Various contractors use these sets. The cost of blueprints is usually figured in addition to the architect's fee.

Then, of course, there is the creative plan-

Fig.
1.7

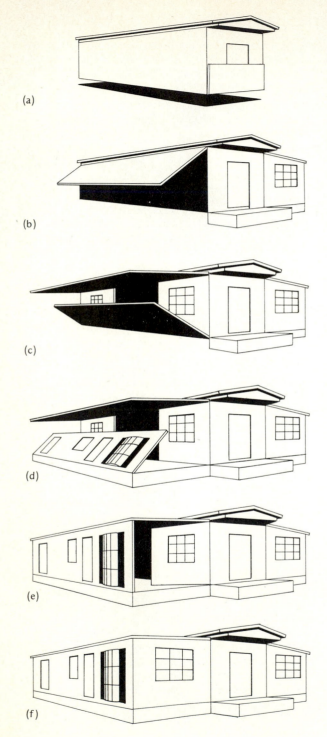

(a)

(b)

(c)

(d)

(e)

(f)

ning and the designing of the house. The difference in "livability" between a plan developed by a good architect and one less expertly conceived by an amateur or a builder is often considerable. Because architect fees are very high today, many families are turning to local draftspeople who are less expensive than architects.

Buying a Plan. Various agencies and organizations offer house plans that one can buy. This approach is cheaper than actually engaging an architect, but it is necessary to engage the builder and rely upon him or her to interpret the plans properly. Keep in mind that it is more expensive to build one house by itself than it is to build a similar house in a development or subdivision in which many similar homes are being built at the same time.

Prefabricated homes and materials. The Home Manufacturers Association, the trade group for the industry, defines a prefabricated house as one whose components have been built in a factory and transported to the site in preassembled parts and sections. One can generally see a sample or a demonstration model and then order another house like it to be erected on one's own land. The house usually consists of exterior walls with windows and doors already installed, roof and floor systems, interior partitions, and exterior siding. Kitchen cabinets, appliances, heating, and plumbing are usually in place. Although the degree of factory "fabrication" varies by manufacturer, the trend is toward more complete house packages, often containing everything except the foundation to eliminate costly on-site labor. Each house is brought to the site on trailers for installation. Prefab houses sitting on a site are difficult to distinguish from conventionally built homes.

A prefabricated house can be purchased and assembled on the site chosen. Housing units purchased this way would seem to be the answer to the high costs of construction; indeed,

Prefabricated homes precision engineered to expand into perfect alignment. *(Courtesy of Guerdon Industries)*

the industry has developed to a point where preconstructed houses are no longer limited to the low-cost economy brackets. They are now acceptable in many areas that would previously approve of homes only in the "luxury" class. There is quite a wide range of types at different cost levels.

Although preconstructed homes may offer an answer to the high costs of building, haulage rates are also high. For the sake of efficiency, the actual manufacturing of the units must take place in a central plant. When the parts are transported for any great distance, the shipping costs mount and sometimes overcome the economic advantages of this method of construction.

A prefabricated house has several advantages. There is a large variety of choice of models, many having been designed by skilled architects. Changes and variations in size, color, style, and type of materials can be made at a fixed rate. The quality of construction is precision-engineered in the factory so that there is less chance of component parts not fitting together well. The manufacturer's bulk purchases of materials reduce the cost of items and assemblage so that the over-all cost of a prefabricated home can be lower than that of houses built on the site.

Another advantage is that after the lot has been staked and the foundation prepared, a packaged house can be installed in a very short period of time.

Financing, however, is more difficult to obtain; because of the poor quality of materials sometimes used in the construction of factory houses, they are often considered a risk.

The development house. Housing developments (in certain areas called *subdivisions* or *track housing*) have become a trend in America. At present, three out of four new houses being built are development houses. In a housing development, a large number of houses are built by the developer according to a master plan. Most features are identical, although the builder may allow for some individuality through variation. Exterior details, including color, awnings, woods, and landscaping, may be some of the features that can be selected by the homeowner. A house is bought or contracted for after the purchaser has examined a model. The lot or the exact house can be examined during or after building. Sometimes an entire community is organized, with such elements as social clubs, new schools, and swimming pools. It may cater to a special interest group. Many communities exclude thru traffic, to assure greater privacy, so that there is some control over the environment. Another feature is that an entire neighborhood can be created to cater to the special needs of the people who will live there.

Several considerations enter into this type of purchase. When examining the "model," one has to realize that it has been furnished by professional decorators who know how to proportion furniture to each room to make the space look larger than it is.

The model will be beautifully landscaped and wallpapered; the house will be loaded with appliances. It must be ascertained which of these features are included in the price of the home. Complete specifications should be written into the contract, to include landscaping, type and amount of insulation, wiring, type of equipment, heating, waterproofing, termite inspection, and appliances. The total sales price of all these features should be specified in the contract.

The site should be checked in advance to determine the size of the terrain and its orientation, and the buyer should find out whether local zoning allows for additions of space if they should become necessary. A final inspection of the house should be made before closing. The completion of all unfinished work should be guaranteed.

The condominium. In certain areas, the condominium is another increasingly popular form of ownership. This type of property fosters a sense of community by the joint ownership of houses.

The individual owns a dwelling unit as well as sharing in the property and facilities held jointly with other owners. The National Housing Act of 1961 (Section 234) authorized the Federal Housing Administration (FHA) to in-

Fig. 1.8 Identical development homes with variations in land-scaping. *(Courtesy of Linda Schneider, Brooklyn, N.Y.)*

sure finances to individual condominium buyers. Condominium ownership is possible for owners of mobile homes, town houses, and single-family dwellings as well as apartments.[4]

Condominium ownership provides an alternative to owning a house and still ensures a sense of pride in ownership. The time and work of having a house built are eliminated. There is group concern over maintenance and management, including landscaping, exterior maintenance, and the upkeep of communal areas as well as facilities that have been paid for by each owner. The individual apartment is the concern of its owner with respect to upkeep and the buying or selling of the unit. In this respect, if one owner defaults, his or her liability does not affect other owners of the condominium.

As in cooperatives, the down payment for the condominium is thought to be a "forced savings" that constitutes a hedge against inflation. All repairs and improvements are tax deductions.

The disadvantage of a condominium is that one is subject to group decisions regarding common property. The individual's interest may not be reflected when group decisions are made about level of upkeep, operation budget, or assessment.[5] Areas of possible disagreement may include issues like the enforcement of clauses such as "no pets allowed" or "for adults only."

Cooperatives. Another option in apartment-house living that has become popular is cooperative ownership. The family becomes a stockholder or member in a nonprofit corporation. Owning a cooperative apartment has many advantages: each owner is concerned with improvements and repairs on an individual apartment as well as the surrounding space that is shared by all tenants. All members, therefore, feel responsible for controlling their own (internal) as well as the immediate (external) environment.

As in a condominium, the initial down payment required for membership in a cooperative

[4] Stephen G. Johnson, "A Second Generation of Condominium Statutes," *Urban Land*, Dec. 1974, pp. 10–13.

[5] James N. Karr, *The Condominium Buyers Guide* (New York: Frederick Fell Publications, 1973).

is thought by many people to represent forced savings. Tax benefits are shared by all tenants when repairs and improvements are made.

Disadvantages to ownership result from the fact that cooperative housing is financed by a single loan to a corporation rather than directly to individual homeowners. Because each tenant is jointly liable, each can be assessed a proportion of another stockholder's share of tax, insurance, utility, management, and maintenance charges in the event of another tenant's defaulting on payments. Before a dwelling can be sold, therefore, the transaction must be approved by all members of the cooperative. All improvements or changes in each apartment are restricted according to the bylaws of the cooperative dwelling.

The townhouse. Townhouses are single houses with individual entrances and private back yards. Units are grouped together and are generally part of a larger development. Developments generally provide recreation areas for communal use. As a large area of land can be planned at one time, land space can be maximized for efficient use. Generally a large developer is able to create a new community, to completely manage an entire area in a single project. Unfortunately, too often look-alike housing laid out in row upon row is reinforced in its sameness by its placement on grid pattern streets. Some new developers are challenging this monotony of design by building townhouses with more flexibility in the appearance of individual units including different types of housing (mixing an apartment house with a townhouse), and varying street arrangements.

The advantage of owning a townhouse is that it has communal recreation spaces generally maintained by the developer. The townhouse concept is part of a contemporary effort to create total environments. One buys not only a house but a community, both of which need to be efficient as well as beautiful. These new environments attempt to provide for a wide range of human activities, to insure well-organized shopping, education, and transportation. At their best, townhouse communities can preserve stately trees, streams, and open spaces and are

distinct, managably-sized entities with their own flavor.

The disadvantages of townhouses include living very closely with other owners, lack of privacy, and limitations on individual choice in life styles. Many townhouse communities lack the vital mixture gained from a variety of housing and the merger of the old and the new. The new community's modern schools and well-paved and landscaped roadways are not always integrated with older, surrounding areas. The townhouse community lacks the interest of aging museums or even of pawnshops or used car lots.

The house trailer. The trailer represents one type of mobile home that has several advantages.

Trailers are comparatively inexpensive and can easily be bought and resold; the buyer knows exactly what he or she is getting and at what price; they are compact and easy to maintain and often come fully equipped; they can follow the family wherever it goes; they have the glamour of newness. The advantages are substantial enough so that trailers are used even when they must be transported by flatcars or large trucks or have to be fixed in place permanently.

But trailers raise some difficult functional problems. Foremost among these is the need for privacy and usable outdoor space: trailers are often small in size. Another point that should be considered is the very sense of mobility that attracts purchasers. Even when the unit is fixed in place for a substantial period of time, there may still be a sense of impermanence. Real or fancied, this "transient" feeling can create many serious community problems in connection with taxation, social relationships, service, and participation.

Shell houses. Shell houses are low-cost, unfinished structures for people who are able to do their own finishing. Windows, doors, exterior walls, and rough flooring are usually complete. The interior is bare except for partitions and roof. All heating, lighting, insulation, cabinets, and equipment have to be bought and installed.

The shell is erected on the buyer's own property. Generally little or no down payment is required. Craftsmanship is not difficult to determine because there is little or no built-in construction. These homes are generally designed for sale in rural areas where there are no minimum building code specifications, and the buyer has to determine whether the house is worth the money being paid for its purchase.

Choosing the Location

Whether one buys or rents a home, the community in which one settles will influence the pattern of living. There will probably be a closer association between one's family and the community if property is owned rather than rented. In either case, the neighbors, the atmosphere, and the spirit of the area will have a direct bearing on whether or not one will be happy in a location. Each town or community has a particular personality, which may be extremely impersonal or extremely group-minded. Those who prefer seclusion may find it difficult to avoid the community spirit. If, on the other hand, one enjoys group activities, a community that has little group-mindedness will be dull and unrewarding.

Beyond the spirit of the community, there are several other practical features that should be evaluated. The general appearance, the accessibility of schools, churches, and shops, and the noise and fumes from factories or other commercial establishments must all be considered. Is public transportation readily available, or must one depend on a car? Are the services that provide electricity, gas, water, and refuse disposal dependable, and what are the costs? Who is responsible for the roads in winter? A community that looks like sheer delight in the summer may be a real problem in the winter if snow plows do not open the roads. Is there a public sewerage system, or must one depend on septic tanks or cesspools? Are there sidewalks, and if not, will they be installed at some future date? Any of these improvements will affect present or future tax rates. Zoning regulations with regard to businesses that may or may not develop in the area should be of concern to the prospective homeowner, because such regulations will affect property values.

Space Between Buildings

Legally speaking, subdivision is the process of dividing land into lots, entailing public rights of way, and providing sites for future individual buildings. Roads, paths, utilities, public facilities, and the shape and position of lots are taken into account. The spaces between buildings should include areas for parking, play, sitting, and disposal facilities. Whether it be private housing or low-cost public housing, a private yard for the ground-floor units may often be included. Tall buildings may provide private balconies, which to some extent serve as substitutes for private yards.

The space between buildings has an important effect on its inhabitants. If structures are too close, noise resonates within. Every room should have adequate light and air; a substantial piece of sky should be visible through a window from a normal standing position in the room. Even where this rule is observed, it may be unpleasant to look directly into opposite windows that are so close as to destroy visual or acoustic privacy. Therefore it is well to avoid any layout in which windows that face one another are closer than 75 feet. It is equally desirable, for visual relief, for at least a few windows in a house to command a long, free view.

Climate

Each site has a general climate that it shares with the surrounding region. The climate is expressed in a set of average data for the region, including ranges of temperature and humidity, precipitation, wind direction and force, and solar angle. This information is broken down according to the major seasons of the year and has a basic influence on the orientation of structures, their being shielded from or exposed to the sun, equipment for cooling and heating, and building materials. In addition, the typical condition of light will have a profound effect on the visual pattern. If human beings are to be comfortable, certain basic ranges of daylight, temperature, and humidity are necessary.

The climate of an area plays an important role in the selection of a home. The general weather pattern affects the structure of the house. For example, if a house is situated in a valley, cellar dampness and humidity may pose a problem when rain gathers from surrounding mountains, so that adequate drainage against water seepage is necessary. A house situated on a mountain might encounter strong winds. In this instance, protection could include trees, fences, or other landscape solutions. Exposure to the sun might result in a light, sunny apartment. The careful orientation of a house on its site and the proper location of windows can admit sun to rooms at the time of day when it is most desired.

Stylistic Traditions

People who are interested in purchasing and perhaps remodeling an older home should be aware of the existence of different styles. The majority of homes built today do not, as a rule, cling to traditional styles of architecture, although any home may interpret the "flavor" of some particular style. Except for houses in the luxury class, where costs are not a primary factor, the expense of duplicating many of the older and more familiar architectural styles is prohibitive. Besides, newer concepts of form and function in small homes have made it more desirable to adapt only certain styles of architecture and to develop new ones that are more suitable to modern building methods and materials. Thus, current home building includes various designs that are inspired by traditional styles but that make no attempt to copy them in an authentic fashion. This approach to house design has given rise to numerous hybrid styles that almost defy classification. It has become the custom, therefore, to refer to the style of a house in several different ways. The architect or the builder may give it a name suggestive of its origin or may merely designate it by a number.

The Colonial Period: 1661 to 1775

In North America, the available materials and the geographic location had a decisive impact on colonial architecture. The first settlers brought with them the knowledge, skills, and tastes of their national backgrounds. Most of the structures were medieval in form, resembling the styles used in Flanders and Holland during the late Middle Ages. Because of the settlers' knowledge and their lack of funds, tools, and time, the buildings had a natural, rough look. These homes were built of wood, brick, or stone; often all three materials were used in the same house. The brick work had a pattern of varicolored pieces. Along the edges the bricks were laid in a mouse-tooth finish. Frequently the roofs were steep, single-pitch, and A-shaped, with end chimneys. The gables were either stepped or straight-line, but always outstanding. Tile roofs predominated in the towns, thatched roofs in the country. Later double-pitch gambrel roofs were used, with or without spring eaves. The stone houses were built with local stones and lime mortar mixed with shells, laid in random widths. Clapboards were used to cover the materials, such as local clay and straw, or mud and oyster-shell lime—substances that would not hold up under inclement weather conditions. A house often grew with the family's needs. An addition would be built in the taste and style of the respective period. Dutch and French windows between 1680 to 1700 were of the casement type and opened inward (English casement windows opened outward). Many times, under the spring eave a stoop was built, generally accessible by one or more steps. Side railings were used, with benches placed alongside them for family use.

The Classical Revival

Georgian Colonial: 1700 to 1780. Georgian architecture was inspired by renewed interest in classical culture and the Renaissance. The Georgian style used Roman forms but expressed these forms in new ways and in novel combinations. Because America, at that time, had few architects, the new design was an outgrowth of the owners' and the carpenters' interpretation of classical forms. The materials used were mostly wood and brick. The brickmakers became so proficient that they even made molded brick, which was used in water tables, chimney caps,

Fig. 1.9

Vernacular

1661 to 1700
Medieval

1561 to 1775 Dutch Colonial (Gambrel, Stoep, Spring Eave)

Mouse-tooth
Dutch Gables

New England
Gambrel Roof

1661 to 1775
Dutch
Colonial
(Gable)

1661
to 1775
Eliza-
bethan-
English
Colonial

Dutch Gambrel
Roof
(Spring Eave)

Swedish
Gambrel Roof

Classical Revival

Doric   Ionic   Corin-   Tuscan   Doric Ionic   Corin- Com-
         (Greek) thian   (Roman) thian   posite

Georgian Door Styles

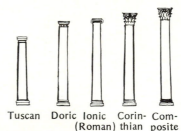

1700 to 1780
Georgian Colonial

1810 to 1855
Gothic Revival

1760 to 1810
Adam or Federal

1800 to 1840
Greek Revival

1760 to 1820 Federal
(Farmhouse)

1840 to 1870
Romanesque Revival

Planning a Home

Victorian Period

Chronological chart of architectural styles. (*Courtesy of Dianna Gabay, Staten Island, N.Y.*)

1835 to 1875
Italian Villa

1853 to 1890
Victorian Italianate

1854 to 1880
Victorian Stick Style

1860 to 1885
French Second Empire

1855 to 1890
Victorian Gothic

1874 to 1890
Queen Anne

1880 to 1895
Shingle Style

Contemporary

1900 to Present
Designer's Unique Style
(Frank Lloyd Wright–1957)

1920 to 1950
Cape Cod

1960 to Present
Matchbox Modern Style
(One or Two Family)

1960 to Present
Matchbox Modern Style
(Duplex)

Space for Living

doorway trim, or belt courses. Wood was used where intricate carved moldings and details were needed to enhance the new classic appearances. Frequently a coat of plaster or stucco was applied over the exterior brick and stone. The Georgian style resulted in well-built structures, planned in regular geometric symmetry. The front door showed a major change from the colonial door, with relief columns on both sides of the entrance, and pediments or classical entablatures at the top of the door. Sliding-sash windows were a new feature; they were framed by an architrave and sometimes topped by a pediment or cornice. Water-table molding brick was used to mark the top of the basement level. A belt course was placed between floor levels to mark the level of the floor joists. Roofs were either hipped or featured the low-pitched classic pediment shape; but in this period of transition, some of the colonial roof styles remained, such as the gable and the gambrel. The eaves were frequently decorated by classical cornices, such as dentils or other moldings. When the peak of the roof was flattened, it was topped by a baluster or railing.

Greek Revival: 1800 to 1840. The Greek Revival represented a rebirth of the traditional Greek temple. Buildings were mainly rectangular in shape, with Doric, Ionic, or Corinthian columns supporting a portico, which either went around the building or was confined to just the front. Sometimes the front of the building had a pediment over the portico. Most roof slopes were pitched low or were almost flat. Doors and windows were less decorative. Plain or dentil cornice designs at the base of the roof could be seen. The construction was of smooth brick or smooth clapboard. As might be expected from the name, columns are the outstanding feature of the Greek Revival.

The Adam or Federal style: 1760 to 1820. The Adam period was inspired by the Georgian Colonial style. Symmetrical, rectangular in form, and abounding in geometrical ornaments, the style is more delicate and light in appearance than Georgian Colonial. The doors were outstanding; they were flanked by slender columns or glass windows or both, with semielliptical leaded-glass transoms. A semicircular porch, supported by slender delicate columns, may appear over the door. Windows may be semicircular at the top with very fine leading; some small, semicircular, recessed windows may have scalloped leading. The roof was normally unobtrusive, sometimes concealed by a balustrade or decorative cornice. Brick was set in the Flemish bond. Some of the houses were still sided by clapboard. The Federal farmhouse style was simpler yet. Most farmhouses may have only one or two features of the Adam style. In both styles, the house was flanked by two end chimneys.

The Gothic Revival

Early Gothic: 1810 to 1855; Late Gothic: 1895 to 1912. Two periods characterize the Gothic Revival; one, the Early Gothic Revival, was popular around the early 1800s. The other style is called the Late Gothic Revival. This period was a rebirth of the earlier revival, blooming around the late 1800s. The differences between the two are characterized by several details.

The Early Gothic Revival had the typical Gothic pointed-arched windows and doors, clover-leaf carvings, dormers with tracery windows, gables, and buttresses with finials; Early Gothic favored the use of crenellations (battlements). All of these forms were borrowed from the medieval style but were applied in a new fashion. Wood, brick, or stone could be used; the wooden bargeboard was often ornamented in the gingerbread pattern. All of these materials were used in either similar shades of the same color, to give the building a monochromatic effect.

The Late Gothic Revival resembled the Early Gothic in the use of pointed-arched windows and doors, clover-leaf carvings, tracery windows, buttresses with finials, and battlements. The major difference was the superior craftsmanship in the use of masonry and stone, with more varied, detailed moldings. The Gothic detail was often of terra-cotta, especially in commercial buildings. (In the Early Gothic Revival homes often had the Gothic details as shown in the drawing.)

Romanesque Revival: 1840 to 1870. More subdued than the Gothic Revival, the Romanesque style predominated in utilitarian or commercial structures. The primary features are the use of rounded-arched windows and doors that had rounded arches around them. Corbel designs are used in an arcade effect around the gables. The wall surfaces are mainly wide areas of unbroken masonry, brick, or stone, giving the building a very simple, yet refined, look.

The Victorian Period

Italian Villa style: 1835 to 1875. The buildings of the Italian Villa style are well-defined rectangular or square blocks, grouped with symmetrical elevation of the individual units. Often there is a square or octagonal glazed cupola or tower somewhere on the structure. Windows may be round-headed or rectangular, often grouped in twos or threes. The roofs are slightly pitched, with very attractive eaves, which are frequently corniced and usually supported by brackets. Most such houses have a veranda or a balustraded balcony. Walls are often brick with a facing of sandstone, but the outside walls may also be of clapboard.

Victorian Italianate: 1853 to 1890. The Italianate style is mainly recognizable by a busy network of accented windows in rows. Each level of the building is divided by an overhanging molding on which the windows rest, giving the style its characteristic vertical look. The windows on each floor are uniform, with outstanding moldings or columns, always topped by an arch that may be rounded, rectangular, flat-topped with rounded sides, or stilted and segmental. On each level the windows are somewhat different from those on other levels, lending variety to the building. The Victorian Italianate windows have a busy, shadow-box aspect.

Victorian Stick style: 1854 to 1880. The diagonal stickwork of some Victorian buildings may have an overlay of other boards, vertically or horizontally, to symbolize the structural frame. The overhanging gables are accented by jigsaw curtain work, large brackets, or exposed frame work, any of which casts a rich shadow on the plain, recessed wall. The main purpose is to show off the wooden structure and its bracing members, as a form of structural "truthfulness."

In some areas, such as New York, the Stick style buildings are hard to find, because they have had their outside structures covered up with another form of siding.

French Second Empire: 1860 to 1885. One can spot Second Empire buildings by the high mansard roof, with the visible curb molding above and below, and the many ornate, characteristic dormers. These conspicuous dormers may take many forms or shapes, including oval or circular. The appearance of the lower level accentuates the mansard roof. Most Second Empire buildings are tall and sturdy looking.

Victorian Gothic: 1855 to 1890. Heavy, thick moldings, chimneys, and carved ornaments with as many different facets as possible give Victorian Gothic buildings an ornate and massive look. Towers, balconies, and ironwork are used at the roof level, often with a topheavy effect. Windows are mostly pointed Gothic, set back from all of the very busy outer wall work.

Queen Anne revival: 1874 to 1890. Queen Anne buildings may look like layered, iced wedding cakes, with many different building materials used on the walls. The chimneys are treated appropriately to give them the sculptured, molded-brick look. Round or polygonal turrets may be another interesting feature. The Queen Anne style presented many high roofs, meeting at right angles or at the turret. It is a combination of many periods, forming a potpourri. The windows' upper parts are treated with colored glass or molded into little squares.

Shingle style: 1880 to 1895. Derived from the Queen Anne trend, the Shingle style's outstanding feature is the use of the shingle on the roof and walls, to give them a uniform color and texture. The gambrel, hipped, or gable roof is seen quite frequently. As the name indicates, shingles may be used on such buildings almost anywhere.

Space for Living

Designer's personalized style: 1900 to the present. Constructed with the same materials used in the Matchbox Modern style, the outstanding feature of personalized houses is that they are built with design in mind, or to express the likes of the affluent individual owners or their architects. Most of the better-designed buildings in this category are not of any revival style, yet they are unusual in design.

Today's architects are trying to understand the spatial problems of a building and to create buildings without using any old styles or schools of thought. New types of material are now available that were not known in past centuries. These materials allow for an approach that is much more daring and risky—and is capable of achieving surprising results. Architects of today tend to think of a building not as an isolated structure but as part of the surrounding area.

Cape Cod style: 1920 to 1950. Cape Cods are very practical buildings. All of them have A-type frame roofs, which house the attic. Cape Cod houses were built with expansion in mind. Most people would purchase them with only the first floor finished; later, when the owners' needs demanded, they would finish the attic area. The outstanding feature of these buildings is windows with six-over-six panes. The house has a simple, compact look. The front can be broadside or gable. The siding materials used are clapboard, shingle, or brick.

Matchbox Modern style: 1960 to present. The Matchbox Modern style is a combination of various current forms; it is also the style that is at present used in many new communities throughout the country. Its basic feature, and the source of its name, is the box form, constructed of new materials, and sidings, with asphalt roofs. These buildings are erected with the idea of utilitarian use, economically constructed for the middle-class owner. All are box-shaped or else resemble two boxes put together. The building fronts have varied textures or balconies put on to decorate the facade. Most of these buildings are constructed by a contract

builder, so that an area may have 25 or more of the same sort of homes. Areas may feature what is called the duplex or townhouse. In areas of the country that are already heavily populated, few unattached homes are being built; if they are, they are two-family units. The package includes ready-to-use windows, doors, siding materials, and decorative ornaments. The siding can be brick veneer, asphalt or wood shingles, aluminum, cedar shake, or stone veneer, placed over plywood.

One-story or ranch type. Although we have come to refer to the one-story house as a ranch-type home, the wide variety of styles often bear little, if any, resemblance to an actual ranch house. Colonial, Oriental, Spanish, and modern styles of architecture have all been interpreted in the single-story home.

Even in a fairly small home, the exterior of the one-story design presents broad, low lines that have popular appeal. However, a ranch house requires a sufficient amount of ground to show it off to best advantage; it is not usually attractive when built on a small lot.

Split-level. A popular style that has developed in recent years has part of the house on the ground floor and the other parts on two or more other levels. There have been many interpretations of the split-level form, including some that are very poorly planned. However, when the house is well designed, the arrangement offers the practical advantages of conserving land and building expenses.

Although the split-level house would seem to be the answer to many problems, it can present problems of its own. The need to climb any steps at all may be a disadvantage in some situations. Also, it is a difficult house to design and to build. Usually, a split-level home looks more attractive on sloping terrain than on flat ground. The exterior proportions may have a chopped-up appearance, especially in small homes built on too little ground.

Two-story. For the economical use of ground and building materials, the house that is built up rather than spread out offers the most advantages. This form lends itself to a wide variety of treatments, ranging from basic economy models to luxurious formal dwellings.

Some of the low-cost houses make use of one-and-one-half-story arrangements, with the upper floor frequently unfinished. The lower floor provides a complete home, and the space in the upper story is available when the owner is ready to finish it.

Architects and builders should stress the importance of relating the style of the house to the site upon which it will be built. The building and the surrounding terrain should enhance and complement each other. Outdoor living areas have become as important as the indoor living space. Although we need and want the enclosure offered by the walls of the house, we like the spirit and atmosphere of the interior flowing to the outside. The surrounding areas that will include terraces, patios, and swimming pools must, therefore, look like a continuation of the house and not just an afterthought.

The materials used to build the house are an integral part of the design. Texture and color must be chosen and arranged to enhance rather than detract from the basic lines. The general spirit or expressiveness of the house is also dependent on the actual substance in relation to the over-all design. Wood, stone, metal, and glass are commonly used. In the future, plastics will probably play an important role.

All houses combine materials in one way or another, and there is a wide variety from which to choose. Just as in any form of art, the success of the design depends on sensitivity in selecting the medium. In housing design, a common mistake is to use too many different materials. Restraint and good taste in this respect separate the good from the mediocre.

The design of a house must be considered in relation to the neighborhood as well as its immediate vicinity. A huge formal mansion would certainly be out of place in a development of low-cost economy homes. A truly modern home looks incongruous when nestled in the peaceful hills of a sleepy country village. Yet does this mean we must be stereotyped in housing design? Not at all. It simply means that experiments with prototypes of future homes are more

Split-level house. (Courtesy of Linda Schneider, Brooklyn, N.Y.)

Fig. 1.10

successful and more interesting if they are isolated enough to be judged on their own merits. We look at any house in relation to its surroundings as well as in terms of its purpose. A house that is exaggerated or completely different may become a sore thumb rather than a pacesetter in spite of all its advantages. A house plan that recognizes the importance of the setting may incorporate many new ideas and innovations without becoming an architectural outcast in the community.

How to Read a Blueprint

Anyone who plans to buy or build a home should learn something about blueprints and about how space is represented on a small sheet of paper.

A blueprint is a photographic reproduction of an original drawing of a floor plan, illustrating the layout of rooms from a bird's-eye view. Floor plans have two dimensions, length and width, giving no indication about the height of the rooms. Perspective drawings—illustrations of a room or a house viewed from a particular point of reference—often accompany floor plans and help to give a three-dimensional impression

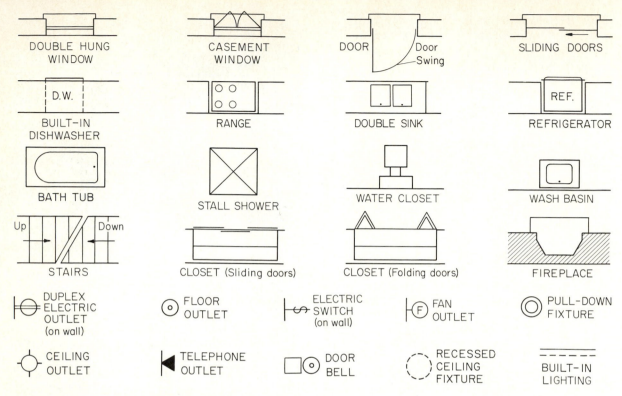

Fig. 1.11 Architectural symbols are useful in understanding floor plans.

of what the room or house will look like. Electrical, mechanical, and plumbing plans are also included.

As a "map" of a house, a blueprint will reveal many things, but until one learns to interpret the plans in terms of *actual* space, they have little meaning. For example, consider a floor plan that includes a bedroom 10' 0" × 10' 0". Is it large or small? One should measure some of one's present rooms, then take a ruler and a plain sheet of paper and draw a scale plan of rooms that one really knows. One-quarter inch on the ruler should equal one foot of the actual measurements. At first, only an outline should be drawn, without any indication of doors, windows, and so on.

Now it is possible to see familiar living quarters represented, after a fashion, in a plan. Next, doors, windows, closets, radiators, juts in the

walls, and electrical outlets should be placed. Figure 1.11 shows some of the symbols used in architectural plans. The space where the doors, windows, stairways, and electrical outlets are placed influences the way a home will function, so it pays to understand and interpret floor plans.

A primary concern in evaluating a floor plan should be the total amount of space, the number of rooms, and the size of each. All these factors should be evaluated in terms of usefulness and costs. The plan should also point up the features of the functionalism of the house. The following points should be checked:

1. Does one have to go through any room to get to another?
2. Is there an entrance from the garage or parking area that facilitates unloading the car and bringing supplies into the kitchen?
3. Is there a closet near the main entrance where guests may deposit coats and hats?

4. Is the wall space in each room flexible for furniture arrangement, or is it broken up by windows and doors that limit the placement of larger pieces?
5. Is there sufficient space to entertain guests for meals or overnight?
6. Is there a utility area that can serve as a laundry, a workroom, and so on?
7. Is there sufficient storage space for both indoor and outdoor needs?
8. If living space is to be added in the future, how can the plan be adapted? Is it feasible to add another room? Can the attic or basement be converted to more useful space?

The House Itself

There are many features one should consider very carefully before buying a new house. The appearance of the house and whether or not it will meet the needs of the new owner are, of course, important. In addition, it pays to seek the unbiased opinions of people who are qualified to judge construction. The advice of reliable appraisers, real estate agents, contractors, architects, and building inspectors may cost money, but their training and experience in the technical aspects of construction can be of inestimable value to the average person.

Evaluating a House Plan

A house has to *work* for you. It should be designed for efficient and convenient living, working, sleeping, playing, entertaining, and just plain relaxing. People should be able to work or play in it without disturbing others who are involved in different activities.

A house should also be cheerful, with plenty of light and a feeling of openness; it should be warm in winter and cool in summer; it should be designed for good living, with privacy and without built-in noise, frustration, or inconvenience. Although today's designs emphasize openness in planning, the individual needs of the people occupying the space should be satisfied. Some people, for example, may not want an open environment.

A house should have a good floor plan and room arrangement. Each room should be designed well for its particular purpose. The house should be located properly on its lot and turned properly in relation to the sun so that it will be warmer and easier to heat in winter, which can mean fuelbill savings; most rooms will be bright with sunshine; and there will be a minimum of condensation on windows. In summer the same house can be 5 to 10 degrees cooler than a house not properly located and receive the benefit from cooling breezes. In general, the kitchen, dining room, and family room should face south so that natural light will flow in.

Areas

Good houses have three main zones: living, sleeping, and working. Each zone should be clearly separate, yet properly related to the others, the street, the sun, and the outdoors.

Are the bedrooms separated from the noise of work and play? Can you entertain guests without waking the children? A buffer zone, not just a partition, is needed between bedrooms and the rest of the house. Such a zone can be a hall, a bathroom, or ingeniously placed closets. Can unwashed laundry be stored without being visible to a chance visitor? Much depends on the internal "zoning"—a term not to be confused with the legal requirements of the same name, which specify the permissible use, size, and so forth of structures in various neighborhoods.

The two-story house is a good example of natural zoning between the second-floor bedrooms and the kitchen and living areas on the first floor. Even better might be a house laid out like an **H** where the living and sleeping areas, at opposite ends of the house, are neatly connected down the middle by the kitchen and the utility work zone; yet all are on one level.

How can one recognize a good floor plan? The main routes in a house, the ones used over and over again, are the key:

1. Does the family entrance lead directly from the garage or the driveway to the kitchen? This is highly important. The main entrance for a family is usually through the kitchen. The garage and driveway should be near the kitchen for quick entry and swift grocery

unloading. The garage-to-kitchen route should be sheltered from rain.

2. Is the kitchen centrally located? This, too, is crucial. From the kitchen, a person should have control over the entire house. The kitchen area should be near the front door and the family entrance. It is also important to be able to watch children playing outside and to be near the dining room, the living room, and the outside patio. The kitchen should be a command post.

3. Does the front door (the main entrance) lead directly to the center of the house? Guests enter here. A center hall or foyer will help greatly. It will shield people inside from casual visitors and protect them from the inrush of wind, snow, and rain. The main entrance should be close to the driveway and the street. A guest closet for coats near the front door is essential.

4. Is the living room shielded from cross traffic? It should not be a main highway for people going in and out of the house. It should be a "dead end," so that it is possible to read, talk, watch television, or entertain guests without people running through every few minutes.

5. Is there good room-to-room circulation? Can you go from any room to any other room without passing through a third room (possibly except the dining room)? Can one get from any entrance to any room without walking through a third room? One bathroom in particular should be accessible from any room (usually through a hall) and should not require passage through another room. It is also necessary to avoid bedrooms in series, which require going through one to reach another.

6. Is there a good indoor–outdoor relationship? Is it easy to reach the patio, terrace, or outdoor play area from the house? Such access normally calls for a door to the outdoors in or near the living room to avoid walking through the kitchen, which is likely to be cluttered, especially when one is entertaining. A desirable feature is to have a door to the patio or terrace near the kitchen, as people often barbecue and eat out of doors.

The Structure of a House

There are certain things that anyone can observe about the construction of a house, but by and large it takes a trained eye to judge hidden aspects. For example, it is easy to see whether or not the house seems to be run down and badly in need of repair. In an old house, peeling paint, cracked masonry, and sagging beams all indicate needed repair work. A more experienced eye is usually needed to evaluate other features.

A person buying a house should have some knowledge of the elements of the house's structure and some idea about what good construction may involve. We shall describe a general structure for a two-story frame building with a basement and an attic; there are homes that use different construction methods, and variations of this design are rather common.

Foundation. A home in the process of construction has its dimensions staked out on the property, the earth excavated, and a "footing" poured. A footing is the continuous concrete stand or base of the house. Its overall dimensions vary according to the building code of the area. Footings are also designed to serve as the bases for the columns that support the floors. There are variations in the size and type of footings, depending upon the condition of the ground and the weight of the house. In cold climates, the footings go below the frost line to be protected in winter.

Drain tiles. Drain tiles are frequently placed around the footing and in some cases around the concrete floor area to reduce the chance of water flow and damage. The tiles drain into soft soil and are sufficiently sloped so that water can drain away quickly from the protected area.

Foundation wall. Generally the foundation wall is poured concrete about 10" to 12" thick. It usually starts at the top of the footing and ends at the beginning of the house frame or sill. Concrete blocks are sometimes used for this purpose. Foundation walls usually extend above the earth to protect the frame of the house from moisture. A basement, or a crawl space that is large enough for routine maintenance, may be used as the house's foundation.

The sill. The sill, a continuous length of wood that varies in size according to the overall dimension of the structure, serves as a base on which to build wooden walls and floors. The sill is anchored on the concrete foundation by steel bolts, which are sunk into the concrete with their threaded ends up. The steel-bolted sill holds the wood frame that is to be constructed on top of it. Concrete blocks loosely assembled with mortar are sometimes used, but they do not hold the steel bolts as well as a poured single-section wall.

Waterproofing. Special material is often applied to the outer surface of the concrete foundation down to and below the house footing to prevent moisture from seeping through the concrete. In the case of concrete blocks, a coat of cement plaster is put on before the waterproofing compound.

Termite guards. A guard should be installed against wood-eating insects that travel from the moist soil to the wood. Termites avoid being exposed to air, so if they cannot reach the wood, they build mud tubes to travel into the wood. Projecting copper guards may be placed just below the wood sill, extending beyond it, so that termites cannot build a wall around the projecting area. Generally, no wooden parts of a building should touch the ground.

Floor slabs. The basement floor consists generally of four or more inches of concrete poured on well-compacted earth. Reinforcement by means of steel mesh is put into the concrete while it is being poured.

First floor. The first floor consists of a floor frame that supports the flooring. Within the frame itself are wood sections called joists, usually spaced 16″ apart, attached to the sill. A subfloor or rough flooring, made of plywood nailed to the joists, is put above this frame. Materials such as hardwood, softwood, vinyl, or ceramic tiles may be used to finish the floor.

Wall framing. The wall framing acts as a support for the ceiling, the upper floors, and the roof and serves as a nailing base for wall finishes. Wall frames consist of vertical studs and horizontal plates and headers (spacing) for doors and windows. Studs are vertical pieces of 2″ × 44″ wood, normally spaced 16″ apart. The studs rest on the sill. Horizontal pieces of wood are nailed across the tops of the studs in order to keep them in a straight line.

Ceiling and roof. Ceiling joists spaced 16″ apart are used both as supports for ceiling finishes and as floor joists for attic floors. In addition, they hold together the roof frame. The ridge is another roof piece that spans to the roof's peak, making it easier for the builder to construct a roof.

Exterior walls. Many people would prefer heavy masonry walls like brick or stone, but these materials are not only expensive to buy and install, but in some respects, they are also less advantageous and require more upkeep than many people realize.

Wood, masonite, and asbestos have become popular alternatives to brick or stone. New long-life exterior paints have been developed that last on wood 50 to 100 per cent longer in low-humidity areas than oil-base paints and reduce the need for frequently repainting. Various new kinds of nonmasonry wall materials, such as aluminum siding and asbestos cement, have become popular in recent years. Because of rising costs, maintenance-free exteriors such as aluminum have become popular. Rising labor costs seem to make this trend even more desirable.

Interior walls. In wood construction, an interior wall or partition usually consists of 2″ × 4″ studs spaced at 14″ intervals with a finish applied to both sides. If the wall supports the floors or roof above, it is known as *load-bearing*. This is important to keep in mind when remodeling and especially when changing the size or shape of a room. The load-bearing interior wall should never be removed unless a beam is substituted to support the upper structure.

Windows. There is a great variety in type and brand of windows. The principal kinds of window frames are aluminum and wood. Aluminum frames get cold in winter, and moisture condensation can be troublesome. The window panes fog up with moisture, and even the frames will drip water. This problem can be minimized if aluminum windows are made so that the inside movable section containing the glass does not touch the cold outside frame. On the other hand aluminum requires less maintenance than wood and little or no painting. Windows made of wood are often selected for homes with wooden exterior walls to continue the feel of the natural look. Contemporary wooden windows are often coated with plastic for easy maintenance.

All windows should come with integral weather stripping. There must be no air leaks around the frame. In the North, storm windows or insulating glass will almost always pay off in increased winter comfort and reduced heating bills. In the South, insulated glass may help in lowering utility costs by maintaining a cool, air-conditioned interior. Insulating glass has two parallel sheets of glass with a sealed air space in between.

Doors. The decorative design of exterior doors should always be coordinated with the architecture of the house. Doors are available in a wide range of designs to fit the style of almost every house.

If there is an entry hall in the house with no source of daylight, the entrance door should have windows to provide light.

Exterior doors are normally hinged so that they swing inward. Enough space should be allowed for the door to swing freely. Interior doors should be hinged in the direction of natural entry. Whenever possible, they should swing against a blank wall, and one door should not be obstructed by another swinging door.

Today, doors are generally made of Douglas fir or ponderosa pine. But as an exception to the above rule, flush doors, flat on both sides, are available with a hardwood veneer suitable for staining or varnishing. They are either solid or hollow. Paneled doors are built of vertical pieces (the stiles) and horizontal pieces (the rails). The set-in thinner sheets of wood are called *panels*. Doors are described according to the number of panels in the design.

Louvered doors have thin slats of wood with open spaces between to permit ventilation. The slats are tilted so that the openings cannot be seen through.

Glazed doors have pieces of glass or windows inserted to permit light to pass through.

Batten doors, generally used in barns or cellars, are roughly constructed; vertical boards are nailed together at the top, bottom, and center with horizontal boards called *battens*.

Dutch doors consist of two sets of doors, one above the other. The upper portion, usually glazed, may be open while the lower portion is kept closed. The two sections may be fastened together so that they may be opened and closed as one door.

A folding door consists of narrow sections hinged together and gliding on an overhead track. The sections fold against each other accordion style at the sides of the door opening.

Sliding doors with large glass surfaces are used in places where open access to an outside view is desirable, such as near an entrance to a porch or garden or balcony. The door frame is generally of lightweight aluminum with shatterproof glass. It is sometimes tinted to filter the sun and for privacy.

Stairways. Stairs consist of three basic parts: tread, riser and stringer. The tread is the horizontal section of the stair. The riser is the vertical section between two treads or between a tread and the floor or landing, and the portion of the tread that extends beyond the face of the riser is the nosing. Stringers, located on the sides of the stairs, carry the treads and risers through the stairwell opening.

The depth of the tread (not including the nosing) is called the *run,* and the height of the riser is termed the *rise.*

Stairs may be "open" or "closed." An open stair is one that is without a wall on either side. If a stair has a wall on one side, it is termed a *semihoused stair.* If a stair is located between two walls, it is then a closed, housed, or box stair.

At times, it may be necessary to place a platform or landing in a straight flight of stairs. This is termed a *straight-run platform.* If the stairway turns 90 degrees with the landing, it is called a *one-turn stair.* A **U**-*stair* is a stairway that turns 180 degrees at the landing. A *double-turn stair* turns 90 degrees at each landing.

Circular or spiral stairs are also found in some contemporary homes. Spiral staircases occupy the least space, but this economy may be offset by the difficulty of moving furniture up and down, as well as the increased danger of accidents on the narrow portion of the treads that is near the center of support. In some local areas spiral staircases are against the law unless there is also a conventional stairway leading to the same upper level. A flight of stairs broken at some point by a landing provides the easiest and most graceful way of bridging the approximately nine feet of space that is typical between two floors.

Folding stairs are often used to reach attics and storage areas. These stairs are manufactured in various lengths suitable for residential ceiling heights.

A well-designed stairway should have three basic characteristics: (1) it should be easy to ascend; (2) all its treads and risers should be uniform; and (3) it should be adequately lighted.

Heating and ventilation. Our forefathers had no central heating or air-conditioning units in the homes that they built, but they did recognize the importance of a comfortable atmosphere in the home. With fireplaces and stoves they managed to keep rooms warm; in climates where hot weather was a major problem, the building materials and the arrangement of space in the home were geared to keeping the interior atmosphere comfortable. We can learn a great deal from people in tropical countries about natural methods of air conditioning. They build houses around central patios, keep roofs shaded with tall trees, and use shutters that are closed tight in the middle of the day to prevent the sun from heating the interior of the house. Stone and marble provide excellent insulating materials. But these methods are not always practical in contemporary building, where costs and the availability of space and materials almost dictate the designs of our houses. We rely, therefore, on mechanical methods of keeping interior atmospheres livable and comfortable.

Heating may be a major expense in the maintenance of a home. The heating unit should utilize the most economical fuel for the particular area of the country. Gas and oil are commonly favored. The construction of walls, floors, and ceilings is closely related to the use of fuel. Poor insulating qualities increase costs in winter; good insulation not only reduces costs in cold weather but keeps the house cool during warm weather.

In some areas, air conditioning has become almost a necessity. Although the cost of a central unit is still prohibitive in many cases, room-size devices and exhaust fans in kitchens and bathrooms are relatively inexpensive.

The value of a house will be increased by the ease and economy of keeping the interior comfortable for year-round living. For areas where both heat and cold are problems, there are units that combine heating and cooling systems. If a house is considered in terms of resale value, it might be wise to invest in a unit that has an adequate control of interior temperatures. There is little doubt that in the future this aspect of housing will assume greater importance.

Plumbing. The source of water supply and the condition of all pipes should be carefully checked. An inadequate or a worn system can be expensive to remedy. Sewerage may be taken care of by a community system or by a private septic tank or cesspool. Whatever the system, it should be properly installed and adequate in size. It should be accessible for periodic cleanings, which will, of course, add to the cost of maintenance.

Wiring. The house must provide adequate current for all major appliances. The local utility company will probably be able to offer some assistance in this respect. If one plans to use electricity for a range or for air conditioning, dependability should be checked. In some areas, the current is often affected by storms. Of course, outlets should be convenient for lamps and appliances.

Acoustics. A noisy home can be a real problem, and location should be a prime consideration; beware of trains, buses, or commercial establishments in the immediate vicinity. A location close to an airport may be a drawback. A house in a busy district has certain property advantages, but it may also have the disadvantages of a nonresidential atmosphere.

Within the house, noise can be controlled in several ways. Some materials are more sound-absorbent than others. Ceiling tiles that absorb sound are a great advantage. Resilient materials on floors, counters, and furniture will also contribute to the "sound conditioning" of a home. Closets placed between bedrooms provide space between the room walls.

Odor. It is interesting to observe that some cultures are extremely aware of the interplay of *all* the senses. We tend to emphasize visual, tactile, and auditory sensations, but in the Orient the importance of the olfactory sensations is equally recognized. Incense, an aromatic substance, is burned to create an agreeable atmosphere. Odors certainly influence one's reactions to a particular home. They may be pleasant, soothing, exotic, or stimulating, or they may be repulsive. Too much of any aroma is not appealing, but a faint, suggestive odor can do wonders in creating an atmosphere. The smells of pine and cedar are familiar to many of us, and they usually have delightful associations.

Building materials sometimes provide the aromatic atmosphere. Natural substances, such as some woods, are noteworthy; certain synthetic materials may have rather clinical odors.

Facts About Financing

The generally accepted standard indicates that a family should purchase a house that costs no more than three to three-and-one-half times its annual income. However, some authorities believe that with increased tax rates and increased costs in other areas, a safer limit is no more than two-and-three-quarters times the annual income. The matter is necessarily one that must be decided by each family. It is wise to stay closer to the lower end of the bracket if family operating expenses are high, if one is saving to give children a college education, if the down payment on the house will be small, and if chances for increased income are slight. On the other hand, if one can afford a sizable down payment, if family income will probably increase, if present living expenses are relatively light, and if there are few serious financial responsibilities for the future of the family, it is probably reasonable to pay more for housing.

Shelter costs should be calculated to include *all* the expenses relative to maintaining a home. If one rents a house or an apartment, costs are rather fixed. If it seems desirable to buy a home, the following expenses must be included:

Payments on the mortgage plus interest charges.
Taxes.
Insurance.
Expenses for heating, lighting, and water.
Services for garbage removal.
Maintenance of house and yard.
Costs of repairs and remodeling.

The initial price of a house should also have added to it some of the fees that will probably be levied against the buyer. The advice and appraisals of trained people will cost money. The actual purchase may involve legal documents, a search of previous history, and certain permits that require fees.

The person with a realistic approach to homeownership is prepared for seasonal expenses and also for those that are unexpected. Mowing the lawn in the summer, removing the snow in the winter, or repairing a leak in the roof or a broken pipe can all be expensive projects. Also, certain equipment may not be included in the initial cost of the house—for example, storm windows, screens, lawn mower, garbage cans, and so on.

Few families can afford to buy a house outright with a full payment of cash, nor would it always be advisable to do so. In some cases there are advantages to partial financing of the purchase of a home. However, a down payment is required, and this should be as large as the family can afford while still retaining reserve funds. The balance of the cost of the house is covered by a mortgage, which is, in effect, a loan. Various types of institutions negotiate mortgage loans—savings banks, commercial banks, insurance companies, mortgage bankers, savings and loan associations, and special associations.

The Federal Housing Authority insures loans made by approved lending agencies when they comply with certain regulations, which include some specifications for the type of home that can be insured. The Veterans Administration also guarantees up to $25,000 of a loan made to a service person borrowing from qualified agencies. On loans made with FHA or VA approval, charges and fees are regulated by the government. It is important, however, for the consumer to shop around for suitable terms when financing the purchase of a home. Interest rates on the amount of money borrowed will vary, and the mortgage may run for different periods of time. Of course, the larger the down payment, the less money one will have to borrow, and interest charges may be less. Also, if the mortgage can be paid off in a shorter period, the total interest will be less.

There are several other aspects of the mortgage that should be of concern to the prospective buyer. Some arrangements include prepayment allowances so that the mortgage may be paid up sooner than anticipated if the homeowner finds it possible. Others give the owner the right to borrow additional money for remodeling.

In addition to the payments on the mortgage, one should remember that expenses for owning a home will include other items listed earlier. It is important to estimate *all* of these expenses in a realistic calculation of the cost of buying a home.

Zoning Assessment Taxes
Zoning regulates land use. Every area has its own regulations concerning the types of buildings that may be constructed on a plot of land.

These may regulate the distance the building has to be from the property line. The height of a building may also be restricted. Certain areas may be set aside where no buildings may be constructed, to allow for space and sunshine. Another zoning consideration may be the number of persons allowed to live in the housing units on the land. Zoning avoids overcrowding by preventing houses from being built where adequate schools and roads are not available. Many small towns are opposed to rapid growth, as taxes usually rise to meet the needs of an increased population.

Each dwelling is affected by zoning, assessment, and taxes. The permissible size, shape, and proximity to other buildings are specified in the area's zoning regulations and affect the assessed worth of that building. Land in different areas affects the building's value as well. Improvements or additions to the interior or the exterior also play a role in determining assessed worth. Taxes are based not only on individual assessments but on the area's recreational and educational facilities as well. Most towns have a place, usually in the town hall, where zoning maps are displayed and are available to interested parties.

Although zoning laws also establish which areas are to serve the business or industrial needs of a neighborhood, we are primarily concerned here with zoning regulations in regard to residential building. In some communities, special zoning regulations meant to keep certain areas reserved for the wealthy have been enacted, although such restrictions are today often challenged.

Conclusion

Housing represents one of the most important personal and aesthetic choices for people, influencing not only their interior furnishings but the overall quality of their lives. Home furnishings, in other words, begins with the decisions we make about housing and our responses to the building's structural and visual qualities. The more we know about a house, the better we are prepared to plan for its interiors.

Space for Living

2
Where to Start

It is interesting to note the dictionary definitions of words such as *shelter, dwelling, house,* and *home.* Most of these words emphasize the physical aspects of protection, but the word *home* has more inclusive implications. One dictionary defines home as "a place or abode of affection, peace and rest; a congenial abiding place." It also distinguishes between the word's denotation and its connotation: ". . . thus home *denotes* the place where one lives with one's family, but it usually *connotes* comfort, intimacy, and privacy." The ideas suggested indicate an atmosphere and a pattern of relationships that are more than a physical environment. This is a good beginning, but a home should also be a place that enriches the spirit, stimulates the mind, and encourages creative growth.

No matter what the physical environment may be, the atmosphere of the home expresses something about the people who live in it. The first visit to a person's home may be quite a revelation, explaining certain facets of a particular personality. We almost always feel as though we know a person better after having visited his or her home. When we travel to other areas or foreign lands, we are usually grateful for an opportunity to visit homes because they tell us so much about people and their way of life.

Beyond creating the spirit or the atmosphere of the home, the owner is also faced with the problem of establishing a household that is truly functional. Electrification and automation have changed our way of life, and there are those who would have us think that various appliances and prepared foods have freed people to do little more than push buttons and open packages. Such is not the case. If anything, modern life makes greater demands upon each individual, but in a different way. True, new conveniences have released the homemaker from much of the drudgery of managing a household. Although one no longer needs to scrub clothes on a washboard, new methods and new ideas have brought with them a host of new responsibilities and new chores.

Improved standards of living have brought more demands on family income, and the wider consumer market makes each choice more difficult. The intelligent use of income and other aspects of running a home not only take time and energy but also require a background of consumer information. As just one example, in the realm of textiles a homemaker at the turn of the century had to choose among cotton, linen, silk, or wool, all of which had been used for centuries and which presented no new problems. Today we are faced with a myriad of fibers, fabrics, and finishes that require careful selection and special handling.

The modern family needs a special kind of household, which is planned and equipped to meet its needs. In view of the importance of the task and the problems involved, it is wise to work on some kind of plan, which is based on certain goals and objectives.

Almost everyone approaches the problem of setting up a new household with limitations of one sort or another—space, money, time, or location, to mention only a few. The project usually requires energy and imagination, but it is a creative experience that should be fun and exciting. Above all, homemaking requires an appreciation of the fact that the decisions that must be made will have a keen influence on personal and family life.

The relationship between the individual and that individual's home carries with it important implications for the future structure and character of our society. These brief observations on the meaning of *home* should make it clear that the goals and objectives that people establish when setting up a home are important factors in patterns of family and community relationships.

The Six Basic Questions

One can begin to formulate a plan for a home by asking six basic questions. Frequently the answers to these questions will be interdependent; frequently one will pose more of a problem than another. Yet a bit of clear analysis of each one will help the homeowner to embark on this important project with a feeling of reassurance.

1. Who will live in the home?
2. Where will the home be?
3. Will this home be a permanent or a temporary residence?
4. What should the home look like?
5. How much will it cost?
6. Where and how should one shop for the best values?

Who Will Live in the Home?

Of course if one plans to live alone, one's own tastes, needs, interests, and activities are the chief concern; but when one plans to share a home, it must be everyone's home. Each person may have to compromise or sacrifice in some respects, but it is only through mutual consideration that there can be any satisfactory solution to this problem.

Individual tastes, individual likes and dislikes, must be carefully discussed. There may also be certain needs that should be considered. For example, if one member of a family works at home or has the kind of career that requires bringing work home from the office, the home must be planned to provide adequate space and equipment.

A young couple would probably have common interests in certain things, such as music, reading, and watching television. However, each one may have individual interests for which special provisions should be made. A man with an interest in a hobby or in a collection of some kind and a woman with another hobby of her own should each have the necessary space and facilities to maintain their interests. Hobbies such as photography, crafts, sewing, or music may require special areas in the home.

How one plans to entertain should also be considered. Some people prefer small, intimate groups, whereas others prefer large parties. Provision for both kinds of entertaining would probably make some difference in planning. Relatives or friends who live out of town may require plans for overnight guests.

At the beginning a young couple might not be influenced by long-range plans for a family, but they would certainly want to discuss this matter in terms of planning a home. If they hoped to have children in the near future, it would probably make a difference in their needs for space.

Where Will the Home Be?

One may be able to make some plans before having an actual place to live. With some notion of the type of home one wants, one can begin to collect some silverware, china, and linens. Before doing much more than that, however, one should know where one wants to live.

The actual geographical location may make a difference in the kind of home one establishes. It may determine whether or not a person will live in a private house or in a apartment.

The architectural style of a house may be an important factor in how it is to be furnished. Although it is not always necessary to follow an obvious line, the structural features of the home, especially in a private house, may lend themselves better to one style or another.

With an actual floor plan of the house or apartment drawn according to scale one can plan for the most efficient use of space and map out the areas of activity. It is important to know the actual measurements of doorways and windows, the height of ceilings, and the size of closets. It is also important to know the exposures and to see the rooms at different times during the day to study the kind and amount of natural light that each one gets.

As soon as one knows where he or she will live, what is provided by the landlord or agent should be explored. For example, many new houses are not equipped with a refrigerator, window shades or blinds, and some lighting fixtures. Screens, storm windows, and landscaping must also be considered.

Some apartment houses have restrictions on the use of certain appliances, such as washing machines and air conditioners. There may also be provisions in the contract concerning the use of wallpaper, colored paint, and pictures and mirrors. Frequently in such contracts the wall must be restored to its original condition if any of these means of decoration have been used.

Will This Home Be a Permanent or a Temporary Residence?

One's plans for the future will certainly influence the way a home is furnished. Many young people plan to rent houses or apartments until they can afford to buy their own. Some start in small homes or apartments with the idea of moving to larger quarters in the future. In any event, whether the home is to be considered temporary or permanent will make a difference in some decisions. In furnishing a temporary home, each major investment should be considered with a view toward how the item might be used under other circumstances. For example, it would be unwise to invest in wall-to-wall carpeting for the living room of an apartment in which one expects to live for a short period. However, the purchase of a good-quality room-sized rug that could be cut down to fit a smaller room later on might be considered. A folding table or a card table might serve as a dining table in a small apartment. If one plans eventually to furnish a dining room, it might be wiser to wait rather than buy an expensive table for use in the apartment. Items such as upholstered chairs, tables, lamps, accessories, and beds could probably be used in either a temporary or a permanent home. Floor coverings, curtains, and draperies present more of a problem.

It is usually a mistake to buy cheap things for a temporary home with the idea of selling them or throwing them away when one moves. Corners can be cut on some needs, but it is more sensible to invest in good furnishings that will be adaptable to different situations. This requires careful evaluation and good judgment.

What Should the Home Look Like?

A home reflects many things about the personalities of the people who live in it. Naturally it should be interesting, but homes, like clothes, should provide a background; they should never submerge people. Sometimes a very unusual home becomes such a fetish that it absorbs the people who live in it and becomes the object of all their interests, activities, money, and—unfortunately—conversation.

A home should be functional as well as beautiful. It is important to keep purposes in mind when making each decision. The manner in which the home works for those who live in it as well as the aesthetic satisfactions derived from it will provide the yardstick for measuring success.

Depending on the type of furnishings selected, the colors chosen, and the way the furniture and accessories are arranged, a home will express some theme or mood. As one thinks of possible adjectives that might be used, some may be more appealing than others. Such a list might include *formal, sophisticated, elegant, lively, casual, exotic, exciting, restful, quaint, cheerful.* A room may have more than one of these characteristics. It may be formal *and* elegant, or sophisticated *and* exotic.

Although some people have very definite preferences for a particular style and know exactly what they want, others are somewhat more vague about their ideas. Often they find that several themes are appealing and that it is difficult to select those that will blend well. Is it possible to plan a room that is both formal and casual or one that is both exciting and restful? Discretion should be used, because trying to express too many ideas in one room may result in a disturbing hodge-podge that spells nothing except confusion. A considerable amount of money, time, and energy is invested in furnishing a home. If it is to be thoroughly satisfying, some preliminary efforts must be made to avoid mistakes.

Those who have only a vague idea about what they really want should analyze their own likes and dislikes. Certainly some styles and colors are more appealing than others. One can begin by clipping pictures from magazines, including definitely disliked qualities as well as the preferred ones. The pictures should be separated into "yes," "no," and "maybe" categories. With a fairly large collection, one should go through each group and make a list of the desirable characteristics and another of those that are not desirable, applying as many adjectives as possible to each illustration. A list should also be made of the colors and textures preferred. Special little notes should be made about particular features, such as furniture arrangements, window treatments, or accessories. Then one should visit a few department stores and even museum exhibits with a notebook in hand and jot down special observations.

Putting ideas in writing helps to clarify them. On sifting through all these notes, one will begin to find the common denominators of all the ideas that are appealing. The pictures and notes in the "yes" category will undoubtedly have certain points in common. Possibly they will have a simplicity or an elegance or a certain type of carefree charm. There may be particular colors and types of patterns that keep recurring. The "no" group will also have common characteristics. Are they mostly cluttered or garish or perhaps too formal? This procedure will lead to far more observant and discriminating choices.

When tastes are somewhat narrowed down, one should begin to probe those styles that one likes. It helps to know something about all the styles. The survey presented later in this text will help the reader get started, but further research and a deeper understanding of two or three styles should prove to be very useful.

Once the purpose is clearly in mind, it is time to formulate more definite plans for a budget, room arrangements, and color schemes. This book is meant to be the preparation for these steps.

When one is actually about to furnish a home, the tasks will be much easier if all the floor plans, measurements, swatches, color chips, pamphlets, and specifications are well organized in a notebook and some sort of filing portfolio or loose-leaf arrangement of large envelopes is kept.

How Much Will It Cost?

It is, of course, impossible to name a certain amount of money necessary for establishing a home. Nor is it possible to propose any one budget formula that will suit all needs. It is possible, however, to point out certain principles and guides that will help to set up a financial plan.

Costs of shelter must be considered in conjunction with various other costs that may or may not be included in regular payments. Taxes, insurance, heating, and lighting may be high in some areas and may have to be added to the basic costs of shelter. The expenses of commuting or of owning a car will also be influenced by where one lives and should be considered in conjunction with the costs of the home. Maintenance is another expense that should not be disregarded.

Realism points out that many young people start out with far less than a desirable amount of money. Some depend in part on relatives and wedding presents to furnish their homes. Others buy furnishings on the installment plan. Still others buy some essentials—a table, chairs, a bed, and a few utensils—and plan to furnish as they can afford to do so. But one young couple with about $1,500 spent $900 for a dinette set, a bed, and a chest of drawers, and the other $600 for sterling-silver place settings, even though there was not one piece of furniture in the living room!

Naturally it is better to have an adequate amount of money saved before one begins to buy furnishings. It means having the kind of a home that will meet needs and be a source of satisfaction. Depending on relatives and friends to furnish a home has serious disadvantages. Many young brides receive six or eight salad bowls as wedding presents. Although it is nice to have a variety, this is not the primary concern in setting up a household. In other words, one can't always depend on receiving the necessary items.

Spending plans and the financial aspects of furnishing a home are discussed in more detail in Chapter 29.

*Where and How Should One Shop
for the Best Values?*

Because even a very modest home requires the investment of a considerable amount of money, it is important to use the available money wisely and to the best advantage.

Perhaps the first caution should be to deal with reliable merchants. A store or a company that takes pride in the good will it establishes with the public caters to satisfied customers. In many areas of furnishings it is extremely difficult to judge quality and one must rely on the honesty of the dealer for information about the products. For example, if a salesperson insists that an upholstered chair has a hardwood frame, there is no way of checking this fact.

It is not always easy to determine how reliable a business concern is until one has had some experience in dealing with it. Usually stores and manufacturers that spend large sums of money promoting their names are interested in maintaining good public relations and will stand behind faulty merchandise, but this generality is no true guarantee for the consumer. Besides, there are many small business concerns that are thoroughly dependable even though they do not invest in wide advertising campaigns.

The decision about where to shop must rest with the buyer. One should have a feeling of confidence in the dealer, who may even be a most helpful adviser. The buyer ought to avoid merchants who make a practice of pressuring their customers into buying things. A good merchant will want a customer to take time to think over decisions before he or she actually makes purchases. One should beware of any dealer who makes all sorts of verbal claims but who refuses to put them in writing or to make any notations on the sales receipts about the information being given.

Actual guarantees of durability present many difficulties. An item of furnishing may stand up very well under normal, proper use and care but not if it is mistreated. Just as the consumer has a right to expect honest information about merchandise, she or he must also be reasonable in demands for guarantees. The family that allows the children to roller skate on the carpeting can hardly expect the manufacturer to be responsible for signs of wear and tear, unless of course a claim is made that the product can withstand such violent treatment.

A price policy that is very flexible does not tend to inspire confidence. Price tags that are not clearly marked or a salesperson who keeps reducing the price while the customer is hesitating should make one immediately skeptical. Bargains are always exciting, but unless an item is unquestionably a bargain, one should be very wary.

The wide choice available in today's market is a blessing, but it also presents many problems for the consumer. Intelligent buying requires study and planning. Because a home is such an individual matter, there is no one source that can answer all questions or give all the necessary information. It is a great advantage to become qualified to make the best choices for one's needs. The following sources of information may be useful:

1. *Newspapers and Magazines.* Most newspapers feature new and interesting ideas on home decoration during the week and in Sunday supplements, and many family-type magazines have monthly decorating articles. Some of the magazines have excellent bulletin services that offer useful information.

Certain magazines specialize in the decorative arts and provide a wealth of information and ideas. These, too, frequently have bulletin services and facilities for handling special requests for readers. Special magazines published for interior decorators and designers may have materials that may be useful.

2. *Extension Services.* Most states have an agricultural extension service that publishes a variety of pamphlets and booklets. Some of these will be helpful in establishing and maintaining a home. One should check the list of offerings in one's own state and request the material that might be helpful.

3. *Local Libraries.* There is a wide variety of books on many phases of home planning, building, and decoration. One should find out what the local library has to offer. It may not have a complete selection, but the range of available information may be pleasantly surprising.

4. *The National Design Center (425 East 53rd Street, New York City 10022).* This institution maintains exhibits related to decoration and displays products of many leading manufacturers of home furnishings. Its information bureau has an extensive file of information about products and distributors and will answer questions about these by mail if one cannot visit the center.

5. *Retail Stores.* Many stores that handle home furnishings maintain trained consultants. Large stores have interior designers on their staffs. There may be no charge to customers for some of the services; in other instances, there may be a flat fee or charges based on a prorated scale. One should find out as much as possible about the stores in her or his locality and what they have to offer.

6. *Decorating Services.* An interior designer is not required to have a license, but a good one who meets a high standard of professional training will probably belong to a professional group that limits its membership to qualified people. One professional organization is:

The American Society of Interior Designers
(A.S.I.D.)
750 Fifth Avenue
New York, N.Y. 10019

Entrance into this organization is through appropriate education, experience, and a written and practical examination.

Professionals use different methods for charging fees. In consulting a decorator, one must be sure to work with a reliable person and to understand fully all the terms of the contract. The A.S.I.D. will provide names of its members upon request.

The intelligent consumer should become acquainted with the publications of two organizations that attempt to provide unbiased information and evaluations of products currently available. Both of these organizations strive to assist consumers in making wise decisions, and both operate independent of industry, business, or government. They are

Consumers Union
256 Washington Street
Mount Vernon, N.Y. 10550
Consumers' Research, Inc.
Washington, N.J. 07882

Local libraries usually subscribe to the publications of these organizations.

Furnishing as a Continuing Process

It must be pointed out that although our discussion up to this point has been concerned mainly with the problems of establishing a new household, furnishing and maintaining a home is actually a continuing process. Even the first home is not always completely furnished all at once, and plans often provide for additions over periods of a few years. By the time furnishing is completed, some replacements may be necessary or the homeowner may be ready to revise a color scheme or a special area. Eventually one may want to replace some or all of the major items. Sometimes, when children have grown and moved to homes of their own, parents find it more suitable to move to smaller quarters or to redesign or redecorate their home.

One doesn't usually get rid of everything all at once in refurnishing. In many instances there are sentimental attachments to certain objects, or there may be others that are still too good or too useful to sell or to give away.

The basic principles of furnishing apply to refurnishing and redecorating. Having a plan is equally important, if not more so, because of the possessions that one already has. It is not always easy to create a new setting that will make them look as if they really belong. The plan should be worked around the things to be kept. If possible, these should be separated from the items to be replaced and then visualized in a new setting. New colors in slipcovers or uphol-stery, new wall colors, different arrangements, different accessories, and a creative imagination will all help the situation. Sometimes upholstered furniture can be redesigned and rugs can be cut down. A problem often makes the project more interesting if it is approached with a creative attitude. One woman who wanted to refurnish her living room in the contemporary style also wanted to keep a beautiful oriental rug that had been chosen to blend with her traditional-style furnishings. She selected her new furnishings with careful attention to colors and textures. She planned her color scheme and chose her accessories with equal care. The final result was a magnificent modern room in which the rug was perfectly at home.

All new additions and replacements must be chosen with great care and skill. New fashions and fads in furnishings may be enticing. With some of them it may be possible to create exciting new effects, but with others the lovely existing effects may be spoiled. One has to exercise a discriminating taste to use the fashions that are just right.

SECTION TWO

Design

3

Design Expression

Perception and the ability to enjoy expression depend, to a large extent, on the degree to which we have developed a sensitivity to people, ideas, and physical surroundings. Quite probably, the home atmosphere in which we began to notice sensations was an important factor in determining our early reactions. In the process of growing up, as our interests, attitudes, likes, and dislikes became more firmly established, our personalities also became more individual. Consequently, we obviously have different ideas about beauty, and it is not possible for one person to impose his or her values on others.

Learning in the field of the arts, therefore, is not a matter of accepting standards set up by other people. It is instead a process of becoming more perceptive and of developing one's own ability in expression.

A study of history shows that we have high esteem for any society that has shown sensitivity to beauty in daily living. Much primitive art intrigues connoisseurs and collectors because it represents honest and uninhibited expression in simple objects. We admire the appreciation of beauty that permeates daily living in many areas of the Orient. The ability of the Japanese to create exquisite compositions with a few simple flowers, or even weeds, reflects an inherent appreciation that has been developed over many years. In the Orient one pauses a moment during the day to admire the form and texture of a teacup. Or a "sand garden," merely a pile of sand that is formed to create lovely effects with light and shadow, may grace an empty courtyard. The Oriental child is frequently trained to appreciate beauty in simple objects and so enriches his or her daily life.

In the Western world we have been accused not only of separating true art appreciation from the simple experiences of everyday living but also of using ineffectual methods of teaching the enjoyment of art. The ubiquitous coloring books and crayons that are so often given to young children have been berated as stifling natural expression. Certainly most of them do very little to develop an appreciation of true beauty.

There is little doubt that we are becoming more aware of the importance of design in all phases of our daily life. Automobiles, typewriters, and telephones, as well as kitchen appliances and numerous other articles, have undergone radical changes in past years. Not all of the changes show true artistic progress, but the trend indicates that we want the more mundane objects to be pleasing to the eye as well as functional.

What Is Design?

The term *design* is used in many ways to convey different meanings. We might speak of the design of a salad bowl or the design of a city. In a broad sense, the word implies selection and organization for some specific purpose or intention. Thus we might also think of the design of a musical composition, in which notes and tones are selected and arranged to create a pattern of sounds that will have a particular effect on the listener.

In the visual arts the designer works with lines, forms, colors, and textures. Elements are selected and arranged to suit a purpose, which might be to create something that is purely functional, or purely ornamental, or both functional and beautiful. In doing so the designer expresses various ideas, moods, or values, and such expressions evoke some response in the viewer.

Unity must be a basic factor in any consideration of design. As we look at a painting, we see it as a whole or a unit. The relationship of form, color, and texture produces the design. We look at the design of a house in terms of its relation to the terrain. We also look at each room in relation to the whole house. But we also see the design of the room itself as a unit. Thus the meaning of the word *design* depends upon what we are talking about, but we might say that *design* refers to a composition produced by the integration of various elements.

Because we are individuals and react to the expressions of others in such different ways, any attempt to define good design is indeed an extremely risky business. The very expressiveness of all forms of art is, in itself, a matter of beauty. But not every individual is perceptive of all kinds of expression. Another very broad term, *taste*, represents what one accepts or rejects. Over the centuries, the popular tastes in what represents true beauty have varied and fluctuated, and different cultures have accepted certain modes of expression as representative. Some have emphasized the spiritual expression afforded through art; others have emphasized craftsmanship and techniques. Functionalism, which is such an important factor in contemporary design, represents a philosophy of art. There is probably no universal appreciation and acceptance of any one form of beauty. Neither are there any simple, basic formulas or rigid rules encompassing all design. We could not, nor would we want to, regulate expression in such a way.

It would be difficult to compile a list of one hundred examples of perfect designs, including buildings, paintings, sculptures, textiles, and ceramics, that would be acceptable to all art connoisseurs and critics. Many masterpieces have survived centuries of general acclaim and appreciation, yet almost every one has also had its adversaries. But popular acclaim cannot be considered a criterion. We have innumerable examples of artistic expression that were rejected by contemporaries of the artist but that are generally accepted as masterpieces today. We also have many examples of "art" that were widely accepted by the populace but that are considered atrocities in this era.

Authorities disagree with each other on almost every aspect of art, and certainly they will disagree on any analysis of it. How do we decide for ourselves what art forms we like or dislike? Perhaps we admire the same qualities in artistic expression that we do in people—sincerity, honesty, courage, and a bit of mysticism. We do not admire those who flout tradition for the sake of change, but we accept changes. Intelligent people are open-minded and eager for ideas that represent constructive and creative thinking. Expressions of such qualities are more likely to be accepted as art and survive the tests of time.

There are certain facts that would be difficult to deny—for example, the concept of optical illusion, the emotional impact of color, and the expressive qualities of textures. The elements of design and the principles of their organization make a design good or poor. An objective analysis of the combination of elements can be made. It is important to note, however, that it is often the deviations from accepted design principles that create an interesting or unusual interior solution. Personal taste also has to be considered because a design that appeals to one person may be distasteful to another. The more familiar one becomes with the language of design, the more pleasure will be gained from those expressions that are honest and sincere. There is a basic truth in something that is really beautiful, but one must develop powers of observation and discrimination to appreciate the message that the artist attempts to convey.

Man-Made Design Objects

Furnishings are objects related to the visual arts. Traditionally, the visual arts have been divided into the fine arts, such as painting and sculpture, and the practical or applied arts, such as crafts, fashion, and industrial design. It is important to note that there is a potential for beauty and for aesthetic pleasure in every man-made object, from a cup to a complete interior. Appreciation of visual forms is similar for all artist-designed objects. Such forms may be viewed as designs for communication, having a formal organization—the result of an artist's skilled manipulation of materials. No designed object can exist without an artist's forming it. The wood or fabric that is to become furniture must be selected, manipulated, and controlled to produce a form that is functionally as well as visually pleasing. Every designer must also be a craftsperson, familiar with materials and expert in working with them. The designer must learn to control the materials, to explore the best qualities of their surfaces, and to organize structures and forms. A well-designed object has a properly defined form and shows an orderly, skilled control of the materials used in its construction.

We often speak of beauty in conjunction with designed objects. One way to consider beauty is to say that an object can stimulate a sense of appreciation within each individual. In other words, something outside of ourselves can make us feel beautiful when we encounter it. A second point of view is that designed objects may have the characteristic of beauty within them. This quality may be in the object's material, in the way solutions are found for its function, or in the manner in which individual pieces are organized and combined. In the second point of view, this quality may be recognized by the viewer. A beautiful object is sometimes described as having a harmony of parts working so well together, with such a sense of proportion, that one feels nothing can be added or removed. Even though beauty may be, to some extent, a personal, subjective matter within each one of us, its stimulus is initiated by experiencing a "beautifully" designed object.

Design and production are two primary human activities. In the process of design, the artist selects the visual quality of the things we use. This selection has a wide and sustained impact on all parts of our lives. In a sense, our entire environment is a work of art. It is not only paintings or sculptures in museums that are works of art, but everyday objects may be as well. Our concern with this experience is important, for the objects that we choose for our homes are around us all the time and are difficult to escape.

What generally distinguishes the design of furnishings from the products of the other fine arts are the practical limits on the designer's freedom. In the creation of a chair, for example, the designer must produce a surface to sit on with relative comfort by the standards of our Western posture and way of sitting. In establishing what the object is to look like, the designer has to determine what it has to do—what needs it must serve—and then incorporate these requirements into the design and the materials used to achieve it. Within these functional limits, an infinite range of forms is possible.

Part of the process of design is a concern for the "look" of the form. Determining an object's function cannot always be separated from considering how to decorate, ornament, embellish, or, in other words, *design* its visual appearance.

Although not useful in itself, this second aspect of design makes our furnishings more interesting and our life more pleasant and varied. Therefore design is the process of making things look pleasing and work properly.

What to Look for in Object Designs

The qualities of a designed object can be examined in several ways. They can speak to the senses by means of qualities of surface that may evoke certain feelings, moods, or associations. All designs are perceived through the senses. Not only may objects have a visual appeal of color, texture, and form, they may also communicate through their size and proportion in relation to the human figure. Surfaces can also be considered in terms of light—that is, the quality of light they absorb, direct, or reflect. An object's surface may be viewed in terms of the movements or energy it suggests. Besides speaking to our visual and tactile senses, some objects may stimulate us by smell, sound, or even taste.

Additional characteristics of form are the medium or material an object is made from and the techniques used to produce it. These qualities may suggest relationships among the object's design features. A work in leather, glass, metal, plastic, or wood suggests a feel, a surface that is characteristic of that material. Objects may look bright or dull, opaque or transparent; they may feel coarse or soft, rigid or flexible, to the touch. Techniques of construction—such as hammering, stitching, casting, or spinning—may create different surfaces and surface impressions. How the materials and surface qualities of a work are organized creates a structure of formal relationships in a work. Features such as symmetry, balance, contrast, complexity, simplicity, harmony, rhythm, and unity can be seen as structural qualities.

A distinctive feature of a designed object is style. Generally, *style* may refer to a tradition or a culture, such as European, Italian, Danish, Navajo, or Egyptian. Style may relate to a school of art or a movement: cubistic, abstract, classical, romantic, Bauhaus, futuristic, or art deco,

for example. Design characteristics in any given period are generally the result of an exchange of ideas among artists. Designs in fashion may relate to design in painting, furnishings, or homes; for example, pop art made its appearance in paintings, furniture, and clothing. Design, therefore, may be examined as a temporal phenomenon related to past traditions or present artistic idioms.

Design also has to do with the function of art objects or the purposes for which a form was created. Becoming familiar with the function of an object may lead to a greater appreciation of the resulting solution. This function can always be looked at as both aesthetic and utilitarian.

Good design often contains an unconscious prediction of future tendencies and appearance. In looking at good design, we may not only see what is now available but also gain an insight into what may exist in the future.

Form Related to Function
According to the axiom "Form follows function," the shape of an object is defined by the work it must do. The object should look like what it is and does; that is, there should be no deceptive appearances—a chair should not look like a table, nor a lamp like a waterfall.

Economic considerations also affect design. The difference between American designs and those of Europe is that a country rich in resources, raw materials, and human ingenuity tends to be wasteful. Therefore, the American economy has allowed for a quick turnover in styles and models, by declaring older models obsolete before they have lost their physical usefulness. In contrast, European design is based upon the preservation of raw materials and the production of long-lasting goods. Europeans also try to avoid buying imports, which are more expensive and negatively affect the economy.

In the past, the essential problem of design was to decide which period or style to follow when building a chair or constructing a house. In the eighteenth and nineteenth centuries, furniture design became increasingly decorative. Form followed, not function, but the prevailing taste in period-styled ornamentation.

Industrial design was able to bring common sense and a distinctive abstract excellence to machine-made objects. As time evolved, however, such objects became subject to an overemphasis on function. Does function mean only the operation of an object? Is there more than one correct solution to a problem? Should the object's appearance also function by being more appealing? If so, an object must not only function; it must compete successfully with the similar products of other producers.

Manufacturers discovered in the 1930s that the clean, functional lines of industrially designed products stimulated sales. Therefore they employed experts to redesign traditionally styled merchandise. Objects had a new value: their new appearance. Older designs became obsolete. When a model of a product is either newly designed or newly packaged, the consumer is led to believe that improvements have been made in the product itself. This may not be true. The consumer, however, will discard the old because novelty has become an important value in our culture. Also, new styling creates a need for different objects and thus has economic implications. Workers are constantly employed to keep up profits; at the same time, these workers can buy new products. Durability becomes less important than rapid turnover.

Mass distribution of goods has had its effect on design as well. For example, the need to package and ship large volumes of goods has inspired the design of products to be put together by the owner instead of by the manufacturer, thus reducing the size of each package. In a mobile society we find modular furnishings, light and easily assembled wall units, and inflatable furniture.

What is unique about contemporary design expression is its emphasis on the function the furniture or interior is to serve, rather than its style or period. How is it to be used? Who will use it? Basically, this open approach to planning, where there is no traditional style or predetermined correct way, means that a totally new form or look can be born. Contemporary designers generally do not work from steadfast rules in creating a successful home environment but recognize the opportunities in each new situation and space as well as the importance of personal choices by the individual who will live in the environment.

Handmade and Machine-Made

Furniture created by hand represents an extension of mankind, a manifestation of the human physical and psychological constitution. In the handmade object, the aesthetic quality results from the personal "touch" the artist has employed in the creation of each piece. In machine-made furniture, every aesthetic quality is included in the design of the object, and all pieces produced are exactly alike. Even though handmade objects are produced with the assistance of the lathe, they are always limited in perfection because they are always in touch with the human hand.

Usually handmade furniture has been planned and executed by the same person, giving the object a certain unity of control and execution. The craftsperson not only does the physical work but also varies and adjusts the design according to the requirements of the client or customer, so that "one-of-a-kind" objects result.

Another factor that distinguishes the two categories of objects is that machine-made objects become outdated sooner than handmade ones. As industrially produced objects are subject to an accelerated mass consumption, the result is a formal instability, which leads to changes that follow the dictates of fashion rather than of true style. Thus machine-made designs can be completely gratuitous because of competition, advertising, or sales.

Furniture today can be designed by artists, or draftspersons. These artists in former times were called craftsmen; today they may be called industrial designers. Throughout history, various types of artists—especially architects, sculptors, and interior designers—have created furniture patterns. These artists may have come to design furniture because of their interest in the creation of three-dimensional forms. With furniture today becoming an object of fashion, many clothing designers have also become involved in the styling of furniture.

Because the design of furnishings is a creative endeavor, selecting, arranging, or grouping these pieces becomes another art within a designed room or space.

The kind of workmanship that is generally associated with handmade objects is becoming increasingly a requirement of machine-made forms. It used to be the craftsperson who controlled the quality of his or her objects from design to finished product; today's designers can get high standards from machine production.

Workmanship is an art and an important part of the success of a designer. It is difficult to separate workmanship from design; the two are closely related. The look of an object does not depend on its design alone. The designer cannot simply put instructions on paper and give them to the maker to follow correctly. As in music, the fine details of the performance result from both the composer's specifications and the performer's excellence. Good workmanship implies good details; it implies well-assembled, well-fitted objects with fine surfaces.

Design of Furniture
Related to Changing Life Styles

Some new furniture design meets the demand for comfort and practicality as well as the need for quality. The result is furniture that is simple, easy to take care of, and comfortable to live with, reflecting the way people want to live today.

As life styles change, so do directions in taste. The American life style has been affected by the changing roles of both men and women. Women are redefining their roles as new career choices open, and men are finding that they are becoming increasingly involved in the areas once reserved for women only. As a result, men want to make decorating decisions and take part in their home environment.

As traditional views on life styles become altered, so do the requirements of successful interior design. Homes must work for the people who live in them without complicating their chores. People do not want to become slaves to their possessions.

Today, no one style clearly predominates. There is a desire for simplification and function. Rooms frequently include a few important objects, plus streamlined furniture and lasting materials that are easy to care for. There are fewer surfaces to clean and dust, fewer pieces to rearrange. Storage spaces are often built into the furniture or the architecture, so that clutter is avoided.

Formerly many pieces were crowded into rooms; today each object selected for a space takes on importance. Lighting, furniture, art objects, and even plants are carefully chosen.

Each element functions as an integral part of the whole. Function and purpose predominate, and how the room will be used determines every successful plan today.

More top designers than ever before are creating products for the home that feature variety, good design, and various prices. In the past, only the rich could afford home furnishings created by the artisan. Today interior items such as furniture, linen, rugs, fabrics, china, and cutlery, designed by well-known artists from every field, are readily available. The result is a wide variety of options in every price range. Interior spaces are designed to promote easier living and to produce beautiful and luxurious appearances. In years past, status was achieved by being able to have household help. Today this concept is outdated. Spaces have to accommodate essential items and still provide comfort and be easy to care for.

After the 1890s, affluent people expressed themselves through "conspicuous waste" evidenced in the furniture and fixtures they selected. Furniture was brought from people's original homes in Europe—sometimes from monasteries and castles—and placed in homes for which they were not originally intended. A few decades later, mass production simulated the originals, and the advertising of low prices proliferated these copies. The results brought about a perpetuation of obsolete functional standards and caused the stagnation of style because the principle of producing *en masse* at low prices could not be as successfully applied to imitations as to designs created specifically for the materials and manufacturing devices available.

(a)

Structural designs with emphasis on form, texture, and color. *(a) (Courtesy of Jens Risom Design, Inc.) (b) (Courtesy of Dunbar/Dux, designed by Roger L. Sprunger, photo by Wesley Pusey) (c) (Courtesy of Thayer Coggin, Inc., designed by Milo Baughman)*

Fig. 3.1

(b)

Types of Design

There is no meaningful classification that would be useful in helping us to evaluate all designs. We must learn to judge the expressiveness of any design by the way all of the elements are blended to create the total effect. It is not possible to study line without color and texture. Neither is it possible to ignore the effects that color and texture have on each other. A small area in a bright color and a shiny texture will appear quite different in the context of another area with dull color and rough texture. Therefore the over-all design effects result from the intermingling of elements, and we must learn to understand how these elements work with one another.

We may be more aware of the inspiration of a design if we understand the methods a designer uses to express ideas. In a very general way we might divide designs into five broad categories: structural, naturalistic, stylized, geometric, and abstract. Within these categories there is much overlapping and it is frequently impossible to draw a hairline mark of division.

Structural Designs

In structural design the structure determines the form, and enrichment comes from the materials used. Much of our modern design is of this type, with form dictated by function. There is little, if any, applied ornament.

(c)

**Fig.
3.2**

(a)

(c)

(b)

Naturalistic designs attempt true representations in different ways. *(a)* Vase. *(Courtesy of Cooper-Hewitt Museum of Design, Smithsonian Institute) (b)* "Wild Rose" wallpaper. *(Courtesy of Scalamandrè) (c)* Wallpaper. *(Courtesy of Cooper-Hewitt Museum of Design, Smithsonian Institute)*

Naturalistic Designs

Naturalistic designs represent subject matter drawn from nature—flowers, leaves, fruits, animals, landscapes. Every effort is made to keep the motif realistic so that it appears as an authentic reproduction. When these designs are used on china and fabrics, the colors are frequently related to those found in nature.

Many different effects are possible in naturalistic design. Pastoral scenes or landscapes are useful for creating perspectives. Some motifs are arranged to form stripes, blocks, or medallions.

(a)

Stylized designs translate old themes into contemporary patterns. (a) "Maze" area rug. *(Courtesy of V'Soske—Creative Communications)* (b) "Cathay" wall covering. *(Courtesy of First Editions—Creative Communications)*

The designs lend themselves to either formal or informal themes. But one must use discretion about how and where to use naturalistic motifs. Roses splashed all over the bedroom draperies may be charming, but it is quite another matter to have them on one's dinner plate as a background for steak and vegetables, even though the plate itself may be very attractive.

Stylized Designs

One can recognize the natural sources of a stylized motif, but the design makes no pretense at actual representation. Flowers, leaves, animals, and figures are favorite themes. They are simplified, exaggerated, rearranged, or even distorted to achieve the purposes of the design. Certain natural aspects may be emphasized out of proportion to make those particular features more pronounced. The coloring of stylized designs may also be unconventional.

Geometric Designs

Ancient civilizations recognized the design values of purely geometric forms, including circles, triangles, and rectangles. The plaids of the Celts, as well as the intricate lacy patterns of the Mohammedans, are all based on geometric forms. Moorish designs used the geometric theme with a high degree of skill and refinement. The Greeks were also skillful in the use of geometric design, but more in border patterns than in all-over patterns.

Design Expression

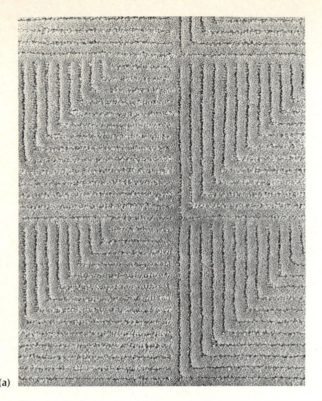

(a)

(b)

Fig. 3.4 Geometric shapes used as an overall pattern.
(a) "Rectilinear Plus." (Courtesy of V'Soske—Creative Communications) (b) "Trimetry." (Courtesy of V'Soske—Creative Communications)

Abstract Designs

Many abstract patterns are based on geometric forms, and some writers do not distinguish between geometric and abstract designs. Yet *abstract* implies a greater freedom than is found in most geometric designs. The shapes and patterns, although derived from geometry, are less rigid and formal than in the popular conception of a geometrical design.

What Price Design?

Fortunately the gap between cost and good design in home furnishings is becoming narrower. Of course one must expect differences in styling and in quality between very low-cost merchandise and high-priced items, but that does not mean that it is impossible to find both good design and good quality in the less expensive categories. Low-priced items may be well designed but poorly executed, simply not well made. Many manufacturers of furnishings in the low and medium price ranges have made sincere efforts to improve both design and quality. Some have hired well-known designers who are interested in improving the general level of design in mass-produced articles for the home. We have seen the results of these efforts in many areas—especially in fabrics, glassware, flatware, and dinnerware.

It is interesting to compare designs at different price levels by browsing in all types of shops, ranging from the low-cost variety and five-and-ten-cent stores to the more exclusive

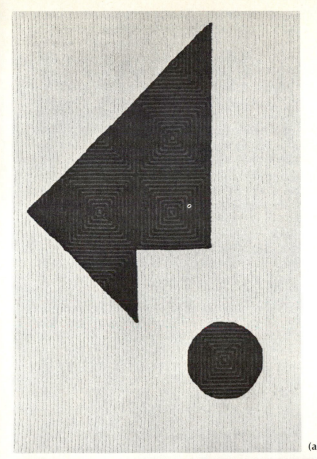

(a) An abstract design making fanciful use of geometric forms called "Mainsail." *(Courtesy of V'Soske—Creative Communications)* (b) Abstract design contrasting geometric forms and free-flowing patterns. *(Courtesy of Westbroadway Gallery, N.Y.)*

Fig. 3.5

(a)

(b)

Fig. 3.6

Designs at different price levels may be similar but not identical. Both plates are plain white; both placemats are green. The total cost of the four items in group (a) was $85.00. The less expensive items in group (b) cost $17.54. Differences in craftsmanship are responsible for differences in cost.

(a)

(b)

Design Expression

department stores. There is quite a difference in the general types of design, but it is possible to create very interesting effects on a low budget by choosing carefully from the less expensive items.

Figure 3.6 shows table appointments that are similar in theme. Both groups have plain white china, green place mats, and simple designs in both glassware and flatware. In group (a) the total cost of the four items shown was $85.00; in group (b) the total cost was $17.54. If the place settings were completed and the tables set for eight people, there would be a difference of several hundred dollars. Of course in the more expensive group there are the fine textures and beauty that often come with very fine quality—for instance, the lovely gleam of the crystal and the beautiful patina of the silverware. But the less expensive setting does not represent cheap ostentation, nor is it obviously of poor quality and design.

It is easier to find good design at budget prices in styles that are simple and free of exces-sive ornamentation. The pretense of elaborate elegance on a low budget will often achieve only pathetic effects. Differences in quality become more obvious in the wide variety of cheap imi-tations. There are some things that are expen-sive to produce and there is no way to copy them exactly at a lower cost, though many at-tempts are made to do just that. A cheap imita-tion of a fine, hand-cut crystal bowl, a beautiful silk brocade fabric, or a fine Oriental rug will not usually satisfy the discriminating taste.

Shopping for good design on a budget means that one must be particularly conscious of quality construction, and it is important to invest in durability. Some inexpensive furniture and floor coverings may have excellent designs, but if quality has been sacrificed for styling, the investment will yield poor returns. The service-ableness of some articles depends on high-quality materials and high standards of con-struction. It is especially important to give design and quality equal emphasis in selecting such items.

One of the most fascinating tools to work with in decorating is the element of color. Because it is relatively inexpensive, it can do wonders for low-level budgets if it is used with imagination. On any cost level, color is often the decorator's favorite element, probably because it is so important in establishing the mood and the personality of a home.

Color can make a room seem warmer or cooler, larger or smaller. It can make bad architectural features seem to fade into the walls, help create a center of interest, and make the room seem unified.

Colors affect moods and attitudes. They can be depressing, irritating, disturbing; they can be restful and soothing; or they can be stimulating and exciting.

What Is Color?

We see color only when there is light. When white light is passed through a suitable prism, the wave lengths that compose the light are diffracted, or bent, at slightly different angles, and are thus separated to form bands of colors collectively called the spectrum. Wave lengths slightly shorter than the violet part of the spectrum are called ultraviolet and are invisible; those slightly longer than the red end of the spectrum are called infrared and are also invisible. If the wave lengths forming the spectrum are recombined by means of a lens, the white light is re-formed.

Objects exhibit color because of the selective manner in which their surfaces reflect and absorb light. As light strikes a colored surface, certain wave lengths are reflected to a greater extent than others, thus determining the color of the object. White surfaces reflect all wave lengths equally and absorb very little energy; thus, white is a mixture of equal parts of all colored wave lengths. A black surface absorbs all wave lengths almost completely and is, therefore, the virtual absence of color.

As wave lengths strike the eye, they stimulate receptor nerves in the retina and create the sensations of color. As children, we learned to associate names with particular sensations.

4
Color

Scientific Approaches to Color

Different groups of people are interested in color for various reasons. The physicist is concerned with wave lengths of light and its physical aspects; the interest lies in the mechanical subdivision of light through a prism to produce the familiar colors of the rainbow. The chemist is concerned with the production of pigments. The psychologist wants to understand the emotional factors involved in the use and perception of color. The physiologist is interested in color as a stimulus of receptor nerves. The artist is concerned with all these aspects, but more particularly with color as pigment and as a medium of expression.

Color Terminology

Color has various dimensions and characteristics that are given special names. We might point out here that there is a difference between working with colored lights and working with colored pigments and dyestuffs. In discussing the spectrum, we noted that white light was the mixture of all wave lengths. Thus, a suitable mixture of colored lights should produce white. Proper proportions of red, yellow, and blue will produce white light through additive mixture, and these colors are called the additive primaries. Similar mixtures of pigments and dyestuffs will not produce white because these colors work on a subtractive principle, selectively absorbing portions of the white light incident upon them. Suitable mixtures of paints or dyes will produce neutral grays but will not produce white. Other pigments or dyes will absorb so much light that in proper mixtures they will produce black.

Hue. *Hue* is the term used for the name of any color. Yellow, green, red, and violet are all hues.

Intensity. *Intensity* is the saturation or purity of a color, its brightness or dullness. The lemon is brighter than the banana. A color in its purest form has greatest brilliance. To dull a color when mixing pigments, add the complement (the color directly opposite it on the color wheel). Gray, black, or white will also dull a color, causing it to lose its brilliance. Thus, we speak of grayed green or grayed yellow. Graying the yellow oranges, orange, and the red oranges will give various copper tones or the colors of saddle leather. A wide range of browns results from the mixture of black and grayed red orange, orange, and yellow orange. Although the beiges and browns are often referred to as "neutral" in the sense that they combine well with many other colors, in true color terminology only black, white, and gray are actually neutral.

Background colors usually are somewhat dull, grayed, or neutralized, because such colors are easier to live with in large amounts. Saturated colors are often reserved for hallways, powder rooms, or other rooms where people do not spend a great deal of time. Intense colors are also used for accessories because they draw more attention than dull colors.

How to Increase the Apparent Intensity of a Hue. If you have a piece of furniture that is dull in color, and you cannot afford to recover it, skillfully place the piece in such a way as to seem to raise the intensity. If it is a faded dull orange chair, you can make it seem brighter by placing the chair next to a light source of bright orange; this can be done with a portable table lamp with an orange shade or with sheer orange curtains that change the daylight to an orange reflection. Placing the dull orange chair next to a dull blue wall will also increase its apparent intensity. Using neutrals next to the dull orange chair will do the same.

Standing next to your taller friend, you look shorter; you look taller standing next to your shorter friend. The same principle can be applied in increasing the apparent intensity of an object. A dull orange chair next to an object or wall that is even duller orange will make it look brighter.

How to Decrease the Apparent Intensity of a Hue. If some object in the room needs to have its intensity lowered, this can be done by illuminating the object with the light of the complementary hue. A blue wall that is too bright can be grayed during the day with sheer orange curtains and with translucent orange lamp shades at night.

Another way to decrease the apparent intensity of the hue is to place the object next to something of the same hue but stronger in intensity. For example, a blue wall that is too bright could have brighter blue draperies, so that the wall would appear more dull.

Introducing something in the room that is more intensely colored than the object will decrease its apparent intensity. A bright yellow sofa will appear duller if a brighter painting is hung over it or if brighter chairs are placed near it.

The Effect of Intensity. Bright objects attract attention and increase the apparent size of an object. Because bright colors advance, using them on the walls will make the room appear smaller.

Value. *Value* is the lightness or darkness of a color. The lightest value of a color is almost white, and the darkest almost black. *Tint* describes the colors that are nearer white in value. Pink is a tint of red; white has been added. A *shade* describes colors that are closer to black in value. Shades are made by mixing the hue with black; navy blue is a shade of blue.

Hues on the color wheel are of different values. Yellow is the lightest color on the wheel, and purple is the darkest. The values in which the hues are shown on the color wheel are known as normal values. The value scale of the color wheel follows:

Value Scale	Value Steps on the Color Wheel	
White	White	
High light	Yellow	
Light	Yellow orange	Yellow green
Low light	Orange	Green
Middle	Orange red	Green blue
High dark	Red	Blue
Dark	Red violet	Blue violet
Low dark	Violet	
Black	Black	

Dissonance means discord in art as well as music. In color, it means that the relative values of the colors used in a combination are the reverse of their value on the standard color wheel.

Dark yellow (mustard) and light orange (peach) are examples of dissonance. When the values are reversed, as they are in dissonance, they may be more difficult to use. The effect, however, is usually more dramatic than that produced by the combination of colors in their standard values.

The Effect of Values. Light values raise the spirits and stimulate us to be active. They also recede and make an object seem farther away. Light values make a room seem larger; they create a sense of spaciousness and airiness. At night, light colors in rooms yield a higher degree of reflection and need less high-wattage illumination. A ceiling painted white will seem considerably higher than one painted a darker color.

Dark walls and floor make a room seem smaller.

(a)

Fig. 4.1

(b)

A small room will appear larger if light pink is used on the walls instead of medium-value rose. A protruding fireplace will recede into the wall when it is painted a lighter color than the rest of the wall area; for example, walls may be painted light yellow and the fireplace a lighter yellow.

Middle values are relaxing and comforting. They are often used in rooms where people must spend a good deal of time.

Dark values are serious, dignified, and often somber in feeling. They can cause a room to have a feeling of restfulness—or one of extreme depression. Dark values tend to advance. In contemporary homes with large areas of windows, dark values are more easily used.

Closely related values are quieting; strong contrasts are stimulating and alerting and call attention to things that are important. Strong contrasts increase the apparent size of the object and bring it visually forward. If a piece of furniture, a vase, or a lamp that has contours that should be noticed, the object should be placed against a background of a contrasting value.

Fig. 4.2

Sharp value contrasts call attention to the forms. *(Courtesy of Monsanto Company)*

Warm, cool, advancing, and receding. The terms *warm* and *cool* are frequently used in connection with color. The warm hues are those that we associate with fire, heat, and the sun: red, yellow, and orange. Warm hues tend to raise the spirits and attract attention. In rooms where much activity is to take place, warm colors should be used; studies show that people are more active in rooms decorated with warm colors.

The cool hues are those we associate with ice, shade, and water: blue and green. In rooms where a restful feeling is desired, cool hues tend to calm the emotions.

Colors often cannot definitely be placed in one or the other of these categories. Green, usually considered a cool color, is a mixture of blue and yellow; therefore a predominance of either hue may change the characteristic of green. A yellow green may have a good deal of warmth, whereas blue green is usually quite cool. True purple, which is a mixture of blue and red, is neither warm nor cool; however, if there is a slight predominance of red, it will have a warm quality, and if it leans toward blue, it might be quite cool.

The terms *advancing* and *receding* are also used in connection with color. Several characteristics determine this color quality. The bright warm hues are more advancing than the bright cool hues. Yet any brilliant color is more advancing than grayed colors, which are said to recede. Cool colors, light values, and lower intensities tend to recede and give a feeling of spaciousness.

Color and Light

Because there is no color without light, it is important to know what light does to color. Any color that is planned for a room should be tested in both natural and artificial light. Colors show their truest characteristics in a northern exposure, which provides the most natural form of blue-white daylight.

For artificial lighting we use electric light from incandescent bulbs or fluorescent tubes. Some of these simulate pure blue-white light, but they are not popular for living areas. We are more likely to select bulbs and tubes that cast soft yellow or pink glows, which are more flattering to people and seem to be more pleasing to live with. Candlelight casts a lovely yellow glow that is flattering to almost everyone.

Ordinary incandescent light bulbs cast a yellow glow, although in recent years bulbs have been manufactured with various other color tones. One can buy bulbs with pink, blue, green, or deep yellow tones. These are interesting for decorative effects in some areas, but they do not produce efficient lighting.

The color and the amount of artificial light that are used will affect the colors in one's rooms. The yellow tones of the incandescent bulbs will emphasize any yellow that might be mixed with a color. For example, a yellow green will appear more yellow under electric light than it will in true daylight. Pinks and reds will seem deeper or richer if the source of light is pink rather than yellow. Blue light will, of course, emphasize blue tones, but blue light is usually rather cool and may seem somewhat harsh.

Under white fluorescent light, cool colors are likely to go gray, although greens and yellows intensify. A soft white fluorescent light warms up reds. To overcome the unpleasant effects caused by fluorescent light, a deluxe warm white fluorescent tube can be used. Fluorescents are also available in a variety of tones ranging from a true blue-white that simulates natural daylight to a soft pink.

Color Systems

Various systems have been devised for working with colors, and some of these systems are more suitable than others for dealing with particular aspects of color. It would be beyond the province of this book to delve into all the color theories and unnecessary to present superfluous technical information that may only confuse the reader rather than clarify the subject of color. It is helpful, however, to understand color systems to develop one's own perception and ability to work with color schemes. We shall therefore briefly discuss two well-known color systems.

The Munsell system. The Munsell color-order system describes and catalogs color in terms of the three visual attributes or dimensions mentioned earlier—hue, chroma (intensity), and value. These attributes are arranged into orderly scales of equal *visual* steps. The color solid so defined is an irregular spheroid, having a central vertical axis representing the neutral value scale, with white at the top, black at the bottom, and the intermediate steps of grays scaled between these two extremes.

There are no primary colors as in the pigment-mixture systems, but there are five principal hues—red, yellow, green, blue, and purple—spaced at equal visual intervals around the outside of the color solid. Spaced between the principal hues are five intermediate hues—yellow red, green yellow, blue green, purple blue, and red purple. Radiating out at 90 degrees from the value axis are scales of chroma, or saturation, for each hue at each value level. The low-chroma colors, which are grayish, are near the gray axis, and the chroma increases until the most intense colors are reached on the surface of the solid.

Each of the ten hue families already listed is divided decimally as the hue gradually changes toward its neighbor, with the central hue in each family having the prefix 5. Numbers below 5 indicate hues inclining toward the hue family next in a counterclockwise direction, whereas those above 5 approach the hue family in the opposite direction. Thus 5GY is middle green yellow; 3GY is more yellow, while 7GY is more green.

On the vertical scale absolute black is N 0/ and absolute white is N 10/. The value notation is always followed by a slant line. The chroma attribute is written following the slant line and departs from the value axis, having a chroma of /0, through a series of visual saturation steps to the maximum that can be produced, in some cases as high as /14 or /16. Thus, 5Y 8/4 is a middle yellow hue (5Y) at high value (8/) and low chroma (/4). It is a tint of a grayed yellow or beige.

Munsell notations are available for forty different hues, at the 2.5, 5, 7.5, and 10 positions of each of the ten hue families. Where possible, colors appear on each full value level from 2/ through 9/, and in some cases at half-value lev-els. Neutrals (white, grays, black) are available in eighteen steps (N 1/, N 1.5/, N 2/, . . . N 9/, N 9.5/).

The Munsell notation is related to the internationally recognized CIE[1] system of color specifications by a series of translational diagrams, making it extremely useful in science and industry.

The Prang system. The system developed by David Brewster is probably the best-known color system and is often referred to as the Prang system. The simplest way to understand color relationships is to study a color wheel based on three primary colors: yellow, blue, and red. These three hues are called primary in the Prang system because they cannot be mixed from other pigments.

Theoretically, starting with five cans or tubes of paint—the three primaries plus black and white—one could build an entire range of colors. However, this is not practical, because to achieve the exact gradations in color requires precise mixing of different pigments.

The color wheel indicates that a mixture of yellow and blue produces green. Blue and red produce purple; yellow and red produce orange. Green, purple, and orange are secondary colors in this system. Each one is made by mixing two primary colors.

By mixing a primary and a secondary color, one will produce the tertiary or intermediate colors: yellow green, blue green, blue purple, red purple, red orange, and yellow orange. There are infinite variations on each primary and secondary color. One may mix a small amount of yellow with a large amount of green, then add a small amount of yellow, and then a little more until there is more yellow than green in the mixture. If an individual were to take a sample of each mixture, there would be a variety of yellow-green hues ranging from one that was almost yellow to one that was almost green. One can produce a similar range of hues by mixing the other primary and secondary hues.

[1] Commission Internationale de l'Eclairage.

Factors That Influence Color Choice

This brief discussion of color indicates that one may choose from thousands of colors and that the possible combinations are infinite. The natural question, then, is where to start. Several factors will guide a selection of colors, and some will be more important than others.

The Emotional Effect of Color

People like color and associate it with different events in life. Receiving compliments or having a good time while wearing a particular color may create a favorable response to it. There are reactions and moods to be associated with color. Most colors have associations that are widely recognized within a given culture; in addition they often produce private, personal reactions.

Man has associated colors with various meanings for centuries. Some of the same reactions hold today. The Chinese and Egyptians, as well as the Greeks, held yellow as a sacred color; it became a symbol of power. Yellow is the sun color. Yellow has stood for wisdom, gaiety, and warmth, but it is also used in the term "yellow coward." As a dominant color, yellow is usually rather easy to use.

Blue was not identified as a separate color for a long time; it was considered a form of black. Blue is a very conservative color. It is a symbol of happiness, hope, truth, honor, and repose. Cézanne was a master of blue, blue green, and violet. Study his paintings, and use them for color combination suggestions. Blue is a restraining, cool, soothing, and peaceful color. Its tranquility is relaxing to most people.

Red is the most vital color. It arouses our senses, stimulates the appetite, attracts attention, and stimulates us to be active. Think of the vast ranges of tints and shades of red: strawberry pink, shocking pink, cherry red, tomato red, fire-engine red, lobster red, and maroon.

Purple is an ancient color and was once costly to produce as a pigment. Hence, for more than two thousand years it was a symbol of royalty. Purple has always been considered dramatic and regal. It has been associated with spiritualism, mystery, pride, and wisdom.

Green is associated with life, spring, hope, and envy. It is cold enough to be restful and warm enough to be interesting. Green is a most useful color, as it fits into almost any scheme. Balanced between warm yellow and cool blue, it is especially pleasing with wood tones—after all, it was chosen as the hue for foliage.

Orange is an earth color. In decorating, orange finds its best uses in copper, shrimp, peach, coral, salmon, and rust. Autumn is the time to get acquainted with orange in the maple leaves, bright gourds, and dull butternut squash.

Black is recognized as a neutral. To the ancient Greeks, black symbolized life, because out of night day is born. During the sixteenth century, Anne of Brittany used black for mourning, a custom that continues in Western civilization today. Black is strong and sophisticated; but it is also associated with evil, old age, and silence.

White is the symbol of purity, innocence, faith, peace, and surrender. It is a color for mourning in some Eastern civilizations. Both black and white have a way of making colors look cleaner and livelier.

How to Choose a Color Scheme

Individual Preferences

The colors chosen should be those that the members of the family enjoy viewing. Most of us lean at least a little toward one color or one group of colors. Even if one is not particularly color-conscious, there may be colors that one intensely dislikes. All colors that evoke unfavorable reactions should be avoided. Color preferences are not always clearly defined; learning what they are may take some probing.

Living rooms, family rooms, and dining rooms should have colors that appeal to all members of the family. Strong preferences of any one individual can be limited to that person's bedroom.

The Style and Purpose of the Room

Although we need not be too restricted by style or purpose in choosing colors, a particular theme can be emphasized by the color scheme.

An informal room may call for colors that are bright, strong, and stimulating. A room that is meant for relaxation and repose should have colors that are quiet and restful. Children's rooms may have colors that are either bright or delicate.

Certain syles, such as Early American or Colonial, are best expressed by the authentic colors of the natural dyes that were used with the original furniture. Much of French decor requires soft, delicate coloring. The luxurious themes of eighteenth-century English styles call for rich, elegant tones of claret red, emerald green, gold, and plum color. The modern style has made use of bold, brilliant colors, often in combination and often as accents against white or neutral backgrounds.

Ready-Made Combinations

Another way to approach the planning of a color scheme is to choose some existing design or pattern and key the various color areas to it. One might select a vase, a picture, a rug, or a fabric with a combination of colors that is appealing. Collections of pop art, sea shells, or pennants may help determine a color scheme or theme. Post cards and cards from museums, as well as photographs of a favorite scene, may suggest colors to use in a room setting. It is not necessary to match colors exactly, but the colors in other areas must be related to those in the design. Different values and different intensities should be used.

Color in nature. There is no better guide to color combinations than nature. Observe the brilliant hues of the butterfly wing, or the plummage of birds. To find colors that appeal to you, arrange flowers or vegetables until a combination satisfies you.

Shibui. The Japanese decorating theme of shibui has become popular in the United States. Rooms that are done in the shibui scheme use nature as a guide in combining colors and textures.

Nature does not duplicate any two things. For example, tree leaves are not alike; the color, shape, and veins are varied. Nature is richly textured. The bark of a tree is not plain brown, but many shades of brown, and sometimes green; when wet it may appear black. It is the subtle use of color that makes nature constantly a challenge to view and study. Nothing is obvious; upon careful observation, every miniscule part of nature has infinite variety.

This technique can be employed in interiors. For example, dining-room chairs may look alike from a distance, but a decorator using shibui as a decorating theme may choose to cover the seats with the same color, but in different textures or weaves.

Shibui echoes nature's use of bright accents in small quantities, against large dull backgrounds. Brilliant tulips are seen in small amounts, and nature usually paints the sky and earth in dull colors. This can be a decorative guideline; large areas of dull colors, dark colors on the floor, light colors used on the ceiling, and bright accents reserved for use in small amounts.

The Color Wheel. To develop another color scheme, use the color wheel. This is more fun and truly an exciting experience if one is equipped with a few jars of ordinary poster paint, a plastic egg container for mixing colors, brushes, a glass of water, and lots of white paper.

Start with the primary colors, plus white and black, and follow the color wheel, mixing secondary and intermediate colors. Then start graying colors by mixing them with small amounts of their complements. Tints and shades can be made by the use of the white and black. Keep the samples of the colors mixed. Now you are ready to work on color combinations.

Color Harmonies

Actually, any colors can be combined with pleasing results if we are conscious of intensity and value. For example, one may not be partial to a brilliant red next to a brilliant orange, but in some primitive art this combination is used most effectively. But if the orange is grayed and mixed with a little black, the result is a rich chocolate brown. Now mix some white with the red to produce a lovely pale pink. Brown and pink is not as shocking a combination as the brilliant orange and red. The intensity and the value of the two hues have simply been varied to produce a more acceptable combination of colors. In working with the color wheel, one must be particularly cognizant of variations in both intensity and value, remembering that black, white, and gray are neutrals that can be parts of any color scheme.

Monochromatic. *Mono* means one, and in working out a true monochromatic harmony, one hue must be the keynote of the whole scheme. The popular scheme of beige, brown, and orange is a truly monochromatic scheme, because the tans and browns are simply tints and shades of grayed orange. A brilliant form of orange may be used as an accent or even for larger areas, but if any other hue is introduced, the harmony is no longer monochromatic. Black and white are neutrals that can be used to add spice and interest to the scheme. In monochromatic schemes, the key to success is to provide enough contrast through either value or intensity to make the combination interesting. Pattern, texture, and furniture shapes add interest to the room.

Analogous. Colors that are next to each other on the color wheel frequently provide the basis of very pleasing combinations. Blue, blue violet, and violet have enjoyed tremendous popularity in recent years. A more standard analogous harmony combines yellow, yellow green, and green. Once again, with different values and intensities, any adjacent colors may be used in combination with interesting effects.

Complementary. More contrast is provided by the use of colors that are opposite each other on the color wheel. A true complementary harmony uses colors that are directly opposite, such as orange and blue, red and green, or yellow and purple. When such colors are used in their fullest intensities, they emphasize each other. A brilliant red held next to a brilliant green will appear more intense than when viewed separately. Such combinations are common when a forceful use of color is desired. Note how often complements are used in advertising posters and flags. Although brilliant complements are frequently used in decoration, more interesting combinations of color result when the hues are varied a bit. A soft maize or pale yellow with a deep plum purple, for example, would probably have more appeal than a brilliant yellow and a brilliant purple used together. Instead of brilliant orange and blue, the grayed oranges or copper tones might be used with a blue that is also decreased in intensity. Using tints of each color would produce a combination of peach or apricot and light blue—still a complementary harmony but one that is easier to live with than the colors used in their most brilliant forms. Pink and dark green is also a softer combination than bright red and green. Neutrals may be added to enhance the color scheme even more.

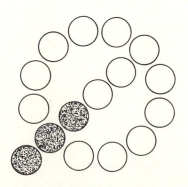

(a) Monochromatic

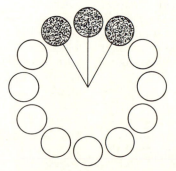

(b) Analogous

(c) Complementary

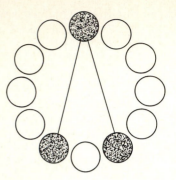
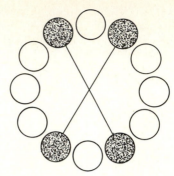
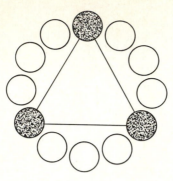

(d) Split Complementary   (e) Double Complementary   (f) Triad

Split complementary. Instead of using colors that are opposite each other on the color wheel, you might select one hue and combine it with the colors that are on either side of its complement as though placing a narrow-angled Y on the color wheel. This provides three colors to work with; by varying their intensities and values you can work out some interesting combinations. For example, if orange is chosen, the split complements are blue green and blue violet. It would be a good idea to experiment with various values and intensities of these three colors to see whether or not a pleasing combination can be worked out.

Double complementary. If a narrow X is superimposed on the color wheel, there will be two sets of complementary colors with which to work. Four colors may be a bit confusing in a small area, but it is fun to test one's skill in combining such a variety. They are good choices for adding variety while coordinating large areas. Use more of one and a tiny amount of another. Use a brilliant form of one in a small area as an accent. Just a touch of it will complete the scheme.

Triad. A triangle placed on the color wheel will point to three colors that form the triad. The primaries—yellow, blue, and red—might be used. In intense tones, such a combination might be suitable for a playroom or a kitchen because these are dashing colors. But if the yellow is subdued to gold, and the red deepened to

claret and the blue to indigo, the combination becomes one that is often found in elegant rooms with colors keyed to the jewel tones of an Oriental rug. Or if all the colors are softened to pastel tints of maize, rose, and light blue, a combination results that is often seen in prints and plaids that might be suitable to a gay but delicate scheme for a young girl's bedroom or a dinette. This triad of the primary colors can lend itself to many adaptations, but triads of other hues can also be the basis of exciting combinations. For example, experiment with green, purple, and orange. In brilliant forms, the combinations may not be attractive, but with different values and intensities some fascinating combinations can be worked out.

Neutrals. The neutrals are black, white, and gray. But in interiors, wheat, beige, off-white, and the high values of each hue are considered neutral.

Color schemes built entirely around neutrals are very restful; but texture and patterns must be used to prevent the scheme from becoming dull.

Black-and-white schemes are highly dramatic because of the strong contrast. For example, a scheme could be developed with more than two thirds of the area white and less than one third black. Some gray could be introduced in a pattern.

Some black-and-white schemes use an addition of one or more fully saturated hues, like yellow, green, turquoise, or red. This would not

**Plate
1**

PRIMARY
YELLOW
YELLOW-ORANGE
YELLOW-GREEN
SECONDARY
ORANGE
SECONDARY
GREEN
RED-ORANGE
BLUE-GREEN
PRIMARY
RED
PRIMARY
BLUE
RED-PURPLE
BLUE-PURPLE
SECONDARY
PURPLE

The color wheel based on three primary colors.

**Plate
2**

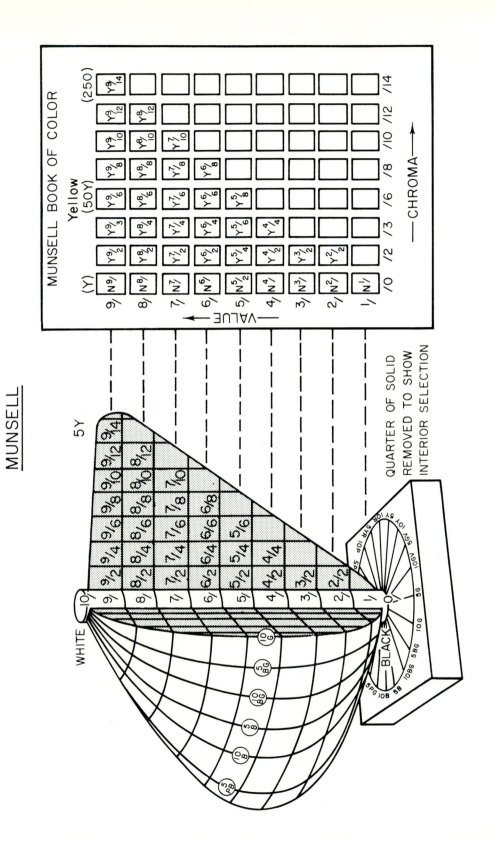

Chart of 2.5 YR in the Munsell System. (*Courtesy of
the Munsell Color Co., Inc.*)

One page from the Munsell Color Co., Inc., color-order system. Variations in value (brightness) and chroma (saturation) are shown for a single hue. *(Courtesy of the Munsell Color Co., Inc.)*

Plate 3

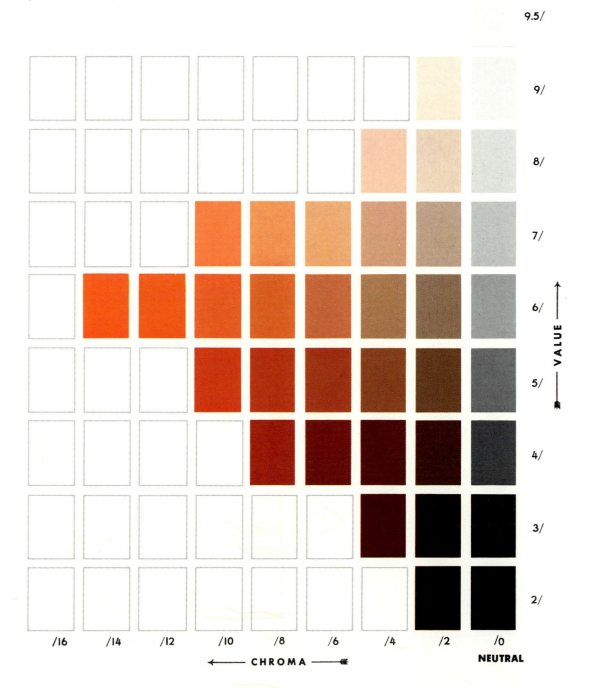

N

9.5/

9/

8/

7/

6/

5/

VALUE

4/

3/

2/

/16 /14 /12 /10 /8 /6 /4 /2 /0

← CHROMA →

NEUTRAL

Plate 4
A monochromatic scheme lends an air of elegance to the drawing room in Celanese House. The Austrian valence combined with plaid shades dramatizes the window. Bamboo armchairs, light in scale, provide comfortable seating without adding heavy proportions to the rather narrow room. *(Courtesy of Celanese Corporation)*

This analogous scheme in the family room of the Ruben House is lively, spacious, and functional. *(Courtesy of Monsanto Company)*

Plate 5

**Plate
6**

Neutral color scheme. Neutrals dominate this color scheme. There is a spacious feeling created by using carpeting over the base of the seating platform, and by the minimum amount of ornamentation on the wall space. There is effective use of African, Indian, and Islamic motifs. The lighted coffee table is an unusual addition to the room. *(Courtesy of Monsanto Company* [House and Garden]*)*

Plate 7

Complementary colors of red and green take on new dimensions in the bedroom setting. The sheer fabric lends itself to the balloon shades at the window as well as to the portiere treatment of the bed. *(Courtesy of The Singer Company)*

Emily Malino, A.I.D., designed this stimulating eclectic room in the triad color scheme with red modular seating, teal blue walls, and yellow gold in the carpeting and wood color. *(Courtesy of Monsanto Company)*

Plate
8

**Plate
9**
The yellow tone of the woods used in this room
blend with the other colors in the scheme. The pattern of the wallpaper repeated on the sofa gives a
unified feeling to the room. *(Courtesy of Monsanto
Company)*

Pattern and color become the dominant note that unifies the room. Two levels differentiate the separate functions in the room. They are clearly marked with carpeting and tile. The use of light bulbs to emphasize the wall hanging lends an unusual atmosphere to the room. *(Courtesy of Monsanto Company)*

Plate 10

**Plate
11**

In a ''mini-budget'' apartment designer Emily Malino
relies on color for interest. Everything was chosen
with cost and practicality in mind for this project to
demonstrate the techniques of low-cost decorating.
(Courtesy of Monsanto Company)

be characterized as a monochromatic scheme because neutrals dominate. It could be called a neutral color scheme with accents.

The Color Plan

Some preliminary paper work is important in the working out of color schemes. In the drawing of floor plans a scale is used in order that each piece of furniture may be accurately represented in relation to the measurements of the room. With color plans, one cannot be quite so accurate about measurements of areas, but one must remember that the amount of each color used is important in the over-all effect. It is essential, therefore, to work with samples and swatches that are somewhat proportionate to the areas they will cover in the room.

Many colors and textures are used in each area of the home. The wood tones of the furniture also contribute to the color scheme. Certain areas, such as a bedroom or a dining room, may have larger areas of wood color. The living room will probably have a certain amount of wood, but the upholstered pieces and the draperies will form major color areas. In every room, the wall and floor areas are considerably larger than the other areas.

When planning a color scheme, one should list the areas of color that will contribute to the decor and mark off proportionate areas that approximate the amounts of space they will cover. This must, of necessity, be guesswork, but the

Plan a color chart for each room. Try to keep areas in relative amounts.

Fig. 4.3

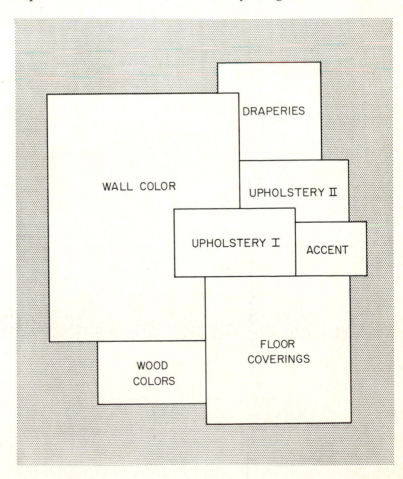

important point is to keep the areas reasonably accurate relative to one another. The samples and swatches should be overlapped as they are arranged, so as to show the effects of having colors next to one another as they will actually be used. If the accent colors will be used in pillows on a sofa, the swatches of accent should be placed next to the swatch that represents the sofa to show the true effect.

Sometimes it is even more useful to draw a large-scale floor plan of the room. Paint the color of the floor covering first. Then paste swatches where they will be used. This method is useful for showing the distribution of colors. Then represent the wood tones with samples cut from magazines or with bits of the adhesive-backed plastic that comes in a variety of wood textures and colors. The piece of paper used should be large enough for pasting generous samples of wall and drapery colors in the margin.

The purpose of either type of color plan is to help visualize the finished room and to present some idea of how the colors will relate to one another. It is important to use actual swatches and colors, or else samples that are as close as possible. Expose the chart to different lighting effects. If the master color chart includes the manufacturer's name, pattern name, color name, and date purchased, reordering will be more accurate.

The Physical Characteristics of the Room

Certain aspects of the room itself may determine the choice of colors. These include:

Exposure. Both the amount and the type of natural light that enters a room may influence the choice of colors. If the room will be used mainly at night, exposure is not such an important consideration, but almost every room will sometimes be used during the day.

Light from the north has a bluish cast that shows colors in their most natural tones. This is the type of light that the artist prefers for the studio, because the light from a northern exposure has a cold quality that intensifies the characteristics of colors. In a home, however, we are more interested in a pleasant atmosphere than in seeing colors at their truest, and it is desirable to select colors that will blend with the natural light to provide the desired effects. To counteract the effects of harsh light, rooms with northern exposures are often decorated with warm colors. Yellow, orange, red, or warm pink may be used to produce a sunshine-like glow.

On the other hand, rooms with a southern or a southwestern exposure receive a warm light. Especially in areas that will be used a great deal during hot weather, these rooms are more pleasant when they are decorated with cool colors. Brilliant colors, especially in the warm group, will seem more intense if the room receives a large amount of natural sunlight.

Preferences for certain colors and the purposes for which a room is to be used may cause one to ignore these effects of exposure, but, because colors vary so much under different conditions of light, it is important that they be examined carefully in the natural setting of the room before they are selected.

Size. It is not always necessary to make small rooms seem larger or large rooms seem smaller, but if one does want to change the apparent size of an area, color is a useful tool. In general, the light colors that are somewhat grayed will make a room appear larger. Pale green, aqua, or pale blue—all cool colors—lend an airy, spacious quality. These receding colors seem to push walls back, whereas brilliant colors and even some tints of the warm colors are more advancing. Dark tones define space and will make a room seem smaller.

Shape. The advancing and receding qualities of color may be used to emphasize or to counteract the shape of a room. A particular wall or an alcove becomes more important if it is decorated in an advancing hue while the other walls and areas are more subdued with colors that recede. Using different colors or textures is a handy technique for treating poorly shaped areas, but it need not be reserved for problem rooms. It is an effective way of adding emphasis or creating a center of interest. However, when a room does have poor proportions it can be made far more attractive by an imaginative use of color and texture. A high ceiling, for example, will seem lower if it is painted a dark color. A brilliant color would also be advancing, but it might serve to draw undue attention to the ceiling and defeat its own purpose.

The short wall in a long, narrow room can be made to advance while the others recede. Different values or different intensities of the same hue can be used; so can colors that contrast with each other. A room that seems too square can be given a more pleasing proportion by using different hues.

Architectural materials. Architectural materials will affect the color scheme. Wood floors and paneling cover large areas, thereby introducing browns into the room. Slate, stone, tiles, or brick also introduce other colors. For example, a wall of old brick may have a pink cast to it; therefore, it will blend better with warm reds or pinks than it will blend with oranges.

Practical Aspects of Color Schemes

For some rooms, it is best to keep in mind a few practical aspects of color planning. In anticipation of the possibility that someday the color scheme may be changed, it is wise to see that the more durable furnishings, such as rugs and upholstered pieces, be of colors that lend themselves to a variety of color combinations. Walls can be refinished, and upholstered pieces can be slipcovered, but a floor covering is not as easy to change. This certainly does not mean that one must be limited to gray or some other neutral or so-called neutral, but if a sizable sum is to be invested in a floor covering, it is wise to think of its adaptability to various other color combinations.

In an area of heavy traffic, the problem of maintenance should be considered too. A very light or a very dark color on the floor will show footprints and soil more readily than the medium values. In general, spots show up more readily on solid colors than they do on figured

rugs and carpets. Upholstered furniture that will receive hard wear should have textures and colors that will not be soiled easily. The lovely light and bright colors are most appealing when they are fresh and clean-looking. If one has to devote a great deal of time to keeping the home spick and span it will soon become a burden rather than a joy. But that does not mean that color schemes must be dreary; it is simply a matter of using interesting but practical colors in the right places. With some forethought, a color scheme can be not only gay, elegant, exciting, or anything else that is wanted, but also very easy to maintain.

Planning the Color Scheme for the Entire Home

There are several advantages to planning a total color scheme. Because space is so valuable today, nothing makes a home look larger than color continuity. A plan will permit the consumer to decorate one room at a time and allow for planned future purchases. With a plan and color swatches available, there is no temptation to buy a piece of furniture on sale if it does not fit in with the plan.

First, establish the basic scheme. Suppose you choose yellow and green. Announce this scheme in the foyer or entry gently but firmly; you might have a painting or wallpaper which is predominately yellow and green. Use the colors throughout in different combinations and proportions. One idea is to reverse the color schemes as you proceed from area to area. If the living room is done in green with yellow accents, in the dining alcove use yellow as the main or background color and repeat green in the chair seats and decorative accessories.

Distribution and proportion of color. There are no hard and fast rules for apportioning colors; it is the almost unlimited freedom to use colors that makes color choice highly personal. However, there are some guidelines in assigning color areas that produce pleasing results.

Decide on the colors for the largest areas: the floors, walls, and ceilings. Generally, the dominant color covers about two thirds of the room's area. It is suggested that the most neutral color in a light value be employed in these areas. For example, if green is the dominant color, use light dull green on the walls, and a high light neutral green on the ceiling. The floors may be predominantly green and yellow figures may be added in the upholstery fabrics.

Floors and walls are big areas that can be unified if they are done in relating colors. If you have yellow walls, both variety and unity can be achieved by using a green rug with yellow motifs.

Next decide on the distribution of color in furniture, draperies, and accessories. Generally, these areas are covered in brighter colors. Pattern and textural contrast add to the impact.

The window area may create contrast, or it may be the center of interest. The drapery fabric is sometimes repeated in chairs used in the living room. If it is a print, a reverse print can create rhythm as well as variety.

In a well-decorated room, the accessories are noticeable. They are strategically placed to create rhythm. The colors chosen may be brighter than the background colors, or, in a room with a predominance of one color, choosing a color that is the true complement can create an accent.

Accent colors are usually bright and intense, and are used in small amounts. Because items used to provide accent are fairly inexpensive and portable, they may be changed with the seasons or for variation.

Wood Tones in the Color Scheme

In popular writings we find a great deal about wood textures but very little about wood colors. Yet woods do have important color tones that should harmonize with the decorative scheme if the furniture is to appear most attractive.

Woods can be bleached or stained to a wide variety of colors. Many of the bleached woods have decided yellow tones. Traditionally, mahogany has a distinct red color, but new finishes sometimes give it a nutmeg cast that reduces or eliminates the red color. Walnut, in its traditional color, is a grayish brown that blends well with many colors. The fruit woods may have distinct colors in grayed form.

A background should be chosen that will either relate or contrast with the tones of the woods used. A deep, rich red mahogany is lovely against a soft pale green or aqua, because the red and green are complementary colors. Against a soft rose-beige background it will be equally attractive because the colors are related. Yet a bleached wood with yellow tones next to a light pinkish beige wall is not usually attractive, because the colors are neither related nor in contrast. Such a wood tone might be lovely against any dark or light contrasting color. Color harmonies can be applied to achieve interesting effects.

In some rooms there will be more exposed wood furniture than in others. Naturally, when the wood tones become a major color area in a room, the background color is particularly important in the color scheme.

Color for a Spacious Look

The more an area is broken up with contrasts of colors, the smaller the area will appear. This is a good case for the use of a monochromatic harmony in a small area to make it look larger. But to keep a monochromatic harmony from becoming dull and monotonous, one must be sensitive to the values and intensities of the basic color. It is necessary to know also how to introduce the neutrals—black, white, and gray—most effectively. In some monochromatic schemes, they may not be wanted at all, but in others they can contribute a great deal to the interest of the color plan.

Let us consider the problem of working out a color scheme for a small living room. It does not necessarily have to be monochromatic harmony to make the room appear larger. We shall use a complementary harmony of red orange and blue green.

Assume that the room is rather dismal, with little natural light and a northern exposure. We want to make the room light and bright; we also

(a)

(b)

Fig.
4.4

Large areas of pattern or strong contrasts make furniture seem more prominent and decrease the apparent size of the room.

want it to seem larger than it really is. Our major color areas include:

Walls.
Floor covering.
Draperies.
Sofa.
Two upholstered chairs.
Accents.

Where shall we begin? Suppose we select a printed fabric that has a warm beige background (a tint of red orange) and a small geometric print in turquoise. The print may have some cocoa brown (also related to the red orange) and perhaps various shades of the turquoise.

Because this is a room with dull light, we shall choose the red orange as the basic color for large areas. But because we do not want brilliant colors that will make the room seem smaller, we gray the red orange and use a tint of the hue to produce a warm beige.

The color plan might evolve as follows:

Walls   Beige, to match the background of the print.
Floor covering   Cocoa brown.
Draperies   Printed fabric.
Sofa   Beige slightly deeper than the walls.
Two chairs   Turquoise or the printed fabric.
Accents   (sofa pillows, ashtrays, and so on): Brilliant blue green and a few small touches of red orange.

How have we applied the theories to planning a color scheme for this room?

1. We do not have large areas of contrast. Although the drapery fabric is a print, the wall color *matches* the background of the fabric, unifying the wall and window areas. A solid-color drapery to match the walls would be better in this respect, but for this particular room we prefer a print for interest.
2. The large area of floor covering is a deeper tone of the wall color, which relates these two large areas. It is a medium value that will not readily show soil and footprints.
3. The sofa, which is a large color area, is not in strong contrast to the wall, so it will not be emphasized as a heavy piece of furniture.

4. The two chairs repeat the turquoise in the print, or the print itself, to provide a feeling of rhythm or unity.
5. The accents of brilliant color are used in small areas to emphasize the print and to provide interest.

It should be noted that no strong contrasts are used for large areas. Also, keeping the wall color closely related to the background of the print provides a unifying effect. A sharp contrast between the drapery and the wall would emphasize the window area by sharpening the vertical line where the drapery meets the wall.

To make a small room seem larger, the major color areas should melt into one another. Bright and more advancing colors may be used in smaller areas and in accessories.

Lighting is an important element in determining the beauty and comfort of the home. Within the past few decades, lighting has developed as both an art and a science. Engineers have devoted a tremendous amount of effort in exploiting the aesthetic as well as the functional possibilities of artificial lighting. We have seen the interesting results in many modern public buildings and in some homes of more progressive design.

Unfortunately, most residential lighting has not kept pace with the advances made in industrial light. Too many people decorate their house or apartment first and then consider lighting as an afterthought. There are many homes with inadequate or improper illumination, and frequently the potentials of decorating with light are sadly neglected. Even when there is an adequate amount, light is used in many homes in a rather stereotyped manner. This is unfortunate because there are so many new ideas and trends in light and lighting fixtures today.

The proper amount and type of light should add beauty to the colors and furnishings in the home. The color scheme can be carefully planned, yet the room can have little effect if the room is poorly lighted. Clever lighting can give an ordinary room character. Good lighting can increase efficiency, relieve eye strain, cut down on accidents, and help set the mood of the room. With the new lighting fixtures and lamps, and with materials that have translucent or diffusing qualities, even the amateur can create beautiful effects.

In recent years, there has been considerable emphasis on adjustable lighting. Dimmer controls that are relatively easy to install make it possible to increase or decrease the amount of light as needed. Ceiling and wall fixtures that adjust to different heights or swing to different positions have also become popular. Lamp poles have several advantages in that they can be moved around, they take up little space, and they provide direct light where it is needed. Although these have been associated with a modern theme, they are now being designed to fit more easily into traditional rooms as well.

5

Lighting

We must understand a few basic facts about light before we can undertake any meaningful discussion of lighting the home. Lighting is an important factor in planning color schemes. It should be remembered that without light, there is no color, and although we may feel textures in the dark, they have no visual significance unless there is some source of light.

As light rays strike a surface they are either absorbed or reflected. The color and the texture of the substance upon which the light rays fall determine the reflective qualities. A dull black surface will absorb all the rays of light; a shiny white surface will reflect all the rays of light.

We see color because of a pigment in the surface material. This surface will absorb some light rays and reflect others. Tints of colors, or the very light colors, reflect most of the light rays that strike the surface. Dark colors will absorb most of the light rays and reflect relatively few. Textures that are dull or uneven tend to reflect fewer light rays than those that are glossy and smooth.

Thus one element of practical lighting depends on how and where we see the light. For example, in a room with dark walls and all other areas in dark, dull textures, most of the light thrown from a light source would be absorbed. In a similar room decorated in white or light tints and glossy surfaces, most of the light from the same lamp would be reflected. Therefore it would seem to emanate from about the room rather than from the lamp alone.

The Effect of Light on Color

The interaction of light and color is a subtle but powerful force in planning lighting for the home. Fabric in a store can seem different in color under fluorescent lighting, as compared to the incandescent lighting at home or to natural light. This is why it is important to test a color under the lighting in the home. Place the samples on the floor and wall during the different daylight hours and when artificial lighting is used. Two colors that contrast pleasingly by natural light or by fluorescent light can look almost identical, or clash appallingly, by incandescent light.

A quick review of the color wheel should explain some of the effects that different colors of light will produce. It has been noted that we can gray a color or decrease its intensity by mixing it with its complement. Colored light will produce similar effects. Therefore, light with pink, orange, or yellow tones will tend to decrease the brilliance of blues and greens. Light with a special color will deepen or intensify similar colors in the room. Pink or red areas viewed under a pink light will take on added depth and richness. Mixed colors will take on added color from light; for example, a yellowish light will emphasize the yellow element in yellow green or yellow orange.

It is often difficult to combine different colors of light in the same room. When both incandescent and fluorescent lighting are used, the warm white or deluxe warm white fluorescent tube is recommended, because it combines pleasantly with the color of incandescent light.

Cool light such as blue does what any cool color will do: it gives more apparent space to the room and adds a chilling effect. Warm light such as yellow or pink takes away from the cool effects of the room and dulls the cool colors.

Light Sources

Light can be generated through three different physical processes: combustion, incandescent, and electric discharge.

Combustion. The oldest way known to man to produce light is combustion. Fire, oil lamps, candles, and gas lamps are a few examples of light produced by combustion. The yellow-orange color of the light from sources of combustion is particularly flattering to skin tones. However, it is impractical to use this method to light the home because it is rather difficult to control, it can be a fire hazard, and it represents an inefficient use of natural resources.

Incandescent. When a substance is heated to incandescence, it produces light. There are two sources of incandescent light: natural daylight (sunlight), and incandescent electric light.

Natural Light (*Sunlight*). The sun is the first and oldest source of light known to us. Its radiation not only permits us to see, but it also allows the life-supporting processes to take place.

Rooms that are illuminated by sunlight have a vitality about them. Areas used early in the day, such as kitchens, breakfast areas, and bedrooms, that face the east are warmed by the awakening rays of the morning sun.

Artists' studios and designers' workshops should not have as wide a variation of illumination as other spaces; therefore, a northern orientation is more suitable. Rooms that face south will have daylight suitable for such areas as family rooms and sewing rooms.

Western exposures can create an uncomfortable glare and heat in some parts of the country. Unless such lighting is carefully controlled by shading devices such as overhangs or blinds, problems arise from the harshness of the direct light of the sun.

Landscaping with deciduous trees may help solve the problem of heat and glare. A deciduous tree has its full foilage during the summer and sheds it during the winter, thus providing the house with shade during the hotter months of the year and allowing the warming rays of the sun to reach the windows during the colder months, resulting in a savings on the heating bill. Conversely, coniferous trees planted on the north side of the house can block some of the piercing northern winds in the colder months of the year.

Incandescent Electric Light. The incandescent light is produced from the heating of a tungsten filament in the light bulb (the bulb is only the glass envelope). The variety of incandescent bulbs available has been increasing at a rapid rate for some years and continues to do so. It is possible to purchase bulbs that provide three levels of brightness. The size varies from three watts to 10,000 watts; light bulbs are available in colors such as blue, pink, yellow, and green. All types of bulbs are made in a wide variety of shapes and finishes, including frosted coatings that soften and diffuse the light as well as minimize the glare. The most familiar incandescent bulb is the standard frosted one that gives a warm light, much warmer than the light produced by the most familar fluorescent tube.

Because bulbs of different wattage can be used in the same socket, and because of the convenient size and shape of the bulbs, incandescent lighting allows more flexibility than fluorescent. Incandescent bulbs are generally less expensive to install, they light immediately when activated and produce more light from a small source than fluorescent light.

It takes more energy to use incandescent lighting than fluorescent lighting. To determine the exact cost of using any size bulb at any electric rate for one hour, multiply the bulb wattage by the electric rate and divide by 1000. For example:

$$\frac{\begin{array}{r} 100 \text{ watt bulb} \\ \times\ 3¢ \end{array}}{300} \qquad 300 \div 1000 = .3¢ \text{ per KWH.}$$

Therefore, it costs three tenths of a cent to burn a 100-watt bulb for one hour at three cents per KWH (kilowatt hour).

Electric discharge sources. An electric discharge lamp produces light by passing electric current through a gas or vapor. Only two types are suitable for use in interiors: fluorescent and neon.

Fluorescent. In fluorescent lighting, a tube is filled with mercury vapor and the inside of the tube is coated with special powders. When the cathodes at each end of the tube activate the vapors, they cause the fluorescent coating to produce light.

The tube can be purchased in tubular, straight, circular, or U shapes. One of the unique advantages of fluorescent sources is their linear quality, which is handy in lighting some architectural elements such as valances, coves, cornices, and brackets, and for installations along the length of a surface such as under kitchen cabinets and shelves.

Because fluorescent installation is more complicated, it is more costly. However, the tubes last longer, are cooler, require fewer fixtures, produce less glare, and use from one third to one fifth less electricity than incandescent light bulbs.

**Table
5.1**

A Guide for Lamp Selection Based on General Color Rendering Properties

Type of Lamp	Efficacy lm/w	Lamp Appearance Effect on Neutral Surfaces	Effect on "Atmosphere"	Colors Strengthened	Colors Grayed	Effect on Complexions	Remarks
Fluorescent Lamps							
Cool[a] white CW	High	White	Neutral to moderately cool	Orange, yellow, blue	Red	Pale pink	Blends with natural daylight—good color acceptance
Deluxe[a] cool white CWX	Medium	White	Neutral to moderately cool	All nearly equal	None appreciably	Most natural	Best overall color rendition; simulates natural daylight
Warm[b] white WW	High	Yellowish white	Warm	Orange, yellow	Red, green, blue	Sallow	Blends with incandescent light—poor color acceptance
Deluxe[b] warm white WWX	Medium	Yellowish white	Warm	Red, orange, yellow, green	Blue	Ruddy	Good color rendition; simulated incandescent light
Daylight	Medium-high	Bluish white	Very cool	Green, blue	Red, orange	Grayed	Usually replaceable with CW
White	High	Pale yellowish white	Moderately warm	Orange, yellow	Red, green, blue	Pale	Usually replaceable with CW or WW
Soft white/ natural	Medium	Purplish white	Warm pinkish	Red, orange	Green, blue	Ruddy pink	Tinted source usually replaceable with CWX or WWX
Incandescent Lamps							
Incandescent filament	Low	Yellowish white	Warm	Red, orange, yellow	Blue	Ruddiest	Good color rendering
High Intensity Discharge Lamps							
Clear mercury	Medium	Greenish blue-white	Very cool, greenish	Yellow, blue, green	Red, orange	Greenish	Very poor color rendering

Design

Table 5.1 A Guide for Lamp Selection Based on General Color Rendering Properties *(Cont.)*

Type of Lamp	Efficacy lm/w	Lamp Appearance Effect on Neutral Surfaces	Effect on "Atmosphere"	Colors Strengthened	Colors Grayed	Effect on Com-plexions	Remarks
High Intensity Discharge Lamps							
White mercury	Medium	Greenish white	Moderately cool, greenish	Yellow, green, blue	Red, orange	Very pale	Moderate color rendering
Deluxe white[a] mercury	Medium	Purplish white	Warm, purplish	Red, blue, yellow	Green	Ruddy	Color acceptance similar to CW fluorescent
Metal halide[a]	High	Greenish white	Moderately cool, greenish	Yellow, green, blue	Red	Grayed	Color acceptance similar to CW fluorescent
High pressure sodium[b]	High	Yellowish	Warm, yellowish	Yellow, green, orange	Red, blue	Yellowish	Color acceptance approaches that of WW fluorescent

[a] Greater preference at higher levels. [b] Greater preference at lower levels.
(General Electric Co.)

Neon Light.   Neon light is technically known as cold-cathode. It is most commonly used for sign making. The greatest advantage of neon light is that it can be shaped into any form. It also has a long life and presents few maintenance problems.

Although this source has not been used often outside the sign industry, its potential for use within architectural spaces is yet to be fully explored. Neon lights could be used to provide extra sparkle and excitement in a room. Recently artists have used neon lights to create light sculpture.

Types of Lighting

Several methods may be used to provide illumination; frequently more than one type of lighting is used in the same room.

Lamps and Fixtures

The most commonly used sources of light are portable lamps and fixtures that are mounted on walls or ceilings.

Lamps provide a certain amount of flexibility in that they can be moved from one place to another. Both lamps and mounted fixtures may be useful in emphasizing a particular decorative theme or in adding some special note of individuality. Fixed lighting makes it possible to conserve table and floor space and to light areas where portable lamps seem impractical. Individual preferences and the requirements for functional light must therefore guide one's choice. There are no rules about where to use lamps or mounted fixtures. The ultimate goals are to provide the type of light needed and to choose designs that are in keeping with the decorative scheme.

Fig.
5.1

AVG. 40"

Choose proper lamp heights.

In choosing lamps the following points might be considered.

1. A sturdy base or one that is heavily weighted at the bottom prevents tipping. With the tall slender bases currently in vogue, this is an important factor.
2. A lamp that has a diffusing bowl will give less glare.
3. A harp makes it possible to adjust the height of the shade or to tilt the shade if necessary.
4. A table lamp intended for reading purposes should have the lower edge of the shade about 40 to 42 inches above the floor. The lower edge of the shade on a floor lamp should be from 47 to 49 inches from the floor.
5. Lampshades should be similar in color and texture or else they should contrast. One beige shade, one white shade, and one pink shade would probably be unattractive. On the other hand, two identical beige shades and one gold metallic-paper shade might provide an interesting combination.
6. For some areas, swing-arm or adjustable gooseneck lamps may be practical.
7. A floor lamp should be placed so that the light comes from behind the shoulder of the reader, near the rear of the chair, at either the right or the left side, but not from directly behind the chair.

In choosing fixtures, these points may be important.

1. Adjustability of position often increases functionalism. Chandeliers that may be raised or lowered and wall units that swing provide a variety of lighting effects.
2. Diffused light is more pleasant. In many fixtures the bulbs may be exposed and present an irritating glare.
3. The design of the fixture should be in harmony with the character of the room.

Architectural Lighting
Glamorous effects for general lighting may be achieved by the mounting of simple fixtures in valances, cornices, or coves, or behind translucent panels. One may light a window area, wall, ceiling, floor, or any special area for emphasis. Fluorescent tubes are useful for such lighting because they provide an even line of light. Incandescent bulbs may be used for many similar effects, but one has to be careful to avoid a spotty appearance.

In *valance* lighting the light source is mounted so that some of the light is directed up toward the ceiling and some down over the draperies or the wall. Fluorescent tubes are installed behind the valance frames, which are painted white to reflect the light. At least a ten-inch space between the top of the valance and the ceiling is recommended. The frame will conceal both the fixtures and the top of the draperies.

Cornice lighting can be used to give general illumination. Usually in cornice lighting, fluorescent tubes are placed behind a cornice, at least six inches in depth, built at the junction of the ceiling and the wall. Fluorescent tubes are recommended as they burn cooler, thus preventing any wall discoloration. For the best light reflection, the faceboard should be painted flat white.

Cornice lighting is most effective for dramatizing a mural, pictures, walls or wall textures. It is particularly desirable in low-ceilinged rooms because it helps to give the impression of greater ceiling height.

Cove lighting implies a troughlike arrangement, usually near the ceiling, with the light directed upward. Cove lighting creates an effect of openness and an atmosphere of serenity. The quality of light is soft.

(a) Valance Lighting

(b) Cornice Lighting

(c) Cove Lighting

(d) Lighted Wall Bracket

(e) Soffit Lighting

(f) Recessed downlighting that gives a spotlight effect.

Brackets are located at a lower height than valances and are not necessarily related to window treatments.

Soffit is the underside of any architectural member. Often the space provides a housing for light sources. This method lights bathrooms, kitchens, bookshelves, mirrors, wall niches, and shelves.

Recessed lighting is a type of lighting that includes built-in panel fixtures that provide concentrated light. The fixtures can be round (eyelid spots), square, or rectangular metal boxes set in a ceiling or wall.

Skylights. A skylight is a glazed opening in the roof of a house constructed to allow natural light into the space.

(g) Wall Washing

(a) Luminous Wall Panel

(c) Luminous panels can be used effectively on the ceiling in various rooms.

(b) Luminous panel lighting can be used as a decorative vertical light.

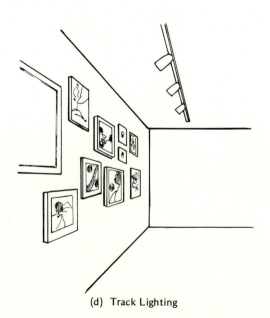

(d) Track Lighting

Design

Translucent panels are set in a surface that reflects light. The light source is concealed under the panel, which may be on the floor or ceiling, or in a free-standing decorative unit. Luminescent ceiling panels, an efficient treatment used in kitchens, bathrooms, or other work areas, provide comfortable, glare-free illuminations.

Today, *track lighting* is not confined to modern interiors. It is easy to install and provides some of the same effects as architectural lighting. The cylinders that are placed in the track are flexible, thus solving many lighting problems.

Kinds of Lighting

Basic lighting makes use of five kinds of lighting: direct, indirect, direct-indirect, semi-direct, and semi-indirect.

Direct lighting. Direct lighting provides the sharpest contrast between light and dark and makes the most dramatic shadows. Because the light shines directly down on the object, it produces a strong glare unless a reflector bulb is used. Gooseneck lamps and track lighting are examples of direct lighting.

A direct light can be pointed down to become a downlight. Downlighting may be used to highlight a group of plants, a piece of sculpture, as well as to provide light for reading and other tasks if a reflector bulb is used.

A downlight can be placed where the chandelier is ordinarily hung, thus illuminating the table or the arrangement on the table, but additional lighting will be needed in the area. Some hanging lamps have a downlight as well as branched lights.

Because track lighting does not require elaborate electrical wiring, this form of direct lighting may be used to throw light on an empty textured wall. This process is called wall-washing. Track lighting can also be used to spotlight a collection of pictures or for task lighting if a reflector bulb is used. If track lighting is not mounted correctly, the light may cause disturbing shadows or a glare. To achieve the best lighting effect, the track should be mounted as follows:

Ceiling Height	Track Distance from Wall
7½'–9'	24"–36"
9'–11'	36"–48"
11'–13'	48"–60"

Indirect lighting. Indirect lighting is produced by a light source that is hidden. The light is directed to a ceiling, to a cove, or to another surface from which it is reflected back into the room. Indirect lighting creates almost no shadows when it is used next to the ceiling, and it is ideal for general illumination. However, when it is used alone it can be flat and uninteresting. Indirect lighting reflected down from the ceiling tends to raise the ceiling height by creating a visual illusion.

Uplighting is another form of indirect lighting. Canister shapes are used in a variety of locations: on the floor in the corners of rooms; at either end of a sofa; under the sofa; or behind plants. Uplighting can be aimed at a piece of sculpture or a plant to create interesting shadows on the wall. The technique of uplighting can add a dramatic mood to the room as well as introducing softness to the room's rectilinear forms.

Direct-indirect lighting. Direct-indirect light uses both direct and indirect light distributed evenly in all directions. A fixture that has bulbs both inside and outside the reflector, as some table and floor lamps do, produces a direct-indirect or diffused light.

Semi-direct. In semi-direct fixtures sixty per cent of the light is directed down to the work surface and the remaining amount directed upward.

Semi-indirect. Conversely, semi-indirect lighting directs sixty to ninety per cent of the light toward the ceiling and upper walls, using the ceiling as the main reflective source; the other forty to ten per cent is directed toward the work plane. A lamp providing semi-indirect lighting with a diffuser is preferred for reading and study. (See Figure 5.4, p. 90.)

Fig.
5.2

(a)

(b)

(d)

(c)

(a) Fluorescent lamps behind a valance accent the timber in the ceiling and provide general room illumination. The bar features built-in soffit lighting overhead. Louvered doors, when closed, allow the light through to present a luminous panel effect. (b) A 250 W PAR spot over the fireplace grazes the surface to accent the texture and pattern of the brick. Recessed downlights around the perimeter of the room give accent to specifics as well as provide general illumination. All light sources are on dimmers. (c) Master bath lighted by 8-foot soffit. (d) An 8-foot lighted bracket provides general lighting. (a–d Courtesy of General Electric Company) (e) Track lighting. (Courtesy of American Plywood Association)

(e)

Plans for home lighting should recognize three important factors:

1. *Function.* Certain specialized activities will require specific amounts and possibly certain kinds of light. Function, therefore, must be evaluated in terms of both quantity and quality of light. Reading, writing, playing a musical instrument, sewing, shaving, and applying makeup all demand proper illumination. Many activities, especially in the kitchen, laundry, and workroom, require special types of light. In all these instances, functional lighting will prevent eyestrain and make it possible to carry on the activities in the most comfortable and efficient manner.

2. *Safety.* In many respects safety is related to functionalism, but it is such an important factor that it should be given special consideration. Improper lighting is a particular hazard in several areas that may easily escape notice—for example, on stairways that lead to a basement or an attic, on patios that have different levels separated by steps, or at any doorway that requires a step up or a step down.

   Another aspect of safety involves adequate wiring and sufficient outlets for all needs. It is dangerous as well as unattractive to use long extension cords. Electric wires should never be placed under rugs where traffic might cause wear on the insulation. A circuit should never be overloaded with equipment that makes excessive demands on the current.

3. *Beauty.* We begin to appreciate light as a decorative medium when we see a room bathed in a pleasing glow of illumination. A dim, dreary type of lighting is as bad as, if not worse than, one that is harsh and glaring. There is also the close relationship between the type of light and the appearance of colors. With the wrong choice of lighting a well-planned scheme may lose its effectiveness.

How to Provide for General, Local (Task), and Accent Lighting

Concentrated light is essential in areas where the eyes will be used for close work, but there should also be a general, over-all illumination to prevent strong contrasts of light.

General lighting may be provided by various means, such as coves, valances, cornices, soffits, or luminous panel lighting. Lamps and fixtures may provide either direct or indirect lighting; many produce both types.

Good local (task) lighting is particularly needed when reading, sewing, cooking, playing a musical instrument, cleaning, carpentering, grooming, and playing indoor games. Without general illumination, local lighting will produce a glare.

Local lighting provides concentrated illumination in a particular area. Various types of portable lamps and wall or ceiling fixtures are now made with adjustable features. These allow considerable flexibility in producing the correct amount of light exactly where it is needed.

Accent lighting is spot lighting that emphasizes a center of interest in the room. It may highlight important furniture groupings, wall hangings, or other accessories. Recessed or track lighting may be used to accent a center of interest in the room.

Avoiding Glare and Shadows

It is usually uncomfortable to have light shine directly from the source to the eye. Some means of diffusing light generally provides a better quality of illumination. Frosted bulbs rather than those made of clear glass, and diffusing bowls that shield the bulbs entirely, are commonly used. Translucent lampshades in light colors allow for considerable diffusion of light, whereas opaque shades such as those made of heavy paper allow none at all. Certain fixtures are equipped with various sorts of diffusing shields to protect the eye from the glare of the light source as well as to eliminate the shadows produced by concentrated light.

Planning an Adequate Amount of Light

The actual light yield in any room or special area will be the product of many factors, including the location and the direction of the light sources, the reflective qualities of the colors and the textures, the number of lamps and fixtures, and, of course, the wattage of the light bulbs or tubes. With so many variable factors, it is difficult to prescribe for specific needs.

It is customary to recommend standards for adequate amounts of light in terms of foot-candles. This is a quantitative unit of measurement, one foot-candle being the amount of illumination produced by a standard plumber's candle at a distance of one foot. With a light meter it is possible to measure the amount of light at any given point in terms of foot-candles.

Experts seem to agree that for general illumination in most areas there should be at least ten foot-candles of light; utility areas require twenty foot-candles.

Specific activities require greater amounts of light:

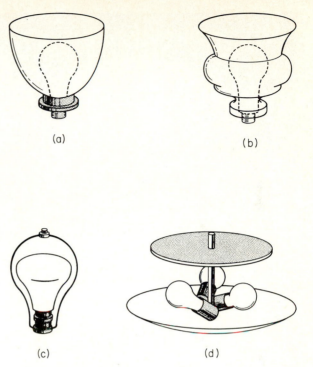

Fig. 5.3

Ways of diffusing and softening light. (a) and (b) Diffusing bowls. (c) Frosted bulb in harp. (d) Translucent and perforated shields.

	(Foot-candles)
Reading	30–70
Desk work	40–70
Sewing	50–100
Sewing on dark fabrics	80–200
Shaving or applying makeup	50
Kitchen activities	50–70
Ironing	50

When there will be prolonged periods of close eyework, the upper limits are recommended. Also, specific conditions will dictate requirements; for example, sewing on dark fabrics with matching thread and working on fine details would require more light than simple work on light-colored fabrics.

Because few families have a light meter to measure the amount of illumination, the above recommendations are not a very practical guide. They are presented merely to indicate the relative needs in specific areas. From a more practical standpoint, the consumer is interested in knowing what size bulbs to provide in specific areas. In view of the variables mentioned above, this is a far more difficult problem. Light sources may be rated in terms of lumens, a quantitative unit for measuring light output. Manufacturers of light sources publish data about output on various products, but once again these figures have little meaning for the average consumer.

Much close work, such as reading, writing, and sewing, is done with portable lamps as the source of illumination. For functional use, the single-socket lamp should have a bulb of 150 to 200 watts. Multiple-socket lamps would require three 60-watt bulbs to provide a comparable amount of light. The lamp used for close work should be equipped with a diffuser, to prevent glare; this is also recommended for other light sources.

Each room should have general illumination and local lighting. This can be interpreted by the decorator in many ways, but a few general suggestions for each room may prove helpful.

This table lamp makes an ideal study lamp or reading light. It provides for a 200 W bulb, and light is evenly diffused. The shade and inner refractor prevent glare and shadows over the entire task area. Vented louver tops prevent glare from above. *(Courtesy of Lightolier)*

Fig. 5.4

Light from the floor represents a new concept in illumination. *(Designed by Barbara D'Arcy, A.I.D., courtesy of Bloomingdale's, N.Y.)*

Fig. 5.5

Fig.
5.6

Living room and family room. Lighting a wall surface improves visual comfort as well as making the walls and ceiling appear lighter and more attractive while providing for general illumination. Wall illumination can be achieved through valance, cornice, cove, track, or recessed lighting. Table and floor lamps provide general illumination as well as doing some task lighting.

Kitchen. Good lighting in the kitchen means both general and task lighting. The ceiling fixture provides general lighting and should fur-

Concealed light sources in a modern room highlight wall panels. *(Designed by Barbara D'Arcy, A.I.D., courtesy of Bloomingdale's, N.Y.)*

nish at least 150 to 200 watts of incandescance or 60 to 80 watts of fluorescence for each fifty square feet of space. Long fluorescent tubes may be attached under the cabinets to light the work surfaces.

Dining room. In the dining room, the use of low-level general illumination will create a serene atmosphere. A dimmer control installed in a hanging lamp over the table can help establish

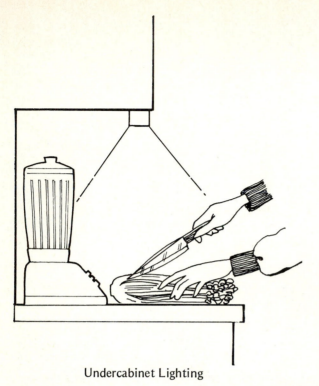

Undercabinet Lighting

moods for the room. However, other lighting should be used in the room; a single dimmed source of light will not provide adequate lighting for dining, and one light source shining down on those sitting at the table can be unflattering. Fluorescent tubes may be used for valance, cornice, or cove lighting to provide the soft concealed general illumination in the room. In lieu of a light fixture hanging over the table, built-in recessed lighting may be used to frame the table with incandescent light and bring out the sparkle of silver, china, and glassware.

Because most dining rooms have fixtures that hang over the table, the bottom of the fixture should be approximately thirty inches above the table if the room has an eight-foot ceiling. In rooms with higher ceilings, the fixture will need to be raised for better proportion.

Chandeliers of 21 to 29 inches in diameter should be chosen unless the dining area is less than ten feet wide, in which case the diameter should be less than 24 inches. These guidelines need to be flexible, however; the chandelier may be massive in design and color, thus appearing heavier than the actual measurements.

Fig. 5.7

Under-the-cabinet fixtures provide light at work areas. A translucent ceiling supplies the necessary over-all illumination in the kitchen. *(Courtesy of Formica Corporation)*

Fig. 5.8

Lytetrough, a product from Lightolier, is designed to eliminate the cost of custom installations. It can be used to focus attention on paintings, wall sculpture, or wall shelving or to enhance draperies or other window treatment. Lytetrough is made of particle board that can be painted and has built-in concealed details that provide for installation of track lighting. *(Courtesy of Lightolier)*

A chandelier with downlights can give more direct lighting for tasks that take place around the table.

Generally speaking, on an 8' ceiling, a chandelier would be hung approximately 30" above the table.

Lighting

Bedroom. Lamps for reading may be on night stands or attached to the wall or ceiling if space is at a premium. High-intensity lighting will allow reading without disturbing the partner; however, this is not recommended, for a glare is created if the rest of the room is dark.

Task lighting for studying, sewing, and grooming should be included in the lighting plan. For applying makeup, table lamps with translucent shades should be on either side of the mirror approximately 36 inches apart. The center of the shades should be the height of the face. Strip lighting can be used on the sides and top of the mirror.

Bathroom. Again, it should be mentioned that it is desirable to have both general and task lighting in bathrooms. The bright light furnished from the task lighting can produce a glare if there is no general lighting such as a ceiling fixture, or soffit lighting. The bathroom mirror may be lighted for grooming with rows of tiny bulbs around three sides of the mirror.

A vapor-proof lighting fixture is useful in the tub and shower area when the shower curtain is closed to natural or artifical light.

Stairways, hallways, and closets. Hallways and stairways must be well lighted for safety

Fig. 5.9

When space is a problem, hanging lamps in the bedroom may provide a solution. (*Courtesy of Monsanto Company, photo by Lisanti, Inc.*)

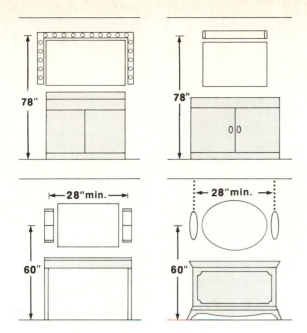

Light for grooming should come from above the top of the head and well below the chin.

Lamps that have three-way switches for lower intensity can create mood and also conserve on electricity. Such lights can be switched to high intensity when needed.

Another mood definer is a device that can be added to the track lighting system which projects patterns on the wall that can be changed when desired. One man projects the changing patterns of light on the wall to simulate falling water while he plays a tape recording of Niagara Falls. Like the stage designer, the decorator can create any atmosphere desired simply by choosing and arranging the light with care and imagination.

Principles of Lighting Design

The use of lighting is visually pleasing when it follows the principles of design. Because prin-

reasons. Lighting near the baseboard in a hallway creates a warm glow and gives a flattering effect to the area. Recessed lighting may be secured to the risers on the stairs and give a feeling of elegance to the room while adding to the safety of the stairs. Closets with automatic switches that activate when the door is opened and deactivate when the door is closed are convenient as well as energy-saving.

Using Lighting to Create a Mood

Lighting can be used to create a mood. High-level lighting can be formal or create a party effect; low-level lighting gives a feeling of intimacy and relaxation. A dimming device can provide illumination from intense brightness to low lighting. The low intensity offers a savings on electricity and is useful as a night light, particularly in children's rooms. The dimmer can be connected to an automatic timer that turns the lights on and off at predesignated times. In the long run, the dimmer could pay for its installation.

Stairway lighting acts as a safety precaution and highlights the shape of the steps.

(a)

Fig. 5.10
(a) One style of profile light in garden fixtures calls attention to steps, paths, walkways, and low plants. *(Courtesy of Shalda Lighting Products, Burbank, Ca.)* *(b)* Fixtures such as the type shown here spread light downward on flowers and pool while giving an upward light to emphasize overhanging foliage. *(Courtesy of Shalda Lighting Products, Burbank, Ca.)*

(b)

ciples of design are mutually reinforcing, it is difficult to speak of one without considering the others.

Balance is achieved by placing light sources throughout the room, avoiding a concentration of light on any side or area of the space. Balance can be symmetrical or asymmetrical.

Unity can be created by duplicating the fixture as well as by repeating the materials, finishes, colors, textures, or lampshades. Using similar, but not identical, fixtures will create *variety*. If the fixtures are the same throughout the room, it will be monotonous, but if they are totally different it will be chaotic. Variety is also created by having general and local lighting, and by changing the level of illumination with dimmers or three-way incandescent bulbs.

As the space is illuminated, there will be a need to highlight certain objects or areas, thus creating *emphasis*. Lack of emphasis in an interior causes boredom, confusion, and uncertainty as to the design intent.

The sequence of lighting will create a luminous *rhythm*, giving the space a dynamic quality. The light fixtures should be in *proportion* and *scale* to the room and to the related objects in the room.

If the contrast between the general lighting and the accent lighting is too strong, there will not be enough luminous transition, and the lighting composition will lack *harmony*.

Outdoor Lighting

A picture window that frames an attractive view all day long can be merely a dark area on the living room wall after sundown. When the garden is lighted, it is possible to have a beautiful view day or night. Locate spot lamps on the house or in a tree twelve to twenty feet above the ground. Aim to light flowers and shrubbery at an angle that is 45 to 90 degrees from the principal viewing angle.

A beautiful tree should be lighted from two or three directions to avoid a flat appearance. Experiment with locations and distances from the lamp to the tree for the best effects.

Lighted steps and walks invite one to tour the gardens after dark as well as preventing dangerous slips and falls. Outdoor lighting also discourages trespassing. Small fixtures need to be near the entrance to welcome guests and allow them to see the house or apartment number.

6

Elements of Design

The relationships among the components of a design give it individuality. It is, therefore, impossible to look at any particular design as a unit or a whole without considering the pattern of interrelationships among color, light line, form, pattern, texture, and space. However, because each of these elements contributes something in its own way to the over-all effect, a discussion of them separately may help one to understand the total effect. Color and light have been discussed in other chapters.

Line

Although most designs are composed of many lines, there is often a predominance of one type that contributes to the character of the design. Lines compel our eyes to follow them. Even simple lines evoke an emotional response, and we associate certain feelings with different types of line. This point is important to remember when trying to create a theme or a mood in any room.

There are two kinds of line: straight and curved.

Straight

Vertical.   An erect, upward line expresses strength and forcefulness. It is likely to be dignified, masculine, and formal. Vertical lines tend to suggest the apparent height of the room. With the low ceilings in today's homes, it is important to consider the use of vertical lines to make the room appear taller.

Horizontal.   The sideways line suggests repose and relaxation. It tends to increase the width of the room and give a feeling of informality. The horizontal line is provided by tables, benches, desks, or sofas in a room.

Diagonal.   Diagonal lines are the most difficult to use. They are lines of action that seem to be pointing into space; therefore they are likely to keep the eye moving. Chevron designs are two diagonal lines meeting, thus stopping the action.

Fig. 6.1

Different effects are achieved by straight and curved lines.

(a) The vertical line is overused.
(b) The vertical line is softened with the use of some horizontal lines.

Fig. 6.2

(a)

(b)

(a)

Fig. 6.3

(b)

(a) The horizontal line is overemphasized. *(b)* The horizontal line has been relieved by using some vertical lines.

Compare diagonal lines that approach the vertical and the horizontal. Each tends to take on the characteristics of the predominating direction.

Curves

The infinite variety of curved lines makes them useful in expressing many different moods or ideas. The circle, or any full, voluptuous curve, may give a feeling of gaiety or buoyancy as, for example, in a wallpaper with a motif of light, iridescent bubbles or a circus scene with balloons and clowns wearing polka dots and pompons. However, baroque designs in dark colors and heavy textures may give the effect of elegance or even opulence.

A softer type of curved line is found in the S curve, which is more likely to express gracefulness and refinement. These curves provide interest without being too dynamic or too ener-

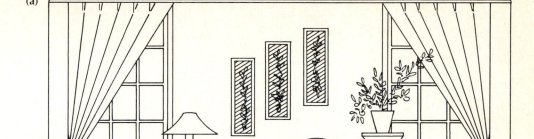

(a)

(b)

(a) In this room, there is an over-use of diagonal lines. (b) The designer has used diagonal lines, but there is judicious use of vertical, horizontal, and curved lines resulting in a more interesting room.

Fig. 6.4

getic. However, too many curved lines in a room can produce a restless effect.

Line combinations in the structural features of a room, the furniture designs, the accessories, and the patterns must be carefully considered to achieve the desired effects. A composition with too much of any one type of line may become uninteresting or unpleasant, but emphasis on one type helps to promote the theme. Thus, in a room meant for relaxation and repose, horizontal lines should predominate.

One may want to emphasize certain structural lines in a room—such as doorways, archways, dados, panels, and moldings. Windows that are long and narrow will, of course, emphasize vertical lines unless a planned treatment is used to produce a different effect.

Both structural and decorative lines in interior design contribute to the theme. Some furniture is composed all of straight lines; other types combine straight and curved lines. Curves in furniture design range from soft, graceful lines to full and voluptuous ones. Frequently, straight

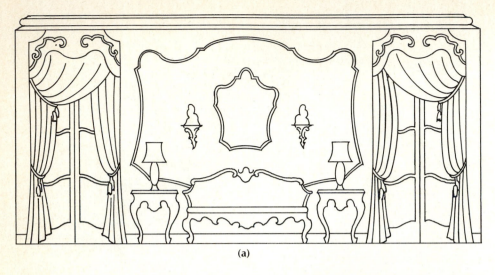

(a)

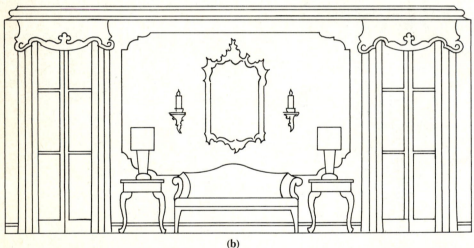

(b)

**Fig.
6.5**

Overused curved lines in room (a) create a busy effect. In room (b), curved lines are used, but they are relieved with vertical and horizontal ones to make the room less busy and more pleasing to the eye.

pieces seem to spell formality; softer curves introduce gracefulness; whereas fuller curves are more exuberant.

Patterned fabrics may be used to introduce emphatic lines. Stripes, plaids, and geometrics might be used for a severe or dramatic effect that would be difficult to achieve with a graceful floral scroll pattern.

Sometimes the mood of a room can be varied by very simple changes in important lines. One should experiment with draperies hanging straight at the windows or tied back to form

graceful, curved lines. Drum-shaped or bell-shaped lampshades may also make quite a difference.

Shape, Form, and Area

Shape and *form* are terms that are used interchangeably; however, there are some differences. When lines are joined to enclose space, they result in an outline, a contour, or a shape. When a two-dimensional shape acquires a third

(a)

(a) A masculine appearance is achieved by emphasizing straight lines. *(Courtesy of DuPont Textile Fibers)* (b) Diagonal lines emphasize a wall and lend a vibrant note to a room that uses line as an important element of design. *(Courtesy of Monsanto Company)*

Fig. 6.6

(b)

Architectural features, furniture, and decorative accents determine space relationships. *(Designed by Patricia Harvey, A.I.D. Photo by Henry S. Fullerton)*

Fig. 6.7

(b)

dimension, it becomes a form. Shape can be understood in terms of pattern, and form in terms of mass. Furniture is perceived as form. The form of an object usually suggests its use. The Charles Eames lounge chair (see Figure 14.8) is a good example of form, suggesting its use by the inviting curves of the seat, back, and arms.

There are basically three categories of form: rectilinear (square or rectangle), angular (triangle, pyramid), curved (circle, sphere, cone, cylinder). Seldom can one find a room with only one form. Most interiors illustrate a combination of forms: curved lamp shades, rectilinear sofa, area rugs, and angular ceiling or staircase, for example.

Although repetition is one way to achieve rhythm, too many of the same forms can become uninteresting. For example, a rectangular mirror over a rectangular desk, placed in front of a rectangular wall space, can seem monotonous because of the excessive repetition of one form.

The first area to be considered is the enclosure of the whole house or apartment. Interesting concepts of spatial relationships are evident in modern residential architecture, where there is a conscious effort to design the house in terms of the geographical terrain. The desire to relate the interior to the exterior has led to the extensive use of window walls and huge picture windows. But this trend has found disfavor among another group of architects, who decry the lack of privacy. One answer has been the use of lacy grille patterns in façades to let in light and air. Those on the inside can see out, but outsiders cannot see in. Apparently there is a need for a feeling of enclosure without one of confinement.

The room itself, the height of the ceiling, the placement of the windows, doorways, and the other structural features—for example, a fireplace—will determine to a large extent how the area is to be utilized. Every form and shape will introduce new area relationships. Furniture groups, pictures on the wall, draperies at the windows, floor coverings, and accessories will all contribute to the space divisions.

It may be desirable to divide a long, narrow room into different functional spaces, such as a living area and a dining or study area. Some rooms have alcoves that will determine such area division. Areas may be separated from one another in many ways. Furniture placement, room dividers, "area" rugs, color, pattern, and texture may all be used to mark certain areas.

Pattern

Pattern is a two-dimensional or three-dimensional ornament arranged in a motif. Because patterns can be created by textures and forms, the entire arrangement of the room creates a pattern. Pattern is found in the shape of individual items of furniture and in their groupings; in wall pantings, parquet floor, architectural detail, and light and shadow in the room.

Pattern has movement and should be arranged so it will flow with the rhythm of the room or the object it adorns. Pattern should not compete with the major focal point in the room, and too much pattern will make a room seem busy. If necessary, try large swatches of the pattern before purchasing it.

How to Use Pattern
- Most often a pattern accent is at its best against a neutral background.
- Usually a bold pattern calls for a large massive area, but this guideline also needs to be viewed in terms of its exceptions. A large chintz can be charming on a small chair; a small print that appears one color from a distance may be attractive on a large sofa.
- Using the same pattern on many pieces is a good way to achieve harmony.
- It is popular today to mix prints, but such mixing must be done with skill and a feeling for color and design. Two patterns of the same color may be effectively combined if they are of related styles and design scales. The same pattern in another related color may combine well.
- Geometric patterns may be combined with florals, if they use the same colors; the dominant color could then be used in solid areas of the room.

Elements of Design

**Fig.
6.8**

Texture

When we mention the word *texture,* we immediately think of touching something. But texture is visual as well as tactile, because we associate past tactile sensations when we look at objects that are smooth or rough, hard or soft. The artist depicts textures on canvas as he paints a woman wearing a beautiful satin dress with glowing folds, or a bowl of flowers with lovely soft petals. The textures he portrays give character to his work and help to express ideas.

Just as lines, shapes, and colors convey messages, so do textures. Those that are rough and coarse have a rugged, sturdy quality. Handcrafts often owe their charm to having a texture that is not pretentious. Textures that are smooth and fine are more likely to suggest formality and elegance.

This room has a combination of patterns, straight lines, and curved lines. Unity is achieved through the use of texture and color and the size of the pattern. *(Courtesy of Simmons Company)*

Rich textures that represent luxury, expert ornamentation, and highly skilled craftsmanship do not, as a rule, combine well with those of a more homespun nature. Although remembering that we must never say "never," we should realize that certain qualities seem to be incongruous when used together. A room furnished with elegant traditional pieces upholstered in brocades and velvets would undoubtedly have a peculiar character if the accessories included modern metal lamps, rough pottery ashtrays, hooked rugs, abstract paintings, and a dash of Spanish wrought iron.

Woods vary in texture and quality to such an

extent that they must be selected and combined with great care. Those that are fine-grained or exotic in grain pattern are not likely to harmonize easily with those that are of a coarser open grain. A lovely figured walnut, therefore, would probably look uncomfortable in the company of rough, sturdy oak.

There are no hard and fast rules about the relationships of color and texture. Certain textural qualities are easier to emphasize with particular colors. Dark red, emerald green, purple, and gold suggest luxury and elegance of texture. The earthy colors of brown, mustard yellow, burnt orange, and yellow green seem to be more suitable with less refined textures. But one should not feel restricted by any definite rules in reference to texture and color. The over-all effect is the most important consideration.

Space

The element called space can be used to increase the size of the room visually and to give the room a quiet feeling of rest and beauty. Large unadorned openings between rooms encourage the eye to explore the distance beyond, especially when the same material or color carries throughout. Cool or light-value colors will add to the spacious feeling. Colors that blend well provide a minimum of contrast and pattern.

Other ways to develop the feeling of spaciousness are to use floor-to-ceiling glass cur-

This room emphasizes textures and contrasts in lines, forms, and colors to produce a warm atmosphere. (Courtesy of Interior Design Studio, B. Altman & Co.)

Fig. 6.9

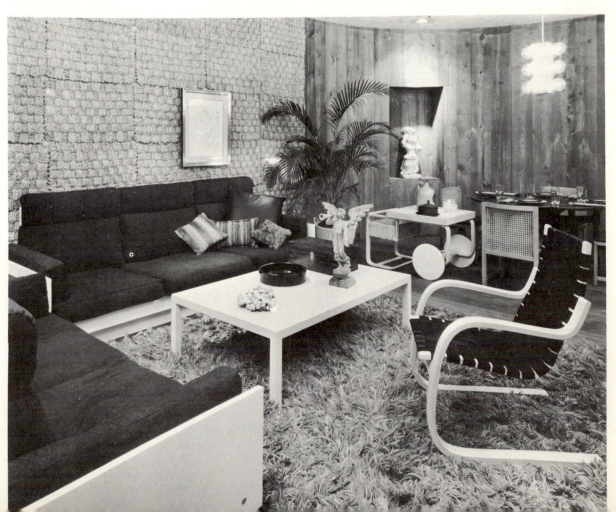

**Fig.
6.10**

Space has quiet beauty and gives a feeling of rest. Large undecorated walls and floors give a feeling of space. Arrange furniture in concentrated groups so that there are some empty silent spaces in the room. Indoor space seems increased by means of fewer partitions and larger openings between rooms. Indoor space seems also to connect with limitless outdoor space by means of glass walls, large openings, and porches. The decorating scheme is keyed to the outdoors—beiges and sky-blue accents that do not distract from nature's colors and low furniture that does not obstruct the view.

tains the color of the wall or illusionistic devices such as mirrors, paintings with deep perspective, and scenic wallpapers to suggest distance.

Lighting is another device that can be used to provide a feeling of space. Lighting that emphasizes the ceiling can make the room look larger. Curtains with valance lighting or a luminous panel on one wall will make a room appear visually larger than it is; hence, more spacious. Lighting placed under the sofa can make it appear to float; thus, less massive.

To preserve a spacious atmosphere, the available space should be divided as little as possible, with a minimum amount of small-scale furniture with few accessories. Furniture on legs will contribute to a more spacious appearance than furniture with bases that extend to the floor. The clear plastic furniture available today creates a feeling of airiness.

Exposing as much floor as possible increases the room's spatial fluidity. If the floor is covered with carpeting, continuing the carpeting over the base of a sofa or window seat will increase the visual size of the room. Some sofas, beds, and coffee tables have an enclosed base of mirror; thus, the visual space is increased.

7

Principles of Design

Because a design is created by the selection and arrangement of forms, colors, and textures, the result is an expression of the person who does the selecting and arranging. In the sense that a home is a "design" it represents the ideas and personalities of the individuals who create it. It is important, therefore, to understand some of the basic principles that might serve as a guide.

There can be no rigid rules or formulas for selecting and arranging the components of a design because these would immediately preclude the spontaneous expressions of the individual. Designs that are stereotyped or imitative lack individuality and soon become tiresome. Yet there are certain fundamentals that should be considered if the design is to achieve its objectives.

Harmony

Harmony is essential to design. All the elements and principles of design blend together to create harmony. Leonardo da Vinci's comment that "every part is disposed to unite with the whole that it may thereby escape its own incompleteness" is an accurate description of harmony. Eero Saarinen has observed that when you are in a building with unity, it "sings with the same message."

Everyone has heard an orchestra tuning up before a concert. When each member is concerned only with one instrument and not with the total effect of all the sounds, the result is anything but pleasant. But the moment the conductor taps the baton, the orchestra becomes a unit and each member directs the notes toward the composite of sounds. So it is in design. The elements or components must blend to present a unified whole, and each must contribute to the theme or the mood of the design.

Of course it would be easy to achieve harmony by keeping all the variables the same, but using forms, colors, textures, patterns, and lines that are all similar would be monotonous. Variety must be introduced to provide interest. Yet too much variety yields to confusion. A good design is neither monotonous nor confused.

When all the elements of a design are harmonious we are aware of an integral whole that is more than merely a sum of the parts. This relationship of the various parts is responsible for the unity of the design, and one discordant note can destroy the totality of the effect. How and where one introduces the interest of variation without disturbing the harmonious blending of the ingredients is a key question. One answer lies in the theme or the idea that the design must express. In other words, variables should enhance the mood rather than contradict it. As one chooses furnishings, therefore, it is important to understand the philosophy and conditions that prompted the style and the reasons for the choice of materials. A common factor of purpose has a unifying effect, even though the modes of expression might be quite different. As an example, there are several fundamentals common to the Early American and the French Provincial styles that make it possible for many of these designs to live together in harmony; on the other hand, Early Colonial and mid-Victorian styles had few common purposes, materials, or conditions of birth. It would be far more difficult to unite these styles, although the experienced decorator might very well do it through a judicious choice of elements.

Contrast is frequently employed to lend interest to a design, but here again, unless the contrasting elements are chosen with great discretion, it is easy to introduce a discordant note. Using contrasting colors is a relatively simple way of adding interest, providing the textures are somewhat similar. It is not quite so easy, however, to contrast textures, because those that are crude and rough suggest an idea that does not blend easily with those that are highly refined as a result of skilled, delicate craftsmanship.

Strong contrast of line and form is sometimes used very successfully to create a startling or an exciting design. We have ample evidence of the effectiveness of this type of contrast in modern art. But in good modern designs, the colors and textures are skillfully selected so that the final result has the unity that comes with the fine blending of the ingredients.

We look at a house, or any building, in conjunction with the surrounding terrain, or with the landscaping. Good architectural designers plan the building in terms of the site and the background. The areas within the building must also be planned in relation to the over-all theme or mood. Thus it would be difficult to imagine a harmonious combination of a Cape Cod saltbox house with very formal, elegant furnishings set in a garden of Oriental style. The contrast would probably be not only confusing but disturbing. Yet a startling contrast planned with skill is often exciting. The unexpected note is stimulating because it defies the stereotype and we like this amount of change if it is not discordant.

Similarity with variation is, then, the keynote of harmony, but no one can dictate when and how to vary. This is the way to express yourself in any design that you create, and it will reflect your own perception, taste, and imagination.

Proportion

The untrained person often has an inherent sense of good proportion. The sofa is almost automatically placed against the long wall in the living room. The tiny woman avoids a huge hat and handbag that will overpower her. A letter typed without regard for margins on the paper is disturbing to the eye. These examples represent space divisions that are either pleasing or disturbing. *Proportion* and *scale* refer to the relationships of various parts of the design to one another and to the whole. In everyday life we are constantly aware of scale and proportion, and we are often applying this principle of design even though we are not always aware of doing so.

Ancient Greek designers were masters of proportions, and their art and architecture have for centuries been considered the epitome of perfection in space divisions. The scholars who have attempted to study these beautiful works realized that Greek proportions were derived from mathematical ratios that have been called the Golden Section. These ratios were based on a series of numbers that progressed by the sum of the two previous numbers. The ratio for a proportion was formed as follows: 2 : 3; 3 : 5; 5 : 8; 8 : 13. Compare in Figure 7.1 the areas formed on the Greek basis with the areas formed using other proportions. Are the basic relationships of the Greeks more pleasing to the eye than other spatial proportions?

Of course, many artists have experimented with more unusual proportions, and we find in

Fig. 7.1

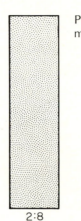

Proportion: Are traditional relationships more pleasing?

| 2:3 | 3:5 | 1:5 | 2:8 |

Proportions

Pleasing proportions are established when all pieces in a group are in proper scale. Having the end table the same height as the armchair is functional as well as creating a continuous line in the room.

Fig. 7.2

Design

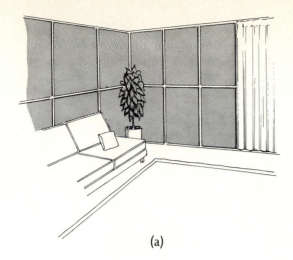

(a)

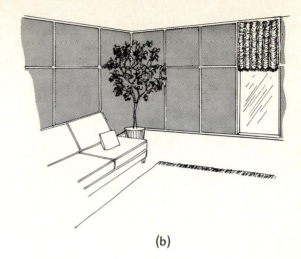

(b)

Fig.
7.3

Problems in the division of wall space. (a) or (b), which one is more appealing?

the modern style a desire to depart from traditional space relationships. Some designers have produced results that are not only pleasing, but stimulating and exciting. Others with less keen perception have used proportions that seem interesting at first but soon lose their appeal.

The Greeks also discovered the Golden Mean—that is, the fact that the most pleasant division of space is somewhere between one-half and one-third. This proportion can be applied in a room when hanging pictures, using molding, or choosing the location of the fireplace mantel.

Most of us do not measure areas in our homes to divide the spaces according to mathematical ratios, but our eyes soon tell us whether or not the proportions are interesting and the scale is pleasing.

Different-sized objects and areas in relationship to one another determine scale. We are constantly applying our sense of proportion when we select and arrange the objects in a room: a rug on the floor, a sofa against a wall, a picture or group of pictures over the sofa, a table and lamp next to a chair. The size and shape of the room will certainly determine the amount of furniture and the size of each piece. A very small room crowded with heavy, massive pieces is not likely to be either pleasing or functional. In modern rooms we tend to use a few pieces of

rather small-scale furniture to preserve an airy, spacious look. But again the design of the room must be carefully considered so that the furniture may not seem lost and insignificant.

Color, texture, and line play a significant part in establishing proportions. Strong, brilliant colors advance and will, therefore, make a particular area more obvious. Textures that reflect light or patterned areas will also tend to increase the importance of an area. Strong contrasts of color and texture will emphasize lines and forms. Vertical lines tend to slenderize an object and make it look taller. Horizontal lines make an object appear shorter and broader.

Proportions, therefore, are subject to the types and amounts of color, line, and texture in different areas. This interrelationship of the elements may be used in many ways to emphasize desirable space divisions or to minimize those that are not so pleasing; for example, the different effects created by the use of draperies that match the wall color and draperies that form a strong contrast (Figure 7.9). We are not so aware of the window as a separate area when the drapery color matches the wall. On the other hand, contrasting draperies create a different space division.

(a)

Fig. 7.4 (a) The forms in the room are out of scale with each other and the room. For example, the pictures are too small for the wall space and the accessories on the mantel are also out of scale. The division of space is uninteresting as can be noticed in the placement of the curtain tie-backs, the size of the cornice, and the molding from the ceiling. (b) This room has interesting division of space readily seen in the proportion of the cornice and drapery length. The furniture is in scale with the room and the accessories.

(b)

Balance

The principle of balance in design appeals to our sense of equilibrium. It is more pleasing to the eye when weights are so adjusted around a central focal point that they appear to be in a state of repose. A feeling of unbalance is almost always disturbing and unpleasant. One of the reasons the Leaning Tower of Pisa is well known is due to the fact that it is out of balance and still stands. One expects it either to balance itself or to fall. Because it does neither, it is visually disturbing.

The "weights" of the furniture and other objects in a room are determined by size, shape, color, and texture, all of which must be considered in adjusting the balance. The seesaw is, of course, a perfect example of physical balance, and the basic laws affecting a seesaw may be applied to artistic balance. When two objects of equal weight are placed at opposite ends of the board, they must be equidistant from the central

Fig. 7.5

(a) The room is not visually balanced as the door has more visual weight than the end table and accessories. (b) This room is a good example of asymmetrical balance. The lines in the room are interesting and in scale with the height of the door. There is an obvious focal point in this room.

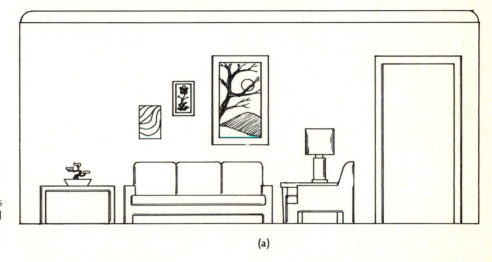

(a)

(b)

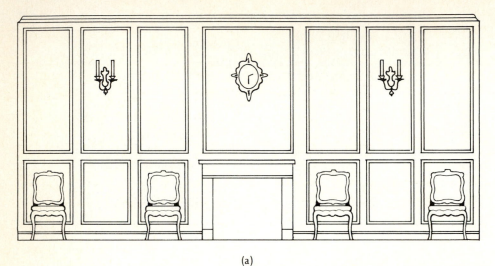

(a)

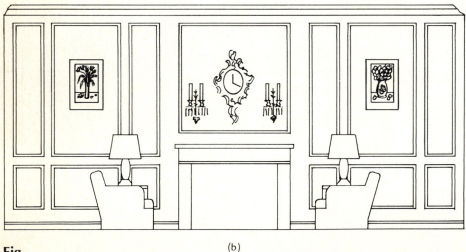

(b)

(a) Symmetrical balance that is repetitious, uninteresting, and out of scale to the wall space. (b) Symmetrical balance that is well used in the room.

Fig. 7.6

point to balance each other. If one object is replaced by a heavier one, it must be moved closer to the center to balance the lighter one at the other end of the board.

When applying this principle to design, one should remember that similar areas will seem lighter or heavier in different colors and textures. On the visual seesaw, therefore, if two objects are the same size but one is bright yellow and the other gray, the brighter one will appear heavier.

Formal Balance

When objects on each side of the center point are alike in every respect, there is no problem in balancing them. The type of balance is called *formal* or *symmetrical balance.*

Frequently the size, shape, and other architectural features of a room will influence the way furniture must be placed and where it will be desirable to use formal or informal balance. On a wall that has identical windows symmetrically placed it would seem logical, although not always necessary, to place furniture in a formally balanced arrangement. When the structural features of the room are asymmetrical, an informal balance is usually more attractive.

The theme of the room will also influence the type of balance that should predominate. A large, elegant room that is formal in character could well stand several groups of furniture arranged in formal balance. Having all the groups arranged this way, however, would be monotonous and would, in addition, lend an air of rigidity that might be unpleasant.

An asymmetrical arrangement (a) requires careful consideration of lines, shapes, and colors to achieve balance. Formal balance (b) is more easily achieved by symmetrical placement of furniture and accessories.

(a)

Fig. 7.7

(b)

Principles of Design

Fig.
7.8

(a)

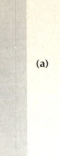

Examples of formal and informal
balance. *(Courtesy of Dunbar/Dux,
photo by Wesley Pusey)*

(b)

Although formal balance has more static and stable qualities, it does not need to be dull and uninteresting. This type of balance may be achieved through arrangements in which the objects on either side of the central line are not identical but are of equal weight and importance.

Informal Balance

Informal, asymmetrical, or *occult* are words used to describe a form of balance in which objects that are not similar are grouped around a focal point to create equilibrium. The principle of the seesaw is used here. In order to balance a heavy object, a lighter-weight object must be placed farther from the center axis.

A number of different factors may cause a form to appear heavier: texture, color, size, decorative pattern, or placement. Because coarse-textured surfaces give a tactile feeling, they are visually heavier than smooth-textured surfaces. Color is important in weight. In general, warmer colors, stronger intensities, and darker values give a feeling of more weight. Size adds to the visual sense of weight. All things being equal, the object that is larger will appear heavier. An object that has more decorative pattern will appear heavier than the same object with very little or no pattern. Placement of objects can affect the visual weight. An object that is placed closer to the eye of the viewer will appear heavier than one placed to the back of the composition.

Large pieces of furniture must usually be distributed around a room so that the walls and various areas of the room balance one another. All heavy pieces at one end and all lightweight pieces at the other would certainly produce an unbalanced design. If function or some other reason dictates such an arrangement, color and texture can be employed to reestablish a more pleasing equilibrium. For example, a dining area at one end of a living room would probably have furniture that is lighter in weight than the heavier upholstered pieces at the other end. In such a case one might use a different wall color, bright accents of color on chair seats, or some emphatic center of interest to add importance to the dining area.

Rhythm

When the elements of a design are arranged to make the eye travel from one part to another, the design has movement. If the eye moves smoothly and easily, the motion is rhythmic. This principle of rhythm is extremely important in producing unity, because it makes the eye sweep over the whole design before it rests at any particular focal point.

The principle of rhythm is an exciting one to work with because the effects are interesting and dramatic. A few simple tricks of decorating will provide an easy, graceful motion. If the eye jumps from one spot to another, the result may be most disturbing.

There are several methods of producing rhythm in a design:

1. Continuous line.
2. Repetition.
3. Progression-gradation.
4. Radiation.
5. Alternation.

Continuous Line

We have already discussed the way that lines compel the eye to follow the directions they take. This powerful quality may be employed in various ways to control the movement of the eye. Of course the design of a room is usually composed of many different lines, but a predominance of one type will cause the eye to move in that direction.

Continuous line has a flowing quality. In interiors it is most often used in baseboards, moldings, borders, chair rails, and framing elements such as cornices, windows, and rugs. The continuity of the line may occasionally be broken, but the gaps are small and the eye moves on to the next section in a rhythmical manner. The top of picture frames may be approximately the same height as major openings in the room. The bottom of the frame may be near the height of the lamp shade. End tables reach some major division of a chair or sofa, either the same height as the seat or the same height as the arm rest. Of course to have this line perfectly measured would make the room look geometric and less

Fig. 7.9

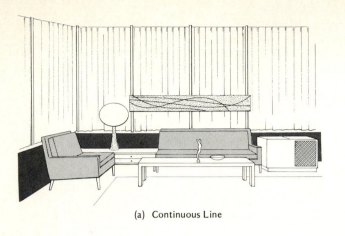

(a) Continuous Line

(b) Repetition

(c) Radiation

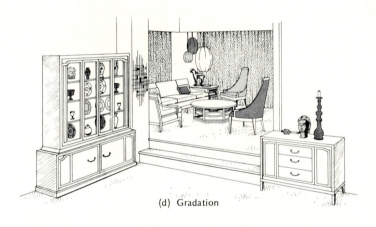

(d) Gradation

Rhythm produced in various ways.

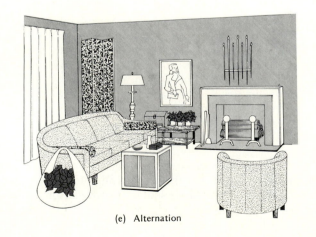

(e) Alternation

interesting, but a sharp variation in the continuous line will call attention to the difference.

Repetition

Some very interesting, simple experiments can be performed in any room of the home to show the power of repetition in creating movement. Through the repetition of line, color, shape, light, texture, pattern, or space, one can control the movement of the eye so that it will move in any desired direction.

Although it has been pointed out that vertical lines carry the eye up and down, a series of vertical lines that are horizontally arranged and evenly spaced can carry the eye from side to side. Various border designs, such as the famil-

Fig.
7.10

The principle of gradation with line and color is used in this rug designed by Marie Creamer. The deep gold color of the rug is repeated on one wall. Textural interest is added by a clear lucite stand and an etagere with tortoise shell finish. There is also rhythm through repetition of rectangular forms in the chair, desk, stool, etagere, mirror, and the lamp and picture, which create a rectangular form. *(Courtesy of Allied Chemical Corporation)*

iar egg-and-dart and fret motifs, illustrate this principle. Repetition of shape will also cause the eye to move in various directions. For example, a series of pictures mounted in frames of similar shape will cause the eye to travel from one point to another.

Color provides an excellent means of producing rhythm. To experiment, one can take any two objects of a bright color that will contrast with the other colors in a room, or use two pieces of bright fabric and place them at different spots in the room. When the effects are viewed from the doorway, the eye goes from one to the other. This experiment should be tried with different locations so that the movement is easy and graceful. Try the same experiment with a patterned fabric.

Repetition can be used without incurring monotony. For example, if the same color is repeated often, variety can be created by using different textures or patterns.

Progression-Gradation

A progression through a series of intermediate steps will carry the eye from one end of the scale to the other. This principle may be applied through gradual changes in line, size, shape, light, pattern, texture, or color.

Progression is more lively and dynamic than repetition; it is perhaps more easily used with accessories than with large pieces of furniture. It is also more difficult to manage, as it carries the eye more daringly than rhythm by repetition. Used unsuccessfully, it may cause the design to look like a stepladder.

Gradations of color are used in some fabrics. The eye will travel from the more dominant tone to the more subdued.

Radiation

Although diverging lines do not tend to carry the eye *smoothly* from one part of a design to another, they are sometimes useful in creating a particular effect. Radiation is frequently employed as a basis of design in lighting fixtures, structural elements, and many decorative objects. Some ski lodges have a fireplace in the center of the room with seating radiating out from it, creating rhythm through radiation.

Alternation

Any element can be alternated: black and white, warm and cool, tall and short, large and small, or light and dark. To name a few examples in nature, we see rhythm created by the alternation of day and night or the dark and light stripes of the zebra. Without destroying the whole, a surprise or difference can give variety. For example, when black and white stripes are alternated, a surprise of two black stripes provides interest without destroying the unity of the design.

Emphasis

A good design needs leadership or some particular note that attracts the interest. Other components of the design enhance the focal point, but they are subordinate to it.

There may be more than one center of interest in a room, but too many points of emphasis will produce a confused effect.

What to Emphasize

What one chooses as the focal point of an arrangement depends on the type and purpose of the room. Occasionally some structural feature of the room will almost automatically become a center of interest. The fireplace offers endless creative possibilities as the focal point. A group of paintings, mirrors, or wall sconces can be used to enhance the fireplace. Shelves to display books or collections may be added on either side. Windows are also natural focal points in a room. Those with spectacular views, such as a cityscape or a country scene, should be decorated to draw attention to the view. The window treatment may be underplayed by using simple curtains or leaving the glass bare. Elaborate window treatments will detract from the view.

When there is no built-in center of attention, it is a simple matter to create one. A particular furniture grouping or even one piece of furniture can be a focal point. In a bedroom, for example, the bed is often the center of interest with all other furnishings subordinate. In a living room the point of emphasis may be the

(a)

(b)

Fig.
7.11

Emphasis. (a) There is no distinct center of interest on the fireplace mantle. (b) The three large pictures make the focal point obvious in the room.

conversation area. However, a large area of pattern might provide a center of interest. An Oriental rug, or any rug with an outstanding pattern or design, may become a focal point when other furnishings are simple and subdued. A scenic wallpaper or a painting might serve the same purpose.

Any wall can be transformed into a focal point. For example, floor-to-ceiling bookcases with decorative objects interspersed on the shelves with the books may be the focal point. Some wall areas can be used to display prints, pictures, or wall hanging. A wall covered with smoked or plain glass makes an effective backdrop for a table holding decorative accessories.

Scenic wallpaper can visually expand the space and serve as a center of interest as well.

Sometimes a special interest or hobby provides individuality when it serves as the dominant note in a room. For example, in one den, a collection of figures of giraffes was displayed on wall shelves. The owner had started the collection quite by accident, but, as her friends traveled around the world, they delighted in finding unusual figures to add to it. Soon there were giraffes of various sizes made of wood, straw,

Principles of Design

(a)

Fig. 7.12

(b)

Emphasis. (a) The cabinets over the television have been given attention by painting them the same color as the couch. Thus, the eye moves around the room, but it never comes to focus at any point of emphasis. (b) The cabinet has been painted the same color as the wall thus making a subdued background area that does not compete for attention. The glass collection has been moved to the divider to allow the light to show off the natural beauty. The room has a focal point—the center of interest is the area rug.

glass, metals, ivory, pottery, and so on. The display provided quite a whimsical touch as well as a conversation piece—quite definitely a center of interest that might not appeal to many other people. Yet such a personalized touch does add interest if it is displayed with imagination and good taste.

How to Emphasize

There are several ways to attract attention to the important part of the room. These include repetition, unusual size, and contrast in texture, hue, value, intensity, line, space, form, or pattern. The arrangement of objects or the use of space and light may help develop a focal point. The unexpected is also a way to draw attention to an area of interest. Sometimes several methods are used to develop the center of interest.

Emphasis through repetition. A simple experiment will clearly show how repetition can be used for emphasis. A patterned fabric that has several colors may be held next to various samples of solid colors that repeat those in the print. If the pattern has both blue and green, the green color in the design will be more prominent when the fabric is held next to a solid green fabric. Next to a blue fabric, the blue in the design will become more pronounced.

Repetition of color, line, shape, or texture can be used to give added emphasis to any element you choose to stress. But repetition should be used in a subtle fashion. Too much is likely to become monotonous.

Emphasis through size. Dominance is most easily achieved by size. A large form draws attention simply because it is big and, therefore;

immediately visible. However, the size of the focal point should be scaled to the proportion of the room. A large, high-ceilinged room needs a dominant focal point that stands on its own and is not lost by the generous size of the room. On the other hand, a small room should not contain a massive center of interest that is too large for the room.

Emphasis through contrast. All the elements of design can be contrasted and, thus, draw attention to the center of interest. For example, in a room dominated with smooth textures, one rough-textured piece will attract attention.

Contrasts in color can create emphasis, too. If all things are equal, the object whose color is the most intense or the warmest will attract the

Fig. 7.13

(a)

(a) There is no center of interest in this room and every surface clamors for attention. (b) This room has a center of interest established through pattern. The other areas are subdued.

(b)

Principles of Design

(a)

Fig. 7.14

(a) The furniture in this room has been arranged without focusing on a center of interest. (b) There is more harmony in this room because the furniture is well grouped.

(b)

viewer's attention. Advertisements use strong color contrast to draw attention to the product; but, of course, color contrasts would be used more subtly in a room.

When a white object is held against a black background, the white seems whiter and the black takes on added depth. Whenever two extremes are used together, they intensify each other. The principle of emphasis through contrast has numerous applications. Draperies in strong contrast to the wall color will emphasize a window treatment.

Space can be used to capture attention through contrast. An individual has the capacity to enjoy only a limited number of things at a time. When too many items compete for attention, the eye cannot choose among them. In a fabric store, one sees many bolts of fabric, and the effect is confusion; however, if a single bolt of fabric is lying alone on the table to be cut for another customer, it becomes a focal point. The same principle can be applied to interiors. For example, one painting surrounded by three empty walls attracts attention; the same painting may be overlooked if it is surrounded by other paintings or art objects.

Emphasis through arrangement.   As you walk into an empty room, certain areas will attract your attention first. Therefore, the shape and the structural features will determine to some extent where the center of interest should be placed. It is important to choose a dominant area rather than some obscure corner of the room. The background and surrounding areas must be carefully planned to recede rather than advance. Furniture may be arranged to point to the center of interest.

Emphasis through the unusual or the unexpected.   Dominance can be achieved by the unexpected or the unusual line, form, texture, pattern, or color. The unusual stands out. If a blue chair appears in a predominantly yellow room, it is viewed as the exception or the emphasized object. Of course, for rhythm, that unusual element should be repeated.

An unusual location for an object may draw attention. A famous dress designer chose to hang Japanese wedding kimonos from the ceiling. Not only is this choice unusual and unexpected, but it also helps establish the character of the room and displays the owner's interest.

Establishing the center of interest in a room can be the most entertaining aspect of design. By using the elements and principles of design to lead the eye easily to the center of interest, the designer can achieve unity and a feeling of completeness.

Emphasis is achieved in this room by the unusual and unexpected use of carpeting curving up the wall. The imaginative multilevel coffee tables are made of nine separate plywood boxes covered with silver paper. ([Photo courtesy of *Family Circle*], courtesy of Monsanto Company)

Fig. 7.15

8
Taste

People who study examples of good taste can acquire good taste. Some people are surrounded by good taste from birth. Others acquire a sense of taste from teachers or knowledgable individuals. Those who improve their taste do it by observing and perceiving objects of good design.

History has placed a stamp of approval on the culture and artifacts of ancient Egypt, Greece, and Rome. The periods of Louis XV and Louis XVI, as well as the designs of the Renaissance period in Europe, are also rated high from the standpoint of good taste.

However, taste is always in a state of flux because new designs are continually being created. Nostalgia also plays an important role in the tastes of many. It accounts for the popularity of traditional or classical decoration, which represents a return to the "good old days," as in the popularity of Early American (handcrafted and antique) furniture today.

Some people favor a traditional period and style. Even when this choice is correct in every aspect, it can produce rooms that lack the imprint of the individual's personality. Other people who desire to break from tradition find expression for their taste in a choice of contemporary designs. Still another group, the eclectics, like a mixture of different styles.

As one looks at the past and contemporary designs with a critical, appraising eye, accepting what is right for a particular life style and rejecting what is not, personal tastes are developed. No one is born with a discerning eye, nor is it acquired overnight, but once acquired most possessions will become more rewarding.

Taste is a purely subjective judgment of what one thinks is beautiful, attractive, or appropriate. What one individual may consider to be good taste another may find in poor taste. Once Victorian homes filled with bric-a-brac were considered appropriate. Today modern society frowns on cluttered environments, as witnessed in our sleek, unadorned skyscrapers and our uncluttered interiors with clean-line furniture.

Taste is also a personal preference, whether or not others feel that it needs improvement. But genuine good taste is discrimination and judgment based on a knowledge of art principles that follow good design. Taste is not acquired by accepting each new trend that becomes fashionable, but rather through a deliberate and continuing process of first becoming aware, then training the eye to discriminate between what is and what is not good design. How is good taste distinguished from bad taste? An item is in good taste if it can be described as well proportioned, integrated, beautiful, original, fine, sincere, appropriate, logical, direct, and efficient, with its form defining its function. An item can be considered in bad taste if the observer feels that it can be fairly described as chaotic, confused, illogical, shoddy, fake, cheap, insincere, ostentatious, or vulgar. There are many degrees of taste, ranging from the abysmally bad through the mediocre to the superlatively good.

Although the arbiters of taste might disagree with a person's individual judgment and classification, whatever they are they represent that person's honest and personal taste. If we are mentally growing—developing finer discrimination, keener perception, and maturer appreciation—our standards of taste are constantly changing. We might discover that our previous taste has become inadequate, and perhaps even abandon it. Thus it is not uncommon for young consumers to rush out and decorate their first apartment with furniture they think they like because they did not understand their own taste. Their purchases were made too hastily.

Our tastes are a result of how we see things aesthetically, the scope of our educational and cultural experiences, our values, and our attitudes. Our tastes make us reject certain styles and accept others. Rejection could even evolve into acceptance as we become more familiar with a style. For example, one may not want to own antiques because they are not understood or appreciated but once a knowledge of antiques is acquired, an individual may become very much interested in using them in the home.

Taste is more than purely subjective. It is an emotional response, and therefore a blend of thinking and feeling. Your emotional reaction may limit your enjoyment of a design.

"Taste is also the orientation of an individual that results in his making judgments about so-cial appropriateness of cultural products— nonmaterial, as well as material. Thus judgments of taste can be directed toward music, manners, and social conduct as well as art, architecture, and interior decoration," according to Roach and Eicher, who also point out that "taste is exhibited within a social context and is judged in relation to standards for taste that have grown out of the behavior patterns of the social group."[1] Taste operates in a sociological context because judgments are applied to an individual's pattern of selection from the alternatives available. But that individual is judged on the basis of how well his or her taste measures with a given group's taste. In other words, one is assessed with regard to the ability to differentiate good from bad taste as measured against arbitrary standards set by the group.

Timing also influences what is considered good or bad taste. James Laver, a British historian, saw the relationship between taste and timing when he said that good taste depends upon the time perspective in judging a particular item. An item, he said, is considered thus:[2]

"indecent"	10 years before its time
"shameless"	5 years before its time
"outre"	1 year before its time
"smart"	in its time
"dowdy"	1 year after its time
"hideous"	10 years after its time
"ridiculous"	20 years after its time

The amount of time covered may be greatly expanded or condensed for different items or styles; but the cycle is still a valid concept. This concept operates in the collecting of antiques. Ten years ago people were not collecting Art Deco items, but today these items are highly prized. A great deal depends on how far removed an item is from the time period in which it is judged.

[1]Mary Ellen Roach, and Jo Anne Eicher, *The Visible Self* (New York: Wiley, 1973), pp. 135–136.
[2]Laver, James, *Taste and Fashion*, revised (London: George G. Harrap and Co., Ltd., 1946), p. 202.

"Personal Preferences." Instructions: Check the preferred items in each category for the home. More than one item may be checked in each category.

Table 8.1

Home

Dwelling Types
☐ Apartment
☐ Condominium
☐ Cooperative
☐ Duplex
☐ Free-standing
☐ Mobile
☐ Modular
☐ Prefabricated

Design

Design Types
☐ Abstract
☐ Applied
☐ Geometric
☐ Naturalistic
☐ Structural
☐ Stylized

Colors
☐ Neutrals
☐ Neutrals with accents
☐ Yellow
☐ Yellow green
☐ Green
☐ Blue green
☐ Blue
☐ Blue purple
☐ Purple
☐ Red purple
☐ Red
☐ Red orange
☐ Orange
☐ Yellow orange

Types of Lines
☐ Curved
☐ Diagonal
☐ Horizontal
☐ Vertical

Styles

Furniture Styles
French styles
☐ Louis XIV
☐ Louis XV
☐ Louis XVI
☐ Empire
☐ French provincial
☐ Directoire
English styles
☐ Tudor
☐ Elizabethan
☐ William and Mary
☐ Early Georgian
☐ Middle Georgian
☐ Late Georgian
☐ Regency
☐ Victorian
☐ Modern
American styles
☐ Colonial
☐ Federal
☐ Pennsylvania Dutch
☐ Shaker
Other
☐ African
☐ Art Nouveau
☐ Biedermeier
☐ Eclectic
☐ Islamic
☐ Italian
☐ Mediterranean
☐ Oriental

Furniture Materials
☐ Glass
☐ Marble
☐ Metals
☐ Plastics
☐ Rattan
☐ Wood
☐ Others_____

Life Styles
☐ Casual
☐ Formal
☐ Functional
☐ Sophisticated

Styles or Periods
☐ Contemporary
☐ Eclectic
☐ Modern
☐ Traditional

Backgrounds

Floor Coverings
Hard
☐ Brick
☐ Ceramic
☐ Concrete
☐ Flagstone
☐ Marble
☐ Pebble
☐ Slate
☐ Terrazzo
☐ Wood

Soft
☐ Area Rugs
☐ Carpets and rugs
☐ Carpet tiles
☐ French rugs
☐ Oriental
☐ Scatter rugs
☐ Shag carpeting
☐ Wall-to-wall
☐ Others_____

Resilient
☐ Asphalt tile
☐ Cork
☐ Linoleum
☐ Rubber
☐ Vinyls
☐ Others_____

Lighting
☐ Architectural treatments
☐ Daylight or natural light
☐ Floor and table lamps
☐ Fluorescent
☐ Incandescent
☐ Track lighting
☐ Combinations
☐ Others_____

Table 8.1 "Personal Preferences" *(Cont.)*   *131*

Wall Coverings
- ☐ Brick
- ☐ Ceramic tile
- ☐ Fabric
- ☐ Laminates
- ☐ Painted
- ☐ Paneling
- ☐ Wallpaper
- ☐ Others_____

Window Treatments
- ☐ Bare look
- ☐ Beads
- ☐ Blinds
- ☐ Curtains
- ☐ Draperies

Styles
- ☐ Contemporary
- ☐ Modern
- ☐ Period
- ☐ Traditional
- ☐ Lambrequins
- ☐ Screens
- ☐ Shades
- ☐ Shutters
- ☐ Others_____

Others

Accessories
- ☐ Antiques
- ☐ Baskets
- ☐ Books and magazines
- ☐ Clocks
- ☐ Collections
- ☐ Flower arrangements
- ☐ Lithographs

- ☐ Mirrors
- ☐ Paintings
- ☐ Photographs
- ☐ Pictures
- ☐ Plants
- ☐ Records
- ☐ Sculpture
- ☐ Wall hangings
- ☐ Others_____

Fabric Constructions
- ☐ Felting
- ☐ Films
- ☐ Knitting
- ☐ Knit sew
- ☐ Laces
- ☐ Multicomponents
- ☐ Nonwovens
- ☐ Pile
- ☐ Tufting
- ☐ Weaving

Types of Fabrics
- ☐ Broadcloth
- ☐ Brocade
- ☐ Burlap
- ☐ Canvas
- ☐ Challis
- ☐ Chintz
- ☐ Cord
- ☐ Crepe
- ☐ Damask
- ☐ Denim
- ☐ Imitation furs
- ☐ Herringbone
- ☐ Muslin
- ☐ Peau de soie
- ☐ Percale
- ☐ Satin
- ☐ Shantung

- ☐ Suede cloth
- ☐ Tapestry
- ☐ Tweed
- ☐ Velvet
- ☐ Others_____

Types of Fibers
- ☐ Acetate
- ☐ Acrylic
- ☐ Cotton
- ☐ Glass
- ☐ Linen
- ☐ Modacrylic
- ☐ Nylon
- ☐ Olefin
- ☐ Polyester
- ☐ Rayon
- ☐ Saran
- ☐ Silk
- ☐ Triacetate
- ☐ Vinyl
- ☐ Wool

Upholstery
- ☐ Fabrics
- ☐ Leathers and suedes
- ☐ Vinyl
- ☐ Others_____

Woods
- ☐ Birch
- ☐ Cherry
- ☐ Elm
- ☐ Mahogany
- ☐ Maple
- ☐ Oak
- ☐ Pine
- ☐ Rosewood
- ☐ Teak
- ☐ Walnut
- ☐ Others_____

There are a few basic recommendations for developing good taste:

1. Observe. Before analyzing personal taste, observe things in your surroundings. Visit museums, historical homes, local furniture departments, and room displays; read newspapers and magazines. With careful observation you will notice color, pattern, line, shape, texture, balance, emphasis, rhythm, scale, and proportion in objects, some of which exhibit good taste, others of which do not. Learn to recognize good design and poor design.

Fig. 8.1

The setting shown blends the various types and elements of design to produce a feeling of harmony. *(Courtesy of Dunbar-Dux, photo by Wesley Pusey)*

2. Examine in detail appealing items. Ask yourself why they exhibit good design. Before commenting "I like it" or "I don't like it," study each item as an achievement or failure in design.
3. Start a notebook of clippings showing examples of design that are appealing. A clipping might be a picture of a room, a piece of furniture, or an accessory. Gradually you will begin to eliminate some ideas and develop a preference for one item over another. Only through observing many objects and comparing them can personal taste be analyzed.
4. Become convinced that the mass acceptability of an item is not always a good criterion of design. Just as fashionable clothing becomes outdated, so do home furnishings. It is

therefore necessary to become discriminating about purchases, however small they may be.

5. Learn that cost is not always a good criterion of design. There are expensive items that are in poor taste and inexpensive, well-designed items that exhibit good taste.

Many people lack confidence when it comes to decorating a room, house, or office. One reason is that they are not familiar with their personal likes and dislikes. The table of decorating alternatives and preferences on pp. 130–131 was compiled to assist you in developing personal tastes. The table lists different items, styles, periods, and so forth. Read through the different categories of items and check those that you like. After doing this for all classifications, compare and compile your choices. You will discover the kinds of decoration that will be most suitable to your needs and desires. Gradually you will find that you begin to eliminate some items and prefer others.

The development of good taste or good design sense has a practical aspect. A person usually receives more enjoyment from an object that follows the principles of good design. The owner of that object learns to appreciate it and enjoy it permanently, whereas a poorly designed object may be enjoyed for only a short time, and then discarded. Good design, therefore, becomes a matter of economy.

SECTION THREE

**Furniture Styles,
Selection,
and Room Arrangement**

Choosing a Style of Home Furniture

The furniture styles of a period relate to the architecture that was designed to house them. The design vocabulary of the building's exterior—its ornamentation, symmetry, simplicity or complexity, color, choice of materials—relates to the appearance of furniture created during the same period. The look of furnishings relates to the larger concept of fashions in design that may be popular at a particular time, expressing how artists of that period perceived society.

In the design of architecture, plans are formulated for the exterior appearance of a building and also for the detailing of interior spaces. A well-designed house integrates all exterior and interior features; this integration includes its furnishings.

Many of our contemporary classics in furniture design were created by architects to carry their ideas of exterior form to interior design. A great architect such as Frank Lloyd Wright worked on every aspect of his homes, relating all details, including furnishings, to his own principles of design. Some of our most exciting pieces of furniture are chairs, tables, and lamps created by Wright and best appreciated when viewed in the context of the original building. Many designers see the furnishings of their buildings as part of an over-all design.

Different styles in homes created during various periods can be identified through distinct forms and details. A Victorian building has not only a distinct set of exterior forms but a unique arrangement of its interior spaces—that is, its ways of dividing and connecting interior spaces and circulating people through them. The unique dimensions and shapes of interior rooms govern the look and arrangement of furnishings within them. In a contemporary building, for example, the geometry, the simplicity, and the modular forms have a distinct relationship to contemporary designs in furniture. The steel, chrome, and glass on the exterior of contemporary buildings are frequently found in the furnishings within them.

When one is furnishing a contemporary or period home, it may be helpful to understand the general fashion and design concepts of the time, looking at many art forms, including the exterior architecture of that period. In this way,

Fig. 9.1

(a)

Victorian interior is coordinated with a Victorian-style home. (a) Victorian home. *(Courtesy of Linda Schneider, Brooklyn, N.Y.)* (b) Downstairs guest room, 1975 Burlington House Award. *(Courtesy of Letitia Baldrige Enterprises, photo by Jack Sink)*

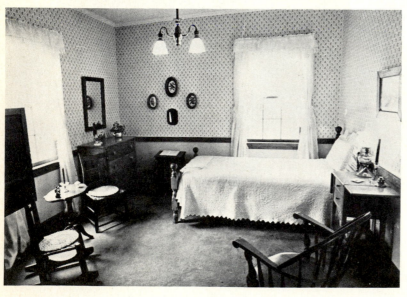

(b)

Furniture Styles, Selection, and Room Arrangement

one can begin to visualize how furnishings may have looked and been arranged.

Although furnishings can be used to relate to and complement the original style of a building, another approach that is commonly utilized today is a free mixture of exterior and interior styles. A visual interest may be found in the contrasts created in a simple contemporary home with ornately decorated interior furnishings or in a Victorian home with the stark simplicity of contemporary furnishings.

In considering home furnishings, one should be aware of the influence of exterior design on the interior forms and their arrangements. One should decide whether one wants to be faithful to the original appearance of a period and re-create it or to use furniture interpretively, reacting freely to whatever the house and its interior inspires one to do.

The consumer today is faced with a wide variety of choices in the area of furnishings. The many styles and types available make it possible to create almost any atmosphere that one desires. This bountiful market, however, may be a paradoxical blessing because it makes decisions more difficult.

Terminology

The terminology relating to furniture styles has become somewhat confusing. Not many years ago one might have asked, "Shall I use 'period' or 'modern'?" Now we are more likely to hear the terms *traditional* and *contemporary*. *Modern* is often used with some qualifying word, such as *Danish* or *organic*. These terms are rather difficult to define, because their connotations and meanings overlap; individuals give them different interpretations, and there is no agency for establishing definitions that clearly mark the differences.

An Egyptian interior entitled "20th Century" designed for a contemporary city dweller. *(Designed by Richard Knapple, courtesy of Bloomingdale's, N.Y.)*

Fig. 9.2

Traditional

Traditional refers to furniture designs that have come to us from past generations. The words *period* and *style* are often used interchangeably with reference to traditional furnishings. Some authorities prefer to use the term *period* to define a particular time and the term *style* to define the work of a particular individual. Thus Chippendale and Hepplewhite would be two styles of the Georgian period. This distinction is by no means a hard-and-fast rule. We often see references to Queen Anne "style" rather than "period," even though the queen did not design furniture.

In the true sense, a period piece would be either the original or an exact reproduction. Very few pieces of furniture made today are exact copies of original designs. Styles have been adapted to present-day living and current methods of production. Changes can be made in scale and ornamentation without destroying the characteristics of the style. We have a variety of furniture that is called *traditional*. The design retains enough characteristics to make its origin unmistakable, yet it is not usually an exact reproduction of any one specific original piece.

However, because of our current interest in restorations there are several manufacturers who do reproduce traditional designs in the most authentic manner possible, and many of these are available to the consumer who desires the more exact copies.

It should be mentioned here that the popular, and sometimes indiscriminate, use of the word *antique* has given it multiple meanings. An Act of Congress stipulates that ". . . Artistic antiquity and objects of art of ornamental character or educational value which shall have been produced prior to the year 1830" may be admitted to the country duty free. Reputable antique dealers, however, reject any theory that something is good simply because it is old. They want examples of the best designs and craftsmanship and accept or reject antiques on the basis of artistic merit as well as age. The government has upheld this view in a decision qualifying the use of the word *artistic* and the phrase *objects of art* and does not allow items to enter duty free merely because they are old.

Modern Adaptations

Modern adaptations refers to a broad array of current designs, many of which draw upon traditional styling for inspiration without actually reproducing any one style in particular. Much contemporary furniture cannot be identified with any previous design, nor can it be associated with the new concepts of the modern style.

In another category, current designers have created various hybrid styles that seem to have popular appeal. Some influences of the past are evident, but the designs are modified and simplified to produce a flavor rather than a true representation. Examples of this type of contemporary design might include Italian Provincial, Mediterranean, and the more recent adaptations of early English styles such as Tudor.

A considerable amount of contemporary furniture is designed for mass production. At the present time there is a growing interest in the use of molded plastic components to develop this new transitional type of design. Some authorities view with horror the simulation of wood carving in plastic. Others seem to find a challenge in adapting new techniques and new methods to bridge the transition between the past and the present. It is probably too early to evaluate these modern methods in terms of design, but there can be little doubt that in the future plastics will become more important in the contemporary style.

Contemporary

The *contemporary* style has been developing since the early part of the twentieth century; it breaks all ties with previous designs. New forms, unusual proportions, and modern materials characterize furnishings that bear little, if any, suggestion of past heritage. This style has gone through periods of growing pains, with abundant examples of poor design that were rejected shortly after they were born. However, the classic examples of contemporary styling have reached a high level of artistic refinement and have recognized the relationship between modern technology and beauty of line, form, color, and texture.

A traditional setting with reproductions of English Georgian Furniture. *(Courtesy of Kittinger Company, photographed in Williamsburg, Va.)*

This living–dining room combines several traditional styles of furniture. *(Designed by Patricia Harvey, A.I.D., photo by Henry S. Fullerton)*

Fig. 9.3

Fig. 9.4

Choosing a Style of Home Furniture

Fig.
9.5

Fig.
9.6

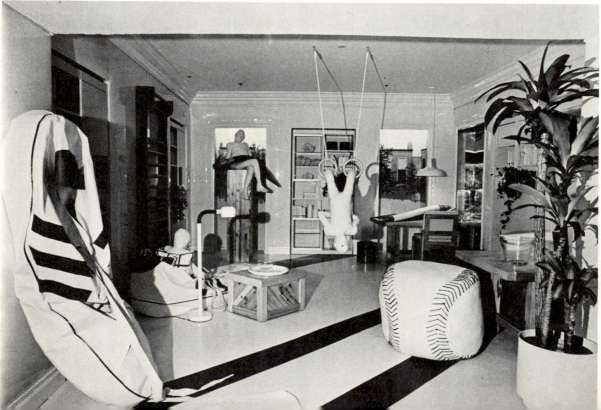

A traditional atmosphere with suggestions of contemporary design is expressed in this living room. *(Designed by Patricia Harvey, A.I.D., photo by Doris Jacoby)*

(bottom, left) Accessories reflecting "upbeat" tastes include an oversized "baseball chair" and "pencil pillows." *(Designed by Richard Knapple, courtesy of Bloomingdale's, N.Y.)*

(top, right) An Early American theme is introduced into an unusual family room with separate nooks. *(Designed by Edmund Motyka, A.I.D.)*

(bottom, right) A contemporary room that represents no authentic period style is given an Oriental feeling by the use of accessories in a setting designed by Lois Kelley, N.S.I.D. (*"Trend East"* room group by Stratford, courtesy of Futorian Mfg. Corp.)

Fig. 9.7

Fig. 9.8

Because a considerable amount of money is involved in establishing a home, a family will usually have to live with furnishings for many years. Before any selections are made, therefore, it is desirable to investigate the various possibilities so that the final selections will provide lasting satisfaction.

Many factors will influence buying decisions. In addition to the theme or the mood one wants to create, problems of space, function, maintenance, and cost may have to be considered. The more familiar one becomes with different types of decoration, the easier it is to understand how certain styles can be used to achieve specific purposes.

Perhaps the first consideration should be the atmosphere of the home. Qualities such as formality, elegance, comfort, cheerfulness, gaiety, or simplicity may be more easily achieved through one style than another. It is important, therefore, to explore the characteristics of various modes of design in terms of such expressiveness.

Many traditional designs have withstood the test of time. The styles that are popular today have been here for many years. They have grown, have developed, and have ultimately proved their worth. They have shown that they are easy to live with and that they are not likely to become boring or obnoxious because they are no longer fashionable. In furnishings, a truly good design is always in fashion. Living with traditional designs may give one a certain sense of security, but some personalities may find this expression of security in their homes rather dull. People who react well to change and to new ideas will probably find the contemporary and the modern styles more stimulating and exciting. Because these styles have grown up with us, they are often more closely keyed to our requirements in modern living. They are designed to cope with the problems of space and care. The furniture is flexible so that it may be adapted to different conditions and situations. It must be remembered, however, that these styles are more vulnerable to fashion changes. Each year new developments, new ideas, and new

A truly modern room that emphasizes new forms and textures. There is little recognition of tradition in the design of this room. *(Designed by Barbara D'Arcy, A.I.D., Bloomingdale's, N.Y., photo by Richard Averill Smith)*

advances in technology threaten the current modes.

Of course, no one can be sure that one's taste will not change in five, or even two, years. The person who chooses traditional styles may become bored with them and suddenly find ultramodern furnishings very exciting. Strangely enough, this sometimes happens to people in their middle years. There has been a trend toward modern furnishings among couples whose families have grown up and moved away from home. Frequently the parents move to smaller quarters and refurnish in the more modern style after having lived with traditional furniture for many years. Simplicity and ease of care seem to be the influencing factors. As one woman pointed out, she had dusted bric-a-brac for twenty-five years and was tired of it. Now she wanted smooth, uncluttered surfaces. On the other hand, there has been a trend among

This room is modern in mood with a hint of the traditional in chest and table. *(Courtesy of Bloomingdale's, photo by Richard Averill Smith)*

Fig. 9.10

Fig.
9.11

Can one mix modern and traditional styles? The room above shows antique Georgian chairs, a modern painting, a steel and glass coffee table, and an Oriental rug in perfect harmony. A Jacobean print on the loveseat accents the blues and greens in the border of the rug which has an ivory background. The background is a subdued champagne color that serves the purposes of contrast in line and color accents.
(Courtesy of Oriental Rug Importers Association)

young people to furnish in traditional styles as well as with antiques. In an age when one must face stark reality and the pressures of daily living in a mechanized society, the repose of soft, graceful lines in a traditional home may be soothing.

From the economic standpoint one usually gets better value by selecting styles that have a minimum of ornamentation. Probably the two best values in this respect are contemporary and Early American. In both styles the emphasis on simplicity, texture, and color make it possible to achieve various effects without undue expense. It should be noted, however, that some manufacturers are experimenting with very new methods of constructing other types of furniture that can provide high quality at low cost. If the application of plastics continues to develop, we may see a much wider variety of better-quality furniture in the low-cost category.

Combining Styles

We are in an eclectic period, and it is common practice to combine various styles of furnishings in the same room. The trained eye of an expert interior designer sees each choice in relation to the final effect. She or he may, there-

An unusual example of eclectic design is found in this room. A Queen Anne chair is combined with a bold wallpaper in striking contrast, yet they seem to complement each other. *(Courtesy of Wallcovering Industry Bureau)*

Fig. 9.12

fore, combine furnishings in a most unorthodox manner with very pleasing results. Sometimes designs of widely different heritages blend well and complement each other in an exciting manner. An example of this might be the use of certain Oriental rugs with very modern furniture. Within recent years, several interior designers who have experimented with such combinations have initiated a trend that seems to have popular appeal. This is not exactly a new idea: seafarers in the eighteenth century brought back rugs and accessories from the Orient, and they blended beautifully with the formal Georgian designs, which were, of course, the "modern" of the time.

It is difficult to achieve a feeling of unity with indiscriminate combinations. The novice, there-fore, may find it more difficult to combine the unusual without creating a feeling of confusion.

Components are more likely to blend well if they express similar ideas or if they have a common spirit. Furnishings that are formal in character may be quite compatible, even though they represent different styles. It is not quite as easy to relate the quaint to the sophisticated or the elegant to the rustic. However, there can be no rigid rules about unusual combinations.

In simple terms, harmony refers to similarity with some variation for interest. Color, texture, and form must all be carefully considered. Although one or another element might be used as the variant, for the sake of unity there must also be some unifying concepts to provide the similarity.

Choosing a Style of Home Furniture

10

Development of Furniture Styles

Study of the decorative styles used by various groups in the development of civilization presents a fascinating approach to history. Throughout the ages, homes have represented a way of life. Customs, beliefs, political interests, economic conditions, new discoveries, and particular personalities have all been influential factors at one time or another in determining decorative modes. In more recent years, technological advances, the development of communications, and the expansion of travel facilities have had important effects on modern tastes.

As one studies the evolution of interior design, it is entertaining to imagine what it might have been like to live with some historic style when it was the "modern" of the age. It is difficult to imagine living in a feudal castle with huge, dreary rooms. There would be no comfortable chairs, no telephone, and no electricity. Visualize a glamorous, but damp, house on a canal in Venice or a lovely formal Georgian mansion. With a good imagination it is hardly possible to become acquainted with any particular period without becoming more aware of the people who lived in such homes.

One approach to our heritage is through a bird's-eye view of the influences on current styles. Table 10.1 (pages 156–159) presents a synopsis of development. By reading both vertically and horizontally, one can see the broad relationships between eras and cultures.

Ancient Designs

Although the inspiration for current furniture designs usually dates back only to about the fifteenth century, we have frequently borrowed ideas and motifs from the ancient Greeks, Romans, and Egyptians. Actually there is very little of their furniture still in existence, but from art and literature we know that they used certain basic forms that we are still using, such as couches, tables, chests, and stools. There was far less variety, however, because some of our more familiar pieces of furniture did not develop until centuries later. Furniture of the ancient civilizations was, nevertheless, quite elegant. It was made of beautiful woods, marbles, and bronze. Decorative detail was supplied through carving, painting, inlay, and veneers.

It is interesting to notice that some of the features characterizing Egyptian furniture are evident in the design of furniture in later years. Many of the chairs and beds were equipped with feet that were carved paws placed on small blocks of wood so that the ornament could be seen. The legs of the furniture were designed to emulate the front and hind legs of animals (often the lion or dog).

The Egyptians designed stools with legs in the form of an **X**. The intersection of the **X** was fitted with a pin and was movable, as on the folding camp stool used today. Many ancient tables were really tripods with tops mounted on three elaborate legs. Some contemporary adaptations seem to indicate a revival of interest in ancient designs.

Greek architecture played an important part in the Renaissance. The revival of the Greek forms in architecture found its way to the furniture. The Greeks contributed the *Klismos* (concave) chair, a lightweight, armless chair constructed of wood that had back rails curved in concave form, roughly following the curve of the human back.

The Roman civilization, following that of the Greeks, copied and adapted many of the Greek forms. The Romans developed the use of the arch, the vault, the niche, and many other architectural forms.

Replica of the "Princess Sitamun Chair" (c. 1400 B.C.) now in the Cairo Museum. The original is made of reddish tropical wood and ornamented with gold leaf. Pieces of this type often used designs representing protective spirits. *(Courtesy of The Baker Furniture Museum)*

Fig. 10.1

Dark Ages

After the decline of the Roman Empire, the era known as the Dark Ages began. From an artistic standpoint we have little to draw upon from this long period. Most people lived in rather crude, simple cottages on feudal estates. There was little interest in the arts, nor were there many significant contributions. There seems to

(a) The form of the Greek Klismos chair.

(b) Roman Folding Stool

(c) Roman Chair

have been no interest in the "home" atmosphere as we know it today. Consequently, this is a long period during which there were few, if any, influences that are important today.

By the eleventh century, some of the nations of Europe had been established. As countries developed, so did national characteristics. Large buildings—chiefly castles, churches, and monasteries—slowly began to take on architectural styles that reflected the artistic environment.

Gothic Style

During the thirteenth and fourteenth centuries, Western Europe became somewhat less rural. As towns grew, new buildings were needed and architecture became an important mode of expression. The Gothic style flourished, and furniture followed the general theme. It was large and heavy, with extensive carving. Gothic design endeavored to accentu-

Fig. 10.2

An English oak stall chair in the Gothic style showing linenfold and tracery carvings. The finial motif is on the top of the chair.

Chair showing linenfold, tracery, and finials.

ate the vertical line. Panels on chests assumed the lines of the tall, pointed Gothic arch, and linenfold (folded linen imitated in wood) and tracery designs were used. Ornamental form consisted of small-scale carved architectural motifs, such as rose windows, buttresses, finials, and crockets.

In France the Gothic style was somewhat more refined than it was in England. There was more expert carving, and the decorative details were more intricate. In addition to foliage and animals, motifs included rosettes and fleurs-de-lis. France also produced many exquisite tapestries during this era.

Renaissance

A new way of life opened with the Renaissance, or "rebirth." It was characterized by an interest in all phases of human activity. The spirit manifested itself in many ways. The new awareness of the individual tended to foster the development of artistic capabilities. The manner of life that evolved was creative, gay, witty, and intellectually stimulating. Social amenities and dress became more important. In such an atmosphere of activity, inquiry, and interest, the arts in particular flourished.

Italy

The new era of appreciation began to develop in Italy during the fourteenth century and reached its height during the first half of the sixteenth century. During this "golden age," great artisans produced many of the finest art treasures the world has ever known. The Renaissance was most fruitful in Italy, but eventually its influence spread to other countries and inspired similar developments.

Furniture designs reflected the new interest in the arts. They became more refined in form and somewhat more graceful in proportion. As one would expect, the techniques of ornamentation followed the development of an appreciation of high levels of artistic achievement.

One of the main chairs of this period was the scissors, or "Savonarola," type, found in Rome and before that in Egypt. The chair was com-

(a) Savonarola Chair

(b) Dante-type Chair

(c) Sgabello

posed of interlacing curved slats and usually had a carved wooden back and arms. Another, the "Dante" type, had heavy curved arms and legs, and usually had a leather or cloth back and seat. A stool chair (*sgabello*), used for dining, was developed from a stool with three splayed legs; it had a small octagonal seat and a stiff back. Some chairs were straight and square, built on flat runners with heavy stretchers.

Chests were used for storing valuables and served as traveling baggage. A typical chest was called a *cassone,* a long flat chest with hinged lids that could be used as a table or for seating. Many times the chests were extremely decorative.

France

By the end of the fifteenth century there were many Renaissance influences in France, but the French were slow to give up their preference for Gothic forms. During the reign of Francis I (1515–1547), the court at Paris attracted many of the Italian artists and their influences continued during the reign of Henry II (1547–1559). However, religious strife in the succeeding years caused a decline in all the arts.

In 1589 the Bourbons took over, and a new era began in the cultural progress of France. There was a very close relationship between the development of the arts and the government. There was no clear-cut style of art during the ensuing years because of the many different

(d) Typical Italian Renaissance Chair

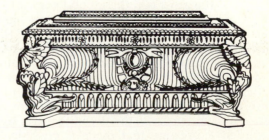

(e) Cassone

Development of Furniture Styles

Fig. 10.3

Caryatids are used to ornament a French armoire in walnut, sixteenth century. *(Courtesy of The Brooklyn Museum, gift of Mrs. J. Fuller Feder)*

One must always bear in mind that the court furniture was quite different from the furniture used by the masses of people. Yet, in an indirect manner, the influences of the court seeped into French national design and provided the basis for styles that have become extremely popular in our current trends of decoration.

England

The Renaissance influence was felt later in England than in other European countries. Feudalism had just about disappeared in England by the end of the fifteenth century, and the feudal lords gave way to a new class of wealthy English merchants who lived in manor houses. Magnificent houses with beautiful gardens became the prized possessions of this new stratum of English aristocracy. England was becoming a sea power with a rapidly developing colonial empire. There were many forces at work in the development of English nationalism.

In the latter part of the fifteenth and the early part of the sixteenth centuries, art in England was dominated by a mixture of Gothic and Flemish influences. All during the Tudor era (1485–1558), the furniture was essentially Gothic in form; but after 1530, Renaissance themes became increasingly important. Furniture was carved and decorated with inlay, although the techniques were not as refined as those employed in other countries. During the reign of Elizabeth I (1559–1603), the Renaissance took hold in England and almost completely supplanted the Gothic style.

The Jacobean period, beginning with the reign of James I (1603–1625), ushered in an era of increasing wealth and expanding trade for England. Renaissance influences became more important during this period, and by the middle of the seventeenth century they were very strong.

Spain

Prior to the Renaissance, almost all art in Spain had been influenced by the dominance of the Moors, who had ruled Spain for almost eight centuries. The Spanish Christians were influenced by the Moorish taste for geometrical designs. It was during the Renaissance that Spain went through her "golden age" in his-

influences, but the prestige and dignity accorded to the artist laid the groundwork for the future development of French artistic achievement. During the reign of Louis XIII (1589–1643), French art showed many Flemish and Italian influences. Furniture was rather heavy, with prolific use of carving and turning. Although this period has not had great influence on present-day styles, it is important because the craftsmen in the decorative arts were accorded a prestige that made it possible for France to develop the glorious court styles that were to follow.

ENGLISH RENAISSANCE

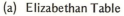

English Renaissance furniture. (a) Oak table in the Elizabethan style with the characteristic bulbous legs. (b) A wainscot chair popular in the seventeenth century under James I rule. The stretchers held the feet off the cold floor. (c) Strapwork carving.

(a) Elizabethan Table   (b) Wainscot Chair   (c) Strapwork Carving

tory. The sixteenth century marked a brilliant era of Spanish power in Europe: it included the reign of Ferdinand and Isabella, the Spanish discoveries in the New World, and flourishing commerce. By the end of the century, however, Spain was almost bankrupt and did not continue to exert important influences in world affairs. Today there seems to be a revival of interest in Spanish art.

The central patio around which the Spanish home was built provided a setting for beautiful iron grillwork. The rooms in the house usually had stark white plastered walls, but the wide use of mosaic-tile work, wood-paneled ceilings, tooled leather, and magnificent fabrics for seat cushions and wall hangings gave the Spanish interior an exotic quality that was different from that of any other European country. The furniture was essentially simple in design and consisted of a few basic pieces, such as tables, benches, stools, chairs, chests, and cupboards.

Practically all the furniture in Spain from

Fig. 10.4

Fig. 10.5

SPANISH RENAISSANCE

(a)

(b)

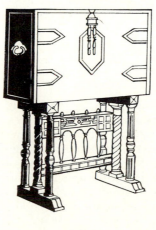

(c)

(d)

Spanish Renaissance furniture. (a) Italian-inspired Spanish Dante chair. (b) Italian-inspired square-backed chair with the use of nail heads for decoration. (c) Vargueño. (d) Geometric ornamentation in Spanish design reflecting the Moorish taste.

1500–1650 was of Italian inspiration. The Spanish developed chairs similar to the Italian scissors chair and the Dante chair. The square-backed chairs were inspired by the Italians, but the Spanish upholstered their chairs with tooled and embossed leathers rather than the velvets that the Italians used.

The Spanish paid more attention to strength of construction than to design, and unnecessarily heavy proportions resulted. The furniture was simple in structure, with elaborate ornamentation. Many pieces were made entirely of metal; others were covered with silver or bound with iron.

The Spanish developed the writing table more extensively than the Italians. The writing cabinet was known as the *vargueño,* a chest of drawers with a front that dropped down to form a desk with elaborate cubbyholes for supplies. The interior was subdivided into many drawers and some secret sections, and the front of each subdivision was elaborately decorated. Handles were placed on each end of the *vargueño,* and the body was separate from the support so that the chest could be quickly transported.

Spanish ornamentation throughout the Renaissance reflected the Moorish tastes for geometrical designs and vivid coloring, giving a distinctly different flavor to the Spanish interpretation of the conventional Renaissance motifs.

Baroque and Rococo

Styles have developed gradually over a long period of time and have reached different areas of the world at widely spaced intervals. Following the Renaissance, a style known as Baroque developed in Italy and eventually spread to other European countries. Although the word *baroque* is French, it comes from the Italian name for a pearl with an uneven shape. The style is characterized by complex curves that are full and vigorous. It developed in different ways in Italy, France, England, and Spain, but the general characteristics were splendor, elegance, and glamour. The first application was in architecture, and the most notable example is St. Peter's

Cathedral in Rome. This magnificent structure was begun in 1506 and completed 120 years later. All during this period and until about 1670, the Baroque style flourished in the Italian architecture of churches, palaces, and villas. Naturally the feeling of the style spread to interior design and furniture. Although the furniture was large and heavy, it was lavish and elaborately decorated with panels, inlay work, painting, and nailheads.

Even while the Baroque style was flourishing in Italy, another style known as Rococo began to appear. It became increasingly popular by the end of the seventeenth century, particularly in France, where it reached its height by the middle of the eighteenth century. France was aspiring toward leadership in the artistic world and there was close association between Italian and French artists.

The Rococo style developed the use of curved lines and shapes, but in a much lighter and more delicate manner than the Baroque style. The word *rococo* comes from two French words meaning "rock" and "cockle shells." These two motifs, along with delicate but elaborate scrolls and foliage, were widely used in wall paneling, woodwork, furniture design, textiles, and ceramics. The Rococo designs of the Louis XV period were characterized by the French creative genius and perfect techniques in craftsmanship. They did not reach the same degree of refinement in Italy, where the work was somewhat coarse and theatrical by comparison with the French. The best examples of Italian Rococo furniture were made in Venice, the center of artistic and social life in Italy during the eighteenth century. The Venetian furniture of this period was notable for its painted decoration, which was applied in a manner that produced exquisite texture. The furniture was extremely ornate, but it also had a delightfully graceful quality.

By the time the Renaissance came to England, the Baroque style had a strong foothold on the Continent. Eventually the English borrowed and adapted both the Baroque and the Rococo themes, but because of the general feeling of English interior designs, the styles were interpreted quite differently.

Post-Renaissance Styles

The furniture designs that developed after the Renaissance are the ones that have the most significance for current home furnishings. As each country went through various periods of affluence or strife, popular tastes were guided by many factors. We must remember, however, that communications were not nearly as advanced as they are today. Influences did spread from one area to another, but not as quickly as they might today. Nationalistic interests and immediate happenings were more potent forces in setting the various styles that developed.

The following chapters contain a brief analysis of the furniture styles we live with today. These chapters represent nothing more than a survey, presented with the hope that the student will find some areas of interest for more intensive study.

Baroque styling is introduced in a room created by Joseph Braswell, A.I.D. Antiques and an elegant window treatment are emphasized by luxurious carpeting in a vibrant spring green color. Accents in coral and pale apricot create a subtle contrast that avoids a heavy appearance. (*Courtesy of Allied Chemical Corporation,* Source *fiber*)

Fig. 10.6

Furniture Styles

Table 10.1

Period	Egyptian (4500 B.C.–7th Century A.D.)	Greek (2000 B.C.–2nd Century B.C.)	Roman (8th Century B.C.–5th Century A.D.)
ANCIENT	High level of craftsmanship. Furniture carved and decorated with inlays of ivory and ebony, gold, enamel, and precious gems. Legs of chairs and couches carved to resemble dog leg with paw on small block of wood. Shaped seats and backs of chairs, sometimes covered with loose cushions. Used metal (gold, silver, bronze), glass, alabaster. Colorful fabrics; painted leather. Pottery used for tableware and personal accessories.	Furniture carved and decorated with painting. Legs were plain graceful curves with turning and animal forms for decoration. Used metals, marble, and beautiful woods. Wide use of tripods or three-legged tables. Exquisite urns and vases pictured daily life, history, beliefs, and customs.	Adapted and borrowed from Greeks but art was more ornate. Furniture quite heavy looking. Used more veneering, especially ebony. Much inlay done with exotic wood, gold, silver, ivory, and tortoise shell.
DARK AGES About 6th–11th centuries	Western Europe in a period of upheaval. Growth of Christian Church. Large buildings were monasteries, churches, feudal estates. People lived in crude cottages on feudal estates. Development of different religious orders; monks chiefly responsible for education. Romanesque style of architecture developed during the 11th century and showed strong Byzantine influences, especially in Italy, where there were principal trade routes between East and West. Long warfare between Christians in Western Europe and Mohammedans. Period has little significance for interior design.		

Period	England	France	Italy	Others
MIDDLE AGES	Norman conquest (1066 A.D.) brought influences of refinement. Large homes had a great hall, which was center of all activity. Gradually began to add more rooms. Gothic style of architecture. Stone walls and floors of earth or stone. Few pieces of furniture in large, solid rectilinear forms. Mostly oak carved with Gothic motifs, panels, foliage, figures, and tracery work in somewhat crude manner. Used chests, trestle tables, benches, and cupboards. Wall hangings of rich, colorful tapestries and other fabrics.	During 12th–14th centuries developed Gothic style of architecture, which reached its height in 14th century. Precise carving of foliage, fleurs-de-lis, rosettes, trefoil and cinquefoil, birds and animals. Art of tapestry weaving developed to height of excellence during 14th century.	Became center of trade routes which brought great wealth. Gothic style did not flourish to same degree that it did in other countries although Venice had some fine examples. During 14th century Renaissance began in Italy. New interest in artistic and scientific pursuits and interest in ancient Roman civilization. Palaces richly decorated and elegantly furnished. Ornate carving, magnificent fabrics, wide use of Venetian glass and lace. Medici family encouraged cultural development and humanist ideas.	**Spain** Centuries of Mohammedan domination resulted in intermingling of Moorish influences with art of Christian Spain. Many geometrical motifs used on furniture and in wrought-iron decorative work. **Dutch and Flemish** Prosperous trade centers. People liked decorative objects. Highly skilled craftsmen produced exquisite work in metal, glass, ceramics, leather, fabrics, lace, and embroidery. Southern areas associated with Catholic art and architecture. Northern parts, chiefly Protestant, did not mix religion and art to same extent.
RENAISSANCE	AGE OF OAK **Tudor Period (1485–1588)** Gothic forms prevailed. Renaissance influences slow to develop. More towns; end of feudal system: Style of domestic architecture developed. Large rambling country	**15th–16th Centuries** Fusion of French Gothic and Italian Renaissance styles. English and Italian influence on Gothic forms. Furniture simple and well constructed. Much of it imported from Italy.	**16th Century** Height of Renaissance. Michaelangelo, Da Vinci, Raphael, and Titian contributed to "golden age" of Italian art. Furniture became more delicate. Various art centers had individual ap-	**Spain** Wealthy, leading world power. Moorish influences in art but applied to Gothic forms. Rich decoration. Homes built around a central courtyard. Much built-in decoration—grille work,

Period	England	France	America	Others
	houses with lawns and gardens instead of castles. More furniture used; gradually became more refined. **Elizabethan Period (1558–1603)** Renaissance influences spread. Transitional period. **Jacobean Period (1603–1649) and Restoration (1660–1689)** Furniture still heavy but new forms introduced. Used sofas, gate-leg tables, round tables; more upholstered pieces. Parquet floors, oriental rugs. Rich fabrics in brilliant colors. Fine embroidery included crewel and needlepoint.	Spain, and the Netherlands. Bourbon regime marked beginning of new emphasis on French artistic and cultural development. Carpet, tapestry, and silk industries encouraged. Paris became center of social and intellectual activities. **17th Century** Strong Italian influences but characteristic French style developed. Baroque designs with short, stopped curves. Court styles with magnificent grandeur and stately elegance. Craftsmen in the decorative arts on a plane with painters, sculptors, and architects.	proaches to all phases of art, including furnishings. Designs became more excessively carved and more pretentious. Furniture mostly walnut. Baroque style developed in late 16th century. Pompous and luxurious; dramatic splendor. Many whirling curves. **17th Century** Baroque influences continued with some influences of French Rococo styles.	painted ceilings; tile in colorful mosaics. Moorish influences persisted throughout the Renaissance. At end of 16th century, furniture was more austere, but during 17th century followed Baroque style with more lavish decoration.
18th CENTURY	AGE OF WALNUT **William and Mary (1687–1702)** Dutch influence. Design showed more refinement and simplicity. Graceful curves with little carving. Cabriole leg originated; highboy made its appearance. Use of lacquered furniture; wallpaper. **Queen Anne (1702–1714)** More emphasis on comfort, hominess. Shell carving, spoon foot. Small tables, lowboys, desks with simple, curved lines. Smaller-scale furniture. **Early Georgian (1714–1750)** Continued style of Queen Anne, but new influences toward middle of century made this a transitional period. Furniture became more elaborate and mahogany became more popular.	**Louis XIV (1643–1715)** Development of Rococo style with flowing serpentine curves. **Louis XV (1715–1774)** Rococo style flourished. Complete emphasis on curves. Ornamentation elaborate and luxurious. Chinese influences fostered by Madame de Pompadour. Wide use of gilt, lacquer, ormolu, fine silk fabrics. Furniture fine in scale, comfortable. Wide use of tables, commodes, writing desks.	**Colonial** **(a) Early American (1608–1770)** Early homes had few pieces of furniture. Styles derived from familiar forms popular in native countries of settlers but executed in woods readily available in America and scaled to smaller rooms. At first, construction simple and crude with little ornamentation. By 1700 more skilled craftsmen and greater interest in comfort and beauty of the home. **(b) American Georgian (1720–1790)** Growth of cities produced more elaborate homes and demand for furniture that followed prevailing styles in Europe. American interpretations of English designs became popular.	

Table 10.1 Furniture Styles (Cont.)

Period	England	France	America	Others
18th CENTURY	AGE OF MAHOGANY **Middle Georgian (1750–1770)** French designs in Rococo mood more popular. Interiors formal and elaborate. *Chippendale (1718–1779)* Designed elegant furniture that showed French, Gothic, and oriental influences. Beautiful carving with emphasis on C curve. Solid and substantial proportions that give style "masculine" appearance. AGE OF SATINWOOD **Late Georgian (1770–1810)** Neoclassic period. Furniture design during this "golden age" was at its height with graceful lines and beautiful proportions. Architecture and interior design blended to produce lovely effects. Fine craftsmanship and appreciation for unusual woods provided exquisite designs. *Robert Adam (1728–1792)* Architect who designed furniture to be made by other craftsmen. Designs were refined and noted for classical simplicity and architectural qualities. Used mahogany and satinwood. *George Hepplewhite (d. 1786)* Delicate furniture that showed modified classical influence. Combined straight and curved lines in skillful manner. Best known for shield-back chair.	**Louis XVI (1774–1793)** Reaction to overuse of curves and emphasis on Neoclassicism; Refined, delicate designs; fine craftsmanship. **French Provincial** Styles that developed in provinces during late 17th, 18th, and early 19th centuries. Influences of court styles uneven. Furniture in cities followed spirit of elegance and splendor but in simplified manner. Country styles graceful but less elegant—used native materials with woods usually waxed or painted. **Directoire (1795–1799)** Political unrest influenced arts but new spirit of freedom combined with interest in classical forms and French heritage of fine design produced graceful style. In general, lines and proportions followed Louis XVI style.	**Federal (1780–1830)** Styles followed English designs, especially those of Sheraton and Hepplewhite. Excellent cabinet work in America but furniture less elaborate than in England. *Duncan Phyfe (1768–1854)* Famous American cabinetmaker. Used graceful, delicate proportions; adapted styles of Sheraton and others. Noted for use of lyre motif, cornucopia legs, and pedestal bases. His work continued into Victorian period.	

Thomas Sheraton (1751–1806) Known for beautiful proportions. Restrained designs on small-scaled slender lines. Extensive inlay. Secret compartments and dual-purpose furniture.

19th CENTURY

Regency (1810–1820) French influences that showed interest in Greek, Roman, and Egyptian designs. Furniture gradually heavier and more elaborate. Eventually exaggerated and bizarre. Period marks end of "golden age" in English furniture design.

Victorian (1837–1901) Long period marked by many diverse influences. Style generally characterized by excessive ornamentation, mixture of unrelated themes and ideas, elaborate and exaggerated forms and motifs. However, the designs can be adapted to present-day living with appealing gracefulness.

Empire (1799–1815) Furniture heavier and more pretentious. Motifs reflected patriotic spirit and influences of Napoleon.

American Directoire and Empire (1805–1830) Some influences of French styles. Patriotic motifs, widespread use of eagle in all phases of design.

Regional Styles Development in different parts of country of Pennsylvania "Dutch," Scandinavian, Shaker, and Spanish Colonial styles.

Post-Federal Period After 1840, designs followed Victorian styles. Many influences. Decorative elaborate furniture. Decoration in general heavy and cluttered. However, some fine examples of American Victorian cabinetwork.

Biedermeier (1815–1860) Style developed in Germany and Austria. Interpreted designs from various sources, including French Empire and Sheraton. Characterized by heavy proportions with simple decorations.

20th CENTURY

DEVELOPMENT OF THE MODERN STYLE

Late 19th Century Evidence of reaction to overelaborate decoration of Victorian era and to use of machines to imitate handcrafts. William Morris, Charles Eastlake, Jr., and E. W. Godwin promoted skilled craftsmanship in design.

19th–20th Centuries L'art Nouveau fostered a new style based on naturalistic themes but rejected traditional forms. Idea of functionalism manifested in work of Louis Sullivan.

Early 20th Century Formation of **Deutsche Werkbund,** group of craftsmen who attempted to design for machine age. Formation of **The Bauhaus,** school led by Walter Gropius, Marcel Breuer, and Ludwig Mies Van der Rohe; continued to emphasize proper use of machines and materials to create good designs.

Work of Le Corbusier and Frank Lloyd Wright in architecture developed theme of functionalism and had important effects on residential design.

1925 The Paris Exposition awakened widespread interest in new ideas, forms, and materials.

CURRENT TRENDS

Wide variety of designs. Some top-level designers working on problems of mass production at various cost levels. Scandinavian designs have had major role in development of style; Italian designs becoming increasingly important.

Modern movement has shown rapid progress in America since 1940.

General features—Functional designs; fresh, new proportions; asymmetrical space divisions. Emphasis on beauty of color and texture; use of new materials. Production of modular furniture to meet individual needs at lowest possible costs.

11

French Styles

For generations, France—and particularly Paris—held a unique position of world leadership in the development of the arts. There are probably many reasons for this predominance, not the least of which is the inherent love of beauty so characteristic of the French people. The national appreciation of the joy and the art of living is sometimes exuberant and sometimes restrained, but it seems to be always present. Art is part of the French life and soul. The spirit of romanticism that pervades the French approach to the business of everyday living is witnessed by French excellence in the culinary arts and in the world of fashion. A close personal association with the arts seems to be a more intrinsic quality in the French people than in many other peoples.

In spite of the dark periods in France's history when creative activity reached low ebbs, the country managed to survive with a certain position of prestige in the arts. Even as France's supremacy in some fields is being challenged today, we tend to harbor a certain sentimentalism for her leadership in design.

Economic, political, and social forces have fostered the interchange of artistic ideas among various countries. France has welcomed and encouraged artists. She has established an atmosphere of freedom for the creative spirit. When France has borrowed ideas from other countries, the results have usually had a distinctive French interpretation—the French "touch," as it has been called. Except in a few outstanding instances, other countries have not been as successful in adapting French ideas to their own particular styles. There have been some excellent designs based on French influences, but the flavor remains French rather than being absorbed in the way that the French use foreign ideas.

The esteem accorded to artists and craftsmen in France may be traced back to the Renaissance. In the latter part of the sixteenth century, the French court began to look with envy at the splendor enjoyed by the Italian rulers. The Renaissance movement had been under way for some time in Italy. During the reign of Francis I (1515–1547), Italian artists, including Leonardo da Vinci and Benvenuto Cellini, had been invited to work at the French court. Catherine de Medici, the wife of Henry II (reigned 1547–1559), was Italian and continued to encourage this Italian influence in the French arts. It was not until the reign of Henry IV (1589–1610), however, that the government actively encouraged the development of the decorative arts. The king wanted the personal glorification of a splendid court and made plans for the development of France as the artistic center of the world. These plans included various programs of sponsorship for artists and craftsmen as well as encouragement of the industries that made tapestries, rugs, and fabrics.

During the reign of Louis XIII (1610–1643), Cardinal Richelieu was a potent factor in encouraging the development of the arts. He urged French artists to travel to other countries and invited foreign artists to work in Paris. The result was a mixture of many influences in French art during the first half of the seventeenth century—mostly Spanish, Flemish, and Italian.

The style of the Louis XIII period was confused by the various foreign influences. In general, the furniture was rectilinear in form and heavy in proportion. But the French craftsmen were learning and adapting new ideas. Gradually a French style was developing. In the characteristic French manner, the new ideas were modified with the stamp of good taste. By the middle of the seventeenth century, the Baroque style was popular; it continued to develop during the following years.

Louis XIV

When Louis XIV was proclaimed king he was only five years old. He reigned from 1643 to 1715, but his mother, Anne of Austria, acted as regent until 1651. Cardinal Mazarin, first minister until he died in 1661, was an enthusiastic patron of the arts. When Louis assumed the responsibilities of the throne he did so with a firm hand. He was an absolute monarch who chose the sun as his emblem—*Le Roi Soleil* ("the Sun King").

LOUIS XIV

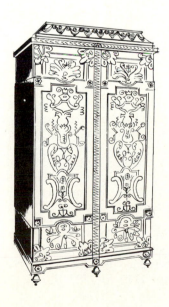

Fig. 11.1

Louis XIV (1643–1715). A baroque style of furniture, developed during the reign of Louis XIV, characterized by large scale and symmetry. Carving was rich and heavy, and plain woods were gilded. The famous cabinetmaker Boulle perfected intricate marquetry of tortoise shell, brass, ivory, bone, and mother-of-pearl. Gorgeous damasks, velvets, and tapestries covered the upholstered pieces.

French Styles

He established a glittering, pompous court. Splendor and magnificence were the keynotes of his reign. Louis XIV was intensely interested in establishing France as the world leader in the arts. His efforts in this direction gave France the position of supremacy that Italy had enjoyed since the Renaissance.

The palace at Versailles is a monument to the pompous splendor of the Sun King's court. The huge building was surrounded by formal gardens, lakes, temples, statues, and fountains. The project was the combined work of many great architects, painters, sculptors, designers, and craftsmen working under the direction of Charles Lebrun, a painter who viewed the decorative arts on a par with the fine arts. Even though Lebrun had the ability to conceive and execute projects on a grandiose scale, he was cognizant of every detail in the design.

Throughout the building were great public rooms, salons, and private apartments that were works of magnificent architectural splendor. Walls and ceilings were decorated with carving, paintings, paneling, mirrors, and tapestries with an extravagance that had never been known before. The famous Hall of Mirrors, 240 feet long, has been the scene of many historic events since the building was made a museum. The beautiful windows, the magnificent ceilings decorated with paintings by Lebrun, and the green marble columns provide an atmosphere of incomparable splendor that is characteristic of the whole palace. Because the walls and ceilings were such magnificent decorative features of each room, the furniture was somewhat secondary; however, it was designed in the elaborate Baroque style to blend with the decor.

The style of furniture that developed during the reign of Louis XIV is important because it was the first of the truly French styles. It was massive, regal, and formal. Because it was so elaborate it was suitable only for the aristocracy. Rich carving, gilding, oriental lacquer, and marquetry were used to produce the elegant pieces. As the period progressed, the lines of the furniture became more curvilinear. Both **S** and **C** scrolls were widely used. The tables, usually placed against the walls, were quite large. Commodes became quite popular and various types of writing desks made their appearance. Armoires were widely used. Huge beds, with much ornamentation and elaborate draperies, were often considered a status symbol. The more elaborate the bed, the more desirable it was as a mark of distinction.

Rich carving, elaborate inlay, and metal mounts were used to produce the elegant pieces. Carved wood was often gilded, and pieces were frequently topped with beautiful colored marble. The upholstery fabrics were richly colored velvets, damasks, satins, and brocades. Tapestries were used for both upholstery and wall hangings. Various types of needlework were also popular.

Although the Louis XIV period was inspired by the Italian Baroque style, the French artists handled the theme with refinement and restraint.

Perhaps the most famous cabinetmaker of the time was André Charles Boulle (1642–1732), the favorite of the king and of the aristocracy. He developed techniques that had been used before but not perfected. "Boulle work" refers to marquetry of tortoiseshell, ebony, and metal, including bronze, copper, silver, and brass. Boulle used bronze mounts and ormolu.

The enthusiasm for Chinese art during this period prompted the development of delightful chinoiseries. The French interpretation of the imaginary Chinese figures and scenes founded this whimsical form of decoration, which was to be copied and adapted in many different forms.

Regency

It must be pointed out that the period referred to as French Regency occurred about a century before the one known as English Regency. The intervening years were marked by technological advances caused by the Industrial Revolution and the resultant sociological changes. The student must be careful not to associate these two periods because of the similarity in names.

Louis XIV died in 1715. The actual period when France was governed by Philippe, the Duke of Orléans, serving as regent for Louis XV, covers only the years 1715 to 1723. From the standpoint of style development, however, the period includes the transitional years from about 1700 to 1720. Many features of the Louis XIV style were disappearing, and new ones associated with the Louis XV style were beginning to appear. Changes in style evolve over a period of years and one supersedes another in a very gradual process.

During the Louis XIV period, furniture had been majestic and elegant. The trend during the Regency period was toward less formality and a lighter spirit. The heavy Baroque features of the earlier style were gradually replaced by the more graceful and exuberant forms of the newly developing Rococo theme. The spirit of gaiety and the preoccupation with fantasy were becoming more marked, although the Regency style managed to retain its dignity.

Architects and painters exerted a tremendous influence on interior designs. The work of Antoine Watteau (1684–1721) and his followers established a new school of painting and was largely responsible for the increasing popularity of the Rococo trend. Watteau, as well as many other great artists, delved into decorative design to produce compositions that were reproduced or executed by skilled craftsmen.

It was quite evident that during this transitional period a new spirit of vivacious gaiety was developing in France. The interest in the Orient continued, and the new spirit stimulated the French imagination to produce compositions that were thoroughly delightful in their amusing fantasia. Turkish, Hindu, and Persian themes were also employed in all forms of decoration. Another favorite subject was the monkey in whimsical motifs known as *singeries*.

The furniture, although lighter in scale and softer in design, was still embellished with carving and marquetry. Much of the furniture was gilded, but beautifully colored woods were also employed. Bronze was popular for mounts and decorative hardware, but frequently it was chased and gilded.

Although chairs and tables became lighter in scale during the Regency period, commodes remained rather heavy. The *bombé* shape was introduced and was to become increasingly popular.

Louis XV

The trends initiated during the Regency were to develop during the reign of Louis XV to establish the style associated with his name.

Several factors contributed to the rather black period for the French monarchy during the reign of Louis XV (1723–1774). The king did not have a talent for ruling the country with a firm hand and instead conducted a court renowned for its frivolity, extravagance, and corrupt behavior. The aristocracy was indifferent to the people and the national problems.

A rather strong middle class had developed and had begun to resent the heavy burden of taxation coupled with the mismanagement of the government. France also fared badly in her efforts toward colonial domination. The general spirit of discontent was fired by the critical writings of French philosophers and economists. Although the seeds of revolution were germinating all during this era it was actually a period that saw the development of a wealthy upper-middle-class bourgeoisie composed of merchants, professional men, bankers, and prosperous farmers. The rise of this group created new demands for homes that were comfortable, refined, and representative of social position.

Most of the palaces and residences of the aristocracy were filled with extremely elaborate furniture that was impossible to reproduce in any large quantity. However, some of the pieces could be adapted or copied in a less sumptuous manner to meet the requirements of the bourgeoisie. Such furniture, with its gracefulness, excellent proportions, and somewhat restrained elegance, was often more beautiful than its more elaborate royal counterpart.

The French Rococo style reached its height of perfection during this era. The skill of the French craftsmen was highly developed during this period. The manner of life, with its emphasis on comfort and convenience, resulted in a desire for smaller rooms designed for special purposes—music rooms, game rooms, sitting rooms, and, later on, dining rooms. Accordingly, furniture became smaller in scale, and a wider variety of small pieces, especially tables, was used.

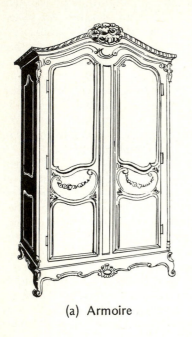

(a) Armoire

(b) Fauteuil

(c) Bergère

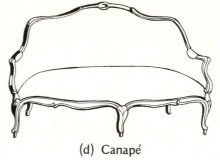
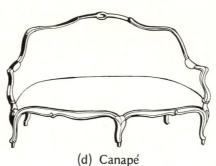

(d) Canapé

(f) Console Table

**Fig.
11.2**

(e) Bombé or Serpentine
Commode

Louis XV. The rococo style that emerged during the reign of Louis XV is considered by many to be the ultimate in decorative furniture. Louis XV furniture is more feminine in character, smaller in scale, and more gracefully proportioned than Louis XIV. Furniture was upholstered with loose down cushions and covered with pretty, delicate fabrics.

Furniture Styles, Selection, and Room Arrangement

The prevailing characteristic of the Louis XV style was the use of curvilinear forms at all times, particularly the cabriole leg. Straight lines were avoided. Much of the case furniture had bulging fronts, known as bombé or serpentine fronts. Corners were rounded, legs were curved, and ornamentation was based on curved motifs. Asymmetrical balance was employed whenever possible. With all of these principles employed in one piece, the resulting beauty of design was indeed a tribute to the French artistic genius, good taste, and technical flare.

A wide variety of different colored woods was used for veneers and in marquetry work. Much of the furniture was painted or gilded. Lacquered work was extremely popular, both for panels and for whole pieces. Some of this work was imported from the Orient, but European craftsmen developed new lacquering techniques. Porcelain plaques or panels of mirrors were often used as embellishments.

Motifs were delicate and feminine. Exquisite floral bouquets were depicted in inlaid panels. Garland and trellis patterns were widely used, as were cupids, hearts, doves, bowknots, ribbons, and musical instruments. Pastoral scenes and motifs were also popular. Leaves and the cockleshell were extensively used.

This was an era of intrigue, and much of the furniture was designed with mechanical devices that transformed the piece in some way or opened up secret compartments.

Madame de Pompadour, favorite mistress of the king, was instrumental in setting many style trends during the period. Her interest in the Orient added impetus to the vogue for Chinese decoration. She is credited with having exquisite taste, which is probably responsible in part, at any rate, for some of the restraints found in design toward the latter part of the reign of Louis XV.

Several eminent architects and artists opposed the Rococo style during the Louis XV period. Derisive publications appeared criticizing the exaggerations of the style, and as the criticism was mounting the importance of the archaeological excavations at Pompeii was beginning to have an impact on all the arts.

Around 1760 the classical influences were beginning to appear in furniture design, and the next decade was a period of transition from the Rococo style to the Neoclassical. The exaggerated curves gradually became softer and more restrained, until a new style evolved with emphasis on rectilinear forms and straight lines. Although these Neoclassical trends are not usually associated with the Louis XV period, the new style was firmly established by the time the king died in 1774.

Louis XVI

The designs that are associated with the Louis XVI style represent classical beauty interpreted with the exquisite taste of the French. The style embodies graceful lines, perfect proportions, and restrained ornamentation. The principles of the style, executed with the superior skill of the French craftsmen, produced the acme in French furniture design. By the time Louis XVI ascended the throne in 1774, the style was well established, and it remained popular until the Revolution in 1789.

The aristocracy of the later eighteenth century continued to live lives of ease and luxurious comfort. It had become the vogue, however, to profess simplicity and to admire the noble virtues of the humble life. Reflecting this, the cabriole leg began to straighten out, with less curvature between the knee and the ankle. By 1770, the legs of all pieces of furniture were straight and tapered, crowned at the top by a square block on which was a carved rosette. The surface of the leg was usually vertical or spiral fluting.

It was fashionable to be interested in antiquity, and the inspiration for the decorative arts was drawn from Roman architectural form. Architectural details, such as colonnettes and miniature pilasters, were frequently used for both structure and decoration. The French designers and craftsmen incorporated the Greek and Roman ideas with grace and delicacy. Although the basic forms were rectangular and the emphasis was on the straight line, they avoided severity and heaviness by skillful incorporation

French Styles

The bed is upholstered in Toile de Jouy.

Fig.
11.3

Louis XVI. A neoclassic style emerged during the reign of Louis XVI. French cabinetmakers, in reaction against the frills of Louis XV and affected by the discoveries of Pompeii and Herculaneum, returned to the symmetry and simplicity of the ancient architectural forms. Furniture took severer straight lines. Upholstery fabrics stressed Toile de Jouy and striped satin.

of graceful curves. The wide variety of ornamental motifs included bouquets of flowers, garlands, swags, wreaths, and festoons. Classical motifs such as the Greek fret, vases, and mythological figures were used, especially in panel moldings and for mounts. The pastoral scenes were used in various forms of decoration and some motifs had an agricultural flavor. The romantic cupids and cherubs continued to find favor. Panels were often used for decoration and sometimes the panel corners were indented and embellished with rosettes.

Marie Antoinette had several favorite cabinetmakers—notably Jean Henri Riesener (1734–1806), one of the outstanding craftsmen of the time. His work typified the finer qualities of

Louis XVI style and is notable for exquisite floral marquetry and bronze mounts. Riesener also excelled in making furniture with mechanical devices and secret compartments, which were still popular.

Mahogany was a very popular wood, although woods such as walnut, satinwood, and sycamore continued to be used. Much of the furniture was painted, usually in tones of ivory or soft gray. Small tables and commodes often had marble tops, but writing desks and tables frequently had tooled leather tops.

Although the beautiful French silk fabrics continued to be used for upholstery, there was widespread use of hand-blocked cottons and linens. The well-known *Toile de Jouy* cottons with pastoral scenic motifs were especially favored. Needlework was also used extensively.

Soft color tones on walls and ceilings and in Oriental, Aubusson, and Savonnerie rugs were the general rule. Delicate shades of blue, gray, green, and pink were popular, and walls were often painted in one of these soft colors or in off-white. Panels of painted fabric or scenic wallpaper were also used.

Accessories included mirrors, crystal chandeliers, lusters, candlesticks, clocks (usually ormolu), statues, and an almost infinite variety of vases and objects in the famous French ceramics.

During this period the interest of the upper middle classes in home decoration continued to spread, partly because of the changes in production methods, with more widespread use of machines and the introduction of new materials that could be used as substitutes for those previously available only to the wealthy. More people began to enjoy the pleasures of homes that were simple but artistically decorated.

Directoire

Although the *Directoire*—the revolutionary government—existed in France for only four years (from 1792 to 1795), the name is given to a style that represents a transition from the Louis XVI style to that of the Empire under Napoleon. Actually the Directoire style began to take form before the Revolution, and some elements continued to exist after the rise of Napoleon. One cannot assign specific dates to style trends, which tend to evolve slowly, but the Directoire period might be considered as lasting from about 1789 to 1804.

Naturally the political upheaval in France during and after the Revolution had its impact on the arts. Many craftsmen were forced to turn to other types of work, and the apprenticeship system—which had been responsible for the development of great skills—was disrupted.

However, the designers and craftsmen who did continue their work developed during this rather short period a style that has found widespread appeal. The furniture retained the graceful lines and beautiful proportions of the Louis XVI style. The classical influences not only continued but developed to the point where structural forms were adopted. The Directoire style employed Greek curves in chairs and sofas. Many chairs took direct inspiration from the Greek *klismos*. Chair backs were often concave and showed a slight roll backward. The legs had gently flowing curves, and the arms on sofas curved outward. Daybeds with both ends of equal height and outward-curved scrolls became very popular.

Egyptian motifs were freely borrowed. In addition to human figures, designs included lotus flowers, sphinxes, papyrus, date palms, and lion heads.

Anything reminiscent of the monarchy was carefully avoided. The spirit of equality, democracy, and freedom prevailed in all modes of life. Ornamental motifs were based on military, revolutionary, and agricultural themes—drums, spears, stars, wheat, and farm tools. Fabric motifs followed these principles, but stripes were also very popular. Color schemes became stronger and were often related to the new flag colors—white was often used with accents of bright red and blue.

Empire

In 1804 Napoleon became Emperor of France. The widespread changes in the political, economic, and social life of France during this era were naturally reflected in the Empire style, which remained very popular while Napoleon was in power, that is, until 1814. The style continued to be fashionable during the succeeding years until about 1830. However, these later years witnessed the decline of French furniture design.

The style associated with this era, reflecting many facets of Napoleon's personality and career, was inspired by militaristic ideas.

The use of Greek, Roman, and Egyptian motifs was fostered by Napoleon's interest and by his successful campaigns. The love of power, grandeur, splendor, and pomp that was characteristic of Napoleon resulted in designs that became heavy and imposing.

Two architects, Pierre Fontaine (1762–1853) and Charles Percier (1764–1838), were largely responsible for establishing the Empire style. Their admiration for the styles of antiquity and their fervent devotion to the authentic reproduction of its principles resulted in designs that were austere and formal. Curved lines were almost completely eliminated, except in chairs

Méridienne

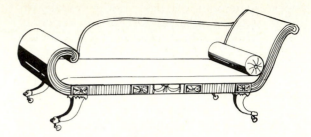

Récamier Sofa

Fig. 11.4

Empire. The French Empire was a style dictated by Napoleon based on Greek and Roman pieces with a strong Egyptian influence. The French Empire style used motifs symbolic of conquest such as Roman eagles, wreaths, torches, lions, the sphinx, the pineapple, the letter *N* framed in a victor's wreath, and the bee. Empire influences may be recognized in German Biedermeier, American Federal, and English Victorian furniture.

and sofas. A severe angularity developed and was sharpened by the use of highly polished flat surfaces, usually unrelieved by any form of carving, paneling, or marquetry. Sometimes carving was used on chairs or sofas, or bands of contrasting woods were used for inlay, but for the most part the decoration of furniture was achieved by the use of gilded bronze appliqués and mounts.

Supports of gilded metals or woods frequently took the form of fantastic figures. Horns, winged lions, the sphinx, a lion's head extending down to a single paw, and various forms of weird figures were combined to produce these decorations. When other motifs were employed they were chosen to represent military power. Napoleon's initial, often encircled by a wreath, was also a favorite motif.

Mahogany was the favorite wood, but marble was widely used for table tops and fireplaces. Other woods—including ebony, rose-wood, yew, elm, pear, and apple—were usually highly polished to emphasize the grain.

Striped fabrics were very popular. Rich brocades, damasks, and velvets often had small conventional motifs. *Toiles de Jouy* with pastoral scenes were also used. Rich, vibrant colors were used, including wine red, purple, bright blue, emerald green, and gold.

Accessories included porcelain vases and urns, and marble and bronze clocks. Candelabra often were supported by caryatids (tall, slender figures). Also used were busts and statues on pedestals or in niches, and mirrors in beautiful Empire frames.

Current adaptations of French styles feature graceful curves and elegant fabrics. In this setting the colors of muted rose and apple green in the taffeta stripe are repeated in the chintz on the sofa and in the colors of the rug in a Savonnerie design. *(Courtesy of Globe Furniture Company)*

Fig. 11.5

The severity and richness of this style depict the spirit of the Roman Empire translated into the mode of nineteenth-century French living. The emphasis on symmetry gives it a feeling of formality; the large proportions make it a masculine style. However, in the early phases, which reflect some of the Directoire trends, the formality is both graceful and unpretentious. Present-day adaptations of the traditional Empire style have scaled down the proportions to provide a style that can be most appealing and suitable to current needs.

In the early part of the nineteenth century the Industrial Revolution was responsible for many changes in France. The country had been essentially agricultural, so the factory system took hold more slowly than it did in England; however, by the middle of the century the use of machines had become somewhat widespread, and the guild system of training fine craftsmen had disappeared. The glorious age of French furniture design had passed, and there was neither the inspiration, the creative genius, nor the skilled craftsmanship to produce another historic style.

French Provincial

Only the nobility and the wealthy class could afford furniture in the French "court" styles described in the preceding sections. Nevertheless, these styles did influence, to a great extent, the furniture used throughout the country. However, geographical position, cultural and economic development, and local customs all influenced the development of furniture styles in the provinces.

Until the seventeenth century, the houses in rural districts, populated chiefly by peasant farmers, were simple cottages that were sparsely furnished with rather crude furniture. Tables, stools, chests, and beds were often built by the people themselves. Where towns and cities had developed, local cabinetmakers with varying degrees of skill met the demands. At about the

FRENCH PROVINCIAL
CITY STYLE

Furniture Styles, Selection, and Room Arrangement

beginning of the seventeenth century, furniture from Italy and the Netherlands started coming into France. It was also during the early half of the seventeenth century that local cabinetmakers became more skillful in adapting the prevailing styles to local modes. The middle class was becoming larger and the farmers were becoming more prosperous. As the various provinces developed economically and culturally, the homes became more completely furnished.

Quite naturally the changes in home furnishings took place much more slowly in rural areas than they did in larger cities. In addition, countryfolk used the materials at hand and whatever native craftsmanship was available. The wealthier bourgeoisie, especially in the cities, could begin to emulate the court styles, but in a highly simplified version. The very fine craftsmen worked in Paris; their labors and the materials with which they worked were available only to the wealthy nobility. As the interest in home surroundings mounted during the seventeenth century, local craftsmen became more skillful and more aware of the changing fashions in furnishings.

The innate French artistry adapted the court styles to a simple manner of living. The result embodied the exquisite proportions and graceful lines of French furniture design at its best. It had the feeling of elegance that comes with the use of beautiful fabrics and woods, and the unpretentious simplicity that is appealing to so many people today. Perhaps no other style of furniture has ever been so successful in combining grace, elegance, and simplicity. No doubt this is why it enjoys phenomenal popularity today.

From this very brief introduction to French Provincial furniture, it should be evident that there are wide diversifications in the style. The crude type made and used by the rural peasants is somewhat akin to our own Early American. The stress was on utility, but with the characteristic French taste and beauty it was charming and even graceful in its sturdiness. The border provinces showed influences from neighboring countries—Germany, Italy, and the Netherlands. Different regions fostered individual customs or wares, but there is a distinctive French touch in the rural French Provincial style. The

woods—mostly the fruit woods, walnut, and oak—were usually waxed. Some furniture was painted, but it was rarely gilded. The fabrics of wool, linen, and cotton were gay and colorful. Toiles, checks, prints, and many forms of needlework were used. The accessories of copper, pewter, and pottery were often useful as well as decorative. Tole candlesticks and *Quimperware*, a pottery with colorful local scenes, were popular.

The furniture made by local cabinetmakers for the wealthier merchants and lesser nobility showed more of the influences of court styles. This type could not be as elaborate as the actual court furniture, but its simplification was an improvement. It was characterized by the elegance that comes with the use of fine materials

French Styles

and the refinement of skilled craftsmanship. This is the style we are likely to associate with the description "French Provincial" and it is the style we frequently use in our homes today. It adapted mostly the Louis XV style, with its graceful curves and excellent proportions, but it eliminated the excessive ornamentation. It represents an interpretation of the Rococo style—which reached its height during the Louis XV period—in a beautifully subdued and restrained version.

Some Louis XVI forms were used, but very few of the Directoire or the Empire themes influenced the Provincial style. Carving and marquetry were used moderately, as were gilding and metal mounts.

Silk fabrics in damask or satin added to the richness and elegance. Whereas in the rural furniture loose cushions of a rough-textured fabric might be merely tied on, this more refined Provincial furniture was beautifully upholstered.

The larger pieces, such as armoires, cupboards, and sideboards, were often decorated with Louis XV–type paneling. The beds were fitted into alcoves, which were curtained with draperies or shut off by paneled doors. Our contemporary version of the Provincial style frequently makes use of upholstered headboards.

The accessories used with the more elaborate type of French Provincial furniture were more in keeping with the feeling of elegance. Crystal, silver, and fine porcelain were popular and added accents to the theme of elegance.

Because England was not closely associated with Italy either geographically or intellectually, Renaissance styles were accepted rather slowly there. In the early stages of Renaissance influence in England, the furniture designers did not understand the correct proportions of classical architecture. Relatively few pieces were used, but the selection included large refectory tables with carved bulbous legs, straight chairs with high backs, benches, stools, cupboards, Welsh dressers, some chests on legs, and large canopied beds. The dignified and solid furniture was usually made of oak.

There has been a revival of interest in early English styles as interpreted by current designers. Of course, the contemporary versions are adapted to current needs, proportions, and methods of manufacturing. The sturdy qualities, however, seem to be becoming increasingly popular.

Jacobean and Restoration

James I, an admirer of Renaissance trends, became a patron of Inigo Jones, a celebrated architect who promoted Renaissance influences in England. During the Jacobean period, which derives its name from the name *James,* furniture was still straight-lined and heavily carved, but it became somewhat smaller in scale. Spiral turns and carved scrolls gradually replaced the heavy bulbous legs. New pieces were introduced, including drop-leaf and gate-leg tables. Chairs and sofas became lighter in weight and began to have upholstered seats and backs nailed to the framework. Until about 1660, oak was still the most popular wood, although walnut had become popular on the Continent. Wood paneling was widely used on walls, and some wallpaper was introduced. Fabrics became more elegant and more brightly colored.

In general, Jacobean trends continued during the reign of Charles I (1625–1649). However, the middle of the seventeenth century was a period of destruction and disorder in England. Charles I was executed in 1649; during the Cromwellian period that followed, neither industry nor the arts made significant progress.

12
English Styles

Fig. 12.1 Jacobean. The period includes the reigns of the Stuart kings James I and Charles I. The furniture was mostly oak, and large, square, rectangular lines dominated the extensively carved forms.

The monarchy was restored in 1660 when Charles II took over the throne. He emulated the lavish French court, and, although his reign was corrupt, he encouraged the arts. Another new era began, and progress in the decorative arts was given new impetus by the interest of the court and the wealthy middle class.

Both French and Flemish influences were strong during the Restoration period. Furniture became more refined and more comfortable. The backs of some chairs were slanted, and the wing chair was introduced. Spiral turning and Flemish curves became much more popular on legs, backs, arms, and stretchers. Some chairs were made with caning. Smaller tables, some of them round, became popular. Game tables and bookcases were introduced.

Oriental themes were popular, and Oriental rugs were used. In accessories there was greater use of marble and ivory, rare woods in inlay work, framed mirrors, and crystal chandeliers.

William and Mary

James II succeeded Charles on the throne but was eventually ousted. Mary, the daughter of James II, and her husband William, Holland's Prince of Orange, were asked to rule.

This period (1689–1702) is significant because the Dutch influence put great emphasis on a happy, comfortable home life. The English people, who had reacted unfavorably to the extravagance and lavishness of the previous court, welcomed the simple tastes of William.

Furniture became much more delicate and graceful. Walnut was used almost exclusively. This was the beginning of the "age of walnut" in English cabinetmaking. Veneers were used in decorative treatment, notably in panels and cross-bandings on borders, with the grain running perpendicular to the main section. In general, there was far less carving of furniture than in the previous styles. Strong French and Dutch influences continued throughout this period. A number of outstanding artists and craftsmen had migrated to England, including Daniel Marot, a French designer, engraver, and architect. He had gone from France to Holland, where he had served William as chief architect. Marot came to England in 1694, and his background was instrumental in promoting both the Dutch and the French influences on the English design of the period. France under Louis XIV had become the leading center for all the arts. As a result, the French influences were widespread throughout Europe.

The legs of William and Mary furniture were the most distinguishing part. They were twisted or scrolled, or shaped like an inverted cup or trumpet with the large part at the top. The bun foot was used. The stretchers were gracefully curved and sometimes met at a central point to form an **X**. The ogee arch was used on highboy aprons. Marquetry in the forms of floral patterns and rambling foliage was popular and lacquered furniture came into wide use.

Although the form of furniture was essentially rectilinear, more curves gradually appeared—for example, in the hooded tops of chests, the aprons of tables, and the splats of chairs. In about 1700 the cabriole leg was introduced in England. This curved leg, which was a decorative adaptation of the foreleg of a four-footed animal, had been incorporated in French furniture design during the Louis XIV period.

During the reign of William and Mary many new types of furniture appeared, including various cabinets, tall case clocks, writing desks,

William and Mary. A style of English furniture made during the reign of Mary Stuart and her Dutch husband, William of Orange. Cabinetmakers from Flanders, Holland, and France were influenced by Louis XIV, while England's Christopher Wren worked in the more chaste Italian mode. These influences produced a distinctive type of furniture that was somewhat comfortable, and light in scale to fit in the new smaller, more intimate, rooms. The legs were turned and braced with serpentine stretchers; the Dutch club foot and the scroll leg were introduced. Chairs were padded and often covered with needlepoint.

dressing tables, and—probably the most important—the tall chest or highboy, which was a chest of drawers supported on a table. Tea drinking as a social custom was popular and resulted in the need for many small tables. There was a much wider use of upholstered furniture, and some pieces were done in over-all upholstery.

Queen Mary had a large collection of porcelain and Delftware. It became quite fashionable to collect china and to display it above doors and chimney pieces. Tiered shelves and china cabinets also became popular.

Needlework was a favorite pastime. Beautiful and subtle coloring was used for crewelwork (wool embroidery on linen). Designs for tapestries and other forms of needlework were often based on Oriental themes.

Queen Anne

The period of prosperity and expansion that England was enjoying was to continue for some time. During the reign of Queen Anne (1702–1714), increased trading and the resulting wealth brought new ways of living and new ideas. Social life developed and the aristocracy enjoyed lives of comfort and culture.

The Queen's name has become associated with a style that really began to develop during the later part of the William and Mary period. It flourished during the reign of Queen Anne, although she personally was not responsible for it, and it found continued popularity well into

WILLIAM AND MARY

(a) Typical Furniture Legs Used During the Period of William and Mary

(b)

(c) Highboy

(d) Lowboy

(e) Side Chair

(f) Side Chair

(g) Armchair

(h) William and Mary Walnut Wing Armchair

Fig. 12.2

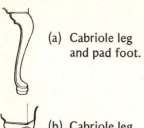

(a) Cabriole leg and pad foot.

(b) Cabriole leg with shell motif and claw and ball foot.

(c) Highboy

(d) Lowboy

(f) Tripod Tier Table

(e) Wing-back Chair

(g) Transitional chair showing curved-splat back, Dutch leg, and Spanish foot.

(h) Side Chair

Fig. 12.3

Queen Anne (1702–1714). A style of period furniture that developed during the reign of Queen Anne of England. It is recognized by its curving lines and fiddle- or vase-shaped chair back. The furniture makers introduced upholstery in the overstuffed manner and the craze for tea drinking brought into being small tea tables.

the reign of the following ruler, George I. The Queen Anne style, therefore, is also characteristic of the Early Georgian period.

The Queen Anne period, which saw the flowering of the "age of walnut," ushered in a golden age in English furniture design. Although there was a fairly rapid succession of different styles, the eighteenth century is notable for the artistry and the exceptionally high standards of craftsmanship in cabinet work.

The rapidly expanding economy during the early years of the century gave rise to widespread activity in building. Inigo Jones had promoted increased interest in the works of Palladio, the famous Italian architect of the Renaissance who had been particularly influenced by structures of ancient Rome. The Venetian influence in English architecture was quite evident in the many Palladian mansions built for the wealthy.

Part of the education of young English aristocrats included travel to the Continent for first-hand study of the arts in Paris, Rome, Florence, and Venice. The interest in the arts and in literature and the familiarity of the wealthy Englishmen with life on the Continent were to influence interior design. The vogue for collecting extended to books, statuary, and all objects of art. Homes were built to display prized possessions. This mixture of the English love of formality, the grandiose style of the Italian Baroque, and the more subtle French Rococo and Oriental influences resulted in a charming elegance in English mansions.

The style of furniture of the Queen Anne period is characterized by a graceful simplicity and excellent proportion. There was a continuation of the Dutch influence, and the trend toward curved contours developed and expanded. The result was a style that has been popular ever since.

A typical Georgian dining room adapted to one of today's more luxurious homes. *(Designed by Barbara D'Arcy, A.I.D., Bloomingdale's, N.Y.)*

Fig. 12.4

Curves were particularly evident in chairs, with fiddle- and vase-shaped center splats, and in the widespread use of cabriole legs. On *early* Queen Anne pieces, the legs were quite plain and usually rested on club feet. **H**-form stretchers were often used but gradually disappeared. As the style developed, a carved shell motif was added to the knee of the leg, and in later adaptations the foot was carved as a ball and claw.

A spoon-shaped profile curved at the back of the chair made it more comfortable. Seats flared so that they were wider at the front than at the back. Perhaps one of the most notable of the chair designs of the period is the upholstered wing chair, which became very popular. It was often upholstered in needlework with a floral design, and it often had a loose seat cushion. As the style developed, the legs became more heavily carved and more massive. The arms of the wing chair as well as of the other forms of easy chairs generally curved outward in a scroll form.

The period is also distinctive for the wider use of many newer pieces of furniture, including the tallboy and the lowboy. Various small tables, secretaries, writing desks, upholstered love seats, and Windsor chairs also became popular during this period.

The highboy, which had been an innovation during the William and Mary period, developed into a much more graceful piece of furniture with the addition of a hooded top and cabriole legs. Queen Anne–style highboys are still popular. Of course, our present-day interpretations have been scaled and adapted to current needs, but the essential style still remains.

English Styles

The simple, graceful lines of Queen Anne furniture, combined with beautiful fabrics, exquisite needlework, rugs and exotic accessories from the Orient, and Dutch, English, and French *objects d'art* produce an atmosphere or flavor in interior design that has remained appealing for generations.

Georgian

The eighteenth century was a glorious period in English cabinetmaking. The period takes its name from the kings who succeeded Queen Anne, but they were not popular rulers and their immediate courts had little influence on the English way of life. The aristocracy and the wealthy class held the power and set the modes.

The style divisions of the period do not coincide with the reigns of the kings. For our purposes we may divide the period as follows:

Early Georgian: 1714–1750
Middle Georgian: 1750–1770
Late Georgian: 1770–1810

Early Georgian

Essentially, the style of the Early Georgian period is that of Queen Anne, and frequently the two periods are treated as one. Much of the furniture that is referred to as "Queen Anne" was designed and made during the Early Georgian period. Although the furniture became somewhat heavier and was decorated with more elaborate carving, the designs actually improved because of their finer proportions and more subtle lines. Some of the more beautiful examples in the Queen Anne style were made during this period. Many of the fine English cabinetmakers continued to follow the Queen Anne style of furniture until almost the middle of the eighteenth century.

During this period, an architect named William Kent was exerting considerable influence in England both in architecture and in furniture design. He was particularly active from about 1725 until 1745, and he initiated several trends that were to be developed in later years. The furniture designs of Kent were done mostly in mahogany, and this period is generally considered the transitional one between England's "age of walnut" and its "age of mahogany." His furniture had architectural features meant to harmonize with the doors, windows, walls, and pediments of the Palladian mansions that he designed. Kent's furniture showed strong influences of the Venetian Baroque style, with much carving, gilding, and heavy ornamentation.

Wood paneling on walls was used extensively during the early part of the eighteenth century. Toward the middle of the century it became fashionable to use fabric or paper on walls. Oriental rugs remained popular. Rich, elegant fabrics were still used, but prints gained in favor.

Middle Georgian

As we have stated, the vogue for mahogany started in the Early Georgian period. The dates for the so-called age of mahogany are generally given as 1710 to 1770. By 1733, mahogany was used almost exclusively. About 1740, a new style of furniture began to evolve. The fact that mahogany lends itself better than walnut to more elaborately carved detail was one contributing factor to the new style.

An important development in the design of this period was the increasing popularity of French designs in England. Rococo was at the height of its popularity in France. In the beginning, English cabinetmakers adapted the Rococo decorative motifs to the typical English forms, but from about 1745 to 1765 the French influence was obvious in both form and ornamentation.

One must remember that there was a pronounced interest in architecture all during the Georgian periods, and that architects were held in very high esteem. Not only were architects interested in furniture designs, but cabinetmakers were serious students of architecture. From these varying influences evolved a style called *Chippendale*, named after the man who was not only the most famous designer of the period but perhaps of all time.

Thomas Chippendale. Much has been written about the genius of Thomas Chippendale (1718–1779). He is renowned as a furniture de-

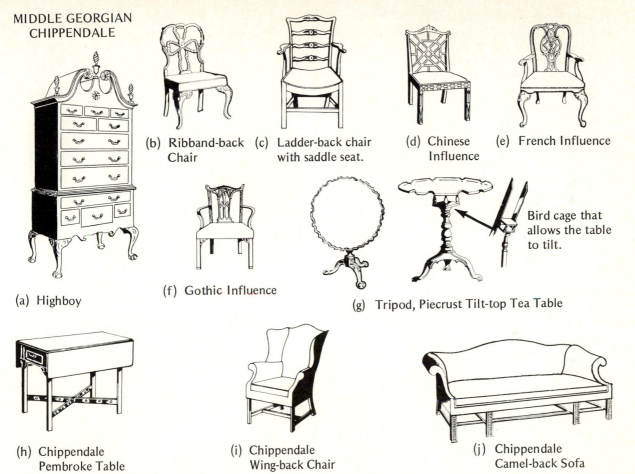

(b) Ribband-back Chair

(c) Ladder-back chair with saddle seat.

(d) Chinese Influence

(e) French Influence

(f) Gothic Influence

(a) Highboy

Bird cage that allows the table to tilt.

(g) Tripod, Piecrust Tilt-top Tea Table

(h) Chippendale Pembroke Table

(i) Chippendale Wing-back Chair

(j) Chippendale Camel-back Sofa

Fig. 12.5

Chippendale. Chippendale derived his inspiration from preceding English, French, and Chinese sources and worked in a variety of styles, but he added a skill and stamp of his own.

signer as well as a master craftsman, and his name is almost exclusively associated with the style of the Middle Georgian period. It seems only fair to point out that research by students of the Chippendale style has punctured some of the bubbles and exploded some of the myths that have created an aura of such greatness about the man himself. This is not meant in any way to discredit the elegance and magnificence of the Chippendale style, which is still popular, or to underestimate the quality of furniture that came from his shop. The studies merely suggest that Thomas Chippendale himself was not personally responsible for a number of the accomplishments that have been attributed to him for many years.

Chippendale's father, also Thomas Chippendale, was a cabinetmaker and woodcarver who opened a shop in London in about 1727. The younger Chippendale opened his own shop in 1749. Four years later he moved his shop to 60 St. Martin's Lane, and for the rest of his life he headed a large firm that decorated a number of important English mansions.

Chippendale was a good businessman and enjoyed an admirable rapport with his clients. He maintained very high standards of workmanship, and his staff included fine designers

English Styles

and craftsmen. In 1754 he published the *Gentleman's and Cabinet Maker's Directoire*, the most impressive book on furniture design that had ever been produced in England.

A question has been raised as to whether or not all of the designs in the directory were those of Chippendale or whether some were done by members of his staff. It has also been pointed out that, although Chippendale has been extolled as a master woodcarver, there is actually no evidence that he did any of the carving himself.

The book published by Chippendale invited many other cabinetmakers to copy his designs, which they did. Because the furniture was not signed or identified in any way, it is difficult now to determine exactly which pieces actually came from the Chippendale shop. There are relatively few authenticated pieces for which bills of sale or other corroborating evidence are available. Other editions of the directory were subsequently published. Although not all the designs were suitable for actual execution, they give us a good idea of the influences that prevailed.

Thomas Chippendale, Jr., carried on his father's business until 1804, when he went bankrupt; so for almost a century the name was esteemed in the circles of British cabinetmaking. Although Chippendale has been questioned as a "leader" in style trends, the fact remains that during the Middle Georgian period, the style of furniture that was made bears his name, and it has been extremely popular ever since.

Basically, the Chippendale style has a masculine quality combined with a graceful elegance. Probably this is why it has been so widely used for over two hundred years. The curves, such as the typical "camel back," are strong and forthright, yet gentle. The proportions are comfortable, and the design is sturdy without being too heavy.

Three important influences have been associated with Chippendale design: French, Oriental, and Gothic.

The Rococo mode, fashionable in France from about 1720 until 1760, was interpreted in English furniture design by the combination of broken curves and straight lines in basic forms and by the carved ornamentation of flowers, foliage, and fruit. Rococo themes were used in heavily carved small tables, sconces, mirrors, and other small pieces. Although these motifs were also used to decorate larger pieces, the English could not quite equal the skill of the French designers in combining form and decorative features to express the Rococo spirit in larger pieces. Nevertheless, the Chippendale designs in the Rococo style are excellent examples of graceful elegance, representing the rather unusual blending of a somewhat solid quality with the fanciful lightness of Rococo themes.

Perhaps some of the best examples of the French Rococo influence in Chippendale designs are in the openwork backs of chairs and settees. These have been copied, adapted, and modified in countless ways. The ribband back is perhaps the best-known Chippendale chair design.

The vogue for Chinese motifs and ideas was very much evidenced in French design during this period. It is not surprising that the interest spread to England, nor that the English designers produced furniture intended to satisfy the British "Chinese tastes." Although the basic forms were still typically mid-Georgian English, they were carved with Oriental motifs such as pagodas and Chinese figures. Fretwork was widely used in moldings and panels as well as for the arms and backs of chairs. The interest in lacquered furniture, which had been so popular earlier in the century, was renewed. Chinoiseries, somewhat whimsical motifs or scenes showing make-believe Chinese figures, were popular decorative themes in lacquered furniture, fabrics, and accessories, Chinese wallpaper was widely used, as were Oriental accessories.

The Gothic influences in Chippendale's work have been somewhat discredited as his merely yielding to the whims of clients during a phase of interest in the Gothic revival. Straight legs, resembling columns, carved details of trefoil and cinquefoil, and tracery work gave the designs a Gothic flavor but that was about all. There was no attempt to adapt or emulate basic Gothic form and proportion. Certainly the Gothic influence was not responsible for Chippendale's best designs. It is generally recognized that the French influences were by far the most important.

It should be pointed out that, although Chippendale's work was mostly in mohogany and his style is best known for the mahogany pieces that came from his shop, during his later years he did produce some furniture in other woods and in designs that were typical of Robert Adam. For almost ten years, from 1770 to 1779, he worked with woods other than mahogany and in a style that was quite different from the one usually associated with his name.

Late Georgian

The later part of the eighteenth century and the early part of the nineteenth century was a period of intense interest in classicism, brought about by archaeological discoveries in Pompeii. The site of this ancient Roman city was discovered in 1748, and excavations were begun of the ruins. Pompeii had been a flourishing city that was also a resort for wealthy Romans. In A.D. 79 it was buried under ashes by an eruption of Vesuvius. The preservation of the complete city, including works of art, during the following centuries was somewhat amazing. When the excavations were under way, it was possible to reconstruct an unprecedented picture of the life of the ancient Romans. The publication of numerous books on the findings of these studies led to a revival of interest in the classics, and this interest led to a Neoclassic movement that permeated the arts. Although the discovery of the Pompeiian ruins served as the trigger for the classic revival, it has been suggested that the movement was certainly fostered by a weary reaction to the Renaissance and the Rococo art forms. The time was ripe for new themes, and the interest in classics provided a suitable basis for new ideas.

The Late Georgian period probably represents the zenith of the "golden age" of English interior design. There was a keen awareness of a room as a blending of furnishings and architectural features. Plaster walls painted in soft colors replaced the wood paneling that had been popular earlier in the century. Plasterwork festoons, garlands, panels, and medallions gave a lightness to the architectural composition.

The Neoclassic mode brought with it a revolt against curves and heavy proportions. Although elegance was still a key theme, it was expressed in a much more formal, restrained type of grandeur than the Rococo themes had produced.

This era is sometimes referred to as the "age of satinwood." Mahogany was still used, but the trend toward lighter colors and more exotic grain patterns resulted in the use of a wide variety of woods, such as satinwood, rosewood, harewood, tulipwood, and holly. Instead of an emphasis on carving as a decorative medium, contrasting veneers were used in many ways. Grain patterns were selected and arranged to lend their intrinsic beauty. Inlay, gilding, and painted decorations were also favored means of decoration.

Although Chippendale's name is more closely associated with designs of the Middle Georgian period, his shop did produce some excellent furniture in the characteristic mode of the earlier years of the Late Georgian period. The names associated with these later years of the eighteenth century include such famous peers in furniture design as Robert Adam, George Hepplewhite, and Thomas Sheraton.

Robert Adam. Probably the strongest force in the application of classical themes to furniture design was an architect named Robert Adam (1728–1792). He and his three brothers received early training from their father, a Scottish architect. Robert enjoyed a most successful career as an architect in London. He and his brother James worked together, designing many public buildings and private homes for wealthy clients. The Adam brothers published their architectural designs and included designs for furnishings. They were not cabinetmakers, and the actual construction of the furniture was done by other firms, including Chippendale.

Although there were many fine architects during the Georgian period, Robert Adam was probably the best known. He was held in high esteem and served as architect for the king for several years. Because Adam was so greatly concerned with final effects, he considered

Fig. 12.6

Room from the Landsdowne House in London, now in the Metropolitan Museum of Art in New York City. The room was designed by Adam who worked in the late Georgian period of eighteenth-century England. *(Courtesy The Metropolitan Museum of Art, Rogers Fund, 1932)*

every detail important. The furniture that he designed to blend with his interiors clearly reflected his architectural styles, and the work of Adam is noted for classic simplicity. He had a remarkable ability to use the motifs and themes found in Roman stuccowork in light and delicate ornamentation. He also used festoons, garlands, and trails of vine.

Adam's work, with its fine proportions and delicate ornamentation, was a source of inspiration for other designers. He catered to the wealthy who could afford large, sumptuous homes, but his work was widely copied and adapted for smaller homes by other architects and designers. Because Adam emphasized the importance of proper scaling and the use of harmonious detail, the modifications and adaptations of his designs for smaller homes produced many interesting effects.

George Hepplewhite. Not very much is known about the personal life of Hepplewhite (d. 1786). He was both a cabinetmaker and a furniture designer, and his shop in London was responsible for a style of furniture that was extremely popular in the latter part of the eighteenth century. His designs have been widely copied and adapted ever since.

The catalog of Hepplewhite's shop, the *Cabinetmaker and Upholsterer's Guide,* was published two years after his death by his widow, Alice. She had continued to conduct the business, and two more editions were published later.

(a) Breakfront Bookcase

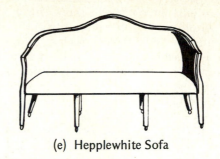

(e) Hepplewhite Sofa

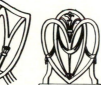

(b) Camel Back   Shield   Heart   Oval   Wheel

(f) Hepplewhite Shield-back
Side Chair

(c) Pier Table

(d) Hepplewhite Sideboard

(g) Poudreuse

English Styles

184

As in the case of Chippendale, it is difficult to tell exactly which pieces were the work of Hepplewhite himself, because only a few of the several hundred designs were actually signed by him. It is reasonable to assume that most of these signed designs were done under his supervision or were approved by him. In the preface to the catalog there is a statement that "we designedly followed the latest or most prevailing fashion." The esteem accorded Hepplewhite has been based on his ability to translate the prevailing tastes for the Neoclassic style into furniture designs that were both elegant and useful.

Probably some of the furniture designed by Robert Adam was made in the Hepplewhite shop. The influences of the Adam brothers and the contemporary French Louis XVI style are clearly seen in the work of Hepplewhite. The style is delicate, light, and refined. The contours of the style are essentially rectilinear, but Hepplewhite used more curved lines in the basic forms than did other designers of the time.

The best examples of Hepplewhite designs were chairs and small pieces, such as pier tables, dressing tables, commodes, and screens. The open backs of the chairs and the settees were almost always shaped in curves to form wheels, camel backs, shields, hearts, or ovals. The famous shield back with which Hepplewhite is always associated was also used by Adam, but Hepplewhite used it more constantly and more successfully. Many of the chair backs were intricate compositions of curving lines. Some of the heart-shaped backs give a rather sentimental, feminine flavor to the designs. The arm supports for the chairs were usually curved. The chests of drawers and sideboards sometimes had bow or serpentine fronts. Curved lines were also introduced in oval table tops and semicircular commodes. Although some cabriole legs were shown in the catalog, the style favored straight, tapered legs, which were either quadrangular or cylindrical and were frequently fluted or reeded.

The furniture was usually mahogany or satinwood, but other woods such as tulipwood, sycamore, harewood, and rosewood were used for decoration. Beautiful colors and grains were carefully selected for use in bands or for exquisite inlay work. Some designs were painted, but gilding was also used for decoration.

Hepplewhite designs display a wide variety of decorative motifs. Of course the classic motifs favored by Adam were used. Acanthus leaves, scrolls, husks, ribbons, bowknots, rosettes, fans, wreaths, vines, garlands, and festoons were all employed in a refined, elegant manner to give the designs their graceful delicacy. Hepplewhite is credited with introducing the Prince of Wales feather as a decorative motif. Basic designs of the chair backs often centered on this feather emblem, but wheat stalks, vines, and urns were also used. Sometimes the furniture was decorated with lovely insets of Angelica Kaufman's painting or medallions made by Josiah Wedgwood, a contemporary who was interpreting the Neoclassic spirit in the field of ceramics.

The fine proportions of the Hepplewhite style, and the lightness and simplicity of his design, have made it a favorite with those who prefer a graceful style with a simple elegance.

Thomas Sheraton. Many people consider Thomas Sheraton (1751–1806) the greatest of all the designers in this "golden age" of English furniture. From what is known about him, it seems that he was a rather peculiar person who led a varied career in the fifty-five years of his life. Although he had some early training as a cabinetmaker, he was also a Baptist preacher, an author of religious works, a drawing teacher, an inventor, and a mechanic. Sheraton came from impoverished surroundings and never enjoyed any degree of financial success. When he settled in London in about 1790 he lived in a humble abode with his wife and two children. It has not been established that he actually carried on a business of cabinetmaking there, but he did publish a book in four parts entitled *Cabinetmaker and Upholsterer's Drawing Book*. The first part appeared in 1791. Later he published a dictionary of terms for cabinetmaking and upholstering and had plans for an encyclopedia, which he did not complete. A book of designs from these works was published posthumously in 1812.

(a) Breakfront

(b) Sheraton Pembroke Table

(c) Tambour Rolltop Secretary

(d) Sheraton Sofa

(e) Sheraton Settee

(f) Sheraton Chair Backs

(g) Sheraton Side Chair

(h) Sheraton-type Mahogany Drum Table

Sheraton may have done some cabinetwork in his early life and perhaps supervised some of the construction of his designs, but his fame is certainly not based on actual cabinetmaking. His books were intended for use by other craftsmen, and they were widely used in both England and America. The Sheraton style is based on the drawings in these publications.

Sheraton's designs interpreting the Neoclassic trends were unsurpassed for their excellent proportions, fine balance, and exquisite ornamentation. His early work showed many adaptations of the Adam, Hepplewhite, and Louis XVI styles. Later his work was undoubtedly influenced by French Directoire and Empire styles. Nevertheless, the designs showed originality and an unusually keen awareness of beautiful lines.

The basic forms were generally rectilinear, with emphasis on the vertical line. Straight lines were favored, but lovely graceful curves were incorporated in a somewhat subtle manner with convex corners on sideboards, gently curved arms on chairs, elongated urns in chair backs, and festoons or garlands used as ornament. The rails across the backs of chairs were usually straight, however, and the legs were mostly straight and tapered.

Sheraton's mechanical ability manifested itself in furniture with secret compartments. He also designed several dual-purpose pieces and was probably the first furniture designer to show twin beds.

Satinwood and mahogany were used for much of the Sheraton-style furniture. Other woods, including tulipwood, harewood, ebony, and rosewood, were frequently used for bands or panels. Techniques for veneering and inlay work were excellent by the late eighteenth century, and Sheraton ornamented his designs with garlands, scrolls, festoons, trailing vines, rosettes, fans, and shells. Marquetry and painted decorations were also used, as well as gilding. Sometimes painted medallions or panels showing classical motifs or figures were used as decoration. Although Sheraton adapted many of the favorite motifs and used all the tricks of reeding, turning, inlay, and painting, his designs never had a gingerbread appearance. His fame as a furniture designer probably stems from the restraint with which he used the techniques of ornamentation and his feeling for beautiful proportions and purity of line. The combination of these qualities produced some of the finest furniture designs ever known.

Regency

George III was declared mentally incompetent, and the Prince of Wales acted as regent from 1810 to 1820, after which he became George IV. This ten-year period is known as the Regency, but the style trends associated with it started in about 1795 and lasted until almost 1837, when Victoria became queen.

Political developments were shaping new styles in France and America. Both of these countries looked upon English designs with disfavor. The "golden age" had come to an end, and furniture designers seemed to lack the creative inspiration that had marked the eighteenth century. Ideas were borrowed from the French Directoire and Empire styles, which reflected a revived interest in ancient Greek, Roman, and Egyptian art. In England, this revived interest was manifest in English adaptations of the Empire styles. With this revival of classicism, however, it was the heavier of the classical forms and motifs that were preferred to the more graceful and delicate themes.

Furniture gradually became heavier in scale and more massive in proportion. Attempts to reproduce and adapt the forms of Greek and Roman furniture resulted in arms with heavy outward scrolls and couches with scrolled headrests. Tripods and adaptations of the characteristic Greek side chair known as the *klismos* also appeared. In the early Regency furniture, these designs were executed with simplicity. The heritage of fine English design and expert workmanship gave them a dignified beauty. Although there are no great designers associated with the Regency period, it should be noted again that in his later years Sheraton showed the French Empire influences. This phase of his work is not closely associated with the so-called Sheraton style and is more representative of early Regency. Thomas Chippendale, Jr., was continuing the business of his father and made some excellent furniture in the Regency style.

A noted English architect, Henry Holland (1746–1806), designed some beautiful interiors and included designs for some lovely, graceful furniture in the Regency style. In addition, a wealthy art collector named Thomas Hope (1769–1831) published a book of furniture designs that reflected the French Empire influences and his own interest in archaeology.

In addition to Greek, Roman, and Egyptian motifs, Chinese and Gothic themes were found in ornamentation. Thus furniture was decorated with cornucopias, Egyptian figures, sphinxes, lotus flowers, and chinoiseries. Animal heads and paws were used in various ways. Furniture legs terminating in paws were popular.

Rosewood, mahogany, and satinwood were widely used. Brass and bronze were used exten-

sively for inlay work and trellis insets in doors, moldings, and fretwork.

As the Regency style developed, it became bizarre. English designers showed a lack of discrimination and taste in applying ornament to form. Exaggerated curves and superfluous decorations marked the decline of the Regency furniture designs.

Victorian

Queen Victoria had the longest reign of any English monarch. The sixty-four years of the Victorian period, from 1837 to 1901, naturally saw many different influences and trends, so it is difficult to generalize about the characteristics of the style. When one must generalize, however, the adjectives usually used are *lavish, ostentatious, eclectic,* and *ugly.* The disdain that most aesthetic souls feel toward the Victorian style is somewhat understandable, because the

decline that had started during the Regency period continued to a point where taste and the appreciation of beauty reached an incredibly low level. But it is unfortunate that there is a widespread trend to associate only the bad with Victoriana. It is true that not many of us would want to be confined to authentic Victorian surroundings today, but we should not dismiss the possibilities that various facets of the style have to offer. Some designers have recognized the elements of charm beneath the rather grotesque clutter of Victorian design and have managed to adapt the Victorian flavor to contemporary interiors. When this is done with taste and discrimination, the effects are not only lovely but livable. There are some basic qualities of the Victorian style that can be extremely appealing. It is something of a challenge to accept the "good" and discard the "bad" in order to create an atmosphere of beauty and functionalism.

The aesthetic sense of the English people reached a low ebb, and they eagerly accepted

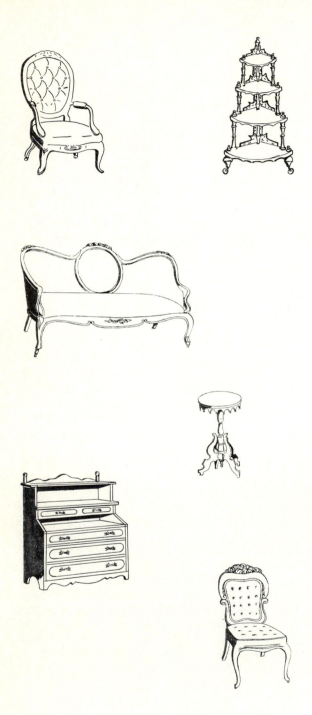

novelties, fakes, and imitations. The abundance of poor-quality merchandise on the market is often attributed to the inception of the technological age and the use of machines. Most of these inferior products were designed to represent lavish luxury at the lowest possible cost. This attempt produced some decorative horrors.

The Victorian period may be divided into three phases: the early period, which lasted until about 1850; the mid-Victorian period, from about 1850 to 1875; and the late Victorian period, from about 1875 to 1901. There was much overlapping of trends in each of these phases, and, because of the general borrowing of ideas from many different sources and the ready acceptance of novelties, it is difficult to define the trends at any particular time. The early period seems to have been most dominated by enthusiasm for Gothic styles. By the middle of the century the taste seems to have leaned toward Renaissance and Rococo forms, with excessive and exaggerated curves and overabundant ornament. The third phase shows some simplification with a rather poor adaptation of medieval themes. Throughout the period the eclectic mood was dominant. Ideas were borrowed from Greek, Gothic, French, Venetian, Turkish, Persian, and Egyptian sources. The adaptation of modes, forms, and motifs was carried out with no semblance of authenticity. Frequently a designer mixed several unrelated ideas and then added a bit of novelty of his own choosing.

By the middle of the nineteenth century the typical Victorian interior was confusing, heavy, and oppressive. Pattern and ornamentation were used everywhere. The motto seemed to be "never use a straight line," and the abundant curves were voluminous. The mania was for bric-a-brac—cluttered rooms with statuary, figurines, artificial flowers, and a wide variety of other such ornaments. The "what-not," a special shelf arrangement that displayed these possessions, was almost mandatory. Windows were covered with curtains and heavy draperies in intricate arrangements, and usually embellished with fringes or tassels—or both. Carpeting of many colors, often in floral patterns, was popular. Walls were covered with patterned paper or fabric. The furniture, often poorly proportioned and massive in scale, was heavily carved and ornamented. Black walnut, rosewood, ebony, and mahogany were popular woods. Mother-of-pearl was often used for inlay work. Marble was used extensively for table tops. Even *papier mâché* was used for furniture.

Chairs, sofas, and love seats—which were especially popular—were upholstered with horsehair. Plush, velvet, satin, and brocade were used extensively and were often tufted. Tidies or antimacassars—small doilies used on the backs and arms of chairs—protected them from soil. Lambrequins or strips of cloth were draped over windows, mantels, and tables. These, too, were decorated with fringes and tassels. Elaborate chandeliers and sconces were fashionable. In some, gas jets replaced candles.

It would seem incredible that we could adapt any part of this mélange of ostentation and poor taste to present-day living. Yet there were some very fine pieces of furniture made by expert craftsmen for wealthy Victorians. In addition, our contemporary designers have modified and adapted the styles to produce furniture that has the Victorian flavor without excessive ornament. These reproductions are often improvements on the originals from the standpoint of design and comfort.

Several men should be mentioned in connection with the Victorian period because of their efforts to instigate reforms. Sir Charles Eastlake (1793–1865) was an English architect and art critic who deplored the lavish designs of the Victorian era and urged a return to simplicity. He preferred the Gothic themes, and furniture manufacturers attempted to comply with demands for furniture in the Eastlake style.

William Morris (1834–1896) was a cabinetmaker, designer (mostly of textiles and wallpaper), weaver, printer, poet, and essayist. He wrote , "Have nothing in your home that you do not know to be useful and believe to be beautiful." Morris, along with John Ruskin and several other leaders, decried mechanization and attempted to revive both purity in design and pride in craftsmanship. The dissatisfactions voiced by these writers and their associates gave impetus to a renewed interest in skills. Their dislikes for machine-made designs could not, of course, stem the forces of mechanization, but they were instrumental in provoking a more discriminating level of taste and a more thoughtful approach to the role of the designer in a mechanized society.

The inspiration for the movement toward modern style might be indirectly traced back to Morris and his associates, although they had no direct relationship to it.

13
American Styles

To understand and appreciate the development of American art, one must remember that many different factors and influences enter the picture. It is hardly possible to present a simple and concise story, because different sections of the country were developed at widely spaced intervals. The settlers came from different countries; in some cases they brought with them strong heritages that significantly influenced their modes of living, and in other cases influences of previous roots yielded to the new life and the new country.

The very early settlers were, of course, concerned with clearing the land and establishing their farms. The hardships and tremendous physical labors left them little time to do much more than build houses that were habitable and utilitarian. Because space on the sailing vessels was extremely limited, they brought very few possessions and very little furniture with them. The homes that they managed to establish were sparsely furnished with bare essentials that were crudely made.

Gradually the industry and the fortitude of the pioneers began to reap dividends. As agriculture flourished, the towns and then the cities began to develop. The growing and expanding colonies attracted new settlers with different financial backgrounds, as well as groups of different national origins. However, the majority of the American settlers were English, and ties to the English culture have always predominated in the evolution of the American pattern. No one can deny the important contributions made by other national groups to the development of America; the very philosophy upon which the American structure is based was certainly influenced by the desires of these groups to find a haven that would transcend national boundaries. Yet we find that the Dutch tended to settle in New York and Pennsylvania, the Spanish in Florida, the French in Louisiana, and the Germans in Pennsylvania. Their tendencies to preserve national roots, at the same time they were absorbing a new way of life, is one of the phenomena of the American scene. In later years, particularly in the nineteenth century, immigration from Ireland, Italy, Russia, and the Balkans had important effects on the economic and industrial conditions in America. From a cultural standpoint, however, these groups have been more or less absorbed by the English tradition in America. In view of the rich aesthetic backgrounds of some of these national groups, this fact is somewhat paradoxical.

As the American pattern evolved, the wealthier settlers, who received their land by royal grants, tended to settle in the South. They built up huge plantations with luxurious homes and imported the furnishings. They adopted a way of life that was in sharp contrast to that in New England, where the settlers who had been attracted to America for political and religious reasons lived a comparatively simple life. In the small New England town the church was the center of activity. In addition, geographical conditions and the nature of the settlers made large estates impractical and undesirable.

The development of the western part of the country was accompanied by strong Spanish and Oriental influences. It is interesting to travel through the United States today to observe how traditions have maintained certain flavors in many areas. Despite a rapidly changing world and speedy communications, which should tend to dissolve and obliterate such characteristics, we still find something of an austerity in New England, the gracious hospitality of luxurious living in the South, the quaintness of the Pennsylvania Dutch, and the modernized Latin atmosphere of the Spaniards in Florida and the West. Somehow these influences have managed to persevere throughout the more than three hundred years of American history.

As the country developed, cities grew, and various industries became concentrated in different localities. Philadelphia eventually became the center for cabinet work, and other industries were more or less localized in other sections.

The student of trends in America, should bear in mind that the different regions of the country were developed by many different groups of people. It should also be remembered that the new ideas and styles that prevailed in other parts of the world were somewhat slow in reaching the United States. It often took several years for foreign trends to become adopted here.

For our purposes, we may divide the American styles of furniture as follows:

1. *Colonial:* The period up to the establishment of the Federal Government.
   a. Early American: 1608–1770.
   b. American Georgian: 1720–1790.
2. *Federal:* 1790–1830.
3. *Regional styles.*
4. *Post-Federal:* American Victorian: 1840–1880.

Colonial

The Colonial period covers over 160 years when the colonies were growing. According to present-day standards, the changes were not rapid, but it was an era of growth and development. The mosaic of American culture was being formed, and the foundations for an American way of life were taking shape. The heritage of America, so different from that of other countries, was formed in a relatively short span of time.

Early American (1608–1770)
The term *Early American* is used rather indiscriminately today to refer to a style that we associate with colonial life. Charming as the modern interpretation is, it is not authentic in its portrayal of the furnishings actually used in the very early days of the colonies.

Because most of the early settlers were from the English middle class, the furnishings with which they were familiar were of the Gothic-Renaissance forms used in the cottages in provincial England. The few simple items of furnishings that they produced here were based on the general lines of Elizabethan and Jacobean forms and those of the period of William and Mary. The American reproductions were smaller than the English originals, in order to fit the small rooms and lower ceilings in the homes.

Even in the native lands there had not yet been a widespread interest in beautifying home surroundings. Because of the struggles and

Fig.
13.1

Early American interior. This multipurpose room from the Hart House (c. 1670) has heavy, centered beam supports. The typical furniture pieces are the sturdy gateleg table, the oak court cupboard, and the carved wainscot chair. The sturdy stool is typical of the Early American period. *(Courtesy of the Henry Francis du Pont Winterthur Museum)*

hardships that faced the newcomers in an undeveloped land, it is not surprising that homes were furnished with only the bare essentials and that there was little concern for beauty or comfort.

The first houses had one room that served all purposes. The fireplace was used for both heating and cooking. Gradually this arrangement gave way to the two-room house and eventually to more complex plans with two chimneys. Sometimes the expansions were made by the addition of wings, and the "saltbox" style of architecture evolved.

These houses were sparsely furnished. The chest, cupboard, and desk-box, the turned and wainscot chair, the stool and settle, the trestle table, and some space-saving articles such as the chair-table and the drop-leaf (butterfly and gateleg types) tables were used in the combination kitchen, living, and dining room.

Four-poster beds, trundle beds, and wooden cradles formed the principal furnishings for the sleeping rooms, with additional chests for storage purposes. Wooden chests played an important role in Early American furnishings. Many had been brought over by the settlers in lieu of trunks. They were copied and reproduced in various forms, and served as seats as well as storage space. Soon they were made with legs and then with drawers. One type, called a desk-box—the prototype of the familiar slant-top desk—was made to hold writing materials and had a slanted top.

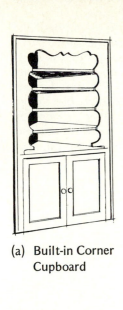

(a) Built-in Corner
Cupboard

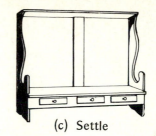

(b) A Bible box. If it is slanted,
it is a writing box.

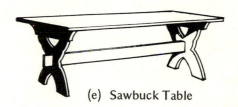

(c) Settle

(d) Trestle Table

(e) Sawbuck Table

(f) Butterfly Table

(g) Wainscot Chair

(h) Banister-back Chair

(i) Slat-back Chair

(j) Chair Table

(k) Court Cupboard

(l) Hadley Chest

American Styles

Chairs made few concessions to the needs of the human body; straight-lined, firm, and often elaborately turned and carved, they did, however, impose a measure of dignity upon the sitter. The back uprights of the chairs sometimes consisted of split spindles or flat bars, called banisters, which gave them the name *banister-back chair*. Horizontal slat-backed or ladder-back chairs, more comfortable than the vertical post chairs, were popular in the late seventeenth century. The chairs had stretchers to support the construction, and either plain or rush seats. The chair-table, a chair with a table-top back, was also used. By the middle of the seventeenth century, loose cushions were used for comfort. Upholstered chairs were introduced later.

When local carpenters were called upon to produce furniture, they had neither the talent nor the tools to do fine cabinetmaking. They could only copy, to the best of their ability, the furniture that had been imported or that they remembered from their homelands. They worked with the woods that were readily available, mostly pine, beech, cherry, maple, ash, elm, and cedar. Ornamentation was simple and crude, consisting of turnings, strapwork patterns, or applied split spindles. Carving, turning, and painting were usually done by amateurs trying to pass long winter evenings.

By the beginning of the eighteenth century, trained cabinetmakers had come to the new country and were making furniture in the William and Mary style. Shaped aprons, flat stretchers, bun feet, and bell turnings on legs appeared in furniture designs. Highboys (sometimes called tallboys), dressing tables (called lowboys), and chests on chests were introduced in simplified designs. A greater interest in beauty and comfort in the home had gradually developed by 1700.

American Georgian (1720–1790)

As the wealthier group in the colonies grew, there was a greater demand for more elaborate houses. More formal architectural design was applied to the interiors as well as to the exteriors. Moldings were used to trim doors, windows, and mantels. Wood paneling became popular in the larger homes, and in the smaller houses walls were often decorated with stenciled designs, murals, or wallpaper.

A more social way of life had developed, and entertaining in the home required more furniture. There was a demand for more tables, especially ones that could be used for serving tea and playing parlor games. Upholstered furniture, desks and secretaries, consoles, pier tables, and roundabout chairs were all very popular. There was greater interest in decorative accessories, including china, mirrors, and tall case clocks.

Those who could afford to import furniture eagerly followed the style trends prevalent in England and on the Continent. However, many skilled craftsmen had emigrated to America in the early years of the eighteenth century, and they began to reproduce the English styles by copying imported models. They avidly used the design books published by the well-known English designers.

Many pieces were accurate reproductions of original designs, but soon the American craftsmen began to vary their interpretations, making changes in the details and in the proportions. It is common practice now to refer to "American Queen Anne" or "American Chippendale" when discussing the furniture that was made in America but was based on English styles.

Many fine cabinetmakers were located in Philadelphia. Beautiful examples of American furniture in the Early Georgian style were produced in that city. The Philadelphia craftsmen followed the Queen Anne, Chippendale, Hepplewhite, and Sheraton styles as each became popular in England.

Two cabinetmakers in Newport, Rhode Island, became well known for furniture with block-front designs. During the second half of the eighteenth century John Goddard and John Townsend made chests, cabinets, and desks with the fronts divided into three panels decorated with shell motifs. The central panel was usually concave, and the outer ones were convex.

By the middle of the eighteenth century, the Windsor chair had become extremely popular and has remained so ever since. Although the design originated in England, the American ad-

Fig. 13.2

Fig. 13.3

Many interpretations of colonial furniture are popular today. This room adapts some modern ideas to an Early American theme. *(Designed by Barbara D'Arcy, A.I.D., Bloomingdale's, N.Y.)*

A revival of interest in colonial styles and in Oriental rugs is shown in this corner of a living room that is keyed to contemporary color schemes. An unusual modern Sarouk has an ivory ground with turquoise, rose, gold, blue, and green in the stylized design. The rich wood tones of the Early American adaptations blend well with these colors. *(Courtesy of Oriental Rug Importers Association, designed by Duke Piner and Harvey Barnett, A.I.D.)*

Fig.
13.4

Mahogany highboy, Philadelphia Style (c. 1765). *(Courtesy of The Metropolitan Museum of Art, Kennedy Fund, 1918.)*

Fig. 13.5 Some fine reproductions of American Georgian furniture.

(a) Tea table. *(Courtesy Pennsylvania House)*

(b) Historic Newport reproduction by Kittinger of a shell-carved, block-front chest by John Townsend, c. 1767.

aptations produced a variety of types. The distinctive characteristics of the chair included a shaped seat and legs slanting outward. Stretchers were always used, and both the legs and the supports were usually decorated with turning. The various forms of the back were made of spindles placed in the rear of the seat. The loop back, one of the more popular versions, had a bent frame. The fan back, with a straight or curved top rail, sometimes had an additional section resembling a ladies' comb. The chairs were often made of several different woods and were painted. Black, red, and green were popular colors.

Rocking chairs were widely used during this period. Of the many different rocking chairs, the Windsor rocker was the most commonly used.

(e) This Queen Anne corner table (sometimes called handkerchief table) is a Williamsburg furniture reproduction by Kittinger.

(c) Hunt table of Sheraton design by Kittinger.

(f) The corner or roundabout chair in the Chippendale style is also a Williamsburg furniture reproduction by Kittinger. (b–f Courtesy of Kittinger Company)

(d) Butler tray table of Chippendale design by Kittinger.

(a) Comb-back Rocker

(b) Bow Back

(c) Fan Back

(d) Loop Back

(e) Arch Back

(f) Rod Back

(g) Arrow Back

(h) Captain's Chair

Federal

In the period following the Revolutionary War there was an increased awakening of interest in the arts. The prevailing spirit of freedom and democracy fostered interest in the classics. Inspiration drawn from Greece and Rome during this period permeated all phases of activity. The politically important figures—Washington, Jefferson, Franklin, and Hamilton—were all men with highly developed cultural tastes, and they undoubtedly influenced artistic standards.

The political spirit strengthened the bonds of understanding between France and America. Also, after the French Revolution, French styles influenced English designs, and these English designs were, in turn, important factors in American production.

During the Federal period (1790–1830) both the Hepplewhite and the Sheraton styles were popular in America. When the war ended, the Hepplewhite style was widely accepted in England; as normal relations between the two countries were resumed, the style was adopted by American cabinetmakers. A little later, the Sheraton style became popular in England; it also was adopted in America. Because the pattern books of both Hepplewhite and Sheraton were extensively used by American cabinetmakers, there was a period at the end of the eighteenth century when much of the furniture combined the characteristics of both styles. By this time cabinetmaking in America had reached a high level, and the Federal era saw the production of many fine pieces of furniture.

The American interpretations of the English styles were notable for their delicacy, refinement, and excellent proportions, but the furniture was not as elaborate as that made for the aristocracy in England. Philadelphia was the center of activity during the Federal era and assumed a position of leadership in setting the fashions; but the great American fortunes had not yet been built up and there were not many Americans of tremendous wealth, so there was no great demand for sumptuous homes and interiors such as Adam was designing for his very wealthy clients in England. Adam's influ-

(a) Dressing Table

(b) Boston Rocker

(c) Hitchcock Chair

American Styles

ences in American design were seen in some decorative work and were important insofar as they were interpreted through Hepplewhite's designs. Although the Hepplewhite style never really flourished in America, it was of considerable influence in the work of Samuel McIntire (1757–1811), an architect and a craftsman of Salem, Massachusetts, during the Federal period. He created beautiful interiors with expert wood carving and paneling. His carved mantels, cornices, dadoes, and stairways were beautifully proportioned and exquisite in detail. McIntire designed and made excellent furniture, and his interiors represent a high level of artistic achievement in the Federal style.

The American designs patterned after those of Hepplewhite and Sheraton reflected the graceful elegance of the originals. Chests of drawers, sideboards, dining tables, secretaries, card tables, shield-back chairs, and settees were all made to follow the styles. Veneer work was carefully done, and the pieces were decorated with carving, inlay work, reeding, and fluting.

From 1805 to 1815, a style of furniture often referred to as American Directoire, characterized by Greek and Roman influences, was popular. Chairs were derived from the Grecian *klismos*, with the tops showing a backward sweep. The legs were frequently concave. Sofas and settees were also inspired by Greek and Roman designs.

The period from 1810 to 1830 marks the American Empire period. It should be noted that the Directoire and Empire styles overlapped. The style of this period did not closely follow the French Empire style, though there were some similarities.

The theme of American ornamentation was patriotic. It glorified the abundance of the land with motifs of fruits, flowers, leaves, and the horn of plenty. The eagle had been adopted as the national emblem and was so widely used as a decorative motif that this era is sometimes referred to as the "American Eagle Period." Brass eagles were imported; others were carved and gilded. They were used as finishes on wall mirrors and clocks, and they were painted on glassware and chinaware. They were used in every conceivable way; there can be little doubt that this was a period when Americans were proud of their insignia.

Duncan Phyfe (1768–1854)

Probably the most famous name in the decorative arts of this period is Duncan Phyfe. He came from Scotland to America as a young man, and after learning cabinetmaking in Albany he moved to New York in the early 1790s. He operated a very successful shop until 1847.

Contrary to the popular conception, Phyfe did not originate a style of furniture. He designed in the Sheraton, Directoire, and Empire styles, although he gave the designs his own interpretation. He was an expert cabinetmaker, but also a good businessman. Although his great ability is generally recognized, his superiority to all other cabinetmakers of the era is questioned by some authorities. Many believe that his eminence is partly caused by his long career and his good business sense. There were many other fine craftsmen working in the decorative arts during the Colonial and Federal periods. Nevertheless, for the first 25 or 30 years of his career, Phyfe made furniture that was graceful and delicate, beautifully proportioned, and exquisite in detail.

Thomas Sheraton had a strong and distinct influence in the work of this period. The lyre motif that he had used was extremely popular with Phyfe, who continued to use it on much of the furniture that he made in the Directoire style. He also used acanthus leaves, swags, tassels, rosettes, cornucopias, and sheaves of wheat. The legs of the furniture often ended in conventionalized animal feet.

The carving and reeding were expertly done, mostly on beautiful mahogany. His most famous designs in chairs, sofas, sideboards, and tables with tripod bases reflect the Greek and Roman influence in the Empire style. The refined curves, excellent proportions, and delicacy of detail gave the pieces an elegance that has kept these designs popular in contemporary interpretations.

After about 1820, the proportions of Phyfe's designs gradually became heavier and more

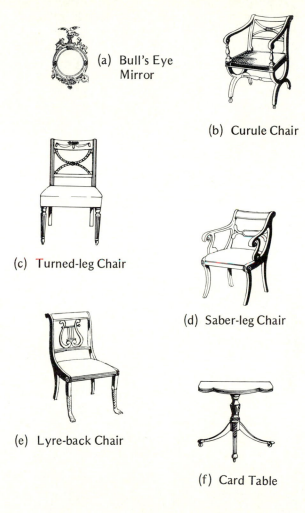

(a) Bull's Eye Mirror

(b) Curule Chair

(c) Turned-leg Chair

(d) Saber-leg Chair

(e) Lyre-back Chair

(f) Card Table

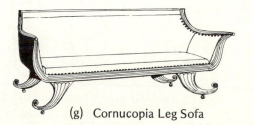

(g) Cornucopia Leg Sofa

cumbersome. The decorative details were coarser and more overdone. In all probability much of Phyfe's work was done to meet the popular demand; it is reported that he himself was unhappy enough about such designs to refer to them as "butcher furniture."

Regional Styles

As America grew and developed, there was a tendency for certain groups of people to settle in particular areas. Frequently the previous customs and traditions were eventually blended into or absorbed by a new American way of life. In other instances, however, past associations and patterns remained dominant, with the result that we have several styles in the American decorative arts that are referred to as "regional." Although some of these styles have spread far beyond their specific regions, and some of them have been very popular, they have not had any great influence on general styles. Their contributions have been so important, however, that they must not be overlooked in any discussion of American styles.

Pennsylvania "Dutch" (miscalled "Dutch" for Deutsch)

The Mennonites, who settled in Pennsylvania toward the end of the seventeenth century, were mostly Germans who were eager to establish themselves in a land where they could find the freedom to follow their religious beliefs. They formed isolated communities where they clung rigidly to their customs and language. Even today these people resist change and have managed to preserve their old ways of life. The Mennonites are a simple and industrious people with an inherent love for beauty and gaiety. They decorate their homes in a delightfully colorful style that is light and cheerful.

The furniture forms followed the simple lines of the country furniture used throughout the colonies, but the severe sturdiness is relieved by a greater use of curves. The Mennonites used ladder-back chairs, drop-leaf tables, sawbuck tables, and many different types of chests, cabi-

American Styles

(a) Painted Dower Chest

(c) Cobbler's Bench Table

(b) Painted Side Chair

nets, and cupboards. The style has merited great popularity, chiefly because of the distinctive painted or stenciled decorations.

Symbolic motifs, such as tulips, hearts, birds, leaves, and hex signs, were painted on furniture and walls in bright gay colors. These designs were often combined with German script and included decorative scrolls showing family histories of births and weddings.

Fabrics and rugs followed a similar colorful pattern. Textile designs were often embroidered or appliquéd. Added to this joyful and pleasant atmosphere were copper, iron, and decorated wooden kitchen equipment.

This simple style has been readily accepted by many people who delight in its gay informality and who welcome its sturdy practicality.

Scandinavian

Many immigrants from Norway, Finland, and Sweden established communities in the Midwest—particularly in Minnesota and Wisconsin. The blending of their heritage with the factors that inspired Colonial furniture produced another regional style that was somewhat similar to the Pennsylvania Dutch.

The furniture was simple and sturdy; it too was painted with designs that were bright and gay. Flowers and leaves decorated the furniture, but there was a tendency to use more animal and human figures than were used in the Pennsylvania Dutch style. Also, these designs were more realistic than the stylized German designs. Possibly for that reason they have not had the same widespread popular appeal in current times.

SHAKER

(a) Pine cabinet that is rectangular and austere. The plain molded base rests directly on the floor.

(b) Three-slat-back chair ornamented with knob finials.

(c) Maple Drop-leaf Sewing Cabinet

(d) Four-slat rail-back rocker. The turned crossbar was used to hold a folded blanket or quilt.

Shaker

The Shakers came to the United States from England during the second half of the eighteenth century in order to pursue a communal religious life style. They were sometimes called the "Shaking Quakers" because of their physical manifestations during worship. The first group settled in New York; other groups were formed later in New England, Kentucky, Ohio, and Indiana. Shakerism began to decline in 1860, but during their active period the Shakers were well known for excellence in agriculture, inventions, and crafts. Before the Civil War, the Shakers invented a flat broom, a wheel-driven washing machine, a circular saw, and a tiltback chair.

Shaker life was based on communal "families" of thirty to ninety people. The members donated possessions and services to the group. Men and women shared equal responsibilities, although they lived and worked separately; even the houses were designed with separate doorways for men and women. Shakers advocated pacifism, separation from the world, celibacy, integrity, frugality, and industry.

A strict but cheerful work ethic, a passion for cleanliness and order, and a compulsion for efficiency contributed to the Shakers' approach to design; they believed that every object made should have a function—a forerunner of the modern concept. Furniture was designed for easy cleaning, and chairs were so light they could be easily moved or hung on pegs when not in use.

The rigid beliefs of the Shakers necessitated furnishings that were functional and completely devoid of ornamentation. They used built-in storage areas and multipurpose pieces. The simple chairs, tables, chests, beds, and candle stands were light in scale so that they could be moved easily, but the sturdy construction was testimony to the skilled craftsmanship of the Shakers. The lines were pure and uncomplicated. The natural grains of the woods were emphasized by light stains and polishing. The result of all this is a refined simplicity that lends a strange air of modernism and contemporary elegance to what is in reality a country style. Many modern designs find their inspiration in Shaker furniture, which was neither modeled after nor openly influenced by preceding styles.

203

Fig. 13.6

A Shaker storeroom. Because the Shakers shunned ornamentation, their furniture has a distinctive character of utter simplicity. *(Courtesy of Henry Francis du Pont Winterthur Museum)*

Walnut armchair with tooled leather back and sling seat.

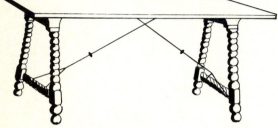

Walnut table with iron stretcher.

Spanish Colonial

The Spanish influence in America is widespread from the standpoint of both distance and time. From the seventeenth century to the present time, and in various locations ranging from Florida to California, there have been important Spanish contributions to the development of regional styles.

The nature of the Spanish styles made them a natural background for the preservation of much American Indian art. There are considerable regional differences throughout Texas, New Mexico, Arizona, California, and Florida, but there are some general themes in the character of the Spanish styles.

Architectural forms, as seen in houses made of thick walls and built around a patio, became common. The interior walls were whitewashed, and the rooms were furnished with a few essential pieces that were heavy and crudely carved.

Some bright colors were used in accessories, but modern interpretations of the Spanish colonial styles have assigned larger areas of more garish colors than were actually used.

Decorative motifs blended Indian symbols with Moorish geometrics. Some Mexican influ-

ences were also seen. Favorite themes included flowers, leaves, and animals such as birds, deer, lambs, and goats.

In the Southwest, particularly in Texas and California, some Spanish influence was evident in the missions, the chapels, and other buildings that were erected by inexpert craftsmen who worked with a few crude tools. The mixture of Mexican, Indian, and Spanish influences did not, in a true sense, represent authentic Spanish detail in either the architecture or the furniture. The crude, heavily proportioned, rectilinear cabinets, chests, tables, and chairs were sturdy and simple, made from woods that were readily available. This type of furniture is sometimes associated with designs that developed during the early stages of the modern movement and were known as Mission style.

Post-Federal

The nineteenth century was marked by periods of rapid expansion. The physical frontiers of the country were broadening through the acquisition of new territories. The new wonders of the machine were fostering an industrial development that had extensive social as well as economic implications. By the middle of the century this pattern had developed to the point where the huge fortunes of America's wealthy class were being built up. The period was also marked by the popular love for ostentation and display, with a resulting disregard for intrinsic artistic merit. It has been pointed out that there is no sharp dividing line between one period and another in furniture styles. The period of 1815 to 1830, generally referred to as American Empire, has already been discussed. The following decade, 1830–1840, is often spoken of as late Empire. The furniture of this era began to assume heavy proportions and cumbersome lines. The gradual decline in taste for fine art was reflected in the concurrent decline of American furniture styles.

American Victorian

After 1840, American designs followed the Victorian style. As in the case of the English

Victorian, much of the furniture was heavily proportioned and far too elaborate. There was much borrowing from Gothic, Turkish, Egyptian, and French Rococo themes. The excessive ornamentation was often inspired by a mixture of unrelated influences that served only to clutter the designs.

The elaborate upholstered furniture was decorated with fringes, cords, tassels, and buttons. The excessively ornamented wood pieces were frequently machine-inspired and decorated with whatever could be produced by the new machine methods. Omnipresent bric-a-brac was displayed on mantels, tables, shelves, and special "what-nots" made for the purpose. Needlework was also displayed everywhere, in framed mottos and embroidered pictures, on chairs in the form of tidies, and draped on windows, tables, and mantels in the form of antimacassars. All of this in the setting of patterned floor coverings, heavy draperies, and gas lighting gives the picture of the Victorian room. Yet it has been pointed out that in the midst of the clutter and the ugly, ostentatious designs there was furniture that merits respect. In America, as in England, some cabinetmakers maintained high standards of workmanship. They worked in the prevailing style but they managed to pro-

Fig. 13.7

The parlor in a New York brownstone house built in the middle of the nineteenth century is graced by Belter sofa and chairs. *(Photo by John T. Hill)*

Fig. 13.8

An asymmetrical Belter sofa with tufting and intricately carved frame. *(Courtesy of Cooper-Hewitt Museum of Design, Smithsonian Institute)*

duce many pieces that had charm and appeal.

In New York during the middle of the nineteenth century, a cabinetmaker named John H. Belter made a considerable amount of outstanding furniture in the Victorian style from about 1844 to 1860. Belter was an expert craftsman who worked with several kinds of wood, but he is best known for pieces made of fine-quality rosewood. He is noted for using a process of building up several layers of thin wood with the grain of each layer at right angles to the grain of the next layer. This type of lamination is commonly used today, but Belter was probably one of the first cabinetmakers to employ the process. The veneers were carved or pierced in lacy openwork patterns and ornamented with motifs of leaves, fruits, and flowers.

Another eminent cabinetmaker was Daniel Pabst, who made some excellent furniture in his Philadelphia shop during the 1860s. Much of his best work was executed in black walnut and showed distinct French influences.

It is interesting to note that certain Victorian accessories hold an appeal for the modern collector who may have no general interest in Victoriana. Popular in this respect is much of the Victorian glassware and ceramic work, as well as bronze statuary, notably that of John Rogers, who was active in this field around the middle of the century.

Currier and Ives prints were made in New York, also around the middle of the century. The originals of these colored lithographs were the work of several artists and they covered a wide range of subjects. The prints were inexpensive and were widely used. It was also about this time that daguerreotypes became very popular, shortly after Louis Daguerre had discovered a new process of photography in France.

The end of the nineteenth century brought more leisure and wealth and an awakened interest in culture and the arts. Increased travel to Europe created a demand for antiques and reproductions of foreign furniture styles. Art publications and the establishment of several art schools indicated a growing aesthetic interest. In 1870, the Metropolitan Museum of Art was founded.

Reactions to the period's debased forms of art were giving rise to the rumblings of the modern movement which by the turn of the century was in the developmental stages. This period will be discussed in a later section.

Choosing American Antiques

In judging furniture that may have antique value, it is important to have an open mind, be willing to observe details, and practice evaluating old pieces. Pay particular attention to the patina, normal signs of wear, tool marks, construction, dimensions, varieties of woods, and the condition of the article.

Patina

Patina is another name for the complexion that cabinet surfaces acquire through age, rubbing, polishing, and use. The patina varies with different woods, such as the brownish-red of mahogany, but the bloom of age is still there. If the antique has been scraped and sandpapered, the patina is practically destroyed.

Normal Signs of Wear

Most old furniture has been used often, and consequently it bears normal signs of wear. These marks or signs vary on pieces. Sharp edges of a piece may have become slightly rounded, and there may be some dents. The sharp edge of any carving on the piece will have dulled over the years.

Some inlaid pieces may have a part missing. It is also common to find warping with old table leaves that are made of single boards. Look at the legs, feet, and drawers to find signs of wear.

Tool Marks

The track of the jack plane is one of the marks most often seen on interior parts and undersides of antique furniture. The cutting edge of its wide blade was always given a slight arc, with the center about an eighth of an inch

higher than the corners. As a result, boards smoothed with it have an irregular series of slight ridges and hollows that follow the grain of the wood and vary according to the size of the plane and the effort taken in planing individual boards. Some of the ridges and hollows can be seen with the naked eye; others can be felt by passing one's fingertips lightly over the surface.

Saw marks are easy to observe. The old cabinetmakers used straight, hand-operated saws with coarse teeth. As the boards were sliced, the saw left a clear pattern of straight parallel scratches.

The power-driven circular saw (buzz saw) was introduced in the United States about 1825. With the buzz saw, there are a series of concentric arclike scratches that form part of a circle six to eighteen inches in diameter. There may be buzz-saw markings on some American Empire furniture in original condition.

The rotary plane came into use during the Victorian years. The smoothness of this machine planing was a mechanical perfection far different from that of handwork.

Construction

The construction details of all the furniture forms show that the old cabinetmakers followed certain standard ways. The mortice and tenon and dovetail joints are the most easily recognized. Prior to 1725 and the use of glue, the parts of the individual joints were large and not snugly fitted. After gluing joints became a standard practice, the parts were made smaller and were fitted with great precision.

Dimensions

There is surprising uniformity of measurement and proportions in the furniture of Early American cabinetmakers. An occasional piece may be found with dimensions greater or lesser, but it will be the exception.

Seats of chairs were from 16 to 18 inches from the floor, with some exceptions: slipper chairs were from 12 to 14 inches high, and early Victorian side chairs were about 14 or 15 inches from the floor. Rocking chair seats were generally 14 to 16 inches high, and the Victorian ones are as low as 12 inches.

Table tops ranged from 27 to 30 inches high. The low chest of drawers was usually about 30 to 40 inches high, 34 to 44 inches wide, and 17 to 20 inches deep. Tall chests of drawers may be 48 to 66 inches high, 36 to 46 inches wide, and 20 to 22 inches deep.

Sofas were almost always too long by present-day standards, especially those of the Hepplewhite, Sheraton, and American Empire periods. The smallest were six feet long, and those of seven and eight feet were not uncommon.

Varieties of Woods

Antique chairs were often made from two or more different woods. The old cabinetmakers used whatever wood happened to be around.

Condition

A genuine antique piece in good condition presents no problems. The antique dealers' term *original finish* means that the piece needs only polish and minor repairs. These are the most desirable pieces and hard to find.

To be worth putting in usable condition, a piece in the rough should be at least three-quarters complete. Otherwise, one ends with a rebuilt article instead of an antique. Check the interior parts of the restored piece to see if the repair person used care in using hand tools for replacing and restoring old wood. If modern machine marks predominate, the chances are that it is either a fake, rebuilt from old wood, or a factory-made copy ten to thirty years old.

It would be impossible to fix the beginning of the modern movement with one date, name, or event. The inception of the modern style might be traced, in a very indirect manner, back to the Industrial Revolution and the beginning of the machine age. The use of machines in the early part of the nineteenth century gradually supplanted most of the fine craftsmanship. But man had not yet learned to cope with the machine or to appreciate fully its potentialities. The attempts to imitate handmade products with machine methods resulted in a glut of poor design and poor construction.

The popular taste during the middle of the nineteenth century was at a low level that readily accepted imitation and ostentation. The pretentious, overelaborate Victorian style was at its height of popularity and in its pendulum swing was reaching extremes of debased designs.

Development of the Modern Style

The Arts and Crafts Movement

One important influence was the British Arts and Crafts Movement, headed by William Morris, designer of the famous chair that bears his name. Here the attempt was to return to basic honesty and simplicity of handmade furniture, as well as to revive the principles of medieval art.

Writers such as John Ruskin, Goethe, Walter Scott, and Victor Hugo supported the cause. In the field of interior design, William Morris and Charles Eastlake, Jr., are notable for their rebellion against the indiscriminate use of the machine. A noted architect, E. W. Godwin, designed furniture in the Jacobean style but also became interested in Japanese art and promoted an Oriental theme in design. Morris worked with a group of skilled craftsmen who became known as "Pre-Raphaelites." Eventually, however, their designs were debased by cheap imitation.

In England the emphasis was on arts and crafts with a deliberate attempt to establish an individual, amateurish quality in design. This movement resulted in a comparable trend in America. One manifestation of this new art was

14
The Modern Style

Morris chair. The nineteenth century (1900–1910) large easy chair was made of heavy solid sections, adjustable back, and loose cushions. Variations of the design appear in contemporary lounging chairs. *(Courtesy of the Brooklyn Museum, gift of William J. Berry)*

an interest in what was called "Mission" furniture, a style that was crude, simple, and heavy in proportion. It became outdated shortly after the first decade of the twentieth century.

Bentwood

An important development in furniture construction was introduced in 1842 by Michael Thonet in Austria. He experimented with a process of steaming solid lengths of beechwood and bending them into curves. Wood treated in this manner remained as strong as or stronger than before. He applied this process to furniture making, producing sturdy, lightweight, economical pieces. Manufactured or mass-produced furniture started with Thonet chairs.

Forty years later, Thonet's beautiful curves were echoed by the Art Nouveau movement. Various chairs that he designed have become internationally famous. At present, Thonet Industries, Inc., still pioneers in modern design.

Art Nouveau

Still another reaction to Victoriana was the Art Nouveau movement in France, England, Belgium, and the United States. Just as it opposed excessive overloading of interiors with unnecessary furniture and ornaments, Art Nouveau also held that the machine was the great symbol of the modern age and that it was useless and illogical to ignore it. Artists were encouraged to use the machine to apply ideas to everyday objects that could be produced at reasonable prices for the benefit of as many users as possible. The Art Nouveau artists wanted the average person to have the benefits of living in a comfortable surrounding. They thought that the beauty of the object should not be derived from the cost of its materials but from its essential artistic merit. The artist's ability for self-expression was emphasized, along with craftsmanship with simplicity and the use of natural forms.

Thonet Vienna cafe chair. *(Courtesy of Thonet Industries)*

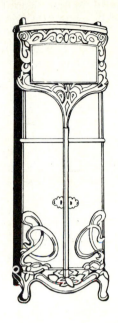

Victor Horta, a Belgian architect, developed the style in the Tassel house in Brussels. Hector Guimard was the leading Art Nouveau architect in France. The Scotsman Charles Rennie Mackintosh was a great leader of the Glasgow school. One of the most original talents in the Art Nouveau movement was Antoni Gaudi of Barcelona. Louis Comfort Tiffany, an American, developed new techniques of working with glass and metallic oxides. He produced vases, lamps, lampshades, glasses, and stained glass windows in the Art Nouveau style. However, it was Henri Van de Velde, of Belgium, who became the spokesman for the Art Nouveau movement. He spoke of the dynamic quality of line and believed that line did not merely ornament form, but developed it.

Many craftsmen tried to create a new style based on ornaments inspired by nature. Leaves, flowers, branches, and sweeping curves were used in a manner that protested against traditional designs. Art Nouveau is characterized by flowing, sinuous, asymmetrical lines ending in a curve like the bud of a plant.

Shortly after the turn of the century, the fanciful designs grew so bold that the style became as romantic and excessive as Victorian, and the movement died rather quickly. However, Art Nouveau was responsible for liberating the arts and design from the long bondage of historicism and tradition.

Functionalism

The theme of functionalism began to find favor toward the end of the nineteenth century. Earlier, in 1840, the American sculptor Horatio Greenough had decreed that function should determine design and that the beauty of any object should result from the form and the material. By the end of the century, the same idea was being promoted in architecture by Louis Sullivan (1856–1924), who rejected all previous stylistic influences. The theme of his work was organic, and the design of his Transportation

Building at the Columbian Exposition in Chicago in 1893 received worldwide acclaim. He designed a number of commercial buildings in Chicago, but died before the public really accepted his ideas. His work was carried on by several followers, notably Frank Lloyd Wright (1869–1959), whose long career in architectural design won him international acclaim.

The work of Frank Lloyd Wright also became very important in the progress of the modern movement. Although he designed public buildings, he applied many commercial techniques to residential structures with the result that his houses were innovations in design. Wright firmly believed in relating his structures to the geography of their settings, but he built from the inside out. The function of the building determined its form. He designed to take maximum advantage of sun, light, and view, but he rejected window walls when they violated privacy. He also made maximum use of the decorative qualities of building materials, both inexpensive and costly ones. He created a style of architecture that has been accepted throughout the world.

Wright's last public building received both acclaim and bitter criticism. The Guggenheim Museum in New York City was completed and opened shortly after his death in 1959. The unusual design of the building caused wide public interest and editorial comment. Some critics noted Wright's dislike for cities and implied that he had played a joke on New York. One referred to the building as an "upturned dish of oatmeal." Those who voiced acclaim hailed the structure as a milestone in modern architectural design. The only point of agreement seems to be that the building is certainly "different."

Another important development in the modern movement was the work of Le Corbusier (the professional name of Charles E. Jeanneret, 1887–1965), a Swiss architect who designed residential buildings in the modern style. He designed structures supported by skeletons of columns that made his buildings seem to be off the ground. Le Corbusier preferred glass walls to allow maximum light and a closer relationship between the exterior and the interior. With many built-in features and only necessary movable furniture, he aimed to create homes that would make living simple, emphasizing the importance of surroundings that are easy to maintain, convenient to use, and healthy. Le Corbusier believed that the intrinsic qualities of the home could be spiritually satisfying. To meet this purpose, he advocated beauty through good proportions, the utilitarian aspects of materials, and the use of only a few accessories of superb quality.

de Stijl

Several important developments in the modern movement took place in the early part of the twentieth century. Following the Art Nouveau, a magazine known as *de Stijl* ("the style") was published in Holland in 1917. It represented new ideas of expression in painting, architecture, sculpture, and other forms of art, with emphasis on the use of cubes, squares, and flat planes. Theo van Doesburg published the magazine and originated this movement, which had considerable influence on new styles of architecture and furniture.

Piet Mondrian was the chief spokesman for this group of artists, who described their theories as an attempt to close the gap between art and life. Their principles were purity of all elements; purity of horizontals and verticals; and the use of pure primary colors with black, white, and grey. The artists were to restrict the elements of painting to an abstract arrangement of lines and geometric shapes or a flat surface using only black, white, and the primary colors.

The *de Stijl* movement declared that the furniture should be composed of simple square elements screwed together. Furniture, at this time, was a series of vertical and horizontal planes, visually weightless in space.

Gerrit Rietvelt (1888–1964), a furniture designer turned architect, translated the principle to a three-dimensional form as early as 1917 in the "Red-Blue Chair." His intention was to design a chair anyone could afford, but it appears that the chair was made almost as a sculpture: the functional aspect was incidental.

Deutsche Werkbund
Bauhaus

In Germany, a group of craftsmen sought to reconcile machine production, good craftsman-

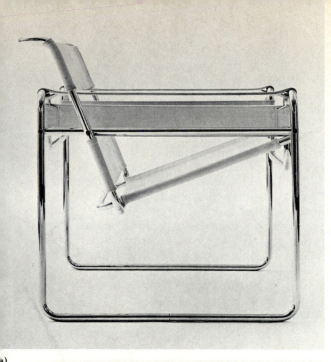

(a)

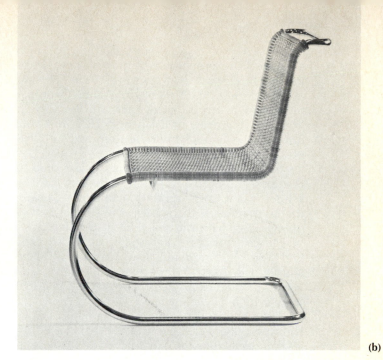

(b)

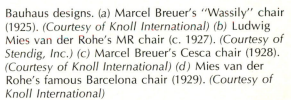

Bauhaus designs. (a) Marcel Breuer's "Wassily" chair (1925). *(Courtesy of Knoll International)* (b) Ludwig Mies van der Rohe's MR chair (c. 1927). *(Courtesy of Stendig, Inc.)* (c) Marcel Breuer's Cesca chair (1928). *(Courtesy of Knoll International)* (d) Mies van der Rohe's famous Barcelona chair (1929). *(Courtesy of Knoll International)*

Fig. 14.3

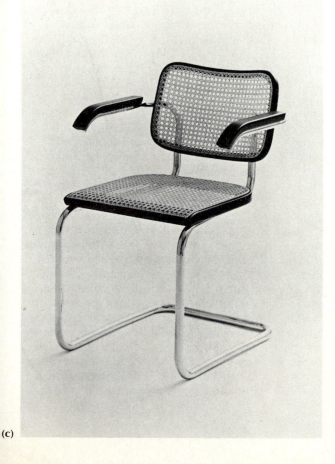

(c)

(d)

ship, and the proper use of materials by establishing the *Deutsche Werkbund* in 1907. In 1919 one of the leaders of this group, Walter Gropius, organized a school known as the *Bauhaus* in Weimar. It moved to Dessau in 1925 and was housed in a famous building designed by Gropius.

In the beginning, the school was devoted to the arts-and-crafts tradition. The aim of the school was to unify art and technology. During the later years of the school, the emphasis was on working with the machine in the design of buildings, furniture, lighting fixtures, textiles, and household articles. The design was to be simple and free of unnecessary elements that would distract from the function or the material from which it was made.

The greatest contribution of Bauhaus was in furniture engineering, and the style is based on a frank revelation of machine-made attributes. The architect Marcel Breuer studied at the Bauhaus and became the first master of the furniture workshop. The Wassily chair (1925), a tubular steel, one-piece design, was Breuer's attempt to use tubular metal to its full potential. Canvas or leather straps are stretched across the metal tubes to provide the seat, back, and arm rests.

Ludwig Mies van der Rohe succeeded Gropius as director of the Bauhaus and spread the machine-oriented aesthetic of the Bauhaus throughout Europe and America. Mies van der Rohe designed the MR chair (1927), the earliest use of the cantilever principle for chairs of tubular steel. The MR chair was originally produced with a continuous seat and back of woven cane. It was later made with a separate seat and back of leather.

In 1928, Marcel Breuer developed the Cesca chair, also designed on the cantilever principle, which was capturing the imagination of architects and engineers at the time. Also in 1928, Le Corbusier, in close association with his partner, Charlotte Perriand, designed the adjustable chaise lounge.

In 1929, Mies van de Rohe designed an exhibition pavilion in Barcelona. He had to design every detail in the house, including all the chairs and tables, as there was no furniture fitting for the building. The Barcelona chair was designed to receive a king, a dictator, or an ambassador. It is almost entirely handmade, except for some machine sewing and the extruded steel sections.

In Europe during the first quarter of the twentieth century, various new ideas for furnishings and home equipment were developed. By 1925, general interest in the new style was widespread. France sponsored an exposition in Paris to display and publicize the advanced ideas. Neither Germany nor the United States participated. After the exposition, many of the exhibits were sent to America, where they awakened public interest in the "international style." Designers and manufacturers were responsive, and the year 1926 marks a milestone in the development of the modern style in America.

Current Modern

At the present time the term *modern* evokes many different interpretations, and perhaps we are too close to the evolution of the style to evaluate it objectively. There is no doubt that much modern art is exciting, forceful, and expressive of our way of life.

The critics of modern style ask, "Must any change be one for the better?" and "Is change without reason necessarily good?" The advocates ask, "Must we be chained to tradition?" and "Are not current technologies and thinking geared to the new and the different?" The answers to such questions may not be simple "yes" or "no" replies, because true artistic expression has deeper implications.

The modern style has gone through a period of growing pains. We like to think, at this point, that it has reached fruition and is really meeting our needs and expressing our way of life. Whether or not it really is and will continue to do so is a matter of conjecture. At the present writing there is considerable interest in styles of the past. Is there some need for association with the past, overlooked by modern designers? Do we need ornament and surface decoration to meet some spiritual need? Only time will tell. Perhaps we must find the meeting ground of the old and the new. Probably the best example of this point can be found in the architecture of Edward Stone, which has won popular acclaim in the last few years. Architecture has often dictated the styles of interior design. Stone's work has answered the need for the functional and the need for embellishment. His openwork facades in magnificent geometric patterns let in light and air but curb intense sunlight. One has privacy, yet the indoors is not alienated from the outdoors. Stone has incorporated this useful but ancient idea into buildings of the most modern design. They meet contemporary needs and tastes, they are functional in every respect, yet they also provide an atmosphere of elegance. In this architecture one senses a respect for tradition mingled with admiration for the present. Perhaps this is one answer to some of the questions about the modern style. Must it be totally and completely different to be effective? Is there not a blend, or a happy medium, of the old and the new that will meet all our current needs? Some will still say no,—that we must break with past tradition to make the new form of expression completely effective; others will say that we must use the experiences of the past in combination with current objectives.

Every style in the past was at one time "modern," and each one had both good and bad examples. So it is with the modern style today. Whether or not it is good design depends on the sensitivity of the designer to forms, proportions, and the materials that are being used. Success depends also on the designer's ability to appreciate true functionalism and modern production.

Although some of the critics of the modern style have felt that there is too much effort to be different without just cause, there are many examples of new ideas in design that now have classic value. There are others that have become tiresome, or even irritating, in just a few years. Much of the furniture manufactured ten years ago now appears terribly dated and out of fashion. Fortunately, most of the top-notch designers in the modern style are striving toward ideals that give some degree of permanency to their work.

Different influences and individual interpretations have produced a variety of designs at different price levels. In furniture and all household accessories, many manufacturers who produce on a national scale have hired competent designers to cope with the problem of designing low-cost items that are well constructed and in good taste. It should be borne in mind that not all expensive articles are necessarily of good design. Some are as grotesque and ostentatious as the worst examples of Victoriana, and in years to come they may be viewed with more horror.

However, modern designers would have the public educated to appreciate a more intrinsic type of beauty, one that is achieved through structure and substance. They admire hand craftsmanship, but they recognize that beauty of form and texture may be achieved even with mass production. We do not believe that contemporary design has reached its pinnacle, but where, how, and when it will must remain matters of conjecture for the time being.

Although American art and industry were rather late in accepting the modern movement, progress has been extremely rapid since 1940. Leaders in design and production have established America in a prominent position on the world scene. It is particularly encouraging that the bonds between art and industry have been steadily growing stronger, and there are many indications that the relationship will continue to grow and to develop. This closer association will no doubt strengthen American contemporary art, especially in the field of interior design.

The manner in which the Scandinavian countries have projected contemporary styles has been widely acclaimed. Keen appreciation for craftsmanship is not new to the Scandinavians, nor is the feeling for simplicity of line and form. This combination of values nurtured the development of the modern style, particularly in Sweden and Denmark. In many phases of the decorative arts, the Scandinavian countries have attained fashion leadership.

There has been a strong Oriental influence in modern decoration. The emphasis on simplicity and beauty of form that has marked so much Oriental art provides the basis for a happy association between modern and ancient styles. The similarity of purpose has been more responsible for supplementation of basic designs rather than direct influence on them, but now that some of the Oriental countries are developing their industries to produce for a world market we shall probably see some interesting interpretations of the modern style.

The fashion world has felt the impact of a fresh, new spirit in Italian design, and the creative exuberance in Italy has spread to the decorative arts. The Italian interpretations of contemporary styles are becoming increasingly important.

General Features

In the discussion of style terminology it was pointed out that it is difficult to draw a fine line of demarcation between "contemporary" and "modern." In the sense that contemporary designs recognize and often draw upon the ideas of the past, we must remember that they are still part of the modern style in its broadest interpretation. The term *organic* is often used to distinguish modern designs that attempt to break with past tradition. Thus there is a variety of ideas represented by the term *modern*. Although the style has a unique character, it is almost impossible to generalize about characteristics. We may, however, point out some of the trends and ideas that seem to have won general favor.

A primary purpose of the modern style is to create beauty in a functional form. In this respect, many of the designs have been highly successful. We have furniture that is sturdy, durable, well constructed, and easy to care for.

Proportions
New shapes and forms have been introduced. In the past, forms were generally square, rectangular, oval, or circular, and certain proportions were generally accepted as being the most pleasing to the eye. Modern furniture has introduced the "free" form, which rejects geometrical stereotypes. Modern materials and technologies make it possible to mold chairs in which the seat, back, and arms are shaped from one piece of material (as we see, for example, in the shell chair).

Much modern furniture is still built on rectilinear lines, but the modern designer is becoming more at ease with the use of curved and sloping lines to create different effects.

Asymmetrical forms are not a new idea, but modern designs have given them fresh interpretations. Desks, sofas, and chests have been unleashed from their traditional symmetry.

Functionalism
The idea of functionalism has been projected into the design of dual-purpose pieces intended to simplify living in small areas where each piece of furniture must earn its keep. Because people are more and more mobile and cannot spend large amounts of money each time they move, there is an even greater demand for well-designed multi-use adjustable furniture. Wall storage systems give flexibility to limited space. Much furniture is designed to take advantage of vertical space. Sofas, chairs, and ottomans that open to form beds have been particularly useful and popular. There are also tables that adjust to different heights so that they may be used as coffee or dining tables. Chests of drawers are made with tops that extend to form long tables or with "drawers" that open to form desk surfaces.

A few words of caution must be injected here with regard to dual-purpose pieces. Sofas that extend to beds must have space in front of them—or tables that are easily moved. A dual-height table cannot serve two purposes at once. Tiny desk surfaces are not useful for certain types of work. It is important to visualize such furniture in actual use and to evaluate the practical values.

Another practical development in home decoration is high-tech, the "industrial style." Industrial objects are moving into the residential scene. However, high-tech is not a new concept, just one that is finally being given recognition. Office bookcases have been looking good in homes for a long time, as have industrial light fixtures. Track lighting and butcher blocks, too, came to the home from industry.

New Materials

Much of the furniture in the modern style has incorporated new materials, or has used old materials in new ways. Wood is still the favorite substance, but glass, metal, and plastics are also used. Laminates and fiberglass have tremendous potentials for new design effects, and the exponents of the modern style are exercising their imagination to incorporate these materials into their creations. An intrinsic beauty of texture in a material that lends itself to the purpose and form of the object is basic to modern design. Leaders in the field have been willing and eager to use new scientific achievements to fulfill this purpose. However, they have not overlooked the fact that more familiar materials, such as wood, marble, glass, straw, and ceramic tile, may achieve the same purpose.

Urethane foam—an extremely versatile man-made product that has found wide application in industry as well as in the home—has become increasingly important in modern furniture. The chemicals from which the foam is made can be varied in the early stages of production to provide a wide range of materials. Thus the manufacturer may vary the recipe to suit the end purposes. It can be produced in flexible, semirigid, or rigid forms, and the degree of softness can be controlled. It resists many of the factors that tend to cause deterioration in other materials, and it is low in cost. The broad advantages of this substance will undoubtedly make it a very important element in future design, especially in the area of modular furniture.

Molded plastic components and impregnated plastic finishes on wood will certainly influence future designs in furniture. As these techniques develop, we may see some interesting ornamentation of contemporary designs and new adaptations of traditional styles. Let us hope, however, that the new technologies will be used with discretion. It is difficult to imagine a beautiful Hepplewhite chair reproduced in plastic. We may shudder at the thought, but it might happen.

An innovation in modern design has been the introduction of inflatable furniture. Chair kits, equipped with small pumps and repair patches, have captured our imaginations as to the advantages of this type of furniture. If one has to move frequently or suddenly, the idea of letting out the air and packing the frame in a shoebox can be most intriguing.

Knock-down (KD) furniture, in some cases referred to as lifestyle furniture, has gained in popularity. It is a bridge between old and new ways of designing, merchandising, and selling to meet the needs of the consumer.

KD furniture is not a new concept, but it has become popular because of the savings to the consumer from its more compact size for shipping and because it offers immediate delivery as the consumer can take it home at the time of purchase. Generally speaking, KD furniture can withstand more abuse than conventional furniture. Because of the interest in do-it-yourself, people often do not mind setting up their own furniture.

Paper is another material that is being explored for possible contributions in furnishings. Rather rigid, inexpensive items have been produced to meet specific needs.

(Courtesy of B and B America)

Fig. 14.4

The computer is now used in furniture construction, from the programming of production, through the molding of the plastics, to the cutting of fabrics. The finish may be applied by hand. One firm using this process of furniture construction is B and B Italia.

Modular Furniture

The production of a relatively few, standardized units that may be combined in various ways has made it possible to achieve arrangements that will suit individual tastes and needs at a comparatively low cost. Modular furniture is flexible: it offers more seating in less space. It

can be arranged and rearranged in different homes and subtracted to or added to as the needs arise.

The idea of unit combinations has been popular for many years in unpainted furniture and in sectional sofas. It has also been applied to finished chest and shelf units that may be stacked or mounted on legs or bases. Small tables that lock together to form larger tables are also used.

Wall-hung furniture has become popular. With brackets mounted on walls it is possible to have a flexible arrangement of shelves and various storage units. This type of furniture has proven particularly appealing to those who live in small quarters and who desire to conserve floor space.

A furniture grouping designed by Matta that is particularly useful for those who move often. *(Courtesy of Knoll International)*

Fig. 14.5

Pit group by Alan White is an example of modular seating. *(Courtesy of Uniroyal, Inc.)*

Fig. 14.6

Designers in the Modern Style

Perhaps one of the most interesting features in the development of the modern style is the manner in which it has transcended national boundaries. Although the Scandinavian countries have assumed leadership in many areas, designers and manufacturers in other countries have accepted the challenge, and there is an international exchange of ideas and methods. Several American concerns have employed foreign designers and have established showrooms throughout the world. On the other hand, foreign manufacturers have established factories in the United States and have drawn upon American technology to advance their ideas.

Because of this international scope, it would be impossible to name all the fine artists and craftsmen who have made major contributions to the special type of classicism that modern design has achieved. We have already discussed some of the earlier leaders, such as Marcel Breuer, who experimented with new chair forms using metal tubing and metal strips. The Barcelona chair, which Mies van der Rohe designed in 1929, has become a famous classic in the modern style.

A few other names must be mentioned because of the outstanding designs that have been associated with them.

Charles Eames (1907–1978) was a versatile designer who had a background in architecture.

(a)

His name has become associated with chair forms, although he designed other pieces as well. The famous LCM chair (molded plywood) by Eames, exhibited in New York in 1946, was a distinct departure from conventional chair construction and one of the first widely accepted designs in the organic modern style. It was made of laminated plywood, bent to provide comfortable contours. The lounge chair 670 by Eames was designed in 1956 to give comfort, both physical and psychological. Its leather, permanently wrinkled by the way the buttons are placed, suggests that it has recently been sat in.

Eames continued to experiment with new forms and new materials and his imaginative

(a) The famous LCM chair (molded plywood) by Charles Eames (1946). The chair has a molded plywood seat and back attached to a frame of metal rods. (Courtesy of Herman Miller, Inc.) (b) The lounge chair and ottoman was designed in 1956, by Eames. (Courtesy of Herman Miller, Inc.)

Fig. 14.7

(b)

use of aluminum won particular acclaim in recent years. He designed many pieces for the line of Herman Miller, Inc.

Eero Saarinen (1911–1961) was another architect whose name is associated with innovations in chair design. He was particularly interested in the possibilities of molded plastics. His early "womb" chair (1945), the "tulip" chair, and the pedestal bases that he introduced in 1956 have sculptural qualities that introduced new dimensions in form. Knoll International, a group of outstanding leaders in design, produces much of the furniture designed by Saarinen.

George Nelson has designed a considerable amount of furniture for Herman Miller, Inc., but he now operates his own firm in New York.

(a) Eero Saarinen designed the comfortable "womb" chair in 1945. *(b)* Saarinen's pedestal chair in 1956 was an effective interpretation of molded plastics. *(Courtesy of Knoll International)*

Fig. 14.8

(a)

(b)

The Modern Style

Another very versatile designer with a background in architecture, Mr. Nelson has created a variety of storage units that indicate a superb ability to combine beauty of form with the highest degree of functionalism. His designs of other pieces are equally beautiful.

Harry Bertoia was a sculptor who designed for Knoll International with an emphasis on airy metal construction. His work in furniture design revealed the sculptural approach as well as an appreciation of the adaptability of new materials to the creation of new forms.

Edward Wormley has designed a great deal of furniture with emphasis on the beautiful colors and grain patterns of wood, although he is equally proficient in the use of other materials.

Many of his designs, which indicate his fine appreciation of form and texture, are produced by The Dunbar Furniture Corporation.

George Nakashima has designed some furniture for Knoll International, but in general his work is more closely associated with handcraft methods. He seems to have a particular ability to create very contemporary forms that have a certain flavor of the past. The slight suggestion of an Early American influence in his modern designs lends a very distinctive quality.

Warren Platner's talent can be seen in his designs of furniture, lighting fixtures, fabrics, china, and flatware. He has designed a style of pedestal and wire furniture for Knoll International.

Fig. 14.9

A classic storage unit designed by George Nelson. *(Courtesy of Herman Miller, Inc.)*

(a) Harry Bertoia's chair of wire and mesh. *(Courtesy of Knoll International)* (b) New wire furniture by designer–architect Warren Platner is akin to contemporary metal sculpture in appearance and intricacy. It took three years to perfect the complex technologies that made this furniture a commercial reality. *(Courtesy of Knoll International)*

Fig. 14.10

The Modern Style

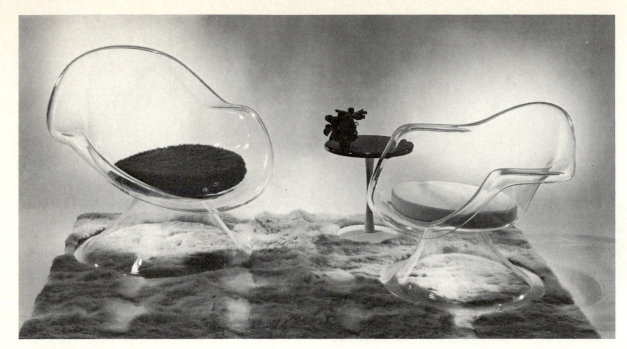

Fig. 14.11

Clear plastic is used to mold "invisible" chairs that can add new dimensions to a room. *(Courtesy of Laverne International Ltd., N.Y.)*

A lightly scaled shell armchair rests on a dramatic cantilevered base of chrome-plated steel. *(Courtesy of Jens Risom Design, Inc.)*

Fig. 14.12

"See-through" furniture has become important in the modern style. Laverne International, Ltd., introduced a plexiglass chair in 1962 that became known as the "invisible chair." Transparent substances for furniture have provided a new dimension of lightness in modern design; they are being adapted in a variety of ways today. The Lavernes also design with great distinction in other areas, including fabrics and wall coverings.

Jens Risom is a designer-manufacturer who came to the United States from Denmark. He produces fine quality furniture with high standards of craftsmanship. Although Risom's designs are suitable for the modern home, a considerable amount of his work is designed for institutional needs.

Isamu Noguchi is associated with several phases of the modern style. He is a sculptor who has designed furniture for Herman Miller, Inc. Noguchi has also done considerable work with lighting fixtures that reflect his interest in sculpture.

A leader in the field of designing good-

An innovation in modern design is inflatable furniture made of a thick, vinyl-like fabric. Each chair is equipped with a foot pump and patches that can be used in case of puncture. *(Courtesy of Selig Manufacturing Co.)*

Fig. 14.13

quality furniture for mass production was Paul McCobb. He died in 1969 at the age of fifty-one, but his designs have had significant influence, especially in the area of modular furniture and coordinated groupings.

Another designer who has shown interest in new methods for mass production is Milo Baughman, who has won several awards for furniture design and is particularly cognizant of craftsmanship as it can be related to modern technology. His use of metals, such as steel and chrome, often combined with wood, his sensitivity to the new materials, and his appreciation of vibrant colors and textures have established a new look in contemporary design.

David Rowland solved the problem of stacking chairs in a close area. He used a very thin, high-tensile steel rod to form the rear support, rear leg, floor rail, front leg and side seat rail. The seat and back are a sheet metal formed to fit the body. This produced an ideal solution to stacking and storage as well as a beautiful and comfortable chair.

Many foreign designers have either initiated trends or have influenced modern design on the international level. Again, it is not possible to cite all of the important leaders but a few must be mentioned.

Cini Boeri, a Milanese architect and industrial designer, designed the Lunario dining, coffee, and end tables for Knoll International. These tables deviated from the rigid geometry of table design.

The cocktail table pictured in Figure 14.18 is a sculptural shape. Its oval glass top is cantilevered from a marble base. Ronald Schmitt, who designed this furniture form, was discovered by the Turners at the Cologne Fair in 1972.

Werner Panton of Switzerland designed the Panton Stacking Chair in the 1960s. This, the first single-form plastic chair, is satisfying and simple. The freedom in plastics and mold-forming technology has been used to the maximum advantage.

The Nordics, long familiar with molded skis, made of many veneers of wood curved under steam or heat, have been prominent in furniture design. Around 1933, Alvar Aalto, a famous

The Modern Style

**Fig.
14.14**

(a)

(a) Milo Baughman uses a frame fence of steel tubing to support blocks of foam rubber covered in a textured fabric. (b) Sides of amber plexiglass give this sofa designed by Milo Baughman a floating effect. (Courtesy of Thayer Coggin, Inc.)

(right) Some chair designs by: (a) Dick Schultz, (b) Don Petit, (c) Bill Stephens, and (d) Takahama. (Courtesy of Knoll International)

(b)

(a)

(b)

(c)

Fig. 14.15

(d)

Fig. 14.16

David Rowland's stacking chairs marketed in 1964. *(Courtesy of General Fireproofing)*

Furniture Styles, Selection, and Room Arrangement

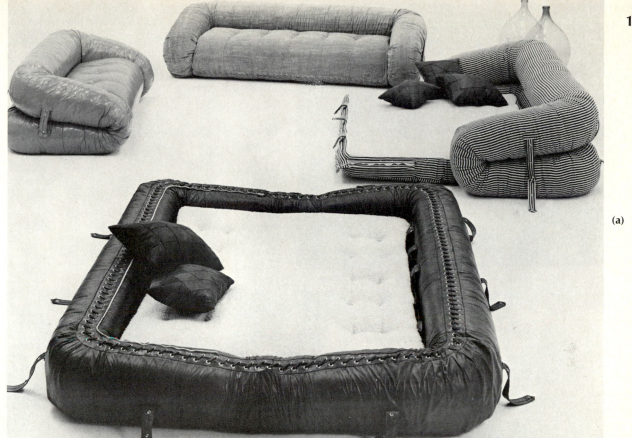

Fig. 14.17

(a)

Some examples of today's interpretation of dual purpose furniture. *(a) (Courtesy of International Contract Furnishings Inc.) (b) (Courtesy of Trianon)*

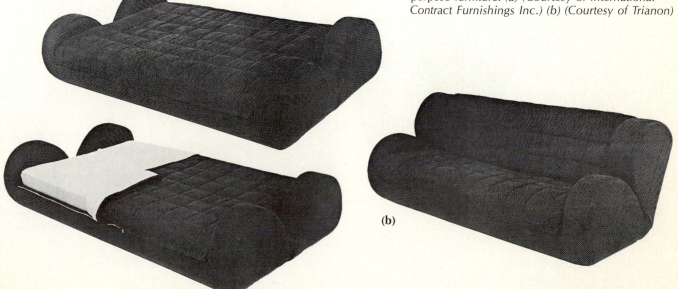

(b)

Cocktail table designed by Ronald Schmitt with a clear crystal glass top and arasbescato or palais royal marble base. *(Courtesy of Turner T. Ltd., N.Y.)*

(a) Molded plastic chair designed by Werner Panton. *(Courtesy of Herman Miller, Inc.) (b)* The Ribbon Lounge chair designed by Pierre Paulin, 1965, is covered with a stretch fabric that lends itself to new forms in upholstered furniture. *(Manufactured by Artifort of Holland, distributed by Turner T. Ltd., N.Y.)*

Fig. 14.18

Fig. 14.19

(a)

(b)

Finnish architect, developed Armchair 406, made of laminated wood. The form was springy, entirely natural, and appropriate to the material. He designed stacking stools of the same material.

Hans Wegner is a Danish designer noted for exquisite simplicity. His chairs and storage units have qualities that combine comfort, functionalism, and a handcrafted appearance. His Classic Chair, 1949, is simple and beautifully proportioned. All the parts seem to flow into each other, making a unifed form.

Several other names must be mentioned in connection with Scandinavian design. Bruno Mathsson of Sweden experimented with laminated wood as Alvar Aalto did in Finland. Ib Kofol-Larson, Karl-Erik Ekselius, and Arne Jacobsen are other designers who have achieved distinction.

Finn Juhl, another Danish designer, has worked with The Baker Company in America. This association has been credited with being an important step in promoting the interest of American industry in developing the interna-

Swedish designer Bruno Mathsson uses a swivel base and neck cushions to give comfort. *(Furniture by Dunbar/Dux, vinyl flooring by Flintkote)*

DANISH MODERN

(a) Alvar Aalto's molded and bent birch plywood lounge chair, designed c. 1934.

(b) Stacking Stools

(c) Hans Wegner's Folding Chair

(d) Hans Wegner's Armchair

Fig. 14.20

tional style. Scandinavian furniture became extremely popular throughout the world during the 30s, 40s, and 50s.

Contemporary furniture produced by Dunbar/Dux, a Swedish company that now has a factory in the United States, represents large-scale manufacturing of fine-quality modern furniture.

Italy has had a revival of spirit in various phases of design. Some authorities believe that the most exciting new ideas for interior design are now coming from Italy but that they are geared to avant-garde tastes and not yet ready for general acceptance.

In the realm of furniture design, Gio Ponti has had a significant influence as a purist. Carlo de Carli, Ico Parisi, and Franco Albini have also had considerable influence. There are a number of young Italian designers who will probably influence future designs because they seem to have a special awareness of beautiful form as it relates to functionalism in all aspects of daily living.

The post-war generation brought in a new era of informality, honesty, and sensuality. In the late 50s and the early 60s Italy brought forth new ideas about furniture. At that time American designs were devoted to the functionalism of the Bauhaus school. Until the 60s, people sat in chairs the way the chair wanted them to sit.

But then the Italians developed designs that answered our yearning for comfort and luxury. Shapes are curved, comfortable, and sometimes humorous. Furniture is more accommodating. The trend toward soft furniture filled with air, water, or polyurethane can be seen in the bean bag chair designed in Italy by Gatti, Poalini, and Teodoro and filled with replaceable polyurethane pellets.

The firm Stendig, Inc., encourages new directions in the modern style. Figure 14.21 represents some examples. Joe Colombo's Elda chair began the post-Bauhaus revolution. The "Gyro" chair and the "Pony" designed by Eero Aarnio are eye-catching designs. DePas, D'Urbino, and Lomazzi designed the "Joe Lounge" chair that can be purchased from Stendig in glove leather or blue denim-like fabric. Stendig's "Marilyn" chair was introduced in 1974.

(a)

(b)

(c)

(d)

(a) The Elda chair, 1959, designed by Joe C. Colombo, has a fiberglas shell; the seat and back are cushioned with foam. (b) The "Pony" chair is easy seating by Eero Aarnio. The reinforced molded urethane foam is upholstered in stretch velour. (c) The "Gyro" chair designed by Eero Aarnio is a whimsical, eye-catching new design. It is made of reinforced molded fiberglas. (d) De Pas, D'Urbino, and Lomazzi designed the "Joe Lounge" chair, 1974. It is made of molded reinforced urethane foam. (e) The "Marilyn" love seat was designed and introduced in 1974. It is an interesting and comfortable design. (a–e Courtesy Stendig, Inc.)

Fig. 14.21

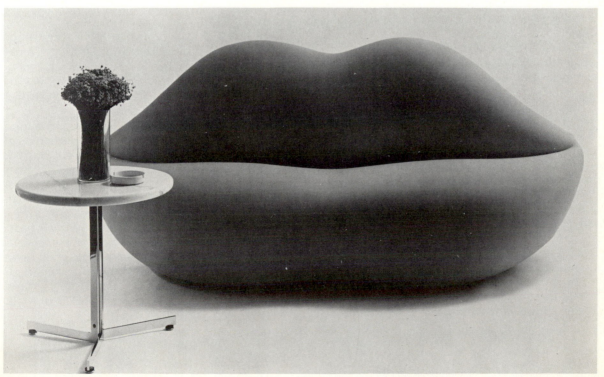

(e)

Because people come in all sizes and shapes, the chair has always been a challenge to the designer. The new trend in chair design is known as *ergonomics*, or biotechnology. Ergonomics in its broadest sense is the study of the relationship between humans and the objects in their environment or the adaptation of humans and their conditions to each other. Its development reflects the worldwide recognition of the importance of health and good environmental conditions.

Many chairs in homes and offices today are uncomfortable and unhealthful. A seat that is too high can impair circulation in the lower legs; when a chair back exerts too much pressure on the back, the result can be neck strain and/or headaches, as well as back problems. Ergonomics has enabled designers to determine the optimum dimensions for nearly every part of the chair, from the height of the seat to the precise amount of finger clearance needed between the arm rests and the underside of the desk.

Ergonomically designed chairs are common in Western Europe. A law was passed in West Germany to protect office workers from dangerous or unsafe chairs that can contribute to bad health. Some European cars have seats that are designed to make the driver more comfortable as well as to make it easier to drive.

William Stumpf, a professor of design at the University of Wisconsin, designed the Ergon chair, introduced in 1976 by Herman Miller. After nearly ten years of studying how people sit, Stumpf found that office workers have three basic postural positions: work-intensive, conversation-reflective, and relaxation-stretching. His chair was designed to fit all these postures in a healthful and comfortable way. A later entry in the field is the Vertebra chair, designed by Emilio Ambasz and Giancarlo Piretti.

A number of other chairs now available share several comfort features: a well-contoured back rest, with support for the lower-back area; a relatively short seat that is rounded at the front edge to avoid impairing leg circulation; and shorter armrests. These chairs join the chair by Charles Eames, preferred by Bobby Fischer in the chess tournament, and the popular Pollack chair, which combines aesthetic appeal with extraordinary comfort.

Any chair could benefit from the understanding of ergonomics; certainly a reading chair or a dining chair could be improved by its application. Hopefully, ergonomics will inspire designers to expand their field from a purely aesthetic technological model to include ergonomics.

Our discussion up to this point has been concerned mostly with furniture, but in the field of textiles several designers have made outstanding contributions.

Dorothy Liebes pioneered in designing fabrics that combine unusual colors and textures in yarns. Much of her work was either handwoven or had similar effects. Her influence on modern textile design has been widespread.

Jack Lenor Larsen has had a background in architecture and interior design but chose to devote his talents to fabric design. With a perceptive appreciation for both handcrafts and the technical aspects of production, Larsen has managed to unite concepts that seem to represent widely divergent ideas. The firm of Jack Lenor Larsen, Inc., established in 1952, has been responsible for numerous innovations in textile design.

Another fabric designer with a background in architecture is Alexander Girard, who designs for Herman Miller, Inc. Girard draws upon a wide variety of sources from all over the world for design inspiration and some of his fabrics are actually woven in foreign countries.

Ben Rose, another textile designer, designs wall coverings as well. He has been particularly known for excellence in printed fabrics, but he also designs plain fabrics with beautiful textures.

For some time, couturier designers have been designing home furnishings. Furniture, accessories, wall coverings, and linens all bear the signatures of individuals usually associated with Seventh Avenue in New York and Paris fashion salons. Halston is designing rugs and Gloria Vanderbilt is designing dishes. Mary McFadden has introduced a collection of wall coverings and fabrics.

parmeter

(a)

(a) William Stumpf's Ergon chair introduced in 1976. *(Courtesy of Herman Miller, Inc.)* (b) Charles Pollock's executive chair. *(Courtesy of Knoll International)*

(b)

Fig. 14.22

Home furnishings manufacturers are realizing that good designers are a valuable asset. Hence, objects with more and more quality design are appearing on the mass home furnishings market.

In other areas of modern interior design it is not quite as easy to name outstanding leaders. In various countries there are many designers who are striving to create lighting fixtures and accessories that combine innovations of form with functionalism. There have been important advances in this direction and several designers have won international recognition for their contributions. However, it is difficult to name leaders who should be cited in a brief survey such as this. In view of the fact that outstanding designers have had backgrounds in architecture, it seems odd that the challenging field of lighting has not attracted more attention. This is in no way meant to discredit those who have made significant contributions but merely to point out that there is an apparent need for more leadership in other areas of interior design.

15
Miscellaneous Styles

Various countries throughout the world have played more or less important roles in influencing our homes today. The arts of different cultures have provided rich inspiration for decorative motifs and accessories. Furniture forms, however, have not been as much affected as one might expect. For example, the vogues for Oriental design during the eighteenth and nineteenth centuries were manifested chiefly in ornamentation. There was some adaptation of Oriental design, but the basic furniture forms drew little from outside sources.

The Scandinavian countries, as well as Spain and Italy, have contributed to present furniture design. Germany and Austria have also contributed to the decorative arts in various ways. It is not within the scope of this book to elaborate on all of them. Perhaps it will suffice to point out that modern interior designers are turning to some of these less-known areas for inspiration and the results have been quite exciting. We have seen in recent years a growing interest in blending Oriental and Near Eastern themes with contemporary styles. When the arts of more primitive cultures are used to add interest and accent to modern styles, the effects can be intriguing and enchanting. The potentials of combining the new with the ancient have had tremendous popular appeal. The growing interest in these somewhat neglected sources has been stimulated by increased travel and by the growing emphasis on cultural interchange as a factor in promoting world peace.

Some of the areas that bear investigation are the arts of the Oriental and Near Eastern cultures and those of the European peasants. There is also a renewed interest in ethnic identity and designs today. The art of the American Indian and African art should not be overlooked.

For our purposes here we shall consider several miscellaneous styles that have been popular during recent years:

Biedermeier.
Oriental.
Italian.
Spanish.

Biedermeier

A style that has found rather popular favor during recent years developed in Germany and Austria during the nineteenth century. The name was taken from a popular fictional character named "Papa Biedermeier," a humorous, corpulent figure who did not hesitate to express his views on any subject.

The furniture was popular from about 1815 to 1860. It was a naïve interpretation of the French Empire style, although it also drew from other sources, such as Sheraton, Regency, Directoire, and even some German peasant styles. In spite of somewhat heavy proportions and unrefined curves, the style had a simple, comfortable appeal. The furniture was neither luxurious nor extravagant. It eliminated the excessive decorative detail of the French Empire mode.

The chair backs were carved in various designs, but the carving was never elaborate; the legs were rarely turned or carved. Decorative detail included simple moldings; some marquetry, often in border designs of contrasting wood; brass ornaments; and painted or stenciled designs. Motifs included simple classical themes, flowers, and human or animal figures. The character of the ornament sometimes introduced a playful note that gave the furniture a spirit of humor and informality.

The typical Empire forms were executed in light woods, usually cherry, birch, walnut, and fruit woods. Some furniture was painted black and decorated with simple gilding.

Favorite fabric patterns were small, flowered designs and stripes. Silk, satin, and taffeta were sometimes trimmed with fringe, but in general the materials were plain and sturdy. The strong Empire colors of yellow, green, red, purple, and blue were popular. Wallpaper in bold patterns and figured Brussels carpeting were used extensively.

Some authorities seem to look upon Biedermeier with an ill-concealed disdain because it was imitative of several styles and did not attain perfection in proportion or purity of line. Yet its

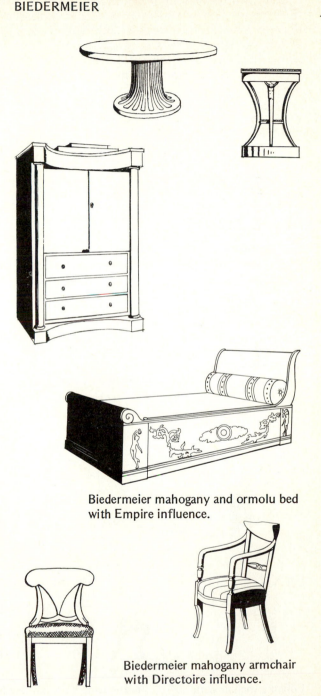

Biedermeier mahogany and ormolu bed with Empire influence.

Biedermeier mahogany armchair with Directoire influence.

Miscellaneous Styles

appeal for others is understandable, because it does express a down-to-earth feeling of comfort and simplicity. It mixes easily with several other styles, notably some of our contemporary designs. It seems to be the answer for those who would prefer the French Empire design in a simplified version.

Oriental

The term *Oriental* covers a vast geographical territory and a long period of time, and it would be impossible within the confines of this text to include an adequate analysis of the complex histories and philosophies of Eastern art. But neither may we overlook the Oriental styles, because they are of such importance today. We must, therefore, limit the discussion to a few significant points. The student should bear in mind that a more realistic approach would cover many different cultures over a broad period of time.

For our purposes we may divide the Orient into the Near East and the Far East. The troubled conditions in this part of the world make it difficult to identify areas by geographical boundaries, but India, Pakistan, Iran, and Israel compose most of the Near East, and China and Japan are considered the Far East.

The patterns used in all branches of Islamic arts have a wide range of origin and subject matter. The Mohammedans were divided into two sects. One, the Sunni, considered the use of living forms as motifs of ornamentation to be pagan idolatry. Their designs developed geometric patterns. The Shi'a doctrines account for the floral, animal, and human subject matter used in their design.

The art styles of the Eastern countries have always been characterized by great beauty and purity of design. Oriental artists have shown an amazing ability of expression in every medium, and the arts reflect the deep appreciation of Oriental culture for all facets of physical and spiritual life. Concepts based on religion, mysticism, and philosophy give the art an intellectual appeal. The imagination and spirit of the Oriental mind, combined with the excellence of expression and execution, lend tremendous emotional appeal.

The expert skills of the Oriental peoples have been evident in long, glorious histories of architecture, sculpture, painting, textiles, ceramics,

ORIENTAL

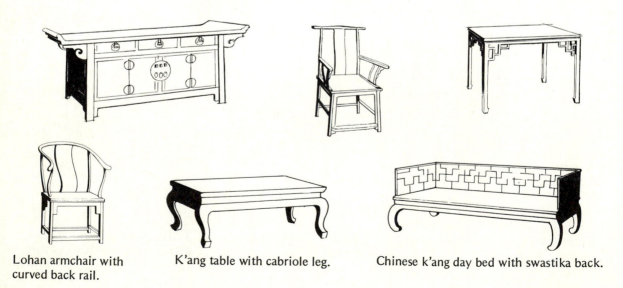

Lohan armchair with curved back rail.

K'ang table with cabriole leg.

Chinese k'ang day bed with swastika back.

A living–dining room completely decorated in the
Oriental style. *(Designed by Patricia Harvey, A.I.D.,
photo by Henry S. Fullerton)*

**Fig.
15.1**

and metalwork. In recent years we have also
come to appreciate more fully their excellence in
cabinetmaking.

Architects and interior designers have drawn
heavily from Oriental themes and concepts in
the past few years. Eastern influences on our
modern furniture are discussed in the section on
modern style. Yet apart from these influences
we have developed a deeper appreciation for
the intrinsic qualities of the Oriental styles. We
have not only drawn inspiration from them in
modern design, but we are adapting some of
their basic concepts to our way of living. Perhaps no other style of art is so successful in
combining the practical with the exotic. The
combination of functionalism and beauty, inherent characteristics of much Oriental art, sat-

isfies modern requirements and taste. For example, current trends in modern architecture show Islamic influences in façades using geometric patterns. Many of these are designed to let in light and air, at the same time protecting interiors from strong sunlight and visibility from outside.

The Western world is becoming more aware of the true art of China and Japan as a source of inspiration for interior design. Although references have been made to the Oriental "mania" in French and English styles of the eighteenth and nineteenth centuries, it must be pointed out here that these adaptations did not represent the true spirit of the Far East. By the time trade relations between the East and the West began to flourish, the art of China had reached a decadent level. Oriental merchants, only too eager to meet a demand for their wares, produced quantities of horrendous items that completely violated their artistic heritage. In the past few years we have had a somewhat analogous situation with the Japanese endeavor to build up native industry. They have been willing to apply their skills to the imitation of almost anything and everything, including German china and Venetian glass.

Chinese history dates back several thousand years before Christ, but the arts went through a period of active development during the Han dynasty (206 B.C.–220 A.D.). They flourished during the "golden age" of the Tang (618–906 A.D.) and Sung (960–1279) dynasties. Strength, vigor, and originality continued during the Ming dynasty (1368–1644), but during the Ching dynasty (1644–1912) art gradually became more imitative. The technical skills and craftsmanship were still superb, but there was a lack of the spontaneity and freshness that were characteristic of Chinese art during the high periods.

Students of Oriental culture have long recognized the fine talents of the Chinese in ceramics, textiles, carving, and lacquer work. It is only recently, however, that the excellence of Chinese cabinet work has been truly appreciated—partly, perhaps, because the Chinese themselves have never held the same regard for cabinetmaking that they have had for other crafts. Also, it is safe to assume that much of the finest furniture was destroyed during several turbulent periods when dynasties were overthrown and great palaces were destroyed.

In recent years some of the ancient tombs of China have been opened as a result of railroad construction. The custom of burying material objects with the dead is responsible for the discovery of numerous works of art. The furniture, household utensils, and decorative objects revealed in the tombs have enabled scholars to reconstruct ideas about ancient Chinese civilization.

At first mats and then low platforms were used in Chinese homes for sitting, eating, and sleeping. Stools and chairs were eventually introduced in most areas of China, but the Chinese adapted all furniture forms to their own distinctive way of life.

Some of the finest furniture was made during the fifteenth and sixteenth centuries during the Ming dynasty, when a classical simplicity pervaded all the arts. Pure and simple lines, restrained ornament, squared proportions, and elegant woods make this furniture refined and forceful. It is severe and formal, but it blends with many contemporary designs with amazing ease. The techniques of construction were superb. Unique methods of joinery dispensed with glue and dowels unless they were absolutely necessary, yet the furniture is sturdy and durable. Most of the woods have a beautiful satin finish that enhances the texture, color, and grain patterns. Metal decorations in hinges and handles were shaped to blend perfectly with the designs of the pieces. The luster of the metal, often an alloy of copper, zinc, and nickel, was always in perfect harmony with the wood finish. Large pieces of furniture were not generally lacquered, but stands made to hold exquisite sculptures and porcelains were frequently lacquered in red.

Ming furniture had a limited amount of carved detail. The Chinese are expert carvers, but during some periods excessive amounts of carved decoration detracted from the basic designs.

Decorative accessories included scrolls, paintings, jades, carved ivory figures, and beautiful porcelains. Richly embroidered silk cushions added to the exquisite blend of colors. All furniture and accessories were placed with a studied decorum that was both rigid and formal, but the Chinese interior reflects a high esteem for home and family life. Theirs is the gift of creating an atmosphere of simplicity with a note of elegance that is never pretentious.

During the seventh and eighth centuries, Japanese culture was in a formative stage and borrowed heavily from the Chinese. The practice of sitting on mats, or *tatami,* is still followed in Japan. It is the custom to remove one's shoes before stepping on the mats, which cover almost the entire floor. Almost every room has an *oshi-ire,* a built-in cabinet with sliding doors. Very little furniture is used in the Japanese home. There may be special cushions for guests to sit on and low tables of various shapes and sizes.

Ceramics and paintings decorate the Japanese interior. Of course, flowers play an important role in decoration, because flower arranging is a highly regarded art. Many schools of flower arrangement in Japan have developed skills in and appreciation of this form of art.

Italian

Although Italy was the scene of the archaeological discoveries that prompted the classical revival in the decorative arts, the Neoclassic style was fairly well established in France and England before it was widely adopted in Italy. The new style was accepted by the Italians with enthusiasm. The interiors of old palaces and villas were redecorated in the classical manner. Large quantities of furniture and decorative accessories were made to interpret the idea. Most of the designs were borrowed from the French and the English styles, but the Italians interpreted them with individuality. They used different techniques and materials, but they incorporated the architectural motifs and the graceful classical curves. Because walnut was plentiful in Italy, it was used to a greater extent. Caned panels were popular for chairs and settees. Some furniture was painted and decorated with

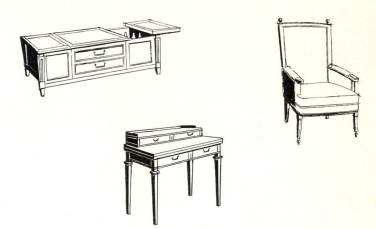

moderate amounts of gilt. Marquetry work was also used for decoration.

The Italians followed both the Directoire and the Empire styles, modifying them to suit their needs and tastes. The results were charming individual interpretations of the classical style, with a dash of the Italian spirit. The craftsmanship in Italy at this time was inferior to that in France and England, but local cabinetmakers did copy and modify the elaborate furniture used by the nobility and the wealthy classes in Venice, Rome, Milan, and Florence.

There is current interest in a mode referred to as "Italian Provincial." Many authorities object to the name because what we see today is not an authentic style but an adaptation of classic Italian furniture designed to meet popular tastes and the requirements of mass production. In the process of adapting the style, current designers have developed a type of furniture that retains a degree of elegance and refinement.

This furniture is somewhat severe in line, yet there is an element of dignity that seems to appeal to us today. It mixes easily with other designs of contemporary inspiration, and with our present eclectic trends this quality is important.

Miscellaneous Styles

Spanish

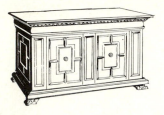

The style of Spanish Renaissance furniture was briefly discussed in Chapter 10. However, the interest in Spanish culture has given rise to a very popular mode that is sometimes referred to as "Spanish Provincial" or "Mediterranean." The latter term is becoming more widely accepted because the style is not pure, but a contemporary adaptation of designs from countries that were influenced by Spain many years ago. Just as "Spanish Provincial" is a misnomer, so is "Mediterranean," because the current mode includes characteristics that were found in both North and South America. At present, there is growing emphasis on some of the style's Mexican characteristics.

With little regard for authenticity, today's furniture designers have interpreted these designs to produce a style that blends well with hybrid architecture, modern decor, and the eclectic trend in furnishings.

Although the furniture is scaled to present-day needs, it is rectilinear in form and somewhat heavy in proportion. With emphasis on geometric design, grillwork, tile, mosaics, leather, and rich colors in sturdy fabrics, the style seems to meet a need to combine the new and the functional with a flavor of the exotic past.

When one arrives at the point of actually purchasing furniture, the natural question is "How do you judge quality?" Unfortunately there is no simple, easy answer. The problem of the consumer is complicated in this respect by several factors. It takes time and effort to acquire the background knowledge that is essential if money is to be spent wisely.

The wide variety of furniture that is available ranges in quality from poor to excellent. Many of the features that determine quality depend upon how the manufacturer selects and handles the materials. There are many things the consumer cannot see or judge when shopping for a piece of furniture. These features are often referred to as "hidden" values. For example, wood must be properly aged or seasoned before it is used. It is impossible to tell just by looking at a piece of furniture whether or not this seasoning process has been done under carefully controlled conditions. In upholstered furniture, it is particularly difficult to judge quality because the filling materials, framework, springs, and so on are completely obscured. Even if they could be seen, it would be difficult to determine whether or not the piece would really meet specific needs.

In addition, the labels that do exist or any that are required by law are of little help because they often state information that has no meaning to the consumer who is questioning serviceability, durability, and performance. Although many reliable stores try to maintain a sales staff that is both well informed and helpful, the word of the salesperson is not always the most reassuring basis on which to buy. In absence of written guarantees, the consumer who returns to complain about merchandise that has not proved satisfactory only too often finds that the glib-talking salesclerk is too busy with other customers to show much interest or concern. Once the furniture is in the home and used, one is at the mercy of the dealer and the manufacturer as to whether or not they will stand behind their product. Reliable merchants will do so because they want to maintain the good will of their customers. Call the Better Business Bureau in your city to find out the rating on the particular store you are visiting. Shop around and

16

Selection and Buying of Furniture

compare prices before purchasing a large piece of furniture.

Although good materials and high standards of workmanship are costly, price is not always an indication of excellent serviceability. Buying the most expensive item does not mean that it will measure up to one's needs.

In spite of all these complications, the intelligent consumer who is well fortified with basic information and who is willing to do some comparative shopping will soon learn to be discriminating.

General Points to Consider

Before any piece of furniture is actually purchased, there are certain points that need to be considered. These include:

Needs
Because a home is an extension of the self, it is necessary to understand needs or preferences before planning furnishings. Window shopping and talking with store decorators can help determine the styles and colors that are appealing to an individual.

Plan
The decorator's plan should include a general theme or type of furniture that is to be purchased. While establishing the plan for the room, consider the activities that will take place in the room. Once the floor plan is determined, make a list of the furniture needed as well as the order of purchase.

Design
The piece must harmonize with the other furnishings of the room. The lines, color, and texture should express the mood or theme of the room and blend well with all the other pieces.

Cost
Furniture is an investment; therefore, consider pieces that may be used in the dining room, later in the living room, and perhaps, with another move, in the bedroom. If the furniture will be used for several years, choose pieces that lend themselves to quick fabric or color changes.

The terms and conditions of a guarantee need to be discussed before purchasing the item. Also ask if the item is in stock; if not determine the delivery time. Often the selling price may not include delivering, uncrating, and setting up the piece.

Size
Measure the space where the furniture is to be placed. Carry these figures on paper, along with a tape measure, while shopping. The furniture should relate to the size of the room and the other furniture in the room. Furniture that is to be placed against the wall should be in proportion to the wall. Keep in mind that the piece may need to fit through the door or around a sharp turn in the hallway. Apartment dwellers may find that the size of the elevator creates a limit on furniture size. As homes continue to decrease in size, it is important to have furniture that fits together snugly or reduces size by folding, stacking, or nesting.

Cost of Maintenance
Cleaning, repairing, and general maintenance add to the cost of the furniture.

Function
How is the piece to be used, and will it serve the purposes for which it is intended? A lounge chair should be comfortable. A table that will be used next to a chair should be about the same level as the arm of the chair. A dining table should be a comfortable height for the people who use it. Coffee tables should be large enough to be useful for entertaining; storage units must be large enough to hold the items to be stored.

Furniture may be divided into two general categories:

1. Case goods, including chests, desks, tables, bookcases, and chairs that have no upholstered parts. Most of this type of furniture is made of wood, although other materials are becoming increasingly popular.
2. Upholstered pieces: sofas and chairs that are wholly or partially upholstered, and bedding.

Case Goods

There are specific features that might be considered when case goods are bought. Some of these can be readily seen by the consumer; others will require answers from the salesperson. Do not hesitate to ask questions about the parts of the furniture that cannot be examined.

Rigidity

One should place a hand firmly on a table or a chest of drawers and try to rock it back and forth. It should be sturdy enough to withstand firm pressure; any piece that wobbles is poorly constructed.

Unexposed Parts

The finishing on the underneath parts of a table or the back panel of a chest is often a clue to the manufacturer's standards. It is quite natural that these areas will not be of the same quality as the exposed parts, but they should be sanded smooth and stained to match the rest of the piece. The back panel of a chest of drawers should match the frame precisely and be fitted in place in an inconspicuous fashion. On poor-quality furniture, these unexposed areas may have little finishing; the wood may be rough and uneven; there may have been only a careless attempt to match the color; and the back panels are often uneven and only roughly nailed in position.

Construction

The style and quality of any particular piece will determine how many steps are necessary for its production from beginning to end. Naturally, the more labor involved, the higher the production costs, and these are always reflected in the retail price.

Furniture construction is a complicated process. It is unnecessary for the consumer to delve in detail into techniques, but there are a few points that should be discussed because they influence quality and cost.

Shaping. For whole pieces that will be made of solid wood or for some parts such as pedestals and legs, the lumber is cut to the desired size by saws. A plane may then be used to shape the edges. If no decorative effects are required, the next step may be sanding. Much of this can be done by machine, but some areas still require hand finishing.

Carving. Certain types of decorative cutting can also be done by machine, but the results are somewhat crude; machine carving is used on mass-produced inexpensive furniture only. For better qualities, the initial work may be done by machine, but hand labor is used for the finishing. Hand carving is found only on expensive furniture because the process is slow and laborious. It must be done by skilled craftsmen who are trained in the art.

Some carved effects are achieved by the use of a wood compound molded to the desired shape. The motif, often a beaded molding, is then glued in place on the piece of furniture.

Turning. Legs, posts, and bases may be shaped by a *turning lathe*, which cuts symmetrical indentations to form a design. The effect of a twisted rope is achieved when the block of wood is moved slowly along the cutting machine.

Fluting. Lengthwise grooves may be cut into posts, legs, and pedestals.

Reeding. The term *reeding* refers to a decorative process of applying parallel rows of beaded mountings that project from the surface. It is the opposite of fluting, and it too is used on legs and posts.

Joining. The various sections of a piece of furniture must be joined firmly and securely. Careful joinery is an art that is of utmost importance to the consumer, yet most of it is hidden from view in the finished piece. You must, therefore, rely on the word of the manufacturer that the piece has been joined with care and precision.

Nails, screws, and glue are also used to hold sections together at points of strain. Nails are the least desirable, but they are quick and cheap to use. Screws and bolts are more desirable when they are inconspicuous. They are fre-

(a) Details of a chair.

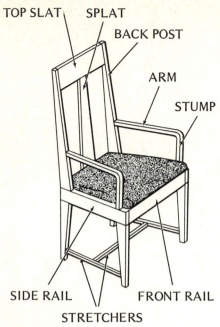

TOP SLAT   SPLAT

BACK POST

ARM

STUMP

SIDE RAIL   FRONT RAIL

STRETCHERS

(b) Types of joints.

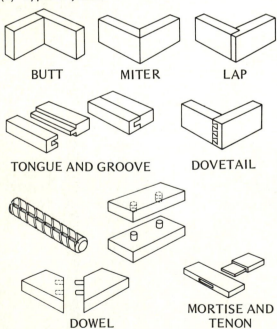

BUTT   MITER   LAP

TONGUE AND GROOVE   DOVETAIL

DOWEL   MORTISE AND TENON

Furniture Styles, Selection, and Room Arrangement

quently used for added security. A metal washer under the head prevents the screw from wearing away at the wood. Good-quality glue is also used to hold surfaces together. Old-fashioned glues would eventually dry out, but new developments have produced glues that are firm, durable bonding agents. They are resistant to the ordinary hazards of use, such as heat and moisture.

Various methods are used to join the frameworks of chairs, chests, tables, desks, and so on. On high-quality furniture the joinings are as near perfectly matched as possible, smooth and tight. One should beware of crevices and gaps that have been filled in with glue or other filler, which reflect a low standard of workmanship.

Butt.   A butt is a simple joining made by nailing or gluing two ends together. It will not withstand much strain.

Dovetail.   A series of projections fit into a series of grooves; the grooves are often fan-shaped. This is a secure joining that usually indicates good craftsmanship.

Dowel.   A small peg of wood is used to join two edges. The dowel pins are used for various types of joining on chairs, frames for upholstered pieces, and so on. Double dowels provide added stability. Sometimes the dowels are grooved so that air can escape when the dowels are driven into place.

Lap.   Two pieces have equal-sized grooves so that they are flush when placed together.

Miter.   Square corners are often mitered. Each edge is cut on a 45-degree angle and the two are held together with glue, nails, or brads. Mitering is used on moldings, picture frames, and so on.

Mortise and Tenon.   One of the strongest joinings for frames of chairs and other case goods is mortise and tenon. A groove (mortise) on one edge is cut to fit a projection (tenon) on the other edge. The projection and the groove may be square or triangular. Sometimes glue or screws are added for extra reinforcement.

Tongue and Groove.   A projection on one edge fits into a matching groove on the other edge. Used on drawer sections and wood panels used for wall coverings.

Corner blocks. Triangular pieces of wood are often used to support and reinforce the frames of tables, case goods, and seating pieces. They are screwed and glued into place to keep one side from pulling away from the other. Corner blocks are usually made of a different wood, stronger than that used in the exposed wood parts.

Drawers and doors. If the piece in question has drawers, they are frequently a good indication of the general level of workmanship.

The drawer should glide back and forth eas-ily. Those mounted on metal tracks often have wheels or ball bearings to ensure easy movement. A drawer-stop, or tiny lock on the back of the drawer, prevents it from pulling all the way out unless the lever is released.

The insides of the drawers on good-quality furniture are smoothly finished and treated with a coat of shellac or varnish. The top edges on the back and sides are rounded for smoother operation.

Drawer sections are joined by dovetailing on better-quality furniture. If the wood used in the drawer is of good quality, this is a secure method of construction. However, if the wood

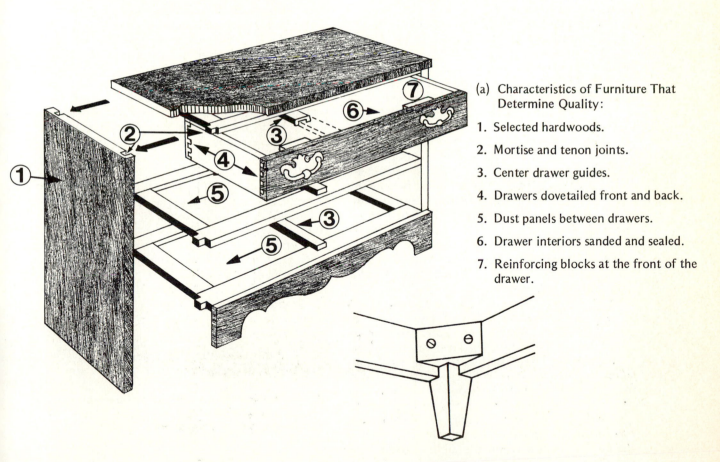

(a) Characteristics of Furniture That Determine Quality:

1. Selected hardwoods.

2. Mortise and tenon joints.

3. Center drawer guides.

4. Drawers dovetailed front and back.

5. Dust panels between drawers.

6. Drawer interiors sanded and sealed.

7. Reinforcing blocks at the front of the drawer.

(b) Screw-on Corner Block

is of poor quality, the tiny projections split away and the drawer will fall apart—another example of quality being dependent on a combination of good material and good craftsmanship.

Drawer pulls also offer some indication of quality. All handles and hardware on any piece of furniture should be in keeping with the design of the piece. They should be firm and substantial enough to withstand strain over a long period of time. Drawer handles should be fastened in place by screws or bolts that go through the drawer panel. On some inferior furniture the hardware is merely nailed in place on the exterior.

On many well-made pieces a panel of plywood or fiber board is used to separate the drawer areas. This *dust partition* may serve a useful purpose in adding some rigidity to the frame. It protects articles placed in the drawer and helps to prevent the jamming of one drawer by material in another drawer.

Glass Doors. Cabinets and breakfronts often have doors made with panes of glass set into a wood frame. On high-quality furniture, the door might be composed of a rather intricate latticework of wood with each piece of glass set in place as an individual section. This process, called *muntin* or *mullion,* is expensive, especially if the glass sections are curved or bent. Less expensive copies of such design often use one panel of glass with a wooden lattice or fret superimposed on it.

Hardware. Naturally the design of the handles and drawer pulls should be in keeping with the style of the piece. Well-made metal hardware is heavy and substantial.

The hinges on doors and drop-leaf tables should be carefully examined. They must be sturdy and firm. Screws are usually more desirable than nails for holding hardware in place.

Supports. Tables and desks that open out often require some sort of support for the surface. In the case of desks, wooden brackets that may be pulled out to support the writing surface are desirable. Extension tables should usually have some sort of extra legs or braces to support the center section when the table is used with several leaves.

Table tops. The joinery on the table top should be barely visible. The table leaves need to fit perfectly when inserted in the table. Some manufacturers will cut corners by using a poor quality of wood or finish on the extension leaves.

Cabinets. Open and close all the doors, making sure that they do not sag; check to see if the doors fit well. High-quality castors will enable case goods to pivot and roll easily.

Finishes

Manufacturers of fine-quality furniture take great pride in selecting materials. The surface of the wood is treated and polished to develop a beautiful color and patina—a mellowness or "glow" that comes from much rubbing and polishing. The grain pattern is carefully placed to enhance the design of the piece; sometimes panels are formed of matched sections to form an intricate design. On poor-quality furniture, the surface color and gloss may be applied in the cheapest and quickest manner possible, often a quick coat of varnish in which even the brush marks are evident. There is a hard shine rather than a subtle sheen.

The initial steps of finishing may be done by machine, but the final operations in high-quality furniture are usually done by hand. Several sandings and applications of stain develop a uniformity of color and bring out the beauty of the grain pattern. Some woods must have a "sealer" to close off the pores of the grain. Any special decorative effects, such as ebony finish or tortoiseshell, would be applied at this stage.

Wood finishes are applied for various reasons:

1. To produce or develop color.
2. To seal off the pores and produce a smooth, level surface.
3. To protect the wood from heat, moisture, alcohol, and so on.
4. To decorate the surface.

In fine finishing, several applications of

stain, glaze, oil, or wax require sanding or rubbing in between. As these processes are repeated a richness and depth of tone develops. Naturally, the number of operations affects retail costs, but high-quality finish must be applied in a series of processes and cannot be hurried.

Some manufacturers of fine furniture maintain that the lovely patina of the wood can be developed only by time-consuming hand methods and that machine polishing simply does not produce the same effects. They use hand rubbing of oil and wax finishes to produce sleek, satiny textures.

Distressing. Distressing is a process used to give an old look to new woods. The surface is beaten and dented with light chains and then rubbed to develop a patina.

Decoration

Those furniture styles that require some form of embellishment, such as inlay or stenciling, are naturally more expensive to produce than the plain, simple forms. Dollar for dollar, one can expect better quality in furniture that is unadorned. In the more elaborate styles, one should be sure to buy furniture that has such decorative details executed with a high degree of skill. There can be elegance in simplicity, but it is difficult to achieve elaborate elegance on a low budget.

Fine carving and inlay work are expensive modes of decoration, and they are rarely found in low-cost quality furniture. Cheap imitations that simulate such skillful craftsmanship are usually crude and unattractive. In addition, the work is done with poor-quality materials, which makes the situation worse. Here is one instance in which price is some indication of quality, and one can develop one's powers of discrimination by carefully examining furniture in all price ranges from very low to very high. In the more expensive types, the decorative detail will be more refined and more tastefully executed. The crudeness of the cheap imitations will soon become obvious.

Materials

Wood always has been and still is the favored material for furniture construction. However, metal, glass, plastic, and various fibers are also used, particularly for furniture in the modern style. Interesting effects are frequently achieved by the use of these various materials in combinations.

Wood. The advantages of wood far outweigh any disadvantages of its use as a medium for creating beautiful furniture. The wide variety of natural color is further increased by the ability of wood to take stains and bleaches. Lovely textures and grain patterns are enhanced by polishing, which develops the mellow glow or patina. Because wood can be carved, it lends itself to a range of decorative effects. When properly treated and handled, most wood is sturdy and durable. The difficulties that arise in the use of wood result from the fact that it absorbs and loses moisture, which sometimes causes warping and splitting if it has not been properly *seasoned*. This process consists of drying the wood after the tree has been cut and it must be done under carefully controlled conditions to ensure excellence of quality. Wood has great strength across the grain, but it is relatively weak along the grain, which accounts for the splitting of improperly handled wood. Modern methods of kiln drying have made it possible to control carefully the moisture content of wood; the problems of warping and splitting are reduced to a minimum when wood is properly treated.

Wood is composed mainly of cellulose in the form of long fibers or cells. The characteristics and arrangement of these fibers are responsible for such qualities as the ability of wood to hold nails and screws and the ability to absorb paints, stains, and lacquers. As new fibers are formed during the growth of the tree, the grain pattern of wood develops. Various species of woods have different types of fibers that affect the texture. Maple and birch have a fine grain; oak has a coarse or open grain. Mahogany and walnut have a medium grain.

Crotch

Quartered

Flat Cut

Stump Wood

Rotary

Burl

Fiber formation varies at different seasons of the year. A cross section of a tree trunk reveals the fibers arranged in annual rings or concentric circles. On some parts of the tree the fiber arrangement is distorted so that an interesting and unusual grain pattern develops. The familiar crotch figures occur at points where the trunk divides to form branches. Swirl patterns are often found just above the roots. Trees that form many small branches have knots that provide an interesting pattern, as does the familiar knotty pine. Abnormal growths on the tree trunk also produce unusual patterns. These growths, known as burls, are often responsible for beautifully figured grains. Other designs formed by fibers that have become twisted, curled, or wrinkled frequently have grain patterns that have lovely textural qualities.

Hardwood and Softwood. A very broad and general classification of furniture woods divides them into hard and soft, referring to a botanical difference rather than to any definite degree of hardness that separates the two categories. Hardwood trees have broad flat leaves that fall off after maturity. The softwood trees have needles or scalelike leaves that they retain all year; they are the evergreens. The two groups differ in cell structure, appearance, and general properties. Most hardwoods are stronger and less likely to dent than the softwoods; they also hold nails and screws more securely. But hardwoods vary considerably in degree of hardness. There are some, such as basswood, aspen, and poplar, that are actually softer than some of the so-called softwoods. Pine, spruce, hemlock, redwood, and cedar are all classified as softwoods. Another softwood—yew—is often as hard as or harder than, oak.

Labeling. In 1963, the Federal Trade Commission promulagated Trade Practice Rules for the Household Furniture Industry. False and misleading representations of the wood and the wood imitations used in furniture are prohibited. The rules also cover leather and leather imitations, the outer coverings and the stuffing of upholstered furniture, as well as certain practices such as deceptive pricing and bait advertising. With regard to wood, the rules are quite specific in defining the practices that are considered unfair or misleading.

In 1974, the F.T.C. put into effect a new set of guidelines for the industry, aimed at giving the shopper more information. Manufacturers must now disclose whether such materials as vinyl, other plastics, or marble dust are being used to give the appearance of leather, wood, or marble. Moreover, if one wood is mentioned, all exposed parts of the furniture must be made of that wood. The guidelines provide that if the surface is veneered, that fact must be indicated on the label.

The guidelines will eliminate the retail practice of removing manufacturer's tags and labels

(a) Growth Rings

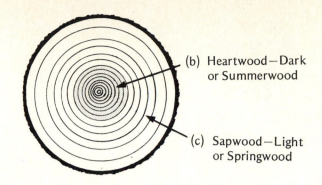

(b) Heartwood—Dark or Summerwood

(c) Sapwood—Light or Springwood

Knife

(d) Flat Cut or Plain Slicing

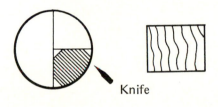

Knife

(e) The Quarter Cut

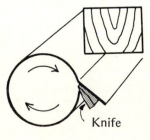

Knife

(f) Rotary Cut

(a) Growth rings. (b) Heartwood, dark or summerwood. (c) Sapwood, light or springwood. (d) Flat cut or plain slicing. The half log or flitch is moved up and down against the knife. Slicing is parallel to the center line. This procedure produces a variegated figure. (e) The quarter cut. The quartered log moves against the blade at right angles to growth rings, which produces a striped veneer pattern, straight in some woods and varied in others. (f) Rotary cut. The whole log revolves against the blade, peeling off a continuous sheet as wide as the log is long. Because this cut follows the log's annular growth rings, a bold variegated grain marking is produced.

Fig. 16.1

Selection and Buying of Furniture

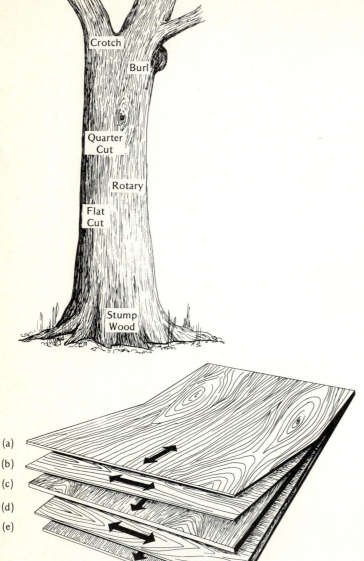

An Example of Five-Ply Veneer Construction:

(a) Face veneer.
(b) Crossband (usually poplar or gum).
(c) Core (lumber, chips).
(d) Crossband (poplar, etc.).
(e) Back veneer.

that disclose information about the construction and composition of the furniture. Furthermore, the name of a country associated with a particular style cannot be used if the furniture was not made there; for example, furniture in the Spanish style manufactured in the United States may not be referred to as "Spanish," but may be described as "Spanish design" or "Spanish style," furniture. However, commonly accepted terms, such as "French Provincial," "Chinese Chippendale," and "Italian Provincial," are permitted. In the future, the consumer will probably find more informative and more meaningful labels on furniture.

Terms. Labels will be of little help unless the terms are understood. The term *solid* means that all exposed wood is made of the wood named. The unexposed parts may be made of another wood, but a solid piece of furniture has no veneer. *Genuine* is a term usually meaning that all exposed parts are veneer.

Veneer refers to a thin slice of wood. Several layers of wood, usually three, five, or seven, are arranged with the lengthwise grain in alternate directions to form *plywood*. The top layer, or face veneer, is often cut from a log selected for beauty of grain, color, and texture; the other layers are made of good-quality wood that is strong and stable but less costly. The center layer, or core, is usually thicker than the others. All layers are glued together with synthetic resin that provides a very secure bond.

The principle of veneering dates back to ancient times. It was also used by the master cabinetmakers of the eighteenth century on exquisite tables and chests. Modern techniques provide plywood that is both stable and durable. Because of the plastic glues and alternating grains, plywood is equally strong lengthwise and crosswise and is therefore often more stable than solid wood. Plywood is used in much of the finest quality of furniture, both in the exposed parts and in the hidden areas. Rare and exotic woods are often used for the exposed surfaces.

Laminated wood is another type of plywood, in which all the layers are placed with the grain—that is, in the same direction. Another term used in the furniture industry is *particle* board. It is made by combining wood flakes, wood scraps, and chips that are heat pressed into sheets and often covered with veneer. Particle board is also known as hardboard and wallboard.

The term *combination* applies if more than one type of wood is used in the exposed parts of furniture. *All-wood construction* means that the parts of the wood exposed is the wood throughout the entire thickness of the piece. Here, manufacturers may save costs on materials by gluing a thin panel of wood to a wood frame, giving the outward appearance of thick wood. An all-wood panel sounds dead when the surface is tapped, whereas a panel on a frame echoes.

Popular Furniture Woods. The use of various woods goes through fashion cycles. At the present time we use a variety of woods, and the designers in the modern style seem to be especially perceptive in choosing colors, textures, and grains that become an integral part of the design. This bond between form and material in contemporary design has served to further strengthen and deepen our appreciation of the beautiful qualities of wood as a medium for fine furniture.

In addition, new techniques for handling wood as a decorative medium are making it even more versatile. It is possible to inject dye into the living tree to obtain interesting color effects in the grain pattern. A relatively new process with the trade name of Fineline produces most unusual textural effects. Sheets of veneer are laminated into a solid block of wood, which is then sliced at right angles to the layers. In this manner it is possible to produce veneers with vertically striped patterns. Countless variations may be produced by alteration of the order and the species of veneers when laying up the block. Different methods of cutting the block also allow for a wide variety of pattern.

Some of the popular furniture woods include the following:

ASH. There are several varieties of ash used in furniture construction, mostly in frames and on unexposed parts. White ash is a hard, strong, durable wood with a grain that resembles oak. The natural color ranges from white to a light brown. Some varieties have pronounced grain patterns, especially the Japanese ash, which is also known as *tamo*.

BIRCH. Another strong, versatile hardwood with a close, even texture comes from the yellow birch tree, also known as the silver or swamp birch. The general characteristics of birch are similar to those of maple. Its durable qualities and relatively low cost make it a popular choice for doors, floors, wood trim, plywood, and the structural parts of furniture.

The natural color of birch is a pale golden brown, but it can be bleached or stained to resemble other woods, including maple, walnut, and mahogany. Most birch has a straight grain, but some varieties have curly figures that are usually reserved for veneers.

Birch takes paints and stains extremely well and can be polished to a lovely glowing luster.

FRUITWOOD. Consumers seem to have the misconception that this term refers to a particular species, but actually there is no *one* fruitwood. Cherry, apple, and pear woods are the most commonly used fruitwoods. Other woods, such as birch and maple, are sometimes given a fruitwood finish. They are colored in the delicate brown tones associated with much of the French Provincial furniture that was actually made of fruitwood. They are also frequently given a distressing treatment to make them simulate old, used, and timeworn woods.

The wild black cherry tree is the most widely used of the fruit woods in present-day furniture construction. Cherry has been used for many centuries in various countries, but we probably associate it most closely with Early American and Colonial furniture. It is strong, durable, and moderately hard. Much cherry has a natural reddish-brown color, but tones vary to amber and to a light yellow that may be almost white. The close grain is suited to a variety of finishes, and although the grain markings are not as dramatic as in some other woods, they do provide textural interest. Cherry furniture is likely to be expensive because there is much waste in cutting the logs.

Both apple and pear are smooth woods that are fine-grained and light in color. They are rarely used today except for decorative trim and inlay work on fine furniture.

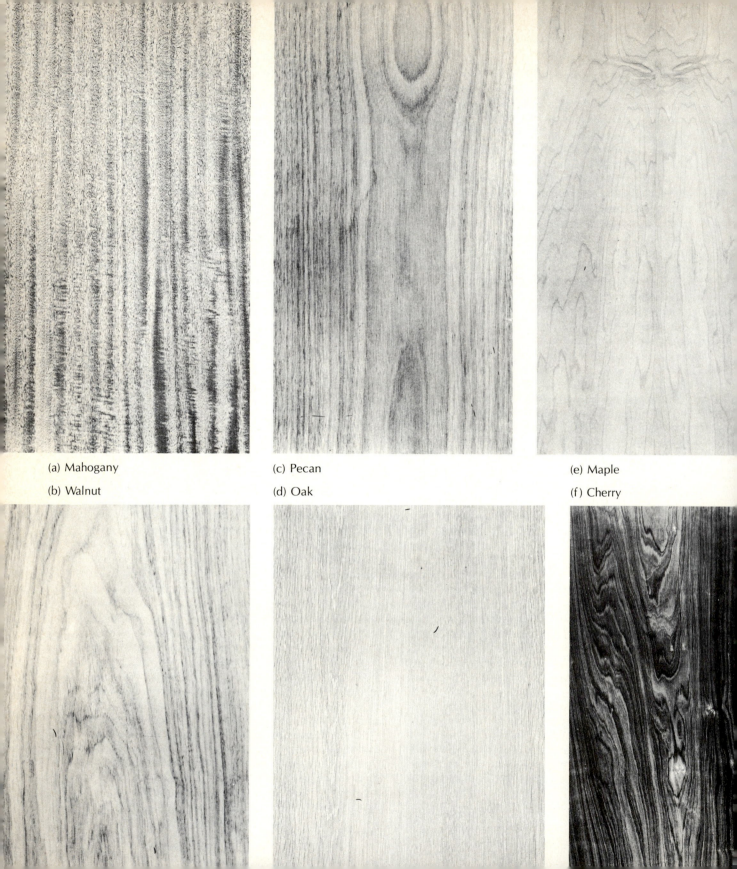

(a) Mahogany   (c) Pecan   (e) Maple

(b) Walnut   (d) Oak   (f) Cherry

(g) Rosewood

(h) Zebrawood

GUM. Since the development of new methods of drying lumber, red gum has become an important addition to the family of furniture woods. If not seasoned under carefully controlled conditions, gumwood has a tendency to split and warp. However, if properly handled it is quite satisfactory and it has several advantages. It is readily available and relatively inexpensive. It is easy to work, and the close, smooth grain takes finishes extremely well. Gumwood is often used for framework, posts, and legs that must be made of solid wood. It can be finished to closely resemble other woods, such as the walnut and mahogany that are used on veneered panels.

MAHOGANY. An excellent hardwood that is favored for fine furniture is mahogany. The best varieties grow in tropical regions of Central America, the West Indies, South America, and Africa. Other woods are similar to genuine mahogany but not botanically related to it: lauan, known also as Philippine mahogany, and primavera, known also as white mahogany, are both used for furniture, but they are not true mahogany.

The master cabinetmakers of the past often preferred to use mahogany because of its strength, its variety of beautiful grain figures, and its workability. It has a uniform texture that is adaptable to many interesting finishes. Natural mahogany varies in color from a light golden brown to a deeper tone with a red cast. The traditional use of mahogany developed the reddish tones through applications of stains and finishes. This deep, rich purple or red came to be accepted as the natural color of the wood. In modern use mahogany is frequently finished to enhance its natural light brown color, or it is bleached to an even lighter tone.

MAPLE. Although maple trees grow in many parts of the world, the sugar maple or rock maple of the northern United States was used so extensively for furniture during colonial times

Selection and Buying of Furniture

Table 16.1

Acacia Hardwood from Australia and Africa. Used in ancient times for ecclesiastical purposes; also used in inlay work.

Amaranth A fine-grained hardwood that develops a red or purple color with age and exposure to air. Used for decorative work and inlay. Imported from Central and South America.

Amboyna Wood from the East Indies. Characterized by rich brown color with burls or mottled patterns in tones of yellow, orange, and red.

Aspen The white poplar of Europe. Simple figured grain; polishes to a satiny texture with high lustre.

Avodire Gold or yellowish-white wood from western Africa. Grain is characterized by a rippled or mottled pattern in attractive designs.

Bamboo Treelike grass with woody stem that is smooth and lustrous. Yellowish tan in color. Characterized by knobby joints. Used for furniture and many decorative purposes.

Basswood Softwood with little or no figure. Used mostly for cores and for inexpensive furniture. Creamy white in color.

Beech A hard, strong wood that is dense in texture. Color ranges from white to slightly reddish tones. Must be carefully seasoned to prevent warping. Lends itself well to turning and polishing. Used in medium-priced furniture for frames, curved sections such as runners on rockers, drawer guides, and bent backs on chairs.

Cedar Various types that range in color from pale to dark reddish brown. Pleasant natural odor repels moth larvae. Used for lining closets, storage chests; also for shingles and sidings.

Chestnut Gray-brown wood with coarse, open grain similar to oak. Not particularly durable although it resists warping. Used for core stock and for some less expensive furniture.

Circassian walnut Highly figured wood from the Black Sea region. Brown color. Expensive. Used for paneling and furniture.

Cypress Light brown wood with close grain. Durable and extremely resistant to warping. Comes from southern and western states. Used for face veneers and for outdoor furniture.

Douglas fir A strong, durable, creamy white or yellow wood from western United States. Similar to pine. Used for paneling, structural parts (and for exposed parts on inexpensive furniture), and for plywood.

Ebony A hard, heavy wood from Africa and tropical Asia. Dark brown or almost black in color; fine grain and smooth texture takes a high polish.

Elm Strong and tough wood from Europe and parts of United States. Color ranges from light to dark reddish brown. Bends well, but it tends to warp and twist. Used for kitchen furniture, interior trim and frames, and decorative veneers.

Hackberry light Colored wood that takes finishes well. Similar to elm.

Harewood (English sycamore) A close, fine-grained wood often dyed a silver-gray color. Figured grain in fiddle design used for veneer work.

Hemlock Similar to white pine. Lightweight and easy to work. Not used extensively for finishing.

Hickory Tough, heavy, and hard. Tree belongs to the walnut family. Not used extensively.

Holly Fine grain. Light in color, sometimes almost white. Used with other woods for marquetry.

Kingwood Used in fine cabinet work because of dark brown color with streaks of black and yellow. Comes from South America and Sumatra.

Koa Figured wood that ranges from a medium tone of golden brown to dark shades. Comes from Hawaii and was formerly called Hawaiian mahogany.

Korina Light-colored wood from the Congo. Available in plain or figured grain patterns. Similar to Primavera.

Lacewood Durable wood from Australia. Polishes to high luster. Ranges in color from pinkish to light brown tones.

Laurel Highly figured with wavy grain pattern. Dark reddish-brown color can be bleached to lighter tones. Takes a high polish. Comes from India.

Limba Another name for *Korina*.

Linden Another name for *Basswood*.

Magnolia Similar to yellow poplar, but harder and heavier. Smooth, fine grain that sometimes has a slight figure.

Makore African cherry. Similar to cherry.

Myrtle Usually light in color with a curly grain pattern. used for veneers and panels. Comes from western United States.

Paldao Ranges in color from grayish to reddish brown. Interesting patterns. Comes from Philippines.

Poplar Several types that grow in eastern and southern United States range in color from white through yellow to light brown. Yellow poplar also known as whitewood. Easy to work, lightweight; takes especially well to paints and finishes.

Primavera Light-colored wood with lovely grain pattern. Comes from Mexico. Sometimes called white mahogany. Takes well to high polish.

Purpleheart Same as *Amaranth*.

Rattan A vine rather than a wood. Used extensively for wicker furniture. Comes from Asia.

Redwood Durable, strong, and lightweight. Attractive red color. Resists weather and insects. Used extensively in the United States for outdoor furniture and some indoor work.

Sandalwood Close grain; yellow-brown, fragrant wood. Used in Oriental furniture and woodwork.

Satinwood Light-colored with lovely texture and grain pattern. Used in inlay work and border designs. Comes from India and West Indies.

Spruce Strong, lightweight wood; holds glue well. Sometimes used for core stock.

Sycamore Color reddish to red brown; may have interesting grain pattern. Dense and hard but some tendency to warp. Comes from eastern United States and England.

Tulipwood Light yellow streaked with red or purple stripes. Used for ornamental work.

Tupelo (Black Gum) Easily worked and may have intricate grain pattern. Tends to warp. Used for same purposes as other gumwoods.

Willow Rather soft wood not used extensively for solid construction. Flexible branches often used for wicker furniture.

Yew Hard and durable; close grained. European evergreen.

Zebrawood Characterized by brown or black stripes on light yellow background. Used mostly for ornamental work.

---

that its color and texture are closely associated with the style of that era. The close-grained wood is hard, strong, and durable. It resists splitting and is easy to shape. The fine texture takes a beautiful, smooth finish, and the color ranges from almost white to a reddish brown.

Although most of the maple used in modern and Colonial-style furniture has a plain, straight grain, some varieties yield a curly, wavy grain figure that is on a par with other woods prized for lovely designs. Bird's-eye maple is quite rare, but it has an interesting grain pattern caused by an abnormal growth of buds that could not get through the bark of the tree. The resulting distortion of the annual rings produces a very interesting design in the wood.

OAK. Many species of oak trees are found in North America, Asia, Europe, and Africa. About fifty varieties of oak are native to the United States, but the best known are white oak and red oak. The natural color ranges from a light yellow to amber-brown.

Oak is characterized by a coarse, open grain, which is particularly suited to various color effects and special finishes. A filler is sometimes rubbed into the wood to emphasize the coarse grain. This limed oak has enjoyed periods of considerable popularity in modern furniture.

The hard, durable qualities of oak plus its resistance to the vagaries of climate have resulted in its wide use for paneling and flooring as well as for furniture. From medieval times, with elaborate methods of hand carving, to the modern era, with machine methods, the sturdy, versatile oak has appealed to craftsmen.

PECAN. Increasing in popularity is pecan, a strong wood that is dense and hard. It is readily available in America but the seasoning requires special skill. The texture, grain, and natural light color of pecan lend themselves with excellent results to a variety of stains and finishes.

PINE. Because pine is a softwood, its uses are not extensive in furniture construction. It is found in unpainted furniture, rustic designs, and some inexpensive cabinetwork. It is used on paneled walls.

ROSEWOOD. Rosewood, an interesting wood, ranges in color from light to dark reddish brown. Various species come from India and Brazil. It is often figured with dark streaks that provide an interesting pattern. Rosewood polishes well and is popular for use in fine furniture and paneling.

TEAK. Furniture designers working in the modern style have favored teak, a wood native to India, Burma, and the surrounding areas. It is dense, durable, moderately hard, and easily worked. The natural color ranges from a light to a dark brown with fine black streaks. The wood darkens with age but it is often finished in a deep brown tone that is almost black. Some teak has a richly figured grain pattern, but most of it is plain.

WALNUT. Ever since the Renaissance, walnut has been an important wood for both furniture and interior architectural designs, because of its great beauty and its practical characteristics.

The various species of walnut differ in color, so that a range of tones is available. The native American walnut, or black walnut, is so named because of the color of the nut shells. The wood ranges from light to dark in rich grayish-brown tones. Butternut, another native American wood, is lighter in color and is often called white walnut. Circassian walnut, from the regions near the Black Sea, is a rich brown color. Its dramatic curly grain makes it ideal for decorative effects, but it is very rare and therefore expensive.

The American walnuts produce a wide variety of beautiful grain patterns. Crotch, burl, and stumpwood are all popular figures.

The wood is hard but not so hard that it cannot be worked easily. It has a natural resistance to shrinking and warping. Its high strength lends it to slim, tapered legs and other parts that must withstand strain. The medium grain is excellent for holding glue and it readily takes a wide variety of finishes, particularly the currently popular oiled finish.

Other woods used in furniture to a lesser extent are listed in Table 16.1 (pp. 256–57). Some of these are rare, exotic woods, used chiefly for decorative purposes; others are less expensive but for one reason or another have not achieved major importance in the furniture industry.

Other materials. Although wood is still by far the favored material for furniture, other materials are becoming increasingly popular, especially in modern designs. Metals, plastics, and glass are favorites; caning is also used for panels and chair seats. Frequently these materials are combined with wood.

Metals. Brass, steel, and wrought iron are all used for legs, frames, and trim on various types of furniture. Copper and aluminum also find favor for certain designs.

(a) A series of molds is necessary to produce simulated wood components.

Metal has a number of advantages as a furniture material. It is strong and durable; it is suitable for indoor and outdoor use; it can be easily molded and shaped. Joining by bolts, rivets, or welding is secure and sturdy. Aluminum outdoor furniture has been extremely popular because it withstands weather conditions; it is easily washed with soap, and it is light in weight. However, surface finishes on metals will sometimes wear off and occasionally they are difficult to repair or replace.

Construction problems with metal are minimal, but the furniture needs to be checked for sturdiness. A piece of furniture should stand level on the floor. The surface areas should be polished smooth and be free of any sharp burrs or bits of metal.

Brass and brass finishes combine beautifully with interesting wood grains. The color and texture of this metal have appealed to designers in the modern style.

Plastics. Synthetics have become a vital part of the home furnishings field in many areas, including the actual construction of furniture. Molded chairs represent for modern design a

(b) Wide design latitudes are possible with the new application of plastics. Chair backs are made of molded polymer.

(c) Testing in a research laboratory indicates high strength of molded components.

Molded components represent a new concept in furniture construction. *(Courtesy of Shell Chemical Company)*

Fig. 16.3

(d) Door panels molded of polymer indicate the versatility of this new technique.

complete break with traditional methods. Sturdy, durable, light in weight, interesting in texture, easily maintained, and relatively inexpensive, the plastics would seem to qualify for a major role in furniture construction. And so they have.

Plastics freed furniture forms from the rigid right angles of conventional construction. Now we see fluid furniture forms, sculptural shapes in hard, smooth plastic or soft polyurethane foam. In plastics color is intrinsic and will not wear or chip off. Plastics are durable, but not all plastics are unbreakable. If enough pressure is applied, plastics may crack or chip.

In previous chapters we have referred to periods such as the "age of walnut," the "age of mahogany." It is quite possible that in the future the twentieth century will be referred to as the "age of plastics" or the "age of the molecule." In Chapter 14 we discussed some of the plastics in connection with the modern style. They are becoming increasingly important in producing molded components and laminated surfaces for other styles as well. That the practical aspects of a surface impervious to moisture, resistant to heat, and easily cleaned with soap and water should appeal to a busy person is understandable. There are numerous pieces that are made with wood as the basic material but finished off with a matching laminated surface to make it more serviceable and easier to maintain.

In a rather short period of time, man-made substances have permeated almost every phase of living, including medicine, construction, transportation, agriculture, and textiles. In spite of the impact that has been made, the plastics industry is still in a stage of infancy. It is difficult to imagine the innovations that will certainly influence our homes in the future; but as one representative phrased it, "the best is yet to come."

Glass. For many years, the top surfaces of tables and chests were protected with glass, but the idea of a protective glass top has become rather old-fashioned. Glass has instead branched out into a more glamorous role in home furnishings. Thick plates of glass are used as tops for dining tables designed for both outdoor and indoor use.

Upholstered Furniture and Bedding

So much of the quality of any upholstered piece is hidden under the covering that it is extremely difficult for the consumer to judge value. There are some features that one can observe and test very carefully, but for the most part one must rely on the word of the dealer and the small amount of information that is found on labels. This is certainly a case where the consumer should have confidence in both the dealer and the manufacturer before investing any money.

Chairs and Sofas

Just as in the matter of case goods, the design of an upholstered chair or sofa must blend into the theme of the room and harmonize with other furnishings. The problem of slipcovering and reupholstering should also be considered. Slipcovers on upholstered furniture not only protect the fabric covering but give a change of pace. As a matter of fact, some people prefer to buy furniture upholstered in muslin and keep two (or more) sets of slipcovers so they can change the color scheme for different seasons of the year. A removable slipcover reduces the problem of care, because it is easier to wash or dry clean a cover than the actual upholstery. Although this is a matter of personal preference, furniture with simple, straight lines is easier and less expensive to cover or to reupholster. Intricate curves such as might be found in fan-back or tub chairs are difficult to fit with slipcovers. Upholstery that is tufted and held with buttons is usually more expensive to replace.

Some modern furniture has been designed with these problems in mind. The "upholstery" is really separate cushions, which are especially easy to recover. Covers on cushions designed with zippers and snaps can be removed for cleaning or replacing. However, some cushions have covers that are not to be removed. The salesperson or the label may provide this information.

Certain other specific points should be checked before the purchase of any upholstered pieces. These would include the following considerations.

Comfort. We depend on upholstered pieces in our home for comfortable sitting and sleeping. It would be foolish, naturally, to buy a chair or a sofa without considering the people who will be using it most. A seat that slants a bit toward the back is usually more comfortable, but again this is a matter of personal preference. Some chairs that are very deep are uncomfortable for short people, whereas others that are too shallow are uncomfortable for tall people. Adequate support for legs, hips, and shoulders is necessary. The height, width, and slant of the seat and back should be tested carefully. The height of the arms will also affect comfort. One should try sitting in chairs and sofas with high sides, compare them with others that have lower arms or no arms at all, and then make a choice in terms of the purpose the piece will have to serve.

The firmness or softness of upholstery is another feature that must be considered for comfort. This too is a matter of personal choice.

Exposed parts of frame. If a piece has legs or a frame that is not covered, the finish should be examined very carefully. The workmanship here may be some indication of inside quality. Wood should have an even color tone and a rich texture. Carving or ornamental work should be refined and smooth.

Welting. A cording or welting is frequently used in the seams of upholstery for added strength and durability as well as for appearance. High-quality upholstery will have welting that is made from a solid piece of fabric with very few seams, and it will be neatly fitted at the corners.

Seams. The construction lines that are evident on the exterior should be firm, smooth, and even. The corners of the arms and backs need to be smooth, not bunched up. A firm clean finish with no projecting thread ends, bumps, or puckers is another sign of good workmanship.

Covering. It may be necessary to purchase a piece covered as it is, but more often the consumer will have a choice of upholstery fabric. If the sample swatches are small, it is not always easy to visualize the whole piece in its finished form, so one must be very careful about color, texture, and pattern. The chair or sofa may take on a completely different appearance when covered in another fabric.

Pieces that will receive hard use should of course be covered with a fabric that resists both soil and wear. Closely woven fabric in a medium color tone is a good choice for pieces that will receive hard wear. In many areas of the home, plastic upholstery fabrics are becoming popular. The newer elegant styling of these easy-care coverings has increased their versatility and made them more generally acceptable. However, in some areas the warmer texture of the more traditional upholstery fabrics may be preferable.

Construction. It is important to know something about the way upholstered furniture is made so that it is possible to ask questions about any pieces being considered. The quality features concealed within the piece determine serviceability, durability, and comfort.

Framework. The basic frame of an upholstered piece must be carefully designed and constructed to withstand stress and strain over a long period of time. A hardwood that is free from imperfections and that has been kiln dried is most desirable. Ash, birch, maple, oak, and gumwood are commonly used. The frame must hold nails and screws securely; any wood that is soft or improperly seasoned will not be satisfactory in this respect.

The joints on good-quality frames are usually double-dowel constructions that employ kiln-dried, grooved pegs. Corners should be reinforced with triangular blocks carefully fitted and fastened with glue and screws. Metal plates are sometimes used for strengthening corners.

The legs and back of the frame need to be made of one piece. If they are separate pieces, one of the better joints should be used: four screw-on legs can become wobbly with use.

Webbing. On most chairs and sofas, bands of webbing are closely interlaced and tacked to the frame. Woven jute is commonly used because it is strong, durable, and resilient. A steel and plastic combination is also used for webbing,

261

Selection and Buying of Furniture

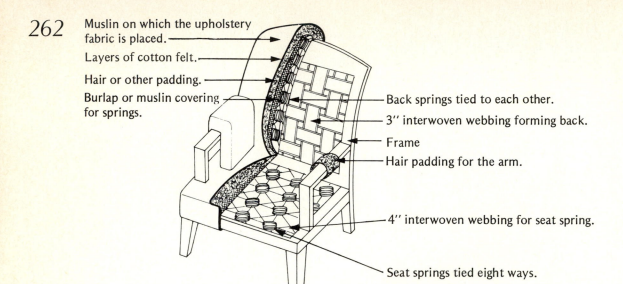

Muslin on which the upholstery fabric is placed.

Layers of cotton felt.

Hair or other padding.

Burlap or muslin covering for springs.

Back springs tied to each other.

3" interwoven webbing forming back.

Frame

Hair padding for the arm.

4" interwoven webbing for seat spring.

Seat springs tied eight ways.

Fig. 16.4

(a)

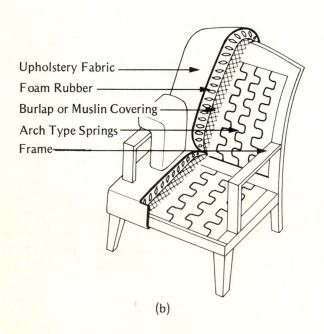

Upholstery Fabric

Foam Rubber

Burlap or Muslin Covering

Arch Type Springs

Frame

(b)

(a) The detailed construction of a quality upholstered seat. *(b)* The detailed construction of an inexpensive but upholstered seat.

and in some constructions plain steel bands form the base.

Springs. The coil springs in better-quality furniture are made of tempered steel and are placed close together. Twelve coils for each seat area is best; there should be no less than eight. In high-quality construction the springs are tied in place with a good grade of twine. Proper tying is important in keeping the springs firmly in place and in providing the correct degree of resiliency. It is desirable to have each spring hand-tied eight times. The coils are anchored to the webbing or to steel bands. In some high-quality pieces, the springs are covered with a muslin jacket. Then a piece of good-quality strong fabric is stretched over the springs and tacked to the frame. Heavy burlap is frequently used to support the filling material.

It may not be possible to use eight-way hand-tied construction in some of the new, lower, upholstered furniture styles that are designed with a minimum of seat thickness. But some of the comfort without the cost of the eight-way hand-tied construction can be gained by using Perelli webbing.

Perelli webbing is an elastic material made of latex interfaced with reinforcing cords to restrict the amount of elongation. The webbing is stapled to the back rail of the piece of furniture and then stretched over the front rail to the point where the webbing has been elongated approximately 15 per cent. This provides the proper tension. Then it is stapled to the front rail and cut off at this point. Any material that the furniture manufacturer desires, such as polyurethane and polyester in combination or a prefabricated seat pad of polyester fibers bonded together with a resin material, can be used over the Perelli webbing.

In some of the smaller-scaled upholstered pieces, flat springs of zigzag strips of steel are used instead of coil springs. These springs do not require the support of webbing, nor do they have to be tied.

Filling. The material used for upholstery filling is as important as the way the piece is constructed. Well-made furniture will have an ample amount of filling selected and applied so that the piece will retain its shape for a long period of time. Poor quality and workmanship will be evident after a relatively short period of use. The filling will shift, mat, and lump to distort the shape of the piece in a most unattractive manner.

Various filling materials are used for upholstered work, sometimes in combinations. Descriptive information about the filling used should be on a label permanently attached to the piece, but these labels usually do not indicate the grade or quality, which may vary considerably for each type.

Foam rubber has become a popular filling material. It is durable, comfortable, and resilient. It retains its shape and is lightweight. Foam rubber may be used as a layer over a spring construction or it may be used alone.

Urethane foam is a test-tube product that has become popular as a filling material. It is resilient and lightweight, and impervious to water, perspiration, and cleaning fluids. Slabs of urethane may be sliced, cut, stitched, or glued. Because of its high tensile strength, urethane may be stretched around furniture frames without tearing. Its lightness is a desirable feature for mattresses. A twin-sized mattress of urethane foam weighs about eleven pounds as compared to thirty-five pounds for an innerspring mattress.

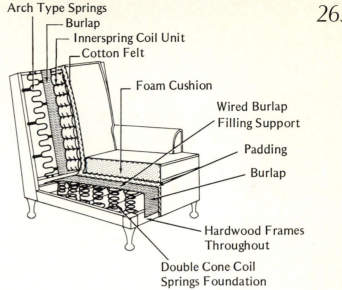

Arch Type Springs
Burlap
Innerspring Coil Unit
Cotton Felt
Foam Cushion
Wired Burlap
Filling Support
Padding
Burlap
Hardwood Frames Throughout
Double Cone Coil Springs Foundation

An upholstered chair may have various types of springs and filling materials.

Fig. 16.5

Polyester is a popular filling material. It may be used by itself or with foam cores or innerspring constructions. It is resilient, lightweight, odorless, and resistant to moths and mildew.

Rubberized hair or rubberized sisal may be used in medium- and low-cost furniture. The mixture is vulcanized and molded so that it has a fair degree of resiliency.

Cotton felt is sometimes used as a protective covering over springs and other filling materials. On medium- and low-priced furniture, cotton felt is often used without another more resilient filling.

Moss and shredded fibers are also used in furniture. Palm leaves, coconut husks, and sisal have some degree of resiliency but are usually found only in less expensive pieces.

The filling material is distributed over the surface of the chair. If the standards of workmanship are high, it is packed firmly and held in place to prevent lumping and shifting. This may be done by securing it to a layer of supporting burlap and placing a covering of cotton felt,

Fig. 16.6

Another concept in construction is demonstrated here. Wide bands of black webbing on chrome-plated tubular seat and back frames are used by George Mulhauser to integrate construction and design. *(Courtesy of Directional Industries, Inc.)*

foam rubber, or rubberized sisal over the filling at the top. On less expensive furniture, the upholstery fabric is the next layer; on better-quality furniture, a firm muslin is used to hold the filling in place and to serve as an interlining for the actual upholstery fabric.

Tufting and Buttons. Sometimes the filling and the upholstery fabric are secured by decorative stitching or by buttons. There are advantages and disadvantages to this type of upholstering. The chief advantage is that the filling is less apt to shift out of position. If well done, it may add interest to the piece. However, it is more costly in the initial construction and also more expensive to reupholster when the piece needs recovering. If it is not used with discretion, the furniture may have a gingerbread appearance. Also, this type of upholstered piece is more difficult to keep clean because dust collects in the crevices.

Separate Cushions. Seats and sometimes backs may have separate cushions. When these are reversible, the wear can be distributed. Such chairs and sofas often seem more comfortable than those having "tight" construction in upholstery (without separate cushions).

The consumer is often given a choice of filling for cushions. Down, foam rubber, or spring constructions are used on better-quality furniture; inexpensive varieties may use cotton batting, cotton felt, kapok, or other fibers, all of which tend to become lumpy.

Down, the soft underfeathers of a goose or duck, provides a soft, luxurious filling. For added body, chopped feathers are mixed with the down. A fifty-fifty combination is commonly used. Seventy-five per cent down is softer and more expensive; less than 25 per cent down has little value so far as comfort is concerned. Many people prefer the luxurious comfort of down cushions, which have the disadvantage of having to be plumped up every time one sits on them. They depress and stay that way until fluffed up again.

Foam rubber cushions require no plumping, but the fabric covering must be firmly woven. Otherwise the covering will lose its shape and wrinkle on the cushion.

Some cushions are made with a spring construction covered with a layer of cotton felt or foam rubber. These are stable and comfortable, although they do not have the soft luxury of down cushions.

One of the newer fire-retardant cushion designs starts with a polyurethane (a synthetic resin simulating foam rubber) core; then the outer edges of a batted layer of polyester are glued to this core. Instead of the traditional muslin cover for the filled cushion, a nonwoven fabric cover of synthetic material is used.

Other fillings for separate cushions include cotton, kapok, flax tow, or other fibers. None of these has the required resiliency for cushions that receive much use. They are found mostly on inexpensive furniture.

Mattresses and Bedsprings

Good beds are such a major item in furnishing a home that they should be selected with special care. Bargains are likely to be dangerous, because mattresses with poor construction and low-quality filling may begin to sag or become lumpy after a few months of use.

There is a wide variety of beds available in different sizes. However, longer and wider beds are becoming more popular. They may present problems in transporting them up stairs or around corners. A king-size mattress may not fold without breaking or bending the metal coils.

265

Of three types of coil construction tested, two proved consistently more durable than the other—the pocketed coil *(upper left),* and the open-end coil *(right).* The least durable type, the knotted-end coil, is shown at lower left. *(Courtesy of Consumers Union of U.S., Inc.)*

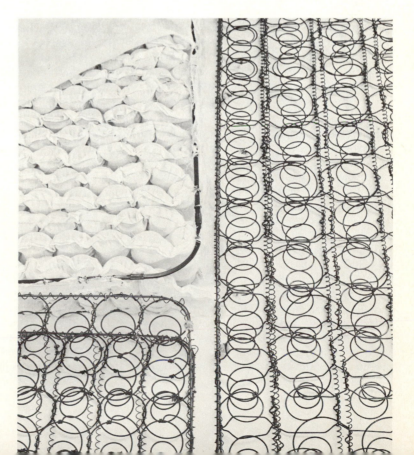

Fig. 16.7

Table 16.2

Beds

Bunk Two beds in a framework in which one bed is directly above the other.

Canopy A drapery or hood decorates the head of the bed. It may be supported on posts or mounted on the wall or ceiling.

Cot A small-scaled narrow bed.

Daybed Various couches. Usually they have two ends of equal height and identical design.

Fourposter Elongated corner posts at each corner of the bed.

Hi-riser A single couch with an under section that can be pulled out and raised to form an extra bed. A latter-day version of the old colonial trundle bed.

Hollywood A mattress and box spring supported on four or six legs. May be used with or without a headboard.

Sleigh The headboard and footboard of the bed curve outward to resemble an old-fashioned sleigh.

Sofa Various sofas that convert into beds. Some pull out from under the seat section; others allow for the back of the sofa to drop down (jackknife).

Spool Posts and spindles of headboard and footboard are turned in a spool design.

Studio couch A couch with loose pillows that rest against a wall. Some form single beds, whereas others can be converted into double beds.

Tester (field bed) A canopy or ruffled valance is supported on four posts to cover the top.

Cabinets, Chests, and Dressers

Armoire Tall cupboard that may be used as a wardrobe or storage chest.

Bachelor Low chest of drawers with small proportions. Top may extend to form a table, or top "drawer" may open to form a desk.

Bookcase Any cabinet designed to hold books; may or may not have glass doors.

Breakfront Tall unit that usually has glass-enclosed shelves on top of drawer cabinet below. Center section usually protrudes from side sections.

Buffet A piece of dining furniture set against a wall to hold food and serving dishes. Originally a fifteenth-century Italian cupboard, but it has developed during the seventeenth and eighteenth centuries into different pieces of furniture and now may be a sideboard, dresser or a simple contemporary storage piece.

Bureau A word that changes meaning according to the country or century. Originally, *bureau* referred to the cover used to protect a table when letters were written. To Sheraton, a bureau was what we call a secretary. In the United States today, a bedroom chest of drawers is commonly called a bureau.

Campaign chest A portable chest of drawers with brass-bound corners and handles at either side that developed in the late eighteenth century to store the gear of officers in the British colonies. The chests were made as both single and stacking units, and the upper portion of a campaign chest was often fitted as a writing desk.

Captain's Sturdy wooden chest with hardware recessed so that surfaces are smooth.

Cassone A large Italian chest decorated with paint, inlays, or carving.

Cedar chest Long, low chest made entirely of cedar or lined with cedar for storage of household items with protection against moth damage.

Cellarette Chest designed for storage of bottles and glasses.

Chest-on-chest American name for the English tallboy, a piggyback combination of the two chests of similar design, with one resting on top of the other. The upper chest is slightly narrower, with a row of smaller drawers over three or four long, graduated drawers. The lower chest usually has three or four long drawers and bracket feet.

Chiffonier Tall chest of drawers.

Chifforobe Combination chest of drawers and wardrobe unit.

China closet Cabinet designed for display of china or glasses. Usually has glass front and sides.

Commode Low cabinet with drawers and compartments. May be used against a wall or as an end table.

Corner Any cabinet designed with a triangular back so that it can stand in a corner.

Court cupboard The word *court* means to show off or to display. It was a seventeenth century sideboard with an enclosed cabinet above for storage and often an open shelf below for the display of plates and pottery vessels.

Credenza A cabinet that usually combines shelves and doors for storage. It was originally intended for use in the dining room but is now frequently used in the living room, library or hall.

Curio Cabinet with glass doors and sides for displaying various types of collections.

Dower Painted dower chests, characteristic of German settlements in Pennsylvania, are traditional American interpretations of designs originating in the Germanic areas of Europe. They were storage chests for the bride's household linens.

Dresser Chest of drawers usually designed for use in a bedroom.

Etagere Series of open shelves, supported by posts or columns.

Hadley chest Early type of New England chest with hinged top and short legs, with one to three drawers. The chest was crudely carved in simple floral designs, often with the owner's initials on the center panel. Hadley chests were made in and around Hadley, Massachusetts, between 1675 and 1740.

Highboy (sometimes called **Tallboy**) A tall chest of drawers mounted on legs that make an important part of the design. Usually crowned with cornice moldings or a pediment.

Hutch A tall cupboard or sideboard that usually has open shelves on the top section and cabinets below.

Kas Cabinet of Dutch origin. May be tall or short with compartments and drawers for storage. Sturdy, generous proportions with carved or painted decorations.

Lowboy Low chest or table with drawers.

Room divider Various types of shelves and cabinets designed to separate one area from another.

Sideboard Long, low cabinet designed to be placed against a wall. May have drawers, compartments, or a combination of both.

Wall-hung units Shelves and cabinets fastened to a wall with brackets.

Wardrobe Free-standing cabinet made for storage of clothes.

Welsh dresser A side table or provincial dresser with enclosed cupboard, drawers and a ceiling-high, shelved upper structure above. Generally in oak and a traditional form in rural England from the 1600s, but associated in America with the Welsh settlers in Pennsylvania.

Whatnot Series of shelves designed for display of bric-a-brac. May hang on the wall or stand against a wall. Corner units often have graduated shelves.

Chairs

Banister-back A back made of spindles, half spindles or similar uprights, found on seventeenth century English and American chairs.

Barrel or tub Chair with circular back, usually upholstered.

Bench Seat with no back; may or may not have arms. During medieval times, chairs were relatively rare, and benches were the principal form of seating.

Bergère (pronounced bear-ZHEHR) An upholstered armchair with closed, upholstered sides perfected in France during the eighteenth century. It usually has a loose seat cushion.

Boston rocker Characterized by wide, decorated top rail and curved seat. Often painted black with gilt design. Evolved from Windsor chair.

Boudoir Small-scale upholstered chair designed for use in bedroom.

Captain's A type of Windsor chair with high legs and a low, round spindle back. The captains of the nineteenth century steamers found the chair to be a sturdy support while on the bridge or in the wheelhouse.

Chair-table Seventeenth-century form of dual-purpose furniture, a chair with a large circular or rectangular back that worked on pivots and could be pulled forward to rest on the arms, making a table. Also called a monk's chair.

Chaise longue An elongated chair designed for reclining.

Club General term for a sturdy upholstered chair in simple lines and generous proportions.

Cobbler's bench An adaptation of the old cobbler's worktable with a raised section at one end. May be used as a table or as a seat.

Cockfight chair A chair for reading, writing, or viewing sports events by straddling the seat and facing the back. The back had a small shelf that opened to store cards or tobacco.

Cogswell Upholstered armchair with open arms and part of the wood frame exposed.

Contour Chair shaped for comfort; may adjust to different positions.

Corner Sometimes called *roundabout*. Diamond-shaped chair with one leg in the middle of the front.

Curule chair A chair with X-shaped legs, derived from ancient Roman and Grecian forms. These chairs were popular in Sheraton's designs and were widely interpreted in the Empire period by Duncan Phyfe.

Dante chair A curule chair of the Italian renaissance having a leather or fabric seat. The four heavy legs curve up to the arms.

Eames Seat and back of molded plywood; named after noted contemporary designer Charles Eames.

Fan-back Upholstered chair with rounded back.

Fauteuil (pronounced foh-TOY) French open-arm chair with either upholstered or caned seat and back, as distinguished from the completely upholstered bergère.

Fiddle back   Chair in the Queen Anne style with a back splat resembling the swelling shape of a violin.

Fireside   Upholstered chair with recessed arms or no arms at all. Usually used in pairs.

Guérite (pronounced gay-RITT)   The French for "sentry box." A hall porter's chair with a high hooded back and closed sides, designed to protect the sitter from drafts. It was widely used during the sixteenth and seventeenth centuries. In the eighteenth century, it was made of wicker and moved outdoors as a piece of garden furniture.

Hassock   Heavily upholstered stool. May have removable top so it can be used for storage.

Hitchcock   American-type straight chair. Lambert Hitchcock, an early nineteenth century cabinetmaker, designed this chair. It was based on a Sheraton original with a broad pillow-back band, turned and splayed legs, and rush or cane seat. It was usually painted and frequently stenciled with fruit, flowers, or patriotic motifs.

Klismos   A Greek type of chair having a concave back rail and legs. It inspired similar styles in the French Directoire and English periods as well as in the twentieth century.

Ladder-back   Chair with horizontal rails or slats forming the back.

Lawson   Sturdy upholstered chair in simple lines of English club furniture.

Lounge   Upholstered chair with deep seat.

Martha Washington   An open-armed chair with a high, straight upholstered back and upholstered seat in the Adam, Sheraton, or Hepplewhite style, named after the wife of the first American president.

Morris   A large chair developed in the nineteenth century by William Morris, an English artist and designer who attempted to bring art and craftsmanship to the masses as a revolt against the sterotyped products of the machine age. The chair has a wood frame, adjustable back, and loose cushions.

Occasional   Small-scale chair usually used in living room.

Ottoman   Upholstered bench or seat with no arms or back.

Peacock   Rattan chair from Hong Kong with a high, lacy fan back and a base that swells out like an hourglass. This style has been popular since mid-Victorian times and is often known as the "Saratoga" chair because of its use in the New York state spa.

Pull-up   Similar to an occasional chair.

Rocker   Chair with curved runners at the base, permitting the chair to tilt backward and forward. A platform rocker has a stationary base upon which the chair rocks back and forth.

Saber leg   A chair design popular in English Regency and used by Duncan Phyfe during the Federal period. The front legs of the chair were curved sharply.

Scissors (Savonarola)   Slats form the side arms and base in an X-shaped arrangement.

Sgabello   A small wooden Renaissance chair, usually having a carved splat back, an octagonal seat, and carved trestle supports. The chair design was based on a three-legged stool.

Shell   Side, back, and seat are molded from plastic or fiberglass.

Side   Small chair without arms.

Stool   Small seat with no arms or back. Usually mounted on legs.

Swivel   Chair with seat that revolves.

Table   Back of chair is hinged so that it can drop down to form a table top.

Thonet   Chair with bent-wood frame.

Tub   Chair with rounded back and sides.

Tubular   Framework of chair is made of bent tubes, usually metal.

Wainscot   Sturdy chair with panel back. Usually decorated with ornate carving.

Windsor   Introduced during the reign of Queen Anne. The original chair was made by wheelwrights in different variations. The various forms have bentwood frames with spindles that form the backs. Seats are shaped; legs are attached directly to the bases of the seats and flare outward.

Wing   Upholstered chair with high back- and side-sections

Desks

Desk box   A legless box that was our first "desk." Desk boxes were rectangular in shape with a slanting, slightly overhanging hinged lid. When closed, the lid served as the writing surface, with the interior of the box as a storage well for writing materials. **Bible boxes** were similar, but had flat lids rather than slanting ones.

Fall front or drop front   Writing cabinet or secretary with a flap that falls to show a series of compartments. The earliest, seventeenth-century models had drawers or doors in the lower section. Later the size of the flap was often reduced, and a glass-doored bookcase section was added above the writing surface.

Flat-top Various desks having broad, flat surfaces.

Kidney-shaped Desk with a curved top and curved drawer sections.

Kneehole Any desk that has a flat top and drawer sections on one or both sides.

Rolltop Desk with a flexible hood that can be drawn down over the writing surface and storage compartments.

Secretary Desk with bookshelves above and storage compartments below. Writing surface is usually a drop-leaf panel.

Slant-top Similar to the lower section of a secretary, with a drop-lid writing section and drawers in the base.

Tambour Desk with flexible-slat shutters or doors that can be drawn closed to hide the storage compartments. Usually has one or more drawers below the writing surface.

Vargueño (pronounced vahr-GAYN-yoh) A Spanish drop-front cabinet desk of the sixteenth, seventeenth, and eighteenth centuries which was set on a separate base, either a table or a chest. The cabinet had many drawers and handles on the side for transporting.

Sofas and Settees

Camel-back Gracefully curved arch back.

Canapé A French sofa or couch with a curved back that continues into arms sloping to the front. Originally covered with a canopy, the canapé may have doubled as a daybed. Associated with Louis XV design period.

Chairback settee Popular in the late seventeenth century, the chairback settee resembles two chairs joined together. It reappeared in the Queen Anne, Chippendale, Sheraton and Hepplewhite styles in both England and America.

Charles of London Upholstered sofa of sturdy club-type proportions. Usually has short, flat arms.

Chesterfield A large, completely upholstered overstuffed sofa, common in England and Canada.

Confidante A three-in-one sofa consisting of a center section that had two smaller, angled seats at either end.

Couch French seventeenth-century forerunner of the daybed, with arms and cushions at one or both ends.

Davenport Originally a small writing desk; now a common United States term for an upholstered sofa. An upholsterer in Boston named Davenport made handsome overstuffed couches, and people began to speak of all similar couches as ''davenports.''

Deacon's bench American name for a Windsor settee with four back divisions contoured like chair backs.

Divan A Turkish term for large, low couches without arms or backs that developed from piles of rugs for reclining.

Lawson Sturdy upholstered club-type sofa with square or key-shaped arms.

Love seat Small sofa designed for seating two people. Originated during the Queen Anne period as a double chair.

Méridienne (pronounced may-ree-d'YEN) A short sofa of the French Empire period, with one arm higher than the other.

Récamier (pronounced ray-kah-M'YEH) or **Grecian couch** French Empire chaise longue that has a highly curved end. Derived from a Roman couch. It was named for Madame Récamier, who was reclining on such a piece as she was being painted by David.

Sectional Separate seating units designed to be used together to form a variety of arrangements.

Settee Lightweight sofa that may have open-work back and arms. Seat may or may not be upholstered.

Settle All-wood settee with solid arms and back, usually built like a box, solid to the floor, with hinged seat.

Sofa From *suffah*, a divanlike seat of Arabic descent. Sofas today assume all shapes and sizes, from cushiony Chesterfield, Lawson, and tuxedo types to those with contemporary contours.

Tete-à-tete Two-seat sofa designed so that seats face in opposite directions.

Tuxedo Sofa with slender proportions. Arms are same height as back.

Tables

Butler's tray In English cabinetwork, a small movable tray-top table used for serving and at tea time. The table has hinged sides that fold up. Cut-out sections form handles.

Butterfly Small folding table with splayed legs, generally turned, and with wing brackets to support leaves on either side. So named because of the resemblance in the shape of the solid wooden wing brackets to the shape of butterfly wings.

Cocktail Low table for use in front of a sofa.

Console The French word for ''table'' or ''bracket.'' Originally, it referred to a bracket or shelf fastened to the wall; it now includes tables designed to be used against the wall.

Corner Square or triangular table. Often used with sectional furniture.

Dinette   Small-scale dining table.

Dressing   Used as vanity or powder table.

Drop-leaf   Hinged sections on table drop down when not in use.

Drum   A round or octagonal table with shelves, drawers, or compartments. The original design included a tooled leather top, which revolved on a column with four splayed legs.

End   Small table designed for use next to a chair or sofa.

Extension   Dining table that can be enlarged by use of extra sections or leaves.

Flip-top   Card or dining table with a fold-over top opening up into facing leaves, like a book, and supported either by pivoting the top to the opposite axis or by a swing-out leg or runner.

Game   Top of table has game board in inlaid or painted design.

Gate-leg   Has drop leaves that are supported by extra legs that are swung away from the base when the leaves are raised.

Handkerchief   An American drop-leaf table with a triangular top, like a handkerchief folded corner to corner. When the drop leaf is raised, the table becomes square.

Harvest   Long, narrow table with drop leaves.

Hunt   Semicircular table. May have short drop leaves at both ends. The original table was tall enough for people to stand around it to eat.

Lazy Susan   Table with raised platform that revolves.

Library   Long, narrow table sometimes used behind a sofa.

Martha Washington   An oval sewing or work table made in America in the Hepplewhite, Sheraton, and American Empire styles during the late eighteenth and early nineteenth century. It has two or three center drawers fitted for sewing gear. The ends have hinged tops that lift to reveal rounded bins for work in progress.

Nest of tables   Set of graduated tables made to form one unit.

Night   The night stand, popular in England during the eighteenth century, was similar to the enclosed washing stand of the period. It was a small oblong table with a removable tray top fitted with hand grips, which was over a cupboard with one or two doors. Today it is a small table used next to a bed.

Parsons   Usually a square or rectangular table with straight legs with the apron and leg width that measures the same. Often finished with high-gloss enamel in bright colors. Developed at the Parsons School of Design in New York City.

Pembroke   Table with a broad bed and narrow drop leaves, and usually with a drawer in the apron. The straight four legs may be connected by an X-shaped stretcher. Named for the Earl of Pembroke, for whom Thomas Chippendale designed and made such a table.

Piecrust   Round table, frequently with a tilt top, with edge raised and carved in fluted or scalloped design.

Pier   Similar to console table. Often used between two windows with mirror hung above.

Poudreuse (pronounced poo-DRUHZ)   French powder table or vanity, usually with a mirror that raises in the midsection.

Refectory   In Renaissance cabinetwork, a long narrow rectangular dining table, used in the monestary refectory. In the early fifteenth century, the table was designed along the lines of a trestle table. Later four or more sturdy legs were used and joined by a continuous stretcher close to the floor.

Sawbuck   Rectangular table top on X-shaped supports. Originally of Gothic design, but associated with early American interiors.

Sewing   Table designed with drawers or compartments to hold sewing equipment. Has a lid top and often a cloth bag for sewing gear.

Step   Table with two or more levels; adapted from library step-stools.

Tavern   In England and America, this small table was of Jacobean style. The rectangular, octagonal, round or oval top extended well over the apron, which may have had drawers. The legs were connected with a box stretcher close to the floor.

Tea   The introduction of tea to Europe in the seventeenth century caused a number of small tables to be developed. A popular one was a single table with pull-out leaves.

Tea wagon   Table on wheels; often has one or more shelves below table top.

Tiered   Small table with two or more levels, it was called a dumbwaiter in early eighteenth-century England.

Tilt-top   Table top is hinged so that it may stand in vertical position.

Trestle   Long table on sturdy bases. The primitive form was composed of boards laid across trestles or sawhorses and removed when not in use.

Tripod   A pedestal table with three legs flaring out at the base. Favored by Adam and Chippendale.

Various kinds of tests are performed to determine how well a mattress may be expected to conform to the body of a sleeper and to stand up under use. *(Courtesy of Consumers Union of U.S., Inc.)*

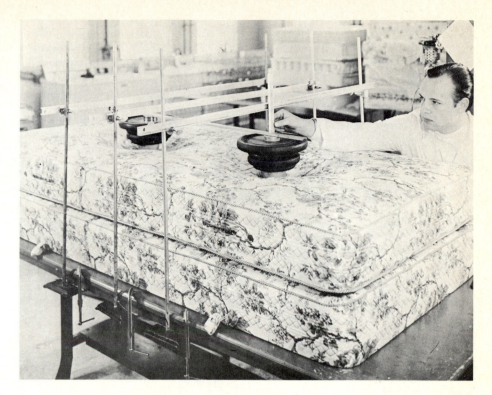

Fig. 16.8

The popular types of high-quality mattresses include innerspring, and urethane foam. Cotton felt is also used, but it is not likely to hold its shape as well as other materials.

There are two major methods of constructing an innerspring mattress. In the open coil method, a group of coils is tied together by helical wires. In the second method, each coil is individually pocketed in some type of material. Both methods have advantages and disadvantages. The guage of the wire used in the coils is an important factor in determining their quality.

Urethane foam mattresses have also become quite popular. They retain their shape well and are light in weight. However, there are different qualities available and one has to be sure to buy from a reliable dealer.

Cotton felt used in layers is often found in less expensive mattresses, and it may be of quite good quality. However, cotton batting or cotton fibers that have not been felted tend to mat and may cause the mattress to become lumpy.

Ticking is used as the outer cover of a mattress. It should be closely woven and strong.

Well-constructed mattresses are stitched through cover and filling to prevent the shifting of materials. This tufting is often secured by buttons. A sturdy reinforced edge will prevent the mattress from sagging at the sides. Firmly attached handles facilitate turning the mattress.

The bedspring used under a mattress provides support and is important for proper comfort. There are various types and qualities on the market, including the box spring, the open-coil spring, and several kinds of flat constructions made of bands and strips of wire.

Bedsprings are generally made of heavier-gauge metal than innerspring coils. In the box spring, the coils are anchored to slats in the base and covered with ticking. Open coils are attached to metal slats and left uncovered. The box spring is usually more expensive, but it is more desirable because it is easier to clean and it has no rough areas to rub against the mattress or to tear sheets and blankets.

Springs with flat constructions do not provide as much support or resiliency as coil springs.

17

Room Plans and Furniture Arrangement

Plan implies purpose, and the success of a home will depend upon how well one can keep purposes in mind when selecting and arranging *all* the furnishings. A comfortable, livable home that is also a joy to behold does not just happen; it must be developed with clearly defined goals. To have a home that is comfortable, convenient, and beautiful, it is essential, therefore, to consider how each area will be used and to integrate usefulness with beauty.

A room plan involves all aspects of furnishing. Colors, furniture, floor coverings, window treatments, and accessories must be chosen and used with definite objectives in mind. Although it is necessary to discuss these various factors in separate chapters, each one is vital to the final result. Here we shall be concerned chiefly with the selection and arrangement of furniture; other aspects of planning rooms are discussed in greater detail throughout the book.

Activity Planning

In furniture arrangement, function supersedes beauty. The furniture arrangement must provide for the occupant's needs and comfort first. Develop an activity planning chart for each room that includes the following: activities, furniture required, floor space required, lighting, color preference, and special conditions.

Determine what activities will be carried on in the area and what furniture will be required. Even in fairly large homes, each room may serve more than one purpose. In small quarters, the most efficient use of space will present a real challenge to the planner's ingenuity.

Drawing the Floor Plan

Planning ahead is the key to an attractive and comfortable room, and planning on paper is the most practical method of furniture arrangement. The plans and drawings will be useful for future remodeling or moving.

A floor plan is an architectural scale drawing of one or more rooms, showing the arrangement

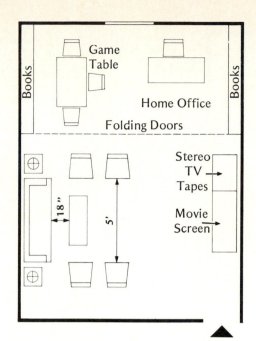

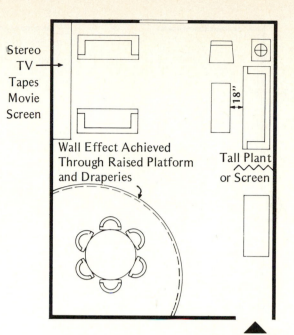

Multipurpose Room 18′ x 24′ (Living Room – Library)

Needs and Activities Include:

a. Entertaining.
b. Home theater, stereo, tapes, TV.
c. Game playing in privacy.
d. Home office.

Multipurpose Room 18′ x 24′ (Living Room – Dining Room)

Needs and Activities Include:

a. Entertaining.
b. Home theater.
c. Dining.

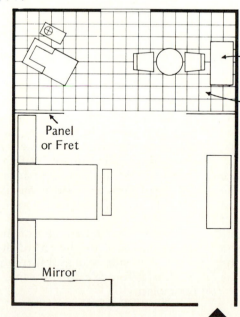

Multipurpose Room 18′ x 24′ (Master Bedroom)

Needs and Activities Include:

a. Sleeping.
b. Dressing.
c. Eating breakfast.
d. Leisure.
e. Home office.

MULTIPURPOSE ROOMS

Room Plans and Furniture Arrangement

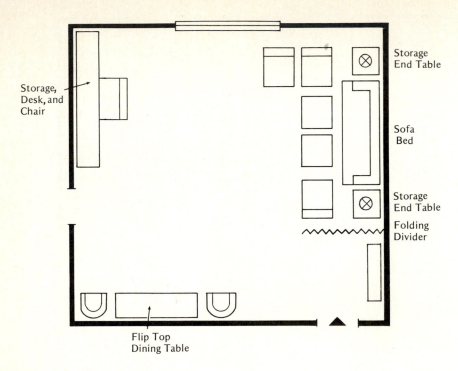

Storage,
Desk, and
Chair

Storage
End Table

Sofa
Bed

Storage
End Table

Folding
Divider

Flip Top
Dining Table

Multipurpose Room (One-Room Apartment)

Needs and Activities Include:

a. Entertaining.
b. Sleeping.
c. Storage.
d. Desk.
e. Dining.

and the horizontal dimensions. It includes the size and arrangement of rooms as well as the locations of all windows, doors, and other architectural features.

Measure every part of the room: the distance between windows on the walls, the width of the doors and windows (inside measurement and frame to frame measurement), and the width of the fireplace and hearth. Do the measuring at floor level to prevent any deviation caused by a sloping tape. Then plot the dimensions of the room on graph paper allowing 1/4 inch per one foot.

After drawing the floor plan, add the architectural symbols that show the windows, the swing of the doors, and the lighting symbols. Show the placement of heating and air-conditioning units. If the room has structural projections, corners, or a break in the wall, make a note of such measurements and add them to the floor plan.

The second dimension of the room may be drawn to see if the height of the furniture balances. The side wall and furniture elevation can be drawn to scale in the same manner as the floor plan.

Measure the space between the doors and
windows and the space between the windows.

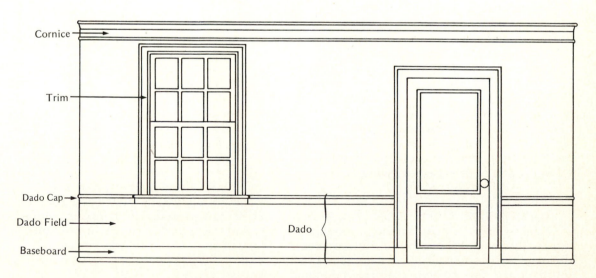

Cornice

Trim

Dado Cap

Dado Field

Dado

Baseboard

Measure all heights on the wall. Get the width
of the baseboard next to the floor. Determine
the height of the dado. Find out the width of
all the moldings used in the room.

Room Plans and Furniture Arrangement

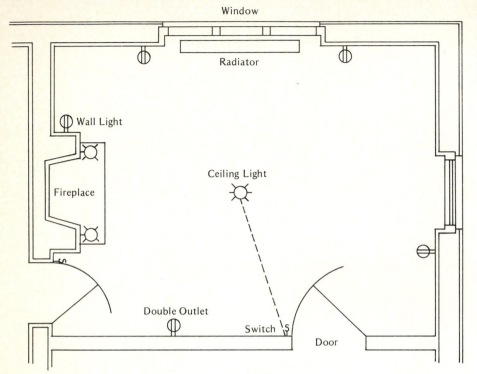

Window

Radiator

Wall Light

Fireplace

Ceiling Light

Double Outlet

Switch S

Door

Standard architectural symbols may vary. Here are some symbols that indicate doors, windows, a radiator, wall lights, a fireplace, double outlets, a ceiling light, and switches.

Traffic Patterns

Traffic patterns should be worked out before any furniture is placed on the graph paper. Starting at the entrance, draw a line to every door in the room. Allow access to windows and built-in bookcases. Arrange for easy entrances, exits, and crossings without having to cut around jutting tables and chairs, or in front of conversations or television viewing.

Zoning the Floor Plan

Imagine an individual standing in the major entry to the room. What is the first area of focus? That may be part of or all of the major focal point in the room. Draw a line to that focal point and one to the other exit in the room. The large zone thus included is probably close to or includes the center of interest. Mark it with numbers and estimate the size; compare this with the needs of the occupants.

Arranging the Furniture

Measure the furnishings that are to be used in the room, including area rugs and lamps (both table and floor). Then make cutouts of each piece of furniture. Trace the templates from those (Figure 17.1) and modify them to the exact size of the furniture used. It is important that all measurements be accurate. Label each piece with the name and measurements. There are some kits on the market that use three-dimensional forms, which are usually done in a scale of $1/2''$ to one foot. The templates should correspond, however, to the scale used on the basic floor plan.

With the development of modern materials and styles, as well as the decrease in space for living, rooms and furniture are seldom limited to one specific use. However, there are specific considerations for some activities related to furniture arrangement. For the sake of convenience, they are listed room by room.

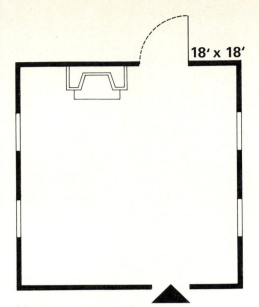

(a) Needs and Activities:

Entertaining—8 people
Reading—provide for books.
Home office—to pay bills.
Music—stereo.

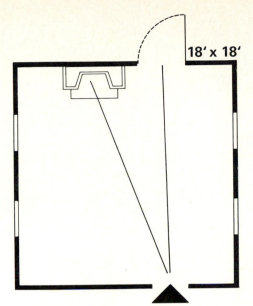

(b) The traffic pattern is drawn and the focal point is determined.

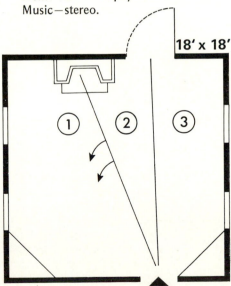

(c) Zones Are Determined:

1. Group zone.
2. Small zone.
3. Medium zone.

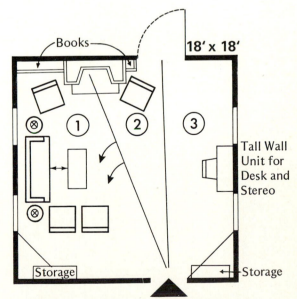

(d) Furniture is placed according to the zones and needs.

Room Plans and Furniture Arrangement

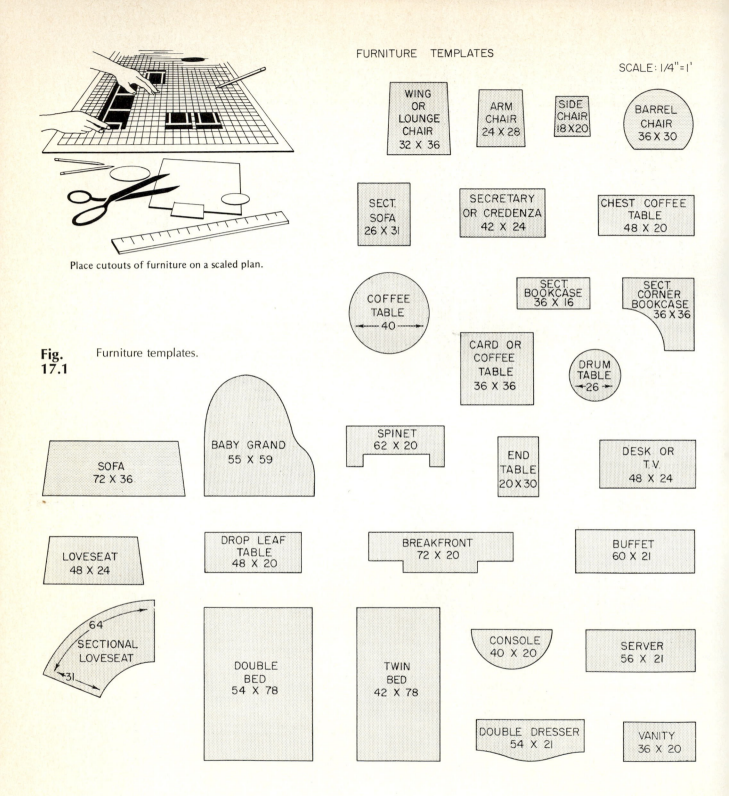

FURNITURE TEMPLATES

SCALE: 1/4"=1'

Place cutouts of furniture on a scaled plan.

Fig. 17.1 Furniture templates.

WING OR LOUNGE CHAIR 32 X 36

ARM CHAIR 24 X 28

SIDE CHAIR 18 X 20

BARREL CHAIR 36 X 30

SECT. SOFA 26 X 31

SECRETARY OR CREDENZA 42 X 24

CHEST COFFEE TABLE 48 X 20

COFFEE TABLE 40

SECT. BOOKCASE 36 X 16

SECT CORNER BOOKCASE 36 X 36

CARD OR COFFEE TABLE 36 X 36

DRUM TABLE 26

SOFA 72 X 36

BABY GRAND 55 X 59

SPINET 62 X 20

END TABLE 20 X 30

DESK OR T.V. 48 X 24

LOVESEAT 48 X 24

DROP LEAF TABLE 48 X 20

BREAKFRONT 72 X 20

BUFFET 60 X 21

64 SECTIONAL LOVESEAT 31

DOUBLE BED 54 X 78

TWIN BED 42 X 78

CONSOLE 40 X 20

SERVER 56 X 21

DOUBLE DRESSER 54 X 21

VANITY 36 X 20

Furniture Styles, Selection, and Room Arrangement

A well-planned living room provides a functional arrangement and recognizes architectural features.

Living Room
Decide on the natural focal point and place the main conversation group first. Experiment with arrangements that bring some pieces of furniture into the center of the room or perpendicular to the wall.

When furniture is arranged for conversation, usually four or five people in a single conversational grouping is the maximum number. Several conversation groupings are desirable if space allows. For ease of conversation, the people should be no more than approximately six to eight feet apart.

After the conversation area is determined, the heavy pieces of furniture need to be placed. Remember to allow space in front of cabinets so they can be opened. Placing all of the large pieces at one end of the room can create a feeling of unbalance.

Keep in mind that regardless of where a

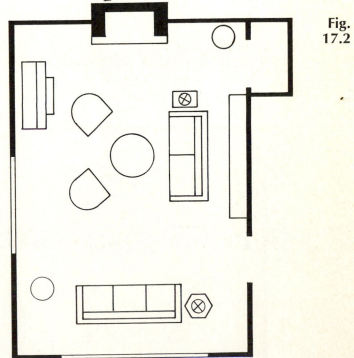

**Fig.
17.2**

Room Plans and Furniture Arrangement

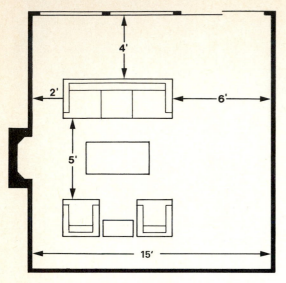

(a) Living Room

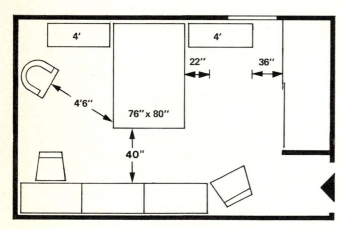

(b) Bedroom

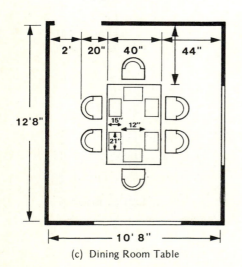

(c) Dining Room Table

person sits, there should be an attractive view. Each person also needs to have a surface for placing a cup or a glass, as well as adequate lighting.

Placing a desk or a sofa at a right angle to the wall will visually separate the living areas; tall plants, sculpture, or screens can achieve the same purpose. One individual used Venetian blinds to separate a study area from the living room.

After you try the various arrangements of furniture on the floor plan, and one seems satisfactory, trace each piece on the floor plan and label it. It should be pointed out that this procedure is of value when planning to use presently owned furnishings in a new location. Furniture that will not fit in the home after it has been moved in can add to the unexpected expenses of moving by making a replacement necessary.

Dining Room

The sideboard or table is usually the center of interest in the dining room. The serving table should be placed as close to the kitchen door as possible for more convenient service.

A good rule of thumb allows a minimum of eight square feet for a dining area for four. In planning seating arrangements, it is wise to be aware of the amount of space needed. These guidelines should help in furniture arrangement.

Table space for each adult	21″–24″ width; 15″ depth
Strip in the center for serving pieces and centerpiece	12″
Space to rise from the table	32″
Space to edge past a seated person	36″

Some houses and apartments are arranged in such a manner as to use part of the living room for dining. When that is the case, furniture needs to be selected with dual purpose in mind. A console table may be enlarged to seat people, or folded to serve as a side table flanked by two side chairs. The chairs may be used in the living room for additional conversation grouping when needed. Various coffee tables can be purchased that increase in height for dining. Parsons tables of dining height can be placed end to end for dining; when not in use, they can serve as desks, tables behind the sofa, or servers next to a wall.

Bedroom

The bedroom serves two major functions: a place to sleep and a place to dress. Therefore a minimum list of furnishings should include a bed, storage pieces, a mirror, good lighting, and a place to sit.

Allow enough space to make the bed, or mount it on castors to make it simple to move. Dressers should be placed close to the closet areas. A full-length mirror close to the closet area would be useful. A large night table the height of the mattress is a functional addition to the bedroom.

If space permits, sewing, hobby, a desk, or morning lounging can be arranged. Here are some guidelines for furniture arrangement in the bedroom that will allow ample space for the tasks.

Space for bed making	22″
Space in front of closet	36″
Space for dressing	36–42″ in both directions
Space in front of dresser	40″

Maintenance

Maintenance of a home is usually done without staffs or servants, and ease of care must be a major factor in planning each room. Modern materials that resist soil, and vacuum cleaners with attachments do simplify the problem of keeping the home clean. However, some locations have excessive amounts of dust and grime that will tax even the most carefree surfaces. Furniture should be easy to move and corners easy to reach.

In planning an easily maintained room, floor coverings need special attention. Heavy traffic areas with a very light or a very dark wall-to-wall carpet installation can present many cleaning problems.

Aesthetic Plans

A room can be both functional and beautiful, although there may be times when one aspect will have to be sacrificed for the other because of specific limitations. When such a problem does arise, creative ability can work out a happy solution. For example, radiators that are not concealed can seriously tax the imagination. One needs them for heating, yet their appearance can mar the beauty of the room. One simple solution is to use bookcases on either side and a metal grille over the front of the radiator. With a shelf over the whole unit, the "problem" may become a very attractive adjunct to a room. Perhaps all problems will not be solved as easily as that, but it is more interesting at least to try some creative approach rather than simply to ignore them. The beauty of a home will depend on how well the principles of design are applied.

To some extent, natural instincts dictate the placement of furniture in a room. Even people who are not well versed in the fundamentals of art place the sofa against the long wall in the living room because it seems to "look right" in that position. But a more refined awareness of design establishes the subtle aesthetics that make a room more beautiful.

Harmony

A room plan blends all the elements so that the whole area expresses a particular theme or mood. The old axiom that the "sum is greater than the total of the parts" can well be applied to the composition of a room. Each object and each element contributes to the whole, but the result must be a unit that has a charm and a personality of its own. The beauty of any room depends

Fig. 17.3

Fig. 17.4

One large room is divided into two with the aid of curtain poles. The living and dining areas are given different but coordinated window treatments. *(Courtesy of The Singer Company)*

A sleeping alcove in an L-shaped room is separated from the living area by a folding screen covered in a vividly striped fabric that matches the bedspread. *(Courtesy of The Englander Company, a subsidiary of Union Carbide Corporation)*

The fireplace in this room is a natural center of interest but another wall is emphasized by the use of a Baroque console and mirror. *(Designed by Patricia Harvey, A.I.D., photo by Alexandre Georges)*

(a)

(b)

Fig. 17.5

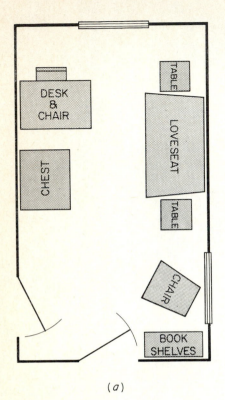

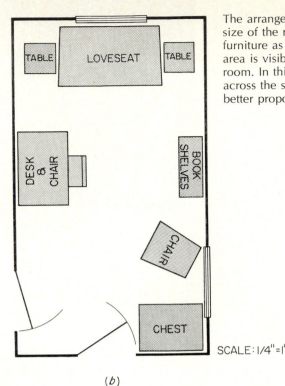

The arrangement in (a) decreases the size of the room. By rearranging the furniture as shown in (b), more floor area is visible as one enters the room. In this case, the love seat across the short wall gives the room better proportions.

SCALE: 1/4"=1'

(a)　　　　　　　　　　　(b)

Fig. 17.6

upon this interrelationship of all the components. The furnishings must look as though they belong in the room and in the company of one another.

Proportion

Because proportion is a matter of spatial relationships, the size of the room and the available wall space will determine the types of furniture and the amount of it that can be used. Furniture should be in scale with the room. A small room will usually appear to best advantage if it has small-scaled pieces and a minimum number of them; a large room can take more massive ones.

A wall area is broken by the outlines of the furniture and the accessories placed against it. Each wall arrangement must, therefore, be considered in terms of divisions that are pleasing to the eye. Pictures or other accessories that are hung on the wall should accord with both the furniture and the wall area.

Scale is also important in grouping pieces of furniture. A tiny, delicate table next to a massive chair becomes insignificant, although the table itself may be charming near a more delicate piece.

Balance

In almost every room there will be some pieces of furniture that are heavier than others. The larger, more important pieces should be distributed around the room in such a way that all areas will be in equilibrium. But the architectural features, such as windows or a fireplace, also bear "weight," and frequently must be balanced by heavier pieces on opposite walls.

Often color can be employed to bring areas into balance. A small area of brilliant color or of a bold pattern takes on an added weight that can often balance a larger area of a more subdued nature. Thus a chair covered in a bright color might balance the more subdued draperies of a large window.

(a) Before

(a) Before. (1) Scattered furniture makes conversation difficult. Furniture placed diagonally makes the room seem cluttered. (2) There is no strong focal point. (3) The pictures are too small for the wall areas. (4) The lamps are not in proportion to the furniture and the tables they serve. (5) The draperies are too small. (6) The room is not in balance as each wall is not balanced with the one directly opposite.

    (b) After. (1) There is a conversation grouping with the sofa and large chairs now placed parallel to the walls, thus relating to the architecture of the room. (2) The fireplace is the strong focal point in the room. There are other areas in the room that are subordinate focal points such as the books, art objects, music equipment, TV, pictures, window treatments, and display of plants. (3) Pictures, mirrors, and picture groupings are in proportion to the size of the areas they occupy and the furniture near them. (4) The lamps are in proportion to the furniture and the tables they serve. (5) Full-length draperies add unity and richness to the room. (6) The room is balanced as the fireplace has a visually heavier piece on the opposite wall. The window treatment balances the heavy conversation grouping on the opposite wall.

Fig. 17.7

(b) After

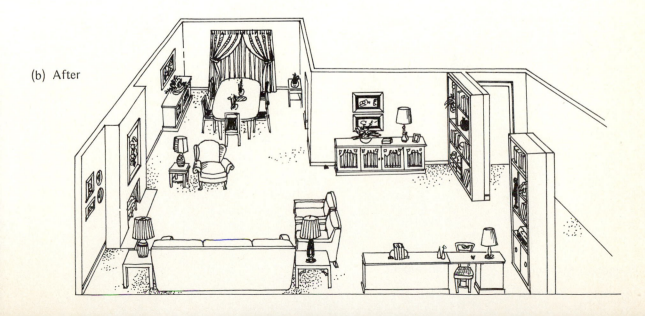

Balance within groupings of furniture is also important. In Chapter 7 we discussed the two principal types of balance—formal and informal, or occult. Most rooms need some of each, but in general, modern style and the more casual traditional styles lend themselves to informal balance. Elegance in a stately traditional room may be expressed by groups that are symmetrically arranged. The mood of the room will determine how much of each type of balance one may want to use. Too much asymmetry may lead to confusion and restlessness; too much symmetry may be stiff and forbidding.

Emphasis

Most rooms are more interesting if there are definite centers of interest that give leadership to their designs. A large room may have more than one dominant center, but in a small room one or perhaps two centers will usually be sufficient.

One should study each room carefully to determine what or where the center of interest might be. Perhaps a fireplace, a large window, a pair of windows, or some other architectural feature can be used as the area of emphasis. One large wall area can be given importance by furniture, accessories, color, or pattern. For example, a wall treated with a mural, painted in a brighter color, or covered with a different texture immediately becomes a dominant note. A large important piece of furniture, a large picture, or a picture grouping may lend added emphasis to an area.

Some special activity, hobby, or interest may provide an interesting basis for a dominant area in a room. A musical instrument or a collection of some sort can be emphasized by the manner in which it is placed or displayed. Such a center of interest frequently gives a room its individuality and may set the theme for the entire plan.

Rhythm

Lines, colors, and textures in the furnishings will cause the eye to move in certain directions. It is usually more pleasing for the eye to move in an easy, graceful manner rather than to move with a jumpy or jerky motion. We have discussed various ways of producing rhythmic sensations, and all of the techniques may be applied in developing a room plan. A pleasing rhythm depends on well-organized relationships of all the elements of design.

The lines of the more important furnishings are generally more attractive if they follow the structural lines of the room. Rectangular pieces will appear to better advantage when placed with the major line parallel to a wall or at right angles to it. Placing furniture on the diagonal, or catercornered, is often disturbing, except for pull-up chairs or even lounge chairs in some rooms.

Continuity of line helps the eye to travel smoothly. Thus tables that are the same height as the arm of a chair are not only more convenient to use but are usually more attractive in relation to the chair. Pictures and other accessories must be arranged to keep eye movements smooth and easy.

Repetition is an excellent means of providing a feeling of rhythm, but it must be employed with discretion. Too much may become dull or monotonous; some contrast is necessary for interest.

Most rooms will have to be planned and equipped to meet a variety of needs. Every aspect of furnishing should be carefully considered to make the available space as functional and attractive as possible. Furniture must be chosen with respect to suitability as well as design; it must be arranged to make the space both useful and beautiful. Thus specific purposes of the area as well as the *mood* or *theme* to be expressed will influence the selection of furnishings.

When space is at a premium, planning for maximum efficiency is particularly important. It is not always possible to foresee the pitfalls that may arise until one actually lives in a home. Wise and careful planning of each area can prevent serious mistakes.

Hallways

A home may have several kinds of halls, which may do no more than provide a passageway from one area to another. Hallways can serve so many useful purposes that they should never be considered wasted space. More and more we are looking at them from the functional as well as the decorative point of view. Storage cabinets and bookshelves are being designed for the narrow proportions of some hallways. Wallpapers, lighting, and carpeting may be used to provide various novelty effects. Imagine, for example, a long, narrow hallway papered with a scenic wall covering that suggests a glen or forest, carpeted in soft velvety green, and illuminated to give a sunshiny glow. Just walking through such a hallway could be a delightful experience.

Entrance Halls

It should be remembered that the front door and the entrance hall create the initial impression of a home. As people leave, the area also creates the final impression. Therefore it should represent the spirit of a household, but it should also be useful. When one arrives there may be packages, books, or mail to deposit. Is there a convenient surface? In stormy weather there is always the problem of wet clothing. Is the hall-

18

Specific Rooms and Areas

287

Fig.
18.1

(left) A narrow hallway can be furnished without furniture. In this case, accessories, a console shelf, a mirror used in a problem corner, and a distinctive floor covering all contribute to a welcoming atmosphere. *(Designed by Patricia Harvey, A. I. D., photo by Dennis Purse)*

A front hallway is converted into a sewing area with the addition of a closet specifically fitted to hold sewing needs. *(Courtesy of The Singer Company, photo by Lisanti, Inc.)*

Fig. 18.2

way equipped to stand the rough treatment of muddy overshoes and dripping umbrellas? Is there a place to hang clothes when guests arrive?

Space in the entrance hall must frequently be used for additional purposes. In private homes this problem may not be as vital, but in apartments the entrance hall might be used as a dining area or a den or for storage. Then functionalism becomes a major concern and requires a most careful utilization of space. Dual-purpose furniture that is small in scale or wall-hung units may be very useful in this respect.

Living Rooms

There is a general trend to plan more than one area in the home for group living. The family room as a second living area has become increasingly popular in modern homes, as has an outdoor "living room." Moreover, we no longer cling to the idea that bedrooms are only for sleeping or that the dining rooms are only for dining. Either room may be furnished to relieve some of the demands on the living room. For example, a bedroom may be furnished to double as a sitting room or as a quiet study area, and a dining room may be planned to function as a second living room. However, there are many homes in which it is not possible to use any other area for the purposes usually served by the living room. In a one-room apartment, for example, there must be provisions not only for sleeping, eating, and storage but also for reading, watching television, entertaining, and any other activities that appeal to the occupants. Even in somewhat larger homes, an all-purpose living room is often a necessity.

How a living area is furnished will, of

Fig.
18.3

A rather formal living room can provide for various types of activities. *(Courtesy of Drexel Heritage Furnishings, Inc.)*

course, depend on how the room is to function and whether or not there will be other areas in the home that might be used for certain activities of the family.

In all probability, the living room will be used for entertaining. The considerate host or hostess plans for the comfort of guests. Furniture is arranged so that people can converse with one another. A table or some other surface convenient for refreshments is provided. Buffet service and informal entertaining have become so popular that there are all sorts of lap trays and small folding tables on the market to ease

the problems of entertaining in the living room. The important point is to plan the living area so that it is possible to entertain graciously in whatever manner is chosen without disrupting the normal arrangements.

If the living room is planned to accommodate guests comfortably, it will probably also take care of the usual family needs. These might include several comfortable chairs with good light for reading, as well as the convenient table surfaces that have been mentioned. But there may also be other family demands upon the living area. The television set, for example, may be in the living room. In the early days of television, this was the logical place for it. Now many families find that either some other area is more to their liking or that two, or more, TV sets are desirable. Watching television, even if only for short periods, has become pretty much a part of our daily lives, and where there is only one set in the home, its location will influence the pattern of family living.

Frequently the living room must also provide for a music center. Hi-fi or stereophonic systems are often combined with TV sets in handsome cabinets that become an important part of the furnishings and may even become major centers of interest. A piano or some other musical instrument may also be located in the living room. Despite its merits, the grand or baby grand piano often does present a problem in arranging a room. Because it is a large, heavy piece of furniture, it should be balanced with another important piece or furniture grouping in another area. The music center will often require some type of storage facilities for records or sheet music. Good lighting is another important consideration when planning such an area.

In many homes the living room must also provide a study or business area. A desk, a chair, and bookshelves may provide all the necessary equipment, but good lighting is also of utmost importance. Whether or not this area of activity is located in the living room will depend on the over-all arrangement of the home, but no matter where it is, well-planned organization can do a great deal to relieve the frustrations of daily living.

Physical Characteristics

Although the living room should be planned primarily for utmost functionalism, its aesthetic qualities are no less important. It should be a pleasant, congenial room that appeals to every member of the family. In a certain sense the living room is synonymous with *home;* we associate it with family life. In some homes, some other area may assume a more important function, but the living room should, nevertheless, contribute to the spirit of family life. It should be a place where members of the family like to gather and enjoy both group and individual interests.

We have discussed some of the functions that the living room must perform; we must also realize that there may be certain limiting factors. The room may be too small or have a peculiar shape. It may have architectural features that become problems even though they also add to the interest of the room.

Fireplaces. A fireplace appeals to many people because it connotes various ideas, such as warmth, elegance, friendliness, and so on. A fireplace seems to add a certain touch to a home even though it may be useless. Few homes today depend on a fireplace for heating, yet many homes include one for other reasons. In some instances a fireplace may be used for cooking informal meals, thereby serving as an indoor barbecue.

However, when a fireplace is included in the living room or some other area of the home, it almost naturally becomes a center of interest. It often determines the character of the room and how furniture will be arranged. Although a fireplace adds character and distinction to a room, it also represents a limitation with respect to the efficient use of wall space.

A built-in fireplace may cost anywhere from six hundred dollars up. Portable models may cost a bit less, but they are still expensive adjuncts in terms of actual contributions to the efficiency of the home.

Window walls. Modern planning favors a relationship between the outdoors and the indoors, and the window wall has been a convenient means of achieving this purpose. Yet a wall of glass, however desirable it may be, will present certain problems of furniture arrangement. Large, heavy pieces will not be attractive when placed against such a wall. The open appearance of this area is one of its chief attractions, so it must be relatively free of furniture. When other walls are cut up with doors or architectural features, there may be little wall space left for placing furniture.

Fig.
18.4

Furniture placed to emphasize the view. *(Courtesy of American Plywood Association)*

Dining Areas

Today a home with one large room devoted exclusively to dining is indeed a luxury. In recent years we have seen various space arrangements that attempt to cope with the problem of the dining area. L-shaped living rooms with the alcove accessible to the kitchen are widely used in both apartments and private homes. Both small houses and apartments are often planned with a breakfast room or dinette adjacent to the kitchen. Or the kitchen itself may be designed to provide space for table, chairs, and serving units. Some apartments utilize a foyer hall as the dining area. Somehow none of these arrangements seems to have really taken the place of the lovely old-fashioned dining room. In many large homes, as well as in small ones, that are designed for construction at medium cost levels, the addition of an adaptable room that can be used as a family room or as an informal dining room is finding increasing favor. Frequently the room is furnished to serve several functions.

Even when a separate room for dining is feasible, there is a trend to furnish it in a more individual manner. We are no longer bound to using matching suites of furniture. Often the chairs do not match the table; they may not even match one another. Contrasting servers, cabinets, and other storage units are also used. In other words, dining-room decoration is following the path of living-room decor, which long ago rejected the idea of conformity.

Although we tend to think of the living room as the center of group activities for the family, in actual practice the dining area may be a more important one in terms of family living. Is not the dinner table the place where conversation really unites the family as a group? How many families actually sit in their living rooms to discuss the happenings of the day or to exchange ideas? At the table, the very physical setup, with each person at his or her place, unites the family group. In a living room or even a family room, the distractions of television and other activities preclude the sense of unity that one finds at the dinner table. Probably for these reasons we have felt the need for an area in the home that provides a pleasant, relaxed atmosphere, fostering a family spirit. Dining areas in the kitchen or closely attached to the kitchen do not seem to do

the same thing, although the practical advantages of such arrangements are obvious.

In view of the above comments it can be readily understood that the spirit of the dining area must be pleasant. It may be happy and cheerful or quiet and restful, but it should be conducive to happy relaxation. Soft light, flowers, plants, and music usually contribute to such an atmosphere.

There is no reason that the dining table must always be placed in the center of the room. With the trends toward dual-purpose dining rooms and greater freedom of expression in decorating, many interesting arrangements have been developed with the table at one end of the room or even projecting from a wall. The important

An elegant, formal dining room can be furnished with excellent reproductions of eighteenth-century furniture, wallpaper, and fabrics. *(Courtesy of The Kittinger Company)*

Fig. 18.5

294

Fig. 18.6

A dining area at one end of the living room must often take the place of a separate room. Here a specially designed corner unit and graceful chairs create a room within a room. *(Designed by John and Earline Brice, A.I.D., courtesy of Harvey Probber, Inc.)*

Fig. 18.7

A relatively small cabinet can serve as a dining area when space is a problem. *(Courtesy of Greatwood Products, Inc.)*

(a)

(b)

points to consider are appearance and comfort. The shape of the table should harmonize with the shape of the area, and the design should express the theme of the room. There should be adequate space at the table for each person. About two feet is a comfortable minimum. The height of dining tables usually ranges from twenty-nine to thirty-one inches, and the seats of chairs range from seventeen to eighteen inches from the floor. A free space of about three feet around the table allows for comfort in sitting and serving.

A serving table on wheels is often useful in the dining area. Some of these are made with surfaces that can be heated and some have storage units or extra shelves below. Cabinets and various types of cupboards are designed to hold silver, dishes, linens, and so on. Sometimes a closet in the dining room is very convenient for storing extra table appointments.

Bedrooms

Because we begin and end each day in the bedroom, the area should certainly be furnished to suit individual tastes and needs. Above all, the bedroom should be comfortable and convenient to use, not only for sleeping but for dressing and all the other personal activities for which it is a haven. A comfortable chair with a table and lamp for reading or a desk for work and study may add considerably to the usefulness of the room. Sometimes a bedroom furnished as an extra sitting room is the solution for families in which teenagers or elderly people require a "living room" of their own. The various types of daybeds and sofa beds that are available make it possible to plan such rooms so that they are both beautiful and functional.

The usual size of a twin bed is at least six feet long and about three feet, three inches wide. A

Fig. 18.8

An air of elegance and relaxation is evident in this room. Commodes used as night tables increase storage space. *(Designed by Patricia Harvey, A.I.D.)*

full-sized bed may be five feet wide. However, headboards and footboards add to the dimensions. In addition, there has been a growing trend toward oversized or king-sized beds that are longer and wider, so it is important to know the exact dimensions of the beds to be used before planning an arrangement. Some beds may require as much as seven-and-one-half by five feet of space. The clearance space for making a bed must be about two feet.

For small bedrooms, various youth beds, daybeds, and bunk beds, and convertible chairs, sofas, and ottomans may conserve space. However, for a bed that is to be used every night, some of these smaller units may not provide the same comfort or convenience that the more standard bed offers. For example, bunk beds are difficult to make, and convertibles frequently require extra storage space for pillows and blankets.

Easy access to closets and chests of drawers is a major consideration in arranging bedroom furniture. Standing in front of a chest and opening the drawers requires about three feet of clearance space. A closet door on hinges should swing back freely. Sliding or folding doors on closets will often conserve space in a small room.

Children's Rooms

Child may mean anything from infancy to teenage, and during these years the individual goes through many stages of development. At each stage the requirements vary, so furnishings should not be static.

We might consider four stages of child development with respect to furnishing: infancy, preschool, school age, and teenage. At each of these levels the requirements of a practical, satisfying room will be quite different.

Infancy
It is believed that young babies are stimulated by colors and patterns. In addition to the concern of meeting the infant's basic needs for food, sleep, and comfort, there is an increasing concern to meet the infant's need for a multi-sensory environment, having beautiful things around for the baby to feel, see, and hear. A room should be bright and cheerful, but the practical aspects should make it possible to take care of the baby's needs with minimum effort. A crib and a storage chest for clothes are essential. A bathinette or a high table will be necessary for changing the baby's clothes.

Any surfaces with which the baby might come in contact should be treated with lead-free paint and should be free from sharp edges and other safety hazards.

Preschool
The toddler has requirements that are quite different from those of the infant. At this stage the youngster is learning to appreciate spaces, shapes, and colors. In all probability, the child has outgrown the crib and a new bed is required. A low table with suitable chairs, and low open shelves are of primary importance.

This is a period when the child is learning to coordinate and is also learning colors and developing habits of neatness. A chest for toys, or shelves that the child can reach, becomes extremely important.

All surfaces should be easily cleaned, because the youngster, in learning to coordinate, may spill beverages or paints. A child should never be made to feel guilty about such accidents, and if the room is carefully planned to allow for development, such accidents do no harm.

School Age
At the school-age stage, as the child is becoming more of an individualist, there will be particular tastes that should be considered. A desk with a good light is important. Bookshelves and a convenient storage space for clothing become more important. The child's room becomes a haven for special interests and activities; there may be pets such as goldfish or turtles that assume major importance. The wise parent recognizes and develops such interests.

When it is necessary or desirable for children to share a room, a plan might be developed to give each one a special area. Narrow shelves or chests of drawers can be used as dividers or

Brother and sister areas can be clearly defined in one large room. (Courtesy of Creslan Acrylic Fiber)

Fig. 18.9

"walls," even though they may be low. Each situation requires special planning, but it is usually desirable to try to provide some feeling of privacy for each child.

Teenage

The transition period between childhood and adulthood often requires a special living area away from the family group. The teenager's room may become a second living room. Couches and sofas that pull out to form beds, along with other dual-purpose furniture, may solve this problem as well as other problems of different family needs at different age levels. Of course the teenager's room should be furnished to provide for his or her interests and activities. It is particularly important at this stage to allow individual expression.

Study Areas

A special room equipped as the home office or as a place where one might go to read or study in quiet solitude is an ideal arrangement, but space limitations frequently preclude the use of an entire room for such purposes. How delightful it must be to have a library or a study, but most of us have to settle for a more economical use of space. The study area, therefore, may be part of the bedroom, the dining room, or the living room. Nevertheless, wise planning can make even a tiny area conducive to comfortable, efficient, and enjoyable work at home.

What are some of the essentials for this type of room or area? Perhaps a comfortable, restful atmosphere would be of prime importance. There must be a good working surface provided by a desk or table, a comfortable chair, and good light. Books might be very important in such an area, so shelves in standing units or wall-hung brackets must also be provided. Storage facilities for records and various papers are essential. The "business of living" has prompted some manufacturers to make desks with file drawers, which can be a great asset to even the simplest household.

Whatever area is chosen as the business or study area of the home, the decor should be restful. Soft colors along with comfortable,

Fig.
18.10

Known as the *home office*, this compact cabinet is designed for ample storage. When opened, an extension leaf provides a useful working surface. *(Courtesy of Greatwood Products, Inc.)*

functional furniture provide the answer. Whether one lives in a small apartment or a huge house, the business of running a household must go on, and life will be simpler if adequate provisions are made for it in some area of the home.

Family Rooms or Dens

The second living room, popularly referred to as the *family room* or den, has become extremely popular today. So many versions of such a room have been proposed that the term defies description. However, it connotes a less formal and more flexible room than the standard living room.

The added space for group living is especially desirable when there are several members of a family at different age levels. Teenagers or elderly people usually have needs that vary from the middle-age group. A home that provides two or more group-living areas helps to solve the problems that arise when several generations attempt to live with one another.

Once again, planning for the most efficient utilization of space is important. A second living room is not always possible. But should the situation require a second living area, a dining room or even an extra bedroom furnished as a family room may provide some solution to the problem. In addition, kitchens may be planned to include living areas or to allow in some way for group activities.

In general, the family room or second living area usually has a more relaxed and casual atmosphere than the actual living room of the house. The less formal furnishings should provide for games and for various kinds of entertainment. It is convenient, therefore, to have this area near the kitchen or to make some provisions for serving meals and refreshments. A wet bar in the den can solve the entertaining problem. In addition, it is useful to have family rooms accessible to outdoor terraces or patios.

The furniture should be comfortable, sturdy, and easy to move; the flooring and fabrics should be easy to maintain; and the color scheme should be compatible with that of the rest of the house.

Kitchens

Perhaps more than any other area of the home, the kitchen has been the subject of intensive research by home economists, builders, and appliance manufacturers. This is understandable in view of the fact that kitchen activities require a considerable amount of time and energy. Also, the relative expense of kitchen equipment contributes to the importance of this area and must be considered as an investment that will satisfy demands for convenience and comfort over a period of years.

We must recognize that there is no one perfect kitchen that will meet the needs of all families. Homemakers differ in personal values concerning the needs that the area must serve. For example, although most families prefer some arrangement for food service in the kitchen, different families regard this area in various ways. Some have all their meals in the kitchen and also entertain guests in this room; others have only certain meals or light snacks in the kitchen and consider another area more desirable for the main meals. Also, homemakers place different amounts of emphasis on convenience and on aesthetics, although it is not always necessary to sacrifice one for the other.

The functionalism of the kitchen will be dependent to some extent upon the composition of the family. The needs, therefore, will vary not only with the type of family unit but also within each family as it goes through different cycles. We might outline four general categories in this respect:

1. The single individual, the young couple, or several adults who live together with no children in the home.
2. The "founding" family in which there are some children younger than eight years of age.
3. The "expanding" family with children between the ages of eight and eighteen.
4. The "contracting" family, in which the parents are older and children have grown and are probably leaving to establish homes of their own.

In addition to the storage of foods and the preparation of meals, it is frequently desirable to plan the kitchen for other needs and activities. The service of meals in the kitchen has already been mentioned. In addition, the kitchen may include:

Planning center. A writing surface with a convenient telephone and storage space for cookbooks, recipes, records, and bills.

Play area. Families with young children sometimes like space for a playpen or a small table and chairs so that they can watch the youngsters while performing duties in the kitchen. Of course, the play area should be far enough away from the main centers of activity so that there is no safety hazard.

Hobby or sewing center. Other activities such as flower arranging, sewing and mending, or some other hobby may require some space and equipment that can be conveniently located in or near the kitchen.

Needs for these areas will vary not only with each family but also at different stages of the family cycle. Some flexibility is desirable, therefore, to allow for the most efficient use of the space.

It is interesting to note that although different families vary in their needs and demands for a useful kitchen, there is a surprising similarity when the matter of storage space is considered. In view of this, planning kitchens that are functional and adaptable to personal preferences and actual needs becomes a rather complex problem in mass-produced homes and apartments. Frequently we are forced to adapt to what is available or to what we can afford to have. Although an original design or even a remodeling project is not always possible, the astute homemaker who understands the basics of kitchen planning can frequently make simple arrangements that will improve conditions in poorly planned areas. Unfortunately, there is such a plethora of poor planning that one often has to accept the challenge of making the best of a bad situation. The only comforting note is that when the planner does figure out some way of making a seemingly impossible kitchen really work, it is a source of great satisfaction. Of course for some problem kitchens the only answer lies in either a partial or a complete remodeling project, but for others a few minor changes may make the room far more functional and more attractive.

Location in Relation to Other Rooms

One basic consideration in evaluating any kitchen plan is how it relates to other areas of the home. Should it be at the front or at the back of the house? Should it be a prominent room where one might entertain guests or should it be relegated to the confines of private family living? Here again, there is no one set answer, because it depends on how the home is to be used. There are some modern apartments where one steps into the entry hall to find himself or herself in the kitchen area. There are also private homes where the first view is of the kitchen. True, the kitchen must be convenient to some entry, but is it the first area that one should see? Authorities agree that the kitchen must be located so that when foods and supplies are brought into the home, they can be easily stored. For this reason, many kitchens in private homes have a doorway that connects with the garage or with a centrally located utility area. In apartments that have only one entrance, the kitchen is often close to the entrance door.

The kitchen must also be convenient to the area for food service. This may be a tiny area in the kitchen itself, a dining room, or several areas, such as a dining room, a family room, and an outdoor living area. Nowadays we are likely to serve food in any one of several areas, depending upon the mood of the moment or the season of the year. Is it possible to have a kitchen that can service all areas of the home with equal convenience? Perhaps not, but it should be located so that it is convenient for most of the meal service in the home.

Doors and Windows

The plan of the kitchen is often determined by the location of doors and windows in the room. Although the kitchen must be convenient for the delivery of foods and for the service of meals, more than two doorways may make the work area a through-passage traffic lane that will impede efficiency. One doorway convenient for delivery and the other convenient for service are usually sufficient.

Although in some modern apartment buildings the kitchens are being designed with no windows at all, for small private homes the window area is considered a major feature of the kitchen for both light and ventilation. In addition, families with young children often prefer a kitchen window that allows them to watch the youngsters at play outdoors. Yet windows and doors do reduce the amount of available wall and floor space in the kitchen. The FHA specifies a minimum window area equal to 10 per cent of the floor area of the kitchen; the Small Homes Council recommends window space that is between 15 and 25 per cent for good light and ventilation.

Amount of Space

Kitchens range from tiny efficiency units to huge rooms, but it is not so much the amount of space as the planning for the use of space that determines how efficient the kitchen will be. A large kitchen that is poorly planned is as bad as, if not worse than, one that is too small.

A kitchen of any size will have three major pieces of equipment: the refrigerator, the sink, and the range. The work centers of activity in the kitchen are related to the placement of the equipment. An analysis of the work areas has shown five major areas of activities:

1. Refrigerator.
2. Mixing and preparation.
3. Sink.
4. Range.
5. Serving.

Kitchen. In addition to a central location, the importance of which has been emphasized, a good kitchen must meet three major requirements. It should conform to the all-important work triangle principle; it should provide adequate storage and counter space; and it should be pleasant to work in and accessible to an eating area, with plenty of light and air. In many places, "kitchens" are very small, but they are practical and there is an eating area close by.

The work triangle means a proper relationship of the refrigerator, the sink, and the cooking range. Kitchen experts generally agree that the distance from refrigerator to sink to range should form a triangle of up to twenty-two feet, from left to right in that order, as preferred by most cooks.

The space near the refrigerator is often called the mix center. The refrigerator door should preferably open toward the sink. A handy countertop space at least 36" wide is needed next to the refrigerator for chopping and cutting.

The sink center, for both preparation and cleanup, is the core of the kitchen and an active area. Dishwasher, garbage disposal, and some supply cabinets go here. Adequate counter space at both sides of the sink is essential. The range or cooking center also requires counter space on both sides, as well as cabinets. Some people say the sink should be placed under a window; this may be desirable, but it is hardly essential, especially if it disrupts the kitchen plan. A separate oven can be located in a less vital area. It should have counter space on one side, at least, for putting down hot dishes.

The kitchen should have good exposure, plenty of air, and ample lighting. An ideal exposure for kitchen and dining room is on the southeast side of a house, providing bright morning sunshine all year round. A kitchen facing the south gets less morning sun, especially in summer, but more afternoon sun. A kitchen on the north gets little morning sun except in summer (suitable if you live in the South) and is exposed to cold winds in winter. A kitchen on the west or southwest is probably worst of all; it gets the heaviest onslaught of sun in late afternoon, which can make it unbearably warm in summer.

Basic Plans

Depending upon the amount of available floor and wall space (determined by the over-all size of the room and the locations of doors and windows), functional kitchens may be worked out on one of several basic plans:

1. The U-shaped kitchen utilizes three walls with corner cabinets and is designed to make the best possible use of space that is inconvenient to begin with.
2. The two-wall or H-shaped kitchen is frequently a corridor. Although there are no difficult corners, the center lane should be between forty-two and fifty-four inches wide for maximum efficiency.
3. The L-shaped kitchen uses two adjacent walls to free other wall space for dining or laundry areas.
4. One-wall kitchens are more suitable for small quarters and limited space.
5. The island kitchen uses the center of a room space to locate food preparation activities and eating area.

There are a number of possible variations on these basic plans, including the peninsular or island versions, in which a unit either projects from one wall or is free-standing in the center.

Guides for Planning

Certain guides may be of great value in making a kitchen more functional. Homeowners must study their own needs and evaluate their own situations, but whatever revisions may be indicated should be based on the following guides for better kitchen planning.

1. Kitchen design must be functional in the sense of minimizing reaching, stooping, and walking.
2. The limit of reaching height should be the height a person can reach with bent fingers while standing in a comfortable working position with both feet flat on the floor.
3. Storage space should be arranged in such a way that items are located close to where the *first* operation involving them will take place.
4. Frequently used items should be stored where they can be taken down and put back without excessive strain.

Fig. 18.11

Basic kitchen plans.

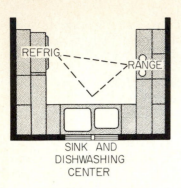

REFRIG.   RANGE

SINK AND
DISHWASHING
CENTER

(a) U-Shaped Kitchen

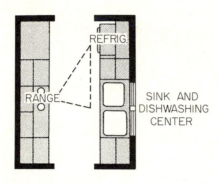

REFRIG.

RANGE

SINK AND
DISHWASHING
CENTER

(b) Two-wall Kitchen

REFRIG.

SINK AND
DISHWASHING
CENTER

RANGE

(c) L-Shaped Kitchen

SINK AND
DISHWASHING
CENTER

REFRIG.

RANGE

(d) One-wall Kitchen

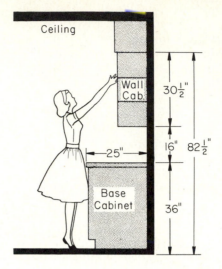

Ceiling

Wall
Cab.

$30\frac{1}{2}$"

25"

16" $82\frac{1}{2}$"

Base
Cabinet

36"

5. Items should be stored so that they can be easily seen, reached, and grasped.
6. Storage space should be sufficiently flexible to permit its adjustment to varying sizes, amounts, and kinds of food, supplies, and utensils.
7. The work surfaces should not require an uncomfortable working posture.
8. The worker should be able to sit while doing certain kitchen work, such as at the sink and the mix center.
9. The work surfaces of some counters should be adjustable to different heights.

Recommendations for adequate counter space and convenient heights and depths of storage units include the following:

Counter Space
Refrigerator   Fifteen to eighteen inches at side where door opens.
Mixing area   Thirty-six inches.
Sink   Thirty to thirty-six inches to the left; thirty-six inches to the right.
Range   Twenty-four inches on both sides.

Cabinets

Height Thirty-six inches counter height; thirty to thirty-two inches for mixing counter.

Wall cabinets Fifteen to eighteen inches above counter (first shelf fifty-two inches from floor).

Depth Twenty-five inches for base cabinets; thirteen inches for wall cabinets.

Pitfalls of Planning

Because of the difficulty of changing kitchen arrangements once they are made, it might be wise at this point to examine some of the common pitfalls of planning this area. Amateurs in the field of kitchen planning frequently make mistakes in the following major areas:

1. Use of space. Improper coordination among appliances, work surfaces, and storage areas.
2. Provisions for changes in family patterns. Needs are different at various stages of family growth. The kitchen is not a static area and must be flexible enough to be adapted to different needs.
3. Actual use of facilities. On-paper measurements may vary considerably from the space required to open doors, pull out chairs, and so on.
4. Safety factors. Many activities in the kitchen affect health and safety. The range area must be large enough to allow pot handles to be turned away from the flame; storage areas for frequently used items must be convenient to reach; edges should be rounded and smooth to prevent injury.
5. Proper illumination, ventilation, and wiring are essential to a well-planned kitchen. Sufficient light over work areas, exhaust fans, and adequate outlets for small appliances all are items that the amateur may forget or overlook.

Lighting and Wiring

The kitchen needs some form of general lighting, and it needs special lighting over counters—usually under wall cabinets—and at each center of activity. Wall outlets must be convenient for small appliances that will be used on counter tops.

Decoration

There are trends toward using the kitchen for more family activities and even for entertaining guests. The concept of the kitchen–family room is not a new idea; kitchens in colonial homes were often the centers of family life, and they reflected the warmth that such a living area should have.

We have become accustomed to color in the kitchen, but now more sophisticated furniture design is being applied to both cabinets and appliances. With lovely textured woods treated for easy maintenance, more decorative hardware, and the growing use of carpeting, the kitchen is taking on an entirely new look. A French Provincial, Mediterranean, or Colonial theme is not unusual, and in some homes where the area is adjacent to another room, it is diffi-

Wallpaper covering for cabinets and appliances coordinated for use as a decorative ceiling. *(Courtesy of Wallcovering Information Bureau)* **Fig. 18.12**

**Fig.
18.13**

A patterned kitchen carpet in a modern setting introduces a traditional theme. *(Courtesy of DuPont Textile Fibers)*

**Fig.
18.14**

Another new concept in designing kitchen appliances is the smooth-surfaced cooking counter that keeps electrical elements out of sight. *(Courtesy of Corning Glass Works)*

A small area can be planned for maximum efficiency in storage. *(Courtesy of Gas Appliance Manufacturers Association)*

Fig. 18.15

cult to tell where the kitchen actually begins and ends.

The well-planned kitchens that look more like living rooms than scientific laboratories have not sacrificed functionalism. Plastic laminates, treated wall coverings, and new counter units that cook are easy to clean as well as attractive in appearance. New designs in utensils and accessories also make it possible to supplement the decorative theme without sacrificing efficiency.

Living Room and Bedrooms

There are several criteria for the living room or any bedroom. Is it big enough? Are there suitable places for furniture? Is there good traffic circulation within? Is it bright, cheerful, and pleasant, with adequate light and air?

The size of the living room depends much on personal needs. The feeling of size can be en-hanced by an extended room, a sloped cathedral ceiling, or the use of glass for mirrors, French doors, and windows. The living room should be free of cross traffic and preferably should have at least two exposures; its design should permit furniture to face the room's main focal points, which might be a fireplace, a television set, or an outdoor view.

Bedrooms for adults should be large enough to hold a desk and chairs as well as bedroom furniture. A child's bedroom needs space for study and play. Windows should be large enough to let in ample light and air.

The Family Room

The family room is an optional room, basically an informal living room. It may also be used as a secondary conversation/entertainment area.

Ideally, the family room should go next to the kitchen, from where children can be watched; preferably it should be on the opposite side of the kitchen from the living room. It should have access to the outdoors. It should have plenty of natural daylight and should not be too small and cramped. In many homes, finished basements have been equipped as family or game rooms, despite the lack of windows.

The Laundry Area

There must be some provision for taking care of the family wash in every household. In most families, an automatic washer and dryer are essential pieces of equipment.

Location

The laundry center is often planned as part of the kitchen or is placed adjacent to the kitchen with some form of division between the two areas. The basement has also been a favorite spot for the laundry, but some homes have special utility rooms on the bedroom floor. Because most of the bulky items in the family wash come from the bedrooms and the bathrooms, there is an increasing trend to place the laundry center closer to these rooms. A location near the bathroom reduces distances in gathering soiled linens and putting away clean ones. It also eliminates the need for clothes chutes and requires little additional cost for plumbing if it is also near a bathroom.

In a two-story house, a second-floor location makes laundering simpler; one is not burdened with the chore of getting clothes up and down two flights of stairs. The total amount of space needed depends on your equipment. The smallest space recommended with an automatic washer, dryer, and ironing area is about six by twelve feet. Ideally, the room should also contain a sink for some hand washing or other special laundry tasks.

Activities

Although automatic washers and dryers have simplified the task of doing the family wash, the myriad new fabrics that require spe-

cial handling have also added something to the complexity of the problem. Some garments must be washed by hand; some respond better to drip-drying. Automatic machines were developed to cope with the various types of fabrics, with special cycles and temperature controls.

All this means that the laundry center must be planned and equipped to keep the expenditure of human energy to the minimum. A large table or counter for sorting the soiled items and folding the clean laundry should be conveniently placed. The automatic equipment is best placed near a deep tub or sink for the hand-washables. Storage cabinets for soaps, detergents, and other supplies must be convenient. Some place to hang the drip-dry items is also an important part of the planning. A place for an ironing board is also desirable.

The laundry must have good light. Although a blue-white light is excellent for showing up spots and scorch marks, it is not a particularly pleasant form of illumination. The person who finds laundry a "problem" chore may want to sacrifice the functional for the aesthetic in this case.

Bathrooms

Although the bathroom is strictly a utility area and above all else must be functional, there is no reason that it cannot also be pleasant and attractive. Modern bathroom planning shows a recognition that this area is more functional if it is large enough and equipped to accommodate two people at once. There must be enough space so that a mother and a young child can move around with ease. When there is illness in the family, the patient may need assistance in the bathroom. Privacy is also essential, so there is a trend toward bathroom compartments with separate areas for tub and/or shower, toilet, and basin. Two basins have become a popular feature of modern design, especially in homes where there is only one bathroom.

Although the equipment and the construction materials in the bathroom must necessarily be designed for cleanliness and easy mainte-

Fig. 18.16

Laundry equipment is concealed behind folding doors at one end of a dining area. *(Courtesy of American Gas Association and American Home Magazine)*

Fig.
18.17

Developments in floor coverings have extended the use of wall-to-wall carpeting into the bathroom. *(Courtesy of Herculon Olefin Fiber)*

nance, it does not follow that this room must have the clinical, scientific type of decoration to which it has been subjected in the past. There seems to be a need for making this room a bit warmer and softer in appearance as evidenced by the interest in colored equipment, washable wall-to-wall floor coverings, and decorative fabrics. Pictures on the wall, growing plants, and other accessories also add to the decorative scheme.

Location

They should be properly located, provide plenty of storage, and have the proper fixtures and accessories sensibly located. One bath and a half-bath (for guests) are adequate for a one-story house of up to about a thousand square feet or for large houses with only two or three people per family. Most larger houses should have a bath for every two bedrooms. A two-story or split-level house should have a half-bath on or near the ground floor. Ideally, the master bedroom would have its own bath. An interior bath location also makes sense; not every bath requires wall windows or a choice outside wall location. Equipped with an exhaust fan and an overhead skylight, it can be relegated to less valuable interior space.

Storage Areas

Well-planned facilities for storage in the home have become almost as much of a status symbol as a swimming pool. So few families have adequate facilities that we are likely to regard a home that does have adequate, well-planned space for all the normal storage problems as something of a luxury. Each year because of soaring inflation the average house size tends to shrink and with this storage becomes more of a problem.

Several factors will influence the needs of homeowners for storage space.

Climate

A family that lives in a changing climate will have more complex storage needs than one living in a constant climate. Seasonal clothing that must be stored is an obvious problem. In addition, outdoor summer furniture, the lawn mower, garden equipment, snow shovels, children's sleds, and other large toys that can be used only at certain times of the year must be stored somewhere. A home in a temperate climate will require storage space of a different nature because the equipment is more likely to have year-round use. For example, there will be no need for sleds and snow shovels, but the lawn mower is used all year round.

Composition of the Family

The number of people living in the home and their ages will influence the type and amount of storage space required. The expanding family with young children may need space for clothes, toys, and play equipment, a carriage, a playpen, and a bathinette.

Activities and Interests

Hobbies and interests demand varying amounts of space. An interest in reading requires bookshelves; an interest in music will probably require record cabinets. Sports enthusiasts require space for both clothing and equipment.

The family that does a considerable amount of entertaining will also have special storage needs. Bridge tables, folding chairs, games, records, and serving pieces such as punch bowls, large platters, extra dishes, large cooking utensils, and so on may all be part of the standard equipment.

An adequate amount of space is important, but planning for the use of space is almost as important. So many homes with storage problems have not used available space in the most efficient manner. To be truly efficient, storage areas must make it possible to place every item

within easy view and accessibility. Either deep, walk-in closets or narrow cabinets with adjustable shelves seem to be the most useful.

Storage walls are often an answer to special problems. Units that allow a certain amount of flexibility can be both functional and decorative.

Guest Rooms

Few homes today can boast of a special room reserved for guests. Space is at such a premium that it must be put to work for more than one purpose, but facilities for entertaining overnight guests are very important in some homeowners' patterns.

A guest room should provide for the comfort and convenience of anyone likely to use it. Various spots in the home may be equipped to fulfill a dual purpose. For example, a sewing room or extra sitting room may also be a guest room. A family room or even a dining room may be equipped to take care of overnight guests by adding a sofa that converts to a bed.

When planning a guest-room area, one should always put oneself in the position of the visitor and try to make the arrangements as convenient as possible, within the limits of the available space. If an extra room for guests cannot be provided, concern should be shown for the special little extras, such as a luggage rack, drawer space, a light for comfortable reading in bed, or a lounge chair.

A guest room should, if possible, be accessible to a bathroom or at least a half-bathroom. Guests should feel as though they have the complete freedom of the home and that they do not interfere with the normal functioning of the household.

Outdoor Living Areas

The terrace, patio, or porch has become another important living area in the home. The cookout for both family meals and the entertainment of guests has a special appeal in our casual, relaxed, and informal pattern of living. When the weather is pleasant, so many of the family activities may be centered on outdoor living space that it really must be considered a room.

Various new pieces of equipment and new types of furniture have been developed to meet the needs of these outdoor activities. Portable barbecue grills range from very simple, inexpensive units to quite complex, luxurious, and of course more expensive arrangements for cooking and serving meals. We not only want outdoor furniture to be comfortable, attractive, and resistant to the elements; we also want it to be easy to maintain. Certain types of wood, such as cypress and redwood, have been popular, but metal, glass, and plastics have also been favorite materials.

The outdoor living area is, of course, unique, but some of the principles of room planning must be applied to the arrangement of outdoor furniture and to the decoration. Because the demands on this room for group living will probably be quite heavy, there should be several comfortable chairs arranged for easy conversation. Many people like to include at least one chaise lounge for relaxation. Some sort of convenient table surface near each chair is usually desirable. Here the imagination may be used to include something different. A low retaining wall with a broad-surfaced top can provide a continuous "end table" around the whole area. A few bricks or cement blocks may be arranged to form convenient tables. There are several types of folding tables that are useful when the outdoor living area is used for large groups.

Accessories in the outdoor living room may not be necessary if the garden or surrounding landscaping provides enough interest. However, statuary, potted plants, or outdoor torchlights may be used to provide interesting effects.

Homes for Elderly People

In recent years we have heard a great deal about the aging population and the special needs of our senior citizens. People are living longer and retiring earlier. As children grow up and marry at an early age, the so-called senior citizens are often faced with the problem of maintaining a home that no longer meets their needs. Therefore the demand for retirement homes is steadily increasing, and the building industry is taking special note of designs that appeal to senior citizens.

In actual fact, the types of homes that appeal to senior citizens have many features that also appeal to younger people. It is a mistake to believe that retirement homes belong in some very special, exclusive category. Senior citizens want houses that are simple, sensible, easy to maintain, and safe to use. True, the retired person or couple may need less space than the expanding family, and certain other features of the home may be of greater importance in the later years than in the early stages of family life. For example, having all rooms on one level with no steps to climb is particularly important to senior citizens, whereas the split-level or two-story house may have more appeal to younger people. Some other desires for convenience and ease of maintenance expressed by senior citizens would certainly appeal to other age groups as well.

In situations where senior citizens must live with other members of their families, every effort should be made to give them a sense of privacy and independence. In small homes this is sometimes difficult, but often a simple structural change can provide a happy solution. If adding a separate wing to the house is inadvisable, a bedroom might be converted to suitable quarters. Whenever possible, senior citizens should have a private bathroom and kitchen. Even a tiny kitchenette unit that is relatively easy to install may simplify some of the problems that arise when several generations attempt to live together. A bed-sitting room that is both comfortable and attractive might be equipped with a private television set and any other equipment that can make it possible for senior citizens to live independently of the rest of the family. Such arrangements should in no sense isolate or exclude the elderly from the family group but should merely make it possible for them to have a certain amount of privacy and independence when they prefer it.

A handicapped person or a senior citizen is greatly affected by the immediate surroundings. Such a person can be made to feel comfortable, secure, and free to move around through the living space. How we see ourselves is always affected by how we function both inside and outside the home. Therefore interior design and decoration is crucial for the well-being of the handicapped or senior citizens.

The ability to enter and leave a home with ease greatly enhances mobility. When entrance-ways are wide enough, a person confined to a wheelchair is made to feel free to come and go at will. Interior furnishings are also important to the handicapped and senior citizens in terms of gaining access to all facilities within an area. A room should have no inaccessible spots. Placing furniture around the edges of the room leaves the center open for traffic flow and allows easy access to all areas of the room.

Entrance for such residents can be defined as a space large enough for a wheelchair; ramps and handrails should be available wherever there are stairs. This includes doors to buildings, individual apartments, rooms, and elevators. Another important feature is the necessity for lightweight doors with lever-type handles located at chair level instead of difficult to manipulate knobs. These are important not only to the physically handicapped but to persons with visual impairments and coordination difficulties as well.

Windows are an important link for the disabled person to the outside environment. They should not only be accessible but also easy to operate. Windows such as sliding or casement types can be pushed or pulled open or shut with a minimum of hand or wrist action. Blinds, heavy draperies, and other elaborate window treatments are generally too difficult for some eldery and handicapped persons to manage.

Bathrooms should be large enough to accommodate wheelchair maneuverability. Nonskid grab bars should be placed near the bathtub, shower, sink, and toilet. Soap dishes should be easily accessible. Nonslip floors are important; shower floors should be the same height as the floor outside, with a slight slope toward the center. For the handicapped person, wall and floor coverings should be easy to maintain.

Floors should be covered with nonslip materials that are not only easy to ride over but eliminate the hazard of falls. Nonskid floorwax should also be used on floor surfaces. For people who are visually impaired, floor materials that are easily detected and defined would be suitable. Persons with hearing problems may benefit from flooring that muffles sounds.

Another feature that is of great aid to the handicapped and senior citizens is having walls that are straight, not unusually angled. Also, light switches should be easily reached from a wheelchair.

There are several areas within a home that should receive special consideration. In the kitchen, for example, storage containers and shelves should be easy to reach. For those in wheelchairs, allowance should be made for space underneath sinks. Open shelves that can be easily reached and revolving pull-out units on cabinet doors are needed for convenience. Sinks should be low, with single-control, level faucets. Special consideration should be given to nonskid flooring. Low work tables with rubber mats to prevent utensils and dishes from sliding are essential. For those who are visually handicapped, knobs identifiable by touch would be helpful. An electric can opener, microwave oven, and toaster can make meal preparation much easier.

Bedroom decorations and designs constitute another major area to be considered. Of course, such rooms should be large enough for a wheelchair to enter and maneuver. There should also be plenty of room around the bed to aid getting in and out of it as well as room for bedmaking. Lighting should be placed at the head of the bed for easy reach. Sliding or swing-out closet doors would assist those who are confined to a wheelchair or people with other handicaps. Furniture such as dressing tables and chests of drawers should be easy to reach. Scatter rugs or carpets should be removed.

SECTION FOUR

Background for Interiors

The basic functions of walls and ceilings are to provide protection and privacy, but these areas are important for many other reasons. They determine spatial relationships within the home, and they have a tremendous effect on light, heat, sound, and odor. In addition, they make a major aesthetic contribution; their color and texture become an integral part of each room.

Modern concepts of interior design have broadened our ideas about what walls and ceilings should and should not do. Even with the open planning favored in so much contemporary architectural design, walls and ceilings remain major areas. But when walls are not necessary for actual enclosure, they are replaced by various types of dividers to separate areas without sacrificing a feeling of spaciousness. Grillwork, panels, screens, open shelves, and cabinets are frequently used in lieu of actual walls. Sliding wall panels and folding walls are used to make rooms more adaptable to a variety of purposes. Storage walls of various types have been utilized to conserve floor space. Wall-hung shelves and cabinets have become decorative as well as functional features. They allow for the maximum expanse of floor area so important in making small rooms seem larger. Also, rooms are easier to clean when furniture does not have to be moved.

In designing a room, one has to consider all architectural elements of the interior. A room is a three-dimensional form; the wall, floor, and ceiling surfaces all have their own colors, textures, and forms, and they envelop the furnishings within them to create the total effect of a unit. In other words, each of the rooms's architectural surfaces creates its own visual statement; it can be designed in a bold manner to become the center of interest, or it can be used in a more subtle way so that it becomes an appropriate background and emphasizes the furnishings in that area.

Walls and Wall Coverings

A distinction should be drawn between the wall itself and wall coverings, which are materials attached to the wall. Contemporary design-

19
Walls, Ceilings, Paints, and Finishes

ers are well aware of the "honesty" of genuine materials and are concerned with maintaining it. Some wall materials, if properly used, need no covering at all. Many interiors, for example, use concrete in its natural texture, showing the pattern left by the wooden forms used to pour the concrete; or brick walls that reveal an interesting pattern may be left in their natural state as a conscious expression of material.

Do-It-Yourself Walls

Today many wall coverings are designed for the homeowner to install. Do-it-yourself walls are generally second wall coverings placed over the original wall surface. Prepasted surfaces for wallpapers, self-adhesive wall tiles, wood planks with interlocking grooves, stick-quick plastic moldings, and modular ceiling tiles make installation easy and practical. Many homeowners welcome this relatively new opportunity to add to the individuality of their homes. In order to meet their needs, there is considerable standardization in the sizes and shapes of interior coverings for walls, ceilings, and floors. People like to experiment with materials and textures reminiscent of natural materials such as stone, brick, or wood. An entire industry is devoted to imitation materials such as artificial brick or stone panels and wood beams that are easily nailed or pasted to existing walls. These products are usually made from plastics or other compounds and come in prepasted, precut standard sizes ready for application. Decorative paneling is available in a range of qualities, from real wood, plastic wood, and compressed sawdust to specially treated paper. Paneling may be decorated in wallpaper patterns, painted or laminated in flat single colors, and stained to emphasize the natural grains of wood. There is a conflict between the tendency in contemporary design to insist on the use of natural materials for surfaces and the vast market of imitation materials available to the homeowner. Working with imitations offers many advantages; for example, stones or heavy beams in their plastic versions are not only lightweight but easy to

install, replace, and maintain. Natural surfaces, however, have a sparkle, color texture, and life that can seldom be duplicated. Both natural and man-made materials can be beautiful, yet neither does well in imitating the other.

Handcrafted Materials versus the Machine-Made Look

Wall treatments today give the buyer a choice between looking machine-made or handmade; new methods of applying paint—for example, with modern applicators and sprays—give wall surfaces an unprecedented shine and smoothness. Plastic laminates, vinyl panels, and metallic wall coverings deliberately give the impression of machine processing rather than hand tooling. On the other hand, the homeowner may want the hand-finished look of natural materials—walls of molded, pressed lumber; areas covered with bark, cork, and hand-textured panels of stucco; jumbles of rock surface set into the wall. The customer must decide among such trends.

The Creative Wall

Another feature of today's walls and ceilings is a new freedom in materials and their creative application. One example is the abundance of materials that were traditionally used on exteriors—rough boards, shingles, and glass building blocks—and that are now imaginatively used indoors. The increasing interest in creating custom-designed walls with an artistic look has led to unusual patterning in ceramic tiles; wall graphics of large, bold, painted numbers and stripes; fabrics stretched to cover walls; or bold, flat colors on individual wall surfaces. Sometimes, different colors are used for ceilings and for walls.

Thus walls can become, in a sense, art objects in themselves. In helping to further this bold creative spirit in walls and ceilings, manufacturers are continuously producing new materials for wall coverings, and designers like to make imaginative use of such products. Today it is not uncommon to see molded plastics, metallic foils, and colored and patterned plexiglass covering walls and ceilings.

Fig.
19.1

Walls

Interior walls constitute the single largest continuous visual surfaces in a room. They not only define the room's size and shape but also determine the feel of its space. In applying color, designs, and materials to walls, one should always be aware that a large span of the room's surface is being used up. Wall coverings define the mood and become the principal setting against which we place all other objects in the room. According to some design experts, the design of the room's walls should be the first consideration in planning for a space. One should decide on the type of wall covering to be used according to how colorful, active, textural, and functional the room is intended to be. Depending on the selection of the wall covering, the room can look larger or smaller, noisy or quiet, formal or informal, light or dark, cluttered or empty, festive or serious.

The scale of walls. Scale must be considered in

This wall provides an unusual backdrop to the room furnishings. *(Courtesy of Environmental Graphics)*

the selection of wall coverings. The scale of the wall covering should be related to the types of furniture selected. Walls with bold patterns—such as large, rough stone or concrete textural surfaces—can be overpowering in a small room with furnishings that are light and delicate in appearance. Wallpaper with a small pattern in a light, single color gives a room the appearance of a larger scale.

Open- or enclosed-looking walls. Another decision regarding wall coverings is whether the walls should appear open and light or massive and heavy, producing a feeling of enclosure. The appearance of walls may be changed through the proper selection of the colors, textures, and materials that are used to cover them. There is an accent on sparseness and openness

Walls, Ceilings, Paints, and Finishes

Fig. 19.2

Glass, a popular wall covering, is used to create a sense of space. *(Designed by Richard Knapple, courtesy of Bloomingdale's, N.Y.)*

in living spaces today because in many cases there is less interior space. A sense of openness may be achieved through the use of simple, inconspicuous wall coverings and flat, textureless finishes, which are thin, light, and unobtrusive. An over-all continuity of colors and wall coverings, even extending into neighboring rooms, tends to give a feeling of space.

In some parts of the country, there is resurgence of the traditional Colonial house with its warm and protected spaces, its low ceilings, and its strong sense of intimate enclosure. Strong wall textures and patterns—such as bold bricks and other natural materials and rough surfaces—create the illusion of a substantial wall space.

The complexity or simplicity of the wall. Is the wall to be an important room element, inviting visual attention to itself, or is it to be a backdrop to the furniture arrangement? A wall of a single neutral or off-white color having a smooth surface may recede into the background, playing a passive role in the room's appearance. Patterned wallpapers, textured wood grains, and colorful tiles suggest a sense of movement that becomes an active part of the room, competing for attention with the furnishings. In general, active wall surfaces should require less furniture and simpler furniture arrangements, for the wall itself acts as a busy space filler and creates visual interest. A simply treated wall can give a sense of cohesiveness to a room in that its neutral color may bring diverse elements and furnishings together. Variations in wall treatment may create contrasts and accentuate different areas of a room.

The texture of walls. In considering the texture of walls, one must recognize that there will be many other textures and patterns (as in rugs and furniture) evident in the room. The walls must be able to work with the other textural surfaces used in the room. The texture of a room's walls can also suggest formality or informality; the smooth white wall, reflecting a great deal of light, has always been considered more formal, whereas textured walls of wood or cork (which also create a darker room in absorbing the light) suggest more intimacy and less formality. Wall textures may range from the glossy, smooth surfaces of ceramic tiles, plastics, or even glass, to rough stony or brick surfaces or textured paint areas, with many possibilities in between.

Durability of the wall covering. In considering durability, we should remember that walls are generally the most often changed elements in a home. We often want to have the flexibility today to change the room's appearance through new types of paints and colors or textures. Coverings may be selected for their durability; but in putting up wood paneling to avoid frequent paint jobs, for example, one must recognize the permanence of such a step.

Wallpaper used as a center of interest. *(Courtesy of the Wallcovering Information Bureau)* **Fig. 19.3**

Wallpaper and painted walls create an interesting sense of space. *(Courtesy of the Wallcovering Information Bureau)* **Fig. 19.4**

Walls, Ceilings, Paints, and Finishes

Sound and light as factors in selecting wall coverings. Noise seems to be a problem in many of today's homes because of the extensive use of sound systems and the greater amount of freedom children have to make noise. Thinner walls and fewer partitions than in the past and less use of the heavy drapery or upholstery fabrics and furnishings that used to absorb noise—all call for some countermeasures. Today we depend more on walls and ceilings for their insulative qualities. Generally speaking soft wall coverings such as cork, padded-fabric, and acoustical materials absorb sound; smooth and hard surfaces such as plastics or wood reflect sound and bounce it around the room.

Light must also be considered in the choice of wall surfaces. For rooms that lack natural lighting and would look better bathed in a great deal of light, smooth and shiny textures may be used. Light-colored walls increase the apparent size of a room and make it easier to illuminate. Smooth and glossy surfaces make the best light reflectors. For more intimate or darker conditions, light-absorbing materials (together with sound-absorbing surfaces such as rough textures) offer interesting combinations.

Fig. 19.5 Changes in pattern directions used as a wall framing device. *(Courtesy of the Wallcovering Information Bureau)*

When thinking of the wall covering to be used, we want to know who will use the room and for what purpose. For a children's room, for example, one may prefer wall tiles or plastic laminates, which are not only quite durable but easy to clean. Of course, the amount of maintenance a wall requires affects the satisfaction that it may give. Generally, masonry, tile, wood, and vinyl plastics are not only easy to maintain but are the most durable. Other more fragile materials, such as wallpapers, may last on walls that do not get hard use. Contemporary paint surfaces are often washable and last for several

Wall Finishes

As far back as the time when people lived in caves, walls have been treated or decorated in some way to add to their beauty and importance. Designs and stories painted on the walls of primitive dwellings have been a valuable source of information for scholarly research.

Just as those who lived in caves wanted to express something by decorating their walls, we do too. We have a wide variety of wall finishes in different colors, textures, and patterns. Modern technology has improved on the old standbys of paint, wallpaper, wood paneling, fabric, and tile, so that today we may have wall surfaces that are both beautiful and easy to maintain.

Paint

Almost any interior wall can be painted in any color. There are many advantages to using paint, especially in certain areas. It is quick and easy to apply, and it is relatively inexpensive. Many paints can be washed; some can be scrubbed with soap and water. When it is necessary or desirable to refinish the wall there is no problem of removing the old finish. In addition to the wide range of available colors, paint can be had in different degrees of gloss, ranging from a dull matte finish to one with a high degree of luster. Various textural effects can be produced by stippling with a stiff brush, a sponge, or a cloth. Variegated color effects can be produced with mottling or spattering. Moreover, certain paints have special extra uses—for example, there are paints that contain insect repellent and some that are phosphorescent.

There are some tricky problems in selecting colors. It should be remembered that a large area of color will look quite different from a small sample or color chip. Walls will reflect each other, and the color will be intensified. Other large color areas in the room will also affect the wall color. The ceiling, the floor, large upholstered pieces, and the wood tones of furniture must all be taken into consideration in choosing the color of the walls. When mixing paints, one should keep in mind that the colors are different when the paint is dry. Some paints will become darker and others lighter when they are thoroughly dry.

The surface to be painted will also affect the texture of the wall. Cracks and serious blemishes may not be easily covered with paint; wallboard and other composition substances may need a sizing coat to prevent the paint from soaking in and producing uneven splotches. However, the original material of the wall may provide an interesting texture when it is refinished with paint. Brick and wallboard are notable in this respect.

Wallpaper

The romantic history of wallpaper dates back to ancient times, but its popular use can be traced back only to about the seventeenth century. Today the diversity of wallpapers presents a real challenge to the imagination. They may be used to create any atmosphere; they may also be used in new and different ways to create an infinite variety of novel effects. The wide range of textures, colors, patterns, and interesting special designs almost defies any attempt at classification. There are wallpapers that simulate wood, marble, and fabric. Flock designs are used to give motifs a fuzzy, raised appearance that adds interesting texture. In these, the design is applied to the paper with some form of glue or adhesive. Short fibers are then embedded in the design, and the background remains smooth. The result is a design of somewhat felted or woven appearance that often has a luxurious texture. Wallpaper with shiny or metallic surfaces can add a sense of high gloss and reflection to wall areas. Bold graphic designs can give one the impression of being in a room surrounded by wall-sized modern paintings.

Some papers introduce architectural features into a room, and still others provide scenic effects. The traditional all-over patterns are ever present, but panels and "spot" motifs have become extremely popular.

Wallpaper is no longer confined to walls. It may be used on folding screens, furniture, and decorative accessories. Closets and other storage areas lined with wallpaper are often more attractive and may even be more useful. For example, cedar wallpaper may make a closet repellent to moth damage.

Advantages of wallpaper. There are many advantages and relatively few disadvantages to using wallpaper as a finish for interior walls. Among the reasons that wallpaper is a popular choice, we might include the following:

1. Color, texture, and pattern lend a distinct individuality to the character of the room.
2. There is a wide variety of designs from which to choose.
3. Wallpaper may be used to emphasize or to minimize architectural features that are either pleasing or unattractive. A large room may be made to appear smaller, a small room may be made to appear larger. The design of

Fig. 19.6   A bold wallpaper emphasizes architectural features.
(Courtesy of DuPont Textile Fibers)

Fig.
19.7

A "new-old" approach is reflected in this setting. The walls, covered in an English crewel-work design, provide an appropriate background for the camel-back sofa covered in gold velvet. *(Courtesy of Latex Foam Rubber)*

the paper may change the apparent proportions of the room; for example, an emphatic treatment of one wall will make it advance.

4. Defects and blemishes in the wall surface can be easily covered or camouflaged.
5. A problem area can be made interesting and attractive. A small foyer or a long, narrow passageway can become a dramatic center of interest without the use of furniture. Difficult or uninteresting alcoves can be given importance.
6. Wallpaper can be used both to separate and to coordinate areas when other means are impractical. One end of a small living room can become the dining area without a room divider simply by the use of a different wall covering.

7. One can try large samples of wallpaper taped to the wall to study the effects of pattern and color in relation to the rest of the furnishings.
8. Wallpaper can emphasize a furniture arrangement or make a center of interest more dramatic. A popular application is a panel or spot design at the headboard of the bed in an otherwise plain bedroom.

Disadvantages of wallpaper. The major disadvantages of wallpaper is that after two or three layers have been applied to a wall, they must be

Walls, Ceilings, Paints, and Finishes

removed before a new finish is applied. With professional steam equipment, old wallpaper can be removed quite easily, but sometimes the amateur without equipment must soak the paper with hot water and scrape it off. This can be very time-consuming.

One other possible disadvantage might be mentioned. The wrong choice of pattern may become tiresome and irritating. Of course, the same objection could be raised for the color of painted walls, but repainting may be easier and less expensive than repapering.

Types of wallpaper. The wallpaper industry has offered to the consumer various kinds of wallpaper at different price levels. With pre-pasted paper that can be simply moistened and applied to the wall, the do-it-yourself amateur can easily develop sufficient skill to paper complete rooms with a professional touch.

The wide variety of materials that are generally categorized as wallpaper almost defies classification. Designs are printed on different grades and weights of paper. Some colors are applied with water-soluble paints, which would, of course, make them nonwashable. Others have various degrees of imperviousness produced by special finishes that set the colors and make it possible to wipe the paper with a damp cloth to remove surface soil. Still others have a design that is impregnated or coated with durable protective finishes that can withstand scrubbing.

In addition to actual wallpapers there are various types of fabric wall coverings and non-woven plastics that have different degrees of permanency and resistance to soil and stains. It behooves the consumer, therefore, to determine the requirements of any particular area in the home and to make the choice accordingly. For example, a kitchen, a bathroom, or a child's room may require a wall covering that is truly scrubbable. A hallway, a dining room, or a guest room may be papered with a less sturdy material.

For our purposes we may classify wallpaper in the following categories:

1. *Nonwashable coverings.* These papers have

Fig. 19.8 A small kitchen assumes a new atmosphere with the use of a bright wallpaper. *(Courtesy of the Wallcovering Information Bureau)*

A fabric panel becomes a headboard and acts as a wall treatment. *(a) (Courtesy of the American Plywood Association) (b) (Courtesy of the Wallcovering Information Bureau)*

been printed with water-soluble dyes, so that any application of water may quickly damage the design. Many of the foil (or metallic looking) wallpapers fall into this category.

2. *Washable coverings.* A thin coating on the paper renders it capable of withstanding cleaning with a damp cloth to remove surface dust. More vigorous treatment of spots and stains will remove the coating and possibly damage the design.

3. *Scrubbable coverings.* Some papers are given a finish that makes them quite resistant to spots and stains. This finish is of a highly protective nature, and therefore it can usually be washed with soap and water. In addition to the coated papers, there are various coated-fabric wall coverings. In general, these tend to be more expensive than the wallpapers, but they are more durable and easier to maintain.

Paper may be given a plastic finish that is quite tough and resistant to scrubbing; however, the more durable scrubbable coverings have a fabric backing. A lightweight canvas may be impregnated with a coating that has the design applied in such a way that it will withstand repeated washings.

Both vinyl coatings on cloth and nonwoven vinyl coverings are available. These are resistant to spots and stains and can withstand constant washing with soap and water.

Selecting a wallpaper. A general rule of thumb is to choose a wallpaper design according to the size of the room—small-scaled patterns for small rooms, medium-scaled patterns for average rooms, large patterns for large rooms. But many other factors must also be considered. In a small room, for example, a dramatic effect can be created with a large-scaled pattern on one wall, or a scenic design can lend perspective and thus

(a)

Fig. 19.9

(b)

increase the apparent size of the area. A large room that has many doors, windows, or other architectural features may have a chopped-off appearance if papered with a large pattern.

The theme of the design and the color tones must, of course, blend with the decoration of the room. Small, delicate, or quaint patterns seem more appropriate for less formal rooms; large motifs and scenic designs lend themselves better to formal and elegant themes.

Wood Paneling

The lovely grain textures of woods make an effective wall finish that is both beautiful and easy to maintain. In modern architecture the

beautiful colors and grain patterns of the more exotic woods have provided an interior finish that meets the requirements of exquisite texture plus easy maintenance.

Wood paneling seems to meet modern requirements for informality or for formality with richness and warmth. The color, texture, and pattern of wood answer a need for beauty in a natural form. Unusual designs are available in which wood is arranged in diagonal, herringbone, and random patterns. Wood paneling looks neither contrived nor man-made. This natural form of elegance has, therefore, found its way into modern buildings that are designed for both public and residential use.

Various types of precut and prefinished panels are available for finishing walls. Sometimes a room may have all the walls finished with

Fig. 19.10 Wall-hung furniture and shelves blend into matching paneling. *(Courtesy of Royal System of Denmark)*

The ease of care makes paneling popular for bathroom use. *(Courtesy of Kohler)* **Fig. 19.11**

Paneling can be used for flooring, wall covering, or ceiling covering. *(Photo by Charles S. Vallone, 1975 Burlington House Award, courtesy of Letitia Baldrige Enterprises)* **Fig. 19.12**

wood, or one wall in a wood finish may be combined with another wall in paint, wallpaper, or a structural material. The familiar pine, walnut, birch, oak, and maple have long been popular. Now the more exotic patterns of rosewood, teak, and zebrawood are in demand, although they are more expensive than the woods that are more readily available.

Laminates

A popular process of bonding layers of various materials together with resins and other plastics has resulted in a number of substances that are extremely useful for wall coverings as well as for counter tops and furniture. Laminated panels are available in a variety of sizes such as in 16″ × 8′ planks and 4′ × 8′ panels for do-it-yourself installation. They are also marketed in premolded units for bathtub and shower areas. These surfaces are usually very durable and resistant to heat and stains. They are easily cleaned with a damp cloth. New techniques of laminating can produce almost any desired effect, so that wood grains, marbleized patterns, cork, and bark can be simulated with an amazing likeness to the natural product. In addition, laminates offer a variety of novelty textures and patterns that resemble no natural materials. The laminates are still rather expensive wall coverings when compared to paint and wallpaper. However, their permanency and ease of maintenance make them desirable for some areas.

Fabrics

Many types of cloth have been used to add interest and warmth to walls. Fabrics may be tacked on frames, pasted directly to the wall, or glued to heavy paper and applied as wallpaper. Open-weave fabrics on metallic papers provide interesting textures and color combinations.

Felt, burlap, canvas, and grass clothes are popular wall fabrics. Damasks and brocades are also used for rich elegance. In recent years a popular trend has been to use bedding sheets as wall fabrics. Sheets are generally less expensive than traditional wall-covering fabrics. There is almost no limit to the variety of color and texture that fabrics can provide. Many of them can be treated or impregnated with plastic so that they will resist soil and can be easily cleaned.

Ceramic Tile

Although it is expensive and time-consuming to apply, true ceramic tile is both durable and easy to maintain. It is a highly desirable finish for floors and counter tops in certain areas, such as the kitchen, the bathroom, and the utility room. Tile table tops have also become increasingly popular because of their high resistance to heat, alcohol, and moisture.

Mosaic tiles produce surfaces with interesting designs and colors. Because of its durability and easy maintenance, ceramic tile is also a favorite finish for certain wall areas that should be both attractive and easily maintained.

Various plastics have simulated tile finishes at considerably less cost. Although many of these are both durable and attractive, they do not have the intrinsic qualities of the real tile. Sheets of simulated tile may be glued or nailed into place. Almost invariably there is something unnatural about the appearance, even though the less expensive substitute may well serve the purpose of the original when cost is a major consideration.

Plastics

Plastic sheets such as vinyls, Formica, Marlite, and similar materials are frequently used for certain sections of interior walls, such as splash boards in kitchens, bathrooms, and laundries. These materials are available in an assortment of colors, patterns, and textures. For more information on these materials, see Chapter 20, "Floors and Floor Coverings."

Ceilings

In some respects the ceiling may be considered the upper wall of a room. The ceiling will affect space, light, heat, and sound, as well as the appearance of a room.

Fabrics and wallpapers are sometimes used to make ceilings more decorative. Acoustical tiles are used to absorb sound, and we have mentioned the contributions that the ceiling area can make toward lighting the room. In general, however, the ceiling has been a somewhat neglected area in modern interior design, particularly in homes of low and average cost—understandably so, because decorated ceilings are expensive. However, the ceiling is a large area that will have considerable influence on the appearance of any room. The height of the ceiling is important in establishing the proportions of the room. It is interesting to note that tall people often feel uncomfortable in rooms with very low ceilings. Although this may seem to be a minor point, it should be considered when one is buying or building a permanent home. Also, utility costs can rise considerably in high-ceilinged areas.

Ceiling Design

It is uncomfortable to have a heavy load overhead unless the weight is obviously supported properly. This, together with the need to reflect illumination, is why ceilings are frequently light and finely textured.

The treatment of floors and ceilings, together with the wall treatment, gives a space its basic shape and character. Ceilings have several important functions. They protect us, and they affect illumination, acoustics, heating, and cooling. A typical ceiling is the same size and shape as the floor it parallels. It is also smooth in surface and is normally painted a light color. A flat, neutral ceiling is inexpensive to build and maintain.

The height of a ceiling is determined by reconciling our needs for head room, air, and economy with our desire for pleasantly proportioned space. Cathedral or beamed ceilings are beautiful and very popular, but rooms with them are considerably more expensive to heat and cool than are rooms with the traditional eight-foot ceiling.

Ceilings can appear to be lower if they are painted a dark color. Horizontal beams also tend to make ceilings appear lower. Moldings, too, can be applied a few inches below the surface to create the illusion of a lower ceiling.

When it is necessary for the ceiling to appear higher, light colors are used or the wall color can

A ceiling used to make a room look larger. The mirrored ceiling highlights the walls as well as the room's furnishings. *(Designed by Richard Knapple, courtesy of Bloomingdale's, N.Y.)*

Fig. 19.13

be extended slightly onto the ceiling perimeter. Another technique is to use mirror ceilings.

Generally, ceilings have to be coordinated with the walls supporting them. They may be complementary and therefore be a continuation of the walls, creating an over-all space, or they may contrast in color, material, texture, or pattern. For example, a wall may be painted an earth color and the ceiling may consist of slats of wood. As in the design of the walls, we may want a ceiling to look inconspicuous; or we may emphasize it as a strong visual element. In the latter case, the ceiling may have unusual light fixtures in different colors and shapes, or it may be covered with unusual materials, such as brick, tile, or fabric, or ceramic tiles. Through special features such as slopes, curves, and indentations, ceilings can give a room an unusual character.

Several types of ceilings may be created to add architectural interest to a space.

Dropped ceilings allow for recessed lighting systems, which can create unusual effects. In systems such as Integrid that allow for easy application, metal suspensions are placed in the ceiling itself, and special-sized tiles are applied close together to form a continuous line. Several types of tiles can be inserted into the ceiling tracks. These are available in a variety of patterns and materials, such as plexiglass sections with lights behind them.

Coved ceilings produce a feeling of expanded space, as ceiling and walls curve into each other and sharp angles are eliminated.

Shed ceilings rise diagonally and give the illusion of space. Gabled ceilings draw the eye upward and accentuate vertical space. Exposed beams follow the line of the ceiling, creating a dramatic effect. Sculptured ceilings, usually made from plaster, fiberglass, or light metal, have low-relief geometric or naturalistic designs.

The most common ceiling materials are plaster and wallboard.

Plaster can be textured, plain, painted, or papered. It provides an uninterrupted surface that meets other plastered walls without joints, thereby unifying the sides and the top of a room.

Fig. 19.14 Modular ceiling tiles provide an ordered patterning of the room space. *(Courtesy of Environmental Graphics)*

Fig. 19.15 Ceiling beams help to create a "rustic" illusion. *(Courtesy of the Wallcovering Information Bureau)*

Fig.
19.16

Gypsum board resembles plaster except that the joints are covered with tape.

Ceiling tiles come in many modular sizes, materials, and patterns. Their advantages include easy application to cover an unattractive ceiling and the property of reducing noise at its source. There are also foil-backed tiles that cut down on air-conditioning costs.

Paints and Finishes

Do-it-yourself projects often require time, patience, and energy, but there is a certain satisfaction that comes with turning something unattractive into something beautiful. With a little imagination and ingenuity, one can sometimes work wonders with what seems like an impossible situation. Whether the project be painting a room, reconverting an old piece of

The coordination of walls and ceilings creates a feeling of spaciousness. *(Courtesy of the Wallcovering Information Bureau)*

furniture, or making a simple table, one's efforts may be well repaid. Many people find this kind of activity so interesting that it actually provides a very rewarding hobby.

Not all such projects have to be time-consuming. Some may require only a few hours or even a few minutes to produce interesting results. At first, such activities should be simple ones that do not require special skills and equipment. New "antiquing kits" and paint in spray cans are fairly simple to use.

One should try to find a local paint store that is well stocked. The dealer will probably be able to offer advice and assistance. A good hardware store will probably have a variety of interesting drawer pulls, knobs, furniture legs, and other equipment for rejuvenating furniture. The new adhesive-backed plastics, available in most paint and hardware stores, have many uses and are particularly suitable for quick and easy projects.

As he or she works up to the somewhat more complicated processes, such as refinishing furniture, the do-it-yourselfer should conduct preliminary research on the proper methods. Extension services often have very useful pamphlets along these lines. The local library will probably have books on the subject. Many paint manufacturers publish directions for using their products.

Major changes in the manufacturing of equipment and supplies for house painting have produced new paints, different colors, and untraditional ways of applying paints to surfaces. Paints produced today generally have less odor; they dry faster and cover almost driplessly without the appearance of brush marks. There is a wider choice of shades and a greater facility for mixing colors at the customer's request. Besides, colors have become brighter, with metallic, wet-look, dayglo, and high-gloss surfaces. Plastic and plastic-looking paints are being produced in a greater variety under names such as epoxy, polyurethanes, and lacquers; these cover a variety of surfaces with all the advantages of a plastic finish covering. There are many new alternatives to applying paints with a brush, such as using sprays and an array of paint applicators. There is a greater choice of paint surfaces—from a flat, matte look to high-gloss or textured surfaces.

Actually, there was a paint revolution in the art world that influenced ways of looking at shades, applying color, and choosing color freely. Color has been the major interest of twentieth-century art, with advances related to chemicals in photography and a concentration on color in paintings and sculpture. Our visual tastes have been influenced by color television as well as by the fashion world's strong interest in color. All this has created a new interest and awareness—a sense of freedom in the use of color in every aspect of home furnishing. Large, flat color fields characterize the schemes of today's homes, with strong color relationships between walls, fabrics, and furniture.

As the contemporary artist in painting, sculpture, and the other visual-arts has relied less on a brush and the look of a handmade surface, new methods have been developed in paint application, such as soaking, spraying, dyeing, and wiping. These new means have become popular for the home as well. The art world's strong interest in color and in novel types of paint is also apparent in the new consumer interest in and the availability of new substances, such as dayglos, lacquers, acrylics, and metallic paints. At this stage, just as many paints and assortments of colors, with different means of applying them, can be found in a paint and hardware store as the artist may find in an art supply store.

With such interest in paints and colors, and with magazines reproducing these ideas, there has developed a new sense of freedom on the part of the homeowner and the decorator in choosing, mixing, and applying colors. The most unusual approaches—such as bright, shiny dayglos—are freely selected, and what may in the past have been considered shocking color combinations are applied to home's interiors and exteriors. Whereas formerly homes may have been white or an inconspicuous pastel, the new owner feels free to redecorate the exterior with bright red window frames, matching railings, and bright green stairs. The traditions dictating "proper" colors for both exterior and interior are being broken.

Types of Paints and Finishes

There is such a wide variety of paints, wood stains, and finishing materials on the market today that the novice may easily become confused. However, paint manufacturers have recognized the interest in home projects among amateurs and have developed products that are easy to use. It always pays to buy good-quality materials: one can be more certain of achieving perfect results.

Essentially, paint is a mixture of three basic ingredients: pigment, binder, and solvent. The pigment determines the color, and the binder holds the pigment particles together to form a film. The solvent or thinner must be a volatile substance that acts as a carrier. It allows the coating to be applied in liquid form, and it then evaporates, leaving the solids affixed to the surface.

Various paints are designed to meet different requirements; for example, a paint for exterior use must be rather heavy and particularly resistant to the elements. Certain paints are made for special surfaces—metal, concrete, wood, or plastic. Also, different degrees of gloss are required for various purposes.

The beginner should understand that paints require different thinners. Some must be thinned with turpentine or mineral spirits; others may be thinned with water. This difference will also determine how one cleans brushes and equipment. It is easier to use a paint that permits the washing of tools in soap and water.

Some of the important terms include:

Alkyd paint Several synthetic resins may be used as vehicles for paint, the usual ones being the alkyds, which represent a most important development in the paint industry and to a large extent have replaced oils in some types of paint. Alkyd paints are usually thinned with turpentine or mineral spirits.

Enamel Somewhat similar to an oil paint, enamel is a special type made with varnish or lacquer to produce a tougher and more durable finish. Much enamel has a high gloss, but it is available in semigloss and low-gloss (or flat).

Epoxy Epoxy paint is also available for interior and exterior use. It is available in cans and sprays and can be bought in a variety of colors, including gold and silver. It looks and feels like procelain and is generally used for household appliances, cabinets, fixtures, and toys, as well as for metal and wood furniture. Epoxy paint adheres to any surface; it is generally nontoxic and lead-free.

Lacquer Lacquer is applied with a brush or a spray. It does not conceal the grain of wood as other finishes do, and it can be used over a painted surface. There are many types of lacquers, ranging from a flat type that dries to a dull matte finish to clear, glossy lacquer that dries to a high-gloss finish. There is also a shading lacquer that produces various shades of white, black, brown, or blond.

Latex paint Another synthetic resin has become extremely popular for interior use. Latex is a resin dispersed in water. As the water evaporates, the extremely fine particles of resin produce a film that is strong and durable. Latex paints have good covering powers, they dry quickly, and they have little or no odor. After drying, they become resistant to water and most of them can be scrubbed. The tools used in painting can be washed easily in soap and water.

Oil-base paint Several kinds of oil may be used as vehicles for binding the pigment particles together and for giving strength to the paint. Linseed oil is most commonly used. Oil-base paints are available for different purposes and in varying degrees of gloss. They are usually thinned with turpentine or mineral spirits.

Polyurethane Polyurethane, has frequent substitute for varnish, is a tough plastic coating, highly resistant to hot and cold water, grease, and most acids. It comes in various finishes, from matte to a high gloss, and can be either sprayed or brushed onto a surface. Used on floors, furniture, and wood paneling, it presents a surface that can be easily maintained.

Sealers and primers New surfaces of plaster, wood, or wallboard sometimes require a preliminary coating that will make the final finishing appear more uniform. Shellac is often useful for this purpose, but paint or special preparations may be used.

Shellac Somewhat similar to varnish, shellac is also a protective coating. However, it is generally less durable and will show water spots. It dries more quickly and is often useful as a primer or wood sealer. Shellac must be thinned with alcohol, and brushes must be cleaned after using this solvent. Different types are available in a clear or an orange finish. The surface to be coated will determine the type to be used. Clear shellac will not darken light-colored surfaces.

Stain Various types of colorants are available

for use on bare wood. These may change the color of the natural wood or merely emphasize the grain pattern. Oil stains penetrate the pores of the wood and must usually be covered with some other protective coating. A stain will react in different ways on different types of wood. It is wise to test the results on some inconspicuous area before staining a piece of furniture.

Varathanes Plastic paints come in cans or sprays. The plastic coating system is used for wood, plaster walls, or metal and is made for both indoor and outdoor use. The plastic finish resists chipping, cracking, or peeling. The high-gloss colors are premixed or can be mixed by the user. Varathane paint is being used regularly by people living near salt water, where rust or corrosion of metal furnishings can present a problem.

Varnish In general, varnish is a transparent protective coating that allows natural surface textures to show through. It is widely used on wood because it does not hide the grain pattern. Various types of varnish are available for different purposes. Some have a high gloss, whereas others have a dull sheen or a satin finish. Certain types of varnish are resistant to moisture and alcohol stains.

A varnish stain may have a colorant mixed with the protective coating. Although these are easy to apply, the results are not usually as attractive as when wood is stained first and then treated with a protective coat of clear varnish.

General Suggestions

A few hints and suggestions may be useful in getting off to a good start.

Assembling the Proper Equipment
Each project will require specific items, and the work will be more enjoyable if one has the right equipment.

Newspapers or drop cloths. Floors and furniture can be protected from spattered paint if they are carefully covered. Cloths are more satis-

factory than newspapers, which tend to crumple and tear. Old plastic tablecloths are good for this purpose. Paint stores sell large plastic or canvas cloths that are very useful.

Mixing pails. Large, clean cans or paper buckets can be used for mixing paint. They must be large enough so that the paint can be stirred easily.

Paddles. Smooth, flat wooden paddles are good for mixing paint. Paint-store dealers often give these to customers. An old ruler or some other piece of flat wood will also serve the purpose.

Clean rags. These are used to wipe up spills and spatters.

Brushes. It pays to invest in good-quality paint brushes and to take good care of them. They will not shed bristles and will probably provide a less streaky effect than cheaper brushes would. One should use a brush that is a convenient size for the job. A three- or four-inch brush is good for walls, but a narrower one will be needed for trim and edges. A width of one and one-half or two inches is usually good for furniture projects.

Rollers and pans. For large flat areas such as walls and ceiling, rollers make a job easier and faster. They come in a variety of sizes and have different types of covers. The paint dealer can help in the selection of the proper roller.

Paint pads. Pads are absorbent spongelike materials that take the place of a roller or brush with the spatter.

Gloves. Old gloves or properly fitted rubber gloves should be worn to protect the hands.

Ladder. A sturdy ladder is essential to the painting of a room. A good one will have a shelf near the top for holding paint cans.

Putty knife. The broad, flat blade of a putty knife is useful for scraping loose flakes of peeling paint before a fresh coat is applied. It is also

Fig.
19.17

essential for removing old finishes when furniture is to be refinished.

Screwdriver. A screwdriver is handy for opening paint cans, removing switch plates, and taking knobs or handles off furniture.

Sandpaper. Sandpaper comes in various degrees of coarseness, and it is important to select the proper grade for the purpose. For most projects a medium coarse (#4/0) and a fine (#6/0) paper will be sufficient.

Steel wool. For some purposes steel wool is more useful than sandpaper. In refinishing furniture, the initial preparation may be done with sandpaper, but a final smoothing with fine steel wool (#0) provides a more pleasing surface.

Selecting Paints and Surfaces

One of the first considerations in the painting of a room or an object is the surface to be painted. Different types of paints for wood, concrete, brick, and aluminum are available for different exteriors; interior surfaces of wood, plaster, vinyl, metals, glass, or ceramic all demand appropriate types of paint.

Another consideration may be the type of use that the surface will get. Areas exposed to heat have to be painted with special metal paints; surfaces that are to be walked on and subjected to heavy wear may require special enamels; surfaces that often get wet or are ex-

A roller and a tray simplify the task of painting large flat surfaces. *(Courtesy of Benjamin Moore & Co.—Paints)*

Fig.
19.18

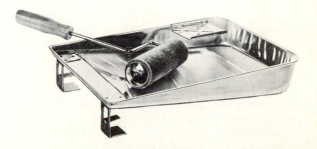

Walls, Ceilings, Paints, and Finishes

posed to moisture may require the use of epoxy-type paints, which cover and seal, or rust-preventing metal paints. Kitchens and bathrooms and their furnishings, which are exposed to moisture or steam, may require enamel paint surfaces. A child's room, where walls face heavy use, may do well with washable paint surfaces such as latex or acrylics, which can be washed with soap and water.

Another consideration may be the condition of the surface to be worked on. For walls that are in a bad state, a heavy or textured paint may be desirable. For those that have surface defects, a thick, hard covering of polyurethane may be desired. For shiny or difficult-to-cover surfaces, such as appliances, fixtures, Formica, or tiles, epoxy paints with a strong adhesive quality may be used.

Another decision in the selection of paints according to surface is the feel or appearance that is desired from the paint job. Often paints are available in flat, shiny, matte, semigloss, gloss, high-gloss, and even textured finishes. A matte area looks and feels different from a high-gloss surface. This decision may be made according to personal preference, based on the surface qualities of the furniture and other objects already in the room. Some of the choices may be visually motivated; for example, shiny paints may be used to emphasize vibrancy or to contrast with soft textures in the room. In terms of safety, some surfaces may have to be non-skid. Glossy hard surfaces may reflect light but are poor sound insulators.

Furthermore, a material can be covered completely with a translucent paint that totally replaces the original color, grain, or material or else gives it a protective coating. One can also apply a finish in such a way that the character of the original wood is emphasized. A protective surface can be obtained through varnishes or polyurethanes (plastic paints).

Deciding on Colors

In deciding on the colors to be used, several things should be considered. Again, some decisions may be practical: how the color selected will cover the surface beneath it (dark colors may require several coats of a lighter hue to cover), or how it will affect the quality of light in the room. Other and more creative decisions may deal with how the shade or tint selected will work within the color scheme of the room. Color not only has to fit into a specific scheme, it should be an exciting addition. One should have a tentative idea as to the color desired and then shop for possibilities. Every brand of paint offers the customer brochures with exact color chips that can be lined up and brought into the home, to assist in decision making. Most of today's stores have paint-mixing machines and can create any color whatever by mixing various shades. Concentrated colors, such as tints can be purchased in cans or tubes and can be added to almost all types of paints to make color changes. Because all of the household members may share the space to be painted (and the choice of color may often influence much of their life), such decisions may involve the members of the home. Because colors change with fashion trends, one could follow trends in such areas as fashion and cars for inspiration. Making a simple diagram of the items in the room can make it easier to visualize and to clarify for oneself what the new color choice will look like in the home.

Prepare the Surface

Much of the success in any home painting project will depend upon how well the surface is prepared for its final finishing. This part of the work may be tedious, but the end results will reflect such efforts.

Before painting a wall, one should repair cracks, holes, and rough spots with plaster, so the surface is smooth and free from blemishes, and remove peeling or cracking paint with a putty knife, sandpaper, or steel wool.

Switch plates, covers of electrical outlets, and any other removable fixture plates should be removed. Handles and knobs that cannot be removed can be covered with masking tape to prevent paint spatters. A little care in this matter makes the cleaning up easier. A paint liner—a gadget with a metal edge that is sometimes useful in the painting of window frames—can be used to keep paint off the glass.

Refinishing furniture is quite another problem. When old finishes or several layers of paint must be removed, a commercial paint and varnish remover can be applied with an old brush and allowed to remain until the surface blisters or crackles. One should have a can or a paint bucket handy and use a putty knife for removing the scum that forms, then use steel wool or a blunt instrument to remove the old finish from corners and crevices. It may be necessary to sandpaper the remains of the old finish or to use a fine steel wool to get down to the bare wood.

All surfaces should be completely free from dust, wax, or grease before any painting or refinishing is attempted. In some cases, merely wiping with a damp cloth will be enough. Greasy kitchen walls may have to be scrubbed with detergent and then rinsed with clear water. Wood surfaces that have been sandpapered should be wiped with a cloth dampened with turpentine. The surface must be completely dry before the new finish is applied.

Paint will adhere better to a surface that is slightly rough. One should sandpaper any very smooth surface and wipe away the dust to be sure the surface is absolutely clean.

Applying Paints

Brushes and rollers have traditionally been the most common means of applying paints to different surfaces. Brushes can be purchased in a variety of sizes (widths and thicknesses) and in different bristle shapes, such as round, flat, or chisel-pointed. The two most common types of brushes are those made of synthetic material, such as acrylic hairs, and bristle brushes. Synthetic brushes are generally used for synthetic water-based paints such as latex or acrylics; bristle brushes are generally used for oil-based enamels and varnishes. There are various brushes for special uses. Some brushes create textural paint surfaces; others, with small bristles, are for fine detail work; still others have special angles for hard-to-reach places.

Rollers, like brushes, can be purchased in different widths and textures. Short-haired rollers are best for oil-based enamels. Thick, long-haired rollers are used for the more absorbent latex paints. There are many types of rubber-textured rollers to create patterns on walls.

Among the new items increasing in popularity with homeowners are paint applicators and spray paints. Although professional house painters still prefer to use a good brush, paint applicators with replaceable pads and sponges in different widths are becoming increasingly popular in the do-it-yourself market. These applicators use the principle of a sponge action in soaking up paint and applying it in a rectangular formation to a wall. Some applicators, in fact, resemble synthetic sponges with handles; others are inserted into plastic handles, and their flat surfaces soak up and apply the paint. Some applicators have edge finders, giving a straight edge and a smooth, controlled surface of paint without the amateur look of a brush job.

Most enamel and plastic-based paints come in spray cans that can be useful to apply over small, detailed areas with an absolutely flat, untouched appearance. Acrylics and latex paints can be premixed and put inside bottles attached to canned air propellants for spraying. Large exterior surfaces are commonly sprayed today with compressed-air spray guns, which can be filled with any type of paint.

Edge guides (rulers for painting) and masking tape, available in different widths, are helpful in painting straight lines and giving crisp color edges.

Applying the Finish

When using paint, one should dip the brush into the paint and wipe it against the rim of the can to remove the excess. Smooth, even strokes will make the paint flow from the brush to the surface. On walls, an up-and-down stroke should be used. On wood, the direction of the grain should be followed. It takes a bit of practice to apply a smooth, even coat that will dry to a uniform finish. With a little practice one can eliminate streaky runs and drips.

Some wood stains should be applied with a cloth or a sponge. One should allow them to penetrate according to the directions on the can and then wipe off the excess with old rags. It may be necessary to experiment a bit, on some inconspicuous part of the piece, to obtain the desired color.

After staining, wood may be finished in a variety of ways. Several coats of wax might be all that is needed. Varnish or shellac may be more desirable in some cases. To develop a beautiful finish, several coats of varnish are often used. One should let each application dry thoroughly, then rub it down with fine steel wool. The surface should be wiped with a clean cloth dampened with turpentine, and then it should be allowed to dry. Then another finishing coat should be applied. The rubbing and polishing between many applications develops a beautiful mellow patina that is far more attractive than the application of one thick coating.

With all painting and refinishing it is important to follow carefully the directions on the label. It may be necessary to experiment a bit on the surface to be refinished, but it pays to develop proper techniques before working on major areas.

Wallpapers

It is so easy to produce interesting and unusual effects with wallpaper that this is one of the most useful means of decorating. One does not always have to paper a whole room to get the desired effect; sometimes merely papering an alcove or one wall will do the trick. Wallpaper can also be used in an interesting manner on folding screens, shelves, accessories, and even on some furniture. Most people who have tried a wallpapering project feel very creative and very proud of the results.

Types of Wallpaper

Two basic types of wallpaper are available, the prepasted variety and the kind to which one must apply the paste oneself. It may be necessary to experiment with each type before deciding which is preferable.

Prepasted papers have a dry paste applied to the wrong side. A strip must be soaked in water for a few seconds until it is thoroughly wet; then the wallpaper is applied directly to a surface. Many dealers sell special cardboard troughs or trays designed for the soaking process, but any tub or vessel that is wider than the roll of paper can be used.

When using a paper without paste, one will need a large table on which to lay the strip and apply the paste. A supply store may rent a special folding paste table. When using a dining room table or two card tables placed together, one should cover the surface with heavy brown paper to protect it from the paste.

Most wallpaper sold today is pretrimmed—that is, the selvage edges are already cut off and do not have to be trimmed. A few special designs may have a protective edge that must be cut off before the paper is hung. One should check this point with the dealer before working with the paper.

The type of design should be carefully studied, especially for a first project. It is easier for the beginner to work with small all-over patterns or textures or with panels that match straight across. Certain designs have "drop-match" patterns with motifs in alternating positions. These require more skill in cutting and applying the paper because the pattern repeat is staggered. With this kind of pattern the motifs on every other strip must be placed at a certain level, with those on the in-between strips dropped to a lower level. This is another point to check with the dealer before buying the paper.

Estimating Amounts

It takes a bit of figuring to determine how much wallpaper will be needed to decorate a specific room or area. With large motifs there may be considerable waste because of the problems of matching the design. The number and sizes of openings in the room will also influence the requirements.

Wallpaper is sold in various widths, usually eighteen, twenty and a half, twenty-four, twenty-eight inches, and so on. A single roll of paper contains about thirty-five square feet (there may be about only thirty square feet of usable paper because of matching problems). The actual length of paper in one roll will vary with the width. Thus the narrower papers will have a greater length per roll than the wider ones.

Ordinarily one will have to buy a "bolt" of paper, which contains either two or three single rolls, depending on the width of the paper. One bolt usually provides five or six floor-to-ceiling strips of paper.

One should approximate the amount of

paper needed by determining the square feet of wall space to be covered, multiplying the length of each wall by the height, and totaling the walls to be covered.

A single roll of paper eighteen inches wide and eight yards long will cover about thirty to thirty-five square feet of wall area. On this basis, a room ten feet wide by fourteen feet long will require about thirteen single rolls. One single roll should be deducted for every two doors or windows of average dimensions.

One should be generous with the estimates. Leftover paper can be used for other purposes; sometimes an unopened package can be returned to the dealer. It is frustrating to run out of paper in the middle of a project and to have to wait until more can be obtained.

Equipment

It has been indicated that equipment needs will depend to some extent upon the type of paper used. With prepasted papers one will not use the large table but will need a vessel for moistening the rolled strips of paper. When applying the paste oneself, one will need a wide brush and a paste bucket. With either type of paper a yardstick will be needed for measuring and shears for cutting. A wheel knife or plenty of sharp razor blades will be necessary for trimming edges. A smoothing brush is used to smooth the paper on the wall. A sponge and cloths will also be needed for wiping away paste drips. A roller or chair caster is useful for pressing edges if one overlaps them at the seams.

Preparing the Walls

New plaster may require a sealer before any finish is applied. A smooth, slick surface is easier to hang paper on than a rough one. Old plaster walls may require patching. A scraper or steel wool should be used to remove rough spots caused by crackling or peeling paint. Holes and cracks should be filled with plaster and the surface should be smoothed.

If a previous layer of wallpaper is firmly attached to the wall, new paper may be applied over it. However, if there are several layers on the wall, it is advisable to remove them by soaking and scraping. Some paint and hardware

stores rent steaming machines, which make the process easier.

Application
Preparing the paper. Because wallpaper is usually tightly rolled, each strip that is cut may curl quite a bit. The paper will be easier to handle if one draws it over the edge of a table, pattern side up, by holding a hand firmly on the paper as it is drawn over the edge. This should be done several times to make the paper lie flat.

When working with a large motif, you should decide how it is to be placed on the wall. A light pencil mark should be put on the paper at the point where the strip is to start at the ceiling or molding. Allowing about four inches above this mark, you cut across, then measure the full length of paper needed from ceiling to floor and, allowing another four inches below this point, cut the strip. Four inches above and below is a generous allowance, which may be reduced once you get started hanging the paper. A yardstick should be used to mark a line where the paper is to be cut.

For the second strip, the paper should be drawn from the roll and held next to the first strip. The pattern should be matched and the top edge marked. The second strip should be cut the same length as the first. Several strips of paper should be cut before the paste is applied.

Pasting. The paste should be mixed according to the directions on the package. It should be about the consistency of cream and entirely free of lumps. One should use a large container so that the wide brush can be easily dipped into the mixture. With the pattern side down, one should place one strip on the table with the edge of the paper along the nearest table edge. The paste should be applied about two thirds of the way down from the top of the strip. About an inch or so should be left unpasted at the top edge. This section should be folded in half with the pasted sides together. Now paste should be applied to the remaining third, and this section should be folded in a similar manner. This folding makes the long strip easier to handle.

Hanging the first strip. It is important to start a

340

(a) Prepare wall surface by filling in cracks and holes and removing loose paint and dust.

Fig. 19.19 **Steps in applying wallpaper.** *(Courtesy of Sunworthy)*

(b) Measure strip length.

(c) Cut strip to the desired length.

(d) Mark a line on the wall for the first strip using a plumb line and ruler.

(e) Apply paste to the back of the wall covering.

(f) Place the strip into position.

(g) Slide strips next to each other to match design.

(h) Smooth strip in position. Trim excess at moldings

papering project with the first strip in a perfectly vertical position, and using a plumb line is the only sure way to accomplish this. The architectural lines of a room are often tilted at a slight angle and may complicate the job unless one uses the plumb line.

You should plan to hang the first strip next to a door or window casing, measuring from the point chosen to a distance about one inch *less* than the width of the pasted strip and placing a tack near the ceiling line at this point. A string is then tied to the tack and a weight is attached to the end of the string near the floor. This line of the string will be a vertical guide for the first strip of paper. You can chalk the string and press it against the wall to mark the vertical guide line.

You should apply the pasted strip of paper by grasping the top edge (about one inch has been left free from paste), unfolding the upper section, and positioning the paper so that the line marking the upper edge is at the ceiling (or molding). The right edge of the strip must follow the plumb line exactly.

The left edge of the strip will extend beyond the starting point about one inch. This will allow for any inaccuracies in the door or window casing.

Holding the right edge in the line, smooth the paper on the wall with a few strokes of the smoothing brush. Working downward, you should be particularly careful to keep the right edge of the strip accurately on the plumb line.

The fold at the lower end of the strip is then opened and the paper is smoothed in place.

When the whole surface is smooth and free from any wrinkles, the top and bottom edges should be trimmed. A *very sharp* razor blade or wheel trimmer must be used. This will make the work easier and help prevent tearing.

At the left edge, where the paper overlaps the window or door casing, the brush should be used to press the paper firmly into the joint. The trimmer or razor blade should then be used to cut away the excess.

Hanging the second strip. The procedure outlined above should be followed in pasting and folding the next strip.

If the paper is pretrimmed, as most of them are, one should butt the seams. This means that there is no overlap; the two edges meet.

Now one is more interested in the left edge of the strip, making sure the pattern matches that of the strip already applied. One slides the paper into place, smooths the surface with the brush, and trims the edges as before.

If the paper has selvage edges, before applying the paste one must trim the edge that will be on top and lay it over the selvage of the preceding strip. The overlap will be less obvious if the seams are gone over with a wallpaper roller.

Corners. When approaching the corner of the room, one should measure the distance from the last strip to the turn of the corner, adding one-half inch to the measurement and cutting a strip that wide. For example, if the last strip ends ten and a half inches from the corner, the next piece should be cut eleven inches wide. You should apply the strip with the half-inch excess extending to the adjoining wall and use the brush to press the paper into the corner.

Next the excess that was cut off should be applied as the next strip. There will be a slight overlap and a mismatch at the corner, but in most cases this will not be obvious. Hanging a new plumb line at the corner will help to keep this strip in proper alignment.

Sponging. Any excess paste should be removed from the surface of the wallpaper and woodwork very quickly. If the paper is water-resistant, one should use a damp sponge; otherwise a dry cloth will do.

Special hints for prepasted papers. There will be directions for moistening the strips before they are applied. Each strip must be thoroughly wet before one attempts to apply it. Also, plenty of *sharp* razor blades must be available for trimming the edges. Wet paper is more likely to tear. Allowing it to dry a few seconds before attempting the trimming process may solve the problem.

You should sponge the surface of prepasted papers with clear water to remove all traces of paste.

Floors, along with walls and ceilings, form the shell of the room. Each one has different functions and should be integrated harmoniously. To develop a total color scheme for interiors, start with the floors and the walls.

Since ancient times people have been concerned with covering the floors of homes and buildings. Floor covering has kept pace with progress in technology and represents our need for comfort and warmth.

The consumer today is faced with a wide range of possible floor coverings. In all probability, color, texture, and price will be the factors that have the strongest influence on one's choice. However, there are three chief reasons why selections should be made with care:

1. The floor is a large, important area. The design, color, and texture of the floor covering will therefore have considerable influence on the appearance of the room.
2. The floor is usually subjected to hard wear from abrasion, pressure, and soil. The surface should be both durable and easy to maintain.
3. Most floor coverings are relatively expensive and represent an investment of a fairly large proportion of the furnishing budget.

Selecting Floor Coverings

Floor coverings fulfill many needs in the home. Consider the following factors in selecting floor coverings:

Comfort includes warmth, sound absorption, resilience, and anti-static features in floor coverings.

Warmth can be desirable or undesirable, depending upon climate. Usually it is desired in all but warm climates. There are basically three visual ways to make floors look warm: to use dark or middle color values, warm hues, or soft textures.

Sound absorption is desirable. Noise can be lessened by the use of rough, porous materials, high-pile rugs, or cork.

Resilience is the degree of springiness with

20
Floors and Floor Coverings

which a carpet returns to its original condition after weight is removed.

Anti-static is the ability of floor coverings to disperse electrostatic charges and prevent a buildup of surface static electricity. Nylon will build up a great deal of static electricity unless an anti-static finish is applied.

Safety from falls, slips, and skidding, as well as flame retardancy, are good features to look for in flooring.

Aesthetics. The principles and elements of design should be used to create the effect you wish to achieve. Floor coverings should harmonize with the furnishings and architecture of the home. Some of the traditional floor coverings,

such as braided, hooked, rag, and needle-punched rugs, harmonize well in a contemporary home as well as in a colonial home. Oriental rugs, which are often thought to be quite formal, look very natural in traditional and colonial as well as in contemporary homes.

Floor coverings can also *control space* through creating optical illusions. The color of floor coverings can expand or diminish the size of the room. The illustrations in Figure 20.1 show how floor covering designs can affect the size of a room.

Personal likes and dislikes are particularly important when selecting floor coverings. Some people cannot bear to live in a room without a soft rug; others enjoy the cool, clean feeling of a smooth, hard floor. Some people dislike having

Floor covering design affects the apparent size of a room.

Fig. 20.1

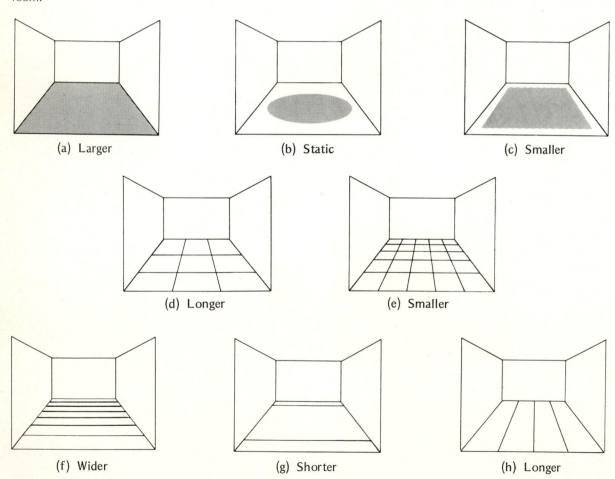

(a) Larger   (b) Static   (c) Smaller

(d) Longer   (e) Smaller

(f) Wider   (g) Shorter   (h) Longer

a floor become an accented area with brilliant color or design; others enjoy a feeling of luxury with a large area of brilliant color or interesting pattern underfoot.

Floor coverings may be divided into two general categories: the soft and the hard. Soft floor coverings include all types of rugs and carpets; hard floor coverings include tile, cork, linoleum, asphalt tile, rubber tile, and vinyl. The structural material of the floor is usually one with a hard surface, such as wood, concrete, or stone. Naturally the merits of each type are of major concern if the floor is to be left uncovered. But because floors are usually covered the advantages and disadvantages of the soft and hard coverings become increasingly important. Soft coverings provide warmth and comfort; they absorb sound; they are often more luxurious than hard coverings. They may, however, be more difficult to keep clean, especially over a long period of time. The hard-surfaced floor coverings are, in general, durable, cool, impervious to stains, and easily cleaned with soap and water. Most homes use both types, with the traditional tile or vinyl in bathroom and kitchen and the soft floor coverings in other areas for comfortable livability. But modern homes are tending to break with such traditions. We find people using the hard-surfaced floorings in many of the living areas and luxurious wall-to-wall carpeting in their kitchens and bathrooms. New developments in both hard and soft floor coverings make it impossible to assign specific roles to each type. The hard-surfaced coverings are becoming more glamorous and more exotic; the soft coverings are becoming more durable and easier to maintain. Many people have resolved the dilemma of a choice by using both types on the same floor, with a background of a hard-surfaced covering accented with areas of a soft covering—a solution that has some obvious merits.

Rugs and Carpets

Soft floor coverings are broadly classified as being either rugs or carpets, although the two terms are often confused. *Rugs* are soft floor coverings that are not fastened to the floor. They

do not cover the entire floor and they are usually cut in standard sizes: $2^{1}/_{4}' \times 4^{1}/_{2}'$, $9' \times 6'$, $9' \times 10^{1}/_{2}'$, $9' \times 12'$, $9' \times 13^{1}/_{2}'$, $9' \times 15'$, $9' \times 18'$, $12' \times 12'$, $12' \times 13^{1}/_{2}'$, $12' \times 15'$, $12' \times 18'$, and $12' \times 21'$. The larger sizes are considered room-size rugs.

A *carpet* is a soft floor covering fastened to the entire floor and sold by the roll in widths of 27 inches to 18 feet or more. It is pieced, if necessary, to fit the room size. Wall-to-wall, stair, and hall carpets are examples.

The term *broadloom* refers to carpeting fifty-

Making the most of limited space: A floating glass shelf serves as an unobtrusive sideboard. The glass and chrome theme is repeated in the sleek dining table and mirrored planter, adding to the open look. (*Anso nylon carpet by Wellco, courtesy of Allied Chemical Corporation*)

Fig. 20.2

345

four inches or wider and describes no other qualities or characteristics except width.

Room-sized rugs can be cut to fit any room. Any length of carpet can be purchased in the standard widths. For example, to cover the floor of a room eleven by sixteen feet a standard finished nine-by-twelve rug would be rather small; a twelve by fifteen would be too wide. One might, therefore, select a fifteen-foot-wide carpet and buy a ten-foot length of it. The rug would then have a six-inch border or floor showing around the edges. Because rugs usually stretch on the floor, it is always desirable to allow a small leeway when ordering such a rug.

Area rugs cover only a small amount of the floor. There are two kinds of area rugs: accent and scatter. *Accent* rugs resemble area rugs but are usually more dramatic in pattern, shape, texture, or color. They are often used for decorative effects. Oriental, hooked, and braided rugs are usually included as accent rugs even though some are room size. *Scatter* rugs are smaller rugs that add spots of color, or texture to make a bare floor look interesting. They are often used to protect areas that are subject to heavy wear or soil; they are usually inexpensive and can be washed.

Carpet tiles are squares of carpet that when laid collectively form a wall-to-wall carpet. They are self-stick-backed squares that can be installed by an amateur. Carpet tiles are available in solid colors, patterns, and various fiber contents. Damaged tiles can be removed and replaced, leaving the spot looking like new, provided the older tiles have not faded or worn out.

An innovation in floor coverings has been the *indoor-outdoor* type of carpeting. This carpeting often has different textural qualities from the more conventional soft floor coverings, but it has opened up new concepts of decorating in various areas of the home. Terraces, swimming pools, playrooms, hallways, and kitchens are achieving an entirely new look with the introduction of a carpet that can withstand weather, stains, and wear. Several synthetic fibers, particularly olefin and acrylic, are being used in either felted or tufted constructions that produce pile effects.

Yarns

The construction of the yarn may affect the durability of the carpet. It is a most important factor in determining styling and appearance. Many novelty textures can be created by the combination of the strands of two or more colors in a ply yarn. Tweed carpets are frequently made this way.

When fibers are given an additional crimp and used in a high-twist ply yarn, the carpet takes on a textural quality that does not readily show marks and footprints. Popularly known as "twist" carpet, this construction has been widely used in recent years.

Yarns can be dyed before they are set in the weaving looms. Sometimes the fiber is dyed before it is spun into the yarn. However, many fine carpets are "piece-dyed" after construction. A reliable manufacturer will guarantee color fastness regardless of the method used for dyeing.

Construction

We might divide soft floor coverings into two categories: the pile weaves and the flat weaves. Either type can be made by machine or by hand, but our discussion here will concentrate mostly on machine-made rugs because these are the ones with which the majority of consumers are

Fig. 20.3

An inexpensive way to have carpeting in one's home is to buy carpet tiles and install them oneself. *(Courtesy of Armstrong)*

concerned. Most of the discussion will be concerned with methods of pile construction.

In past years the method of construction was a more reliable indication of quality than it is today. Now various grades are produced by each method, although to some extent construction processes will still affect costs.

Pile construction means that an extra set of yarns forms either loops or tufts on the surface of a background fabric. Loops, or an uncut pile, are generally more durable, but for appearance most people prefer tufts, or cut pile. This latter construction can be extremely durable if the quality of raw material is high, the yarns are tightly twisted, and the weave is close and tight. *Flat weaving* is just what the term implies.

The following terms are associated with pile construction:

Loop pile. A pile surface with the looped yarns left uncut. The yarn loop can be varied to any height depending upon the pattern desired. In woven carpets, loop pile is often referred to as "round wire."

Two-level-loop patterns. The two-level-loop construction is an extension of the single level loop. The second level of loops is added to create interest. The additional loops make the carpet bulkier and heavier in feel and hand.

Cut pile. Cut pile can be simply described as loop pile that has been cut while it is being tufted. The two most popular types of cut pile today are plush and shag carpeting. A plush carpet is cut pile with a very dense construction. The yarns are usually packed in so tightly that the yarn ends stand straight up and support each other. A shag is a tall, loose plush with a deep pile texture and long cut surface yarns. The pile usually ranges from three-fourths to three inches in height.

Cut and loop pile. Cut and loop pile is a plush with a pattern cut through it, and tightly looped yarns. Cut and loop pile creates a sculptured effect in attractive designs.

Random shear. Random shear is created by

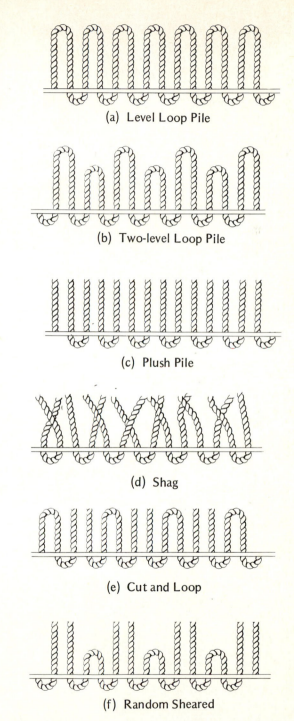

(a) Level Loop Pile

(b) Two-level Loop Pile

(c) Plush Pile

(d) Shag

(e) Cut and Loop

(f) Random Sheared

Fig. 20.4

Different types of carpet constructions.

having two or more levels of loops, with the highest loop area sheared.

Carved shear. A pile may have a design applied by shearing parts of the surface. The pile carving results in beautiful textural effects that have been especially popular in area rugs, in which the design is carefully related to the shape of the rug or carpet. It is also referred to as sculptured.

Density of pile. The terms *pitch* and *wires* are used to indicate the closeness of the weave in carpets or rugs with traditional pile construction. *Pitch* is the number of loops or tufts in a 27″ width; *wires* refers to the rows of loops or tufts in one inch lengthwise. The latter term refers to the method of forming loops on the surface of the pile fabric. Extra warp yarns are strung over wires that are held across the warp and parallel to the filling yarns. As the backing yarns are interlaced, they hold the pile warp in place. Then the wires are withdrawn, leaving loops of the pile warp on the surface. Sometimes a knife is placed on the end of the wire. As the wire is withdrawn, the blade cuts each loop of the pile to form a tuft.

The closest construction has a pitch of 256 tufts or loops in a 27″ width of carpet. A poor-quality carpet may have a pitch of 120. Some rugs may have as many as 13 rows of tufts, or wires, in the lengthwise inch. It should be pointed out that the standards for pitch and wires will vary with the method of construction.

Height of pile. Another factor that is important to both durability and appearance is the height of the pile, which can vary from about one-quarter to five-eighths inches or more. The higher pile will give greater serviceability, a richer appearance, and a more luxurious texture if all other factors are equal. However, unless the weave is also tight and close, a high pile adds none of these desirable qualities.

Backing yarns. The underside or backing of a carpet is usually made of firm yarns that provide a sturdy foundation. They may be made of jute, cotton, rayon, or kraft cord (a special yarn made

The floor is an important area in every room. Texture of a carpet should be chosen with care. *(a)* Plush. *(b)* Short-pile shag. *(c)* Three levels of loop pile in a sculptured effect. *(d)* Long-pile shag. *(Courtesy of Bigelow-Sanford, Inc.)*

from wood pulp). These yarns serve to hold the pile in place as well as to form the backing of the carpet. On some carpets, the warp yarns of the backing may interloop in a chain effect. The crosswise or filling yarns, called *shot*, interlace with the warp yarns. Supplementary yarns called *stuffer warps* are frequently used to give added body to the foundation.

Much carpet is treated with a latex coating on the back. Because this seals the yarns in position, the edges will not ravel and binding is not necessary. Worn or damaged areas of well-constructed pile rugs of this type can be replaced without conspicuous seams. Moreover, because sections of carpet can be joined without traditional seams, it is possible to achieve special design effects with two or more colors.

Types of Soft Floor Coverings

It has already been pointed out that quality in carpet depends on the combination of several factors. In the past the method of construction was a more important indication of quality than it is today, yet it is still important for the consumer to know something about how carpets are made, because such knowledge simplifies comparative shopping. Let us examine some of the types of pile construction.

Axminster. A special and very complex carpet loom is used to weave Axminster carpet, which derives its name from a town in England. Its chief advantage is that almost any pattern can be woven into the carpet. The yarns are set in the loom so that each tuft in a crosswise row can be controlled individually for color. This allows for unlimited variety in both design and color. The initial setting up of a pattern is a slow and expensive process, but once this is done the design may be repeated over and over again with relative ease.

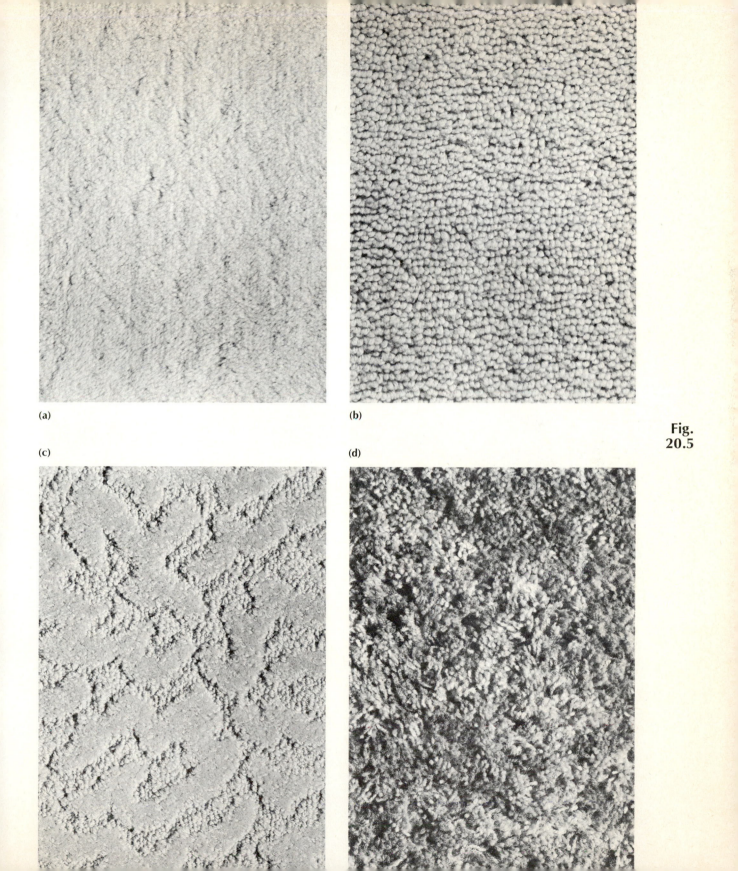

(a)

(b)

(c)

(d)

Fig. 20.5

Fig.
20.6

A zebra rug forms a base for the glass coffee table and emphasizes the primitive and modern art displayed on the wall. *(Courtesy of 1969 Rooms of Tomorrow, designed by Roland Wm. Jutras, N.S.I.D.)*

It is easy to identify an Axminister rug because the crosswise backing yarns are stiff and heavy. Thus the rug will not roll crosswise, but it can be rolled lengthwise.

A standard-quality Axminster carpet has a pitch of 189 (seven tufts per inch crosswise) and at least seven wires or tufts per inch lengthwise. Better qualities have a closer weave. The pile, which is almost always cut, is deeper in the better qualities than it is in poor grades.

Chenille.   There are actually two weaving processes required for the construction of chenille carpet. The first weaving process produces a "blanket," made with strong warp yarns widely spaced and softer yarns in the filling. The blanket is then cut into lengthwise strips, which are pressed into a **V** shape. These furry strips are responsible for the name *chenille*—the French word for "caterpillar." In the second weaving operation, the strips of chenille are placed over the background warp yarns of the carpet, and each strip is held in place with several shots (filling yarns).

This method of construction is expensive, and today it is used mostly for custom-made carpeting. Any pattern or design can be woven into the rug. Naturally, special effects are expensive.

Computer.   The Deering Milliken Company has

devised a new process to make carpets by using the computer. It is the fastest method of making carpets and rugs on the market today.

Knitted. Knitted carpets are made in one operation (similar to hand knitting) by using three sets of needles to loop together the backing, stitching, and pile yarns. Latex is then applied to the backing for body. The pile can be cut or uncut.

Needlepunched. Carpets made by the needle-punch construction are made with layers or batts of loose fiber needled into a core, or scrim, fabric to form a felted or flat-textured carpet material. They have no pile and are usually made of olefin fibers. Needlepunched carpets are harsh and stiff; however they are suitable for outdoor as well as indoor uses. They are good for heavy traffic areas and they resist moisture, so that they are a good choice for pool side.

Rya. *Rya* is the Swedish word for "rug." It is now a popular type of Finnish rug with linen or wool yarns of various lengths and thicknesses. Yarns are knotted and secured into a backing to produce deep shaggy rugs in which the patterns are usually expressionistic or bold in design and color. In Finland, they provide the warmth and color needed for the long winters; in other countries they are usually used with modern furniture.

Tufting. This process of carpet construction has made a significant contribution to the industry in recent years. Now it accounts for over ninety percent of the total production of carpets. The method of tufting represents a departure from traditional pile weaving in that the pile yarns are stitched to a woven cotton or jute backing by a multiple-needle machine. The process has the advantages of being relatively quick and inexpensive. Although it does not permit all types of design, it does permit a wide range of striped, rippled, and tweed patterns as well as various textured effects. All the major carpet fibers can be used in the tufting process. The backing of the carpet is always coated with latex to secure the yarns and to add body. Tufted carpeting is

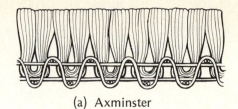

(a) Axminster

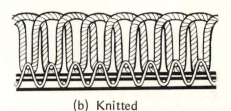

(b) Knitted

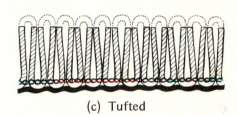

(c) Tufted

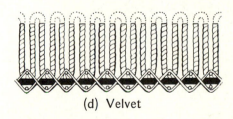

(d) Velvet

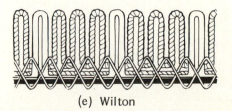

(e) Wilton

Fig. 20.7

Cross-section drawings of the most popular varieties of machine-made carpets.

(left) Carpeting is no longer confined to the floors. The carpeted wall continues the sweep of color and adds acoustical and energy-efficient insulation. Carpet and area rug by Milliken. *(Courtesy of Allied Chemical Corporation)*

(below, left) This contemporary bedroom offers many levels of relaxation and comfort. The carpet texture introduces architectural interest used as an upholstery material and permits lounging and seating possibilities in a simple environment. Easy maintenance and quiet acoustics are other factors offered by carpeting. *(Courtesy of Allied Chemical Corporation)*

(right) Seating can be increased by pitching it at different levels in a series of steps. It is the seventies extension of the old nonfurniture conversation pit. This kind of seating can be built from plywood and covered with carpeting. *(Courtesy of Monsanto)*

(below) The platform room is made with minimal furnishings and lots of carpeting. The platforms provide seating and display space in what would otherwise be a less interesting area. *(Courtesy of E. I. du Pont de Nemours and Company)*

Fig. 20.8

Fig. 20.10

Fig. 20.9

generally available in widths of nine, twelve, and fifteen feet.

As with other types of carpet, the tufted varieties differ in quality. With good-quality yarn, a thick, close pile, and a sturdy backing, tufted rugs will be luxurious and durable.

Velvet. One of the simplest methods of making carpet is by the velvet weave. Some striped and variegated color designs are possible, but the method is used mostly for solid colors. Many different texture effects are possible using various types of yarn. For example, a frieze surface is produced by the use of tightly twisted yarns in a cut pile, whereas a plush surface is produced by the use of straight yarns. Various pebble textures can be achieved by the use of tightly twisted yarns in an uncut pile. Tweed effects are achieved by the use of yarns of two or more colors in either a cut or an uncut pile. Further variations in surface texture are possible when both cut and uncut piles are combined to form a pattern; pile woven in different heights yields still another type of sculptured effect.

The velvet weave is used for carpet at all price levels. Because the method of construction is relatively inexpensive, it is possible to produce carpet that will be durable, serviceable, and attractive at a comparatively low cost.

The velvet method is also called a tapestry weave when it is used with a low uncut pile for a special effect.

Wilton. Wilton carpet is named after the town in England where it originated. It is woven on a special type of Jacquard loom that has a series of cards perforated to control the pattern. They regulate the way the different colors of yarn appear on the surface of the carpet. Each yarn is drawn to the surface as it is needed to form a loop, then it is carried along in the background of the carpet until it is needed again in the design. Wilton carpets have a considerable amount of the high-quality pile yarns actually buried beneath the surface. This feature adds strength, body, and resilience, and because of it, Wilton is commonly known as the weave with "hidden value."

The yarns that form the pile are held in

Fig. 20.11

frames, so there is some limitation to the number of colors that can be used, but intricate patterns can be accurately reproduced. This method is also used for carpet in solid colors.

The pile in Wilton rugs may or may not be cut. The popular sculptured designs often combine both types of pile.

A good-quality Wilton is often made on a loom with five or six frames, and usually a fine, tightly twisted yarn forms the pile, although other fibers may also be used. In the better qualities, Wilton rugs have a dense, luxurious pile that is both durable and attractive. This is an extremely expensive carpet-making process.

Special Types of Rugs

Oriental rugs. The symbolism and mysticism of Oriental floor coverings hold an allure for many people who associate romance and tradition with the exquisite patterns and superb colors of Oriental rugs. The subtle history of Oriental rugs is so intricate that it would require volumes to treat the subject adequately. Yet we hope that even a cursory introduction will open a few avenues of a fascinating study.

Today, even in the Orient, the production of rugs has become commercialized. Although Oriental rugs are still made by hand, machine-made yarns, synthetic dyes, and a flaunting of traditional designs have impaired the intrinsic beauty of the ancient rugs. The older rugs were usually made in the homes of families, with designs and methods passed down from one generation to the next. For some people, any attempt to commercialize or to mass-produce such products destroys the value.

The reaction to all of this discussion may be reduced to the question, ''Does the end justify the means?'' A few of the high-quality modern Oriental rugs simulate the lovely design and textures of the originals to such an extent that only experts can tell the difference; but these will not suit the sort of person who must have an original work, regardless of the beauty of any copy. On the other hand, a *good* reproduction of a work of art will appeal to other people. Perhaps one answer lies in the fact that so many artistic reproductions are not of the best quality.

Some typical designs in Oriental rugs. *(Courtesy of Oriental Rug Importers Association)*

Certainly this has been the case with Oriental rugs. Attempts to reproduce them for a mass market have resulted in many cheap imitations that offend any discriminating taste. We therefore tend to reject any imitation, good or bad. Because the fine originals in Oriental rugs are beyond the economic means of most families, the question reduces to whether or not one will accept and enjoy a good reproduction. The cheap, poor-quality imitations are neither beautiful nor satisfying in any respect, and these should certainly be rejected.

Pile-surfaced Oriental rugs made by hand employ either the Ghiordes knot (Turkish) or the Senna knot (Persian). Rugs made with the Senna knot usually have a deeper, more uniform pile. Some of the fine old examples of Oriental rugs have as many as five hundred knots per square inch, but a good-quality modern rug would have about two hundred knots to the square inch.

Most Oriental rugs are made of wool, although camel's hair and silk are sometimes used.

Caucasian. Rugs from the Caucasus are bold in design and color. Elaborate geometric motifs are done in brilliant yellows, blues, greens, and reds, with some black. Characteristic patterns include the eight-pointed star, the swastika, crosses, and linear figures of both humans and animals. In some respects, the patterns of the rugs resemble those of the American Indians.

Chinese. Perhaps the outstanding difference between Chinese rugs and other Oriental rugs is the plainer background. The borders are usually narrow; the central medallions or small spaced motifs are almost always symbolic. The patterns include flowers—especially the peony—clouds, waves, and dragons. Soft yellow, gold, cream, and apricot are favorite colors, with designs frequently in blue. Modern copies of antique Chinese rugs often violate the traditions of the originals.

Persian. Probably the most popular Oriental rugs are the various types of Persian rug, which

(a) Sarouk

(b) Bokhara

(c) Kerman

(d) Chinese

Fig. 20.12

Fig. 20.13

Persian rug, crystal finials, and Georgian columns harmonize in this elegant but small living room. Oriental rugs confer richness in any interior. *(Courtesy of Uniroyal, Inc.)*

are noted for expert craftsmanship, magnificent designs, and beautiful coloring. Rugs tend to differ in theme and interpretation depending on the town or province in which they are made. Some of the best known include:

Feraghan Small stylized flowers in rows on a deep blue ground.

Ispahan Intricate all-over design on deep red background.

Kerman Light background of cream, rose, blue, with designs in other pastels.

Saraband Palm leaves on a rose or blue background.

Sarouk (Saruk, Sarook) Dark reds and blues with floral designs in lighter colors.

In general, Persian rugs are covered with a variety of floral patterns, vines, and sometimes animals. Some types are characterized by large, geometric medallions in the center and stately borders. The designs are graceful and delicate.

Turkish. Designs in Turkish rugs tend to be more geometric in character, but they use floral patterns and adopt the botanical themes used in Persian rugs. In the small sizes used as prayer rugs by the Mohammedans, the design includes a *mihrab* or niche, which is always pointed toward Mecca when the owner kneels on the rug.

Turkoman. Tribes in Central Asia make rugs with a short, close pile. The designs are geometric and the dominant color is a blood red, often combined with cream, brown, blue, or black. The best-known of these rugs are the Bokhara and those from Afghanistan and Beluchistan (now Pakistan).

Other Oriental Rugs. The term *Oriental rug* usually refers to the pile-weave constructions discussed earlier. However, there are several other types of hand-crafted rugs made in the Orient.

Khilims Hand-loomed Oriental tapestries that are thin enough to be used as wall decorations or table covers as well as durable enough to be used as rugs.

Numdahs Felted rugs from India, frequently made of cow's hair. The rugs are often embroidered with vines and floral designs in bright colors. They are familiar to us as the Indian druggets.

Soumaks Flat-surfaced rugs from the Caucasus, with a pattern woven in by means of an extra filling thread.

French rugs. Several types of handloomed rugs originated in France and became so popular that they deserve special mention.

Aubusson. This type of rug bears the name of a small town in France where it is believed to have originated. It is made with a heavy tapestry weave in colors that are, in general, light and delicate, with a somewhat faded tone.

The designs have followed the prevailing mode in France. The early patterns were probably all-over designs. Then, during the reign of Louis XIV, the motifs became more grandiose with the sunburst, acanthus scrolls, shells, and rosettes. The classical period brought more restraint, with daintier flowers, garlands, ribbands, and latticework. The rugs followed also the Empire themes of the sphinx, drum, laurel wreath, and, of course, *N* for Napoleon. In modern times, Aubusson rugs have been reproduced in the best traditions of French design.

Moquette. Moquette carpeting is not at all on a par with the Aubussons and Savonneries, which were made for the courts and palaces. Moquette was more widely used by the French people who could afford carpeting, and it was woven on a 27″ loom in a manner that was somewhat similar to the English Wilton.

Louis XVI sent a Moquette carpet to George Washington for the banquet room at Mount Vernon. This rug was in storage for a number of years, but has now been returned to its original place in Mount Vernon.

Modern methods of weaving Axminster rugs developed chiefly from the principles involved in the Moquette looms.

Savonnerie. The aristocrats of French rugs began in an abandoned soap factory (*savon* in French means "soap"). In the seventeenth century, the government took over ownership and in the early nineteenth century the looms were moved and the factory became part of Gobelins.

Large, luxurious rugs were usually made for the French palaces, but production was always at the discretion of the reigning king. Huge, elegant rugs with exquisite detail were made for the Louvre at the Savonnerie factory.

Throughout the years, the patterns followed French styles, and the colors were rich and deep. Lovely floral patterns in gold, turquoise, rose, blue, and green were often worked on a velvety black background. Frequently the pile around each motif was carved away so that the design would stand out in relief.

Handmade rugs. Rug making as a handcraft has been practiced throughout the world by many groups of people with different materials, methods, and designs. As with any handicraft, the designs represent the artistic development of the people as well as their customs, beliefs, and values. Many rug designs that originated as handmade products are now reproduced by machine.

Braided Rugs. Strips of cloth were twisted and braided to form a thick strand that was stitched in a round or oval shape. Today, handmade, braided rugs are also made from strips of

358 felt. Design is introduced by the use of contrasting bands of color.

Hooked Rugs. A coarse fabric such as burlap or canvas is stretched on a frame and strips of cloth or yarn are drawn through it to form loops. Although the method has been used in various other countries, hooked rugs have become associated with New England, where they became extremely popular during the nineteenth century. The patterns varied considerably and included geometric, scenic, and floral motifs as well as mottoes and proverbs. In some rugs the looped pile was cut for a varied textural effect. Many of the more beautiful designs, especially floral patterns, have been reproduced on modern machines.

Navajo Rugs. Blankets, mats, and rugs woven by the Navajo Indians are characterized by geometrical designs and symbolic figures in gray, white, and black, with accents in bright reds. Later, other brilliant colors were introduced. Modern reproductions use many strong color combinations.

Needlepoint Rugs. The process of embroidering on heavy net or canvas with thick wool yarn has been used for some of the finest handmade rugs. Simple cross-stitches are used as the basis of construction, but the designs are often complex floral motifs with beautiful delicate shading.

Rag Rugs. Strips of twisted cloth were used as the filling yarn on a loom. Simple rag rugs were made in a plain weave with cotton or linen warp yarns.

Modern Handmade Rugs. The high costs of labor naturally limit the production of handmade rugs, particularly in the Western world. However, there are a few in the luxury class that are being made in contemporary design. In the Scandinavian countries, the typical adaptation of native designs that has characterized other modern handicrafts has been evident in rug weaving. Both pile and flat weaves are used in modern handmade rugs. The current use of area rugs has encouraged modern designers to work on handcrafted products.

Flat-woven rugs. Many kinds of flat-surfaced rugs are made by machine. In general, these

A whole new assortment of floor coverings are becoming available. The newly designed rugs may inspire new decorating ideas. *(a)* Modern and primitive art. *(b)* Flower pattern by Milliken. *(c)* Pulsating circles recalling the Op Art trend of the sixties. *(d)* Interpretation of the classic tree of life pattern. *(Courtesy of Allied Chemical Corporation)*

tend to be less expensive than carpets made with pile construction. Although they are not usually as soft and luxurious as the pile rugs, they have been popular as cool, summer rugs or as starters where a low budget prohibits investment in costly carpet, but where some form of floor covering seems desirable.

Linen Rugs. Coarse, sturdy flax fibers have been used for a variety of textures and patterns. Linen rugs are usually reversible and durable.

Fiber Rugs. Paper pulp, or "kraft" fiber, is twisted into yarn and used in plain, twill, or Jacquard weaves. Some fiber rugs combine fiber with cotton or sisal.

Natural-Strand Rugs. Sisal (related to hemp), coconut, and various other types of rush and grass are also used for rugs. They have been popular in rugs in the form of squares that are of one foot, that can be sewn together to form a rug of the desired size and shape. The texture and color lend themselves to year-round use as an inexpensive floor covering in modern interiors. Full-sized rugs are also made from these natural fibers.

Choosing Carpets and Rugs

How Much Carpeting to Buy?

How much of the floor should be covered? There is no one answer, but here are some of the factors to be considered. A solid, unbroken floor surface, even though there is a pattern or design in the covering, will add to the apparent size of the room. Wall-to-wall carpeting is a good choice for any room that one wants to appear larger. If the same carpeting is extended throughout adjoining areas and rooms, the effect of spaciousness is increased still further and the floor will provide a feeling of unity.

If a rug seems to be more desirable than

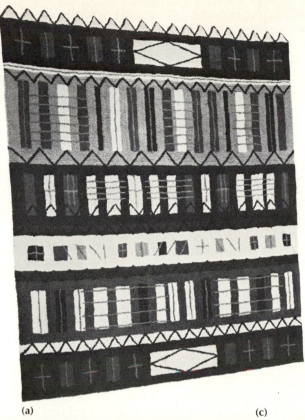
(a)

(b)

(c)

**Fig.
20.14**

(d)

wall-to-wall carpeting, it should be chosen in relation to the size of the room. It may extend almost to the walls for an effect that is similar to carpeting. When some of the floor will show around the edges of the rug, the border and the rug should be in pleasing proportion to each other. There are no hard and fast rules about this, but usually in a small room it is not attractive to have more than about eight inches of floor showing. In a large room, about a twelve-inch border of floor might be a good proportion. Of course, scatter rugs and area rugs are another matter. In a large room, several small Oriental rugs might be extremely attractive even with a fairly large proportion of the floor exposed. It is impossible, therefore, to make general rules that apply to all situations. But usually an ordinary nine-by-twelve rug sitting in the middle of a twelve-by-twenty-two room will seem sad and lost. Rugs should look as though they are at home on floors, and only when they are the correct size and shape for the room will they appear that way.

Because carpeting is sold by the square yard, there will sometimes be waste in cutting a length of carpet to fit a room. Sometimes one can reduce the amount of waste by using the *width* of the carpet lengthwise in the room. For example, if the area to be covered is seven and one-half by fourteen feet, purchasing a fifteen-foot width of carpet means that one foot would have to be cut off the width, and one would buy seven and one-half feet of it. Buying fifteen feet of a nine-foot width and having it cut to seven and a half feet wide would cause more waste.

To figure the amount of carpeting needed to cover an area, one multiplies length by width to obtain the number of square feet; for example, a room twelve by fifteen = 180 square feet. Because there are nine square feet in a square yard, one divides by nine ($180 \div 9 = 20$ square yards). Covering the floor with carpeting that costs $15 a square yard would cost $300 for the twenty square yards. In addition, there may be costs for binding the edges or installing the carpet wall to wall.

Certain areas in a room will receive more wear than others, so it is always an advantage to be able to reverse the position of the rug or carpet. Floor covering cut exactly to fit the shape of the room presents an attractive appearance, but it does mean that the traffic lanes will show signs of wear more quickly. A rug that extends almost to the wall provides an effect similar to wall-to-wall carpeting and is more practical in that it can be turned to distribute the wear.

Color

Because the floor is a relatively large area of any room, the color decision is indeed an important one. Besides, the rug will probably remain longer than other color areas. One may change walls, draperies, and slipcovers before changing the floor covering. It is wise, therefore, to choose a versatile color that will lend itself to a variety of color combinations. This does not mean that the rug must be one of the ubiquitous neutrals, but some colors are definitely more limiting than others. Certain rug colors lend themselves to a wider range of color combinations than others. A deep, rich cherry red, for example, combines beautifully with white, pale blue, pale green, beige, gray, or light pink. On the other hand, lavender or avocado are somewhat more limited colors. Actually they can be used with a variety of colors in that they will not clash, but they need certain tones to bring out their true beauty. Color schemes should look as though they were meant to be. They should not merely be an offensive combination of colors. The choice of color may also be influenced by whether or not this will be the permanent place for the rug. For example, a young couple in a tiny apartment may have plans to move into a house at some future date. The current living-room rug may be purchased with the idea of using it in a bedroom or a guest room later on. Of course, the neutrals are always safe in a situation like this, but if people in such a situation decide on a color with a strong character they must carefully consider its possibilities in other places.

The practical aspects of color should also influence choice. Very light and very dark colors will show footmarks and soil more quickly than the medium hues. Any area that will receive heavy traffic can be a problem in this respect. A foyer hall, for instance, is bound to have many footprints on the floor covering. This can become an irritating, bothersome eyesore.

Some people seem to live *for* their homes rather than *in* them. Consider the case of the young woman, mother of two children, who set her heart on a pale cream-colored carpet throughout her hallway, living room, and dining room even though she knew it was impractical. As soon as the carpeting was on the floor, she tore up a few old sheets and used them as runners on all the traffic lanes. The runners were always left in place, even for company. Of course, the carpeting was beautiful without the sheets, but no one ever saw it that way; and everyone felt rather uncomfortable. Those plastic runners designed to protect carpets from footmarks have the same effect and are equally unattractive. It is more pleasant to have a home that does not present such problems. In all areas that receive heavy traffic one should choose floor covering that does not show soil and can be easily maintained.

Pattern

Whether or not one wants to emphasize or dramatize the floor with pattern is purely a matter of personal preference, but there are some practical points that should be considered. Patterned rugs and carpets have advantages and disadvantages. Within the framework of personal likes and dislikes, pattern and texture should be considered in relation to the purpose and theme of the room.

Advantages of using pattern. Designs in floor coverings range from subdued, small, tone-on-tone texture to large, bold, colorful motifs. Any patterned rug usually has less tendency to show soil and foot marks; therefore, from a practical point of view, such a rug may be desirable for certain areas. The size of the pattern, the type, and the amount of diversified coloring should certainly be in keeping with the room, but frequently a rug or carpet with some pattern lends character to a decorative scheme.

Some people feel that the design in a rug should have architectural qualities. They object to stepping on floral bouquets and delicate motifs, because a floor must be a support and any

Fig. 20.15

(a)

(b)

Pattern predominates in these modern rooms. The controlling factor is the use of only two primary colors for the floor and furnishings. Patterned carpeting limits decorating possibilities because the items that best coordinate with it are usually in solid colors. (a) (Courtesy of Monsanto) (b) (Courtesy of E. I. du Pont de Nemours and Company)

Floors and Floor Coverings

suggestion of delicacy seems incongruous. Yet floral designs may provide a charming atmosphere that is both interesting and tasteful.

The idea that only one pattern may be used in a room is old-fashioned. Many patterned fabrics blend with one another very nicely. It is a matter of selecting those that enhance one another rather than those that compete for attention. A small, all-over pattern will often blend beautifully with a large, bold design if other factors, such as color, texture, and theme, pull the two together. Sometimes even large designs harmonize extremely well. Elegant dining rooms have been decorated with scenic wallpaper or murals and Oriental rugs, certainly two large patterned areas but not at all disturbing if they are well chosen. However, large designs, especially in floor covering, are usually more attractive in large rooms.

Disadvantages of using pattern. Floor coverings with bold designs do tend to be more limiting than solid colors, although, as pointed out above, they are not as restricting as is commonly believed. Also, if the pattern establishes a particular mood, refurnishing the room becomes more of a problem. It is not impossible to change the character of the decoration completely, but it requires more careful planning and selection. In an earlier chapter we mentioned a traditional room with an Oriental rug that was retained when the owner refurnished in the modern style. Through careful choice of colors, textures, and accessories, the result was an extremely beautiful room that was altogether different from its predecessor. Some patterns will be more limiting than others in this respect. In choosing a design, one should consider how it might be used in other settings.

A good rug or carpet may last fifteen years or longer. There is always the possibility that a pattern that is most appealing in the beginning will become tiresome after a few years. Of course, one might also tire of a solid color, but there is a greater chance that a figured rug will become wearisome.

Finishing. Unlike other fabrics, carpets do not go through extensive finishing processes. The coating on the backs of rugs might be considered a finish. Dyeing or printing is sometimes done after the rug is woven, but the majority of carpets have color applied before the weaving stage.

A rug with a somewhat soft cotton backing may be washed in a chemical bath of caustic soda to impart a high sheen or luster finish to the pile yarns. Machine-made "Oriental" rugs are sometimes given this treatment to make them simulate the silky appearance of true handmade originals. The process must be carefully controlled to prevent loss of color and to develop a luxurious sheen rather than a hard, shiny gloss.

Spending Floor Covering Money Wisely
When buying soft floor coverings, it is best to choose better-quality carpeting for high-traffic areas. Use economical and sturdy carpets in kitchens, bathrooms, children's rooms, and playrooms. Avoid faddish designs and patterns that will be quickly dated. Take a piece of carpet sample home and examine it under natural and artificial light in the room in which it is to be used. It should blend with the furnishings in the room. Certain patterns, tweeds, multicolors, uneven weaves, and medium tones show the least amount of dirt and footprints. Light carpets show dirt quickly; dark ones show lint and footprints. Shag piles can flatten with footsteps.

Cost. The consumer should know whether the cost of the carpeting includes delivery, padding, and installation. If you are buying used carpeting, include the cost of cleaning and installation in the price.

Quality. There is no one factor that is responsible for high quality in rugs and carpets; there must be a combination of good materials and excellent construction to assure durability and attractive appearance. The variety of materials used in rugs and the variety of constructions present a complex problem for the consumer who is anxious to receive maximum dollar value. There are some hidden values in rugs and carpets that even the most astute shopper cannot easily judge.

The four chief factors that influence appearance and quality are

1. Type and grade of fiber.
2. Construction of yarn.
3. Height of pile.
4. Closeness of pile.

Fiber. New developments in synthetic fiber production have expanded the variety of soft floor coverings to the extent that they are now practical in every area of the home and in outdoor areas as well. The phenomenal changes in floor coverings within the past few years can be attributed chiefly to the recent developments in the man-made fiber industry.

The most commonly used fibers include wool, nylon, acrylics, olefin, polyesters, cotton, and rayon.

The fibers used in floor coverings must be either carefully selected or specially manufactured to withstand the rigors of wear. Resilience, the ability to retain color, and ease of maintenance are also extremely important factors.

The chapter on decorative fabric has a detailed discussion of fibers. Here, there will only be a brief description of the advantages and disadvantages of fibers used for soft floor coverings. Keep in mind that the construction of the floor covering, as well as the fiber, will influence how the carpet wears.

Acrylics and modacrylics Acrylic and modacrylic fibers look like wool and have some similar qualities. They wear well and have good stain- and spot-removal properties.

Cotton Cotton is seldom used in carpeting today because it has only fair resistance to wear. It soils easily and loses its appearance rapidly, but washes easily.

Nylon Nylon resists abrasion and will not show signs of wear rapidly. It may pill and has the tendency to build up static electricity charges if no anti-static finish has been applied.

Olefin Olefin is a non-absorbant, easy-to-clean fiber that is very strong. It has good abrasion resistance and is available in many colors.

Qualities of Widely Used Soft Flooring Fibers

Table 20.1

Fiber	Wear or Abrasion Resistance	Texture Retention	Resilence (ability to bounce back to life)	Moisture Absorbancy	Soil Resistance	Cleanability	Flammability Resistance
Wool	Good	Good	Very good	Little	Very good	Very good	Good
Cotton	Fair	Fair	Poor	Most	Poor	Very good	Poor
Acrylics/ modacrylics	Medium	Good	Very good	Little	Very good	Very good	Poor
Nylons	Very good	Exceptional	High Very good	Little	Good	Excellent	Fair
Polyesters	Very good	Good	Medium	Little	Medium	Good	Fair
Olefins	Excellent	Medium good	Medium	Least	Very good	Very good	Fair

Olefin is used in kitchens, bathrooms, and outdoor carpeting. It is economical.

Polyester The look and feel of wool can be achieved with polyester. It gives good wear, but lacks resilience when used for carpeting.

Rayon Although it has been greatly improved, rayon performs much like cotton when used for carpeting. It has fair resistance to wear, but little resilience. Rayon carpets have good luster and take dyes well; but they show signs of wear rapidly.

Sisal, flax, grass, jute, and straw The novelty, natural fibers used for carpeting have prices, texture, and a unique appearance that make them attractive purchases. They are usually coarse and do not feel good to bare feet.

Wool A good wool carpet is an excellent buy for long hard wear. It is resistant to soil, cleans easily, and looks good for many years. It is also the most expensive of the carpet fibers. Refer to the chart in the next chapter for additional information on fibers.

Carpet cushions (padding). Padding functions as the shock absorber system for carpets and rugs. It provides insulation, additional resilience, and reduces wear on the carpet. Padding can extend carpet life by as much as thirty to fifty per cent.

Padding is available in several types. The hair padding made of cattle hair is resilient and expensive. The combination hair and jute is less expensive and less resilient, but gives good service. Rubberized hair padding is a combination of a rubber-coated top and bottom with a center layer of blended hair and fiber. Rubber padding is available in a wide variety of types and prices. It may, however, lose resilience with age.

The price of padding increases with the weight and type chosen. For general use, lower weights are sufficient; for stairs, hallways, and heavy traffic areas, heavier weights are recommended.

Installation of floor coverings. The cost of installation should be included in the budget for floor covering because it is not always included in the price of the carpeting. Most wall-to-wall carpeting is installed by the tackless method. Strips of wood with holding nails are put around the edges of the room. Then the carpet is stretched into place and hooked onto the nail-studded strips.

Carpets can also be tacked to the floors, or left loose. The loose-lay method applies to carpets that are used as rugs, either room-size or area types. Carpets can be removed easily for moving or cleaning when they are not tacked to the floor.

The care of soft floor covering. Good care extends the life of soft floor coverings. Where and how you live determines the amount of cleaning needed. Such things as the cleanliness of the air, the condition of the grounds around your home, and the number in your family—as well as the family activities—will affect the amount of soiling. Minimize soil by using scatter rugs or mats near doorways and in heavy traffic areas, or use hard floor covering in the entry. For average carpet wear, the following care is suggested:

1. *Daily.* Once over lightly with a hand-push sweeper.
2. *Weekly.* Thorough cleaning with a vacuum cleaner to remove deeply imbedded soil and grit.
3. *Periodically.* Depending upon traffic, most carpets need to be cleaned by professionals. You can clean your carpets by yourself with wet or dry treatments; but home cleaning cannot equal professional cleaning.

Smooth- and Hard-Surface Floor Coverings

In the past few years, smooth and hard floor coverings have become more glamorous as well as serviceable. Floors are usually made of wood, cement, or stone. When this flooring is attractive and easily maintained, it can be desirable to leave it uncovered. However, in many instances—for either practical or decorative purposes—it is a good idea to cover the flooring with something other than a rug or carpet. The smooth- and hard-surfaced floor coverings offer advantages in that they are durable and easily maintained.

*Factors to Consider in Selecting
Smooth and Hard Floor Coverings*

When selecting any smooth or hard floor covering, be sure that the material is dent-resistant. A flooring that is marked by shoe heels or by an object dropped on it will almost immediately look unattractive. The flooring chosen should feel good to bare feet. Choose a floor covering that is economical to maintain, as well as being unaffected by moisture or grease.

Smooth-Surface Floor Coverings

Smooth-surface floor coverings (also called "resilient" floor coverings) are practical and versatile. They are sold in rolls and tile forms. In essence, most resilient flooring is a mixture composed of a plastic material, fillers, and pigments. Some types give good performance anywhere they are used. Read the floor covering catalogue, or ask a salesperson to be sure that the smooth-surface floor covering you are considering can be used in the location desired. (Rubber, linoleum, cork, and asphalt are also considered resilient, but are not necessarily made of plastic mixes.)

The following are types of smooth-surface floor coverings:

Asphalt tile. Asphalt tile is a serviceable and relatively inexpensive floor covering that is damage-resistant and easy to maintain. It has been widely used in kitchens and other floor areas exposed to grease and oil. It is available in a wide range of colors and patterns, and is generally less expensive than linoleum or rubber tile, but it is more likely to crack or to show scratches.

Cork. Shavings and granules of cork are compressed into sheets and treated with sealers to form a cork flooring. It may be colored, but it is usually used in various natural tones of light and dark brown. The chief advantages of cork

are a lovely texture, high resilience, and good sound absorption. Some types are difficult to maintain and need frequent waxing to preserve color and texture.

Linoleum. A mixture of flour, cork, and oil is applied to some sort of a backing, such as jute or fiber, to form linoleum. There are many different grades, ranging from a heavy inlaid quality to a printed variety whose design wears off rather quickly. In inlaid linoleum, the pattern is impregnated through the thickness of the substance and will stand up under many years of hard wear. Thin linoleum with the pattern applied to the surface is, of course, much less expensive, but it cannot stand heavy use.

Rubber tile. In general characteristics, rubber tile is somewhat similar to linoleum, but it is more resilient. It may be used on almost any type of floor, and the range of color and design is practically unlimited. Often the colors are brighter than those in linoleum. It is extremely durable and attractive.

Vinyl. Available in either rolls or tiles, vinyl floor coverings have branched out into the glamourous areas of interior design. To a large extent, they have removed the stigma of kitchen-and-laundry from hard-surfaced floor coverings, because luxurious vinyls in magnificent designs and colors are now used in the most elegant rooms.

Vinyl is a synthetic that resists abrasion, scratching, denting, and spotting from acids and grease. Different types of vinyl flooring vary in durability as well as in cost; good quality and high style are not at all cheap, but the cost of vinyl compares favorably to other floor coverings of equal beauty and durability.

Vinyl asbestos. The tile made of vinyl and asbestos fillers is similar to asphalt tile, but more resilient; it can be laid over concrete and basement floors. It is tough, and easy to maintain.

Rotovinyl. Rotovinyl is produced through the use of photography and printing. The design and color are printed onto a sheet of vinyl, and

Fig. 20.16

Fig. 20.17

Vinyl floors today are made to look like various luxurious floors. *(Courtesy of Armstrong)*

A vacation home, depending on location and season, should take snow-covered boots, wet bathing suits, and après-ski entertaining in stride. Here the hearth, a tile interpretation of the barbecue pit, is the heart of the retreat. More tile surrounds the fireplace, covers the base of the circular banquette, and solves problems of flying sparks and wet boots or feet. *(Courtesy of Lis King Inc. and Tile Council of America)*

then heavily coated with clear vinyl. It is exceptionally durable.

Sheet vinyl. Sheet vinyl may be purchased with a cushion backing that gives a quieter, more comfortable floor surface. It is available in large sheets and a wide variety of thicknesses; the prices vary accordingly.

Hard-Surface Floor Coverings
Several materials represent this classification of flooring. They are hard-wearing and have decorative properties that make them versatile to use with many different furniture styles.

Brick. Brick is a molded clay, made in block shapes and available in many textures and sizes. Floor brick is frequently glazed. It is extremely durable and easy to clean if it is sealed.

Ceramic tile. One of the world's oldest building and design materials, it still consists of earth clays that are hardened at high temperatures. It can be glazed or unglazed. A glaze gives the tile its surface color and texture and is fused on the tile during firing. Today more than one thousand different types, designs, colors, and shapes of ceramic tile are available. Tiles are easy to maintain especially if they are glazed. They are, however, nonresilient, cold, and often expensive, and slippery when wet.

Concrete. Concrete made of sand and cement mixed with gravel. It is often used for basement flooring. It can be painted, textured, or otherwise ornamented.

Flagstone. Made from a flat stone in irregular sizes, thicknesses, qualities, and colors, flagstone is versatile and durable.

Glass brick. Like the glass brick used for walls, this floor covering is translucent, easy to clean, and adaptable to various kinds of effects.

Marble. A classic floor covering that is elegant but expensive, marble is durable; but it can be damaged by acids and alkaline cleaning solutions, creating dull, rough spots.

Ceramic tile makes this bath look special. Tile can be useful for people with limited space to work with. *(Courtesy of Lis King Inc. and Tile Council of America)*

Fig. 20.18

Mosaic. Mosaic tiles are usually made of glass silica, clay, or marble chips that are mounted on paper, making them easy to lay.

Pebble. Stones are laid in concrete, then polished to look smooth, even though the surface remains rough.

Quarry. Quarry tile is one of the most durable hard floor coverings: it is formed and fired as it comes from the earth. It is very resistant to grease and chemicals.

Slate. Slate is a dense, fine-grained rock produced by the compression of clays and shales, with a characteristic splitting of layers. Its colors range from black to gray.

Terra cotta. Terra cotta is hard baked clay tile which is available in reddish or red-yellow colors. When it has been glazed it is very durable.

Terrazzo. Terrazzo is a floor made of concrete with chips of stone or marble introduced into it. The surface is polished to a smooth finish for very elegant effects. It is durable and easy to maintain, but nonresilient and quite expensive.

Wood. A variety of woods such as oak, walnut, pecan, maple, birch, and pine are all used for hard-surface flooring. Wood has great natural beauty of colors and grain. It is durable and easy to maintain, if cared for properly. Each kind of wood has its own natural color; but different stains and finishes are often applied for different effects. The most popular types of wood flooring today are parquet and plank.

Fabrics are an integral part of every room in the home; they contribute so much to the general decorative atmosphere that they should be chosen carefully. Every note of texture and color, from the lowly dish towel hanging in the kitchen to the most elegant draperies in a formal living room, adds to the personality of a home.

The basic requirements for the various fabrics that are selected will differ, because each one will be used under a different set of conditions. Few if any fabrics have every desirable characteristic; therefore it is important to know how a fabric will be used in order to select one that has the most appropriate properties.

The textile industry and most department stores tend to separate decorative fabrics from regular yard goods, but there is some overlapping. For example, gingham and percale are considered dress materials, but they are useful in several areas of the home; a few decorative fabrics may be used for certain articles of clothing. Sheeting, wide muslin, padding, and toweling are often sold by the yard in still another division of the store. It may be necessary to look in several departments to find exactly the right fabric for a specific purpose.

Widths vary considerably in fabrics. In general, decorative fabrics tend to be wider. Dress-weight cottons and linens are usually forty-five inches wide, but in decorative fabrics forty-eight to seventy-two inches is a more standard width. Of course it is important to know the width of a fabric when figuring yardage for anything one plans to make.

Terminology

To choose wisely from the available textile products on the market, it is important to know textile terminology. With the vast number of textiles that are available, consumers are often bewildered by different trade names and generic names.

To simplify the study of textiles, we will distinguish among four areas: fibers, construction methods, the application of color and patterns, and finishes. The following table shows the components of these four areas, of which it is essential that the consumer have an understanding in order to use textile products to their

21
Decorative Fabrics

best advantage. The table also shows how the different textile elements relate to one another.

Textile terminology can be confusing; refer to the glossary of commonly used textile terms so that the properties of different textile products can be adequately defined.

Fibers—Natural, Man-Mades, and Synthetics

As seen in Table 21.1, fibers are classified as naturals, man-mades, or synthetics. Natural fibers are found in nature, and only their physical form is changed. There are two natural protein fibers of major importance: silk, produced by the silkworm, and wool from animals. The natural cellulosic fibers include seed hairs and stem and leaf fibers. Cotton and linen are in this classification.

Man-made fibers include the regenerated cellulosic fibers as well as the synthetics. Regenerated fibers are produced from something in nature; but their physical and chemical formation has been changed. Rayon, acetate, and triacetate are examples of regenerated cellulosics.

Synthetic fibers, produced from chemicals,

Table 21.1
Textile Fibers, Constructions, Coloring, and Finishes

Fibers		Constructions	Colors and Patterns		Finishes
Naturals	Man-Made and	Weaving	Dyes	Patterns created	Aesthetic
Cellulosics	Synthetics	Brocade	Acid	by Color	Calendering
Cotton	Azlon	Damask	Azoic	Fiber dyeing	Glazed
Flax	Glass	Dobby	Basic	Piece dyeing	Luster
Hemp	Metal	Double cloth	Developed	Yarn dyeing	Napping
Jute	Metallic	Jacquard	Disperse	Printing	Sizing
Kapok	Man-Made	Leno	Fiber reactive	Block	Durable
Ramie	Cellulosics	Pile	Mordant	Direct roller	Abrasion resistant
Sisal	Acetate	Plain	Sulphur	Duplex	Antisnag
Proteins	Rayon	Satin	Pigments	Stencil	Comfort
Silk	Triacetate	Tapestry	Solution Dyeing	Warp	Antistatic
Animal hair	Synthetics	Twill		Resist or discharge	Water repellent
(wools)	Acrylic	Knitting		Batik	Water proof
Alpaca	Anidex	Warp		Discharge	Safety
Angora	Aramid	Weft		Resist	Flame resistant
Cashmere	Modacrylic	Other		Tie dye	Flame retardant
Camel hair	Novoloid	Braids			Care Performance
Asbestos	Nylon	Felted			Crease resistant
Rubber	Olefin	Knit-sew			Durable press
	Polyester	Laces			Sanforized
	Rubber	Multicomponents			Shrink resistant
	Saran	Nonwovens			Soil Release
	Spandex				Biological Resistance
	Vinal				Antiseptic
	Vinyon				Mildew
					Moth resistant
					General
					Bleaching
					Carbonizing
					Mercerization
					Tentering

are made from carbon compounds; they do not include the regenerated fibers. Remember that *all synthetic fibers are man-made, but not all man-made fibers are synthetic.*

The fibers within each class have certain properties in common. Classifications make it easier for the consumer to learn how each fiber behaves with use. For example, the cellulosic fibers are all absorbent and are good conductors of heat. The protein fibers can all be harmed by heat, alkali, and mildew. The synthetic fibers, which are thermoplastics, can all be thermoset (or molded) and be given permanent shapes, such as pleats or crimp.

Some brief explanation of the terminology used on labels seems to be in order before we present a more detailed analysis of decorative fabrics. The Federal Trade Commission (FTC) has promulgated Rules and Regulations under the Textile Fiber Products Identification Act.

Generic names are established for manufactured fibers and each one is defined in specific terms. Table 21.3 lists the classifications and definitions recognized by the FTC. Certain familiar names appear as trademarks owned by particular companies. The regulations stipulate that trademarks may be used on a label along with the generic name of the related fiber.

Fibers

No one fiber has all the desirable qualities that would make it useful for every type of fabric used in the home. Raw materials may be selected on the basis of cost, availability, texture, strength, resilience, resistance to abrasion, ability to take dyes, resistance to soil, ease of care, and so on. In many cases the manufacturer finds that several desirable qualities can be incorporated into the fabric by blending two or more major fibers.

The Natural Fibers

The position of the natural fibers has certainly been challenged by the synthetics, but natural fibers still play a major role in fabrics for home use. That natural fibers are still widely used is an indication that they have advantages for certain purposes.

Abrasion Resistance. The degree to which a fiber is able to withstand surface wear and other frictions, such as rubbing or chafing.

Absorbancy. The ability to absorb moisture.

Denier. The size or thickness of a filament, or yarn. The higher the denier number, the heavier the yarn.

Elasticity. The ability to stretch.

Fabrics. Woven, knitted, braided, felted, or nonwoven material used to make cloth, lace, or upholstery.

Filaments. Fibers of continuous long length. Silk is a natural filament fiber.

Fibers. The smallest structural units in a fabric.

Hand. The way a fiber feels—hard, soft, moist, dry, limp, or silky.

Hydrophilic. Refers to a fiber (yarn or fabric) that absorbs water and is sensitive to moisture.

Hydrophobic. Refers to a fiber (yarn or fabric) that does not absorb water and is insensitive to moisture.

Luster. The shine or glow reflected from the surface of a fiber or fabric.

Monomer. The simple chemical constituent of polymers.

Nonthermoplastic materials. Materials that will not soften with heat or melt. The natural fibers are nonthermoplastic.

Pilling. Small collections of fiber ends on fabric surfaces, forming balls.

Polymer. Many monomers, joined together into a larger unit.

Polymerization. Procedure for converting monomers into polymers, used in producing manufactured fibers.

Resiliency. Ability to spring back to original shape and size after being compressed.

Staple fibers. Short lengths of fibers that must be twisted to form a yarn. All natural fibers except silk are staple fibers.

Textiles. The science of fibers and their end products—fabrics.

Thermoplastic materials. Materials that will soften with heat and take a permanent shape, such as pleats.

Thread. Type of tightly twisted yarn used for sewing.

Trademark. A symbol used to identify merchandise (fibers or fabric) with a specific manufacturer.

Trade name. The name a manufacturer gives to a product to distinguish it from other products.

Yarns. An assemblage of fibers or filaments twisted together to form a continuous strand to make textile fabrics.

Table 21.3

Generic Term and Description*	Registered Trademarks
Acetate A manufactured fiber in which the fiber-forming substance is cellulose acetate. Where not less than 92% by weight of the cellulose is acetylated, the term *Triacetate* may be used as a generic description. (See Triacetate)	Acelet (du Pont) Celaloft Celanese } (Celanese Corp.) Celapermt Chromspunt (Tenn. Eastman) Estron (Tenn. Eastman) —and many in Canada, Europe, and Japan.
Acrylic A manufactured fiber in which the fiber-forming substance is any long-chain synthetic polymer composed of at least 85% by weight of acrylonitrile units.	Acrilan (Monsanto) Creslan (Amer. Cyanamid) Orlon (du Pont) Zefran (Dow Chemical) The acrylics are also being mass-produced under various trade names in Ireland, Belgium, Sweden, France, Italy, Holland, the Iron Curtain countries, and Japan.
Anidex A manufactured fiber in which the fiber-forming substance is any long-chain synthetic polymer composed of at least 50% by weight of one or more esters of a monohydric alcohol and acrylic acid. $CH_2{=}CH{-}COOH$	Anim/8 (Rohm & Haas Co.)
Aramid A manufactured fiber in which the fiber-forming substance is a long chain of synthetic polyamide in which at least 85% of the amides $-\overset{\text{O}}{\underset{\|}{C}}-NH$ linkages are attached directly to the aromatic rings.	Kevlar (du Pont) Nomex (du Pont)
Azlon A manufactured fiber in which the fiber-forming substance is composed of any regenerated naturally occurring proteins, as in corn (zein), milk (casein), peanuts, soy beans, and other natural products.	Ardil (England) Lanital (Belgium) Merinova (Italy) There is considerable Azlon production in Europe and Japan, but none is known of at present in the U.S., which formerly produced fibers known as Aralac and Vicara.
Glass A manufactured fiber in which the fiber-forming substance is glass. The special kind of glass used in making fibers is made by combining molten silica, stone, and certain chemicals and extruding filaments through a spinneret.	Aerocor Fiberglas (Owens-Corning) PPG Fiber Glass (Pittsburgh Plate Glass) Unifab Unirove (Ferro Corp.) Vitron (Libby-Owens-Ford)

Characteristics, Uses, and Care Required

Acetate is manufactured in staple and filament form and produces fabrics of silklike hand and good draping quality. It is moderately hydrophobic (non–water-absorbing) and resistant to moths and mildew.

Acetate dyes are subject to atmospheric fading unless protected by a special finish. Solution-dyed acetates, marked by a dagger in the listing of trademarks resistant to all kinds of fading.

Its pleasing texture and moderate cost make acetate desirable for wearing apparel and for household textiles.

Fabrics containing acetate should be dry-cleaned unless washability is specifically indicated. The fibers themselves are washable, but the finish may be vulnerable to water. Acetates must be ironed at a moderate temperature (325°F.) Contact with acetone (nail polish and remover) and other solvents should be avoided; they dissolve acetate fibers.

The acrylic fibers make light, bulky fabrics with a soft, resilient hand similar to wool. They retain pressed pleats and have good crease recovery, as well as being resistant to wrinkling. Acrylics take well to dyeing in bright colors.

The filament yarn is used for draperies; the staple in knitwear, blankets, rugs, and pile fabrics. Fabrics made of the acrylics are easy to wash and dry, but need moderate temperatures; heat is likely to cause yellowing. Rinse thoroughly; hard-water scum that adheres to the surface will cause graying. Ironing temperature should not exceed 325°F.

A fiber that imparts permanent stretch and recovery properties to fabrics after several launderings and dry cleanings. It improves the comfort of home-furnishing fabrics, provides good shape control, and has excellent resistance to gas fading, sunlight, oils, and chlorine bleach. Used for slipcovers and upholstered items.

A fiber that does not have a melting point. It has high strength and low flammability and is not affected by moisture. Used in hot-air filtration fabrics, protective clothing, and carpets.

A resilient fiber that contributes a soft, woollike hand and excellent draping qualities to fabric.

It is naturally wrinkle resistant. In strength, however, it is so limited that its chief use is as a blend with other fibers used in making woven, knitted, and napped goods. It helps to retard pilling when combined with fibers that have this fault.

Glass fibers and the fabrics made from them are extremely strong; resistant to weather, water, and sunlight; and are not combustible.

The dimensional stability of glass makes it excellent for curtains and draperies; it is also used to reinforce plastics in boat hulls, fishing rods, and golf clubs.

Glass curtains are hand washable, but they should not be rubbed, wrung, folded, or crushed. They drip dry quickly and smoothly and therefore need not to be ironed.

Generic Term and Description*	Registered Trademarks
Metallic A manufactured fiber composed of metal, plastic-coated metal, metal-coated plastic, or a core completely covered by metal.	Lurex (Dow Badische Co.) Metlon (Metlon Corp.) Reymet (Reynolds Metals)
Modacrylic A manufactured fiber in which the fiber-forming substance is any long-chain synthetic polymer composed of less than 85%, but more than 35%, by weight, of acrylonitrile units.	Dynel (Union Carbide) Verel (Tenn. Eastman) Modacrylics are also produced in Canada, Germany, Russia, and Japan.
Novoloid A manufactured fiber containing at least 85% by weight of a cross-linked novolar.	Kynol (Carbarundum Co.)
Nylon A manufactured fiber in which the fiber-forming substance is any long-chain polyamide having recurring amide groups as an integral part of the polymer chain.	A.C.E. (Allied Chemical) Antron (du Pont) Caprolan (Allied Chemical) Nyloft (Hercules Powder) Nylon (du Pont, American Enka, Allied Chemical, Beaunit) Nylon, under various trademarks, is also produced in Mexico, South America, Europe (including the Iron Curtain countries), Egypt, India, and Japan.
Nytril A manufactured fiber containing at least 85% of a long-chain polymer of vinylidene dinitrile, where the vinylidene dinitrile content is no less than that of any other unit in the polymer chain.	Not manufactured in U.S.
Olefin A manufactured fiber in which the fiber-forming substance is any long-chain synthetic polymer composed of at least 85% by weight of ethylene, propylene, or other olefin units.	Durel (Celanese Corp. [polypropylene]) Herculon (Hercules, Inc.) Marvess (Phillips Fibers Corp.) Vectra (Enjay Fibers and Laminates Company)
Polyester A manufactured fiber in which the fiber-forming substance is any long-chain synthetic polymer composed of at least 85% by weight of an ester of dihydric alcohol and terephthalic acid.	Dacron (du Pont) Fortrel (Celanese Fibers Co.) Kodel (Tenn. Eastman) Vycron (Beaunit Mills) Polysters under various trade names are also produced in Holland, Germany, Italy, Russia, Israel, and Japan.

Metallic yarns are usually made with clear polyester films, although acetate and butyrate films are also used, depending on what the yarn is going to be used for.

Metallic yarns in merchandise that is normally washable, such as sheets and bath towels, do not affect the washability.

Modacrylics have a soft hand similar to that of the acrylics. They are resistant to chemicals and are nonflammable, but their heat resistance is poor; ironing temperature must be at 225°F. or lower. Principally used in synthetic furs and carpeting. When blended with acrylic fibers for carpeting, the flammability level is lowered.

A flame-resistant fiber that does not melt and has minimum shrinkage when exposed to flame. It is acid- and alkali-resistant, insoluble in an organic solvent, and easily laundered. Used for upholstered items and draperies.

Nylon is an extremely strong, abrasion-resistant fiber that washes and dries easily. It is thermoplastic; holds heat-set pleats. It has natural wrinkle resistance and crease recovery, and is both moth and mildew resistant. Stretch nylon yarns give elasticity to fabrics. Nylon is much used in blends with other fibers, imparting to the fabrics the strength and wash-and wear characteristics of the nylon.

It should be laundered at moderate temperatures to avoid yellowing; thorough rinsing is essential.

Nylon scavenges color from even normally colorfast items, and white should be washed only with other white items. Low ironing setting is recommended, no more than 325°F.

It is used for curtains, draperies, upholstery fabrics, and carpeting.

Nytril is a soft, springy fiber with much of the feel of cashmere.

Fabrics of nytril are used for knitwear, fashion coatings, and for blending with worsted in men's suitings. Heat sensitive; must be laundered in warm water and ironed at no higher temperatures than 325°F.

A hydrophobic thermoplastic fiber somewhat like Dacron, but with a waxy feel. It is used for carpeting, blankets, robes, seat covers, upholstery fabrics, and marine cordage.

It is highly heat sensitive and should not be exposed to temperatures over 200°F.

This hydrophobic fiber is strong, easy to launder, and quick drying. It holds heat-set pleats, and resists wrinkling, sunlight, mildew and moths.

It may be produced in fabrics that resemble silk, worsted, wool, or cotton.

Some types are more resistant to pilling than others.

Household items made from the polyesters require little ironing because of this fiber's shape-retention properties.

Generic Term and Description*	Registered Trademarks
Rayon A manufactured fiber composed of regenerated cellulose, including that composed of regenerated cellulose in which substituents have replaced not more than 15% of the hydrogens of the hydroxyl groups.	Coloray (Courtaulds Alabama) Colorspun (Amer. Viscose) Cupioni (Beaunit Corp.) Bemberg (Beaunit Corp.) Cordura (du Pont) Fortisan (Celanese Corp.) Kolorbon‡ (American Enka Corp.) Avril (Amer. Viscose) Zantrel (American Euka Corp.) Also many foreign producers in Europe and Japan.
Rubber A manufactured fiber in which the fiber-forming substance is an elastomer composed of natural or synthetic rubber.	Contro (Firestone) Filatex (Filatex Co.) Lastex (U.S. Rubber)
Saran A manufactured fiber in which the fiber-forming substance is any long-chain synthetic polymer composed of at least 80% by weight of vinylidene chloride units.	National (National Plastics) Rovana (Dow Chemical) Saran (Dow Chemical) Velon (Firestone Plastic)
Spandex A manufactured fiber in which the fiber-forming substance is a long-chain synthetic polymer composed of at least 85% of a segmented polyurethane.	Curel (Reeves Bros.) Lycra (du Pont) Vyrene (U.S. Rubber)
Triacetate A subdivision of the acetate group. The designation *Triacetate* may be used where not less than 92% by weight of the cellulose is acetylated.	Arnel (Celanese Corp.)
Vinal A manufactured fiber in which the fiber-forming substance is any long-chain synthetic polymer composed of at least 50% by weight of vinyl alcohol units, and in which the total of the vinyl alcohol units and any one or more of the various acetal units is at least 85% by weight of the fiber.	Not currently produced in U.S.
Vinyon A manufactured fiber in which the fiber-forming substance is any long-chain synthetic polymer composed of at least 85% by weight of vinyl chloride units.	Vinyon HH (Amer. Viscose) Vinyon is also produced in Europe and Japan.

Available in filament and staple. Characteristics similar to cotton. It is a hydrophilic fiber; loses some strength when wet, regains it on drying. Used in blends to produce a great variety of fabrics; lends itself well to special finishes.

When properly finished, rayon can be washed and ironed like cotton. Chlorine bleaches should be avoided on resin-finished rayons to prevent yellowing and tendering.

Rubber is produced neither in staple nor in tow; the yarn is extruded from the spinneret in the desired size. It is used in stretch fabrics, webbings, and rubber thread.

Fabrics containing rubber should not be subjected to heat strong sunlight, oils (lotions, creams, body oils), or constant overstretching.

A tough, flexible fiber that resists stains, chemicals, insects, and flame. Its water repellency makes it useful for outdoor furniture; it is important in carpets, drapery, and upholstery fabrics.

It is highly heat sensitive and cannot be pressed. May be laundered or dry-cleaned depending on nature of material.

Combines light weight with good restoring force. The filament yarn is usually wrapped with another textile fiber or blend, but can be used bare. Makes foundation garments, swimsuits, and other items that demand high elongation, good flex recovery, and durability. It has better resistance than rubber to perspiration, body oils, and cosmetic oils.

Triacetate has excellent draping qualities, is wrinkle resistant, and retains heat-set pleats even in high humidity. It is not as sensitive to heat nor to acetone as the acetates. Dyes well in strong colors but is also susceptible to atmospheric fading. Good wet strength.

An extremely strong fiber, resistant to abrasion and tearing. It is water resistant, but not as impervious to moisture as other synthetics. It is currently being used in rainwear and swimwear, but can be woven to look and feel like silk or wool. Because it is so easily wrinkled, its use in fashion fabrics is limited. It is heat sensitive and should not be exposed to heat over 250°F.

Vinyon is resistant to acids and alkalies, which makes it suitable for fishing nets and industrial uses. It is highly water repellent, strong, and has considerable resiliency. It is so heat sensitive that it melts at normal ironing temperatures.

---

* According to the Federal Trade Commission.
† Solution-dyed acetates.
‡ Indicates solution-dyed.

Cotton. The versatile fiber from the seed of the cotton plant is used in fabrics that range from sheer, delicate textures to heavy industrial materials. The quality of the fiber varies with the type of cotton plant. Sea Island, Egyptian, and Pima (Egyptian cotton plants cultivated in the United States) are the finest kinds of cotton. There are many different grades of fiber depending on length, luster, and natural color. The poorer grades are short, dull, and creamy tan, a color frequently seen in unbleached muslin.

Cotton has the advantages of being relatively inexpensive and readily available. It can be laundered and bleached with little detriment. It takes dyes easily and retains color. On the negative side, the fiber has several disadvantages, but some of these can be overcome in processing and finishing. The length of the fiber, for example, presents problems. The shorter fibers produce a fuzzy yarn. To obtain a smooth yarn, the fibers must be of the longer variety and they must be combed or made more parallel before the spinning process. Mercerizing or treating the fibers with a caustic soda will increase strength and absorbency and will give the fibers a glossy appearance. Continuous exposure to light will cause cotton fibers to weaken and eventually disintegrate, but it is still used for draperies or curtains. Lack of resiliency is one of the chief problems of cotton used as a carpet fiber, but to some extent this difficulty can be overcome by the use of a close, dense pile, which of course increases production costs.

Flax. Linen is made from flax fibers. The lovely textural qualities of real linen have never been equaled by the synthetics, although many attempts have been made. The flax fiber has strength, luster, and a natural unevenness that gives the characteristic "linen" appearance. Qualities vary, and the best types require time and energy to produce. Linen has a natural body and crispness, but it is neither resilient nor elastic. It does not accept dyes readily, and the more interesting and expensive linen fabrics are usually printed by hand blocking. The natural color of linen can be bleached, but the process must be carefully controlled to prevent damage.

Wool. For centuries the excellent qualities of wool have made it a most important fiber for both decorative and clothing fabrics. Technically, *wool* refers to the hair of the sheep, but mohair from the Angora goat and fibers from various other animals, such as the alpaca, llama, and camel, are considered in the same category. The various breeds of sheep produce fibers with different qualities. The desirable characteristics of wool vary considerably with the type and the grade of the fiber. Resiliency and durability are two chief advantages that account for the use of the coarser types of wool in rugs and upholstery fabrics. The fiber takes dyes readily and holds color. The chief difficulties involve care. Most wool fabrics cannot be laundered easily. Strong alkalies damage the fiber. Processes involving heat and moisture may be used to advantage in making felted fabrics, but on other wool fabrics heat and moisture create an undesirable matted appearance. Wool is inherently more flame resistant than other natural fibers.

Silk. For centuries silk has been used for luxurious and exquisite fabrics so it is naturally associated with elegance.

The silk filament is produced by the silkworm, which spins a cocoon. There are various grades of silk, depending upon the type of silkworm and several other factors. The finest qualities come from cultivated silkworms, which are reared with great care and fed on the tender leaves of the mulberry tree. Silk filaments are smooth, even in diameter, and creamy white. When the natural gum is removed the fiber has a beautiful luster. Wild silkworms produce a fiber that is more coarse and uneven. Known as *tussah*, the wild silk has a natural grayish-tan color. It is not usually bleached or degummed, so fabrics made from this type of silk have a texture that is rather dull and rough but not at all unattractive.

Silk is an especially sensitive fiber because it is easily damaged by alkalies, bleaches, and sunlight, causing it to turn yellow and rot. Most silk items should be dry cleaned to maintain a new look.

Minor fibers. Several other natural fibers are

used in the home to a more limited extent than the familiar ones mentioned above. *Jute* is a fiber that is in some ways similar to the coarser grades of linen. It is usually used in its natural state or dyed. It is used chiefly for twine, burlap, furniture webbing, and backings for rugs and carpets. *Hemp,* another coarse fiber, comes from various types of plants that grow in the temperate zone. It is strong and harsh; the natural color ranges from pale yellow to brown. It is used mainly in cord and to some extent for mats and fiber floor coverings. *Sisal* is closely related to hemp and used often for rugs. *Ramie* is sometimes used as a linen substitute. The fiber is coarse and durable. *Kapok* is a silky vegetable fiber that is not suitable for spinning into yarn but does have some advantages for use as a filling material in pillows, mattresses, and upholstery. It is not as durable or as resilient as hair, but it is much cheaper. *Grasses* and *rushes* from a variety of plants can be used in the form of thick ropes to make floor coverings.

Asbestos is an interesting mineral fiber that is difficult to spin into yarn unless it is mixed with some other fiber. Its chief advantage is that it is fireproof.

Man-Made Fibers

There are many reasons why the synthetic fibers are becoming increasingly important in fabrics for the home. Because production can be carefully controlled it is possible to achieve uniform quality and to make fibers that are specifically designed for particular purposes. More uniform production costs are another important factor. At the present time some products made from synthetic fibers are more expensive than similar ones made from natural fibers; others are less expensive. It is difficult to compare products on this basis, because the fabrics will have different characteristics. However, it is expected that with an increased supply of some of the new man-made fibers, the costs of production will decrease. It may well be that in the future differences in cost will become a more important factor.

Ease of care is an important advantage that many man-made fibers have over some of the natural fibers. In general, they tend to resist soil, spots, and stains, and damage from moths and mildew. Many of the washable fabrics need little if any ironing.

Man-made fibers offer a wide variety of textural possibilities. Because the diameter of the fiber can be controlled there is a wide range. Very fine fibers can have considerable strength, so delicate fabrics that are quite durable can be produced.

Length can also be controlled. Filaments can be as long as desired or cut into short pieces and spun in the same manner as the natural fibers. Different degrees of luster can be produced, which further increases the versatility.

Refer to Table 21.3 for the descriptions and characteristics of the man-made fibers.

Yarns

Fibers are spun into yarns in preparation for the weaving or knitting of fabrics. The construction of the yarn influences the appearance, durability, and serviceability of the fabric. Shorter fibers need more twisting to form the yarn than do long filaments, and the way the fibers are twisted as well as the amount of twist will influence performance. In some cases a high twist is desirable for strength and durability, but because twisting decreases the luster of the yarn, the long, smooth fibers sometimes are given very little twist. Unless a strong, durable fiber is used, such low-twist yarns will quickly show signs of wear.

Ply

When two or more single yarns are twisted together in a *ply* construction, the resulting yarn usually has added strength and durability. However, a ply construction may also be used for producing a novelty effect.

Combed

Cotton fabrics are sometimes made with combed yarns. This means that only the longer cotton fibers are used, and they are made as nearly parallel as possible before the actual spinning process. Because there are fewer fiber ends projecting from the surface, a combed yarn will be smoother and usually more lustrous than one that is not combed.

Woolen and Worsted

In fabrics made of wool a distinction is frequently made between woolen and worsted yarns. In woolen yarns the fibers are shorter and in a more random arrangement. Worsted yarns are made of longer fibers in a more parallel position. The cloths made from woolen and worsted yarns will, of course, have different characteristics. The soft woolen yarns will be fuzzy and lighter in weight. Little air spaces trapped in the yarn have excellent insulating value, so this type of yarn is desirable for blankets, but it is not suitable for fabrics that will receive hard wear from abrasion. The smooth surface and the tighter twist of a worsted yarn will produce a more compact fiber, one that is geared to harder use.

Novelty. An infinite variety of textural effects can be produced in fabrics by the use of special yarns. A slub yarn that is thick in some spots and thin in others is frequently used. A ply yarn of one dull strand and one glossy strand, or perhaps two different colors, will produce another effect. Sometimes the two strands are held at different tensions so that the looser one will form little curlicues on the surface for a bouclé texture. The possibilities are infinite, but the consumer must always be sure that the use of a novelty yarn will not detract from the serviceability of the fabric. Frequently the durability of a fabric is sacrificed for interesting texture. In drapery fabrics, this may not be so important, but in upholstery and slipcover fabrics it certainly should be a major consideration.

Metallic. Some of the most fascinating textiles in history were richly decorated with strands of real gold or silver, but these are impractical according to modern standards. We do have instead various metallic yarns that add a touch of luxury along with such practical characteristics as being washable and nontarnishable. Towels and sheets can go through the rigor of the washing machine; and there are lovely durable decorative fabrics that require no special care.

There are several ways of producing metallic yarns. Some employ a core yarn that is impregnated with a metallic film. Most of them have proved to be very satisfactory in service.

Construction of Cloth

There are various ways of constructing a fabric, and the method used will affect not only the appearance but also the purposes for which the cloth can be used. The major methods of construction are weaving and knitting. There are less usual construction methods, which will also be discussed.

Weaving. By far the most common method of producing cloth is by using a loom to interlace at least two sets of yarns. Some looms are quite simple, whereas others are complicated machines that are capable of weaving intricate patterns.

The lengthwise yarns, called *warps*, are wound on rollers and strung through a device that makes it possible to raise and lower the yarns. As certain warp yarns are raised, others remain in the lower position and a *shed* is formed. The crosswise yarn, called *weft* or *filling*, is carried through the shed by a shuttle. The raised warps are returned to the lowered position and another set of warp yarns is raised. The filling yarn is returned through the shed by the shuttle. Thus the filling passes over some warps and under others. The warp yarns at each side of the cloth are often thicker or closer together, so in the finished fabric they appear as a narrow taped edge known as the *selvage*.

There are three basic weaves, and they are used singly or in various combinations to form patterns. There are also other methods of interlacing yarns, and these are known as *fancy* weaves.

The basic weaves include:
Plain Weave. The simplest way of interlacing the warp and filling yarns is an over-and-under arrangement of alternate warps crossing each line of the filling thread. A diagram of this weave looks like a checkerboard.

The plain weave is sturdy and durable if strong yarns are used in a compact construction, but not if weak yarns are used in a widely spaced, open construction.

Fig.
21.1

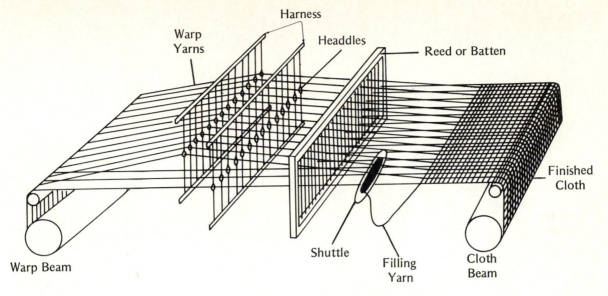

A two-harness weaving loom.

Various effects can be achieved by using yarns of different colors or of different types. Stripes, checks, and plaids are frequently woven in the plain weave. Ribbed effects are easily obtained by using a thick filling yarn.

The *basket* weave, a variation of the plain weave, uses two or more yarns as one in the same pattern of alternate interlacing.

Twill Weave. A wide variety of diagonal ridged effects can be produced by the twill weave. In the simplest pattern, the filling yarn passes over one warp and under two, in the next line passes over and under different sets of warps, and so on. In some variations the filling may go over two and under three warps. As long as there is a progression at each crossing, the interlacing will provide the diagonal effect.

The *herringbone* weave is produced by reversing the direction of the twill at regular intervals.

Fabrics made with the twill weave can be extremely durable—depending, again, on the type of yarn and the compactness of the cloth.

Satin Weave. In the true satin weave, the surface of the cloth is composed mostly of warp yarns. The crosswise yarns are not usually visible on the right side of the finished fabric. The long sections of warp yarns on the right side of the fabric are called *floats.* When glossy yarns are used for the warp, this weave produces the characteristic shiny texture of satin fabric. When the floats are exceptionally long and the warp yarns are not very sturdy, the surface of the fabric will tend to show signs of wear rather quickly. Some upholstery fabrics with designs in the satin weave may be a problem in this respect.

A variation of the satin weave reverses the positions of warp and filling so that long floats of the crosswise yarns appear on the surface. This is known as the *sateen* weave. It is frequently used with cotton yarns, and the resulting fabric is called *sateen.* However, cotton is sometimes used in the true satin construction, and this fabric is known as *warp-faced sateen.*

Fancy Weaves. The fancy weaves are in general more complex than the basic weaves. Some of these include:

DOBBY. An attachment to the loom makes it possible to weave a small all-over pattern in the cloth. The design and the background are, in effect, formed by combinations of the basic weaves.

JACQUARD. Many decorative fabrics are made with rather complex designs woven in the cloth. On the Jacquard looms, each warp yarn

Decorative Fabrics

382

■ Filling

□ Warp

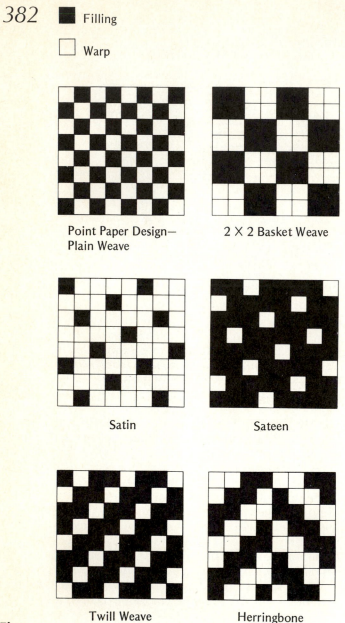

Point Paper Design—
Plain Weave

2 X 2 Basket Weave

Satin

Sateen

Twill Weave

Herringbone

Fig. 21.2 Illustrations of the basic weaving constructions.

there is a separate card for each crosswise thread of the design. As each card comes into place, certain warps are raised and the filling yarn slides across the loom. The warps are returned to position and the next card moves into place to raise another set of warp yarns. In this manner, any desired design can be woven into the cloth.

PILE WEAVES. In addition to the regular warp and weft yarns, a third set of yarns is used to form loops on the surface of the fabric. There are several methods of constructing pile fabrics, and in some of them the pile can be cut so that tiny tufts of yarn project from the surface instead of the uncut loops. Most pile-woven fabrics are constructed by the use of extra warp yarns to form the pile.

In good-quality fabrics, the pile construction often produces a rich, luxurious effect. If the weave is close and the pile is dense, this can be durable construction, but serviceability will, of course, be influenced by fiber and yarn construction.

LENO WEAVE. For sheer, lightweight fabrics, the leno weave is sometimes used. Warp yarns cross over one another between the filling yarns. This construction, often seen in marquisette, prevents the yarns from sliding out of place and provides a more durable quality than that of similar sheer fabrics made with plain weaving.

Other constructions

Braids. A material from textile fibers used for binding or trimming in widths up to three or four inches is considered a braid. Yarns are interlaced diagonally and lengthwise. Braids shape easily; they are usually unstable and extremely stretchy.

Bonding. A bonded (also called laminated) fabric is made by adhering two fabrics together by an adhesive. One is the fashion fabric (or

can be controlled individually so that it may appear on the surface of the cloth at any desired point. Raising the warp yarns is governed by a series of punched cards attached to the loom;

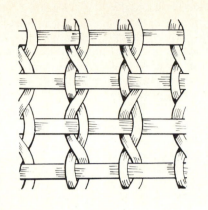

(a) Pile Weave

(b) Leno Knit

Bonded Fabric

Foam Laminate

Quilted

(c) Multicomponent

(d) Chenille Yarns

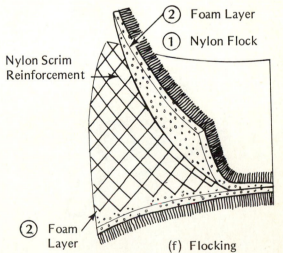

(e) Tufting

Basic Fabric

Tufted Loops

③ Nylon Scrim Reinforcement

② Foam Layer

① Nylon Flock

② Foam Layer

(f) Flocking

Fig. 21.3

Decorative Fabrics

face); the second is the backing, which is usually a knit. The advantages are that inexpensive fabrics can be stabilized by having another fabric bonded to them. The disadvantages are that there can be uneven shrinkage of the two fabrics, the face fabric may be bonded off grain, or the two layers may separate in washing or dry cleaning.

Felt. There are no yarns in fabrics that are felted. In felting, a mass of fibers is subjected to heat, moisture, and pressure, causing them to interlock and cling together and producing a compact felt sheet that has no grain, does not fray or ravel, and absorbs sound. Felt is often used for table covers and for other decorative purposes. Wool fibers have excellent felting properties.

Fig.
21.4

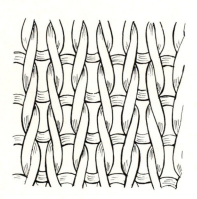

(a) Weft

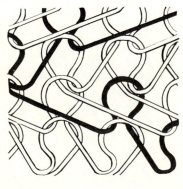

(b) Warp

Weft and warp knit constructions.

Knitting. Knitting is a process using needles to form a series of interlocking loops from a single yarn or from a set of yarns. There are no warp or filling yarns in the same sense as in woven fabrics. Woven fabrics fill the large majority of home furnishings needs, but knitted fabrics are also being used in the home. Ready-made slipcovers frequently are made of knitted fabric to allow for better fit.

Warp and weft are the two basic knitting methods. Warp knits can be manufactured rapidly. They have parallel yarns, running lengthwise, that are locked into a series of loops. Warp-knit fabrics have a great deal of crosswise stretch. A weft knit has loops formed in a circular direction, with one continuous yarn running across the fabric. Knitted fabrics are easy to care for and resist wrinkling. However, they are not always dimensionally stable and have a tendency to stretch, as well as snag.

Multicomponents. Some fabrics are composed of at least two components (fabrics, foams, or films) that are held together by quilting adhesives, foam-flame bonding, embossing, or other techniques. The most popular fabrics made by this method are quilts, blankets, and upholstery fabrics.

Nets and Laces. Various types of fabrics are made with a mesh construction in which yarns are knotted and twisted to form the cloth. Lace usually has a design worked into the mesh background. Net fabrics may have square, diamond-shaped, or hexagonal meshes. Laces have low durability and low stability; they require careful handling. Their principal function is to adorn.

Nonwovens. A textile structure produced by the interlocking of fibers, accomplished by mechanical, chemical, thermal, or solvent means and combinations thereof. The properties of nonwovens include low strength, stiffness, inelasticity, lack of drape, and stretch recovery. Nonwoven fabrics are found in draperies, disposable towels, linens, and diapers.

Tufting. To produce tufted materials, yarns are carried by needles and forced into an already existing fabric. The yarns form loops that may be cut, or left uncut. Tufting is an inexpensive method of making pilelike fabrics; it is an extremely fast process that involves less labor.

Finishes

A finish is a treatment given to a fiber, yarn, or fabric before or after it has been constructed to change the appearance, the hand, or the performance of a textile product. All fabric finishes increase the cost of the fabric. Sometimes finishes are applied to the fabric by the mills that construct the fabric. More often the finish is applied by a converter. The material or unfinished cloth is called *gray* or *greige goods* before finishes have been applied.

There are three ways in which finishes are classified: preparatory, aesthetic, and functional. Preparatory finishes prepare the fabric and are applied to the cloth before aesthetic or functional finishes. Some of the preparatory finishes are bleaching, degumming (for silk), and scouring and singing (for wool). Preparatory finishes help to prepare the fabric for more beautiful finishes to be applied later. After preparatory finishing, the aesthetic and functional finishes are applied. An aesthetic finish makes the cloth look attractive; functional finishes, such as permanent press or sanforization, make the fabric perform better. The finishes applied to make fabric aesthetically appealing or functional may be additive, chemical, or mechanical in nature. In *additive* finishes, a compound or substance is held mechanically to the fiber or fabric. *Chemical* finishes involve a chemical reaction that causes a permanent change in the fabric. *Mechanical* finishes are finishes that cause a physical change only. The following chart is an alphabetical description of finishes and their trade names.

Finishes and Trademarks*

Table 21.4

Antibacterial A finish applied to prevent the growth of bacteria.

Avril A cross-linked rayon with similarity to cotton that takes readily to being Sanforized, mercerized, and treated with wash-and wear finishes. (American Viscose Corp.)

Ban-Dew A process for making fabrics mildew-resistant. (Joseph Bancroft & Sons)

Ban-Lon Garments and fabrics, knitted or woven, made from yarns produced by a hot crimping process that gives a desirable degree of stretch and bulk. (Joseph Bancroft & Sons)

Beetling A preparatory finish, applied to linen fabric, that gives a flattened appearance to the cloth, by the use of beetlers or rollers.

Belfast A finishing process for cotton that permanently modifies the fibers to make the fabric dry wrinkle-free. (Deering-Milliken)

Brushing Bringing the yarns of the fabric up to the surface to create a napped finish.

Burnt-out-prints Process that shows raised motifs on a sheer ground fabric.

Calendering Factory pressing of the fabric.

Carbonizing The chemical elimination of burrs and vegetable matter from wool.

Cadon A specialized type of multifilament nylon yarn. (Chemstrand Corp.)

Carpet nylon A heavy denier nylon yarn with crimp and resiliency, designed especially for floor coverings.

Coronized A process for heat-treating Fiberglas cloth to set the weave and release strain in the glass yarn. (Owens-Corning Fiberglas)

Cotron A yarn that combines cotton and Avisco rayon. (American Viscose Corp.)

Crease retention Ability of a fabric to retain a fold or pleat.

Cumuloft Texturized nylon filament for use in carpets and upholstery fabrics. (Chemstrand Corp.)

Everglaze Designation for various types of fabric with a glazed finish. (Joseph Bancroft & Sons)

Fire proofing A fabric that is 100 per cent fireproof.

Fire retardant treatment A finish to decrease fabric flammability.

Flame resistant A fabric treated with special chemical agents to prevent the spread of fire.

Flocking A decorative treatment that is applied to both fabrics and wall coverings. A pattern is applied to the surface with a form of glue; then short fibers are sprinkled over the area and embedded in the adhesive, often by an electromagnetic force. When insoluble adhesives are used, flocked fabrics are quite durable. The design is raised and has a felted appearance.

Glazing A coating on the surface of the fabric produces a smooth glaze, which adds luster and stiffness to the fabric as well as resistance to soil. Chintz is the favorite fabric for glazing, and now we have glazed chintzes

Table 21.4 Finishes and Trademarks* (*Cont.*)

386

that will retain their finishes through repeated washings. The finishes do gradually disappear, however— even the "permanent" one.

Heat setting Heat finishing treatment that stabilizes thermoplastic fibers, so that there will not be any subsequent change in shape or size.

Mercerization Process used exclusively on cotton yarn and cloth. The material is impregnated with a solution that increases the strength and luster of the fiber.

Metallizing A process used in plating plastic film with a continuous film of metal to produce a brilliant reflecting surface. Used on Mylar polyester film to produce metallic yarns for use in textiles.

Mildew resistant A finish applied to textiles to make them resistant to mildew and mold.

Milium Coating of aluminum flakes in a resin binder applied to fabrics to make them resistant to wind penetration. (Deering-Milliken)

Moth repellent Chemical treatment applied to wool to make it resistant to moth attack.

Napping Some fabrics are made with low-twist yarns and the surface is brushed by rollers covered with tiny wires to produce a fuzzy nap. This finish is desirable in certain articles, such as blankets, because the fibers trap tiny air pockets that act as insulators, yet the weight of the fabric is not increased. When napped fabrics are subjected to abrasion, they tend to show signs of wear rather quickly.

Permanent press Term used to describe a garment or fabric that will retain its flat seams, smooth surface, texture, and appearance for the life of the item.

Preshrunk The familiar "Sanforized" label on cotton fabrics indicates that there is no more than one per cent residual shrinkage in the fabric. With other fabrics we have not been quite so successful in controlling shrinkage. Some will not shrink at all; others will shrink a considerable amount. With any washable fabric that does not have the Sanforized label, the consumer should make some allowance for possible shrinkage.

Sanforized A process applied to fabrics to control shrinkage to within 1% in length and width. (Cluett, Peabody & Co.)

Sanforized Plus A term applied to fabrics finished for wash-and-wear performance in a controlled program. The use of the name is rigidly controlled by the trademark owners, and sample yardage must be submitted periodically to be sure it meets the required wash-and-wear standards. (Cluett, Peabody & Co.)

Sanitized A chemical treatment that renders fabrics and leathers hygienically clean and helps to resist the development of perspiration odors and bacteria. (Sanitized Sales Co.)

Schreinerizing Finishing method that improves luster.

Scotchgard A fluorochemical textile finish used to make fabrics resistant to water-borne and oil-borne stains. (Minnesota Mining & Mfg. Co.)

Silicone A chemical compound in which the element silicon has replaced the element carbon. Textile finishes of the silicone resins render fabrics water repellent and resistant to water-borne stains.

Sizing A certain amount of added substance is sometimes used to give fabrics body. In the past, excessive sizing was frequently used to make a sleazy fabric appear heavy. After one or two launderings, the consumer would realize that it was a sleazy, loosely woven fabric. Today this malpractice is not quite as widespread. the sizing that disappears in laundering can often be replaced by starch to renew the original texture.

Soil release finish A finish that permits the removal of most oil and waterborne stains.

Soil retardant Chemical agents applied to fabrics to enable them to resist soiling.

Special finishes One or more special finishes may be applied to fabrics to improve them in particular ways. Wool fabrics can be made moth repellent; cotton fabrics can be treated to resist mildew.

Starchless finishes Some fabrics, such as organdy, must have crispness in order to retain the desired effect. In the past, these fabrics had to be starched each time they were laundered, but now a finish can be applied that keeps the fabrics stiff through several launderings. It may disappear gradually as the fabric is laundered many times, but soon we shall have fabrics that are truly starchless. Some of the synthetics and blends of synthetics and natural fibers have already achieved this.

Syl-Mer Silicone finish for cottons that makes them resistant to water and water-borne stains. Can withstand machine washing at 160°F.

Water resistant Fabric chemically treated to resist water.

Zelan A chemical finish for water repellency used on cotton and rayon. (du Pont)

Zepel Stain-resistant finish for clothing and home furnishings fabrics. (du Pont)

* Adapted from *Modern Fibers and Fabrics* (New York: J. C. Penney Co., Inc.).

Dyeing and Printing

Color can be applied at any stage of manufacturing. Some of the synthetics have coloring added to them before the fibers are formed, a process that has been extremely successful with acetates. This is called *solution dyeing*. Natural fibers, especially wool, can be dyed before they are spun into yarns (*stock dyeing*). Other yarns are dyed before they are used on the loom (*skein dyeing*). In any of these methods, the cloth is, of course, colored when it comes from the loom. But many fabrics are piece-dyed after weaving, or they are printed. Stock dyeing and skein dyeing are often preferred for more uniform distribution and for deeper color penetration, which will, in general, make the fabric more colorfast. However, many factors influence the permanency of color and it is possible to produce highly desirable fabrics with both piece dyeing and printing.

Colorfastness is a difficult quality for the manufacturer to guarantee. Almost any fabric will eventually change somewhat in color. As consumers, we are concerned about perceptible changes during normal use, but who is to say what constitutes "normal" use? A drapery fabric might be perfectly satisfactory under most conditions, but if it is exposed to very strong sunlight for many hours each day and to excessive soil and fumes so that it needs frequent laundering, such harsh conditions could cause a color change faster than more normal conditions.

Rather than actually guaranteeing a fabric to be colorfast, the manufacturer will often merely assert that the fabric is vat dyed. The *vat dyes* are extremely colorfast; they are insoluble but can be made soluble for the process of dyeing the fabric. Once affixed to the fibers, they again become insoluble. They will not readily change color, but under extreme conditions they might.

Various methods can be used to print designs on fabrics, and each one has advantages as well as disadvantages.

Block printing. Wood or linoleum blocks are carved with a design and a paste dye is applied to the raised areas. When the blocks are placed against the fabric there is a direct application of color to specific areas. This method is used for printing some wallpapers as well as fabrics.

Blocking is a favorite method for printing linen fabrics because it allows for deeper and more uniform penetration of the dye. Linen does not absorb dyes readily, and when it is printed with the roller method—which is faster—the color is more uneven.

Photoengraving. Interesting specialized designs can be transferred to fabrics through the use of photographic film. The photographed designs are transferred to rollers and printed on fabric.

Resist printing. Certain parts of the fabric can be treated in some way to make them resist dyes. An ancient method of coating certain areas with wax is called *batik* dyeing. *Tie dyeing*, in which sections of the fabric are knotted or twisted with cord, is another old hand-dyeing method. Any method that prevents dye from penetrating certain parts of the fabric might be called resist dyeing or printing.

Discharge printing. The discharge printing method is a reverse of the resist process. A cloth is dyed, after which parts of it have the color removed or lightened by the application of some chemical.

Roller printing. Most printed fabrics have the design applied by etched or engraved copper rollers. Each color in the pattern requires a separate roller. As a fabric runs through a series of rollers, each one applies the dye paste in the proper areas.

The initial expense of setting up the rollers is high, but once that is accomplished many yards of fabric can be printed very quickly. Furthermore the same rollers can be used for different color combinations. Also known as direct printing.

Screen printing. A slower and more expensive method of printing fabrics is through the use of large screens, one for each color to be applied. The screen consists of a frame covered with a fine-meshed fabric through which paste dye can be forced. Part of the screen fabric is covered with a film that will resist the dye. All parts of the design that will be applied in one color are left free. Each screen is placed on top of the fabric and the dye is forced through the open-mesh areas. The initial cost of screen printing is lower than for roller printing, but the actual process of applying the dye is slower and therefore more costly. This method is useful for more unique and unusual designs to be printed on limited amounts of fabric. It is also used for much custom work.

Warp printing. Although warp printing is somewhat out of favor at the present time, it occasionally appears in some very interesting fabrics. A design is printed only on the warp threads before the fabric is woven. A solid-color filling thread is used, with the result that the design appears in the finished fabric in a rather shadowy or hazy form.

Plastic Film and Coated Fabrics

A whole group of materials in the plastics category is becoming more important for home use. Many of these are not fabrics in the true sense of the word. Some are sheets or films of plastic materials; others are made of traditional types of woven or knitted fabric with coatings of plastic on the surface.

The plastic-type materials range from thin, lightweight varieties that are particularly useful for shower curtains and table coverings to heavy upholstery fabrics. Coverings in the latter group are now widely used in the home on dinette chairs. New developments in this field have produced a wide variety of upholstery materials that are exciting and extremely practical. Beautiful colors and interesting textures are making these fabrics more suitable for other areas in the home. They are low cost, waterproofed, soil resistant, durable, and easy to maintain. The good-quality materials do not peel, crack, or chip, even with hard use. They may be easily washed with soap and water and they retain their original colors.

The leather look has become very important in upholstery films. It is now possible to make synthetic fabrics that closely resemble suede, doeskin, and other leathers.

Fig. 21.5

Soft white kid would be an impractical choice to upholster loveseats in a city apartment. These are covered in Naugahyde vinyl fabric that looks like kid, but can be cleaned with soap and water, unlike real leather. *(Courtesy of Uniroyal, Inc.)*

Design in Fabrics

The color, texture, and pattern in a fabric must be keyed to the basic theme and to the purpose of the room. Certain fabric designs will express very definite characteristics, perhaps a formal elegance, perhaps a more rustic charm. For example, intricate patterns woven or embroidered with smooth, lustrous yarns in deep, rich colors will relate the idea of skilled craftsmanship and perfection of detail. Other fabrics with coarse, nubby yarns, earthy colors, and little or no pattern may suggest a more simple kind of hand craftsmanship that is less formal in appearance. Different fabrics are appropriate for different styles of furniture. In general, graceful, delicate patterns are suitable for furniture that is graceful and dainty; the more rugged and forceful designs seem better suited to furniture that is more substantial looking. It is not always necessary to follow the letter of the law in choosing authentic designs for a particular style; in fact, rooms may become trite and dull if one tries to do so. We have a wide range of choice today. Many modern fabrics are extremely adaptable to different types and styles of furnishings. Also, there are lovely adaptations and interpretations of traditional fabrics scaled to our contemporary versions of traditional styles. But because there is such a wide variety from which to choose, it is important to select those that do the most to complement and enhance the expressiveness of the furnishings.

The size of the room will certainly influence the color, texture, and scale of the designs used. When shopping for fabrics, one should look closely at quality, but view the pattern from a distance. Is it subdued or advancing? Does it have a great deal of movement or is it a static type of design? It is often wise to purchase a large enough sample, a half yard or so, to try out at home before making a major investment. The color and the scale of the design may appear quite different in a particular room than in a store. A large design, if it has perspective, may even be quite attractive in a small room, but if it is advancing, it may completely overshadow everything else in the room. Seeing the pattern, texture, and color in one's own home will help in making decisions. One should look at the fabric in both natural and artificial light, and see it next to the other colors, textures, and patterns in the room to be certain that the effect will be right. Of course, the amount of any particular color or pattern will influence the effect, and this is difficult to visualize even with a fairly large sample. One should drape the sample on the furniture or fasten it to the wall and use imagination. It should be remembered that strong contrasts will tend to make an area seem smaller whereas related colors will tend to blend and make an area seem larger.

Considerations of Quality

The performance characteristics of fabrics are very important, and should be borne in mind by consumers when selecting different types of fabrics. Some woven fabrics should be chosen for their durability and their strength; the plain and twill weaves are the best choices. The satin and sateen weaves are usually chosen for their richness, luster, and beauty. Close, firm weaves of smooth, strong fibers are best for fabrics that need repeated laundering, or those that are exposed to friction. Looser weaves and rough, uneven-textured fibers provide many interesting effects and are often durable enough in places that are not subject to hard wear.

When selecting pile weave fabrics, examine the loop of the pile. Are the loops held firmly in place, so that they will not pull out with wear or laundering? Is the ground fabric tightly or loosely woven? If loosely woven, will it wear well? Will the selvages pull out? Will the fabric fray a great deal? Try to pull a few loose ends to test it.

Examine knits closely to see that the loops are tightly packed together so that they will not snag easily. Stretch the fabric and see if it goes back to its original size; if not, do not consider it for any purpose.

Determine if the fabric is washable, or preshrunk. Is it colorfast—particularly to sunlight, if it is to be used for curtains or draperies? (It is not always practical to use sheets as window curtains, as some may not be colorfast to sun-

One-room living requires using space imaginatively with an eye for aesthetics. With the clever use of fabrics and wall coverings in one overall design, the alcove of this studio apartment was transformed into a dramatic and functional bedroom by designer John Elmo, FASID. A large-scale Orient-inspired print on linen used as drapery, wall covering and quilted bedspread, helps to unify this small intimate area. The earthtone colors of the rattan furniture and accessories coupled with the burnt orange on white colors of the print sets the mood for a very warm, cozy, relaxing sleep area. A touch of nature is provided by the green plants. *(Courtesy of Belgian Linen Association)*

Turn a bathroom into an oasis of luxury. Here a tented ceiling, wall covering, and shower curtain are created with Springmaid no-iron sheets. *(Designed by Bill Blass, courtesy of Kohler Company)*

Fig. 21.6

Fig. 21.7

Fig.
21.8

With the new technological advances in fiber science, fabrics may have finishes applied that make them useful for different locations. This room has the same fabric on the upholstered pieces and on the screen. *(Courtesy Burlington House, designer, Patricia Crane, A.S.I.D.)*

light.) Sheet manufacturers have promoted their sheets by advocating that sheets be used to make window curtains. This is not always practical, because sheets are not manufactured to be colorfast to sunlight and will fade when used as curtains. Read and save all the labels on textile products. Then, when laundering fabrics, the care label can be checked.

Fabrics play a pre-eminent role in decorating a home. With all of the man-made fibers on the market, it is usually possible to find a fiber that will meet most of your needs. First determine what is most important to you, and then choose a fabric and fiber that meet this need most effectively.

Fabrics are used in every room of the house—for draperies, curtains, upholstery, slipcovers, lamp shades, walls, beds, tables, and floors. Because of modern textile technology, there has never been a greater variety of fabrics available to the consumer.

In draperies and curtains, look for such fabric characteristics as ease of cleaning, minimum shrinkage, drapability, dimensional stability (not loosing shape) and enough opacity to provide privacy but enough translucency to permit light to enter the room.

Upholstery and slipcover materials should be stain repellent, easy to clean, durable, tightly woven, and—in the case of pile fabrics—resistant to crushing.

Wall coverings should have good body and a close, compact weave so that the fabric will not stretch or shrink while on the wall. Fabrics for tables, beds, and floors are discussed in other chapters.

Decorative Fabrics

Table 21.5

Antique satin Nubby yarns are added to give satin or heavy cotton sateen a textural effect.

Appliqué One fabric stitched or pasted to another in the form of a design.

Armure Fabric used for draperies and upholstery. Usually rep or twill background with small raised patterns, often in a satin weave.

Aubusson District in France famous for tapestries and rugs.

Awning stripe Heavy, firm-woven cotton, duck, or canvas with either yarn-dyed, printed, or painted stripes.

Bark cloth Cotton fabric with uneven yarns.

Basket weave Plain-weave fabric made by interlacing one or more sets of warp yarns over and under one or more filling yarns.

Batik Fabric-dyeing method that originated in Java. Wax is applied to certain areas to make them resist dye. After dyeing, wax is removed and may be reapplied in several successive stages to build up intricate patterns in several colors.

Batiste Fine, sheer cotton in plain weave.

Bedford cord Fabric with heavy corded yarn.

Birdseye Cotton or linen cloth with a small geometric pattern that has a center dot resembling a bird's eye.

Blanket fabric Broad term for some woolen overcoating fabrics with a soft hand and a napped finish.

Block print Design applied to fabrics or wallpaper with wood or linoleum blocks.

Bobbinet Net fabric with round or hexagonal mesh.

Bouclé Novelty yarn with curly loops on the surface. Imparts a distinctive texture when used in a fabric.

Broadcloth (1) Cotton or silk; a slightly heavier crosswise yarn gives the effect of a very fine rib. (2) Wool: surface is napped and pressed to impart a sheen.

Brocade Woven pattern, made with an extra filling yarn; brocade often resembles embroidery.

Buckram Strong plain-weave cotton with glue sizing. Used for stiffening.

Burlap Coarse, loosely woven fabric in a plain weave. Usually made of jute or hemp.

Calico Plain-weave cotton fabric printed with small designs.

Cambric Lightweight fabric of cotton or linen in a plain weave.

Candlewick Tufts of yarn stitched to a plain cotton fabric such as muslin. Used for bedspreads.

Canvas Heavy plain-weave fabric in cotton or linen. May be dyed or printed. Popular for outdoor use.

Casement cloth Term used for a variety of fabrics made for use in curtains and draperies. May be any fiber. Weave often has a small design on plain, twill, or leno background.

Challis Soft fabric of silk, wool, or rayon. Challis is available in plain colors or printed with small figures.

Chambray Plain woven fabric with colored warp and white filling that gives a muted colored surface.

Cheesecloth Plain, woven, soft, low-count cotton, also known as gauze. Used for dust cloths and, in finer grades, for table cloths.

Chenille Special type of yarn made by the cutting of strips of a woven cloth. Each strip has a fuzzy surface that produces a pile when used in a fabric.

Chinoiserie French term denoting fabrics influenced by Oriental or Chinese design.

Chintz Fine cotton cloth in a plain weave, often with a printed design. Much of it has a glaze applied to the surface. Unglazed chintz is soft and pliable; glazed chintz is stiff and shiny, but the glaze may gradually disappear in laundering.

Clipped-spot Ornamental embroidered effect in which extra filling yarn is used at regular intervals while weaving the cloth.

Corduroy Cotton fabric with pile in ridges or "wales" running lengthwise. Pinwale has pile in narrow, corded effect.

Crash Term used for various types of fabric that have plain weaves and coarse, uneven yarns.

Crewel Type of embroidery worked in various colors of wool yarn on a fabric of cotton or linen in its natural color. Designs often include trailing vines and floral motifs.

Damask Patterned fabric of any fiber, made on Jacquard loom. Design is flat; fabric can often be used on either side.

Denim Heavy cotton fabric in twill weave.

Dimity Plain-weave cotton fabric that is crisp and sheer. Often has stripe or crossbar design formed by heavier threads.

Dotted Swiss Sheer, plain-weave cotton fabric with woven or embroidered dots. A similar fabric sometimes has tiny flocked dots.

Drill Heavy fabric, usually cotton, in twill weave. Often used as backing for coated fabrics.

Table 21.5 Glossary of Fabrics and Constructions (*Cont.*) 393

Duck   Heavy cotton fabric in plain weave, but often with a ribbed effect. Similar to canvas.

Embroidery   Ornamental needlework executed by hand or machine on fabric that is already woven.

Faille   Plain weave with ribbed effect caused by heavy crosswise yarns. Warp is usually silk or a synthetic such as rayon; filling is usually cotton.

Felt   Fabric formed by matting and interlocking a mass of fibers. Has no yarns.

Flannel   Fabric of wool or cotton with a napped surface.

Flock   Short, clipped fibers glued to fabric or ribbon to provide a suedelike surface.

Fortuny prints   Cotton fabrics in basic weaves with rich textural effects printed upon them.

Friezé   Pile fabric with uncut loops. Made of wool, mohair, cotton, and sometimes linen. When the same construction is used with silk, the fabric is called *uncut velvet*. Mohair friezé is extremely durable but not very popular at the present time.

Gabardine   Durable, compactly woven cloth, showing a diagonal line on the face of the fabric.

Gauze   Thin sheer fabric in an open weave, either plain or leno; sometimes a combination of the two. Made in almost any fiber. Useful for curtains.

Gingham   Lightweight, plain-weave cotton fabric, in which the yarn has been skein-dyed to produce checks, plaids, stripes.

Gobelins   Name associated with hand-loomed tapestries produced in France.

Glazed chints   See *chintz.*

Grass cloth   Fabric made of coarse reeds or other vegetable fibers in a loose, open weave to show texture. Often impregnated to backing for wall coverings or panels on furniture.

Grosgrain   Ribbed fabric with heavy crosswise yarns and close, lustrous warps. Often made in narrow widths for trimmings and ribbons.

Gros-point   See *needlepoint.*

Haircloth   Originally made with a warp of wool, cotton, or linen and a filling thread of horsehair. Frequently synthetics are now used in place of hair. May have small patterns.

Herringbone twill   Broken twill weave giving a zigzag effect by alternating the direction of the twill.

Homespun   Fabrics in a plain loose weave with soft yarns, made to imitate original hand-loomed Colonial textiles.

Honeycomb   Pattern in small squares on a plain or twill background.

Huckaback (Huck)   A cloth with a honeycomb effect. The filling yarns are loosely twisted to aid in absorption. Used primarily for towels.

Indian head   Although this is actually a trade name, the fabric is well known and widely used. A medium-weight cotton in a plain weave. Has a linenlike appearance; available in a wide range of colors.

Jersey   Lightweight knitted fabric.

Lace   Fabric produced by various methods of knotting and twisting yarns or threads. Originally laces were always made by hand, but now machines can reproduce some exquisite effects. Some laces are knitted or crocheted; others are made with pins, bobbins, or shuttles. Intricate designs are often worked into an open-mesh background.

Lamé   Fabric with metallic threads or yarns interspersed throughout.

Lawn   Lightweight fabric in plain weave. May be cotton or linen (handkerchief linen).

Madras   Cotton shirting fabric with small woven pattern. Also a curtain fabric in a leno weave with an all-over design.

Malimo   Fabric for which a layer of warp yarns is placed over a layer of filling yarns, but is not interlaced. The layers are locked together with a chain stitch.

Marquisette   Sheer curtain fabric in the leno weave. Made of cotton, silk, or synthetic.

Matelasse   Double cloth in the Jacquard weave. Pattern has a quilted appearance. Used for upholstery.

Metal cloth   Fabric of any material with decorative interwoven metallic threads.

Moire   Finish produced by engraved rollers to give a fabric a watermarked appearance. Usually applied to fabrics with ribbed weaves.

Monk's cloth   Fabric of loosely twisted coarse yarns in a basket-weave construction.

Muslin   Plain-weave cotton fabric in a variety of weights and grades. Available in bleached or unbleached state, also in wide widths for sheeting.

Needlepoint   A half cross-stitch hand-embroidered with wool yarns on net, coarse linen, or canvas. Petit-point has a small fine stitch; gros-point has a large stitch. Fabrics with similar appearance can be woven by machine.

Net   Sheer fabric used for glass curtains. Often appears

Decorative Fabrics

in plain weave made of rayon, but other weaves and fibers are also used.

Ninon   A smooth, transparent type of voile fabric. Glass fibers are used when the fabric is to serve as curtains.

Oilcloth   Plain-weave cotton fabric coated with mixture of oil, clay, gum, and pigments to provide a waterproof surface.

Organdy   Lightweight muslin fabric with crisp finish.

Organza   A very thin, but stiff, plain-woven fabric made of silk, nylon, acrylic, or polyester.

Osnaburg   Plain-weave cotton fabric with coarse yarns.

Paisley   Design printed or woven to imitate Scotch shawls formerly woven by hand in town of Paisley. Designs adopted from Indian Kashmir shawls.

Panne   Pile fabrics that have been steam pressed to flatten the pile and produce a lustrous surface.

Percale   Plain-weave cotton fabric. Used in fine-quality sheetings. Can be dyed and printed.

Petit-point   See *needlepoint*.

Piqué   Fabric with raised wales or ridges that usually run lengthwise. Also woven with honeycomb pattern (waffle piqué) and diamond pattern (birdseye piqué).

Plissé   Finish applied to fabrics to produce a crinkled surface.

Plush   Fabric similar to velvet but with deeper pile. Used for upholstery.

Point d'esprit   Net with small embroidered design.

Pongee   Plain-weave fabric of wild silk. Usually appears in natural tan color.

Poplin   Fabric in plain weave with crosswise ribbed effect. Heavier than broadcloth, lighter than rep.

Quilted fabrics   Two layers of fabric stitched together, with padding between.

Ratiné   Ply yarn with rough nubby surface. Term also applies to fabric made with these irregular yarns in plain or twill weave and having irregular surface.

Rep   Fabric with horizontal ribs produced by heavy filling threads.

Sailcloth   Heavy cotton fabric in a plain weave. Similar to lightweight canvas.

Sateen   Cotton fabric in a sateen weave.

Satin   Fabric woven in satin weave with glossy warp threads. May be all silk or synthetic. For heavier upholstery weights, a cotton filling yarn is sometimes used.

Scrim   Plain-weave fabric with open construction and somewhat coarse yarns. Used for curtains.

Seersucker   Plain-weave fabric that has a puckered surface texture caused by warp threads being held under different degrees of tension.

Shade cloth   Opaque stiffened cloth used for window shades because of its capacity for light deflection.

Shantung   Fabric with irregular texture produced by uneven yarns. Originally made of wild silk, but heavier than pongee.

Sheeting   Plain weave cloth available in wide widths and light, medium, and heavy weights.

Shepherd's check (also called **shepherd's plaid**)   A small check or plaid-patterned fabric, usually in black and white.

Suede cloth   Cloth with a napped surface made to resemble suede.

Taffeta   Plain-weave fabric; may be made of synthetic, silk, cotton, or wool. Crosswise yarns are sometimes slightly thicker than warps to produce fine ridges.

Tambour   Embroidery done on tambour frames. Now reproduced by machine on Swiss, lawn, or batiste for curtains.

Tapa   Cloth made from tree barks in the South Sea islands. Characterized by block-printed designs applied with vegetable dyes.

Tapestry   Fabric frequently made by machine to imitate original hand-woven tapestries. Made with two sets of warps and two sets of filling yarns. Has ribbed effect.

Tarlatan   Thin cotton fabric in an open plain weave. Sized or glazed to make it stiff.

Tarpaulin   Canvas or nylon fabric usually coated to make it waterproof so that it may serve as a protection against inclement weather.

Tattersal   Heavy, fancy-woolen material with a checkered pattern.

Terry cloth   Fabric with uncut pile loops, usually on both sides. Made of cotton.

Ticking   Heavy, closely woven fabric of cotton. Twill weave, but sometimes varied by satin stripes or small patterns.

Toiles de Jouy   Fabrics made originally in the French town of Jouy with delicate printed designs showing landscapes and figures in monotones on cream-colored backgrounds. Modern adaptations effectively vary the themes and the colors.

Tricot   A type of warp-knitted fabric made from fine yarns to create a thin, lightweight fabric.

Tweed   Broad term applied to fabrics woven from rough,

Table 21.5   Glossary of Fabrics and Constructions (*Cont.*)   395

heavy yarns in two or more colors in plain, twill, or herringbone weaves.

Ultrasuede   A man-made nonwoven fabric created to look and feel like suede, made of 60 per cent polyester and 40 per cent nonfibrous polyurethane. It is color-fast; it will not crock, pill, fray, wrinkle, or water spot. It is distributed by Skinner, a division of Spring Mills.

Upholstery satin   A heavyweight satin fabric made with a cotton back construction. Used in upholstery, drapes, curtains.

Velour   Closely woven pile fabric that resembles velvet but is heavier and has a shorter pile.

Velvet   Broad term for pile fabrics made with the velvet weave.

Velveteen   A cotton velvet made with filling yarns forming the pile. Made on a plain- or twill-weave back. Twill back is stronger and more durable.

Vinyl   A nonwoven material capable of being embossed or printed to produce any desired finish such as leather-grain, floral, or textured designs. Vinyl is used for upholstery applications.

Visa   This is an effective soil release polyester (Deering Milliken).

Voile   Sheer lightweight fabric with tightly twisted yarns. Plain weave. Made in cotton, silk, wool, and synthetics.

Waffle cloth   Fabric with a characteristic honeycomb weave. When made in cotton, it is called waffle piqué. Used for draperies and towels. Same as honeycomb cloth.

Webbing   Tightly woven fabric made of jute yarns. Used for furniture bases and spring supports.

Whipcord   Twill-weave fabric with pronounced wale on right side.

Textile Legislation to Protect the Consumer

To protect the consumer from unscrupulous manufacturers and retailers, Congress has passed several textile and fur acts since the 1930s: the Wool Products Labeling Act, the Fur Products Labeling Act, the Textile Fiber Products Identification Act, and the Flammable Fabrics Act.

*Wool Products Labeling Act of
1939 as Amended to 1965*

The principal objective of the Wool Products Labeling Act is to define three types of wool fiber derived from sheep's wool, reprocessed wool, and reused wool.

- *Wool* is the fiber from the fleece of the sheep, lamb, or hair of the angora or cashmere goat. As so defined, it has never been reclaimed from a woven, or felted wool product.
- *Reprocessed wool* results from wool that has been woven or felted into a wool product, but has not been worn or used by the consumer.
- *Reused wool* results from wool or reprocessed wool that has been made into a wool product and used by the consumer.

- *Wool product* is any product, or portion of a product, that contains wool, reprocessed wool, or reused wool.

The act does not require that speciality hair fibers such as angora, cashmere, camel, or vicuna be indicated on the label. Unfortunately, the act specifically exempts rugs, carpets, and upholstery fabrics.

*Fur Products Labeling Act of 1951
as Amended to 1969*

The purpose of this act is to protect consumers from misbranding, false advertising, and false invoicing of furs and fur byproducts. The act requires that consumers be informed—through labels and in advertising—of the true English name of the animal from which the fur came, its country of origin, and whether the fur product is composed of used, damaged, or scrap fur. The following definitions are included in this act:

- *Fur* is any animal skin.
- *Used fur* is fur that has been used by the consumer.
- *Waste fur* is fur that has come from the ears, throat, or scrap pieces of the animal pelt.

Decorative Fabrics

This act covers all kinds of fur products, including those used in the home for bedspreads and pillows.

Textile Fiber Products Identification Act of 1958 as Amended to 1969

This act requires mandatory fiber content labeling for draperies, floor coverings, furnishings, bedding, and other household goods in addition to apparel products. The provisions follow:

- That a stamp, tag, or label be attached to the product.
- The name or identification number of the manufacturer must be specified.
- If the item is imported, the country where the item was manufactured must be stated on the label.
- The names of the fibers in the products should be listed on the label.
- The percentage, by weight, of each fiber present must be specified.

- If there is less than five per cent of any fiber, it can be listed as "other."
- If an upholstered product, mattress, or cushion contains used stuffing, there must be a labeled statement to that effect.

Flammable Fabrics Act of 1953 as Amended to 1967

The 1953 act prohibits the marketing and importation of dangerously flammable fabrics for apparel. The 1967 amendments continued these standards and promulgated additional flammability standards as follows:

- Standard for carpets and rugs, effective April 1971.
- Standard for small carpets and rugs, effective December 1971.
- Standard for mattresses, effective December 1973.

In addition, there are proposed standards for blankets and upholstered furniture, but they have not been promulgated to date.

We think of windows as being essential for letting light and air into the home. Actually they are not necessary for either purpose, because we can control both light and ventilation in other ways. Natural light during the daytime and fresh air when the weather is pleasant provides a far more desirable indoor atmosphere than one controlled by artificial means.

Windows perform another major function in that they allow for the indoor-outdoor relationship that is so important in modern living. A room with a view appeals to almost everyone, but even when a beautiful view is not possible we still need the psychological association with the outdoors that windows provide.

In many cases it is necessary to consider doors as well as windows in furnishing a room. The placement of these openings will influence the arrangement of furniture as well as the decoration of the room. When a door is part of a window wall or is in close proximity to a window, it may be a very important factor in determining how the window will be treated. The more usual situation, however, calls for a window treatment without any specific relationship to doorways.

Types of Windows

The treatment of windows may be determined to a large extent by the type of a window, as well as by its placement and size. It is important to study each window in order to choose a treatment that will allow for maximum use and also emphasize the desirable features. Decoration should be planned to minimize any undesirable characteristics that the windows may have.

For most windows, a *casing* is built into the wall structure. This is a fixed part of the window, designed to hold the *sash,* which is the wood or metal frame that holds the glass and that is usually the movable part. On some windows there is a *sill,* or ledge at the bottom. An *apron* is a strip of casing below the sill. The *mutins* hold the small individual panes.

The various types of windows include:

22

Window Treatments

Arched A curved arch arrangement at the top of the window may have glass panes or be part of the design of the wall. In either case, the arch adds interest but also adds problems to treating the window.

Awning Wide horizontal panels that open outward from the bottom to any desired angle. Hopper windows are similar to awning windows, except that they are fixed at the bottom, and the top of the frame is pushed out to open the window.

Bay A group of three or more windows is set at angles projecting to the outside to form a recessed area in the room. A bay window usually provides a dominant architectural feature that must be treated as a center of interest.

Bow Somewhat similar to a bay window, the bow is built on a curve rather than with angled sections.

Cathedral A slanted window set high in the wall close to a cathedral ceiling. This window is often found in A-frame houses. Because of its size and shape, the cathedral window is difficult to treat.

Clerestory Shallow windows that are set high on the wall, usually near the ceiling. Sometimes they are part of a slanted construction or the ''cathedral'' window popular in modern architecture. Such windows almost always present problems in decorating, although they do add interest and provide for additional light without reducing wall space.

Corner Various types of windows are designed to form the corners of rooms. These have the advantage of increased light and view, and such an arrangement may be an interesting architectural feature to emphasize in decoration. However, it may be difficult to provide a treatment that is both functional and attractive.

Dormer When a small alcove projects from the room a window is often placed at the end. This construction is frequently but not always found in attics. The window and walls of the dormer often require special treatment to integrate them into the room.

Double-hung Probably the most commonly used type of window, with sashes that slide up and down.

French doors These can be used wherever ordinary doors can be used, and they also can serve as windows. They are useful when easy access to another area is important but when ordinary doors would cut off too much light. They allow for privacy, yet the separation of two rooms is less definitive with translucent doors than it is with other types.

Hopper Windows that are similar to awning windows except that they are fixed at the bottom, and the top of the frame is pushed out to open the window.

Jalousie Narrow strips of glass mounted so that they can assume different angles have become popular. They may be used in ordinary windows, window walls, or even in all the walls of an indoor-outdoor room.

Picture Various types of large windows are designed to allow for an increased view of the outdoors. The window may be one large pane of glass that remains fixed or it may have sections that slide or pivot. Movable sections might be placed alongside of, above, or below the stationary panel of glass.

Ranch Sometimes referred to as *strip windows,* this type is usually wide and placed high on the wall. They are popular because they allow for more usable wall space, but they do limit the easy view of the outdoors and they sometimes present problems of decoration. They may also be a safety hazard in case of fire, especially in children's rooms.

Skylight Small window of one or more fixed panes of glass set into the roof or ceiling of a room. A skylight can be left bare when privacy is not essential; otherwise window shades or Austrian shades are a good choice because both can be set flush to the glass.

Slanting window A window that follows the line of a slanting roof.

Sliding casement Window panels that operate by sliding from side to side in horizontal sashes, thus combining the interesting proportions usually found in casement windows with the weather tightness usually found in double-hung windows. However, to provide equal ventilation, they require more lateral wall space than standard double-hung windows.

Sliding glass doors Doors that have large sheets of glass mounted in wood or aluminum sashes. They slide back and forth to open and close.

Swinging casement Window panels hinged at the side so that the full area of the window is opened when the panel is moved. Casement windows that swing out are relatively easy to decorate; those that swing into the room present problems. Some are operated by mechanical cranks, whereas others are merely moved by hand.

Window wall A favorite feature in modern architecture. An entire wall of glass may be sectioned in various ways so that some panels are stationary, others act as windows, and still others act as doors. A window wall is particularly desirable in areas where the indoor-outdoor relationship is important.

**Fig.
22.1**

Types of windows. *(Courtesy of Kirsch Company)*

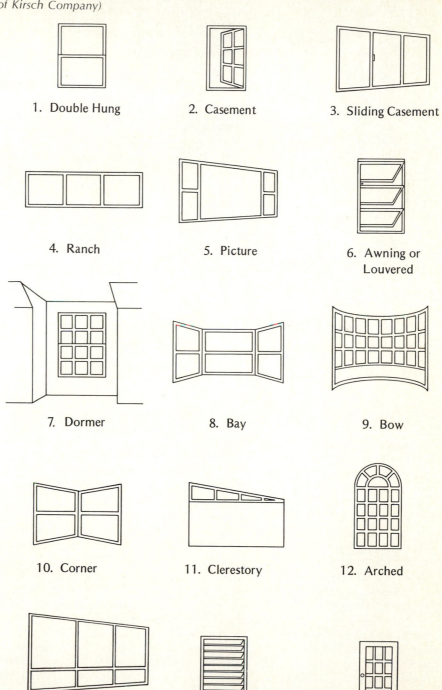

1. Double Hung   2. Casement   3. Sliding Casement

4. Ranch   5. Picture   6. Awning or Louvered

7. Dormer   8. Bay   9. Bow

10. Corner   11. Clerestory   12. Arched

13. Window Wall   14. Jalousie   15. French Door

These windows frame a beautiful view, and the decorator decided to cover them with plants instead of cloth or blinds. *(Courtesy of American Plywood Association)*

Fig. 22.2

Decorative Treatments

Window treatments have the potential for ranking at the top among the home's decorative assets. Even when they are less than ideal in size and shape, they have the power to add character to a room. Window treatments can set a mood, cover faults, create illusions, or become a focal point. Perhaps most important, they can stage-set any mood: quietly reserved, wild as a night club, luxuriously formal, contemporary, or classically charming, and nostalgic. Window treatments offer large units of color, texture, and styling in a room.

With this in mind it is dangerous to state that one must "always do this" or "never do that." Nor is it possible to say that one method is correct and another is not if both are equally functional and pleasing to the eye. We have broken with tradition in many areas of furnishings.

People also differ in their ideas about the exterior appearances of windows. Some consider uniformity from the outside extremely important and will choose shades, blinds, or curtains for the entire home on this basis. A uniform treatment often does add to the neatness of the exterior, but other factors may be more important for interior appearance.

The ultimate purposes of any window treatment should be to make the window functional and to make it attractive from both the outside and the inside. In most rooms control of the amounts of light and air that enter is important. At times it may be desirable for sunshine to flood the room; at other times it may be appropriate to block out strong sunlight. Also, at times privacy may be particularly important.

Exterior Window Treatments

Exterior window treatments are usually not emphasized or decorative in nature. Some of these treatments are awnings, which protect windows from rain, sun, and wind. Outside shutters are seldom used in the United States but are very popular in Mediterranean countries to temper light, heat, and cold. Grilles made of wood, plastic, aluminum, or steel are also used; they control privacy, sun, and wind. Overhanging roofs are exterior shading devices that do not control privacy, but do offer some protection from the sun.

Hard Indoor Window Treatments

Hard indoor window treatments combine function with beauty and are available in a wide variety of styles and colors. Any one of them can provide a complete window treatment or can be used with draperies, curtains, valances, or cornices. How they are to be used in a room de-pends on the style of furnishings and amount of money available.

Blinds. Venetian blinds—which actually origi-nated in China—are available in a variety of styles and materials and adapt well to new and glamorous decorative treatments. Blinds are popular for their light-filtering and room-darken-ing qualities, as well as for providing privacy and controlling air. Today they have undergone vast improvements and are available in many colors, textures, and thicknesses. Blinds can be used with or without draperies. Venetian blinds have been supplemented by newer versions—called shade-cloth vertical blinds—which consist of vanes of shade cloth. There are also varieties made of metal, wood, or plastics. Approxi-mately one and one-half to six inches wide, they can be cut to fit regular silled windows or the floor-to-ceiling type. They can be wall- or ceil-ing-hung. Blinds in general are available with

Fig. 22.3

Update an old porch by enclosing it in insulated glass and installing heat to gain an extra living room that's a real sun porch. Vertical blinds that rotate 180 degrees give plants and people just the amount of light needed. *(Courtesy of Window Shade Manufacturers Association)*

Fig. 22.4

Fig. 22.5

Movable wooden shutters can be a variable in design composition. In this eclectic living room the lines and texture of the shutters relate to the molding on the ceiling. *(Courtesy of Hercules Incorporated)*

A shade-and-shutter combination window treatment acts as the focal point in this bedroom and conceals the heating element when the shutters are closed. *(Courtesy of Window Shade Manufacturers Association)*

Background for Interiors

horizontal or vertical slats in wood, metal, or plastic. There are also split bamboo and matchstick blinds.

Shutters. Although shutters are expensive, they have a long life and require little maintenance. As well as being decorative, they can disguise problem windows, conceal air conditioners and radiators, and enhance the architectural elements of a window. They allow maximum flexibility in light control and ventilation; they insure privacy. Shutters can be purchased painted, with natural wood finishes, or unfinished.

Shutter panels are designed with movable or fixed louvers (sloping slats), or with cane, mesh, solid panel, stained glass, perforated hardboard, or fabric inserts. Shutters may be used with draperies or in place of draperies. They come in a wide variety of stock sizes, or can be ordered for windows of unique dimensions.

Shades. Shades fit windows of all sizes and can be made to suit any decorative finish. There are four basic types: the pull-down shade; the Austrian shade; the Roman shade; and the bottom-up shade. All of them come in plain or textured material that is either opaque or translucent. The opaque material ensures complete room-darkening qualities; the translucent material allows light to filter through.

Shades come in striped, patterned, or solid colors that range all the way from the most unobtrusive, subtle, neutral tints to vivid decorator shades. They can be simply tailored, accented with a decorative trim, or have a custom look with shaped hems, scalloped borders, or matching cornices.

Austrian and Roman shades are not attached to shade rollers, but are regulated with a cord and a pulley. The Austrian shade is shirred and draped when lowered or raised; the Roman shade falls into pleats when it is raised.

Bottom-up shades are mounted at the base of the window and draw up from the sill on a smooth pulley mechanism, which provides flexibility in light control, privacy, and ventilation. These shades are recommended for cathedral windows, or for covering an air conditioner.

Customizing Window Shades. The pull-down or pull-up shade can be trimmed with a precut, pre-scalloped, self-adhesive fringed skirt by pressing it onto the shade. One or more rows of press-on braid or fringe in matching or contrasting colors can be added to create a border effect that harmonizes with the furnishings in the room. Designs can be applied on shades and valances by cutting out coated wall coverings or tightly woven fabric and gluing them firmly in place on the shade. Stencils can also be painted onto the shades with a sun-resistant marker or textile paint. There are also adhesive-coated and heat-sensitive shades that are especially designed for laminating. The roller is designed to hold the added weight of the fabric and glue. Almost any type of fabric can be ironed on with an adhesive.

For energy conservation, the Illinois Institute of Technology studied the amount of energy saved by using window shades. It was found that the use of window shades in a typical residence in a moderate climate would reduce temperature control costs by as much as 8 cents per dollar spent on heating and 21 cents per dollar spent on cooling. These conclusions were based on a well-insulated home with an average amount of glass and no shading devices prior to the installation of roller shades.[1]

Beads. Strands of beads can be purchased in many colors in opaque or gem-cut crystal and in wood. They are permanently fused to nylon cord and can be cut to any length and mounted on a bead track. They make interesting window treatments as well as room dividers.

Lambrequins. Lambrequins can provide a decorative frame for a window. They are usually made of wood and covered with fabric or adhesive paper. They can be cut in interesting shapes.

Shoji screens. Shoji screens, originating in the Orient, are paper screens serving as wall partitions or sliding windows. They are used in

[1] Dix Rollin and Lavan Zalman, *Window Shades and Energy Conservation* (Chicago: Illinois Institute of Technology, 1974), p. ii.

Fig. 22.6

Attic turns apartment with the addition of a skylight. Vinyl shades pull up from the bottom to control light. *(Courtesy of Window Shade Manufacturers Association)*

Below left: For a no-sew window treatment in this alcove window, a floral print is laminated to the window shade. The shade, specially designed for laminating, is adhesive-coated and heat-sensitive so that any fabric can be ironed onto it. The iron's heat activates the adhesive. The shade is trimmed with a border of pressure-sensitive velvet ribbon. The fabric is repeated in the cushions. *(Courtesy of Window Shade Manufacturers Association)*

Below center: At the windows, white frames show off three translucent shades that allow light to filter through. Sash curtains under the shades are secured with spring tension rods. *(Courtesy of Window Shade Manufacturers Association)*

Fig
22

Fig. 22.7

Fig.
22.9

405

Interior designer Shirley Regendahl used an unusual window treatment as catalyst for a skilled blending of old and new. An overall shade cloth valance and matching laminated shades serve to dress up this window niche. *(Courtesy of Window Shade Manufacturers Association)*

For a stunning wall-to-wall effect, designer John Hayden hid an old-fashioned, one-window wall behind a structural frame that houses three shades, laminated in a handsome, floral design. To produce this attractive window treatment in a do-it-yourself manner, use an adhesive-coated and heat-sensitive shade cloth so that fabric can be ironed on with ease. *(Courtesy of Window Shade Manufacturers Association)*

Fig.
22.10

To create an interesting effect build a lambrequin around a window. The lambrequin can be enhanced by framing it in fabric. For one window the project will need one piece of 1″ × 6″ pine the width of the window, two pieces of 1″ × 6″ pine the height of the window, one-inch thick padding, tacks, or staples, plus fabric. (Courtesy of Window Shade Manufacturers Association)

Fig. 22.11

many Oriental homes, and Westerners use the shoji screen to establish an Oriental theme in a room.

Paneltrac. Paneltrac is a sliding fabric panel that looks like a shoji screen. Flat fabric panels are attached to slides in a multi-channel track with Velcro fastening tape. Paneltrac is ideal for use with contemporary or Oriental furnishings.

Curtains and Draperies

There are so many different types of curtains and draperies currently popular that these two terms have rather broad meanings. It is almost impossible to assign any concise, clear-cut definition to each one, nor is it possible to classify types in a consistent, well-organized fashion.

In general, we think of curtains as being made of sheer, semisheer, and lightweight fabrics, and of draperies as being made of heavier fabrics. Draperies may be used alone or over some type of curtain. Either curtains or draperies may be used with or without shades or Venetian blinds, but some windows have all three—shades or blinds, curtains, and draperies.

In general usage the term *curtain* refers to various types of fabric coverings that may extend over only part of the window, all of it, or from the top of the window to the floor; usually, we think of them as being hung next to the

For a pair of difficult corner windows, Edmund Motyka, A.I.D., trimmed white shades with a self-adhering printed wall covering border. The same border frames the windows as lambrequins, and café curtains of matching fabric create an appealing and effective treatment for the sun porch mood of the living room. (Courtesy of Window Shade Manufacturers Association)

Fig. 22.12

glass. On the other hand, *draperies* as a rule extend at least from the top of the window to the sill. More usually they extend below the sill to cover an apron if there is one, or they reach the floor. Both curtains and draperies can be designed to draw back and leave the window completely uncovered.

The broad coverage of these two terms indicates the wide variety of possible window treatments. Individual selections, therefore, will be guided by what the curtains and draperies are to do in the room. Some will be useful in controlling light and air and in providing privacy; others may be purely decorative. We sometimes use curtains and draperies only to add a feeling of warmth to a room. Draperies frequently do contribute to the actual insulation of a room, and some are lined with a special fabric that helps to keep interior temperatures at an even level. Nevertheless, whether or not they make any significant contribution to the actual heat control, fabrics at the window lend softness to the atmosphere. They may also be useful for reducing noise in some areas.

Perhaps one of the most appealing arguments for using curtains and draperies lies in the fact that one can do so much with so little expense. Ready-mades are available in a wide variety of types, colors, and textures.

The person who sews can achieve rich, elegant effects with comparatively little outlay of time or money. Making curtains and draperies that have a professional touch does not require a great deal of skill or practice. In view of the economy and the small amount of time involved, the saving is usually well worth the effort. The availability of fabrics and trimmings stimulates the imagination. The various types of fixtures, hooks, tapes, and pins that are currently on the market further simplify the process. Creating effects that are beautiful, functional, and economical can be a source of great pride and satisfaction. A few simple directions for making curtains and draperies are included in Chapter 29.

The style of curtains and draperies should be in keeping with the spirit of the room. However, texture, color, and pattern in the fabric play such an important role in determining the ap-

In the Orient, this look is achieved with sliding shoji screens. In this picture it is done with Paneltrac. Flat panels cover the most area with the least yardage. They work like sliding screens and stack back compactly. Paneltrac is custom tailored to the windows and width of fabric chosen. Paneltrac has Velcro surfaced sliders and additional Velcro to hold the fabric to these sliders, which are pulled by a baton. *(Courtesy of Kirsch Company)*

Fig. 22.13

pearance of the window that once again it is difficult, if not impossible, to draw up any hard and fast rules that must be followed. For example, plain curtains that hang straight at the windows are suitable for many types of rooms. They may be cheerful, or they may be rich and elegant, depending on the fabric.

Different curtain styles suggest different degrees of formality. For example, short curtains tend to be more informal than those that extend to the floor. Also, some special treatment at the top of the window may provide a particular note of interest. A draped swag or a cornice might be used to emphasize the window, especially if some form of contrast is used. Frequently the top of the window is used for a concealed source of light. Fluorescent tubes inside a cornice may highlight the window and also contribute to the general illumination of a room.

Types of curtains and draperies. Some of the basic forms of window decoration include:

Café curtains Short curtains that cover a portion of window. Often hung on decorative rods by means of rings, clips, loops, or hooks. Usually rather informal but with use of over-draperies may be adapted to more formal treatments.

Cornice Stiff boxlike treatment at top of window. May be wood, metal, or any other decorative material. Fabric-covered cornices are sometimes decorated with fringe or braid.

Criss-cross curtains Wide panels mounted so that they overlap and then tie back. Usually made of sheer fabric and trimmed with ruffles. Also called Priscilla curtains.

Draw curtains (or **draw draperies**) Mounted on traverse rod so they can be drawn open or closed. Different types of traverse rods permit wide variety of treatments. Some draw curtain panels draw so that they meet at center of the window (two-way draw); others draw one panel across an entire window area (one-way draw). Curved traverse rods are also available.

Glass curtains Made of sheer fabric in simple straight lines. May be used alone or with draperies. Usually cover the whole window area. (Tailored.)

Jabots Pleated or draped lengths of fabric that hang down the side of the window. Jabots can be floor length or only a foot long.

Pinch-pleated (or **French**) **draperies** Draperies that are pleated at the heading. They are custom made or made with pleater tape.

Sash curtains Similar to glass curtains, but mounted on rod attached to sash or frame. May cover only part of window. Sometimes held taut with rods at top and bottom.

Shirred curtain A shirred heading that is used when there is no valance. A five-inch crinoline in-heading should be used. This consists of four rows of shirring and gives the appearance of smocking.

Swag Draped section of fabric at top of window. Usually used with short pieces at sides to form cascades. Suitable for more formal window treatments.

Tie-back curtains Panels draped aside and held to frame or wall with extra pieces of fabric or special fixtures. Tie-back curtains are often made of sheer fabric and decorated with ruffles.

Tier curtains Two or more horizontal rows of short curtains mounted so that they overlap.

Valance Decorative finish at top of window. May be gathered or pleated flounce of fabric.

Fig. 22.14

The sheer valence is an unusual pouf-style that runs around the corner to top both windows with the poufs repeated below to silhouette the straight curtains. Tassels tie the scoop-ups and all the colors are repeated in the print on the bedspread, bolsters, wing chair, and laminated shades. The bedspread's box quilting can be done on a home sewing machine. The shades are laminated with matching fabric. (*Courtesy of Window Shade Manufacturers Association*)

Electrac is not another look for draperies, but a way to make them work. Instead of pulling cords, flip a switch. Electromagnetic motors in the rod draw the draperies. A switch can be more practical than cords for wide, long, or heavy draperies. One can draw draperies from the bed. Electrac wiring can go inside the walls of a home being built or installed in a ready-made home. *(Courtesy of Kirsch Company)*

For a different look in draperies, try accordian pleats. The look is slim and trim and tailored. The function is conventional. Like pinch-pleated draperies, these panels are controlled by cords. Draperies of Accordia-Fold snap off and on the rod. This treatment must be custom made. *(Courtesy of Kirsch Company)*

If pinch pleats is not your look, try Ripplefold, a custom system for both draperies and the traverse track. Whether fabric or woven wood, treatments made with Ripplefold are in every sense draw draperies, with all their practicality. There is less fabric in a ripple than in a triple pleat so there is less to stack back when draperies are open. Hanging them is fast; they snap in place with no hooks. But when the panels are unsnapped, they are flat. They are easy to clean. *(Courtesy of Kirsch Company)*

Window Treatments

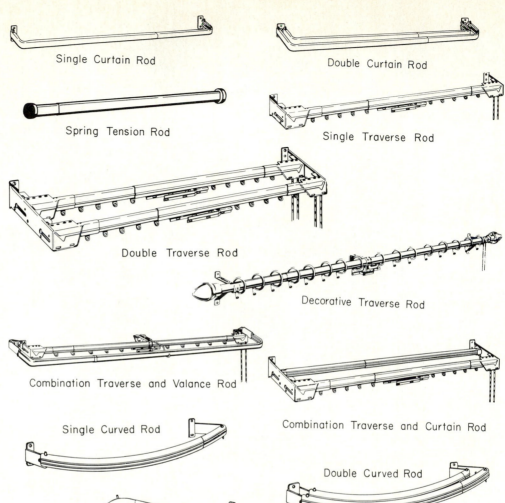

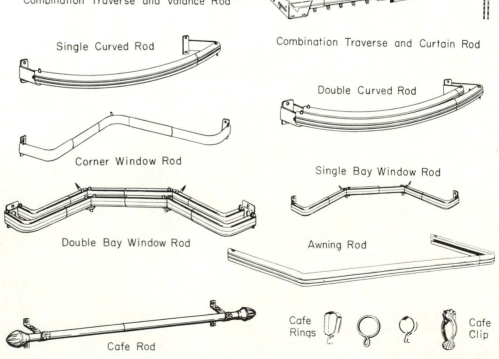

Fig. 22.18
Types of rods and fixtures.

Single Curtain Rod

Double Curtain Rod

Spring Tension Rod

Single Traverse Rod

Double Traverse Rod

Decorative Traverse Rod

Combination Traverse and Valance Rod

Combination Traverse and Curtain Rod

Single Curved Rod

Double Curved Rod

Corner Window Rod

Single Bay Window Rod

Double Bay Window Rod

Awning Rod

Cafe Rod

Cafe Rings

Cafe Clip

Buying ready-made and custom window treatments. Look for good construction features such as fabric on grain, straight hems, full ruffles, square corners, and covered raw edges. Select suitable widths and lengths. Buy draperies sixteen inches wider than the area to be covered if you are using traverse rods, thus allowing fabric for overlaps and returns. Ready-made shirred curtains need to be twice the rod length.

The pleats of custom-made draperies are closer together, creating a luxurious fullness. To make your own curtains and draperies, refer to the chapter on sewing for the home.

Fixtures. There are so many different kinds of curtain and drapery rods on the market that it is important to plan the window treatment carefully and to choose the fixtures that are most suitable for the effect you are trying to achieve. Traverse rods allow one to draw curtains and draperies across the window. On a two-way draw rod, the curtains will meet at the center. However, for some openings—such as a corner window—one-way draw rods are more useful. If it is desirable to clear the window glass when the draw drapery is open, the drapery rod should be one third again as wide as the window.

Fabrics for window treatments. The fabrics used for windows contribute to the character of the room. The new era of textile technology has produced creative fabrics for window treatments. Of all the new fabrics, man-mades such as nylon, acrylic, rayon, polyester, plastic, and fiber glass are the most popular. Fabrics made from man-made fibers are improving all the time.

Consider fabric durability, resistance to sunlight and soil, possible insect damage, suitability, total cost, problems of construction, shape stability, maintenance, and ease of laundering and cleaning.

Finishes affect appearance and performance. Excess starch and sizing are undesirable: they are removed after the first cleaning. Chemical treatments are available for fabrics that are permanently crisp, crease resistant, moisture and

A few of the many accessories that add a finishing touch to window treatments. *(Courtesy of Kirsch Company)*

Fig. 22.19

stain repellent, resistant to yarn slippage, washable, shrinkage controlled, nonflammable, fade resistant, and wash-and-wear. This information can be found on the label.

Lined draperies are used less frequently today than in the past. They cost more than those that are unlined, but they have more body and afford greater privacy, and protect the fabric from the sun's rays. Lined draperies also produce a uniform appearance when viewed from the outside of the home. When an insulated lining is used, it can lower the utility bill.

Before making a final decision on a window treatment fabric, it is recommended that you buy at least a yard of the fabric you are considering (small swatches can be deceptive). Take the fabric home and tape it to the wall in folds, then stand far back to get the effect of the fabric in the room. Allow the sample to hang in the room for a few days to see if it is pleasing.

Hold the fabrics being considered for window treatments up to the light and check translucency or opaqueness. A sheer fabric that will transmit daylight is a good choice for a north-facing kitchen window.

To create a private living or dining room in the evening when the lights are bright, consider a tightly woven opaque fabric. Tightly woven draw draperies are a good choice for a bedroom to keep out the morning sun.

Design

Pattern. The pattern is another factor to consider in selecting window treatments. The pattern or lack of pattern in the fabric should depend on the amount of pattern already in the room. The color of the draperies may be white, off-white, cream, beige, ecru, or a color that blends with the background walls; the tint or shade should be somewhat lighter or darker in value. Duplicating the exact wall color in draperies may be monotonous, or it may give a unified and spacious look to the room. The texture of the drapery must agree with the mood and style of the room.

Window treatment may add pattern to the room. Patterned treatments may be suitable for large rooms, or for wall spaces that need to be broken, or for rooms that need color, design, or pattern. Colorful, highly patterned draperies may help to balance large furnishings elsewhere in the room.

Inconspicuous window treatments may increase the spaciousness of the room. Plain fabrics and colors that blend with the wall make windows less conspicuous. Inconspicuous curtains and draperies can be used to achieve a restful effect. If the room is small, or the windows are poorly placed, inconspicuous curtains can be used effectively. A room with a large number of windows may need to be treated with curtains that do not draw attention to the number of windows. Modern decorators may use two different patterns in the room, and the treatment can be stimulating and exciting if it is well done.

Fabrics should be suited to other furnishings in texture, color, and character. Some fabrics may state formality or informality. Loosely woven woolens, burlap, checked ginghams, organdy, plaids, tweeds, and calicos are suitable choices for informal rooms. Sheer or smooth-textured fabrics blend well with formal furnishings. For this purpose voiles, rayons, marquisettes, brocades, satins, damasks, velvets, and tapestry prints are more appropriate for the formal setting. Some fabrics, such as chintzes, linens, and plain-colored fabrics, will go in either formal or informal settings. Modern rooms can use fabrics with boldly figured, colorful prints, as well as textured and novelty materials.

Line. Line is significant in selecting a window treatment. The number of windows in a room is important because window treatment should be repeated throughout the room. A striking window treatment that would be successful for a

To enlarge a small area and camouflage a poor view, use one design from floor to ceiling and wall to wall. This flower and grille design works ideally for complete coverage and is used in the draperies, wall covering, and window shade. To complement and contrast, another print is used to encase the chair. *(Courtesy of the Belgian Linen Association)*

Prints play wonderful decorative tricks in this garden-fresh living room. Window shades, bordered with two tones of green, fill the arches made from plywood. Matching textured shade cloth backs the lattice-work of the treillage for unity and hides the unattractive details of the old window frames. *(Courtesy of Window Shade Manufacturers Association)*

Fig. 22.20

Fig. 22.21

Fig. 22.22

How to mask or disguise two thin windows on one wall is a common problem. Generally speaking, the windows are not close enough together to be treated as one. The same fabric as on the wall is laminated on a double set of window shades. In addition to light control, the bottom set of shades rolls up from the sill for privacy or to mask a dull view. Shades mounted this way are a good device to hide a window air conditioning unit, too. Sheer curtains are tied loosely at sill height. *(Courtesy of Window Shade Manufacturers Association)*

single window group forming a center of interest may be too striking for repetition. In a room with many windows, the draperies may be treated as part of the background by repeating the color of the wall. The shape of the window affects the curtain design, particularly if that shape is unusual or difficult.

The length of curtains and draperies should begin and end at some architectural feature such as the window frame, sill, apron, or baseboard to enable the eye to move smoothly over the composition.

Glass curtains used alone need to have a heading to cover the wood frame. To make the curtain seem full rather than skimpy, use two, three, or four times the width of the window to be covered. The final amount will be determined by the weight of the fabric. Draperies should use at least a full width of fabric—36″ to 39″ for average windows and 50″ for large ones. Draw draperies may require about 2¼ times the width of the window.

The trained eye can sense the proportion needed for the valance relative to the length of the draperies. As a guide, use 1½ inches for the valance for every foot of height of the draperies. For example, if the draperies are nine feet, multiply 9 by 1½ to total a valance depth of 13½ inches.

Scale and balance. When choosing a window treatment that will keep a room balanced, consider the size of the window and the size of the room. The window and its treatment may be the focal point; thus it will have weight, and should be balanced both on the window wall and the wall opposite the window wall.

The window treatment should be scaled to the window size and room size. A small window in a small room should have a simple treatment to keep the room from being overpowered by the window treatment. It is possible for a large window in a large room to have a heavy elaborate treatment and still be in scale with the rest of the room. The window treatment should also be scaled to the length and height of the walls to produce a harmonious effect.

Consideration of styles. It is essential that the window treatment blend with the character of the room and the furniture style used. When the window treatment and room character clash, the effect of the room is impaired.

For example, an African-inspired room that combines brocade or damask draw draperies with African accessories and furniture represents two different styles; the draperies do not fit the theme of the room. Some kind of window treatment with bamboo or straw shades, macramé, beads, shutters, or blinds would be more harmonious and repeat the African theme. When there are several windows in the same room they should be stylisticly unified.

Problem windows. The architectural deficiencies of windows that are poorly spaced or poorly shaped can often be easily camouflaged with curtains and draperies. Two windows separated by a narrow wall section might be treated as one with a unifying cornice or valance and draw draperies. Short windows may have to be given the effects of added height by the placement of fixtures above the actual window openings. Narrow windows will seem wider if the draperies extend beyond the sides. Various types of cornices and valances may be used to add height or width, the amount of dimension added depending on the manner in which these fixtures are mounted. Deep cornices and swags may be used to give tall, narrow windows more pleasing proportions.

Arched windows and slanting clerestory windows frequently present problems of decoration. Curved rods or flexible tapes can be used to mount curtains on curved frames. On clerestory windows, the rod can follow the slant of the frame. In this case, the curtain will have to be carefully measured, because it will be shorter on one side than on the other. With both these problems it is often more attractive to leave the unusually shaped area uncovered than to use a treatment that seems contrived or awkward.

Maintenance

Modern living seems to demand homes that are easy to maintain. Yet we do not always want to sacrifice warmth or a touch of elegance in decorating our homes. With modern materials and careful planning, we can easily furnish a

Fig. 22.23

Priscilla

Cafe

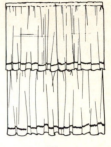

Tier

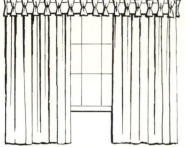

Draw Draperies,
Valance

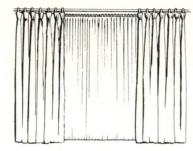

Double-hung
Traverse

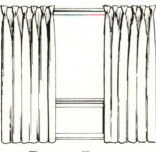

Two-way Traverse

One-way Draw Traverse

Shirred Glass
Curtains

Panel Draperies
with Cornice

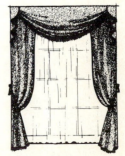

Tie-back Draperies
with Swag

Basic window treatments.

Window Treatments

How to Correlate Decorative Elements[1]

Table 22.1

Period or Style	Associated Styles	Walls and Ceilings	Floors
English			
Early English Tudor Jacobean Charles	Italian Renaissance; Spanish Renaissance William & Mary Larger pieces of Queen Anne	Oak panels Rough plaster with oak trim Parquetry ceilings	Hardwood stained dark, may be planks or flooring Stone, tiles
William & Mary Queen Anne	Chippendale Early Georgian Louis XIV Smaller pieces of Jacobean such as gate-leg table or Windsor chair	Papered Painted (in light tones) Hung with fabrics Paneled	Hardwood flooring Parquetry
Georgian Chippendale	Chippendale Early Georgian Louis XIV Smaller pieces of Jacobean such as gate-leg table or Windsor chair	Paneled dado Painted, paneled, or papered upper section in Chinese motifs.	Hardwood flooring Parquetry
Late Georgian Adam Hepplewhite Sheraton	Chippendale (in Chinese manner) Louis XVI Duncan Phyfe Directoire	Plain plaster. Painted. Papered. Large wood panels, painted. Gesso-ceilings	Hardwood flooring Parquetry
Spanish			
Spanish Renaissance	Italian Renaissance Early English Louis XIV	Rough plaster Painted Ceilings, same or beamed	Hardwood Tiles Linoleum in tile pattern
French			
Louis XVI	All Late Georgian styles 1 or 2 pieces of Louis XV and Directoire	Large wood panels, painted and decorated Wallpaper in Chinese motifs	Hardwood flooring Parquetry
French Provincial	18th Century American Colonial, Federal Biedermeier	Smooth plaster Wallpaper in scenic or geometric designs	Hardwood Parquetry

Background for Interiors

| Floor Coverings | Draperies | | | Upholstery Fabrics |
	Fabric	Colors	Design	
Oriental and large-pattern domestic rugs Plain rug	Crewel embroideries, hand-blocked linen, silk and worsted damask, velvet, brocade	Full-bodied crimson, green and yellow	Large bold patterns: tree branch, fruits, flowers, oak leaf, animals, heraldic designs	Tapestry Leather Needlework Velvet Brocade
Oriental and large-pattern domestic rugs Plain rug	Crewel embroideries, hand-blocked linen, silk and worsted damask, velvet, brocade, India prints	Full-bodied crimson, green and yellow	Large bold patterns: tree branch, fruits, flowers, oak leaf, animals, heraldic design	Tapestry Leather Needlework Velvet Brocade
Plain or small patterned rugs or carpets Oriental rugs	Crewel embroideries, hand-blocked linen, silk and worsted damask, velvet, brocade, India prints	Full-bodied crimson, green and yellow	Jacobean motifs; also classic medallions and garlands	Tapestry Leather Needlework Velvet Brocade
Plain or small-patterned rugs or carpets Oriental rugs	Brocades, damask, chintz, taffeta, satins, toile de jouy	Delicate subdued hues of rose, yellow, mauve, green and gray	Classic designs, small in scale: garlands, urns, floral, animals, etc.	Damask, brocade, velour, satin, petit point, leather (in libraries)
Spanish or Oriental rugs	Velvet, damask, crewel work, India prints, printed and emb. linen	Rich, vigorous colors; red, green and gold	Bold patterns in classic and heraldic designs; also arabesques	Leather Tapestry Velvet Linen Brocatelle
Plain or small-patterned rugs or carpets Oriental rugs	Silks, satin, damask, taffeta, muslins, brocade, toile de jouy	Delicate powder blue, oyster white, pearl, rose, pale greens, mauve, yellow	Stripes sprinkled with ribbons, flowers, medallions, lyres and other classic motifs	Petit point, satin moire, velours, chintz, damask, brocade, tapestry
Aubussons Homespun carpet. Small-pattern Orientals	Chintz, cretonne, blocked linen, velvet	Subdued colors. Pastel shades	Screen prints, block print	Solid colors Textured weaves Tapestry

Table 22.1 How to Correlate Decorative Elements[1] *(Cont.)*

Period or Style		Associated Styles	Walls and Ceilings	Floors
American	Early Colonial	All Early English styles William & Mary Queen Anne wing chair	Oak panels Rough plaster with oak trim Parquetry ceilings	Hardwood flooring or planks Linoleum in jaspe pattern
	Late Colonial	Late Georgian Chippendale Queen Anne Duncan Phyfe French Provincial	Smooth plaster light trim Wallpaper, scenic and Chinese designs Paneling Ceiling, plaster	Dark hardwood flooring Linoleum in plain or jaspe patterns
	Victorian	Colonial William & Mary Queen Anne	Large pattern paper	Hardwood
	Modern	Swedish modern	Painted solid colors. Stripe, figured, plain papers. Combinations of above	Hardwood Parquetry Linoleum in modern pattern

[1] Adapted from *Hoover-Seng Furniture Facts* (Georgetown, Kentucky: Hoover-Seng, 1974), pp. 154–155. Courtesy of Hoover-Seng Co.

home that requires a minimum amount of care and we can make it both functional and attractive. If easy maintenance were the primary consideration, however, we would probably have somewhat clinical-looking homes that would not appeal to most of us. The dilemma may be resolved in part, at least, by the choice of fabrics for interesting, glamorous windows. For example, simple, straight curtains in a lovely shimmering texture may add exactly the note of richness that a modern room needs. True, the curtains will have to be washed sometimes, but if the fabric is one that resists soil, it can be washed in a machine, and needs no ironing, the problem is not serious. Without the curtains, the windows may be completely functional and reasonably attractive, but the room may lack the ingredient of warmth that woven fabrics seem to provide.

Fortunately, fabric manufacturers are providing materials that have rich textures and lovely colors but that require little care. Fabrics

| Floor Coverings | Draperies | | | Upholstery Fabrics |
	Fabric	Colors	Design	
Braided or hooked rugs	Crewel embroideries, hand-blocked linen, silk and worsted damask, velvet, brocade	Full-bodied crimson, green and yellow	Large bold patterns: tree branch, fruits, flowers, oak leaf, animals, heraldic	Tapestry Leather Needlework Velvet Brocade
Hooked, braided, Oriental rugs. Domestic rugs or carpet, plain, two-toned or patterned	Toile de jouy, damask, chintz, organdy, cretonne	All colors, but more subdued than in early period	Scenic Birds Animals Floral	Haircloth Mohair Rep Linen Chintz Velours
Carpeting in large patterns Orientals	Velvet brocades, damask	Turkey Red. Other rich colors	Solid colors Formal patterns	Haircloth Needlework
Carpeting Rugs in solid colors, geometric patterns	Textured and novelty weaves All fabrics	All colors, bright to pastel	Solid colors Modern designs Stripes	All fabrics, novelty weaves, plastics

that can be washed without being ironed, finishes that resist soil, and metallic yarns that do not tarnish have all been combined to produce materials that are both elegant and easy to maintain.

It still takes careful shopping and a certain amount of knowledge to choose fabrics that meet all demands, but the results are well worth the effort. The beautiful effects and the little time required to maintain them will be most satisfying to the creative homemaker.

Coordinating Decorative Elements

The different elements that are used in a home have been discussed throughout this book. Table 22.1, which begins on page 416, has been added to help you coordinate these different elements in a room if you are trying to adhere to one kind of period. We are not recommending that you follow it exactly, but it will give you suggestions for what kinds of elements relate well to one another.

23
Mechanical Systems

Introduction: The Interior and Its Systems

Contemporary homes can be viewed as mechanically controlled environments. The respective systems provide such services as heat, light, air, ventilation, and communication. Properly planned interior systems must be integrated into the design of the home through hidden or inconspicuously placed devices and channels. A house may be lit through an electrical system that has no actual fixtures or open wiring. It may be heated or cooled through means that are not readily detectable in the room's interior. These mechanical appliances—often invisible within the room—have been among the major advances in the architecture of interiors. Other nonmechanical provisions have continued the process of systematization: we now perceive floors or ceilings not as conspicuous surfaces but as unified grid patterns of tiles, for example. Floors may contain heating elements, and ceilings may conceal fixtures that provide air and light. Mechanical systems are more and more often being hidden and integrated into the function of the room's design, allowing a great freedom in the interior arrangements.

A second feature of the contemporary home is a trend toward a totally independent setting with its own provisions for a comfortable, private, weather-controlled environment. This striving for climate control has provided us with many new and interesting systems, such as solar heating, tinted window glass to filter out the sunlight, and acoustical materials that can make the interior appear free from noise, even in the most urban location, while providing built-in music and fine acoustical qualities.

With all these efforts toward total environmental control came an unprecedented increase in energy consumption, reflected in the higher cost of buying and running a home. Machines are becoming a more complex and important part of the building's design and construction, as well as of its maintenance. These factors require all who are seriously concerned with planning to view the house increasingly as a machine. Today, with most interior alterations, some form of mechanical servicing is involved. What is important is that at present outer structures, interior space, and mechanical functions cannot be designed separately. Both structural and mechanical house planning work together to provide a comfortable climate in the house, whereas other elements (intercoms, built-in television wiring, and elevators, for example) allow for the smooth circulation of people and their communication through the interior. In planning a building and its interior, we cannot simply deal with geometric forms or volumes of space; we must consider the many mechanical elements that go into a home. In the design of homes during the past, some basic provisions were always made for the control of environments: there were fireplaces for heat, chimneys to eliminate smoke, and channels for water. But today's systems are more automated, less conspicuous, greater in number, and more complex in their interplay.

Interior environments have to be considered in the design of home structures. Many of our contemporary comforts come from our ability to control our immediate environment. In the rooms of our homes, we can supply heat in winter, cool temperatures in summer, and acoustical and visual privacy. It is interesting to remember that societies with less sophisticated environmental controls, especially our earliest communities in history, had to center their lives around a water hole, a shady tree, or a fire, and their living arrangements were always open to the changes and upsetting interruptions of the elements. There are two essential factors in our society that promote a high standard of living in our homes: we build permanent shelters, and we strive toward power-controlled environments.

Today technological changes are rapid, generally running ahead of the architect and the interior designer. Commercial structures—greenhouses, factories, inflatable tennis courts, and even our cars—have certain environmental facilities that many homes have still not caught up with. In looking toward the future, we can probably see home environments that rely less on structural features, such as large buildings and massive walls, and more on designs centered on the family's mechanical needs. One clear step in this direction that we can already

note is the change of interior walls from brick to major areas of thin siding or open glass; these walls no longer need to serve as sole protectors from the elements, because the mechanical systems inside control the environment in the house.

Today homes are becoming more open and lighter in appearance, with fewer heavy permanent wall or interior divisions. Homes are more flexible in their interior spaces, furniture is lighter, and arrangements are simpler, less cluttered, and more open to change.

The Basics of Heating

Our heating systems may be classified in a number of ways; by fuel, by heat-producing equipment, or by various heating media.

The purpose of the system is to heat the medium utilized (water, air, or steam) and convey it to the target space. For example, hot water is heated in the basement or in a utility room, then travels through pipes to the room, where it gives off heat in the radiator. After it has cooled, it returns to the boiler to be reheated. In steam systems, water is heated until it turns to steam, travels through pipes to radiators, and gives off its heat. It then changes back to water as it cools and flows back to repeat the cycle.

In hot-air systems, air is heated and transported to various rooms through ducts. It gives off heat, and then returns to be reheated and reused.

In the case of electrical heating units, coils are heated; water or air may further preserve the heat for a while.

The different heating systems use different equipment, but the theory remains the same: there is a heating source and a way of transporting the heat to the desired area. Generally, the designer should make the choice of which type to select, with the advice of a heating engineer if necessary.

Heating costs. Providing heat is one of the most expensive services in a house. A poor system causes large heating bills without necessarily eliminating cold drafts in winter.

The two most common kinds of central heating are forced warm-air heat and hot-water heat. Various types of electric heat are also available.

Warm-air heat. A warm-air heat system consists of a furnace, a blower for pushing air under pressure to rooms, and ducts for channeling the air. The presence of ducts and air outlets (vents), rather than radiators, characterizes a warm-air system. The advantages of this method are that central air conditioning can easily be provided through the same duct system and that there is a quick response to calls for heat from the thermostat. The furnace filter cleans the air. If the system is located in the basement, a disadvantage is that openings may have to be cut in the carpeting for outlets in the floor. (In many homes where heating systems are either located in a central part of the house or in the attic, the problem of floor vents is avoided.) Also, furniture placement may be limited to prevent interference with warm air coming through floor outlets.

Hot-water heat. Water is heated in a boiler and flows through pipes to radiators in each room; a pump forces air around under pressure. The tendency today is to build simple radiators, close to the floor and as inconspicuous as possible.

Baseboard heaters are one type of unit. Such a unit cannot go flush up against the wall. It is low, long, and streamlined and rests close to the floor; usually it is only seven to nine inches high. No matter how inconspicuous, baseboards are unsightly and disturb the geometric pattern of floors meeting walls. Furniture should be placed to deemphasize the units.

Radiant hot-water heat uses the same kind of heating as the regular hot-water system. The house is heated by pipes embedded in the floor, through which hot water flows from the boiler. Steam heat is rarely used any more in new houses. Stand-up radiators work the same way as hot-water heat.

With baseboard or radiator heating, however, one wall of the house (often under the windows) is generally the source of comfort, and the heat is not evenly distributed throughout the room. The decorator or designer has to consider the heat source in placing or rearranging furniture and other items.

Electric heat. Electric heat is often called "clean heat"; no boiler or furnace is used in the system. Each room is controlled by a thermostat. Heat is generated by current passing through copper electrodes; air passes over the electrodes and circulates, and the room is then heated with that air.

Electric heat systems have a tendency to age quickly, and the designer has to be aware that permanent fixtures within interiors may have to be removed for repair or replacement of parts. Furthermore, furniture and draperies must be kept away from the heating elements for safety reasons. The tight construction of buildings with central heating gives rise to complaints of stuffiness or excessive moisture buildup. The decorator has to be knowledgeable about this danger when selecting and choosing interior decorations.

For reasons of safety, heating units must be covered and should not be exposed. The problem for the interior designer is to select appropriate coverings that are safe and work well with the room decor.

Houses of the past focused on the fireplace. Furniture groupings and other arrangements were placed around a central fireplace. Today, the purpose of heating and cooling is to condition the entire space. Now there is interest in electrical fireplaces, which give off heat and still offer the visual excitement of the fireplace.

Heating can become part of the invisible systems of a home. With electric heat becoming more and more common, the homes of the future may be heated by elements built into the floor or ceiling of a room, requiring no visible outlets. In many custom homes, this ultimate type of invisible heating already exists.

Solar heat. Energy derived from the sun is becoming an increasingly attractive alternative or supplement to gas, oil, and electric heating. It is becoming more popular in the United States as the concern about the cost and availability of existing energy grows. Solar energy is practical to tap, clean, nonpolluting, and readily available. To make a solar heat system work, the following components are required:

A collector, which may be mounted either on the roof or adjacent to the house, is installed to face south to collect as much sunlight as possible. A collector is a device or structure that is heated by the sun's rays. There are many different types of collectors, such as "flat-plate air," in which air is blown over or under a hot flat surface, "flat-plate liquid," in which liquid is passed over or under the hot flat surface; and "concentrators" of the sun's heat rays which work as a magnifying glass or a reflecting telescope. The air or water moves across the collector, picking up heat as it passes.

A storage chamber filled with a heat-absorbing material stores heat for use at night or during periods of cloudy weather. To transfer the heat from collector to storage or to the home, pumps or fans are required. Generally in a home, some kind of backup heating system is used when excessive demands on the system occur.

For a family of four, for example, using eighty gallons of hot water every day, a large portion of home heating needs (approximately 60 to 80 per cent) can be met by present solar systems. In terms of cost, for example, in one of the more popular models the calculation is that the system will pay for itself in energy savings over a six-year period.

Air Conditioning: Introduction

Modern air conditioning provides almost complete control over the atmospheric variables of temperature, humidity, and purity. Such environmental conditioning is usually part of modern architecture and promotes human health and comfort. Today's home builders usually include facilities for some type of air conditioning.

Air conditioning is a system of complete year-round climate control: heating, cooling, humidity, dehumidifying, cleaning, and air circulation and purification. There is a certain combination of air temperature and humidity

Interior climate control devices for air, light, and heat, including a wall-mounted air conditioner, picture window, and steam heat radiator. *(Courtesy of G. Szekely)*

Fig. 23.1

that is most favorable to human comfort. Air-conditioning systems distribute these factors throughout the home to individual areas. If properly designed, an efficient system will provide good air distribution and individual room control.

Air conditioning has overcome most of the environmental constraints on design that have survived the earlier uses of electricity, such as lighting and heating. For anyone prepared to pay for the power consumed, it is now possible to live anywhere in the world in any type of house. For example, one can have warmth in the Arctic in houses with comparatively thin walls, or one can live in the desert and in tropical areas without suffering from heat.

Air conditioning is a sophisticated device for environmental management; it requires only basic skills to install and very little know-how to operate.

There are a number of methods for making our air more pleasant. Some air conditioners merely blow the air around or bring the fresh air inside. Some are only for summer use to cool and dehumidify the air; others are for year-around use.

Fans are one source of taking hot air out and allowing cooler air to enter. Because the air next to the ground is coolest, basement or first-floor windows can sometimes be left open; but in the attic, fans are needed to draw the hot air out. It is important to ventilate bathrooms, kitchens, closets, garages, and furnace rooms for odors as well as comfort.

There are two types of individual units that can be selected. One is a window unit; the other is a wall unit, designed to be put into a box-shaped opening in the wall.

Small air-conditioning units are for summer cooling only. They are installed in windows or appropriate wall openings. They take up hardly any floor space and require no plumbing connections. Newer units can be moved easily from room to room. However, these appliances cause an uneven drafty cooling effect and are sometimes quite noisy.

An air-conditioning unit basically consists of two devices: an indoor part, visible from inside the room, and an external section that can be seen only from a standing position near the window.

Fig. 23.2 Contemporary styling in a wall-mounted air conditioner. *(Courtesy of G. Szekely)*

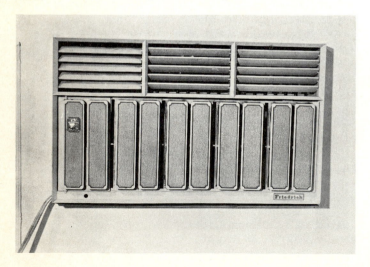

In older wall units, not only is an unsightly hole made in the wall, but the front of the unit itself is often an eyesore. There have been improvements in wall or window air contitioners in terms of size and style. Units now come in various colors and styles to make them more compatible with interiors.

Because no furniture can be placed in front of the air conditioner, the wall in which it is placed should be considered. Seating arrangements should be planned so that there are no uncomfortable drafts. Window units cause another problem: part of the window's function is ventilation and another is an unblocked view of the outside. A window unit not only mars the original design but limits both functions of the window. Advances have been made in portable models that can actually be inserted in and taken out of windows easily when not in use. These new designs in air conditioners are, however, functional only for small rooms, for their cooling capacity is limited.

Generally, in suburbia, the outside part of the air conditioner does not pose visual or architectural problems if there are trees growing in front of the units so that they cannot be seen. In city apartments, however, such installations can bring these environmental improvements into direct conflict with the visual intentions of the architect. The visual appearance of the internal unit has definite effects on the interior design and decoration of the room.

Central air conditioning. A more ambitious type of air conditioning is called the *central* system. Because of its growing popularity, it is incorporated into the original building plans of many new houses. The cost is considerably lower if it is installed while the house is being built.

Central air conditioning is generally designed as part of the house and not as a later addition. Its individual units are concealed in the ceilings, walls, or floors of each room, with only the grilles and/or diffusers showing. Because they are hidden, these units usually do not interfere with the designer's plan.

Air-conditioning cost is lowest in central air conditioning when the house has adequate thermal insulation. Furthermore, large window areas should be shaded from direct sunshine in summer. A large amount of heat enters through glass. Protection can be afforded through trees or awnings.

Major amounts of heat can also enter a house through the roof. In addition to the use of the proper type of shingles and roofing materials, the attic should be thoroughly ventilated to prevent intense heat buildup.

How to buy an air-conditioning system. One important factor when buying either a unit or a central system is to check on the dealer's experience in home cooling services. The customer can ensure satisfaction by asking for a list of people served during the past and contacting them for references.

In purchasing a unit or system it is best to stay with the equipment of a well-known national manufacturer. A certification seal of the Air Conditioning and Refrigeration Institute (ARI) should be mandatory on all equipment purchased. Also, the Better Business Bureau and issues of *Consumer Reports* magazine can be checked for details. It is very important to purchase an air conditioner with a capacity for cooling the home or room for which it is intended. To cut building cost, today many builders are installing air-conditioning units that do not have enough cooling capacity for the space intended.

Central cooling versus individual room air conditioners. In the climate control of a whole house, central air conditioning provides more cooling capacity per dollar than several small units. One large unit is more efficient. Operating costs are generally lower, and service and maintenance may be less expensive. One drawback is that if the system breaks down, the entire house is affected until repairs have been made.

Benefits of air conditioning. We must remember that air conditioning not only cools; it dehumidifies the air so that the inhabitants as well as the house are kept dry. Air conditioning also means a quieter and cleaner house, because the closed windows shut out noise and dirt. It brings relief to people with allergies because air-conditioning filters remove 99 per cent of the pollen in summer air. People with heart conditions also feel less strain.

Other benefits include reduced house cleaning, less hot-weather fatigue, better sleep at night, and more effective refrigeration. Controlled humidity and filtered air also help preserve a room's furniture, fabrics, and paintings.

Air-conditioning checklist
1. Is the cooling system properly sized for the room and house?
2. Does the unit or system carry a certification seal from the ARI?
3. Is the unit or system being installed by a reputable firm? How long has it been in business? Are well-known brands sold? How is their reputation for service?
4. Is the system air cooled or water cooled? Insist on air cooled unless there is plenty of inexpensive water available.
5. In a central system, are the ducts working efficiently, and have they been properly installed? (These questions must be answered by an expert.)
6. Is there an automatic thermostatic control for heating and air conditioning on each floor—preferably in each room?
7. Is the system guaranteed for at least one year in writing for satisfactory operation and repairs at no charge?

Air distribution ducts. It is crucial that ducts be properly designed and installed. Poor ducts result in poor warm-air heating systems. In general, the best duct system is called *perimeter duct distribution*. Warm air is discharged via outlets located around the exterior walls of the house, generally under windows, which are the major source of cold.

In general, one warm-air outlet should be placed in every exposed wall, except in the bathroom and kitchen, where exterior outlets may not be possible. Hot air is generally discharged from near the floor, as warm air rises and helps to counteract cold down-drafts from windows. Two exposures in a room require two warm-air outlets. A perimeter duct system is usually crucial for a house in the North without a basement, especially to warm up cold floors. Sometimes outlets are provided in the floor when floors are made from marble or stone. In any case, the person designing the interior must be aware of which system has been applied in order to place furnishings away from the outlets.

The mechanical system of the older home. In most instances the interior designer is faced with the difficulty of adapting mechanical systems to existing buildings erected long before such systems had been invented.

In decorating or remodeling older homes, it is important for the interior designer to understand and check the mechanical plans against the architectural drawings, so that the mechanical system does not conflict with the design.

For example, flooring and wall systems must be considered carefully for their ability to house conduits for electricity and telephone systems and to provide connections for small pipings leading to and from plumbing fixtures. In older homes, the depth of floors and walls is usually inadequate for concealing air-conditioning ducts unless the floor or wall is especially designed to include plumbing and air-conditioning lines.

In planning the interior, the interior designer must remember that easy access should be provided to those parts of the mechanical system that may have to be adjusted or repaired. Openings for access through ceilings, closets, and so on must be devised.

Vacuum Systems

Openings for air suction ducts can be built into walls when houses are constructed today. Generally, outlets similar to lighting sockets can be put into various rooms. The advantage of a built-in vacuum system is that one can attach a lightweight "electrical broom" to the central system instead of pulling or pushing a heavy vacuum unit. The extraction of dirt can be done from one central location. The popularity of the vacuum system has been limited, however, because its installation is quite costly.

Wiring Systems

Utility lines entering the house from the street supply a home with electrical power. A meter registers the amount that is used. A panel or fuse box regulates the distribution of the electricity to the home wiring system.

Circuits carry electricity to appliances, lights, and other fixtures. It is necessary to know how the wiring runs and to consider the placement of outlets when planning for the electrical appliances and furnishings in a room.

Lighting Systems

Each source of light is part of a system, which should be designed for the specific building and its interiors. We can look at lighting not only in terms of individual windows or lamps but as part of a total system that brings daylight and night illumination to a space. In a sense, therefore, a lighting system is partly mechanical (dealing with lighting fixtures) and partly architectural (in the design of openings such as windows and skylights and the arrangement of control for these openings). In looking at contemporary lighting systems, we begin to see the different qualities of light made possible by such devices as tinted windows, a variety of louver controls, and all of the possible sources of artificial illumination (lighting set into ceilings, walls, and columns). Contemporary lighting illuminates an entire room and may be achieved through screens, reflectors, and diffusors of light for different wall surfaces. In the past, chandeliers or ceiling light fixtures or individual floor units were used to illuminate the room. Contemporary lighting systems cannot only bathe the entire room in light, they can diffuse or reflect light from wall surfaces. Lens, grille, and spot lighting are frequently used in contemporary home planning to shape the lighting of spaces. Mechanical devices such as dimmers and timer switches are becoming popular ways to gain control of the amount and mood of lighting. Translucent ceiling panels may be used to diffuse light in rooms without windows.

A systems approach to lighting does not, therefore, depend on portable light fixtures; instead it determines how light can become an integral part of the design of an interior.

Concealed Power

Acoustic tiling, air conditioning, and fluorescent lighting resulted in the need for a recent invention called the *suspended ceiling*. In older buildings, ceilings have been suspended to close the top of the room and thus reduce volume; but now the same method is frequently used to carry environmental power over an entire area. The ceiling encloses ducts or other parts of heating, cooling, light, and sound systems. Acoustic tiles join with air conditioning to form a "system ceiling" that not only deadens sound but also forms a surface to diffuse and ventilate air and to heat the room.

In addition to the concealed machinery of a modern home, there is a growing number of appliances in our present-day kitchens. Devices of different colors and shapes perform various functions. The homes of today often have complex equipment: intercoms between rooms and the outside, alarm devices, and telephone units; we must, in short, view a house not only as a building arrangement but as a machine we live in.

SECTION five

Finishing Touches

Eclecticism

The term *eclectic* comes from the Greek word "Eclectics," originated by a school of ancient Greek philosophers who believed in borrowing from several systems of thought and rearranging them to form a new philosophic composite. Today eclecticism is the marriage of the old with the new, the past with the present, the native with the foreign. It combines art forms and furnishings from various periods and adapts them to today's living. It is a part of America's heritage, reflecting the influence of many different countries and cultures on the nation. It is a challenging approach that immediately expresses the owner's personality. In decorating terms, it is the art of selecting the best from several sources; applied to interior design, it is an uninhibited mixture of the styles of previous periods with the styles of today.

It was not too long ago that styles from different periods were not used together in a room. The dictates of good taste and good design determined that an acceptable presentation of a certain period (be it modern, or one of a specific period) had to maintain a positive consistency. Only items from the same period could be used together for floors, walls, furniture coverings, and assorted elements such as lighting fixtures and accessories. Even the fabric had to be derived from a single period—either past or present.

For example, to achieve the provincial look, the rules dictated the use of natural finishes of chestnut, walnut, oak, or fruitwood for furniture, and floors; curved furniture lines; rough-textured materials; peasant patterns; copper, brass, or pewter accessories; and bright yellows, blues, and greens. A Queen Anne dining room had to be decorated in Queen Anne furnishings, colors, and accessories, or it did not meet critical approval. If the chairs were upholstered in crimson antique satin, then the carpet had to be in the same color. A chair of another color that did not conform did not belong.

Today we are living in a casual, dissonant world, and many regulations have been abandoned. We no longer say "you cannot do that" or "you must do this." Strict adherence to rules

24
Eclectic Decorating

Fig. 24.1

Ray Kindell, A.I.D., decorated a Victorian room freshly tailored to today's taste without destroying its original charm. A baroque pattern printed on beige linen was used for classic valances, tie-back curtains, and laminated window shades. Together these create a nostalgic atmosphere. Most of the quaint antique pieces were found on serious scavenger hunts. The glass coffee table affords "invisible" service for the conversation group above the nineteenth-century marble fireplace. Above the mantel, a striking abstract contributes a splash of avant-garde imagery. Opposite, a red leather Parsons end table follows the clean lines of an upholstered sleep-divan. Underfoot, a patterned rug gives the room extra special definiton. *(Courtesy of Window Shade Manufacturers Association)*

This room combines many styles from different eras in an eclectic approach. Note the antique trunk used as a coffee table, the antique silver tea service, the Art Nouveau table lamp, Empire chest, Victorian couch, and zebra rug. *(Courtesy of Window Shade Manufacturers Association)*

The old and new are combined in this sophisticated room designed by Angelo Donghia. A neutral background of shades and shutters play host to a modern sofa. Matching chairs are flanked by Chinese porcelain end tables. A pair of water buffalo horns decorates the window sill, and the point they make is repeated by a curious, antique chair built of horns. The room is finished with exquisite antique touches. *(Courtesy of Window Shade Manufacturers Association)*

Fig.
24.2

Fig.
24.3

Fig. 24.4

Using Parsons tables, modern sofas, an Oriental lacquered desk, and Chinese accents in a carefully selected cross-section of design and variety makes for a sophisticated eclectic decor. *(Courtesy of Armstrong)*

is no longer the fashion and we are expressing this freedom in eclectic decorating.

Possibly one of the most exciting things to happen in the field of decoration in recent years is the acceptance of eclecticism for a good sense of color, proportion, and consistency, not expressive of period taste, but of a personal taste that can prevail to make our life styles more suitable to our daily circumstances. Eclecticism allows homeowners to furnish their homes by combining the tastes and personalities of individual family members. The concept makes possible the visual excitement of combining the old rocker found in grandmother's attic with

the contemporary sofa and oriental rug recently purchased for the home.

Suitability is a key word in eclectic decorating—the suitability of an object or a design to the style and purpose of a room, or to a person's lifestyle. It is not the custom today to maintain the same period furnishings within a house or even within the same room. Some professional decorators urge their clients "to let go"—to satisfy their own standards of beauty and taste, instead of being confined by strict adherence to the guidelines of decorating. Many famous decorators even frown on a room decorated with a suite of matching period or contemporary furniture because it may be boring and lacking in creativity. Because it is possible to mix freely (within the constraints of good taste) items from any period, one must not get the impression that eclecticism is organized clutter. It is not. To be successful, an eclectic room should have common elements throughout. One style may dominate, with others used for accent. Antiques are mixed with modern, and there are no set rules except that pieces should be compatible in scale and degree of formality. A well-planned color scheme will tie the different styles together.

Different fabrics such as florals, geometrics, and solids may also be combined in a room. If two or three patterns are combined, it is recommended that they all have something in common like color, flowers, or being derived from the same historical period. Fabrics can be coordinated if the same sized (scale) patterns are used together.

Other examples are the selection of different furniture styles of the same wood, or the combination of the sleek lines of glass and steel combined with a Shaker chair (which also is unadorned). The choice of styles depends on many factors. The final goal is to decorate so that the home will be functional as well as satisfying to all the people who live in it.

Previously the purchase of a particular item might mean the expense and problem of total redecoration in order to accommodate it; today the consumer can collect individual pieces and use them together to convey a personal statement. In order to achieve an eclectic approach, follow these guidelines:

- Do not separate contemporary pieces from traditional. Freely group them together to produce a complementary blend.
- Combine straight and curved lines together, rather than all straight-line items in one area and all curved-line items in another.

The old and the new are combined in a room designed by Paul Kraus, A.I.D. A modern chaise upholstered in scarlet seems at home with the precise geometric design of the Bokhara in black and red on an ivory background. *(Courtesy of The Oriental Rug Importers Association)*

Fig. 24.5

- Use a variety of different materials such as wicker, glass, wood, brass, chrome, and fabric. Be sure to distribute them carefully to avoid the predominance of one material in any given area.
- Achieve a visually pleasing balance of size and scale. Do not use all large, heavy pieces or small, delicate items in one area.

When these guidelines are used, the result is an exciting mixture of old and new.

Our Victorian ancestors attempted eclecticism by combining strangely inconsistent combinations, but later generations faulted them for doing so. Today, however, it is possible to pick and choose to suit one's life style and personality. Mix or match interesting combinations of periods and accessories, if you are so inclined. This is the eclectic approach. It represents a growing sophistication of our own times, and it is not only acceptable but inevitable as the world grows smaller.

Try to visualize a page of a book without capital letters or punctuation marks. It would be extremely difficult to read such a page, and meanings would not be clear. A room without accessories would be equally uninteresting; we might consider accessories as the punctuation marks of decorating. They not only add meaning, they lend personality and individuality to a room that might otherwise be prosaic.

Because the choice of accessories is such an individual matter of expression, it is difficult to formulate rules about them. Each person's selection and arrangement will reflect his or her own interests and sensitivity to good design. But accessories should follow the theme of the room. In a dainty bedroom they should be light and delicate; in a masculine room they may be heavier and more sturdy.

Too many little mementos or pieces of bric-a-brac placed indiscriminately around a room spell confusion and indecision. Accessories should represent interests and tastes, but they should also contribute to the unity of the room. Sometimes a collection, whatever it may be, grouped and displayed with a bit of flair can become a focal point. By all means, one should choose a few accessories that add to the expressiveness of a design rather than a conglomeration of objects dispersed here and there.

A logical question may be raised with regard to what constitute accessories. Some will have specific functions; others will be purely decorative. The functional group might include ashtrays, clocks, and lamps; decorative accessories might include pictures, sculptures, mirrors, flower arrangements, and bric-a-brac.

In the functional category, accessories should first of all be useful. Lamps should provide adequate light where it is needed. Clocks must keep time and have faces that are easy to read. In all cases, the line, shape, color, and texture should harmonize with the spirit of the room.

In selecting nonfunctional accessories, one should remember that a room is often more appealing if these pieces represent interests of the family. Otherwise the effects may seem forced or contrived and the interest will be considerably lessened.

25
Accessories

**Fig.
25.1**

**Fig.
25.2**

This bathroom is accessorized in unusual ways with a ceiling fan, leather elephant, Peacock rattan chair, antique globe, and tortoise shell mirror. *(Courtesy of Kohler Company)*

Decorating a room in a conventional way is often more costly and less appealing than putting together touches of the unexpected to make personal decorating statements. For economy and impact a simple built-in headboard, mattress, and box springs sit on a red painted plywood platform. For imagination rows of hubcaps and coiled lights made from flexible conduit. *(Courtesy of Monsanto [photo courtesy of Family Circle]*

Finishing Touches

Accessories often express the owner's personality. Personal memorabilia and sports equipment serve as accessories for this bedroom. *(Courtesy of E. I. du Pont de Nemours and Company)*

Fig. 25.3

Modern interiors have broken with tradition in the selection and placement of accessories. Almost any selection, combination, or arrangement is acceptable as long as it is pleasing to the eye. Thus we see modern paintings prominently displayed in rather traditional settings, or Oriental art completely at home in the most contemporary settings. The eclectic designs of modern homes preclude any rules; we live with the things we like to look at. Somehow, the most diverse and unauthorized extremes can become interesting companions that add interest and sparkle to one another. Yet an indiscriminate use of accessories can result in a hodge-podge of design. It takes a perceptive eye to combine the unusual in a pleasing manner.

Books and Magazines

Books and magazines are not actually accessories, but are classified as such when used decoratively or in any large quantities in a room. Displaying books adds depth as well as character to a room and reveals the interests of the owner.

Most books are placed on bookshelves, which allow some flexibility in handling. Bookshelves can often be adjusted to accommodate both tall and short books. Place heavier books on the bottom shelves. Not all books need to be placed vertically; position some horizontally for interest. A neat arrangement is to group books according to their size or color. Books with the same binding, or a set of books, may be used as a unit. Any small objects that are on the bookshelves with the books should complement each other and provide an attractive setting. Plants, bric-a-brac, and collections can be dispersed among the books for added interest.

Units or sets of books can also be placed on desks or tables. Using books with the same bindings helps to unify the display. Attractive bookends that are decorative as well as functional can also be purchased as accessories.

Magazines are usually temporary accessories; most of them are read and rapidly discarded. For the magazine collector various receptacles are available; such holders add to the attractiveness of the room in addition to being functional. Plexiglass, wood, and metal are among the most widely used magazine receptacle materials.

When arranged on shelves and tables, books and magazines form striated patterns that enrich the room. *(Courtesy of Drexel Heritage Furnishings, Inc.)*

A storage wall system costing $4,000 may sound extravagant, but not when considered as a lifetime investment. In a one-room apartment, a series of modular units in off-white lacquer finishes eliminate the need for many separate pieces of furniture. One space-saving wall has specialized storage for table linens, flatware, clothes, music, and books. Some of these units have a built-in desk, bed, and lighted display shelves. The units can be used separately in different rooms of a house or apartment. *(Courtesy of International Contract Furnishings, Inc.)*

Fig. 25.4

Fig. 25.5

Finishing Touches

Clocks

An interesting clock may be not only a major accessory but a real center of interest. In traditional homes, a tall-case or grandfather's clock is an elegant note, but another type used on the mantel or on the wall may be equally impressive. Clocks that chime have a special appeal for some people, although others find them bothersome. They should be used far enough from bedrooms so that they are not disturbing at night.

Some traditional clocks are extremely elaborate, with hand-painted panels and ornate cases. Modern clocks tend toward severe simplicity.

Collections

If you have a penchant for collecting, make the collection a vital part of your decor. Your room will have an individual style that reflects your personality and interests. If the collection is an interesting one, arrange it attractively and give yourself the pleasure of displaying it. Collections should be displayed in an organized, significant fashion—adding to the appearance of the room, not distracting from it. Organize collections in one area rather than scattering them

Accessories such as the Columbian masks emphasize the theme of a room. *(Courtesy of Belgian Linen Association)*

Fig. 25.6

Fig. 25.7 Display the baskets you have purchased over the years and group them on the wall. *(Courtesy of Drexel Heritage Furnishings, Inc.)*

Fig. 25.8

A tiny corner of a study–bedroom takes on an Early American atmosphere with a collection of tins, bins, and semi-antique pictures. *(Courtesy of Window Shade Manufacturers Association)*

Finishing Touches

Fig. 25.9

Oriental pieces enhance the French theme in this room and emphasize the formal window treatment. *(Designed by Patricia Harvey, A.I.D., photo by Henry S. Fullerton)*

Trophies, awards, newspaper clippings, prints, and photographs become decorative assets when displayed in this den–study–guest room designed by Mary Davis Gillies for a well-known sportsman. *(Courtesy of Allied Chemical Corporation)*

Fig. 25.10

around the room, which may create confusion. Give your collection importance by emphasizing it with lighting.

If the collection is inherently beautiful it can serve as the center of interest in a room. Be sure that the collection harmonizes in both color and form with the room background. Collections can be grouped on tables or bookshelves designed to display them. The case should be compatible with the furniture style in the room. There are many interesting ways to display collections:

- House a small collection in a large picture frame which holds velvet-covered plywood.
- Build a mirror-backed shadow box to display fragile items.
- Build a glass-covered coffee table, and arrange shells or butterflies in it.
- Use an old-fashioned barbershop rack to house old mugs.
- Place a shelf above a doorway.

Lamps

Well-chosen lamps and lighting fixtures are extremely important in determining the character of a room. Although the functional aspects should be the primary consideration in selecting them, it is no less important to choose designs that emphasize the spirit of the room. With the wide variety available today, it is possible to find useful lamps and fixtures that are suitable for any type of room.

Because they do play such a major role in lighting a room, lamps assume a special importance as accessories. The trend toward using tall lamps has also contributed to making them more important as accessories; either height or large scale can command attention. It is especially important to choose lamps carefully.

The style of the room and the spirit that it will express should suggest certain guides for selection. More formal rooms will usually require lamps with a certain amount of elegance. They may be extremely simple, but the colors and textures should have the richness that we associate with formal treatments. Fine china, glass, metals such as chrome, pewter, and brass, and rattans are all popular. Formal lamps often represent candelabra, graceful vases or urns, or simple columns mounted on heavy bases. Lamps with ornately painted designs or with elaborate figures may be suitable for certain rooms, but they must be chosen with discrimination.

Rooms furnished in the more informal styles should have lamps that are less suggestive of luxury. Materials with a more homespun character, such as wood, pottery, copper, and pewter, are usually suitable. Certain types of glass and some tole bases are also rather informal. Modern rooms may be either formal or informal in character, and the texture of the lamps should be selected accordingly. In either case, the lamps will probably be somewhat simple in design. Polished woods with lovely colors and grain patterns, metals, china, pottery, glass, and leather have all been used in modern lamps. Various types of pole lamps and wall lamps that allow for adjustable lighting often replace the more traditional forms of lighting in modern decoration. Some of these newer types have been adapted for use in traditional rooms.

When several lamps are chosen for use in the same room, they should harmonize with one another. It would probably be monotonous to have all lamps exactly alike, but there should be some similarity of expressiveness. It is usually advisable to have all the lampshades of similar color. For example, two white shades and one of rose-beige might not be attractive. However, a strong contrast may be of interest.

Mirrors

In some areas, such as bedrooms and dressing rooms, mirrors are essential. They are also extremely useful in most entrance halls. In other rooms they are more decorative than functional. However, because mirrors increase the apparent spaciousness of an area, they are particularly suitable for use in small rooms. Sometimes a whole wall is covered with a mirror for this purpose as well as for the decorative effect.

There is considerable variation in the quaility

Space is maximized with a mirrored wall visually expanding the view. White beams and vertical shades framing a dark brown painted ceiling call attention to the unusual height of this apartment in the city. Below, built-in chest of drawers provides access to the wardrobe without wasting space. *(Courtesy of Allied Chemical Corporation, Hollytex carpet)*

Fig. 25.11

of mirrors. The best grades are made of plate glass; less expensive mirrors are made of window glass. The polishing and grinding of plate glass result in a smooth surface that prevents distortion and gives the glass more sparkle. In plate-glass mirrors of high quality, the silvered surface of the back is protected by a copper coating. It is then treated with a coat of shellac and another coat of protective paint. Copper backing renders the mirror more durable and prevents discoloration. High-quality mirrors also have the edges ground to an angle or beveled.

Various techniques are used for decorating mirrors. Some have designs cut or etched into the glass. Others are given an antique finish that provides a mottled, aged appearance. Although

such mirrors have low reflective qualities, they are highly decorative and are often used on large areas of a wall. A tint of some color in the mirror backing may also be used on decorative mirrors.

In modern decoration mirrors are often used without frames. Traditional styles usually have a frame of wood or metal in characteristic design. The girandole mirror, popular during the eighteenth century, has holders for candlesticks attached to the frame.

Mirrors should be selected with respect to wall area and furniture. Because a mirror is often placed over a mantel, a couch, a chest, or a table, the size and shape should be chosen to create a unified grouping that has pleasing spatial relationships.

Fig.
25.12

Paintings become the dominant note in a room designed by Renny B. Saltzman, A.I.D. Walls covered with fabric stretched from ceiling to floor provide a background that emphasizes the collection. *(Courtesy of DuPont Textile Fibers)*

Fig.
25.13

A variety of pictures becomes a unit when they are carefully arranged. *(Courtesy of New York Antiques Fair)*

Pictures

Whether or not one hangs pictures on the walls is purely a matter of taste. They are not necessary, but they can add considerably to the personality of the room if they are well chosen and well placed. However, some people prefer other types of wall decoration or even bare walls.

Choosing suitable pictures that one will enjoy living with is perhaps one of the most difficult problems in planning a room. The art chosen should certainly represent the owner's tastes, but it should also add interest to the room. It is usually safer to select themes and colors that are in keeping with the spirit of the room. Although some people can violate this principle by electing to use the unexpected or the unusual, it is not easy to achieve happy results.

Landscapes, seascapes, street scenes, flower prints, and still-life pictures are all popular choices for traditional rooms. They can be used in formal or informal settings, depending on their interpretation and color. Other types seem to be more appropriate for special rooms. For example, portraits are frequently quite formal, whereas pictures with animals are more likely to express informality. Oriental themes often lend themselves to a variety of backgrounds, including some traditional and many modern settings.

Personal taste again determines whether or not one will use only originals or include some reproductions. Good originals are likely to be quite expensive. Even reproductions are sometimes costly, but many of them are extremely well done. If the artistic qualities of a picture are appealing and suitable, whether it is an original or a copy should not be important.

The colors and textures of pictures should harmonize with those used in the room. Often a picture is useful for emphasizing some other element in a room either by repeating it or by providing a sharp contrast.

The size and shape of a picture must relate to the wall area on which it will be hung and also to the furniture placed against the wall. The outline of the picture will produce a spatial division that should establish pleasing proportions. It is frequently more interesting to group several pictures rather than to use only one. When pictures are exactly alike in shape and size, a group arrangement is usually symmetrical and presents few problems. It is far more difficult to assemble a group of unrelated sizes and shapes in a pleasing arrangement, but once this is accomplished it can be extremely interesting. In this case it is wise to experiment with the pictures to be used by trying different arrangements on the floor or on a large table in order to produce the most effective grouping.

Factors Involved in Choosing a Picture
When deciding to accessorize a room with pictures, think about the following questions:

- Does the wall space need a picture to complete its composition?
- Will a single, vertical, horizontal, square, round, or oval shape fill the need, or is a group of pictures a better solution?
- What is the shape of the wall space needing a picture?
- What subject matter would give you the greatest pleasure and be most suitable for the room?
- What style and medium will fit best in the room? Consider the furnishings and other pictures in the room.

Picture Placement
Use the following suggested guidelines when deciding where to place pictures:

- Picture placement should be planned and arranged in an orderly fashion.
- Hang pictures at eye level, that is, between five and six feet from the floor. In children's rooms, pictures should be hung at their level.
- Hang pictures where they will be enjoyed.
- When hanging a picture over a sofa, it should be low enough to be a part of a grouping and high enough to avoid contact with a person's head when leaning back or sitting on the sofa.

448

- Vertical wall spaces are enhanced by vertical pictures.
- Avoid hanging pictures in stair-step fashion; the eye is carried away from the picture and the composition.
- A large picture may be hung alone, but it should relate to a large piece of furniture.
- A pair of smaller pictures may be used instead of a larger one.
- A horizontal row of pictures may be used over any long, low furniture grouping.
- Most small pictures are effective if they are hung as a composite group. Put them on the floor to determine the desired arrangement. The one that is the center of interest should be hung at eye level. Pictures hung in groups should be similar in character, medium, color, frame, or mats.
- A picture will seem to float in space if there is no furniture underneath it.
- A painting should hang alone only when it is large and important enough to hold interest.

When mounting displays, posters, or pictures follow the "law of margins," which states: In a vertical oblong, the bottom margin should be the widest, the top margin the next widest, and the sides narrower; for the horizontal oblong the bottom should be the widest, the sides the next widest, and the top, narrower; in a square, the bottom should be the widest and the sides and top equal to each other. (Harriet and Vetta Goldstein. *Art in Everyday Life*, New York: Macmillan, 1954, p. 241.)

Choosing the Right Picture Frame

Because the frame of a picture is very important, consider the following guidelines when selecting:

- Consider the frame as an actual part of the picture.
- The frame should complement the theme and technique of the picture.
- Do not choose a wide, massive frame for a delicate floral print.
- A large, dark frame will overpower a picture that is painted in delicate tones.
- The frame material should blend with the furniture in the room.

Choosing a Picture or Painting Mat

When choosing a mat, think of it as a frame within a frame. The mat should blend with the colors in the item to be framed, or an accent color in the room. Matboard, burlap, heavy linen, ultrasuede, or velvet are popular mat materials. Refer to Figure 25.14 for how to mat a picture.

Plants and Indoor Trees

Because Americans are very conscious of nature and their environment, plants and indoor trees have today become more popular than ever in decorating. Plants are living things

Fig. 25.14

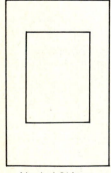

Vertical Oblong

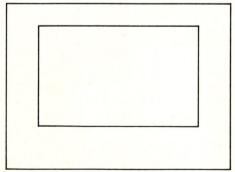

Horizontal Oblong

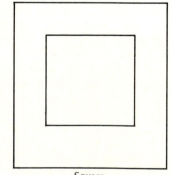

Square

that grow and change, and using them in the decorating scheme can be very satisfying.

Plants and indoor trees can be placed almost anywhere in a home or apartment provided they receive adequate light and the environment is favorable to their growth. Plants usually grow profusely in bathrooms because of the high humidity. They can be used to fill a window space and double as window treatments, or they can be used as room dividers when placed on etageres. There are many different ways of using them. Plants should be chosen as accessories based upon their variety, shape, and interest. They should be placed in attractive containers that complement the color scheme of a room. Each year there are more attractive plant stands, planters, and other plant accessories on the market for use in the home.

If possible, avoid artificial plants and artificial trees unless desperate as they are not very beautiful and when dust collects on them they look bad.

Sculpture

Sculpture has always had an important place in the home, as well as in civic buildings. Reproductions of historic sculpture are very effective, and they are available from museums as well as retail stores and artist showrooms. Many are quite reasonable in price. When choosing sculpture look for good design, honest use of materials, and quality in reproductions if applicable.

Wall Hangings

Wall hangings can be made of a number of materials or types. Printed fabric, carpets, tapestries, macramé, needlework, and tapa cloth have all served as wall hangings. Wall hangings are often used to fill large, plain, empty areas. They can also be the focal point of a room. Stretching a piece of fabric over a wooden frame can be an inexpensive way to add color, texture,

and pattern to a wall. The versatility of wall hangings should not be overlooked.

Miscellaneous Accessories

Various areas in the home will lend themselves to the use of other accessories. A hallway, living room, den, or bedroom may be suitable for shelves or cabinets. The lovely colors of book bindings and jackets may be utilized to form a

Fine porcelain is a favorite item of collectors. This figure may be skillfully placed in a variety of room settings. (Courtesy of Creative Communications—Cybis Porcelains) **Fig. 25.15**

A scattering of pillows adds both pattern and comfort to this informal room. Note how emphasis is achieved by the use of the same fabric for the draperies and pillows.

mosaic that becomes an interesting accessory. As mentioned earlier, collections can become an integral part of a particular room.

Throw pillows can add a dramatic accent note to the color scheme in a living room, bedroom, or den.

A folding screen may serve a useful purpose as an area divider, or it may be used for purely decorative purposes. An inexpensive screen covered with wallpaper of fabric might be used as a background for some particular arrangement of furniture or accessories.

A fireplace in a room requires some equipment. The screen, andirons, poker, tongs, and shovel should all be considered as useful accessories.

A desk in any area of the home will need certain accessories. A lamp is probably the first requirement. The primary purpose is function, but it should also blend with the decor of the room. Desk accessories can be attractive as well as useful.

Fig. 25.16

Fig. 25.17

Cooking paraphernalia can be displayed. This way things are easily reached, and storage space is increased. *(Courtesy of E. I. du Pont de Nemours and Company)*

Trays are useful accessories. Serving trays have become popular with the trend toward informal meals. Many trays are now made to resist heat and alcohol. Sets of lap trays or tray-tables are extremely useful accessories for buffet meals. One interesting or unusual tray may well become part of the decorative scheme in either a living room or dining area. It may be mounted on the wall or placed on a desk or table. Frequently a beautiful tray is placed on a folding rack or stand and used as a permanent table.

How to Arrange a Wall Grouping

Wall groupings are usually arranged symmetrically or asymmetrically. In symmetrical balance, imagine a vertical line in the center of the composition. Arrange the grouping so that an equal amount of area is covered on both sides of the vertical line. The objects used should be in pairs, or else one large thing should be balanced by an equal amount of smaller items. Symmetrical balance is easier to achieve, and generally creates a more formal, dignified feeling.

To form asymmetrical balance, again imagine the vertical line in the center of the composition and arrange an odd number of objects on both sides of the line. Then add the rest of the objects on each side of the arrangement. Make sure that at least one edge of each object lines up with an adjacent edge. Asymmetrical balance requires more skill, but it offers more freedom and individuality.

Some suggestions for arranging objects follow:

- If one side of the arrangement is heavier than the other, add a lamp or plant to achieve visual balance. A mixture of color and texture can also contribute to better balance.
- Leave large spaces between large objects and less space between smaller ones.
- An odd number of objects is often more exciting in an asymmetrical grouping.
- Determine your arrangements on the floor before hanging them.

Balance, emphasis, and harmony are the three basic requirements of an artistic arrangement of accessories. Balance is an attractive grouping which is neither lopsided nor top-heavy. Emphasis is the extent to which the accessory or arrangement is eye-catching. Harmony is the pleasing effect of items seeming to belong together. Form and texture are important to good arrangement of accessories; but they are secondary to color—generally, one key color should predominate.

Accessory Selection and Arrangement

When arranging and choosing accessories, follow these guidelines:

- Accessories should be placed at important points in the room so that the eye is led to a focal point of interest. By choosing the same colors, shapes, or period, the decorator can use accessories to create unity in a room.
- Accessories need to be related to the furniture or furniture groupings.
- Accessories are more interesting if they are not all placed in a straight line.
- Accessories need to be placed with space between individual items, so that they can be enjoyed separately while still forming part of a unit.
- Groups of accessories are more interesting if the shapes and heights are varied. Too many items of one shape may seem monotonous. For continuity, moreover, accessories should be arranged so that the eye goes from one to another. However, if accessories are grouped together, each must have something in common with the next. It may be size, shape, material, or color.
- Accessories that are figured or decorated can be enjoyed best if they are placed against a plain background.
- Inexpensive accessories can look very important if they are grouped together and displayed well. Irregular-shaped bottles displayed in front of a window on shelves can be more dramatically effective than an expensive painting placed in an obscure part of the room.

Fig. 25.18 Artful accessorizing can furnish a dining area. Designer Peg Walker turned empty walls into art themselves. The design rug continues the motif with bands of the same colors as on the wall graphic. *(Courtesy of Monsanto)*

Flower Arrangements

Plants, leaves, and flowers provide most effective and economical accessories for any type of decorative scheme. When used with taste and discretion, they add a warm, livable quality to almost any room. Just as with any other accessory, their overuse can defeat the purpose of accent and become monotonous. The selection of suitable arrangements that truly complement the spirit of the room is just as important here as it is with other accessories.

Flowers should be used in a thoughtful and imaginative manner. When one entertains, a flower arrangement in the entrance hall makes a delightful impression on guests as they arrive. In a guest room, even a tiny bouquet in a miniature holder seems to spell "welcome" to the visitor. At the dining table, fresh flowers or growing plants are usually more attractive than silk arrangements. The centerpiece should be kept low so that it does not impede conversation. A plant or a tiny bouquet of flowers in the bathroom may add an effective touch to an area that is otherwise difficult to decorate.

In the Orient flower arrangement is considered an art form. It is characterized by a severe, stylized line, and formal restraint. Today, in the West, flower arranging is very popular. Although we are not as restricted as the Orientals in our principles of arrangement, we still try to keep harmony, rhythm, focus, balance, and scale in our arrangements. In this chapter, we will explore the Western style of flower arrangement.

Basic Tools of Flower Arrangement

There are certain basic tools that anyone interested in flower arrangements should always have on hand. They might be found in the home, a hardware store, or a florist's shop.

Several sharp cutting utensils are necessary tools for flower arranging. A very sharp paring knife or shears may be used to trim the stems, to pare off any leaves below the water line, and to scrape or split the stems to allow more water to be absorbed by the flower. A pair of wire cutters or heavy-duty shears, and a small pair of scissors, will find various uses in cutting tapes or ribbons and in preparing flower holders.

Flower holders are small devices placed inside the flower container to keep the flowers securely in place. Waterproof clay or styrofoam forms placed in the bottom of the container may satisfactorily hold flower arrangements.

Chicken wire can be bent and shaped to fit inside the container, and flowers may be anchored to it. Fine wire or parafilm may be used to tie stems in a bud vase or a narrow vertical container.

Flower containers come in various shapes and sizes. Remember to take into consideration the type of flower selected when choosing the container. Fragile violets could look absurd in a heavy crock bowl, just as tiger lilies may look odd in a delicate china bud vase. The container should blend with the flowers but not detract from them. An ornate, highly decorated vase should not be used in flower arrangements; its beauty would attract attention away from the flowers.

There are certain basic shapes to flower containers: circular bowls and trays, cylindrical (bud) vases, triangular vases, classical urns, and flared bowls. However, one can use almost any household object as a suitable container as long as it blends with the flower arrangement and the room decor and holds water.

Choosing Flowers for the Arrangement

The mood that you wish to convey should be of prime importance in flower selection. A modern flower arrangement might consist of tropical leaves and flowers in a teakwood bowl. A formal arrangement could feature camellias in a black porcelain urn. An informal arrangement might require a copper bowl and several dozen asters. The mood should be conveyed by the flowers and the container. Everything should harmonize.

When selecting your flowers and container, be certain that everything is related in size.

> An arrangement's proportions should be at least one and a half times a tall container's height, or about one and a half times a low container's width.[1]

Color is important in flower selection as well. Whether you plan a monochromatic scheme of shades of one color or an analogous scheme of either warm or cool colors, the colors should harmonize with one another. The darker, richer

[1] *Good Housekeeping's Book of Flower Arrangements* (New York: The Hearst Corporation, 1958), p. 20.

hues should be used in the center of the arrangement to provide a focal point and give the arrangement a sense of balance. The lighter, more delicate hues may be used at the outer edges of the arrangement. You may, of course, select flowers that appeal to you; but be careful of complementary or mixed color schemes. They may appear too "busy" to be appealing in a small flower arrangement.

Obtaining Flowers for Arrangements

Once you have decided upon the flowers you wish to use in your arrangement, you may either pick them from a garden, buy them at a florist's shop, or use artificial or dried flowers.

Plants are a keynote to the decorating scheme. *(Courtesy of American Plywood Association)*

Fig. 25.19

If you decide to pick the flowers in a garden, gather the flowers either very early in the morning or after sundown, when evaporation is at its lowest ebb. Remember to carry a sharp knife or a pair of shears and a bucket of water in which you can place the cut flowers. Cut the stem slantwise and cut off any excess leaves before placing the flowers in the water.

Several types of stems demand special treatment to ensure the long life and beauty of their flowers. If the flowers have a woody stem, split and scrape the ends to allow them to absorb greater moisture. If the stem ends emit a milky substance, seal the ends before you place them in the bucket by either dipping the ends in an inch or two of boiling water or by burning the ends with a candle.

After you have picked the flowers, fill the bucket up to the blossom of the flower with cold water and place the bucket in a cool, dark place overnight. If you have picked tulips, wrap the stems in newspaper before placing them in the cold water. This process "hardens" the stem, making it easier to arrange the flowers and giving them a long life. Leaves that are to be used in your arrangement should be placed horizontally in a long, flat container and covered with cold water overnight.

If you decide upon flowers from your florist, recut the stems and place them neck-deep in cold water overnight to harden them. Florists can provide you with flowers in or out of season, and give you many types of long-lasting beautiful greens.

Basic Principles of Arranging Flowers

No matter how you intend to arrange your flowers, you must create a sense of balance.

There are several basic designs in flower arrangements: the triangle, the side triangle, the circle, the half-circle, the oval, the crescent, the Hogarth line, the perpendicular, the horizontal, the swirl, or the spiral. The triangle is the basis of many designs. A full triangle has a tall center line, flanked on both sides by equally spaced lines. The triangular shape may be defined by long-stemmed flowers, the buds at the top apex of the triangle and the full blossoms at the bottom edges of the triangular shape. The shape of the triangle might also be defined by foliage, with open blossoms in the center of the triangle to provide a focal point. This shape is attractively arranged in a low circular or rectangular bowl.

The side triangle is probably the most popular design. It is an **L**-shaped arrangement with the focal weight concentrated at the base of the vertical line. Usually one long-stemmed flower acts as the vertical line of the shape. Buds and small flowers could fill in the vertical line. The base of the side triangle can be filled with larger blooms. A long, low tray is the most popular container for the side triangle; however, almost any container may accommodate this design.

The circle has curving lines, with the focal point in the lower half of the circle. The circle can be informally arranged—as an assortment of field flowers, for example, placed casually in a pottery crock. It can also be formally arranged in a tall urn, with the lines of the circle going down over the edges of the container.

The half circle consists of a low center line with the length of the line stretched horizontally down over the sides of the container. The focal point of this design should be in the center of the arrangement. One usually sees this arrangement made with flowers in full bloom in the center while ferns or other greens fall horizontally out over the sides of the container.

The oval design is similar to the circle, but it is higher at the top and narrower at the sides. The outer edges of the oval usually consist of light flowers, buds, or greens. The low center of the oval, which acts as the focal point, usually consists of flowers in full bloom.

The crescent arrangement is a good design for fruits and leaves, as well as flowers. The focal point is low and contains the heaviest material. Tall ferns, greens, or flowers jut out horizontally from the focal point. The arrangement may be tipped to either side or even on both sides as long as it is balanced. A crescent design usually looks best in a low container.

The Hogarth line is done by building an **S**-shaped curve with flowers. It is based on seven blossoms in an asymmetrical balance with

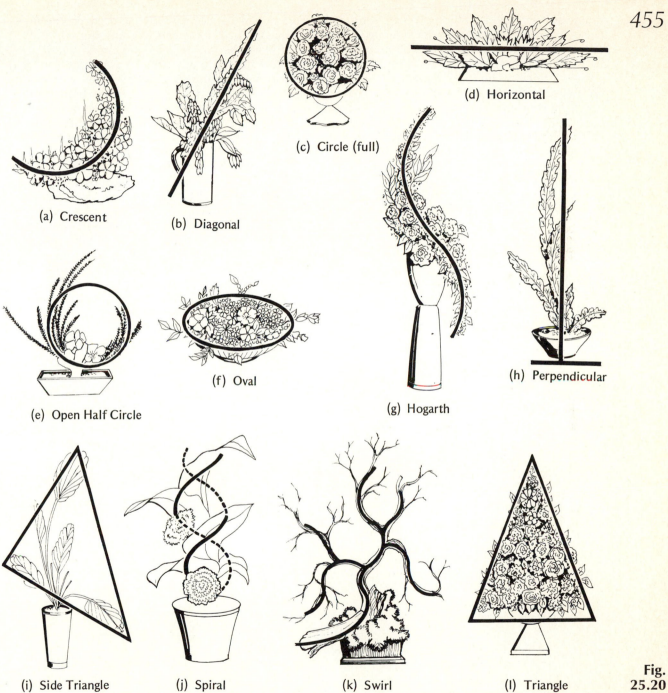

(a) Crescent

(b) Diagonal

(c) Circle (full)

(d) Horizontal

(e) Open Half Circle

(f) Oval

(g) Hogarth

(h) Perpendicular

(i) Side Triangle

(j) Spiral

(k) Swirl

(l) Triangle

Fig. 25.20

Basic flower arrangement designs.

Accessories

seven different levels. When properly arranged, all seven blossoms appear to stem from one stalk to form the **S**-shape. The bottom swing of the Hogarth line should extend below the edges of the container. The focal point of this arrangement should be the center of the **S**-shape.

The perpendicular design is good to use with a slender container or bud vase. The arrangement is high and very narrow. The focal point should rest about halfway between the edges of the container and the tip of the tallest leaf or flower.

The horizontal arrangement is low and extends out in both directions. The horizontal line suggests calm and repose. The Bird-of-Paradise flower is very attractive in this arrangement.

The swirl design is a dramatic, rhythmic line. Bonsai trees are an example of this arrangement.

The spiral arrangement is an upsweeping design that curves like the figure eight. Funkia or Pandanus leaves are often used in this arrangement.

No matter which shape you decide to use, make sure that it is appropriate to the mood you wish to convey, the flowers you wish to use, and the container you have selected.

Keeping the Arrangement Fresh

Basically, the life of the arrangement depends upon two factors: the condition of the flowers when selected for the arrangement and the replenishment of water in the flowers' cells at the same rate at which evaporation takes place. Do not change the water every day. This increased handling will only damage the flowers. Add water instead of changing it.

Place the flower arrangement in a cool position in full light, out of direct sunlight. The ideal conditions for flower arrangements are high humidity and forty to fifty degree temperature. Keeping flowers in a refrigerator may not allow them the necessary light or humidity. Just be sure that the flowers are kept away from drafts, direct sunlight, and intense heat.

Many substances may be added to the water to help keep the flowers fresher longer. A small piece of charcoal keeps the water clean and does not hurt the flowers. An aspirin tablet added to a gallon of water should lengthen the life of tulips and chrysanthemums. A tablespoon of sugar may benefit tulips and lilacs. Copper coins placed in containers are believed to lengthen the lives of some flowers, particularly tulips. Do not add disinfectants to the water as they may kill the flowers while purifying the water.

Summary

There are several basic steps to flower arrangement:

1. Organize your tools.
2. Decide upon the container.
3. Choose the flowers.
4. Properly prepare the flowers for the arrangement.
5. Choose a design to compliment your container and flowers.
6. Make sure that your arrangement stays fresh as long as possible.

26

Table Appointments

Modern living has demanded many changes in the traditionally accepted standards and routines of serving meals. Television, outdoor barbecue pits, prepared foods, and buffet service have all had their impact on our way of life. We have accepted a more casual, informal, and perhaps a much more creative attitude toward both family meals and entertaining. However, the words *casual* and *informal* must never in any sense be confused with *sloppy* and *careless*. Food should always be served with meticulous care and in the most attractive way possible.

Years ago it would have been almost unthinkable to invite guests for a special dinner party without having a regular dining table fully equipped with matched china. Now such traditional standards have been relaxed in several ways. Just as we have come to reject matched suites of furniture in favor of more individual combinations, we have also become more creative about tableware. It is often more interesting to mix and coordinate pieces that harmonize with one another than to use things that exactly match.

We have also become more adventuresome with table decorations. Floral centerpieces are always popular, but more imaginative arrangements and the use of other items to express particular themes are gaining in favor. Colored cloths in a variety of materials and interesting new placemats have also, to a large extent, replaced traditional tablecloths. (Table linens are discussed in Chapter 27.)

An artistically planned table and attractive service contribute to the enjoyment of good food and pleasant conversation. There is a wide choice of tableware, and selections must be made with care. The various items should be chosen to harmonize with one another so that the table presents an interesting design.

Dinnerware

The so-called china department in any large store will probably display dinnerware in a variety of materials and in a wide range of prices. Several types of ceramics are widely popular, but plastics, glass, woods, and metals are also used.

(a)

(b)

Fig. 26.1 Table appointments should relate to the theme of decoration. *(a) (Courtesy of Tiffany and Company) (b) (Courtesy of The Silversmiths Guild of America) (c) and (d) (Courtesy of The Belgian Linen Association)*

(c)

(d)

Finishing Touches

Ceramics

The history of ceramics represents an interesting study of cultural development; and ceramics have provided us with much historical source material, because designs frequently depict the beliefs, customs, and daily activities of the ancient civilizations.

Ceramics are made from a base of clay mixed with other materials, such as flint and feldspar. Water is added to produce a creamy consistency and the mixture is known as *slip.* For fine products, the slip may go through several processes of refining and screening. Excess water is removed and the clay mixture may be allowed to age. Then it is kneaded to remove air bubbles.

Shaping may be done on a potter's wheel or in a mold. Most dinnerware is made by the pressing of clay in molds. Finishing is done on a *jigger* machine.

The *firing* of ceramics is done in a kiln. When the clay form emerges from the firing it is in the *biscuit* stage. Some pottery is used with no further treatment; however, dinnerware and many other ceramics are usually dipped in a milky liquid after the first firing and then fired again in another kiln. This gives the pieces a glaze, providing luster and making the pieces more sanitary. A high-quality glaze fuses with the clay body; it is hard, durable, and resistant to tiny surface cracks (*crazing*).

Decoration may be applied before or after the glazing. When applied on top of the glaze, another firing in a decorating kiln melts the design into the glaze so that it will remain permanent with ordinary care.

It should be obvious that within this rather oversimplified account of pottery making there is room for a tremendous amount of variation. Perhaps because there are so many different types, there is some confusion about the terms associated with ceramics. For example, the word *pottery* technically refers to all types of ceramics, including fine china. In popular usage, the word designates only opaque wares, usually of the coarser types and the heavier shapes. Also, because the first porcelain was made in China, we have incorrectly referred to all dinnerware as *china.*

Today china is used in informal buffet settings. *(Courtesy of The Belgian Linen Association)*

Fig. 26.2

Porcelain. Porcelain is the finest type of china. For centuries the making of fine porcelain was a closely guarded secret in China.

Porcelain is translucent. When a plate is held up to the light, the shadow of the hand can be seen through it. It is also nonporous, or *vitrified.* Even without the glaze, high-quality porcelain will not absorb foreign materials to any appreciable degree. For this reason chipped porcelain is not unsanitary even though it may be unattractive.

Bone china. English potters developed a clay mixture by adding bone ash to kaolin, a white pottery clay. The resulting product was a strong, highly translucent white china that was particularly suitable for decoration under the glaze. Bone ash is used in some china from other countries, but England has several well-established firms associated with the manufacture of fine bone china:

Spode	Minton
Royal Worcester	Royal Doulton
Wedgwood	Royal Crown Derby

Earthenware. In general, earthenware ceramics are opaque when held to a light, and they are also more porous than fine porcelain. However, there are many different grades and types of earthenware. It must be noted that at least two distinguished English pottery firms, Spode and Wedgwood, manufacture high-quality earthenware. The term *earthenware* includes materials that have various degrees of porosity, from the lowest-grade pottery to a fine quality that almost equals that of china.

Semivitreous ware. Semiporous clays have been developed and are sometimes sold in competition with true china. A high-quality semivitreous earthenware may cost more than a poor-quality china, but insofar as classification is concerned these semiporous materials must be grouped with earthenware products.

Stoneware. Certain clay mixtures can be fired to high temperatures that cause them to become quite hard and nonporous. Ironstone is such a product.

Pottery. We have mentioned that this term really refers to all ceramics, but the more popular connotation leans toward the heavier forms of earthenware. We also tend to associate pottery with rougher textures and more earthy colors.

Names and terms. Some well-known names and terms associated with ceramics include:

Arzberg Bavarian china.

Basalt ware Unglazed stoneware, usually black, popularized by Wedgwood factory.

Belleek Highly translucent ivory-colored china characterized by iridescent glaze. Appears mostly in tea sets and small decorative objects. Made in Ireland.

Castleton American china made in various types; suitable for home or institutional use.

Coalport English bone china.

Delftware Various types of ceramics made in Holland. Usually associated with blue and white coloring.

Dresden Name of china made in Meissen, Germany. Frequently associated with delicate figurines.

Faïence Term that refers to various kinds of faïence pottery. Usually earthenware with an opaque lead glaze. Name derived from the Italian town of Faenza.

Haviland China originally made in France but now produced in the United States.

Jasper ware Famous Wedgwood pottery made in blue, green, lilac, and other colors. Characterized by Greek motifs in relief designs.

Lenox Fine-quality American china.

Limoges Ancient town in France renowned for manufacturing fine china.

Majolica Faïence from Spain and Italy, usually enameled in bright colors.

Minton Famous family of English potters. Business established at Stoke-on-Trent.

Queen's ware Famous cream-colored earthenware made by Wedgwood potteries.

Rosenthal Fine Bavarian china.

Royal Copenhagen Fine Danish china.

Royal Crown Derby English china produced at potteries established in the mid-eighteenth century by William Duesbury. Decoration is rich and delicate, often on ivory-colored background.

Royal Doulton Ceramic wares of various types, including fine china, made at potteries in Lambeth, England.

Royal Worcester Wares made at the Lowdin pottery in Worcester, England.

Salt glaze Finish used in making pottery.

Sèvres Fine porcelain named after town in France where it is made. Characterized by delicate but elegant designs.

Spode Wares manufactured at potteries established in England by Josiah Spode, who in 1799 produced the first fine bone china.

Staffordshire County in England famous for its potteries district, centered at Stoke-on-Trent. Among famous factories were those owned by Thomas Minton, Josiah Wedgwood, and Josiah Spode.

Syracuse Fine American china.

Wedgwood Famous wares made at the potteries founded by Josiah Wedgwood in Staffordshire. Designs are most notable for interpretations of neoclassic motifs in jasper ware, especially the white figures applied to delicate, colored backgrounds.

Plastic dinnerware. Within recent years, plastics have become more widely accepted for use at the table. Plastics do not break or chip as easily as ceramic dinnerware; however, some do require special cleaning to remove stains.

Most plastic dinnerware on the market today has been improved to overcome some of the earlier objections to its use. It can be washed in automatic dishwashers, and the styling of the patterns has become far more glamorous than in the first plastic dishes. Quite probably the plastics will continue to grow in popularity as consumers become more aware of the wide range of colors, patterns, and styles now available.

Selection of Dinnerware

Traditional practice called for one everyday set of dishes and another "good" set for company meals. Once again people have broken with tradition, depending upon their fancy; they may choose one set that can be adapted to different situations. Plain white china, for example, may be as formal or as informal as one makes it with table decorations. Another school of thought leans toward having several types of dinnerware suitable for different kinds of entertaining. The available storage space as well as the pattern of living will influence decisions in this respect. One word of caution might be offered here about choosing several types. There may be times when it is desirable to mix dishes. Choose patterns and colors that will harmonize if they must be used together. One set with little or no pattern is usually a good choice.

Pattern. Choosing a design in dinnerware is perhaps one of the most difficult decisions for the consumer. When dishes have to be seen three times a day, it is important that the pattern not become tiresome. It should also be remembered that the design of the dinnerware should be in keeping with the spirit of the home.

Try to visualize food on each plate. Profusely decorated plates are lovely for display, but the plain, simple designs are more adaptable and more generally appealing for the service of food. Embossed motifs or raised effects provide interesting designs, but they do require extra care in washing to prevent food from sticking in the crevices.

Open stock. Some patterns may be purchased in open stock as opposed to complete sets. With open stock any quantity may be purchased. As long as the manufacturer makes the pattern, pieces may be added or replaced. The price may be cheaper by the set, but when breakage occurs, odd pieces will have to replace the broken ones, so selecting an open-stock pattern is advantageous even though you may be initially purchasing an entire set.

Sets may be purchased for four, six, eight, or twelve. These vary in the number of serving pieces included. "Starter" sets for four are popular, and there is sometimes a variety of extra pieces that may be purchased separately.

A popular practice is to buy china in place settings and then to fill in with extra serving pieces. One five-piece place setting generally includes:

1 dinner plate
1 salad plate
1 bread-and-butter plate
1 cup
1 saucer

Glassware

Glass is created by the fusion of silica (sand) and other chemicals into a molten substance that has a thick, viscous consistency. In this stage it may be molded, pressed, or blown into various forms, after which it is carefully cooled by a process called *annealing*.

Types of Glass

There are hundreds of different kinds of glass produced by variations of the raw materials and the methods of heating and cooling. The term *crystal* is sometimes used to refer to any clear glass, but more traditionally it denotes fine-quality, highly refractive glass. For our purposes here we may consider three general categories of glass in common use:

462

Lime glass. Sand, soda, and lime are the basic ingredients of the everyday type known as *lime glass.* It is used for commonplace purposes when high durability and low cost are desirable. Window panes, jars, bottles, and inexpensive glassware for table use are all made of lime glass.

Lead glass. Far more expensive and far more beautiful is a glass made from a mixture of sand, potash, and lead. These ingredients produce a glass that has luster and sparkle. When gently tapped on the rim, lead glass has a bell-like tone.

Borosilicate glass. Boric oxide added to the sand and soda mixture for glass produces a substance that is resistant to heat and cracking. This type of glass is useful for cooking utensils. Because glass holds heat and is attractive in appearance, food is often served in a dish in which it has been cooked. Color and decorative motifs have made glass utensils even more adaptable for use as serving dishes. Pyrex is a trade name.

Shaping Glass

Molten glass may be shaped by several methods:

Blowing. It is indeed a fascinating experience to watch a skilled workman blow a piece of molten glass into a beautiful form. On the end of a simple hollow pipe known as a *blow iron,* he gathers a mass of the hot glass mixture. As he twirls and blows into the pipe, the shaping of the glass seems almost miraculous. The experienced artisan shapes the ball of molten glass with unbelievable symmetry and refinement of form.

Machines have been developed for blowing glass for various items including electric light bulbs, some bottles, and miscellaneous containers. Hand blowing in the commercial field must usually be restricted to the production of high-quality objects.

Molding. Some types of glass are molded either by hand or by machine. Quality products may be *blown-molded,* which means blowing glass into a mold. In some cases mold marks are left on the finished items, but there are methods of rotating the glass within the mold to remove any such markings.

Pressing. Somewhat similar to molding, pressing employs a plunger to shape the inside of the object. It is a fast and inexpensive means of shaping glass items. The molten glass is poured into a mold that forms the outer contours; the plunger presses on the inner surface to shape flat bowls, lids, saucers, and similar forms.

Decorating Glass

Many fine examples of modern glassware depend on exquisite form and intrinsic beauty of high-quality glass for their excellence. A lovely, graceful form fashioned in clear sparkling glass needs little, if any, additional decoration. There are, however, a variety of processes that further enhance the decorative qualities of glass. At almost any stage of manufacture there may be some treatment intended to make the finished product more attractive.

Color may be added to the molten glass by the mixing of mineral salts into the basic blend of ingredients. Milk glass has a colorant that renders the finished product opaque. White milk glass is probably the most widely used, but other colors, especially turquoise, have become popular.

Bubbles injected into molten glass also have a decorative effect. This method is used in manufacturing glass of all qualities, but the "teardrop" designs in some glassware clearly reflect special skills.

Ornamental designs may be applied to glass in the form of enamels or metals encrusted on the surface. Gold, platinum, and silver are favorite forms of enrichment.

Frosted designs are popular for decorating glassware. Clear glass may be given a rough, grayed finish by sandblasting or by treatment with acids. Etching, a widely used means of decorating glass at all levels of quality, employs hydrofluoric acid to produce a frosted effect. Intricate lacy designs may be etched by coating parts of the glass surface with wax and leaving other areas exposed to the acid.

The choice of table covering gives character to a setting. *(Courtesy of The Belgian Linen Association)*

Fig. 26.3

Cutting is another popular method of decorating glass. Hand-cut grooves on lead crystal may be polished to sparkling brilliance. On high-quality pieces the cut designs may be extremely complex. However, machine methods of cutting have been responsible for much of the inexpensive cut glass on the current market. These low-cost items attempt to simulate the finer examples, but they lack the brilliant luster, the sharp edges, and the intricate patterns found on cut glass produced by hand craftsmanship.

Names of Glass

Glassworks in various parts of the world are producing interesting designs that are noteworthy for high quality. In France, the names Daum and Baccarat both represent outstanding firms. Orrefors in Sweden, Leerdam in Holland, and Val Saint Lambert in Belgium are other well-known manufacturers of beautiful glassware. England, Ireland, and Italy also produce considerable amounts of high-quality glass. Venetian glass with its intricate shapes and exquisite colors has been extremely popular.

Several manufacturers in America produce fine glassware for a mass market. Perhaps the most outstanding producer in America is the Corning glassworks, which makes Steuben glass. Exquisite examples of Steuben designs are often exhibited in museums or are presented as gifts to foreign dignitaries. Some other well-known names include Blenco, Fostoria, Libby, Westmoreland, Tiffany, and Waterford.

Choosing Glassware

Glass accessories may be found in any room, and of course they should complement the decor. Bowls, vases, pitchers, ashtrays, and the like may be simple or elegant. They may express formality or informality.

Glassware for entertaining and for table use must be chosen with regard for usefulness as well as design. Glasses are made in a wide variety of sizes and shapes, but modern concepts of living demand fewer types than were often demanded in the past, and it is not uncommon to see glasses that are adaptable to different uses—for example, wine glasses that may also be used for cocktails. Figure 26.4 shows some of the popular sizes of glassware.

The formality or informality of the dining area should have some influence on the types of glasses selected for table use. Tall, long-stemmed water goblets are lovely in a full-sized dining room where there is plenty of space at the table, but they may be a real problem on a small table in a tiny dining area. A short-

Table Appointments

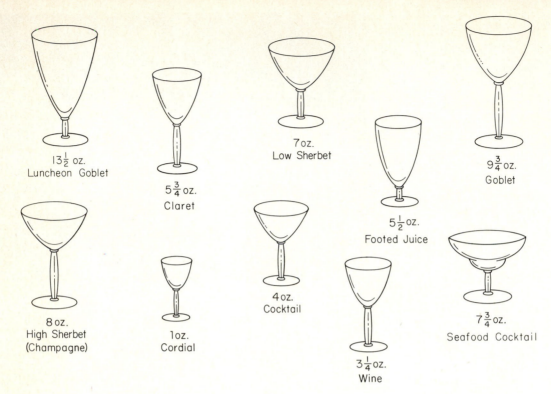

$13\frac{1}{2}$ oz.
Luncheon Goblet

$5\frac{3}{4}$ oz.
Claret

7 oz.
Low Sherbet

$9\frac{3}{4}$ oz.
Goblet

8 oz.
High Sherbet
(Champagne)

1 oz.
Cordial

4 oz.
Cocktail

$5\frac{1}{2}$ oz.
Footed Juice

$3\frac{1}{4}$ oz.
Wine

$7\frac{3}{4}$ oz.
Seafood Cocktail

Fig. 26.4 Basic sizes and shapes in stemware. *(Courtesy of Fostoria Glass Company)*

stemmed glass or some type that is not so likely to tip over would be much more practical.

The design of the glassware for table use should harmonize with the other table appointments. Simple china and plain silver usually call for glassware that is unadorned, although it should be beautiful in form. Graceful curving designs on glassware blend with similar designs on china and silverware. Plain surfaces and geometric and abstract designs have a common denominator that produces a unifying effect.

Flatware

The various types of knives, forks, and spoons are called *flatware*. Ladles, cake servers, and other special serving utensils would also come under this category.

There is a certain symbolism associated with flatware. Sometimes the family silver is passed down from one generation to another. Whether or not it involves sentiment, tradition, or prestige, flatware is a major item in table decoration and has a peculiar role in representing the spirit of the home.

For those who do not inherit beautiful silver, the choice will probably be either sterling, silver plate, or stainless steel. There are several other variations, such as Dirilite, a gold-colored flatware, and combinations of wood, ivory, and similar materials, which have a more limited appeal.

Sterling Silver
The most expensive and generally the most prized silver is sterling. Because silver by itself is too soft to be useful, another metal, usually

copper, is added for durability. By law, a product marked sterling must have 925 parts of pure silver in every 1,000 parts of the finished metal. A sterling silver product will be stamped *925* or *sterling.*

Silver Plate

During the eighteenth century it was discovered that a layer of sterling silver could be fused to a copper base. Objects made by this method were first made in the town of Sheffield, England. Old Sheffield plate is prized by the collector today. Plated ware is made by the use of a base metal of nickel, copper, and zinc. Electrolytic methods are employed to fuse a coating of silver to the surface. The durability depends upon the thickness of the silver coating and also upon how carefully the process is controlled. Some manufacturers reinforce the areas that will receive hard use with inlays of sterling silver.

Naturally, silver plate is much less expensive than sterling silver. Because there is variation in the quality of plated silver, it is wise to deal with reputable firms that take pride in high-quality products. With proper care, well-made silver plate will give many years of satisfactory service. Poor-quality silver plate will soon become unsightly as the plating wears off.

Stainless Steel

Stainless steel is a solid alloy that must contain at least eleven and one-half per cent chromium or it may not be called stainless steel. Within recent years stainless steel has developed wide popularity for table service. Although it does not carry the same sentimental attachment that silver table service does, stainless steel has several practical advantages. It requires less care than silver. It does not tarnish and therefore does not need polishing, and it resists stains from foods that ordinarily discolor silver. Although it is available in a rather wide price range, stainless steel costs less than sterling silver.

Until recently, stainless steel seemed more suitable for contemporary settings. Now, however, there are many traditional designs. In some cases, the same design is made in both silver and stainless steel.

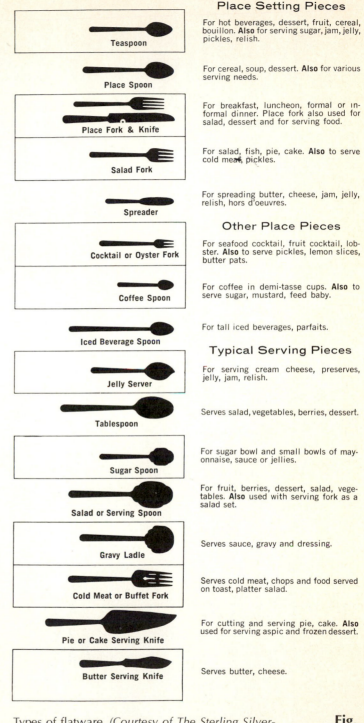

Place Setting Pieces

Teaspoon — For hot beverages, dessert, fruit, cereal, bouillon. **Also** for serving sugar, jam, jelly, pickles, relish.

Place Spoon — For cereal, soup, dessert. **Also** for various serving needs.

Place Fork & Knife — For breakfast, luncheon, formal or informal dinner. Place fork also used for salad, dessert and for serving food.

Salad Fork — For salad, fish, pie, cake. **Also** to serve cold meat, pickles.

Spreader — For spreading butter, cheese, jam, jelly, relish, hors d'oeuvres.

Other Place Pieces

Cocktail or Oyster Fork — For seafood cocktail, fruit cocktail, lobster. **Also** to serve pickles, lemon slices, butter pats.

Coffee Spoon — For coffee in demi-tasse cups. **Also** to serve sugar, mustard, feed baby.

Iced Beverage Spoon — For tall iced beverages, parfaits.

Typical Serving Pieces

Jelly Server — For serving cream cheese, preserves, jelly, jam, relish.

Tablespoon — Serves salad, vegetables, berries, dessert.

Sugar Spoon — For sugar bowl and small bowls of mayonnaise, sauce or jellies.

Salad or Serving Spoon — For fruit, berries, dessert, salad, vegetables. **Also** used with serving fork as a salad set.

Gravy Ladle — Serves sauce, gravy and dressing.

Cold Meat or Buffet Fork — Serves cold meat, chops and food served on toast, platter salad.

Pie or Cake Serving Knife — For cutting and serving pie, cake. **Also** used for serving aspic and frozen dessert.

Butter Serving Knife — Serves butter, cheese.

Types of flatware. (*Courtesy of The Sterling Silversmiths Guild of America*)

Fig. 26.5

Table 26.1 Styles of Table Appointments

Style	Definitions	General Characteristics	Dinnerware	Glassware	Flatware and Hollowware	Table Linens
Classic	Designs have survived from past generations	Delicate, refined lines	Gold leaf trim Scrolled rims or classic borders Patterns include leaves, rosettes, laurel leaves, urns, torches, scrolls, and pastoral scenes	Gold or silver trim Elaborate etching on glasses with long stems	Very ornate urns, flowers, scrolls, and classic curves	Elegant, refined, smooth textures White damask, lace or linen, highly embellished
Country	Suggests rustic designs, often hand-crafted with simple ornamentation	Simple forms, bulky shapes, and rough textures	Weight, color, and pattern emphasized Prints and florals Pottery, melamine	Sturdy-looking, heavy, and often colored Goblets have short stems and tumblers are sturdy Milk glass appropriate	Plain or semiornate reproductions of antique patterns	Interesting weaves with rough textural effects Plain and floral prints popular as well as colored damask
Contemporary	Broad category of current designs with simple lines	Purity of line, form, and materials Use of woods, steel, glass, and plastics Clean-cut, simple, functional designs	Emphasis is on plate, color, and interesting glaze	Bold, clean-cut shapes May be clear or colored, cut or uncut	Simple, plain patterns, lacking in ornamentation Graceful flower sprays on plate rims	Any kind of textures acceptable, including straw and plastic

"Styles of Table Appointments" reprinted from Darlene Kness, *The Butterick Kitchen Equipment Handbook* (1977), courtesy of Butterick Publishing, 161 Sixth Ave., New York, New York 10013.

Pewter

Pewter is a soft, grayish alloy composed chiefly of tin. Originally it was used as an alternative to sterling prior to the invention of silver plate. Today pewter is expensive.

Gold Electroplate

When an article is made of a nonprecious metal and then covered with gold, the process is called gold electroplating. Federal standards require a thickness of at least 7 millionths of an inch of at least 10K gold. This plating usually wears off with age.

Choosing Flatware

Pattern is probably the primary consideration when choosing flatware. In silver, the design may be extremely ornate or very simple. It should be chosen to harmonize with other table equipment. There is such a wide range of patterns that the choice is a matter of individual preference, but it is often a difficult decision to make.

Unusual shapes and proportions are sometimes interesting to look at but not as functional as they might be. Note the balance of each piece while holding it. Well-balanced flatware rests comfortably in the hand when held as it would normally be held. Also study the types and shapes of serving pieces to be sure they will be functional.

It should also be remembered that silver will tarnish and must be cleaned. Ornate designs require more time for careful polishing in all the crevices, although they do add elegance to the table.

Various designs in both flatware and hollowware are intended to blend with particular styles in furnishings. We need not always be consistent in this matter, but usually a design that harmonizes with the general theme of the home will be more attractive. Very modern designs in a home that is traditional in all other respects may seem incongruous. Ornate traditional designs in a modern home may seem equally out of place.

There are several ways to purchase flatware. You may buy individual place settings or a set of four, six, eight, or twelve.

A basic place setting of five pieces would consist of a knife, a fork, a teaspoon, a soup spoon, and a butter spreader. However, a four-piece place setting is sometimes chosen as a starter, with the idea of adding the spreader and

Some motifs designed to blend with traditional styles. *(Courtesy of The Sterling Silversmiths Guild of America)*

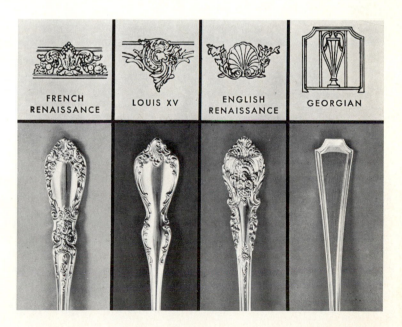

FRENCH RENAISSANCE LOUIS XV ENGLISH RENAISSANCE GEORGIAN

Fig. 26.6

Table Appointments

Stainless steel designed to coordinate with silver in a *Matchmakers* group. *(Courtesy of Matchmakers, Dover by Oneida Silversmiths)*

Fig.
26.7

a salad fork later. In some of the older patterns, knives and forks are made in both a dinner size and a smaller luncheon size. Newer designs are made in one all-purpose size called the *place* size. Many people find extra teaspoons very useful.

Hollowware

Bowls, trays, pitchers, serving dishes, and the like are classified as hollowware. These do not as a rule match the designs in flatware, but they should harmonize with all table appointments. Silver, silver plate, and stainless steel are used for hollowware, sometimes in combination

with crystal. Decide on the metal which best suits your lifestyle.

Designs in hollowware may be as ornate (highly decorative); semiornate (plainer, usually classic patterns); and plain (with minimal or no decoration).

In choosing hollowware, look for the following quality features: pewter spouts on coffee- and teapots (pewter is long lasting); sturdy hinges on covers; insulated handles; and smooth solder seams. When coordinating table appointments, refer to Table 26.1 for suggestions. There will not be the same diversified range of patterns to choose from in hollowware as in flatware, but the general features and characteristics should blend with the china and flatware as much as possible.

Today relatively few of the items in the linen closet are actually made of linen. The term *household linens* dates back to a time when linen was widely used for sheets, pillowcases, towels, and tablecloths. Now, although linen sheets are still available, cotton and synthetic fibers are more widely used. Nevertheless, linen is still popular for table coverings and for certain kinds of towels.

Several items that come under the category of household linens are likely to receive hard use, and they should therefore be selected for durability. However, many items have become more glamorous in recent years, and color and styling have become as important as durability in influencing decisions. Nevertheless, frequent laundering does exert wear and tear, so both styling and durability should be important factors in making selections.

Bed Linens

It pays to invest in good-quality bed linens because they wear longer and present a more attractive appearance. Sheets, pillowcases, mattress covers, and mattress pads must be laundered frequently. Poor-quality products become limp and sleazy after a few washings.

Sizes
Before buying bed linens it is most important to know the exact size of the mattresses on which they are to be used. There is considerable variation in this respect.

Sheets may be either fitted or the more traditional flat type. The fitted or so-called contour types are shaped to fit the mattress. Bottom sheets are fitted or shaped at four corners; top sheets are shaped only at the two bottom corners. Innerspring mattresses are usually six to seven inches deep; foam rubber mattresses are generally four and one-half to six inches deep. Fitted sheets are made for both types.

Sizes for flat sheets are usually expressed as the torn size before hemming. The actual length of the finished sheet will be several inches less than the measurement on the label. It is important to use a flat sheet large enough for the bed.

27
Household Linens

(a)

(b)

Sheets and pillowcases are accessories in the bedroom and should be selected to emphasize a theme. *(a) (Courtesy of Simmons Co.) (b) and (c) (Courtesy of Fieldcrest) (d) (Courtesy of J. P. Stevens and Co., Inc.)*

(d)

Fig.
27.1

(c)

For a bottom sheet there should be a sufficient amount to tuck under the mattress, at least five inches at the foot and at the head of the bed. For a top sheet there should be sufficient length for a five-inch tuck-in at the foot and an eighteen-inch turn-back over the top of the blanket. A twelve- to fifteen-inch overhang at each side is necessary for comfort. Some standard mattress sizes and recommended sizes for flat sheets are shown in Table 27.1.

Pillowcases should be large enough to slip over the pillow with ease, but they should fit smoothly; they should be about ten inches longer than the pillow. For a pillow 20 by 26 inches a pillowcase 36 by 42 inches should be used. Regular size pillow cases fit the pillows for a twin, double, or queen-size bed. For a king-size pillow 20 X 36 inches, use a king size pillow case. Refer to Table 27.2 for pillow sizes and the size of cases they need.

Types of Sheets and Pillowcases

The difference between fitted and flat sheets has been mentioned. Fitted sheets provide a smooth, wrinkle-free surface, which many people find most comfortable. Because they stay in place, less time is required for making the bed. They may require no ironing because they stretch taut over the mattress and wrinkles disappear. However, they are more expensive and may not be adapted to beds that vary slightly from standard sizes.

Sheets are available in a variety of fabrics— some woven, some knitted. Cotton is the most widely used fiber because it is very comfortable for sleeping, but the man-made fibers are becoming more important. Nylon tricot sheets have a silky texture and they are easy to launder. The blends of cotton and polyester are becoming very popular because they require little or no ironing. Combinations of 50/50 per cent

Sheet, Blanket, and Bedspread Sizes

Table 27.1

Type of Bed	Standard Mattress Size (Inches)	Recommended Flat-Sheet Size (Inches)	Blanket Size (Inches)	Finished Bedspread Size (Inches)
Crib	27 × 52	42 × 72	36 × 56	36 × 50
Standard twin	39 × 75	72 × 108	66 × 90	81 × 108
Long twin	39 × 80	72 × 108	66 × 90	81 × 108
Three-quarter	48 × 76	81 × 108	72 × 90	
Standard double	54 × 75	90 × 108	80 × 90	96 × 108
Queen-size	60 × 80	90 × 108	90 × 90	102 × 120
King-size	72 × 84	108 × 120	90 × 108	114 × 120

Pillow and Pillowcase Sizes

Table 27.2

Type of Pillow	Size of Pillow (Inches)	Pillowcase Size Needed (Inches)
Standard	20 × 26	42 × 36
Queen	20 × 30	42 × 40
King	20 × 36	42 × 46

cotton/polyester and 65/35 per cent cotton/polyester have produced fabrics that seem to meet the demands of durability and easy care.

Cotton sheets may be muslin or percale. The basic differences between the two types are weight, type of yarn, and texture. Muslin sheets are heavier and woven with thicker carded yarns. The thread count, or the number of threads in one square inch of fabric, is one way of designating different types of sheeting. A heavy muslin would have 140 threads to the square inch; a medium weight would have a thread count of 128. Lightweight muslin with a thread count of 112 is available but not generally recommended.

Percale sheets are lighter in weight and generally made of smooth combed yarns. Percales vary in the quality of yarn and the closeness of the weave. Fine-quality percale has a thread count of 180; an even finer quality has a thread count of 200 or more. Top-grade percale is expensive, but it has a smooth, luxurious texture.

The choice between muslin and percale may depend on several factors. A medium-weight muslin sheet is strong, long wearing, and economical. Good-quality muslin stands up well in commercial laundering, but when charges are based on pound rates, the upkeep of a heavy muslin sheet will be comparatively high. If sheets are laundered at home, percale may be easier to handle because of its lighter weight.

Well-made sheets will have strong taped selvages at the side edges. Hems will be smooth, with small, firm, even stitches. It is customary to have a one-inch hem at the bottom and a three- or four-inch hem at the top. However, some sheets are made with equal-sized hems at the ends, which makes it possible to reverse the position of the sheet. If these hems are narrow, however, they are not usually as attractive as the one deep hem at the top.

If one has sheets of different sizes and different types in the linen closet it is helpful to have some identifying label stitched at a bottom corner. Many manufacturers provide some sort of a marking, or sheets can be easily marked with colored tape, thread, or a laundry marking pencil.

Design
Color and pattern have become important style features of bed linens. Fashion has moved into bed linens. In fact, many consumers buy extra sets of sheets that they really do not need because they like the printed design or the color

of the sheet. In most cases reliable manufacturers use dyes that stand up well even with commerical laundering. However, in poor-quality sheets the colors may fade. Bright, fresh designs on bed linens often contribute to the attractiveness of a bedroom, but this is another matter of personal preference. Of course the design and the color scheme should blend with the decor of the room for the most charming effects.

Requirements

Specific needs for bed linens will vary for each household, depending on the number of beds, the number of different sized beds, the types of sheets (flat or fitted, white or colored, and so on.), and how the laundry is done. A good basic rule to follow, however, is to allow six sheets for each bed and three cases for each pillow. Thus there will be two sheets in use, two in the laundry, and two in reserve. Linens will wear longer if they are rotated in use, so the reserve supply should be used as frequently as the others.

Many homemakers like to protect mattresses with heavy muslin covers and pads. These are especially desirable in times of illness, when food or medicine may spill and spot a mattress.

Blankets

Comfort, appearance, and durability are major factors in choosing blankets. To be comfortable, the blanket should be of desirable weight and provide adequate warmth. Most people prefer lightweight blankets. A deep fluffy nap will encase many little air spaces that provide good insulating qualities. A firmly woven heavy blanket may not be as warm as a well-made lighter type.

Sizes

Blankets range from small crib sizes to extra-large sizes designed for king-sized beds. Refer to Table 27.1 for sizes.

Types

Blankets are available in a variety of weights and in several fibers. In addition, comforters

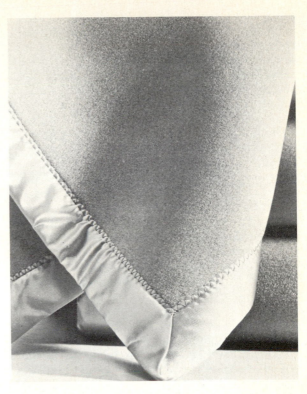

Fig. 27.2

A nonwoven blanket made by bonding nylon yarns to a core of urethane foam. The result is light, soft, and warm. *(Courtesy of West Point Pepperell)*

filled with feathers and down are sometimes used in place of blankets.

Good wool blankets are warm and durable. The nap remains fluffy if the blanket is properly cleaned. Synthetic fibers, including nylon, acrylic, and modacrylic, have become popular in blankets and are often used in blends. If well constructed, blankets made of synthetics retain their light fluffy qualities. They are easy to launder and require no special care to prevent moth damage.

Thermal blankets, constructed so that tiny pockets of air provide excellent insulating qualities, have become very popular. They are very light in weight and easy to care for.

Various finishes are used on the ends of blankets. A machine-made blanket stitch is sometimes used on lightweight blankets. If the thread is firm and the stitches are close together

474 this may be a durable finish. Binding is usually a more attractive and more luxurious finish. Bands of silk, rayon, nylon, or cotton sateen are used to bind edges. These should be of good quality and firmly stitched. They should not interfere with the launderability of a washable blanket.

Designs
Most blankets depend on soft fluffy texture and rich colors for their beauty. However, some do have designs woven into the fabric, and printed designs have become extremely popular. Quilts and comforters may have coverings of printed fabrics or they may be decorated with appliquéd motifs. Some comforters are covered with smooth taffeta or satin. Although rather elegant in appearance, this type of covering tends to slip and slide more than a fuzzy blanket.

Requirements
In some climates at least two blankets may be needed for each bed—one lightweight summer blanket and one heavier-weight winter blanket. Some people prefer more. Electric blankets have become popular for several reasons, but especially because the one blanket can be regulated for various degrees of warmth. Thus they are always comfortable and the owner does not have the problem of storing extra blankets.

Towel and Accessory Types and Sizes

Table 27.3

Type	Size (Inches)
Regular bath	22 × 44
Queen-size	27 × 52
King-size	36 × 70
Bath sheet	44 × 72
Hand towel	16 × 26
Guest towel	11 × 18
Washcloth	12 × 12
Dish towel	16 × 29
Dishcloth	12 × 12
Kitchen towel	16 × 30

Comforters and Quilts

Comforters and quilts consist of two layers of fabric with a layer of stuffing in between. The stuffing may be feathers, down, kapok, fiberfil, or polyester. The fabrics and fibers in them vary in quality and price. Because comforters or quilts are often used in place of bedspreads, they may be available with matching pillow covers or draperies. Like other bed coverings, they are available in various sizes. When choosing them, look for warmth, attractiveness, durability, and ease of care. If possible, choose a comforter of a slightly rough-textured fabric; slippery fabrics usually cause the comforter to slide off the bed.

Bedspreads

Bedspreads cover the top, sides, and foot of the bed. They come in a variety of styles, fabrics, sizes, and constructions such as quilted, chenille, plush, and novelty types. Quilted bedspreads usually have a layer of stuffing in between. Bedspreads are usually selected for decorativeness and durability. Because bedspreads can be expensive, choose one that will coordinate with the other room colors and be durable.

Towels

New fashions in towels have added glamour to both the kitchen and the bathroom. Style trends in both types have followed the prevailing tastes in color and pattern. Towels, therefore, have become important accessories in the decorative scheme, especially because they are always on view. Refer to Table 27.3 for the size that best fits your needs.

Types
Cotton terry cloth is the popular choice for toweling because it is very absorbent. Cotton terry cloth is used for bath towels, hand towels, and kitchen towels. However, other fabrics are

used for some face and hand towels. Huck in either linen or cotton is widely used. Sometimes rayon and cotton mixtures are used. Polyester towels have become very popular because they are less expensive than cotton. However, they are not as absorbent as cotton towels.

Linen is a preferred fiber for kitchen towels because it is so absorbent and because linen towels do not leave lint on dishes and glassware. Some kitchen towels made of cotton are specially constructed and treated to make them free of lint.

Judging quality in towels requires careful observation and comparison. In terry cloth the underweave should be firm and close for strength and durability. The loops of yarn that form the pile provide absorbency; they should be closely packed. More loops mean greater absorbency and a more luxurious texture. The twist of the yarn will influence texture and absorbency. Loosely twisted pile yarns soak up more moisture and feel softer to the touch. However, some people prefer a towel with a slightly hard, rough texture for mild stimulation of the skin.

It is important to compare terry towels of different weights, textures, and qualities to observe the differences before making selections.

The side edges of a towel may be finished in different ways. A woven-taped selvage should be firm and sturdy. An over-edged selvage uses an overcast stitch, which should be close and tight for maximum durability. A hemmed selvage should be stitched with small firm stitches.

The stitching at the hemmed ends of the towel is a good indication of quality. Small stitches and backstitching at the corners provide sturdy hems. The towel should be free from loose thread ends.

Designs

Pile loops are responsible for absorbency in terry coth. Any pattern that reduces the area of the pile will make the towel less functional; for example, some designs are woven with flat areas, and other towels are decorated with large appliquéd motifs. Metallic yarns are sometimes used for added glamour. In most cases these are quite

(a)

Good quality towels have a close, thick pile; the underweave is firm and the hems are stitched with close, even stitches. They are very important in accessorizing bathrooms today. *(a) (Courtesy of Fieldcrest) (b) (Courtesy of Monsanto)*

Fig. 27.3

(b)

durable, but can scratch the skin. Nevertheless any added decoration should not interfere with the chief function of the towel.

Coordinated colors and patterns often add interest in the decoration of the bathroom. Various solid colors may be combined with related prints or stripes.

Requirements

Minimum quantities of towels are difficult to determine, because requirements vary with individuals. Also, if the laundry is done at home in an automatic washer and dryer there will be less need for large reserves. However, there should be a supply adequate to meet extra demands should there be illness in the family or should one entertain overnight guests; moreover, towels wear better if they are rotated in use. A suggested estimate includes:

Six face towels per person.
Six bath towels per person.
Four washcloths per person.

The bathroom linen closet should also include at least two bath mats.

Table Linens

In the selection of table linens there is far more freedom of choice than for other household linens. It has already been pointed out that standards for meal service are individually set. With a trend toward informal service and many easy-care materials on the market, there is no reason why table settings should not be both attractive and functional.

With laminated table tops that require only wiping with a damp cloth, and with paper napkins, there may be no need for any kind of table covering. This kind of table service, however, lacks a certain warm and gracious quality. Various place mats and tablecloths require little or no care, yet they lend a charm and an aura of hospitality to meal service. This is an area where individuality may certainly be exercised, but today it requires little effort to set tables that are gracious and inviting.

Fig. 27.4 Coordinated towels and sheets can unify the home. In these pictures sheets are used for nontraditional purposes. *(a)* and *(b)* *(Courtesy of Fieldcrest)*

Today, one can unify a room with two functions by choosing coordinated linens. *(Courtesy of Fieldcrest)*

Fig. 27.5

Sizes

Placemats are available in new and interesting shapes, but the traditional rectangle measures about twelve by eighteen inches. A cloth that covers the entire table should usually extend about six or eight inches beyond the edges of the table. Naturally the size and shape of the table will determine the size of the cloth. Popular standard sizes for small tables include 36″ × 36″ for a card table, 54″ × 54″ for a dinette table, and 54″ × 72″ for a dinette table with leaves extended. Regular dining tables usually require wider cloths. Popular sizes are 64″ × 72″, 72″ × 90″, and 90″ × 108″. Cloths for round tables are available in a variety of sizes.

Napkins range in size from small cocktail napkins to large dinner napkins. Tea or luncheon napkins may be 12″ × 12″ or 15″ × 15″. Dinner napkins are more usually 18″ × 18″, 22″ × 22″, or 24″ × 24″, although other sizes are available.

Types

There is such a wide range of table coverings on the market that it is difficult to classify them in any useful manner. Perhaps the use, the appearance, and the amount of care required will

The correct-sized tablecloth is very important to the look of the table. Tablecloths are made in all sizes to fit different tables, from the popular square bridge table to the lovely oval, oblong, and round tables. Remember, the larger the table, the longer the overhang should be—a 5″ to 10″ overhang for a small table and a 10″ to 15″ for a larger table. Select napkins in a variety of solid colors, plain, embroidered, or appliqued to mix and match. Napkins are a decorative touch and also subtly indicate formality or informality of the setting. *(Courtesy of Belgian Linen Association)*

Fig. 27.6

be the most important factors in making a selection.

Placemats and even tablecloths in plastic or plastic-coated fabrics have become more glamorous and more sophisticated in styling. Lovely textural effects and interesting color combinations are rapidly removing the stigma that has for so long been associated with plastic. If these are chosen with care and discretion, there should be no objection to their use even on special occasions. For everyday use, especially for breakfast and lunch, they are attractive and require minimum care.

The more traditional mats and cloths are made of linen, cotton, and rayon, along with synthetic fibers. Linen damask cloths have, for many years, been the most desirable cloths for rather formal, elegant settings. The lovely texture of linen provides a suitable background for beautiful china, glassware, and silver. Linen cloths do not become fuzzy with use, they do not absorb stains quickly, and they launder easily. Cotton and rayon have been widely used because they are less expensive, but neither of these fibers offers the beauty and the lasting quality of linen.

Lace is often used for tablecloths that may be either formal or informal. A good lace cloth has many practical advantages. It can be laundered easily, it requires little or no ironing, and it is elegant enough for very special occasions. Spots do not become immediately prominent. A lovely handmade lace cloth is indeed a family treasure. Machine-made lace cloths, although not usually as beautiful, do offer similar advantages.

The synthetics in modern table coverings present beauty and elegance with appealing minimum-care features. Most of the synthetics do not spot easily and require little or no ironing. All of these characteristics are making them more important in the field of table "linens." Be sure to choose these "linens" with a soil release finish.

Requirements

Naturally the requirements for table linens will depend on how family meals will be served, the kind of entertaining that will be done, the size of the tables, and the general decor of the home. However, table linens might be considered as accessories in that they complement the decorative scheme of the room. From this standpoint, they should be chosen with care so that they will provide a suitable background for the other table appointments.

Finishing Touches

Vibrant, warm, and familiar, table linens enhance the pleasant moments of everyday living. Table linens are the background for every setting . . . setting the theme with texture, color, and pattern. The look can be modern, provincial, traditional, or a combination. As the background for all table treasures, china, glassware, and favorite decorations and centerpieces, one chooses linens as one selects wardrobe accessories, to complement, to accent, or to dramatize. For that special occasion formal table, the classic "white" linen tablecloth is no longer the rule. Although white is always in good taste, today we have adapted color throughout the home. Now the finest decorative linens come in colors that range from cool pastels to brilliant jewel tones. In using color, pastels tend to lend dignity and a more quiet look, deep colors a dramatic effect.

(a), *(b)*, and *(c) (Courtesy of The Belgian Linen Association)*

(c)

Fig. 27.7

Household Linens

28

Sewing for the Home

A sewing machine will soon pay for itself if one enjoys making lovely things for the home. Many consumers prefer making decorative items rather than clothing, because in general the sewing of these items is quick and easy. There is a wide variety of beautiful fabrics and exciting trimmings. Also, the many simple labor-saving devices help to provide a custom-made appearance with relatively little expense. There seems to be renewed interest in the various types of needlework that can provide attractive accessories for almost any room. Kits with all the necessary materials are readily available for hooked and braided rugs, needlepoint, and embroidery, especially crewelwork. In many cases designs have become modernized or highly stylized.

General Suggestions

Naturally, every new trend in home decoration will not be suitable for every home, but magazines and department stores are full of ideas that can be adapted. Rooms need never be dull or monotonous, nor need they be static. Often a simple little change, such as new chair covers or a few new decorative pillows, will add fresh interest and sparkle. Curtains and slipcovers need not be expensive to be interesting.

Careful Planning

Successful decoration does require careful and long-range planning. Before investing time and money in sewing for the home, one should be sure to select colors and textures that are exactly what is wanted. Even with inexpensive fabrics, mistakes are costly. If possible, when buying any new fabric, it is wise to take samples of the colors already used in the room. If that is not possible, it is worth investing in one-third or one-half yard of fabric to try out at home. In a different setting, and under different kinds of lights, the colors may look altogether different from their appearance in the store.

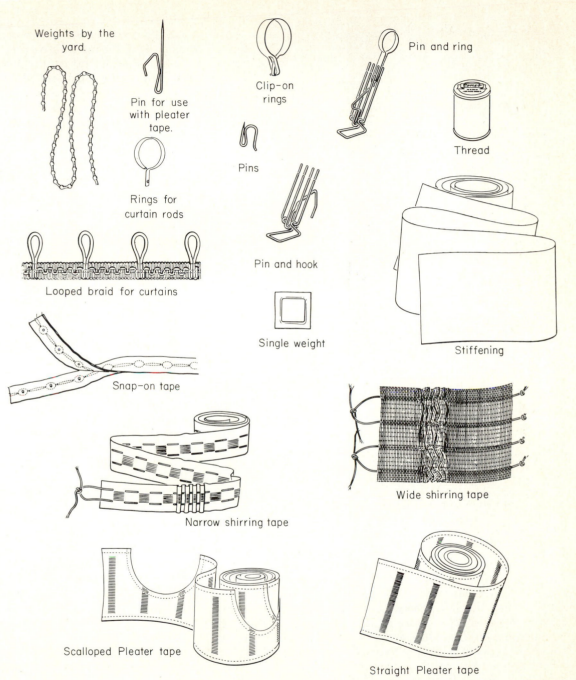

Weights by the yard.

Pin for use with pleater tape.

Rings for curtain rods

Clip-on rings

Pins

Pin and ring

Thread

Pin and hook

Single weight

Stiffening

Looped braid for curtains

Snap-on tape

Wide shirring tape

Narrow shirring tape

Scalloped Pleater tape

Straight Pleater tape

Fig. 28.1

Various tapes and supplies that simplify sewing for the home. *(Courtesy of Conso Products, Inc.)*

Sewing for the Home

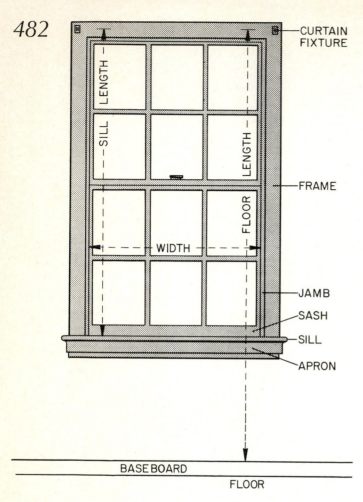

LENGTH

SILL

LENGTH

FLOOR

WIDTH

CURTAIN FIXTURE

FRAME

JAMB

SASH

SILL

APRON

BASEBOARD

FLOOR

Fig. 28.2 Measure from the fixture for the desired length. Allow ample fabric for headings and hems. *(Courtesy of Conso Products, Inc.)*

One should think in terms of the amounts of each color and pattern to be used. It should be remembered that large areas of brilliant colors tend to decrease the apparent size of the room. So does too much bold pattern and too much contrast. Repeating certain colors, textures, and prints tends to unify the effect; but too much repetition can be monotonous. Thus, one must try to visualize the room as a whole and plan the areas of color and pattern for a pleasing result.

Careful Shopping

You should compare qualities very carefully before buying, and check information about shrinkage, colorfastness, and care. You should also deal with stores that will stand behind their products.

It may be necessary to shop in several stores to become familiar with all the different types of curtain rods, drapery hooks, and trimmings. There are also many useful notions and patterns that will make projects easier, such as corded shirring tape, snap tape, and press-on tape; there are various uses for all of these.

Careful Measurement

One must be sure to have complete and accurate measurements for any decorating necessary. Projects like draperies and slipcovers often require large amounts of fabric, and one can get into serious difficulties by not knowing the exact dimensions of windows, sofas, chairs, and so on. Ample fullness in curtains, draperies, bedspreads, and slipcovers should be planned for. Rather than skimp with a costly fabric, it is better to be generous with one that is less expensive. Also, calculations should be generous, allowing for full ruffles and deep pleats, headings, and hems.

Most decorative fabrics are 48 to 54 inches wide, but some are only 36 inches wide. The exact width must be known before the yardage can be figured. If the fabric has a printed or woven design, the size of the motif is important. (This is spoken of as the *repeat.*) When several lengths of fabric are seamed for draperies, the motifs must be evenly matched and they must be placed exactly alike at both sides of a window. When a large motif is used for slipcovers, the design must be attractively placed on the chair; otherwise it will have a chopped-up appearance. The larger the motif, the more fabric will be required for matching and placing the design.

Ruffles, skirts, and pleated flounces are usually cut on the crosswise grain of the fabric. For adequate fullness in gathering, fabric should usually be at least twice as long as the finished measurement; lightweight, sheer fabrics may require two-and-a-half to three times the finished measurement for ample fullness after gathering.

Curtains and Draperies

Only a few simple hems are needed to make plain, tailored curtains, but they can be taken out of the ordinary class with a little trimming, such as a few tucks parallel to the bottom hem, or bands of braid or fringe for a border effect. It is all simple, straight stitching with no complicated fitting. Even the measuring is easy. With the use of lots of fabric and interesting colors, in no time at all a dowdy room can be converted into one that has character.

Curtains and draperies should be planned so that they can be used on either side of the window. This is just a matter of making all the side hems the same depth. Light weakens some fabrics, so they will last longer if the panels are reversed periodically.

The window must be measured accurately. In a patterned fabric, the panels should be cut so that the motif will be spaced the same way across all windows. The lengths of fabric should be cut allowing for headings and bottom hems. A three-inch hem at the bottom may be enough, but on some fabrics a deeper hem looks more attractive and hangs better. Six inches, or even nine inches, may not be too much for a nice solid look at the lower edge. A double hem is sometimes used to add body and to allow for shrinkage. One should be generous with hem allowances, because it is much easier to cut fabric off if the hem is too deep than it is to add on if the curtains have to be lengthened.

Weights are sometimes used at the bottom edges of curtains and draperies to make them hang nicely. There are tiny weights that come by the yard. A length of this type of weighting can be inserted in the bottom hem and tacked in place. Larger single weights can be covered with fabric and tacked on the inside at the lower corners.

The required fullness in the width of the curtain or drapery depends on the weight of the fabric. Sheer, lightweight fabrics should be cut with greater fullness. One should seam together as many lengths as will be needed to give the desired width. If selvages pull or draw, they should be clipped every four or five inches. They may have to be cut off completely and the seam edges finished with a machine stitch to prevent fraying.

The side edges of each curtain should now be hemmed. About one to two inches for this hem is enough, but that depends on the fabric and the width of the whole panel.

Headings
The way the top of the curtain should be finished depends on the kind of rod and hooks to be used. If the curtain or drapery will be covered by a cornice or valance, one can turn a simple hem, leaving both ends open so the rod can be inserted. If the top will be exposed, it is usually more attractive to have some decorative type of heading. For a simple one, one can turn a deep hem, then put in another row of machine stitching to form a casing and a heading at the top of the curtain. When measuring for this type of finish, one must remember that the top row of stitching will rest on the rod. The heading will be in addition to the length of the curtain from rod to hem.

Allow ample amounts for casing and standing heading.

Fig. 28.3

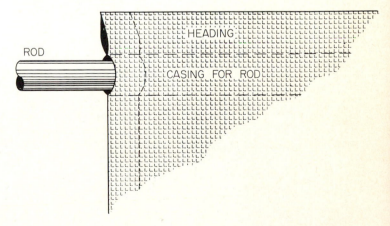

(a)

WRONG SIDE
OF MATERIAL

(b)

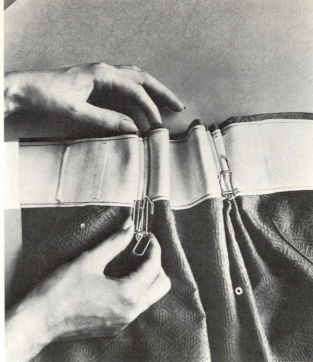

**Fig.
28.4**

Stitch pleater tape to tops of curtains or draperies.
Insert hooks for even, professional-looking pleats.
(Courtesy of Conso Products, Inc.)

Pleater tape. Pinch pleats at the tops of curtains and draperies provide a more finished, custom-made appearance, especially on curtains or draperies that will be mounted on traverse rods and on those that will be exposed at the top.

One could use a strip of stiffening, such as buckram, at the top of the curtain, then measure and stitch the pleats. However, there is on the market a pleater tape that makes the whole process very simple. The tape is made with narrow pockets or casings at regularly spaced intervals; special hooks are inserted to form the pleats.

About three quarters of an inch of fabric should be allowed for turning under at the upper edge. Then the pleater tape is stitched to the wrong side of the fabric. The top edge of the tape must be at the top edge of the curtain so

that the pockets will be in the proper position. Then one inserts hooks to form pleats, spacing the pleats by skipping one casing between pleats. Single hooks should be used at the ends. (Note: The pleats may also be spaced with two casings in between if desired. However, this results in fewer pleats and the effect is not quite as attractive.)

This method of making pinch pleats has several advantages. The tape is easy to apply and requires no complicated measurements. Also, when the hooks are removed the curtains spread out flat, which simplifies cleaning, pressing, and storage.

Shirring tape. Another interesting finish for the tops of curtains is possible through the use of shirring tape that has woven-in cords. The tape is stitched to the top edge of the curtain on the wrong side. The cords are then drawn to provide the desired fullness and tied back at the ends. They can be released so that the curtain will spread out flat for laundering. Regular drapery pins are used for mounting the curtain on the rod.

Valances and Cornices

The top of the window may be covered by a valance or a cornice to lend a more interesting decorative note. The type of finish and trimming chosen will, of course, be influenced by the style of the curtains or draperies. There is almost unlimited variety. The depth of the valance will also be determined by the proportions of the window. A tall, narrow window will seem shorter if a deeper valance is used.

Cornices are usually made of wood or metal, but there is available a special stiffening that can be covered with fabric and mounted on a curtain rod. It can be cut to any desired shape and trimmed to give the effect of a cornice. Wide tape should be stitched across the top on the inside to hold the rod.

Pleater tape can be used at the top of the valance. For a more formal and elegant valance, vertical strips of shirring tape might be used. In this case about three times the length of the finished valance should be allowed when the fabric is measured and cut.

Café Curtains

Short curtains are very popular, and attractive ones can be made quickly and easily. Although café curtains are in general rather informal in appearance, they have been adapted to more formal rooms in some interesting window treatments.

Various finishes can be used on the top edges of the curtains. One can make a plain hem and a casing for the rod just as for plain tailored curtains. There is also a tape with loops that will slide over the rod. Loops of braid or tape can be stitched to the top of the curtain at intervals.

Pleater tape and special hooks are also available for café curtains. This tape for short curtains is not quite as deep as that used for long curtains and draperies.

Some pleater tape also comes in a scalloped design. With this one must allow for side hems

Fig. 28.5

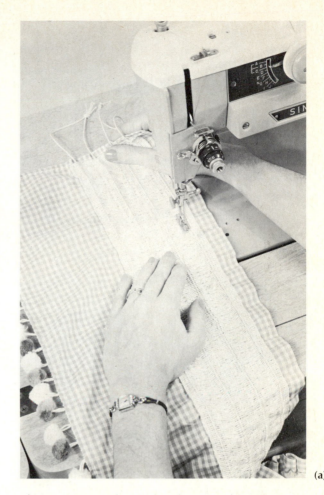

(a)

Shirring tape may be used at the tops of curtains, draperies, or valances. *(Courtesy of Conso Products, Inc.)*

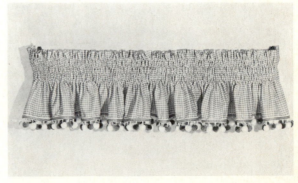

(b)

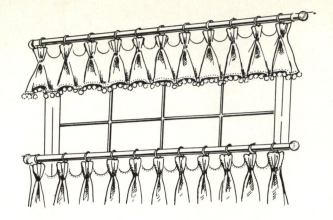

Fig. 28.6

Shirring tape and scalloped pleater tape may be used for a variety of effects. *(Courtesy of Conso Products, Inc.)*

Fig. 28.7

Draperies and café curtains trimmed with braid lend an elegant touch to this window treatment. *(Courtesy of Conso Products, Inc.)*

and stitch the right side of the tape to the right side of the curtain. The top edge should be trimmed close to the line of stitching, and the tape should be turned to the wrong side. When the hems are finished, the lower edge of the tape should be stitched to the curtain, and hooks should be inserted to make pleats between the scallops.

Café curtains are often plain, but a simple trimming frequently adds an interesting touch. Tucks, ruffles, decorative stitching, braid, fringe, or appliqué might be used.

Lined Draperies

Drapery fabrics will usually hang better at the windows if they are lined. Cotton sateen is the popular choice for drapery linings because it lends body without being too stiff. Other fabrics that have a coating of metallic powder are also used, and they act as insulators. For a large picture window that gets a lot of sun these treated fabrics should be investigated. They will make the room cooler in the summer and warmer in the winter.

It is not difficult to line draperies. One makes the drapery panel the desired width by seaming together the required number of panels. The lining should be about three inches narrower and about one inch shorter than the drapery panel. The hems are then turned on the lower edges. With the top edges even and the right sides of the two fabrics together, the two pieces should be seamed together. The panels should

A new press-on fringe adds a smart decorative finish to the window treatment shown. *(Courtesy of Window Shade Manufacturers Association)*

Fig. 28.8

then be turned right side out and pressed along the lengthwise edges so that the drapery fabric folds over to form a hem on each side.

If the depth of the hem at the lower edge has not been determined, the side seams may be left free at the bottom and the hems on the drapery fabric and on the lining may be turned after the side edges have been seamed. The lining should be slip-stitched to the drapery at the lower end after the bottom hems are turned.

At the top edge, the lining should be stitched to the drapery fabric after they have been turned right side out and pressed. Then one turns under one-half inch along the top edge, presses the crease, and applies pleater tape as it is applied for unlined draperies.

Sewing for the Home

For both functional and decorative reasons, slipcovers play a major role in furnishing a home. They protect upholstered pieces, they are easy to keep clean, and they provide a variety of effects. Some people use slipcovers all year round, with one set for winter and another for summer. Others prefer to cover the upholstered pieces only at certain times of the year.

Actually, slipcovers are not difficult to make, but they do require time, patience, and accuracy. With some experience in clothing construction, one can make beautiful covers for any type of chair. Of course, the techniques for cutting and fitting slipcovers are quite different from those used in making clothes. Here we shall present a few of the basic techniques. The extension service in your state will probably have some pamphlets that will be helpful.

Because the first slipcover will be a new experience, it is wise to keep the project as simple as possible so that the results will be letter perfect. The beginner should note the following suggestions.

1. Choose a simple, basic chair with straight lines, if possible.
2. Select a fabric in a solid color or one with a very small all-over pattern. Large motifs, stripes, plaids, and so on must be either placed in a special way or matched.
3. If possible, work first with an old sheet or inexpensive muslin. Using the test pieces as a pattern will increase confidence in cutting the fabric.

Study the Chair

Furniture varies so much in design that one must plan a cover that will fit well and enhance the contours of the chair. In general the seams of the slipcover will follow the basic lines of the chair, but at the back and the sides of the seat, the cover must be tucked down into the crevices to be held in place. It will therefore have to be larger in this area than the chair itself.

Fig. 28.9

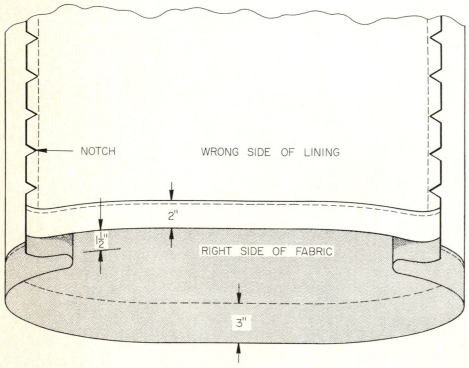

Cut lining narrower and shorter than drapery material.

NOTCH   WRONG SIDE OF LINING

2"

$\frac{1}{2}$"

RIGHT SIDE OF FABRIC

3"

Yardage Chart for Slipcovers*

Table
28.1

Type	Cushions	48" Wide Fabric		36" Wide Fabric		Welting or Trimming (Feet)
		Plain (Feet)	Figured or Striped (Feet)	Plain (Feet)	Figured or Striped (Feet)	
Sofa	2–3	14	15½	21	23	36
6–7 ft.	1 LC	13½	15	20½	22½	33
	0	10	11	15	17	21
3-ft. sectional						
1 arm	1	6½	7½	12	12½	25
no arm	1	5	6	11	11½	20
4-ft. sectional						
1 arm	1	9½	10	13	13½	28
no arm	1	8	9	12	12½	22
5-ft. sectional						
1 arm	1	10½	10½	14	14½	31
no arm	1	9	9	13	13½	24
Sofa bed	2	14½	16	20	21	40
Love seat	2	10½	12	15	16½	24
	1	10½	11	15	16½	23
	0	8½	9½	13	14½	14
Arm, club, lounge,	1	7½	8¼	11¼	12¼	18
and Cogswell	0	6½	7	8½	9½	13
Fanback, wing,	1	8	8½	12	13½	18
and barrel	0	7	7½	10	11	13
Boudoir	1	5	6½	8	9	15
	0	4½	5½	6½	7½	12
Chaise longue	2	11½	12½	16	17	23
	1	10½	11	13	14	20
	0	8	9	12	13¼	16
Ottoman	0	2	2½	3	3½	6
Cushion	1	1¼	1¾	2	2¼	5

*With 54-inch goods, yardage should be reduced 10 per cent for solids and 5 per cent for prints. If the repeat is over 24 inches, the salesperson should be consulted for yardage. (Courtesy of Conso Products, Inc.)

Plan the Cover

How should the lower edge of the chair look? Most slipcovers have a flounce that may be pleated at the corners, pleated all around, or gathered. However, the chair to be covered may be more attractive if the lower edges of the cover are carried under the chair, giving it an upholstered look.

An opening must be provided either at the side seam or at the center back so that the slipcover can be easily removed and replaced. A zipper or snap tape is usually used for the closure. The cover for a separate cushion will have an opening along the back, and possibly it will extend a few inches along the sides to allow for easy removal.

Smooth each section into position. Allow for generous seams and tuck-ins.

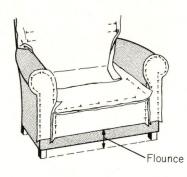

Flounce

Fig. 28.10

The exposed seams of slipcovers are usually reinforced with a welting or some form of trimming, such as fringe. Cable cord can be bought and covered with bias strips of fabric, or welting may be bought ready made in a solid color that blends with the fabric.

Prepare the Fabric

One must be sure the fabric has a true grain line before cutting it. Ends can be straightened by pulling a crosswise thread, always working with the lengthwise thread perpendicular to the floor. Grain line is just as important for the proper appearance of slipcovers as it is in garments.

Cut the Fabric

First the length of fabric needed for each major area of the chair should be measured, allowing for at least one-inch seams wherever sections must be joined and for a generous tuck-in at the back and sides of the seat. A minimum of five inches on each piece is recommended, but a more generous allowance is sometimes advisable to provide for a better fit.

If there is to be some sort of a flounce at the lower edge of the slipcover, a tape or a cord should be pinned around the chair to mark a line for it. A depth of about eight inches is usually attractive for a plain or a pleated flounce; one with gathers might be slightly deeper.

Fit Each Section

While the fabric is held wrong side out, each piece should be smoothed in position. The lengthwise grain line must be kept perpendicular to the floor and the crosswise grain line parallel to the floor. A bit of care here will make the sewing much easier and will also yield better results.

Each piece should now be placed in position on the chair. Whenever possible, pins should be placed exactly at the seam line, and the seam line of one piece should be matched to another. One should pat and smooth the fabric while working, and trim the fabric, allowing for generous one-inch seams.

A few tricky points require special care. Where the inside arm section joins the back section, there is usually a curved seam that must fit smoothly on the arm of the chair. It tapers outward to form the tuck-in at the base of the seat. The seam line should be pinned and the fabric trimmed. Making notches in the seam allowance will make it easier to manipulate the fabric in this area.

The tuck-in allowance at the seat will taper off toward the front on most chairs. Then the seam line must exactly meet the front armpanel. Some chairs or sofas have rounded contours or T-shaped cushions that require different fitting.

When fitting the fabric over a rounded edge, one must make notches in the seam allowance and distribute the fullness with either gathers or darts.

Mark Seam Lines

Using a colored pencil or chalk to mark all seam lines, one should make definite marks that will not rub off during work with the different sections of fabric.

Stitch the Seams

The seams of the tuck-in allowance will not have any cording or trimming. These seams should be joined first, and should be trimmed and pressed as the project continues.

For other seams it is easier to stitch the welting or trimming to the right side of one section of fabric before joining the seam. It is best to baste it in position, completing one section before attempting to join it to another. On the back seam left free for the opening, the welting should be applied along one edge so that the finished effect will be consistent with the other seams.

Fit sections to the chair. Pin and mark seam lines.

Fig. 28.11

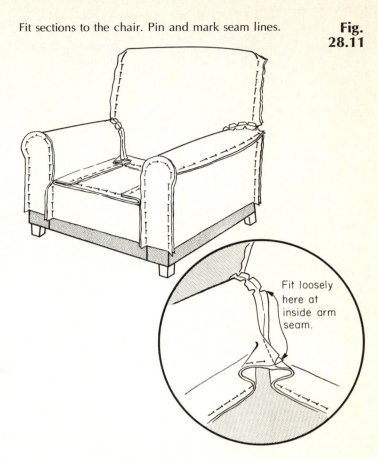

Fit loosely here at inside arm seam.

Keep fabric smooth over rounded parts with gathers or darts.

Fig. 28.12

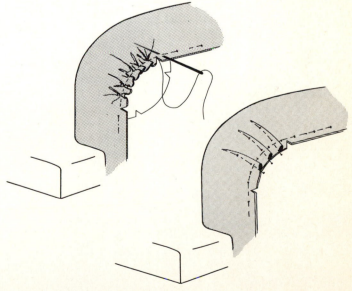

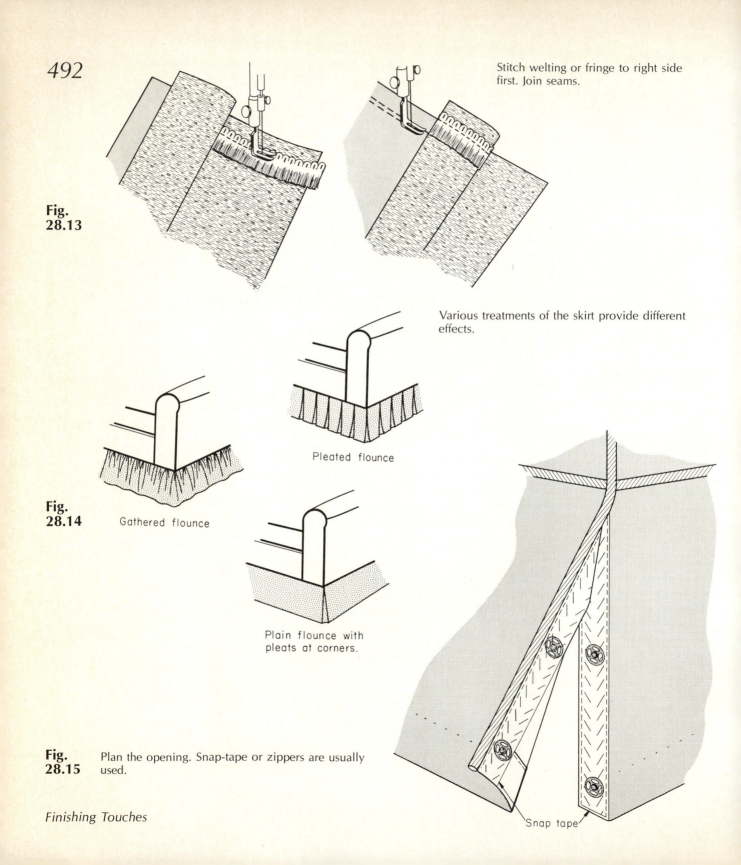

492

Stitch welting or fringe to right side first. Join seams.

Fig. 28.13

Various treatments of the skirt provide different effects.

Gathered flounce

Pleated flounce

Plain flounce with pleats at corners.

Fig. 28.14

Fig. 28.15 Plan the opening. Snap-tape or zippers are usually used.

Snap tape

Finishing Touches

Make the Skirt or Flounce

The sections of fabric that will form the skirt should be joined with plain seams, and the lower edge should be hemmed. A hem of about one or one-and-a-half inches is usually attractive. The skirt should now be pleated or gathered as planned. A kick-pleat at each corner of the chair should have an allowance of at least eight inches. The skirt should be joined to the chair cover with a reinforced seam similar to the other seams. This seam should begin and end at the line of the opening so that the zipper or snap tape may extend to the lower edge of the cover.

Finish the Opening

The raw edges can now be turned under along the lines of the opening. The two finished edges should meet along the seam line. The zipper or the tape can now be stitched into position.

Cover the Cushion

The cushion should be placed on a double thickness of fabric and the outline marked with chalk. One-inch seams should be allowed in cutting the sections for the top and the bottom. Bands should then be cut for boxing the cushion. The band that extends along the front and sides of the cushion should be cut the depth of the cushion plus two inches for seams. Four inches should be added to the length for finishing ends. Some opening along the back band must be provided so that the cover may be removed easily. One method of doing this is to cut

Fig. 28.16

Cover the cushion. The opening should be long enough to allow for easy removal of the cover.

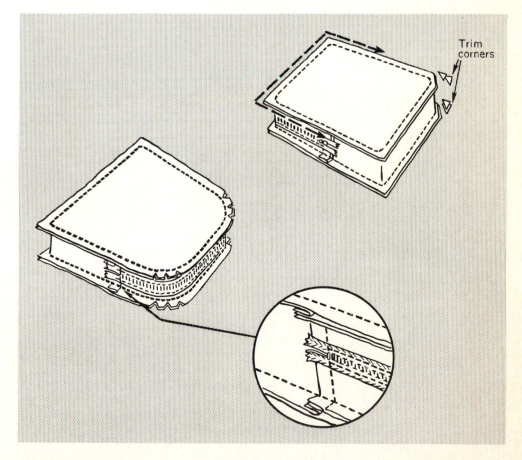

Trim corners

Fig. 28.17

The finished product should be trim and smooth.

section of fabric down the center and another length for the two side sections necessary to cover the surface of the bed. A pleasing proportion should be planned for these sections, even if the fabric must be cut narrower for the center section. For example, if the bed is fifty-four inches wide and a fifty-inch fabric is being used, the center section might be cut thirty-four to thirty-eight inches wide. Some fabric may be wasted, but very narrow strips on either side of the fifty-inch width would not provide pleasing proportions.

Some decorative finish may be used, such as cording, piping, braid, or bands of fabric for the seams. Lace insertions or French seams turned to the outside may also be used. With a striped fabric, one might cut the middle section short and plan a border with mitered corners.

There are various ways of treating the pillows on the bed. The spread can be cut long enough to cover them and tuck in under the pillow edges, or a separate pillow cover can be made to match the spread.

Flounces

The skirt or flounce of the spread is usually attached to the top section with decorative seams. Welting, fringe, or French seams can be used. The flounce may be straight, pleated, gathered, or circular.

Pleated skirt. The fabric is cut on the crosswise grain. The measurement for the depth of the skirt must allow for seams and a hem at the lower edge. Enough strips should be joined to give ample fullness. After the lower edge of the skirt is hemmed, the sewing machine's ruffler attachment can be used to pleat the top edge, or box pleats can be folded with the use of a gauge to keep the pleats uniform and evenly spaced. There should be a pleat at each corner of the bed. This is a pretty effect but it does require patience and arithmetic.

Gathered skirt. The fabric is cut on the crosswise grain with allowance for hems and seams. At least twice the finished measurement of the bed is needed for sufficient fullness. Hem the

two bands the length of the back edge, keeping each band the same width as the front band. Each one should be folded lengthwise and pinned along the fold. One band should be sewn to the cushion top and the other band to the cushion bottom along the back edge. The zipper is then inserted between the folded edges and the under ends of the front band are turned under one inch. These ends should overlap the ends of the back bands. The band should then be seamed to top and the bottom of the cover, as shown in Figure 28.16.

The finished cover should fit smoothly and follow the lines of the chair.

Bedspreads

It is possible to make lovely coordinated ensembles for the bedroom with curtains, bedspreads, and a dressing-table skirt. Closet accessories that go with the bedroom decoration lend a real custom-made touch.

Plan the Spread

Because the fabric used will probably be either thirty-six inches or fifty inches wide, some seams on part of the spread that goes on the surface of the bed may be necessary, such as one

A small room looks more spacious when it is decorated in white. In this teenage girl's bed-sitting room, café curtains, daybed cover, and cushions are fashioned of white cotton corduroy, trimmed with gold and white braid. Walls are pale yellow. Although the room is light and bright, everything in it can be easily washed or wiped clean. *(Courtesy of The Singer Company)*

Fig. 28.18

lower edge. The sewing machine's gathering foot or ruffler attachment should be used on the top edge.

Two-Piece Spreads

The unique attractiveness of a two-piece spread is that the lower section, or dust ruffle, stays on the bed. The top section, or coverlet, covers only the mattress and extends over the dust ruffle about two or three inches. The two parts may match, but often they are made to contrast with each other.

First a pleated or gathered flounce is made for the dust ruffle. There are several ways of attaching it to the bed. One may use preshrunk muslin or cut an old sheet to fit the top of the box spring and seam the dust ruffle to the edge of this piece. One may also fasten the ruffle to the box spring with snap tape, attaching one side of the tape to the spring and the other side to the inside of the dust ruffle.

Dressing Tables

Almost any ordinary small table or even a simple shelf can be converted into an attractive vanity with a few yards of fabric. It can be as tailored or as frilly as desired, but it should add an interesting note to the decoration of the room. The top of the table should be covered with mirror, glass, or a plastic that will not be marred by perfume and cosmetics.

On a plain table or shelf that has no drawers, one might cut a piece of fabric to fit the top, and seam a flounce, or even a simple ruffle, to the

Fig.
28.19

A simple dressing table can become a center of interest in a small area. *(Courtesy of The Singer Company)*

edges. Also, snap-on tape can be used to hold the skirt in place. One side is tacked to the table and the other side is sewed to the inside of the skirt.

A regular vanity table usually has drawers and swing-out arms, so the skirt must be made with a center front opening. One can use either snap-on tape to attach the skirt as already suggested or stitch a plain strip of tape inside the top edge of the skirt and tack it to the table.

The top of the skirt can be pleated or gathered. The ruffler or the gathering foot may be used to stitch a firm cotton tape to the inside.

Shirring tape also provides an attractive heading. The cords at the back of the skirt should be pulled but not cut off. If they are rolled and then tacked to the bottom of the table, the fabric can be drawn out flat when it is laundered.

A bench or stool that matches the table will emphasize the pretty effect.

Bathroom Decoration

Plastic film is available in widths up to seventy-two inches and in some very attractive colors and designs. However, other fabrics are frequently used for decorating bathrooms, and can be used with plastic under-curtains for the shower.

The window curtains might be tailored, tiered, café, or ruffled. If plastic film is used, the edges of ruffles can be pinked instead of hemmed because there is no danger of fraying. Curtains can also be trimmed with braid, tape, or fringe.

Shower curtains should be made with ample length and fullness. If the shower is over a tub, the curtain should extend at least eight inches

Fig.
28.20

Fabric and trimming add a decorative note to an ordinary bathroom. *(Courtesy of Conso Publishing Company)*

below the top of the tub. Narrow felled seams should be used to join panels of fabric if the curtain requires more than one panel.

One-inch side hems are made first. The top hem can be finished with a special tape made with eyelets, or with metal eyelets that can be bought and are easily applied.

If the shower curtain will hang inside the tub the bottom hem should be turned to the *outside* of the curtain so that water running down the curtain does not catch in the hem. A two- or three-inch hem is usually sufficient.

A vanity shelf or table in a bathroom is also useful, and it can be made quite attractive with trimming that blends with the other bathroom decorations.

Decorating with Sheets

Sheets are an inexpensive fabric source for sewing projects. They are very versatile; they come in a wide range of colors and patterns; and they are usually less expensive than most yard goods. Another advantage of sheets is that they are available in large widths, which reduces the amount of fabric needed. However, they will fade easily and should not be used in direct sunlight. Therefore, sheets do not represent a long-term decorating investment. Some suggestions follow for using sheets or other decorative fabrics to decorate your home.[1]

About Sheet Sizes

Today's decorator sheets have two different hem styles. One is a separate attached hem, usually in contrasting color or design. The other is the traditional self hem (turned under). The length before hemming is slightly different, depending on hem type. Of course, it is easy and economical to incorporate the hems into projects whenever possible.

You may wish to refer to the following charts of sizes *before hemming* when planning your decorating projects with sheets.

[1] The following pages on sewing with sheets have been adapted from a booklet by Judy Lindahl, *Fieldcrest Decorating Digest* (New York: Fieldcrest Mills Inc. 1975), pp. 5–26, 41–58. Courtesy of Fieldcrest.

Flat Sheet Size	Approx. Yardage in		
	36"	45"	58" Fabric
Twin	5	4	$3^1/8$
Full (Double)	6	$4^3/4$	$3^7/8$
Queen	7	$5^7/8$	$4^1/2$
King	$8^3/4$	7	$5^3/8$

Flat Sheet Size	Attached Hem (Separate)	Self Hem (Turned Under)
Twin	66" × 94"	66" × 104"
Full (Double)	81" × 94"	81" × 104"
Queen	90" × 100"	90" × 110"
King	108" × 100"	108" × 110"

Fitted Sheets	Mattress Size
Twin	39" × 75"
Full (Double)	54" × 75"
Queen	60" × 80"
King	72" × 84"

NOTE: If seams are let out on all four corners, this allows an additional 8 or 9 inches on each side.

Dust Ruffles

You will need one fitted sheet* (to form the sheets indicated on the chart on page 499. Amounts are figured for 18" or 24" strips, which include a 1" top seam, 1" for turnback, and 2" bottom hem. If your bed requires slightly more or less, make a narrower or deeper hem to adjust for the difference. To determine width of strip you need, measure from top of your box spring to the floor. Add 4".

* If you prefer you may cut a flat sheet the same size as the top of the box spring and use this as the base.

Double fullness allows for:

1. Gathered ruffle, or
2. Box pleated ruffle with $2^1/2$" deep pleats 10" apart.

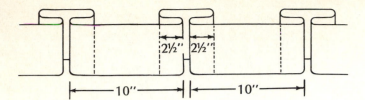

Fig. 28.21

Triple fullness "plus" allows for:

1. *Full* gathered ruffle, or
2. Box pleated ruffle with 2½" deep pleats 5" apart.

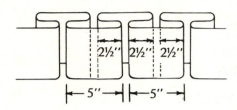

Fig. 28.22

To assemble dust ruffle:

1. Measure from top of spring to floor. Add 1" for top hem, 1" for turnback, and 2" for bottom hem. Compare measurements to 18" or 24" strips on chart. Adjust if necessary.
2. Cut strips from sheets. Seam strips with ½" seams. Make a narrow hem at each end of the strip. For gathered ruffle, run two rows of basting stitches along top edge. Make one row 1" from raw edge, and the other ¾" from raw edge.
3. Turn up a 1" double hem on bottom edge. Stitch.
4. Place fitted sheet on box spring. It may be necessary to open corners at head of the bed to get sheet to fit. (Add ties at open corners to attach sheet firmly to bed if needed.) Be sure sheet fits snugly and smoothly.
5. Draw up gathering threads. Pin ruffle to sheet, right sides together, side hems at head of bed, edge of ruffle even with edge of spring. Remove sheet and ruffle and stitch ruffle in place, 1" from raw edge.
6. Flip ruffle over into position, stitch again next to seam to hold gathers in place.

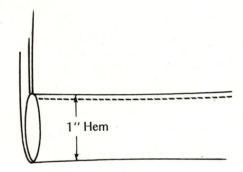

Fig. 28.23

NOTE: If you are making a pleated "ruffle," start at center bottom and pin pleats in place working around to the head of the bed. Stitch as above.

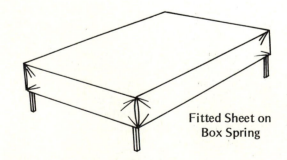

Fitted Sheet on Box Spring

Fig. 28.24

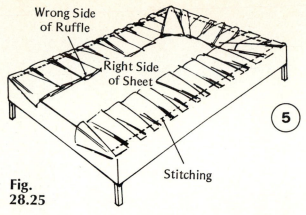

Wrong Side of Ruffle
Right Side of Sheet
Stitching

Fig. 28.25

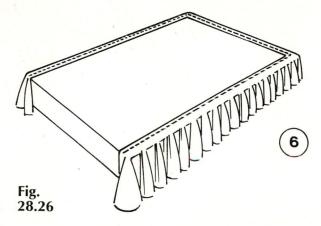

Fig. 28.26

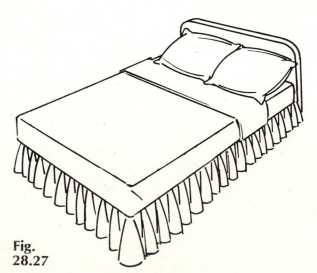

Fig. 28.27

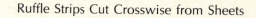

Ruffle Strips Cut Crosswise from Sheets

⑤

| | Double Fullness | |
	18" Strips	24" Strips
Twin	1 Full	1 King
Full (Double)	1 Queen	1 King
Queen	1 Queen	*2 Twin
King	1 Queen	*1 Twin, 1 Full
	**1 King	

| | Triple "plus" Fullness | |
	18" Strips	24" Strips
Twin	2 Twin	1 Full, 1 Queen
Full (Double)	2 Twin	*2 Full
Queen	2 Twin	1 Twin, 1 King
King	1 Twin, 1 Full	*1 Full, 1 King

Ruffle Strips Cut Lengthwise from Sheets

⑥

| | Double Fullness | |
	18" Strips	24" Strips
Twin	1 Full	1 King
Full (Double)	1 Full	2 Twin
	**1 Full, 1 Queen	**1 Twin, 1 Full
Queen	1 Queen	1 Twin, 1 Full
		**2 Full
King	1 Queen	1 Twin, 1 Full
		**2 Full

| | Triple "plus" Fullness | |
	18" Strips	24" Strips
Twin	1 King	2 Full
Full (Double)	2 Twin	2 Full
	**1 Twin, 1 Full	**1 Full, 1 King
Queen	1 Twin, 1 Full	1 Full, 1 King
	**2 Full	
King	1 Twin, 1 Full	1 Queen, 1 King
	**2 Full	**2 King

*Use 23" strips for separate hem sheets, 24" for self-hem sheets.
**Use this amount for sheets which have separate (sewn-on) hems.

NOTE: Amounts allow for best use of sheets, but do NOT allow for pattern match. If sheets require definite match, additional yardage may be required.

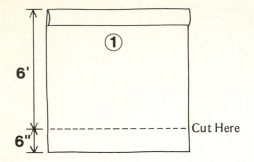

**Fig.
28.28**

Shower Curtains
    A twin flat sheet will make a shower curtain for most baths, and a king size sheet will make a whole bathroom-full of accessories.

    To assemble:

1. Use a twin flat sheet (or full sheet if longer curtain is needed). Leave the top hem in place. Measure 6 ft. along the side edge (selvage) of the sheet, plus 6″ for hem. Cut the sheet at this point. Use extra fabric for valance over tub, curtains, or pad it to make bath accessories (See Figure 28.28–1.)
2. Press in a double 3″ hem and stitch with sewing machine or by hand.
3. Apply grommets or large eyelets (available in fabric stores, or leather craft stores) *or* make machine buttonholes to coincide with eyelets on plastic curtain liner you hang behind.
4. Lay curtain and liner together. Put shower curtain hooks through both. Hang on shower curtain rod.

    NOTE: If you desire a stiffer top hem, open stitching at edges and slip a piece of stiff pellon or drapery header through. Anchor ends. Then apply grommets, which will help hold the stiffener in place.

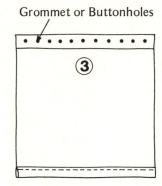

**Fig.
28.29**

The harem pillow is a favorite of decorators and perfect with the softer look in interiors. Best of all, they are simple to construct yourself from sheets, towels, or bedspreads. Try small ones for sofa throw pillows, or larger ones for creating your own sofa or extra floor seating. You'll love the easy care and durability of these easy-to-make pillows.

1. Cut out two squares or rectangles of fabric and sew a knife edge pillow, inserting a zipper in one side. Zipper must be at least 5" shorter than the seam so corners can be tied later (see Figure 28.30–1.)
2. Wrap and tie string securely around each corner about 2" in from the seams. Turn pillow right side out.
3. Sew a liner pillow from muslin or a plain sheet—making it an inch or two larger than the outer case. Because the liner is larger than the outside case, the pillow will be fatter and plumper. Do not tie corners. The corners of the liner will stuff into the shape of the outer pillow. Stuff the liner with shredded foam or polyester fiber fill (from fabric stores). Close liner. Insert in harem cover.

Fig. 28.30

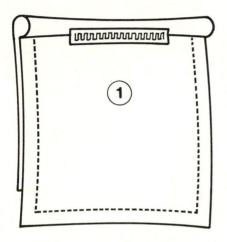

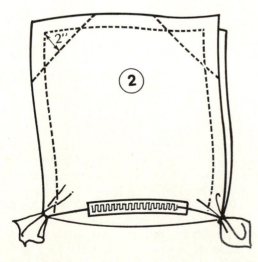

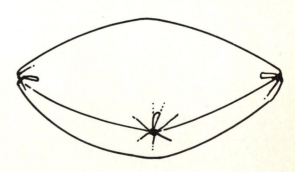

Fig. 28.31

Fabric Walls

Ever wondered just why so many people are busily covering walls with their favorite sheets? It's not *just* the pure beauty of a fabric-covered wall, though that is one of the best reasons. Sheets are economical because of their low price per yard, and the fabric is retrievable. You may leave the sheets on walls for years, then strip them off (re-use them in another way), and put up a new pattern. You need not make marks on the wall—if this is an important concern. Sheets can conceal color, texture, unevenness, even the poor condition of walls beneath.

Determining the number of sheets you need

1. Add the corner to corner measurements of the walls to be covered (see Figure 28.32).

   A. _____ inches
   B. _____ inches
   C. _____ inches
   D. _____ inches
   E. _____ Total inches needed

2. (E) total inches
   (F) width of sheet you are using
   (G) number of sheets needed* $F \overline{)E}^{\,G}$

   Add an extra sheet if the answer above is uneven.

   Example: 5 + 30" = 6 sheets

Fig. 28.32

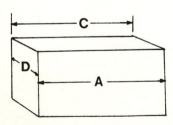

Determining sheet length

Measure ceiling
    to baseboard _____ inches
Add 3" for
    handling ease   3   inches
             _____ Panel length in inches**

    ***Match design before cutting (see Figure 28.32).*

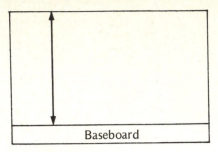

Baseboard

Fig. 28.33

Making a test sample. It is always advisable to make a test sample to determine which method will work best with your walls. Try the ones you are considering in an inconspicuous spot—in a closet, a hall, basement, low on the wall—wherever the wall surface is the same as the walls you will cover.

Two pieces of sheet, each approximately a foot square (or use a pillowcase), will help you test for how well the sheet conceals texture, covers old color or pattern, holds to the wall, resists shrinking or fading, conceals staples, etc.

Plan to include a seam or two in the test samples so you can check for ease of cutting, overlapping, or backtacking a seam.

Stapling. Stapling is the fastest way to put sheets on walls. If your walls are sheetrock, wood, or plaster that will accept staples readily, consider this method. Stapling also conceals a moderate amount of texture and unevenness in wall surface. (Remember a coat of paint will fill staple holes—so fabric now, paint later!)

1. Start by cutting panels the height of the wall plus 3" for handling ease. The extra at top and bottom will either be turned under as you go, or trimmed off later. If you desire, leave a contrasting hem in place and it will act as a border at the top of the wall.
2. Establish a plumb line as a guide for keeping the edge of the sheet straight. Attach a string to a plumb bob or heavy object such as a pair of scissors. Rub the cord with chalk and attach it to the top of the wall along the edge of

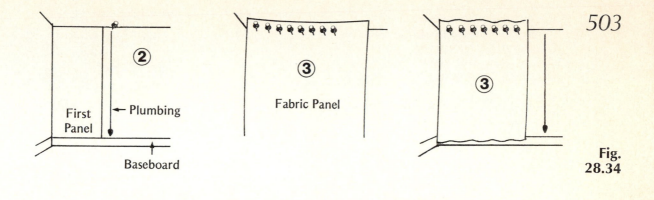

Fig.
28.34

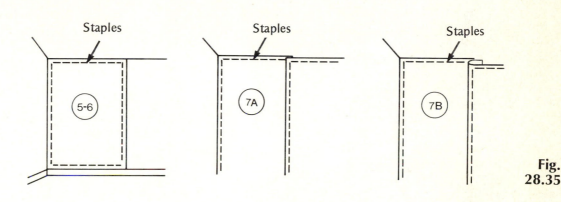

Fig.
28.35

the first panel. Hold the weight at the base-board and snap the line against the wall. The vertical mark is your guide. (You do not have to chalk the string, but it is helpful to do so. You may just hang the line along the panel and leave it as you work.)

3. Push pins hold the fabric in place while you get it straight, and as you apply it to the wall. A strip of double-face tape may work if walls are too hard for push pins. (When you work alone with starch or paste methods, it helps to move the pins down the wall as you work. Keeps the fabric from coming down on your head if you tug too hard on occasion.)

4. Staple at top every 2″ to 3″ close to ceiling, leaving the excess to be trimmed.

5. When fabric is secure, pull at bottom opposite each staple at top, keeping fabric taut and smooth, but not overstretched.

6. Staple one side, then the other.

7. Push pin and overlap the next panel flat (A), or with edge folded under (B), staple seam. Staple top, bottom, and side. Continue with succeeding panels.

8. Cut off excess at ceiling and floor with a sharp razor blade and a metal edge ruler as a guide.

9. Edges and seams may be covered with braid trim, moldings, or wood strips if desired.

HINT: Painting staples the background color of the sheets before loading them in gun may make them inconspicuous so that there is no need to cover them.

504   *Concealing Seams—Backtacking.*   If you wish to keep all staples in seams concealed, use this technique. It gives professional results, easily. It is neat, fast, and economical since you do not need trim or molding to cover seams.

1. The first sheet is applied the same as in the previous directions (steps 1 through 6) above.
2. The second panel is positioned *face down* on the first panel. (Be sure to match pattern.)
3. To make a firm edge that will distribute tension evenly, place a piece of upholsterer's tape (see glossary) or plastic package strapping tape along the seam and staple it in place.
4. Pull the panel back against the edge of the upholsterer's tape and staple it in place.
5. Continue to backtack the panels as you work your way around the room.
6. At the last edge fold the fabric over a piece of upholsterer's tape and fasten the edge up snugly to the wall by pounding ³/₄″ wire brads (see glossary) in place.

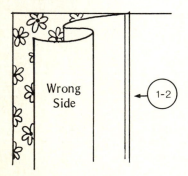

Fig. 28.36

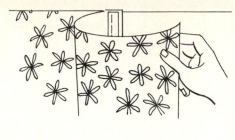

Fig. 28.37

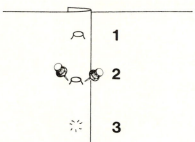

Fig. 28.38

7. If brads are not noticeable, pound them flat. If they show, you can conceal them: (1) Pound them down until about ¹/₁₆″ is exposed. (2) Take a couple of pins and lift and pick at the threads until they open and "swallow" the brad. (3) Pound the brad down flat.

Furring Strips.   Furring strips are thin wood strips that can be purchased at lumber yards; or you can cut a board into thin strips (¹/₄″ thick) on a table saw. They are used as a "buffer" so fabric can be stretched and stapled to them, thus allowing rough or uneven walls to be covered. They can also be attached to hard plaster or concrete walls (with nails or paneling adhesive).

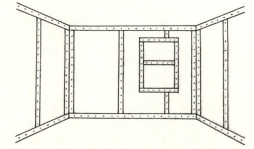

Fig. 28.39

Starching. Some people prefer cellulose wallpaper paste or vinyl wallpaper paste, but *starching* is an excellent way to apply sheets directly to walls if the wall is nearly smooth and can tolerate moisture. Perhaps the biggest advantage is that it can be peeled off the wall, when you want to remove it. The starch can be washed out of the sheets, which can be reused. One half gallon of liquid starch will often do a whole wall. Latex, enamel, paneling, glass, plastic, tile, wood, smooth concrete, and metal can all be starched. Try a test sample.

Read the label to see if the starch contains a mildew inhibitor, especially if you plan to put sheets in a bath or other potentially damp area. If it does not, the addition of a small amount of disinfectant would be wise, or you can purchase a product from wallpaper stores that will do the job. Some brands of liquid starch contain salt, which can cause pitting of scissors, razor blades and metals if the starch is not rinsed off occasionally as you work. (Take care near hinges, door stops, metal trim near formica, etc.)

Read the following directions carefully, all the way through before you start.

1. Wash the wall if it is very soiled or to remove greasy film.
2. Cut panels the desired length plus 1½″ on the top and the bottom. Be sure to match the design before you cut each panel. (Trim off the firmly woven portion of the selvage if it has been pulled or distorted in the printing process.)
3. Determine placement of first panel; establish a plumb line. Protect floor with plastic. Note: It is a good idea to plumb each panel.
4. Pour starch into a pan (use undiluted from bottle). Dip sponge in to saturate with starch, then apply liberally to the wall for the first few feet.
5. Smooth fabric into place at the top of the wall, leaving about 1″ to be trimmed later. Use push pins to hold fabric temporarily as you work your way down the panel, adding starch underneath by lifting the panel when needed.

6. Now apply starch to the top of the sheet panel, brushing and smoothing the fabric in place to remove bubbles and wrinkles. Be sure the starch penetrates the sheet evenly. This step creates a smooth application and soil-resistant finish. Do not be surprised if some bubbles are evident when the sheet has dried. Simply soak them with starch and smooth them out.
7. Work your way down the panel, continuing to sponge starch on the wall, smoothing the sheet, and applying more starch.

505

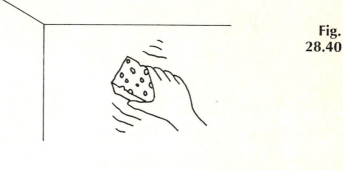

Fig. 28.40

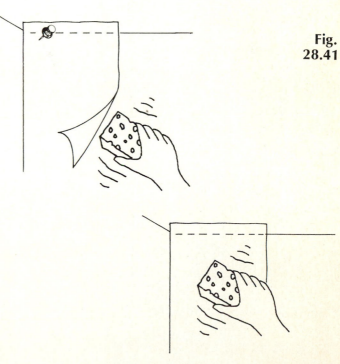

Fig. 28.41

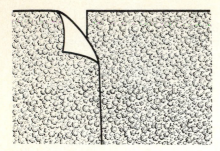

Fig. 28.42

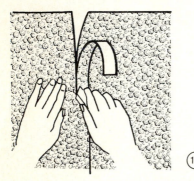

Fig. 28.43

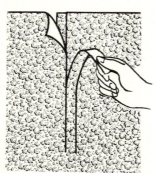

⑩

⑪

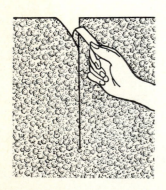

⑫

8. Position the second panel, matching the design. On most sheets you will be able to see through the top layer while it is wet, thus making it easier to align it with the design beneath. Smooth the overlap into place. You can leave seams overlapped if you prefer. It makes no marks on walls, although there will be a small ridge.

9. Or else, allow the seam to "set" about half an hour before cutting. This allows time for some shrinkage and relaxation. The seam must be cut while it is still damp and flexible, but there will be ample time. Meanwhile you can proceed with succeeding panels. (The "cut" seam is very smooth—a nice finish and technique.)

10. To cut the seam use a *sharp* single-edge razor blade. Discard blades as they dull to prevent "chewing" the fabric. Cut through the middle of the overlap with firm pressure. You must cut through both layers of sheet.

11. Peel off the top overlap strip of sheet and discard it.

12. Slightly lift the top layer, reach inside and gently peel out the underlap.

13. Smooth the cut edges together—applying a little starch if needed. If a little shrinkage occurs and edges separate a bit, apply a little more starch and push them back. If you can get them to dry together, they stay together.

14. Seams are cut while sheets are *damp*. However, the sheets should be cut at the floor, ceiling, and around doors and windows when it has *dried completely*. It will then cut clean—like paper. Any shrinkage will have occurred before you cut.

15. Continue with succeeding panels. It is easier to wipe up excess starch from ceiling, baseboards, or window frames as you go—before it dries.

Removing sheets. When you decide to remove the sheets from a wall, if you move or redecorate, peel one corner loose, then gently begin to peel the panel off. If the sheet is holding very snugly and you are concerned that it might pull some paint, just moisten it with a damp sponge and continue to peel it loose. When the sheeting is damp, it will strip smoothly and evenly.

Shirring. Shirred sheets will create the most elegant look of all. They are the most concealing, too. Architectural faults, color, and texture will all disappear beneath the sumptuous folds. Sheets need not be seamed; the edges can easily be hidden in the gathers.

Measuring
Number of Sheets:
1. (Width of wall)″ × (Fullness desired)*

$$= \frac{\rule{5cm}{0.4pt}}{\text{Total Width}}''$$

  *2x is fairly standard, many prefer 2½x, 3x is quite full
2. (Total width)″ ÷ (Width of sheet)
   = _____ No. of sheets
                    needed

Length of sheet panels
  Floor to ceiling
    measurement   _____″
  Allowance for top and
    bottom hems   + 6″
  Take-up when rods are
    inserted in casings   + 1
                         _____″ Sheet
                                  Panel
                                  Length

  NOTE: *Utilize sheet hems where possible to save time and effort.*

Preparing Sheets
1. Turn hem edge over 3″. Press. Turn raw edge under ½″ and machine stitch hem in place. Run another row of stitches across the panel 1½″ from fold.
2. Repeat at bottom hem.
   Installation.   Café curtain brackets and rods are installed at intervals 1½″ down from ceiling and 1½″ up from floor. Sheet panels are shirred onto rods. Hang rods in brackets and adjust the gathers for evenness. Cup hooks and dowels or rods may be used as above. (It is a more economical method.)
   Or else, measure and cut same as for above method, except fold under ¾″, thus making a ¾″ casing. Run cord through casing. Nail cord to wall. Nail cord firmly to opposite wall. Sheets can be stapled directly to the wall at intervals after gathers are distributed evenly.

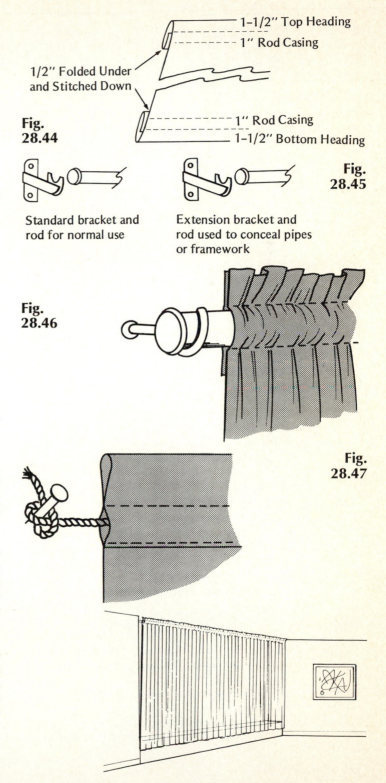

Fig. 28.44
1–1/2″ Top Heading
1″ Rod Casing
1/2″ Folded Under and Stitched Down
1″ Rod Casing
1–1/2″ Bottom Heading

Fig. 28.45
Standard bracket and rod for normal use
Extension bracket and rod used to conceal pipes or framework

Fig. 28.46

Fig. 28.47

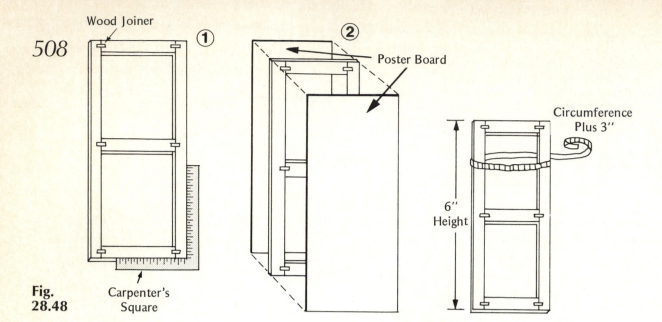

Fig. 28.48

Wood Joiner

① ②

Poster Board

Circumference Plus 3″

6″ Height

Carpenter's Square

Folding Screens

Versatile folding screens are often overlooked as an important decorating tool. They can serve many functions, and will

- Add color and design to a room.
- Conceal storage.
- Screen off a view.
- Create a focal point.
- Serve as room dividers.

Framework

1. An economical screen can be made with 1″ × 2″ boards (available from lumber supply) which can be joined together with corrugated fasteners or Skotch wood joiners (see glossary).

   Use a carpenter's square to keep work straight, and add short strips for braces at intervals.

2. Add thin cardboard, upsom board (see glossary), or poster board by tacking or gluing to each side of framework. It gives a firm surface to work on, and prevents light from showing through.

3. Cut sheet or bedspread to fit screen panels as follows:

   Height—Height of panel + 6″
   Width—Circumference of panel + 3″

Wrapping the screen panels. Wrap the panels in the following manner: In step three above a cardboard strip ½″ wide (upholsterer's tape) is placed near raw edge of fabric. Fabric is wrapped around the strip, then stapled. Or use brads driving them in so heads go through fabric, but not through the cardboard. Or glue or fuse the last fold in place.

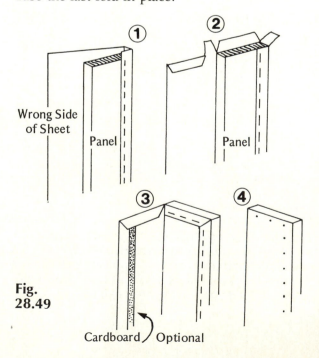

Wrong Side of Sheet

① ②

Panel Panel

③ ④

Cardboard / Optional

Fig. 28.49

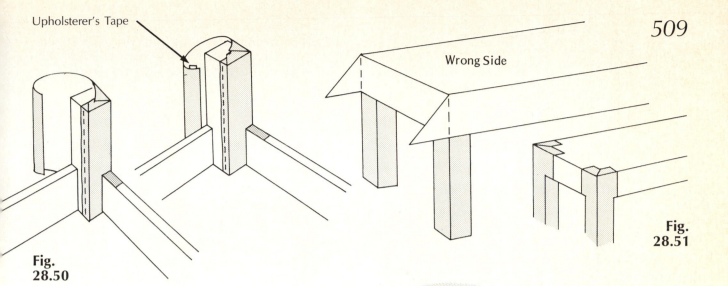

Upholsterer's Tape

Fig. 28.50

Wrong Side

Fig. 28.51

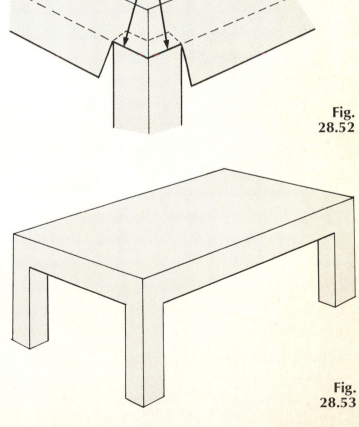

Fold

Fig. 28.52

Fig. 28.53

Parsons Table

Create a special impact by wrapping a table in your favorite sheet or bedspread. It takes less than two square yards for an 18″ × 18″ table.

For a custom touch, cover the table first with a layer of polyester fleece.

1. Cut fabric 10″ longer and wider than table top. Cut four strips for the legs to go around leg plus 3″, and length of leg plus 3″.
2. Starting at inside corner, wrap leg, clipping as needed where leg meets apron of table. Turn edge back over upholsterer's tape and tack with brads. Tack brads through fabric, but not through cardboard, or fuse edge in place with fusible webbing.
3. Place top on table wrong side up and pin darts at each corner so top fits over table like a slipcover. Stitch darts, cut away excess sheet and turn right side out.
4. Clip top piece where apron meets table legs, fold sheet under and tack or fuse underneath table.
5. For added protection for the table it is a good idea to have a piece of glass or plexiglass cut to fit the top. A light spraying with Scotch-guard will help resist soiling, and metal glides on the legs will keep sheet off the floor.

Sewing for the Home

Fig. 28.54

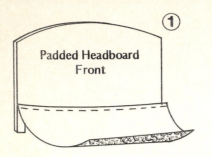

① Padded Headboard Front

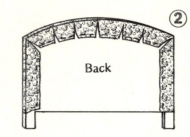

② Back

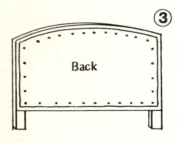

③ Back

Fig. 28.55

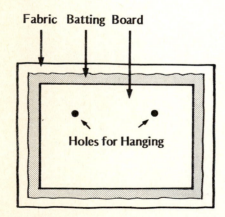

Fabric Batting Board

Holes for Hanging

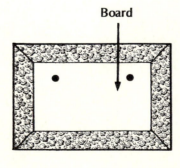

Board

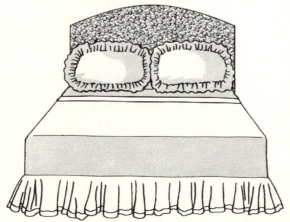

Headboard

Padded headboard. You can use your staple gun and turn a piece of plywood or an old headboard into a new decorator accessory.

1. Cover headboard with layers of polyester quilt batting or poly foam first. Then staple sheet along lower edge.
2. Pull sheet up and over headboard. Staple in place starting at center and working your way to the sides alternating back and forth and keeping sheet taut and grain straight.
3. Finish back with a piece of sheet or muslin tacked in place.

Hanging headboard. This headboard can be on the wall like a picture. Coordinate it with your sheets and comforter for a total look.

1. Cut a piece of ¹/₂″ thick plywood or upsom board in a square or rectangle to desired size. Both are available at lumber or building supply dealers. (See Figure 28.54–1.)
2. Cut three layers of quilt batting to fit the board. Allow additional 2″ on each edge.
3. Cut one layer of sheet to fit the board. Allow additional 3″ on each edge.
4. Place batting, then board on top of sheet. Staple batting in place. Then wrap sheet snugly around.
5. To hang, use picture hangers or drill two holes through the board *before wrapping*, and hang on two screws anchored to wall studs at head of bed.

Finishing Touches

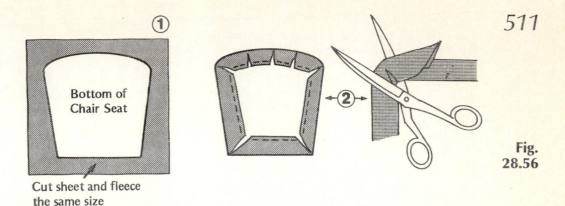

① Bottom of
Chair Seat

Cut sheet and fleece
the same size

②

**Fig.
28.56**

Chair Seats

Whether you cover the chair seats directly or make tie-on pillows, you can cover a whole set from just one sheet or bedspread. Towels are also perfect for this technique.

1. Measure depth and width of chair seat. Add 3″ all around. (See Figure 28.56–1.)
2. Staple polyester fleece (optional under towels) to seat first for opaquing and light padding. Clip to fit as needed and remove excess from corners. (See Figure 28.56–2.)
3. Wrap and staple fabric in place. Wrap ends first, then sides. Pull fabric snug at corners and staple. Do not cut excess from corners of fabric. (See Figure 28.57.)

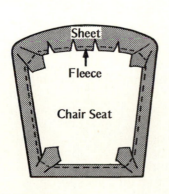

Sheet

Fleece

Chair Seat

**Fig.
28.57**

Planter Stand

Make a quick and easy plant stand using cardboard concrete forms called sono tubes. They can be located at concrete companies and building construction supply outlets. The tubes, which come in 4″ to 48″ diameters, are sold by the foot. There may be a nominal cutting charge to have them sawed to desired lengths. The 8″ and 10″ sizes are just right for planters.

Cut sono tube about 3 feet long, or any length you prefer. Cover it with the sheet by wrapping and stapling, or gluing. Add a plastic pot for a liner, and set your favorite fern or plant in place.

Try grouping several plant stands of various heights.

Fig. 28.58

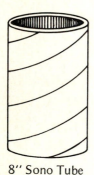

8″ Sono Tube

Glue or staple fabric to sono tube.

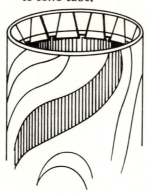

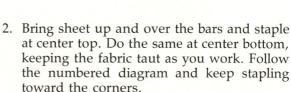

Stretcher Bar Art

Whether you frame a 5′ × 5′ sheet masterpiece or a 16″ × 24″ pillowcase picture, stretcher bars can help you bring "new art" into your home. These soft wood strips are available in pre-measured and premitered lengths from art supply or art needle departments. All you do is push them together to create your frame.

1. Cut sheet or pillowcase at least 2″ wider and longer on each side for wrapping. Lay the fabric face down on smooth surface and center the frame on top. Use push pins to hold the sheet while you check from the side to be sure everything is straight and centered.

2. Bring sheet up and over the bars and staple at center top. Do the same at center bottom, keeping the fabric taut as you work. Follow the numbered diagram and keep stapling toward the corners.

3. Finishing the corners is a two-step process. First smooth the fabric along the stretcher bar, then pull it into a mitered fold and staple it in place.

4. Pick up the remaining fabric and smooth it into a sharp corner, wrap it to the back side and staple it in place on top of the first step.

5. To "shadowproof" your work place a piece of plain sheeting underneath the top design. Cut both the same size. Wrap.

Fig. 28.59

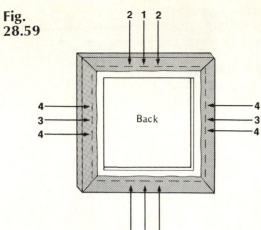

2 1 2

4 → 4
3 → Back 3
4 → 4

2 1 2

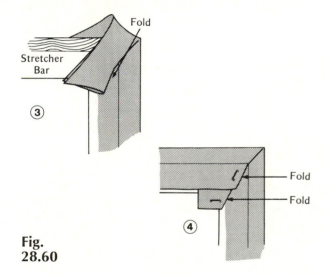

Fold

Stretcher Bar

③

Fold
Fold

④

Fig. 28.60

Fig. 28.61

Gathered Lampshade 513

Make a cover to slip over a lampshade, wastebasket, a flower pot, or plant stand made from a sono tube.

1. Measure the height of your shade, basket or pot. Add 4″. Measure circumference and multiply times 2. Cut a strip of sheet to these dimensions.
2. Seam the short ends together. Fold the raw edge under ⅛″. Turn the folded edge down ⅝″ to form casing. Stitch close to folded edge, leaving an opening to insert elastic. Repeat the bottom edge.
3. Cut ⅜″ elastic and run it through the casing, drawing it up so the cover fits the shade snugly. Cut off the excess elastic, sew ends together. Close the opening by stitching by machine or by hand.

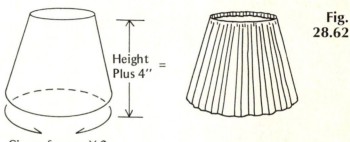

Height Plus 4″ =

Circumference × 2

Fig. 28.62

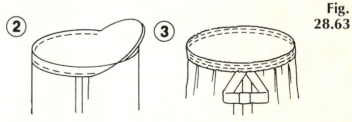

② ③

Fig. 28.63

Fig. 28.64

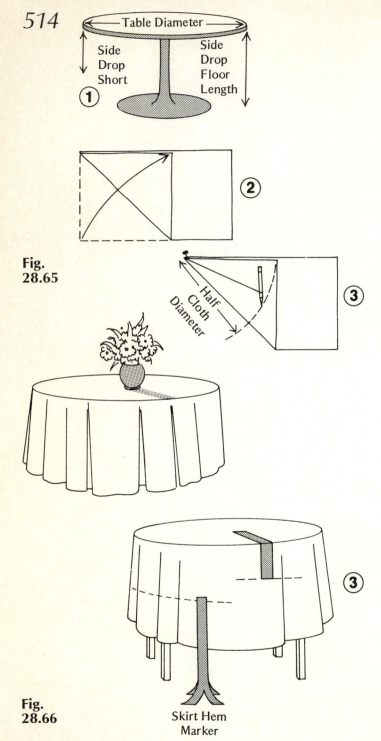

Fig. 28.65

Fig. 28.66

Skirt Hem Marker

Tablecloths and Placemats

A tablecloth without seams is easy and economical when you use your favorite sheets.

Round tablecloths

1. To determine size of cloth:

Diameter of table	=	_____''
Side drop × 2	=	_____''
Plus 1'' for hem	=	___1___''
Diameter of Cloth		_____''

2. Fold flat sheet in half lengthwise then fold crosswise to form a rectangle four layers thick. Fold once again as illustrated.
3. Cut nonstretchy cord to serve as a compass. Knot one end and pin with corsage pin to fabric. Tie a pencil to the other end. Length should be half of diameter of tablecloth plus 1/2''. Mark the outer edge of the cloth. Cut. Make a 1/2'' hem by machine or hand. Press cloth.

Sheets for Round Tablecloths

Diameter of Cloth (Add 1'' for hem)	Flat Sheet Required
Up to 65''	Twin
Up to 80''	Full (Double)
Up to 89''	Queen
Up to 99''	King (Separate hem)
Up to 107''	King (Self hem)

Oval tablecloths. Because oval tables vary a great deal in the shape and size of the oval, cloths must be cut to fit.

1. To mark hem, place cloth on table and weight with heavy objects to prevent shifting.
2. Mark a floor length cloth with chalk or pins 1/2'' from the floor.
3. For shorter overhang use a carpenter's square (see glossary), make a cardboard gauge, or use a skirt hem marker. Be sure to add 1'' to the gauge length for the hem.
4. Cut bottom edge. Hem by machine or hand.

NOTE: Floor-length cloths for large oval tables may require seaming.

Napkins. The extra fabric from the corners and edges can be quickly turned into a set of matching napkins. Cut fabric into squares 16″ × 16″ or preferred size. Press a ¼″ hem all around. Turn hem ¼″ more and stitch by machine or hand.

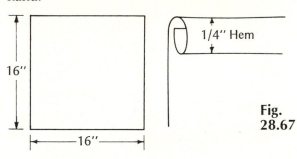

16″

16″

1/4″ Hem

Fig. 28.67

(a)

(b)

Fig. 28.68

(c)

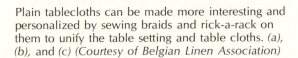

Plain tablecloths can be made more interesting and personalized by sewing braids and rick-a-rack on them to unify the table setting and table cloths. *(a), (b), and (c) (Courtesy of Belgian Linen Association)*

Sewing for the Home

Fig. 28.69 Sewing with fabric, trimmings, and towels adds a decorative note to ordinary bathrooms. *(Courtesy of Fieldcrest)*

Fig. 28.70

Sewing with sheets need not be dull. Here sheets are used to rig the mast and a matching blanket covers the deck of the boat-bed to give a young child's room a South Sea Island flavor. *(Courtesy of Window Shade Manufacturers Association)*

Fig. 28.71

Valance window treatment, fabric laminated shades, dust ruffle, comforter, bedside table, and walls all resplendent in the traditionally inspired design can be created by do-it-yourselfers with sheets. This bedroom boasts practical features in the washable sheeting, also treated with fabric protector. *(Carpet by Karastan, courtesy of Allied Chemical Corporation)*

Table
28.2

Bi-fold hinges These hinges flex in both directions. Use for folding screens, shutters, etc. Available in hardware stores.

Brad Short, sharp, fine nail with small head. Used for finishing edges, as at ends of walls, screens, table legs, etc. From hardware store.

Carpenter's square Metal L-shaped ruler. Used to determine if edges are "true" and for perfect 90° angles. Use to square up stretcher bars, folding screens, picture mats, roller shades, drapes, curtains, etc. From hardware store. Also available is rafter framing square.

Corrugated fastener (or wiggle tail) Small grooved metal strip. Used to form joints, as in screens and window frames, or to tighten loose joints. From hardware store.

Cup hook Round hook that screws into surface. Use for shirred walls, curtain tie-backs for draperies, etc. From hardware and kitchen hardware departments.

Decorator craft glue (Wilhold, Super Tacky) Dries faster than regular white glue, does not soak through as readily. Use for trims on roller shades or lampshades, picture frames, etc. Art supply or craft supply.

Furring strips Thin wood strips attached to wall when surface is rough or uneven. Fabric panels may then be attached to furring strips. From lumber supply.

Fusible webs (Stitch Witchery, Pellon Fusible Web) Heat-sensitive web of synthetic fibers. Placed between objects, heated with steam, pressure applied—they melt and fuse the materials together. Available in fabric stores by the yard in 18″ widths.

Grommets, eyelets Metal ring reinforcements used on shower curtains. Available at fabric stores, leather craft stores.

Hot iron cleaner (Clean and Glide, Bottoms Up) Takes off fusible web and burned-on fabric finish or starch. Fabric stores; notions department.

Plumb line A line attached to a weight. Line is rubbed with chalk, then snapped against the wall to mark true vertical.

Polyester fiberfill Loose fibers of polyester used for stuffing pillows, toys, etc. From fabric stores. Washable and cleanable.

Polyester fleece Washable, cleanable ⅛″ thick polyester. Use for padding and opaquing. By the yard in fabric stores.

Polyester quilt batting 1″ thick glazed ployester fibers. Keeps its shape when washed or cleaned. Available from fabric stores in twin, full, queen, and king sizes.

Skotch wood joiner Same uses as corrugated fasteners. These sharp-toothed clips hold two pieces of wood securely and are easy to pound into wood. Available at hardware stores.

Spray adhesive (SpraMent, P-77 from 3M) Aerosol glues found in art supply stores. Use with lots of ventilation, and put down plenty of newspapers to prevent spray from settling on furnishings.

Staple gun Shoots staples with force. Use to apply fabric to walls, screens, tables, etc. From hardware and some fabric stores. The lightweight "tacker" model is sufficient for most decorating projects.

Upholsterer's tape ½″ wide cardboard strips. Available in either single strips or rolls from upholstery supply. Use for finishing seams and final edge on walls, table legs, folding screens, etc.

Upsom board Cardboard composition board can be sawed easily into shapes. Use for cornices, headboards, and wall treatments. From lumber supply in ¼″, ³/₁₆″, and ½″ thicknesses.

29

Spending Plans, Shopping, and Budget Decorating

During periods of inflation and soaring prices, most consumers become more conscious of price. It is important to budget your decorating dollar. First determine your needs and your furniture style; then plan your budget. Some people may not have a great deal of money to spend for decorating; others have little money so they need to spend it wisely. The home may be temporary because the occupants are transients, changing jobs, continuously being transferred, single, or unsure of their tastes. The home may be a second or vacation home. Some parts of the home may be temporary—for example, the nursery, which will be changed as the child grows. For any of these reasons, one may wish to economize.

Spending Plans

It is not wise to exceed your basic budget. Do not buy a bargain unless it can be used effectively in your decorating scheme. A bargain item may be the most expensive item you buy—it could ruin the effect of your carefully planned room.

The money spent on furnishings should be considered as an investment. It is expensive in the long run to assume that one will buy something for temporary use until there is money for something better.

Major items, such as upholstered furniture, mattresses, chests of drawers, cabinets, and floor coverings, are usually expensive even in the cheapest varieties. To decide, for instance, to buy a cheap living room rug to use for a year or two is not a wise investment. However, it is not always possible to invest in top quality for every item. There will be many factors influencing decisions about each major purchase, including cost, purpose, and appearance. When buying something with the idea of selling it later, it should be remembered that used furnishings usually have a low resale value. It is difficult, and often impossible, to receive a fair return on such an investment. Someone may even have to be paid to remove the article when it is to be replaced.

The most interesting homes are not necessarily the ones that are the most expensive, but neither do they have masses of poor-quality furnishings. Imagination, taste, skill, and intelligence are the prime supports of a budget.

It is incorrect to assume that all low-cost furniture is of poor quality. There is some excellent furniture made in the low and medium price ranges, but the novice must be extremely cautious when judging value. In some items the quality features are hidden, so that it is hardly possible to tell which offers the best value for the money. In mattresses and upholstered furniture, the "insides" are what count. It is difficult to judge the difference between a $60 mattress and a $120 one by looking at them.

Floor coverings are also difficult to judge. In carpets and rugs, the quality of material and construction is a hidden value. It takes years of practice to develop discrimination in judging quality, and sometimes even the experts can be fooled.

It is not possible to establish rules for all consumers; everyone's needs and desires differ. It is unlikely that there are two individuals or two families who are in identical situations and have the same needs, resources, values, and tastes. However, for those who need assistance, here are some guidelines that may be useful:

Home furnishings usually cost about one fourth of the value of a home. A further breakdown on spending for each room follows:

Living room 40%
Dining room 20%
Master bedroom 15%
Second bedroom 15%
Kitchen, bathroom, and halls 10%

For individual items within each room a rational guide is

Furniture and bedding 45%
Flooring 15%
Walls 10%
Windows 15%
Accessories 15%

Although there are certain things necessary for all homes, there are also items that might be considered essential by some people but superfluous by others. A piano or a stereo set may be very important to the person who likes music; in a private house landscaping and outdoor furniture may be big items in the budget. Appliances such as an electric mixer, an electric broiler, or a pressure cooker may be more important in one household than in another. If the homemaker plans to work, certain time- and labor-saving devices simplify the problem of a dual career, but they are not absolutely necessary.

The abundance of consumer goods on the market presents a constant challenge for people trying to live within the boundaries of their incomes. We all want to live as comfortably and as efficiently as possible, but in establishing a household we should never lose sight of the importance of the spiritual values in the home. A family that goes into debt for material items and is under constant economic pressure may find it difficult to keep their values in proper perspective.

Resources

With reference to resources we are likely to think of finances, but it should be noted that resources of time and ability are important factors in setting up a budget plan. A person who has the time and the ability to install fixtures and to build or refinish furniture adds considerably to the family resources. So does someone who has the ability and desire to make curtains and slipcovers. If such projects are not appealing, the cost of having them done by others makes a household more expensive to establish and to operate.

It should be borne in mind that buying furnishings on the installment plan has serious drawbacks. This is an expensive way to buy anything, because the service or interest charges must be added to the costs of purchases.

If one buys a $400 sofa, paying the service charge each month in addition to a $22 monthly payment, and the charge is one and one-half per

Table
29.1

Assume that you purchase a sofa for $400 and pay $22 at the start. Your record of payments would be as follows.

Month	Unpaid Balance	Service Charge		Your Payment
1	$378	$5.67 +	$22.00 =	$27.67
2	356	5.34 +	22.00 =	27.34
3	334	5.01 +	22.00 =	27.01
4	312	4.68 +	22.00 =	26.68
5	290	4.35 +	22.00 =	26.35
6	268	4.02 +	22.00 =	26.02
7	246	3.69 +	22.00 =	25.69
8	224	3.36 +	22.00 =	25.36
9	202	3.03 +	22.00 =	25.03
10	180	2.70 +	22.00 =	24.70
11	158	2.37 +	22.00 =	24.37
12	136	2.04 +	22.00 =	24.04
13	114	1.71 +	22.00 =	23.71
14	92	1.38 +	22.00 =	23.38
15	70	1.05 +	22.00 =	23.05
16	48	.72 +	22.00 =	22.72
17	26	.39 +	22.00 =	22.39
18	4	.06 +	4.00 =	4.06
		Total $51.57		

cent of the unpaid balance, the payments in a year and a half will be those shown in Table 29.1. At the end of eighteen months the $400 sofa would have cost $451.57.

Buying the major portion of furnishings in this manner would be extremely expensive. However, not all installment buying must be frowned upon in such disapproving terms. There are situations in which it may be worth the cost to have the convenience of an article. For example, a mother with several young children may not be able to afford a washing machine, and by the time she saves enough money to buy one, the "period of crisis" may be over. The cost of buying a machine on the installment plan may be well worth the saving of her time and energy during the period when a family has the problem of caring for young children. Nevertheless, it is important to know the cost of using credit plans. The Truth in Lending Law now makes it mandatory for the creditor to pro-vide specific information about the conditions of a contract and the methods of calculating charges.

Making a Budget and Inventory

First, determine the place of residence, then draw a floor plan according to scale with accurate measurements of windows, doors, and wall areas. Now it is time to make a list of household needs. It may or may not be necessary to include in the budget such things as kitchen flooring, window shades, blinds, certain appliances such as an air conditioner, paint, and wallpaper if they are not included in the purchase price of the home.

Next, develop a budget notebook, allowing a section for each room that is to be decorated. At this time, make a list of all the basic needs you can foresee. Then make a list of all the items that appear on the floor plan. Also indicate the items that do not appear on the plan, such as draperies, fixtures, and accessories. Any other items may be added later. Make separate lists, one for essential buys and another for things to be added at a later date.

After that, formulate a second floor plan showing the room arrangement with only the items you can afford initially. At this time, it may be necessary to regroup furniture arrangements.

Once equipped with a list of needs, do some comparison shopping and record the prices. Do not make any purchases, but visit different stores: department, discount, factory outlets, second-hand shops, even junk shops. Total the prices of the desired items. This price list should include furniture, fabrics, wall coverings, floor coverings, lamps, accessories, and paints. This paperwork should be done before anything is actually purchased.

The total of the prices will give an accurate cost of the finished room. Then choose the essential items, and compare this cost with the budget allotment. If the items chosen are not within the budget, decide which items can be eliminated or where money can be saved with do-it-yourself decorating.

Fresh color and pattern used with imagination and do-it-yourself ingenuity transform an attic room into a delightfully feminine retreat under the eaves. Matching fabric, gathered in a short ceiling valance and shirred, floor-to-ceiling on the bed wall, creates an old-fashioned canopy effect. An old childhood sled treated to a new coat of paint and stenciling makes a charming surface for plants and accessories. Vintage sewing machine, electrified for convenience, plus antique rocker, bureau, and needlepoint stand complete a cosy setting for quiet, at-home projects. *(Courtesy of Allied Chemical Corporation)*

Fig. 29.1

Your notebook, price lists, and floor plans will serve as your guide for your decorating plans. Keep these records; all the information will prove useful in future buying.

Because it is not always possible to find items that fit your price range, keep your budget flexible. Consider the consequences of exceeding the budget for any item and know how you will reallocate funds to absorb the unexpected costs.

There are a number of less obvious costs that should not be overlooked when preparing a budget. The maintenance of a home will require some equipment, particularly a vacuum cleaner if there is carpeting on the floors. The cost of drapery hardware will add to the expense of the room.

The following lists suggest some of the items you may wish to include in your decorating plans (the * indicates the essentials).

Living-Dining Area
* Sofa or love seat
  Upholstered chairs
* Tables
  Side chairs
  Desk
* Lamps
  Accessories
* Draperies and fixtures
  Television and radio
  Floor covering
  Slipcovers
  Dinette

Spending Plans, Shopping, and Budget Decorating

Each Bedroom
  * Beds, mattresses, and springs
    Chests of drawers
    Mirror
  * Nightstands
    Bench or chair
    Floor covering
  * Lamps
    Accessories
  * Draperies and fixtures
  * Pillows
    Bedspreads and blankets

Linens
    Table linens
    Bedding:
  * Sheets
  * Pillowcases
    Mattress pads
  * Towels:
      Large bath towels
      Hand towels
      Wash cloths
      Dish towels

Closet Accessories
    Hangers
    Shoe bags
    Storage boxes

General Equipment
    Vacuum
    Mop
    Broom
    Pail
    Basin
    Tool kit
    Curtain rods
    Sewing kit
    Light bulbs
    Clocks
    Iron and ironing board
    Sewing machine—if you sew

Each person develops an individual method of working in the kitchen. Certain utensils and gadgets will undoubtedly become more useful than others. The following list of food-preparation and service equipment is merely suggested as a basis, although not all of these pieces would be absolutely essential initially.

  * Dinnerware
  * Glassware
  * Flatware
    Kettle
  * Saucepans (two small; one large)
  * Skillets
    Roasting pan
    Baking pans
    Cookie sheets
  * Measuring cups
  * Measuring spoons
    Mixing bowls
    Colander
    Strainer
    Grater
    Cutting board
    Pitcher
    Lemon juicer
    Funnel
    Carving set
  * Set of five utensils—large spoon, masher, pancake turner, tonged fork, spatula
    Food chopper
  * Can opener
    Minute timer
    Meat thermometer
  * Potholders
    Canisters
    Salt and pepper shakers
    Toaster
    Coffemaker
    Hand mixer
    Trays
  * Knives

There are several other items that may be useful:

Dutch oven or pressure cooker
Electric fry pan
Electric blender
Muffin pans
Cookie cutters
Ring mold
Fluted mold
Baster
Tongs

These lists are merely suggestions. It is important to develop one's own lists designed to meet specific needs. For example, a spice rack, a chafing dish, a salad basket, and an egg poacher may be important items in one person's kitchen, but they might be useless to someone else. You should decide which items are the most essential as basic equipment. The requirements will depend upon how one manages and operates a home.

The budget developed will serve as long as the home exists. It should include a yearly allowance for additions, replacements, and repair. One may begin with a small amount of furniture in a first apartment, and later buy more upon moving to a larger location.

Personal taste is likely to change with passing years. The furniture liked so much today may seem less attractive in later years. But it is human nature to desire change. After ten or fifteen years, fashion changes may bring about new designs that suit one's tastes and needs more fully than what one presently owns. Perhaps it is good that many people cannot afford to buy all necessary items at once. It takes the experience of living with purchases to become aware of personal likes and dislikes.

Shopping for Value

Here are some guidelines that may be useful in helping to get your money's worth while shopping.

Cost
Comparison shopping is a must, and so is patience. Be familiar with prices in different stores. Some stores charge more than others because their overhead expenses are higher.

Quality
Today quality in design can be found in all price ranges because synthetic products such as man-made fibers, plastics, and inexpensive metals are available. However, it is often expensive to get quality construction work. Some items should have quality construction; for others it may not be so important. A kitchen table or a desk that will be used every day should have sound construction, whereas a table in the foyer that will not get heavy use does not necessarily need quality construction. Sometimes second-hand furniture gives better service and quality than newer furniture of shoddy construction.

Some designs are classics. Others are not. For example, much modern furniture can be very expensive, is dated very quickly, and goes out of style, making it necessary to replace it to be fashionable.

Adaptability
Furnishings should be appropriate to use in future residences, and be easy to move. It is useful if the furnishings can serve several different functions. For example, can the apartment living-room furniture be used in the family room in a future move? Will the baby grand piano fit into the next apartment's elevator? Can the wall-to-wall carpeting be made into area rugs? Can your bookshelves be disassembled easily and rearranged in a different room? Some mobile people only buy things that fold, deflate, roll up, or disassemble.

Maintenance
Consider the maintenance in the cost of a purchase. Draperies that need to be dry cleaned can increase the final cost by as much as fifty per cent. Carpeting that soils easily and needs to be cleaned often is not a thrifty purchase. The same is true for delicate, light-colored upholstery fabrics. Also consider the cost of replacing fragile items.

Functionalism
An item that can be used for two purposes is functional as well as space-saving and economical. For example, there are sofas that convert to beds, tables that double as desks, trunks that serve as tables, and wall units that are decorative as well as serving as storage units.

Creativity
Find uses for items that may otherwise be discarded. For example, use parts of an item, cut the legs off, refinish, repaint, or use contact paper to refurbish.

Spending Plans, Shopping, and Budget Decorating

False Economies

If you have something that you feel is wasteful to discard because it was once expensive or someone gave it to you, and if you will not enjoy using it, do not use it. Avoid building a room and color scheme around a sofa that you do not enjoy, because you will never be satisfied with the total look of the room. This is false economy. Sometimes reupholstering sofas or chairs can be as expensive as buying new ones. Unless the item has an exceptional design, frame, or construction, do not reupholster it unless you can do it yourself; then it may be economical. However, it is wise to have antiques in good condition reupholstered.

Bargains

Inexpensive items may also be of value. Often it is far better to invest in one piece of furniture that will last a long time than buy three pieces of junk with a short life. If you are unsure about an item, do not buy it. A compromise or an inferior product for the ''time being'' is expensive. It will need to be replaced in the near future.

Where to Find Bargains

Business people want to make a profit; learn to differentiate between a real bargain and an illusionary one.

Illusionary bargains. More decorating budgets are ruined by purchasing false bargains than any other way. Therefore, adhere to these common-sense guidelines:

- Unless an item can be used it is not a bargain. Impulse buying can turn a home into a hodge-podge with clashing colors and effects.
- Beware of bait and switch advertising, which entices one into the store to buy an advertised item, whereupon the salesperson tries to sell the customer another, more expensive item.
- Retailers usually sell at wholesale prices only when they are going out of business.

- Some items are fair traded; that is, the manufacturer, not the retailer, controls the price.
- Beware of boraxing; retailers may promise bargain merchandise that is never delivered, then sell an impatient customer a more expensive item that can be delivered immediately.

The real bargains. Occasionally merchants do pass on substantial savings to their customers. Look for the following:

- Discontinued styles. The manufacturer is no longer producing an item, so the retailer sells the remaining incomplete stock at a reduced price.
- Manufacturers' errors. Manufacturers overproduce, or produce irregular items, or need to sell their damaged merchandise. Then they sell it to retailers who in turn may sell it to consumers below retail prices.
- Mill ends and remnants are pieces at the end of rolls of carpeting, fabric, wallpaper, etc. Be sure, however, that there is enough of the item to complete the job.
- Floor samples. If an item is in good condition and fits into your decorating scheme, it may be a good buy. If the item is damaged when you buy it, do not expect the store to repair it free of charge.
- Warehouses, showrooms, clearance centers, and some new kinds of retailers may cut the extras such as delivery, assembly, and unboxing of items, thus trimming their cost considerably and passing the savings on to the consumer.
- Outlet stores. Adjacent to home furnishings factories, there are other outlet stores that sell items below cost, although these items may be irregular or otherwise damaged.
- Classified ads. When customers want to sell new merchandise such as items that they may have won on quiz shows or at raffles, they sell them in the classified ads.
- Unfinished furniture. It is necessary to spend time, energy, and money to finish it yourself.

- Seasonal shopping. Wise shoppers can save a tremendous amount of money by shopping at the right place and at the right time. If you have a knowledge of different kinds of stores and their sales, you can use this to your financial advantage. Look for preclearance, clearance, and special item sales.

At preclearance sales a wide range of merchandise is offered, but the savings are generally not significant. The consumer can wait until later in the season for further reductions, but the items desired may have been sold by the later date.

Clearance sales are held at the end of the season and savings can be significant on regular-price merchandise. Some of this merchandise, however, may be damaged.

Because the merchandising of furnishings is a seasonal business, consumers can often save as much as fifty per cent or more if they buy off-season (such as buying outdoor furniture in the fall instead of the spring) or at special item annual sales. Learn what times of the year stores have their traditional sales. For example, furniture sales take place in January and August; carpet sales in August; white (household linen) sales in January and August; appliances in February; and housewares in March. The above items are also often reduced during Washington's Birthday, Columbus Day, and Thanksgiving Day sales, or whenever the retailer decides to reduce the stock.

Investigate second-hand merchandise sources such as thrift shops, church bazaars, flea markets, garage sales, and moving and storage companies.

Maximizing Shopping Effort
To use time most effectively:

- Call ahead to inquire if the store has what you want and if it is in stock. At this time check business hours and addresses.
- Measure ahead of time. Know the quantity of merchandise you need by taking exact measurements before your shopping trip.
- Read the tags and labels on merchandise. Do not wait until your dining-room table is delivered to discover that the chairs were not included in the price of the table or that a bookcase must be uncrated and assembled by you.

Fig. 29.2

Decorating on a budget does not have to be dull and drab. Colorful fabrics and pillows can add a lively touch to any room. All the furnishings in this room cost under $1,000. *(Courtesy of Sears)*

Bargain hunting, improvising, and making things do can go only so far in decorating satisfaction. Sometimes there is good reason to splurge on some item that will give great satisfaction when owned—be it an oriental rug, a wall storage system, an antique, or a painting—because the eye-catching quality of one outstanding object can make a room look better than the sum of its parts. A wall storage system can be a very good investment even though a system can cost several thousand dollars. It may sound like an extravagance, but not when considered as a lifetime investment as well as a functional piece of furniture. A wall storage system eliminates the need for many pieces of furniture, and it gives specialized storage space for a variety of household items. Many storage systems include a built-in bar, a bed, a desk, and a table, as well as display shelves. When redecorating or moving, the units can be used separately in different rooms in the next home.

Often money spent for beautiful background materials is a good investment because luxurious materials can do a great deal for improving an otherwise dull expanse of space in a room. An oriental rug may be a good investment because it makes other items in the room look better by association. Such rugs usually have good resale value; they mellow with age; and they go with a wide variety of styles and periods.

Budget Decorating

People usually have two limitations when it comes to decorating: not enough space and not enough money. But one does not need to be limited because of a lack of money: there are many ways to save money by using imagination and ingenuity. There are many decorating tasks for the do-it-yourself individual. People often discover that decorating on a budget can be very rewarding because it forces creativity. Remember that there is no price tag on good decorating. Let your imagination be your guide. Study budget decorating magazines for useful ideas.

The current interest in the antipoverty program and in the problems of the low-income

Fig. 29.3

An alternative to expensive furniture is to hand build furniture, like the owner of this apartment did, by using plywood for the platform of the sofa and upholstering the sofa covers with fabric of the owner's choice. *(Courtesy of E. I. du Pont de Nemours and Company)*

Fabric stretched over a wooden frame effectively fills the need for a painting. *(Courtesy of The Belgian Linen Association)*

Fig. 29.4

family has prompted several well-known interior designers to apply their talents to creating attractive homes with the minimum amount of money. The ideas that have resulted from pilot projects and demonstrations are useful for any family that must cut corners on their budget.

Antipoverty studies stress imagination, simple do-it-yourself ideas, color, and functionalism. In both cases the intent is to suggest new ideas and to promote an interest in creating attractive homes even though funds are limited.

A number of manufacturers in the home furnishings field are devoting their attentions to sturdy, useful, attractive items that can be mass-produced at relatively low cost. Many of these are already widely available in stores throughout the country. The demonstration projects indicated some of the ways that modular units, shelving, self-adhesive trimmings, window shades, and printed sheets might be used.

There is also a new interest in rejuvenating good-quality second-hand furniture. Some of the new products, such as spray paints, antiquing kits, self-adhesive plastics, and a wide variety of hardware, make it possible to convert an old eyesore into an attractive and useful piece of furniture with relatively little effort.

Applying wallpaper yourself is extremely useful in stretching a budget. The variety of patterns, colors, and textures can create almost any desired effect. Panels, screens, table tops, and accessories decorated with wall coverings are effective ways of adding interest.

A new emphasis on window shades as an important element in decorating offers a multitude of possibilities for low-cost decorating. The self-adhesive motifs, fringes, braids, and plastics require imagination but very little time and skill to transform an ordinary shade into an attractive window treatment. There are also new products that make it possible to apply fabrics to window shades with relatively little time and expense.

Accessories in the minimum budget are a true challenge to creativity and imagination.

Spending Plans, Shopping, and Budget Decorating

If after decorating the upstairs of a home one has little money left for decorating the basement, one can start a do-it-yourself project. *(Courtesy of Armstrong Cork Co.)*

Converting unused basement space need only involve painting of cinder block walls and the simplest of do-it-yourself ceiling and floor installation projects. (left) Ceiling planks are merely stapled to furring strips. (right) Self-stick floor tile is installed just as it comes from the carton. *(Courtesy of Armstrong Cork Co.)*

Fig. 29.5

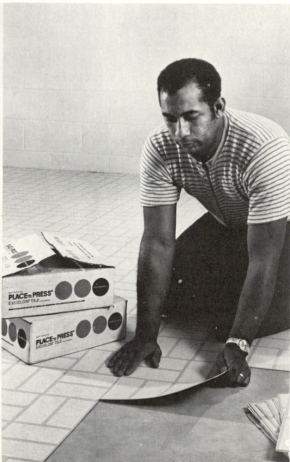

Fig. 29.6

Finishing Touches

Fig.
29.7

With Place 'n Press flooring, Temlock ceiling plank, and an area rug of Epilogue
shag by Armstrong, a long-neglected source of space—the basement—is turned into
a comfortable place to relax by a couple using a lot of imagination and a minimum
of money. *(Courtesy of Armstrong Cork Co.)*

Plants, huge paper flowers, collections—seashells, family pictures, or memorabilia of one type or another—can all be used to provide individuality. Individual interests and skills can add the important ingredient in producing the necessary touch of emphasis. You may begin by following some suggestions given below:

- Assess what you already own and decide how it can be improved. Determine what needs to be purchased and what kind of do-it-yourself projects can be accomplished. Keep a notebook of creative ideas to expand resources.

- Use color to enhance what is already owned; color is one of the least expensive resources.
- Refinish old or damaged furniture by antiquing, painting, or stenciling.
- Use unfinished furniture, or less expensive types of materials like wicker, plastics, or rattan.
- Build your own furniture.
- Use plants to enrich a room's interior.
- Use fabrics, prints, or lithographs in place of expensive paintings.
- Make accent rugs by braiding, hooking, or crocheting.
- Install do-it-yourself flooring by using carpet or resilient flooring tiles.

Spending Plans, Shopping, and Budget Decorating

- Use easy-to-build and -assemble storage units.
- Use sheets and fabrics to cover walls; make curtains, bedspreads, and pillows.
- Build screens and use them as room dividers.
- Make an office in an unused closet.
- Build out-of-the-ordinary lamps and lighting fixtures from materials on hand.

Summary

Creativity, taste, imagination and an eye for value create interesting decoration more often than money. To avoid overspending and impulse buying, keep these things in mind:

- Keep a budget notebook on what is needed, and how much can be spent.
- Decide where and how money will be spent.
- Stay within an established budget.
- Do not overspend on one room and then have to skimp on other rooms.
- Do much comparative shopping—it can save money and prevent mistakes.
- Do not buy something just because it is a bargain; it is no bargain if it does not fit into a decorating scheme.
- Buy quality. Good-quality merchandise lasts longer and wears better than poor-quality items. Buy the best possible within a determined budget range.
- Shop at seasonal sales and other savings events.

In order to make the best use of the concepts and information covered in this text, one must regard the design of interiors as a creative endeavor involving each person who will live in the house or apartment. Many of the necessary ingredients for interior decorating have been laid out here; but it is the unique qualities and creativity of the individual that make a home a personal expression. The choices, interests, and life styles of the people who live there are vividly reflected in every home. Unique qualities are present in every object and arrangement. A home is a revealing portrait of its inhabitants. What is included, what is excluded, how things are displayed—all these are as important as the furnishing objects themselves.

The idea of home furnishings as a creative art form cannot be underestimated: it remains one of the few areas of personal choice and creative expression in a society where most of our choices and environments have been preordained. When a child is born, the parents decide on the room's contents and arrangement. The teacher in school arranges the learning environment before the students enter. In most work settings, we are expected to fit into our environment. It is no wonder that when children grow up and leave the home, they are so concerned with establishing and furnishing their own space.

Decorating a home or apartment can be called one of the last truly popular art forms in which most of us participate. In our concern for our homes and their appearance, the pride we take in our choices or design arrangements raises our level of humanity and provides us with infinite pleasure. This concern with our own environments and their furnishings is a necessary step in our concern for the appearance of our total human environment.

Most people are eager to participate in the selection and arrangement involved in furnishing their home. We see our home as a private space, an enclosure of comfort where we want objects of interest and satisfaction to help us relax and find enjoyment. We want our home to be a source of aesthetic pleasure; we want to be surrounded by objects that are beautiful and entertaining. Besides the physical, psychologi-

30
In Conclusion

cal, and aesthetic comforts and satisfaction, we may look at the home and its furnishings as a source of investment, where unique objects can be assembled for financial security or as something to hand down to our children. No matter which function of the home and its furnishings is considered most important, we want the home to fit our own needs as well as to present a self-image that we want others to see. The home is a special place for most of us, no matter who helps us to design it or what guidance we seek. The ultimate criteria are how it fits the person, how it feels to live in, and how it serves individual needs.

A home and its furnishings are always open to change. To keep our living spaces from stagnating, we can add, regroup, and rearrange to set new moods, serve different needs, and express new visions. The changes in our living areas give us new inspiration, energy, and interest in our lives. If we stop re-creating our personal environments, we become stale and uninterested in life.

Homes are usually open to additions; a house and its furnishings may be seen as a showplace for displaying one's personal collections. There is a little of the collector in every one of us—anxious to trade, add to, share any objects of interest. We like to participate in seeing our home and collection of furnishings grow, all the while knowing that we are never satisfied, because the home really is never complete. With real pleasure, we take stock of the things that we have accumulated, and we often look with great interest at objects that we would like to acquire. Furnishing a home can be seen as a lifelong pursuit and as a basic part of our life style.

It is necessary for those who are interested in interior decoration to survey the best this field has to offer. Museums and galleries are excellent sources of historical and contemporary design in home furnishings. Today's furniture showrooms are often set up as galleries or model rooms: one can look around, even without the immediate intention of buying. Occasionally visiting home improvement centers, looking at new items, collecting samples, and surveying literature may be other ways to keep up with the fast pace of changes in home furnishing.

While watching the changes of trends in fashion in terms of such elements as colors, styles, themes, and materials, one can continuously plan new items for one's own needs. As we develop our senses and are influenced by the standards of taste that we view, we also have to trust our intuition and listen to our own ideas, for a sense of honesty is perhaps the most important quality in creating a design that represents oneself.

Through our interest in the home and its environment, we begin to see our past and the present, and we are sometimes afforded a glimpse into the future. We may gain respect for unusual handicrafts, for traditions in rare antiques; from our past we may acquire an understanding of what designers are doing today. A glimpse at the present-day art world will show us the best designs in home furnishings.

Homes and their furnishings can be seen as sources of communication. They may help us to understand past generations and contemporary ways of life. We may also learn to understand others, as they demonstrate their ideas and show us how they feel and think through the personal expression revealed in their homes. In arranging our homes, we are expressing our thoughts and desires, as well as our fantasies, in a private and public display that can be communicated and perceived by other people. Residences and their interior furnishings are not only sources of pleasure for their designers but also a way to share pleasure with the others who perceive their qualities.

As we become more knowledgeable about the history and current solutions of home furnishing problems, we begin to develop our own taste; we find out what is right for us and discuss our own systems and preferences. In employing ideas for home design, we become aware that personal ideas are both inherited and of our own invention. While reading these pages, we have to look at the furnishing process as a phenomenon related to a particular time, place, and attitude, and we must adapt the ideas and objects available to our own lives and our own needs.

Besides reviewing the theoretical base, it is recommended that the reader practice the process of interior decoration and frequently redesign the furnishings in whatever space may be available. Practical experience comes from such activities as making decisions, selecting forms, and creating arrangements; deciding on how this will be done and what process will be used; and discovering a new need or function within the home. With additional experience, we come up with more artistic ideas and discover the excitement of creating something new.

We know of the great beauty and pleasure that can be found in nature, and we admire the perfection of the natural order. Human-made things are less perfect, sometimes poorly de-signed or manufactured. Unlike the harmonious beauty of the natural environment, our home furnishings need a sophisticated process of careful selection. Involvement in home furnishings means the development and exercising of one's taste and judgments. Because we spend most of our time today not in natural settings but in man-made environments, homes and their furnishings become not only practical shelters with functional objects but take on the role of providing many of the visual and other sensory pleasures by adding a harmonious touch to our lives.

Bibliography

Agan, Tessie, and **Elaine Luchsinger.** *The House.* New York: J. B. Lippincott Company, 1965.

Albers, Josef. *Interaction of Color.* New Haven: Yale University Press, 1975.

Alexander, Harold. *Design: Criteria for Decisions.* New York: Macmillan Publishing Co., Inc., 1976.

Alexander, Patsy. *Textile Fabrics and Their Selection.* Boston: Houghton Mifflin Company, 1976.

Amaya, Mario. *Art Nouveau.* New York: E. P. Dutton and Co., 1960.

Aronson, Joseph. *New Encyclopedia of Furniture.* New York: Crown Publishers, Inc., 1967.

Banheim, Reyner. *The Architecture of the Well Tempered Environment.* Chicago: University of Chicago Press, 1973.

Barnes, Joanna. *Starting from Scratch.* New York: Tower, 1970.

Barrows, Claire M. *Living Walls.* New York: Wallcoverings Council, 1968.

Beitler, Ethel Jane, and **Bill Lockhart.** *Design for You.* New York: John Wiley & Sons, Inc., 1961.

Berger, Robert. *All About Antiquing and Restoring Furniture.* New York: Hawthorn Books, Inc., 1972.

Better Homes and Gardens. *Creative Decorating on a Budget.* New York: Better Homes and Garden Books, 1970.

Bevlin, Marjorie Elliot. *Design Through Discovery.* New York: Holt, Rinehart and Winston, 1970.

Birren, Faber, ed. *A Basic Treatise on the Color System of Wilhelm Ostwald.* New York: Van Nostrand Reinhold, 1969.

Birren, Faber. *Light, Color and Environment.* New York: Van Nostrand Reinhold, 1969.

Birren, Faber. *Creative Color.* New York: Van Nostrand Reinhold, 1965.

Boger, Louise Ade. *Complete Guide to Furniture Styles.* New York: Charles Scribner's Sons, 1969.

Boger, Louise, and **Batterson Boger.** *The Dictionary of Antiques and the Decorative Arts.* New York: Charles Scribner's Sons, 1967.

Bradford, Barbara Taylor. *Easy Steps to Successful Decorating.* New York: Simon & Schuster, Inc., 1971.

Bradford, Barbara Taylor. *How to Solve Your Decorating Problems.* New York: Simon & Schuster, Inc., 1976.

Brown, Jan. *Buy It Right.* Munndelein, Ill.: Career Institute, Consumer Services Division, 1974.

Cary, Jane Randolph. *How to Create Interiors for the Disabled.* New York: Pantheon Books, 1978.

Cobb, Hubbard H. *How to Paint Anything: The Complete Guide to Painting and Refinishing.* New York: Macmillan Publishing Co., Inc., 1972.

Con, J. M. *Carpets from the Orient.* New York: Universe, 1966.

Conran, Terrence. *The House Book.* New York: Crown Publishers, Inc., 1976.

Conran, Terrence. *The Kitchen Book.* New York: Crown Publishers, Inc., 1977.

Corbman, Bernard. *Textiles: Fiber to Fabric* (fifth edition). New York: McGraw-Hill, 1975.

Coysh, A. W., and **J. King.** *Buying Antiques: A Beginner's Guide to English Antiques.* New York: Praeger Publishers, Inc., 1968.

D'Arcy, Barbara. *Bloomingdales Book of Home Decorating.* New York: Harper & Row, Publishers, 1973.

Davidson, Marshall B. *The American Heritage History of Notable American Houses.* New York: American Heritage, 1971.

De Forrest, Michael. *How to Buy at Auction.* New York: Simon & Schuster, Inc., 1972.

Diflow, Donna. *How to Buy Furniture.* New York: Macmillan Publishing Co., Inc., 1972.

Dorfman, John. *Consumer Survival Kit.* New York: Praeger Publishers, Inc., 1975.

Dorn, Sylvia O'Neill. *The How to Collect Anything Book.* New York: Doubleday & Company, Inc., 1976.

Du Bois, M. J. *Curtains and Draperies: A Survey of the Classic Periods.* New York: Viking Press, 1967.

Evans, Ralph M. *An Introduction to Color.* New York: John Wiley & Sons, Inc., 1959.

Faulkner, Ray, and **Sarah Faulkner.** *Inside Today's Homes.* New York: Holt, Rinehart and Winston, 1975.

Faust, Joan Lee. *The New York Times Book of House Plants.* New York: Quandrangle/The New York Times Book Co., 1973.

Feldmen, Edmund. *Art As Image and Ideas.* Englewood Cliffs, New Jersey: Prentice-Hall, Inc., 1967.

Fetterman, Elsie, and **Charles Klamkin.** *Consumer Education in Practice.* New York: John Wiley & Sons, Inc., 1976.

Fiarotta, Phylis. *Nostalgia Crafts Book.* New York: Workman, 1974.

Fitch, James Marston. *American Building.* Boston: Houghton Mifflin, 1972.

Flynn, John E., and **Arthur W. Segil.** *Architectural Interior Systems.* New York: Van Nostrand Reinhold, 1970.

Formenton, Fabio. *Oriental Rugs and Carpets.* New York: McGraw-Hill Book Company, 1972.

Frankel, Virginia. *Interior Space—Interior Design: Livability and Function with Flair.* Garden City, New York: Doubleday & Company, Inc., 1973.

Friedman, Arnold, John Pile, and **Forrest Wilson.** *Interior Design.* New York: American Elsevier Publishing Co., Inc., 1976.

Furniture Facts. Chicago: Hoover-Seng, 1976.

Gakuyo, Shobo, ed. *Japanese Interiors.* San Francisco: Japan Publications Trading Center, 1970.

Gilliat, Mary. *Kitchens and Dining Rooms.* New York: Viking Press, 1970.

Gloag, John. *A Social History of Furniture Design from* B.C. *1300 to* A.D. *1960.* New York: Bonanza Books, 1966.

Goldstein, Vetta, and **Harriet Goldstein.** *Art In Everyday Life.* New York: Macmillan Publishing Co., Inc., 1954.

Gottlieb, Lois Davidson. *Environment and Design in Housing.* New York: Macmillan Publishing Co., Inc., 1965.

Graves, Maitland. *The Art of Color and Design.* New York: McGraw-Hill Book Company, 1951.

Grillo, Paul Jacques. *What Is Design?* Chicago: Paul Theobald, 1962.

Gutman, Robert, ed. *People and Buildings.* New York: Basic Books, Inc., Publishers, 1972.

Hall, Edward T. *The Hidden Dimension.* Garden City, New York: Doubleday & Company, Inc., 1966.

Halse, Albert O. *The Use of Color in Interiors.* New York: McGraw-Hill Book Company, 1968.

Hennessey, James, and **Victor Papanek.** *Nomadic Furniture.* New York: Pantheon, 1973.

Hicks, David. *David Hicks on Decoration.* New York: Macmillan Publishing Co., Inc., 1967.

Hollen, Norma, and **Jane Saddler.** *Textiles* (fifth edition). New York: Macmillan Publishing Co., Inc., 1979.

Hornung, Clarence P. *Treasury of American Design.* New York: Harry N. Abrams, Inc., 1973.

House and Garden's Complete Guide to Decoration. New York: Simon & Schuster, Inc., 1970.

536 Itten, Johannes. *Design and Form*. New York: Van Nostrand Reinhold Company, 1964.

Itten, Johannes. *The Art of Color*. New York: Van Nostrand Reinhold Company, 1973.

Jordan, Furneaux. *A Concise History of Western Architecture*. New York: Harcourt Brace Jovanovich, Inc., 1974.

Jung, Carl G. *Man and His Symbols*. Garden City, New York: Doubleday & Company, Inc., 1959.

Kaufman, John E., and Jack F. Christensen, eds. *Illuminating Engineering Society Lighting Handbook* (fifth edition). New York: I.E.S., 1973.

Kira, Alexander. *The Bathroom*. New York: The Viking Press, Inc., 1976.

Kness, Darlene. *The Butterick Kitchen Equipment Handbook*. New York: Butterick Publishing Company, 1977.

Kuppers, Harold. *Color: Origin, Systems, Uses*. New York: Van Nostrand Reinhold Company, 1973.

Lang, Burnette, Moleski, and Vachon, eds. *Designing for Human Behavior*. Stroudsburg, Pennsylvania: Dowden, Hutchenson and Ross, 1974.

Larson, Jack Lenor, and Jeanne Weeks. *Fabrics For Interiors: A Guide for Architects, Designers and Consumers*. New York: Van Nostrand Reinhold Company, 1975.

Larson, Leslie. *Lighting and Its Design*. New York: Whitney Library of Design, 1964.

Libby, William Charles. *Color and the Structural Sense*. Englewood Cliffs, New Jersey: Prentice-Hall, Inc., 1974.

Lindahl, Judy. *Fieldcrest Decorating Digest*. New York: Fieldcrest Mills, Inc., 1975.

Lyle, Dorthy Siegert. *Modern Textiles*. New York: John Wiley and Sons, Inc., 1976.

Mace, Robert L. *An Illustrated Hand Book of the Handicapped Section of the North Carolina State Building Code*. Raleigh, N.C.: North Carolina Dept. of Insurance, 1976.

Magnani, Franco, ed. *Interiors for Today*. New York: Whitney Library of Design, 1975.

Marsh, Betty. *All About Furniture*. High Point, N.C.: Southern Furniture Manufacturers Association, 1969.

May, Elizabeth, Neva Waggoner, and Eleanor Hotte. *Independent Living for the Elderly and Handicapped*. Boston: Houghton Mifflin Company, 1974.

McClinton, Katharine Morrison. *An Outline of Period Furniture*. New York: Clarkson N. Potter, Inc., 1972.

McClinton, Katharine Morrison. *Antiques Past and Present*. New York: Crown Publishers, Inc., 1971.

Meadmore, Clement. *How to Make Furniture Without Tools*. New York: Pantheon Books, Inc., 1975.

Meadmore, Clement. *The Modern Chair—Classics In Production*. New York: Van Nostrand Reinhold Company, 1975.

Money Management Institute. *Your Home Furnishings Dollar*. Chicago: Household Finance Corporation, 1973.

Moody, Ella. *Modern Furniture*. New York: E. P. Dutton and Co., Inc., 1966.

Moore, Charles, Gerald Allen, and Donlyn Lyndon. *The Place of Houses*. New York: Holt, Rinehart and Winston, 1974.

Naar, Jon, and Molly Siple. *Living In One Room*. New York: Random House, Inc., 1976.

1,001 Decorating Ideas. Consolidated Trimming Corporation, 27 West 23rd Street, New York, 10011.

Ormsbee, Thomas H. *Field Guide to Early American Furniture*. New York: Bantam Books, 1966.

Panero, Julius. *Anatomy For Interior Designers*. New York: Whitney Library of Design, 1962.

Parker, Harry, et al. *Materials and Methods of Architectural Construction*. New York: John Wiley & Sons, Inc., 1966.

Parks, Luciana. *Groovy Guide to Decorating Your Room*. New York: New American Library, 1971.

Percivall, Julia, and Pixie Burger. *Household Ecology*. Englewood Cliffs, New Jersey: Prentice-Hall Inc., 1971.

Phillips, Derek. *Lighting in Architectural Design*. New York: Holt, Reinhart and Winston, 1968.

Phillips, Derek. *Lighting in Architectural Design*. New York: McGraw-Hill, 1963.

Plumb, Barbara. *Young Design in Color*. New York: The Viking Press, Inc., 1972.

Rapoport, Amos. *House Form and Culture*. Englewood Cliffs, New Jersey: Prentice-Hall, Inc., 1969.

Schofield, Maria, ed. *Decorative Art and Modern Interiors*. New York: The Viking Press, Inc., 1975.

Schremp, William E. *Designer Furniture Anyone Can Make*. New York: Simon & Schuster, Inc., 1972.

Schwartz, Marvin, and Betsy Wade. *The New York Times Book of Antiques*. New York: Quadrangle Books, 1972.

Scobey, Jean. *Rugs and Wall Hangings*. New York: The Dial Press, 1974.

Skurka, Norma, and Oberto Gili. *Underground Interiors.* New York: Quandrangle Books, 1972.

Sloane, Patricia. *Color: Basic Principles and New Directions.* London: Studio Vista, 1968.

Smith, R. C. *Materials of Construction* (second edition). New York: McGraw-Hill Book Company, 1973.

Sommer, Robert. *Design Awareness.* Corte Madera, California: Rinehart Press, 1972.

Sommer, Robert. *Personal Space: The Behavioral Basis of Design.* Englewood Cliffs, New Jersey: Prentice-Hall, Inc., 1969.

Steidl, Rose E. *Functional Kitchens.* Ithaca, New York: Cooperative Extension, Bulletin 1166.

Steir, Olga, and J. E. Schuler. *Decorating Small Apartments.* New York: William Morrow & Co., Inc., 1969.

St. Marie, Satnig. *Homes Are for People.* New York: John Wiley & Sons, Inc., 1973.

Stoddard, Alexandra. *Style for Living.* Garden City, New York: Doubleday & Company, Inc., 1974.

Sulahria, Julie, and Ruby Diamond. *Inside Design.* New York: Harper & Row, Publishers, 1977.

Sylvania. *Guide to Indoor Garden Lighting with Sylvania Gro-Lux Lamps.* Danvers, Massachusetts: Sylvania Co., Lighting Center, 1976.

Toben, Bob. *Time-Space and Beyond.* New York: E. P. Dutton & Co., Inc., 1975.

Van Dommelen, David B. *Designing and Decorating Interiors.* New York: John Wiley & Sons, Inc., 1965.

Varney, Carlton. *You and Your Apartment.* Indianapolis: The Bobbs-Merrill Co., Inc., 1967.

Wagner, Dorothy. *What You Should Know About Carpet.* New York: Popular Library, 1967.

Walton, Diana. *Decorating Ideas for Under $10.00.* New York: Award Books, 1971.

Warner, Esther S. *Art: An Everyday Experience.* New York: Harper & Row, Publishers, 1963.

What To Know When You Buy Floor Covering. New York: Montgomery Ward and Company, Inc., 1970.

Whiton, Sherrill. *Interior Design and Decoration.* New York: J. B. Lippincott Company, 1974.

Williams, Adele. *Thrift Shop Decorating.* New York: Arbor House, 1976.

Wilson, José, and Arthur Leamon. *Decorating Defined: A Dictionary of Decoration and Design.* New York: Simon & Schuster, Inc., 1970.

Windows Beautiful. Vol. 6. Sturgis, Michigan: Kirsch Company, 1977.

Wingate, Isabel B., Karen Gillespie, and Betty Mildram. *Know Your Merchandise For Retailers and Consumers* (fourth edition). New York: McGraw-Hill Company, 1975.

Wright, Frank Lloyd. *The Future of Architecture.* New York: Horizon Press, 1953.

Wright, Frank Lloyd. *The Natural House.* New York: Horizon Press, 1954.

Periodicals

American Home
  641 Lexington Avenue
  New York, New York 10022
American Home Crafts
  641 Lexington Avenue
  New York, New York 10022
Antiques Magazine
  551 Fifth Avenue
  New York, New York 10036
Apartment Life
  750 Third Avenue
  New York, New York 10022
Architectural Digest
  680 Fifth Avenue
  New York, New York 10019
Architectural Forum
  130 East 59th Street
  New York, New York 10022
Architectural Record
  1221 Avenue of the Americas
  New York, New York 10019
Better Homes and Gardens
  750 Third Avenue
  New York, New York 10017
Contract
  1515 Broadway
  New York, New York 10036
Curtain, Drapery and Bedspread
  370 Lexington Avenue
  New York, New York 10017
Daily News Record
  7 East 12th Street
  New York, New York 10003
Design and Environment
  355 Lexington Avenue
  New York, New York 10017
The Designer Magazine
  1010 Third Avenue
  New York, New York 10020
Floor Covering Weekly
  919 Third Avenue
  New York, New York 10022
Flooring
  757 Third Avenue
  New York, New York 10017
Furniture Retailer Magazine
  804 Church Street
  Nashville, Tennessee 37203

Furniture South
127 East 31st Street
New York, New York 10016

Furniture World and
Furniture Buyer and Decorator
127 East 31st Street
New York, New York 10016

Home Furnishings Daily
7 East 12th Street
New York, New York 100

Home Sewing Trade News
1440 Broadway
New York, New York 10018

House Beautiful Magazine
250 West 55th Street
New York, New York 10019

Interior Design
850 Third Avenue
New York, New York 10022

Interiors
1515 Broadway
New York, New York 10036

Linens, Domestics and Bath Products
370 Lexington Avenue
New York, New York 10017

Modern Floor Coverings
124 East 40th Street
New York, New York 10016

Modern Textiles Magazine
303 Fifth Avenue
New York, New York 10001

National Furniture Review
666 Lake Shore Drive
Chicago, Illinois 60611

1001 Decorating Ideas
Family Media Inc.
149 Fifth Avenue
New York, New York 10010

Progressive Architecture
600 Summer
Stamford, Connecticut 06504

Southwest Furniture News
Box 4667
Dallas, Texas 78406

Western Fabrics, Curtains and Draperies
1516 Westwood Boulevard
Los Angeles, California 90024

Western Furniture Manufacturing
Suite 102
1516 Westwood Boulevard
Los Angeles, California 90024

Appendix: Careers in Interior Design

Who Is the Interior Decorator?

Many people enjoy decorating their homes, and some are quite good at it. There is a great general interest in looking at illustrations or reading about the latest in furnishings, and most people have direct experience in this area. Some people feel that they can successfully use their interest and experience to further their training and to find a position in the design profession.

As this text clearly indicates, a knowledge of interior design is important to everyone; we all utilize such expertise to some degree many times in our lives. This section may be essential for those who may wish to make a career in this field.

There are two areas of jobs related to interior design; one is *interior decoration*, practiced by people who plan furniture arrangements and assist in the selection of fabrics, materials, and colors. Interior decorators may be free-lance artists or people who own or operate a shop.

A person who has a formal education and is properly trained as an *interior designer* is in a sense an architect of interior space. An interior designer may be a member of the American Society of Interior Designers[1] (A.S.I.D.). This membership is determined by examination after educational and experience requirements have been met.

The architect plans and organizes the features of a building; but the building's interior needs further specific organization, according to the requirements of a particular occupant. The interior designer may work with the architect in considering the divisions and details of space, or she or he may begin where an architect has left off in designing spaces for particular uses. The interior designer is an expert (generally with a good background in the arts) and must also have mechanical and engineering knowledge concerning the building's structure, so that wall spaces can be altered, wiring and mechanical systems reorganized, and other work properly

[1] A.S.I.D. was formed in January 1975 by the consolidation of the American Institute of Interior Designers (A.I.D.) and the National Society of Interior Designers (N.S.I.D.). It is the largest organization of professional interior designers in the world.

planned. In the capacity of an artist, the designer works with forms, colors, and textures in space (which is the task of all artists) having her or his own individual ideas and stylistic preferences. The designer's uniqueness lies in the ability to function according to the specific requirements of each job and the needs of each client.

Both decorators and designers may be retained by individual clients or by businesses interested in an organized, comfortable, and interesting interior.

Creating Interiors

Occupations connected with interiors are both creative and service oriented. People in these fields assist others in making their homes functional, interesting, and personal places to live. Especially today, when more and more people are boxed into smaller and outwardly less individualized units of housing, interior designers can be particularly useful. They assist clients in bringing out their own interests and try to reflect their individuality in their homes.

The job of designing interiors has several facets. One entails educating people to the varieties of spaces, to the ways these affect their lives, so that they may see their environment as made up not only of functional objects but also of forms and colors that affect the mood and quality of the setting. Designers are engaged in educating the customer to the range of furnishing items, materials, and styles. They attempt to inform people about current trends and fashions. In the process, the designer transforms people's needs, ideas, and fantasies into concrete and visual form. The designer must have a broad knowledge of the home designer's field and the ability to understand and interpret the plans and ideas of architects. This ability requires a familiarity with interior and exterior building styles, as well as with the design of home furnishing items and the construction of products. The designer's knowledge and sensitivity must be focused on today's times and life styles, as well as the ability to help people to express their specific needs and *organize* their requirements for their homes.

The designer must be able to adapt to the client's needs and to see each job as a fresh, new problem requiring its own solutions and ideas, while maintaining his or her own convictions and artistic standards.

The designer has to be a resourceful person who knows where to look for things, often unusual items, and where to look for a good selection of furnishings—perhaps a small hidden shop, a less expensive wholesaler, or an importer across the country.

The designer has to be willing to play and experiment, to try new possibilities, all the while knowing what colors go with certain plans and what forms match and may work with other forms.

A designer must be informed of the historical and contemporary trends in building, the qualities and appearances of old and new spaces and objects—not only to be aware of the shapes of objects but to use imagination in arranging them for a specific purpose. She or he may also need to be an expert concerning the prices and values of objects and artworks.

The designer has to be a coordinator, working with other professionals, such as architects, landscape artists, house painters, plumbers, and electricians. In each case, a familiarity with materials and their potentials is important.

The designer has to be a smart consumer for the client, knowing the values of objects and the construction that underlies design; finding materials that are durable and easily maintained at a fair price; recommending reliable craftsmen; giving dependable estimates; and sticking to budgets.

The designer has to be a collector, a shopper for the unusual; it is necessary to have an eye for interesting detail. In terms of selection, the designer has to emphasize practicality and yet please the aesthetic sense.

The designer has to be a synthesizer and an organizer, aware of the visions, amounts, scales, and proportions that help to constitute and simplify life spaces.

Above all, the designer should be a good listener, empathetic with the desires and needs of the client. The good designer recognizes that part of the job is fulfilling dreams.

An over-all view of careers in interior design offers a fascinating glimpse into the world of decorating. This section will attempt to outline some specializations within the field, "careers within a career." To evaluate a career in any area, one should know what these individual jobs are like and also, taken together, what they represent in terms of a life's work. Getting the whole picture is important when one is making the basic decisions in choosing a career.

Before making a decision, one will want to know about the environment, the kinds of people one may work with, and the nature of one's associations with them. How important is the interior designer to the success of an operation? What is the future? How far can one go?

Sales for Interior Design

One major part of interior decoration and design includes jobs in promotion. Because home furnishings are visual objects, the advertising, publicity, and display connected with them should present them in the best possible light. Advertising can be directed both to the public and to the home furnishings industry. Newspapers, magazines, television, and direct mail are some of the media through which the consumer can become aware of a product. The home furnishings industry has its own trade publications, such as *Interior Design,* where a product is seen by the most influential people in the industry. Advertising can be done nationally to build brand identity so that the product becomes widely known, or locally, to lure consumers to a specific purchasing outlet.

Companies doing a large amount of advertising are usually assisted by publicity specialists and public relations personnel who help prepare materials in an interesting and innovative way. These specialists and their departments might arrange interviews or invite celebrities to work up events in order to embellish the firm's image. In a large department, programs for advertising people can be lined up by certain staff members—advertising managers, account executives, art directors assisted by graphic artists, publicity directors, production managers, and promotional and direct mail specialists. Not all of these jobs are found in each company, but there is a need for personnel from varied disciplines in every major advertising division.

Sales Personnel

Marketing specialist—wholesale selling. Sales personnel may represent design houses, manufacturers, or specialty stores. They must have a congenial personality, which is effective in displaying the company's line to the customer. The marketing specialist must be familiar with a great variety of merchandise and know everything about the product being sold, so as to facilitate dealing with the difficult needs and problems of the company's clients.

Part of the job may include visiting clients both near and far, dealing with customer complaints, visiting showrooms, answering correspondence, writing orders, or scanning magazines and trade news publications.

Retail selling. Jobs in the retail area may entail individual sales work or management and merchandising. The manager's job may include ordering supplies and checking deliveries. Merchandising involves the purchasing of products from wholesalers and then selling to customers. *Buyer* is the general term applied to the purchaser of products in a department store; *salesperson* is the term used for the seller of merchandise.

A congenial personality can make or break a sale. It can create an atmosphere of good will and trust. Being a good listener will assist the salesperson in helping the client make the selection that best suits his or her needs.

Complete familiarity with the products is essential in helping to answer customers' questions. If she or he is working with people from the industry, they may be just as well-informed about the product as the salesperson is. A familiarity with sales and marketing strategies is an asset in a sales career.

Friendliness and patience, along with a willingness to work hard, will help guarantee success in this field. Personal satisfaction results from pleasing the customer.

Wholesale showrooms open to the interior design trade are another source of work. A job might include duties ranging from preparing and displaying samples to assisting designers in their selection and introducing new products or techniques to following up on orders placed.

Rendering Artist

Rendering artists do illustration work for interior designers, architects, and contractors, or for individual artists. The artist translates the idea or concept to the client. Renderings are used for promotion and publicity.

The rendering artist must make meticulous plans, using rulers and ruling pens to create a three-dimensional drawing that accurately describes all details of the object in space. A rendering artist can work with a draftsperson, who first prepares a two-dimensional plan or view of the space or object.

Resource Specialist

A resource specialist may work for a manufacturer, a design firm, a museum, or a school. This specialist links a firm with suppliers, manufacturers, and representatives of the goods and services that a company might require. The line-up of colors, price lists, and material samples must be organized and kept up to date so that it can be used effectively.

This specialist needs to be aware of the current trends and follow all aspects of the industry closely. The ability to find the unusual as well as the readily available merchandise will add to job success.

Instructor

An instructor is generally a specialist who has worked as an interior decorator or has been educated in a related area such as home economics or human resources. Some of the sources of employment where one can teach are a four-year college or university, various professional schools, community colleges, or adult education classes. Many people teach part time while pursuing their professional design careers.

Working for the
Home Furnishings Industry

In the home furnishings industry one of the personal rewards is the satisfaction derived from serving the public. What do the customers hope to gain by shopping in one's establishment? What can be achieved by serving them?

An important part of this job is locating some of the newest products and presenting them to the public. The customers will know that by shopping in one's establishment, they can save and spend their money more wisely.

The variety of goods presented to the public allows the purchasers the freedom to explore and experiment with numerous items and settings, expressing themselves through what most appeals to them. One is constantly satisfying the customer's desire for goods, fulfilling the drive to be appealing.

Personal Ingredients

What basic qualifications are needed in the area of interior design? People who have had a long, successful career in the field may caution a newcomer to evaluate her or his personal qualifications, creativity, and academic abilities before seriously considering embarking on a career in interior design.

There is little room for the trial-and-error method. One must be able to absorb information quickly, interpret it properly, and put it to use intelligently.

The very beginning of the first year of college is the time to ask yourself, "Will I be able to develop into the kind of person the industry needs? Do I have the basic qualities to do a job well?" Now is the time to begin laying the groundwork; the more professional aspects of your preparation will come later. Understanding the target population and the factors that influence consumer demand is essential in this business.

There are three general characteristics that are required in this field. One is creativity and a sense of visual awareness. Second is a sense of good business and the ability to deal with various customers. Third is the confidence your personality imparts.

Having formal training in the arts is extremely important. There are few absolute rules or guidelines in this profession. Being visually alert and artistically honest are perhaps the most important qualities. One must know the function of spaces and objects as well as their usefulness, yet depend on intuition to come up with new meanings and new solutions. It is important to understand people's needs, but it

544 is also essential to be sensitive to feelings; interior design has to be practical as well as refreshing and inspiring. Contemporary trends try to fulfill an appetite for simplification, but there is always another need in every effort for detail, for ornament, and for the fanciful.

Over the years, people we have spoken to in this field agree that among the first characteristics they look for in the prospective employee is that the applicant be personable, bright, and eager to learn. It is easy to see why. People in this business come in contact with different kinds of personalities throughout the day. Appearance, style, and self-assurance are some determinants of a successful career person. Other qualities include stamina, fortitude, an eye for details, and an underlying interest in learning about new developments in the field.

Among the characteristics that career-minded people should possess is the ability to understand the drives and desires of the customer and to react by offering merchandise to satisfy his or her needs. The ability to stimulate interest and attract attention and a talent for getting a message across to clients are both connected with this trait.

Education

After World War II, a demand for well-trained interior designers developed. Schools began offering curricula for professional training. A number of designers and architects came from the famous Bauhaus school in Germany and helped establish new trends in design.

Today there are many professional and semi-professional schools, as well as two- and four-year universities that offer interior design programs. There are also a few graduate schools that offer advanced interior design degrees as well.

Until a few years ago, there were few universities offering degrees in interior design, although many offered interior design courses. Many great designers and artists in the early part of the century had no formal training. The increasing trend toward college education in all fields of learning makes it essential for any person seriously interested in a career in interior design to seek formal preparation.

Interior design is a creative field. In essence, all forms of design are creative. However, they differ considerably from the fine arts. Design is concerned with problem-solving in aesthetic terms. Art, in its many forms, is a personal and emotive expression. No matter how design is defined, the fact that it is a creative activity makes it impossible to establish rigid rules for education and practice.

Educational requirements. A knowledge and an understanding of several areas are necessary in interior design careers. The most appropriate type of course work would include:

A. Training in Interior Design
   Knowledge of fibers and fabrics.
   Course work in textile science.
      Crafts.
      Design.
   Course work in construction.
      Furniture construction.
      Sewing construction.
   Course work in careers.
      Field study (museums, showrooms, home building centers, trade shows).
      Orientation to careers.
   Course work in the social sciences and liberal arts.
      Consumerism.
      The family.
      Historical and contemporary architecture.
      Historical furniture.
      Interior design.
      Twentieth-century furniture design.
B. Art Training (Developing Creativity).
   Course work in the fine arts.
      Color theory.
      Drawing.
      Painting.
      Two- and three-dimensional design.
      Visual communication.
   Course work in specific areas.
      Carpentry.
      Environmental design.
      Lighting design.
      Rendering.
      Stagecraft.

C. Business.
   Course work in buying and merchandising.
      Accounting.
      Business law.
      Computer technology.
      Economics.
      Fashion merchandising.
      Management.
      Marketing.
D. Shop Crafts.
   Course work in wood and metal construction (joining, shaping).
   Carpentry and shop experience.
E. Presentation Skills.
   Course work in media workshops.
      Advertising design.
      Display design.
      Photography.

Thorough college preparation is one of the first steps in acquiring the basic knowledge that may contribute to career success. It is on the campus that the opportunity is given not only to learn technical skills but to explore each field in a supervised, structured atmosphere. In this way, one benefits from the experience of well-qualified instructors with suitable backgrounds. Field work has always been an integral part of the practical preparation needed by students. Taking advantage of such opportunities and acquiring on-the-job experience working with experts contribute to knowledge and aid in the transition period from school to the world of work.

In each institution of higher learning, expert counseling is available. Career guidance offered by professionals can be of great value in answering questions and assisting one in achieving maximum experience.

Some students believe that formal schooling is not necessary for finding a position and working in this field. But with the competition in today's job market keener than ever, education is certainly of great value. When moving "up the ladder," the time for advancement is reduced when one has a thorough educational background and degree. The combination of what formal education and what is acquired through on-the-job experience will increase one's chances of getting a better position. The ability to perform at one's best is enhanced by the sense of security derived from previous experience. Expectations based on past performance are realistic. Higher education can prepare the individual to enter the world of professional designing.

Starting a Career

The first item you need to get started in the design field is a portfolio of work. This visual presentation represents evidence of ability. A portfolio should begin in school and represent continuous growth and improvement. In addition, a résumé and references from jobs or field experiences in the area should be included. In other words, it is vital to keep a permanent record of all design work that has been completed. Begin by working for an established firm, or free-lance, and eventually become self-employed if that is your goal.

Selecting Careers

There are many types of specialties within this area. A designer who has specific knowledge of floor plans, storage space, plumbing, or electricity may join the ranks of kitchen and bathroom specialists. Another designer may do only office and commerical spaces. Lighting specialists may work for manufacturers, engineering firms, and builders. Part of the job may be to test new equipment and work with advertising people.

Product designers are involved in the design of both two- and three-dimensional items and models. Two-dimensional products may include textiles, tile, or floor coverings. Three-dimensional products may involve furniture, appliances, lighting, and so on. The work will concern the appearance as well as the function of a product. Profit for the manufacturer is also, of course, a strong consideration.

Technical skills in drafting, design, graphics, rendering, and model construction, based on a thorough knowledge of manufacturing methods, will enhance job success. Knowledge of consumer attitudes and psychology will also help in this work. Most product designers must understand how products are utilized by the consumer and what methods of marketing such products will require. Good technical sense and creative ability will produce a product in the best way possible.

Many interior furnishings manufacturers seek free-lance consultants who have special training for each aspect of product design. When deciding on a home furnishings career, ask yourself: Do you wish to decorate personal dwellings or commercial establishments? Work on a free-lance basis or be employed by a firm? Do general design work or decoration work, or specialize in any one phase of design? Be involved with the technical and business aspects or the creative aspects of designing? Work with interiors or design or merchandise a product?

The Setting of Activities

There are two basic categories of work done by interior decorators and designers: commercial and residential. The residential designer is concerned with creating spaces in private homes, apartments, and model homes. The commercial designer works in offices, hotels, hospitals, and stores; commercial design also includes window displays for various kinds of business establishments.

Interior decorators and designers may work for interior design firms, manufacturers' showrooms, home furnishing departments of stores, fabric shops, or home products industries. Others may be in business for themselves.

Although inspiration may come at various places and odd times, the designer needs three types of places for work. A studio, in the home or in an office, where artwork, plans, and presentations may be prepared is a must. The second work place will be where furnishings can be viewed—galleries, fabric houses, showrooms, or museums. Finally, there is the actual site of decoration.

A Typical Day in the Career of a Decorator or Designer

The decorator's or designer's day may begin with a preliminary meeting with the client for examining the space to be decorated. The designer's main concern at this point is to get a general understanding of the client's likes, dislikes, needs, and tastes, along with budget considerations. Aided by knowledge of past and developing fashions, the designer should advise the client about popular themes and tastes. Harmonious personal relations are necessary when one is working with people, and the designer tries to be open to their needs and desires and to work to meet them.

At the office, a letter of agreement must be drawn. In it is included the retail markup for work and expense plus compensation for the job if it is commercial. It should include the scope of services and the purchasing provisions. If this is contract work, the letter includes provisions for space planning and related services, for interior design furnishings, and for the preparation and issuance of confirmations and purchase orders.

Following the preliminary meeting and after the contract (letter of agreement) has been signed, the designer meets with the client and they have a question-and-answer session in order to explore details about tastes and living preferences and to determine the differences between what is desired and what is actually needed. Some questions asked a client before designing a home may be: What do you do when you get up in the morning? Do you read at night? How frequently are the children in your room? Do you entertain with outside help? Do you have a laundry on the premises? Do you have any physical ailments (important if the designer will be doing a bathroom or buying a chair)? The strategy of asking specific questions should allow the client to feel relaxed and comfortable about the designer's approach and work.

In the office, the designer makes tentative sketches of solutions, as well as preparing materials for a more formal presentation for the client's approval. She or he communicates visions as clearly as possible, using swatches of materials, photographs, colors, and sketches, including three-dimensional renderings and the room from a bird's-eye view, so that the client can visualize the space as realistically as possible. A designer may work together with other people from the firm who have expertise in specific areas of presentation. The final work is then presented to the client in a portfolio.

Depending upon the designer's ability to coordinate efforts and produce satisfactory results, there is no limit to the type of gratification and salary that can be received. Achievements may be publicized by people in the home furnishings industry, who come to know and appreciate the designer's work. Recommendations and word-of-mouth are most important in determining success. The ability to meet deadlines and to work with builders, electricians, painters, and suppliers is important. Strong organizational ability and good judgment as to priorities will allow the designer enough time to get the work done satisfactorily.

Why Is Interior Design an Exciting Area?

Life in the interior design industry today does not necessarily entail regular hours or working from nine to five. During seasonal promotions or holidays, there may be no set hours; the work day may be very long.

As a decorator or representative, one may have to attend furniture showings at any time of the day. Training sessions, advertising meetings, conferences, courses, and client meetings may be part of the daily schedule.

Interior design is an exciting area for those who like to be involved in creating change. Each home, each new space, each new client presents a fresh challenge. In each situation one is able to see a full design process in action, from the investigation of a problem to various stages of planning and inspiration to the solution and the finished product. One may be involved in a variety of functions, such as antique and furnishings shows and going on buying trips and scouting exhibitions. In these endeavors one gets to see the latest in design, to examine beautiful items such as artwork and antiques, and to confer with artists and experts in various fields.

The professional designer is able to select and buy from among many of these beautiful items on behalf of the client, which often may be the next best thing to owning them personally. Designers see their own ideas taking shape in the finished rooms, exemplifying their own convictions and design ideals. If a finished design works and is well liked, one feels a personal sense of pride in being able to come up with good ideas and interesting choices.

Opportunities for Everyone

Prospects for careers in this field have never been brighter. The population is rising despite the lowered birth-rate in the past few years. There is a demand for goods and services with expanding store operations. The fewer choices there are, the more cramped we feel in our complex environments, and the more concerned people seem to be about the qualities of their own homes. According to a leading magazine, people are spending more time and money on items related to their homes than ever before. This is evident in the many new magazines and media advertisements related to home furnishings.

A leading design firm in New York City stated that 39 per cent of their interior designers are under the age of thirty-five. The company's president is forty-one. These data vary from firm to firm, but the emphasis in careers involving decoration and design is definitely on youth.

Women workers have always been welcome in this profession. One remarkable fact about the home furnishings industry is that more and more women have been entering top-level positions each year. A top executive in one of the large department stores in New York City says that almost 30 per cent more women have been hired in the last five years and have moved to executive positions than ever before, and that the future seems even brighter for educated and creative persons who want to enter and move up in a company.

A